"A Peep into the Past."

Copyright.

DR. RICHARD RUSSELL, F.R.S. 1687—1759.

From a Copy of the Original Painting by ZOFFANY, in the Old Ship
 Hotel, made by HENRY WILKIN, Esq., with the permission of MR.
 J. STRACHAN; formerly in the possession of the late CRAWFORD J.
 POCOCK, Esq.

"A Peep into the Past:"

BRIGHTON

IN THE OLDEN TIME,

WITH

GLANCES AT THE PRESENT.

BY

JOHN GEORGE BISHOP,

Author of "The Brighton Pavilion and its Royal Associations," "Strolls in the Extra-Mural Cemetery," &c.

WITH NUMEROUS ILLUSTRATIONS.

BRIGHTON:
PRINTED AND PUBLISHED BY J. G. BISHOP, "HERALD" OFFICE.
1892.

Entered at Stationers' Hall.—All Rights Reserved.

Preface.

IN compliance with the request of many esteemed friends, the Author has been induced to issue, in a cheap form, a "People's Edition" of "A PEEP INTO THE PAST: BRIGHTON IN THE OLDEN TIME." This issue is a complete reprint of the matter in the original Work, with occasional notes and alterations necessitated by lapse of time. In some instances, such as the statistics relating to the Railway, the Post Office, the Free Library and Museum, and the details of the development of Hove and Preston, it was deemed desirable to afford information up to date. To facilitate reference, such new matter has been bracketed. Several new illustrations (unavailable for the original Edition) have been inserted, which should give the Work additional interest. For kind assistance, freely rendered, the Author's grateful acknowledgments are due to Mr. H. Humphriss, Assistant General Manager of the Railway, and to Mr. Wilson A. Hetherington, Postmaster of Brighton; also to Mr. John Haines (for the loan of selections from his fine collection of old Brighton prints and drawings), to Mr. Thomas Tugwell, Mr. Gresham Bacon, Mr. W. Potter, and other Gentlemen. He has only to add that he trusts the present Edition may be as cordially received as was the first.

June, 1892.

PREFACE TO THE ORIGINAL EDITION.

In the Prospectus of this Work the Author stated,—"'A PEEP INTO THE PAST' is in no way intended to be a History of Brighton." In fact, the subjects treated of, though of historical interest, are such as lie to a great extent out of the domain of the historian proper. The Work originated in this wise. The Author, having contributed to the *Brighton Herald* some articles relating to Brighton in 1800, he, at the request of several esteemed friends, was induced to publish them, with additional matter of a kindred character, in a book form. Foremost among these friends was Crawford J. Pocock, Esq., to whom the Author's warmest acknowledgments are due ; that gentleman not only gave him the free use of his fine collection of drawings, prints, &c., relating to Brighton in the Olden Time, and access to his valuable collection of local historical memoranda, but also at all times the benefit of his judgment on important matters which arose during the progress of the Work through the Press. To other friends, the Author likewise tenders his best thanks, and especially to the Proprietors of the *Sussex Advertiser*, Lewes ; to Messrs. Crunden and Sons, of Brighton ; and to J. O. Halliwell-Phillipps, Esq., of Hollingbury Copse, Brighton.

With this brief Preface, the Author sends forth his Work to the public ; and, while asking for indulgence for any sins of omission or commission, trusts that it may serve to throw some new light upon what is regarded by many as an obscure and barren subject, namely, the History of Brighton in the Olden Time.

Brighton, November, 1880.

Contents.

	PAGE
THE BRIGHTHELMSTON DIRECTORY FOR 1800— Introduction—The Town—The Professional and Trading Community—Lodging Houses and Lodging Letting..	1
FASHIONABLE AND POPULAR AMUSEMENTS— Introduction—The Assembly Rooms: The "M.C." Dynasty—The Old Theatres: "Near the Stein"; The Theatre in North-street; The Theatre in Duke-street; The Theatre in New-road—The Promenade Grove—Loyal Festivities, Sports, &c. Horse Racing: Brighton Races—Cricket-Cock Fighting, &c.	25
THE STEINE AND ITS ASSOCIATIONS— Stag Hunting—Royal Visits—the Original Libraries—"Brighton Beauties"—Aristocratic "Amusements"—Fashions, &c.	109
NOTABLE HOUSES ON THE STEINE— The Manor House: The York Hotel—Russell House: The Albion Hotel—"Single Speech" Hamilton's—the Mansion of Mrs. Fitzherbert.	147
THE INNS OF BRIGHTON IN 1800 AND THEIR ASSOCIATIONS— The old East End Inns—Ye Haunte of Olde Strike-a-Lighte—the Great Storm of July, 1850—"The Old Ship," "The Castle," and other well-known Inns	171
SEA BATHING— Visit of Dr. Russell—Wood's "Original" Baths—the Old Bathers:—Martha Gunn, "Smoaker" Miles, and others	223
THE COACHING ERA— The old Sussex "Carrier"—"The Flying Machines," &c.—Post Coaches—Coach travelling in 1790 - Coaching in its Meridian and in its Decline—Castle-square in the Coaching Days	241
THE RAILWAY AND ITS GROWTH— Its Early History—Details of Development—the Resources of the Company—Traffic Returns—System of Lines, &c.	267
THE POST OFFICE— First Brighton Post Office—the Post Office in 1800—the "Off the Stones" period—Development of the Office—Telegraphy in Brighton.	289
NORTH STREET— Its Early History—the first Tradesman in the Street—the Occupiers, Rating, &c., in 1784, in 1800, and in 1814—the earlier Tradesmen—Old Houses in North Street	307
RELIGIOUS EDIFICES IN NORTH STREET— The Friends' Meeting House — The Chapel Royal — The Countess of Huntingdon's.	329
A PIONEER IN LOCAL JOURNALISM—MR. WILLIAM FLEET	355
A RETROSPECT OF TWENTY YEARS—Brighton in 1850 and in 1870.	365
HOVE— Its early History—the old Church—Captain Codlin and the "Adventure"—Fall of the Antheum—Hove's later Development	377
PRESTON— Its early History—Anne of Cleves and Preston Manor—the Shirleys of Preston—William Stanford and the Manor—Tea Gardens at Preston—the old Turnpike, and its removal—the old Church—Purchase of Preston Park; Presentation of Clock Tower.	399

Illustrations.

	PAGE
1. PORTRAIT OF DR. RUSSELL *(facing title)*	
2. Brighthelmston in 1799—(Frontispiece to " Directory for 1800")	
3. Mrs Thrale's House in West-street	7
4. Map of Brighton in 1779	11
5. Old Rocks – Brighton, 1809 (formerly opposite Rock Gardens)	14
6. Lieut.-Col. Eld (the last ' M.C." of Brighton)	37
7. The Theatre in Duke-street, Brighton. 1804.	51
8. Plan of the Promenade Grove, Pavilion, &c. 1803	67
9. The Celebration of a Royal Birthday in Brighton	82
10. Brighton Race Course and Stand. 1790	86
11. Ireland's Royal Pleasure and Cricket Grounds.	102
12. Lambert's Perspective View of Brighton, 1765	112
13. A Perspective View of the Steine, Brighthelmston. 1778	120
14. Portrait of George Prince of Wales. 1791	125
15. The Steine Promenade in 1805	139
16. Russell House, Brighton. 1786	150
17. View of West Side of the Steine, Brighton (showing Lady Anne Murray's and Mrs. Fitzherbert's Mansions)	160
18. Portrait of Mrs. Fitzherbert	165
19. The Block House. Brighton. 1761	173
20. Mahomed's Baths	175
21. The White Horse Hotel	176
22. Pool Valley during the Storm of July 17, 1850	182
23. The Black Lion Brewery	186
24. Original Front of Old Ship Hotel in Ship Street	187
25. The Old Ship Hotel (Sea Front) 50 years ago.	189
26. The Royal Suspension Pier—about 1825	191
27. Ditto—about 1870.	191
28. The White Lion Inn	202
29. The Unicorn Inn	204
30. The New Inn (Clarence Hotel), 1818	208
31. The Castle Tavern, Brighton. 1814	217
32. The Baths at Brighton. 1803	227
33. Martha Gunn, the old Brighton Bather	235
34. The old " Age " and Castle-square	258
35. South Gate of Pavilion : the Blue Coach Office, &c.	259
36. Opening of the Shoreham Branch of the Railway. May, 1840	270
37. Portrait of Mr. Samuel Laing, Chairman of L.B. and S.C. Railway	273
38. Railway " Chalk Hill," about 1860	274
39. Miss Widgett's Library, South of the Steine. (The Post Office).	291
30. The Post Office, New-road, 1848	295
41. Old Houses in North-street (North-West Corner of West-street)	318
42. Ditto (North-East Corner of West-street)	324
43. Portrait of the Countess of Huntingdon	337
44. Portrait of Rev. Joseph Sortain	340
45. The Chapel Royal, with Old Houses formerly on the South, in North-street	344
46. Portrait of Mr. William Fleet	355
47. West Battery, about 1830	369
48. Ruins of Hove Parish Church, about 1780	380
49. The Hove Fishery, 1814	385
50. The Antheum	387
51. Front of Hove, 1833, with old Church	389
52. Lillywhite " at home "	393
53. London-road Viaduct, from " Chalk Hill "	410
54. Preston Church (before restoration)	411

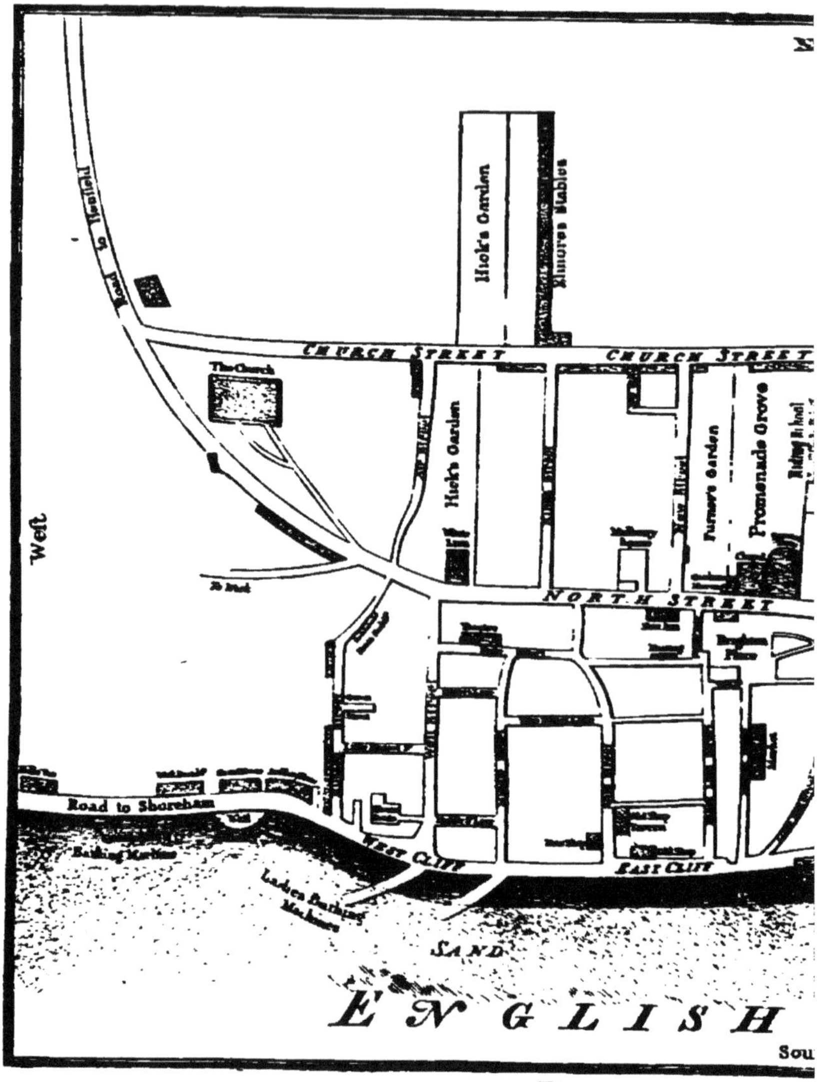
Road to Henfield
Hick's Garden
CHURCH STREET
CHURCH STREET
The Church
Hick's Garden
Furner's Garden
Promenade Grove
West
NORTH STREET
Road to Shoreham
Bathing Machines
WEST CLIFF
EAST CLIFF
Ladies Bathing Machines
SAND
ENGLISH

BRIGHTH

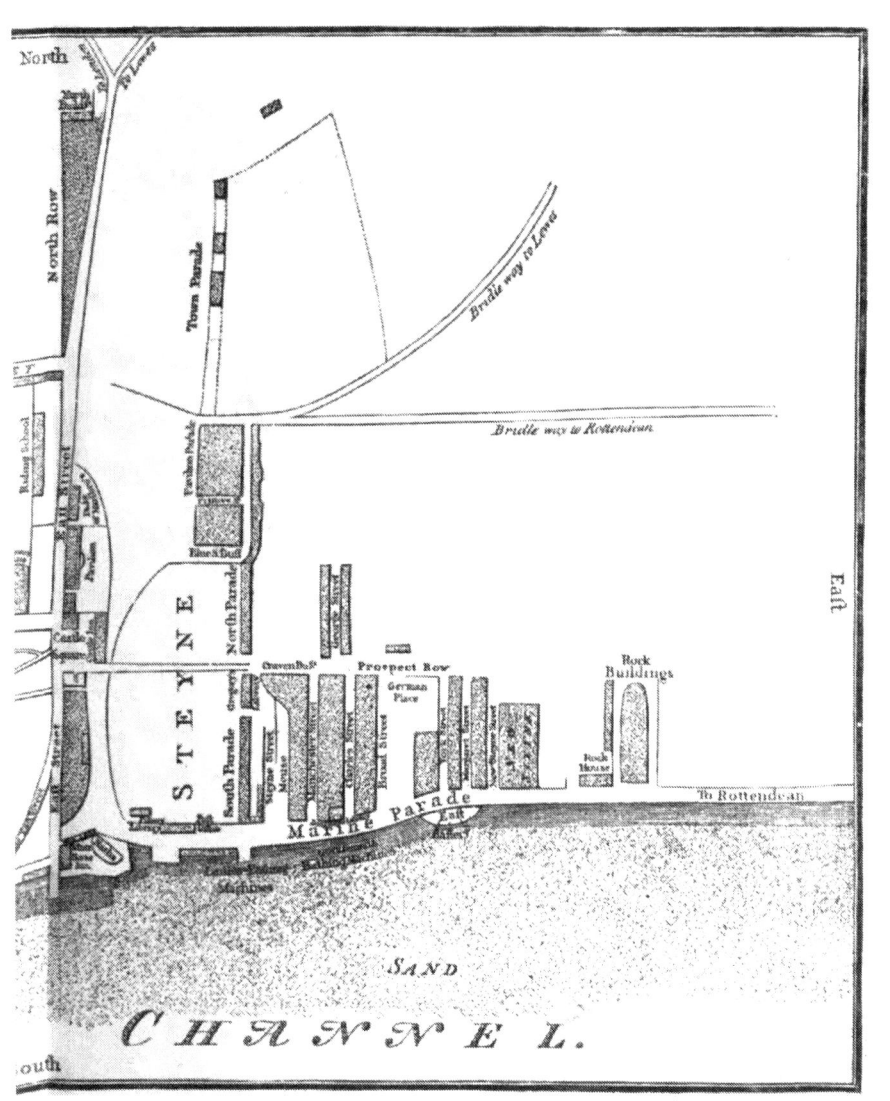

HELMSTON.

THE

𝔅𝔯𝔦𝔤𝔥𝔱𝔥𝔢𝔩𝔪𝔰𝔱𝔬𝔫

DIRECTORY

FOR

1800.

·o══o·

By *EDWARD COBBY.*

BRIGHTON: PRINTED BY W. AND A. LEE.

-(o)(═════)(o)-

Published by the COMPILER; and sold at the Libraries on the Steyne;
at DONALDSON's and WILKS's Library,
Brighthelmston; W. LEE's and A. LEE's, *Lewes;*
and at WRIGHT's, *Piccadilly, London.*

Price TWO SHILLINGS AND SIX-PENCE.

𝔈𝔫𝔱𝔢𝔯𝔢𝔡 𝔞𝔱 𝔖𝔱𝔞𝔱𝔦𝔬𝔫𝔢𝔯𝔰-ℌ𝔞𝔩𝔩.

CONTENTS.

		PAGE.
Town,		iii.
Market,		ibid.
Streets, Houses, &c.,		ib.
Public Buildings,		ib.
Public Rooms,		ib.
Theatre,		ib.
Baths,		iv.
Public Gardens,		ib.
Chalybeate Spring,		ib.
Races,		ib.
Pleasure Boats,		ib.
Principal Residents, &c.,		v.
Principal Inhabitants,		ib.
Professions,		ib.
Parish Officers, &c.		vi.
Tradesmen,		ib.
Lodging Houses,		12
Boarding-Houses,		14
Lodgings,		15
Posts,		18
Coaches,		19
Waggons,		ib.
Carts,		20
Roads,		21

INTRODUCTION.

BRIGHTHELMSTON, the Object of this DIRECTORY, is a Market Town in the County of Sussex, situated on the Coast of that County, which forms a Part of the Southern Boundary of this Island of Great Britain.

It is distant from Rye, the Eastern Extremity of the County, 45 Miles ; from Emsworth, the Western Extremity, 38 Miles ; from Crawley, the Northern Extremity, 23 Miles ; from Chichester, the Metropolis of the County, about 30 Miles ; and from London, the Metropolis of the Kingdom, 54 Miles.

Brighthelmston is situated in 50 deg. 55 min. North Latitude, and nearly 3 min. Westward of the Meridian of London ; distant from Dieppe, the nearest French Port, about 75 miles ; and from Paris, the Metropolis of France, 195 miles.

The Ancient History of the Town. of Brighthelmston is but imperfect and uncertain ; much of what is perfect and certain, is contained in the History of it ; a Work of considerable Credit and Information, edited in 1794, by one of the Printers of this Directory : the Modern History of it, is contained in the same Work, to which the Enquirer is referred, as superseding the Necessity or Utility of any regular historical Detail in these Pages.

In the year 1313, a Charter was obtained to hold a Weekly Market in the Town of Brighthelmston on a Thursday, and in 1772, an Act of Parliament for a Daily Market (Sunday excepted), which it is now, and certainly the best Market in the County.

Previous to the Year 1770, the Town consisted of only Seven principal Streets, and of less than 600 Houses the number of Inhabitants was then about 2500. In 1794, there were Fifteen Streets, the number of Houses was upwards of 1200, and the number of Inhabitants 5600. The present Town consists of Eighteen Streets, containing about 1500 Houses, and the number of Inhabitants is estimated at 7000 and upwards.

The principal Public Buildings in Brighthelmston are, the Public Assembly Rooms, the Theatre, and the Baths.

The PUBLIC ROOMS at the Castle Tavern, in Castle-square, and the Old Ship Tavern, in Ship-street, open early in JULY for the season.

Sunday,	—	Tea and Promenade,	at Tilt's.
Monday,	—	an Undressed Ball,	at Tilt's.
Tuesday,	—	an Assembly,	at Hicks's.
Wednesday,	—	an Assembly,	at Tilt's.
Thursday,	—	an Undress Ball,	at Hicks's.
Friday,	—	an Assembly,	at Tilt's.
Saturday,	—	an Assembly,	at Hicks's.

The first Dress Ball is the Monday next after Lewes Races ; and Dress Balls are continued occasionally on Mondays and Thursdays throughout the Season.

The Terms of Admission to the Balls, Assemblies, and to Tea and Promenade, are as follows :—A Gentleman's Subscription for the Season, 10s. 6d.—A Lady's Subscription for the Season, 10s. 6d.—For each Ball, 3s. — Tea and Promenade, 1s. — Non-Subscribers for each Ball, 5s.— Sunday Tea and Promenade, 2s.—Card Assembly Nights, 1s.

The THEATRE, in Duke-street, opens early in JULY, and closes about the End of SEPTEMBER. The Days of performing are Tuesdays, Wednesdays, Fridays, and Saturdays. The Doors open at Six o'clock, and the Performance begins at Seven o'Clock. Boxes, 4s.—Pit, 2s.—Gallery, 1s.

INTRODUCTION.

The BATHS.—They were built in the Year 1768, from a Plan of Doctor Awsiter's; they consist of two Cold Baths,—four Hot Baths, and a Showering Bath.

The Subscription to the Hot Bath is, for Three Months, £10 10s.—Two Months, £7 7s.—One Month, £4 4s.

The Subscription to the Cold Bath is, for Three Months, £3 3s.—One Month, £1 11s. 6d.

Non-Subscribers pay for Cold-Bathing, 1s 6d., and for Hot-Bathing, 4s.

Subscriptions are not admitted for the Showering Bath—each Person pays for the use of it, 1s 6d each Time.

If any Bath be wanted at any particular Hour, Notice for it may be given at the Bath House, where Persons are always in waiting.

The SEA-BATHING from the Machines, both at the East and West End of the Town, is particularly safe and pleasant—the Expence is, 1s.

At Wick, which is distant little more than Half a Mile Westward from the Town of Brighthelmston, there is a Spring of Chalybeate Water, which has been found particularly serviceable in most Cases of Debility and Indigestion, and in other Cases, where tonic remedies are required. There is a small Building over it, where Attendance is constantly given from the beginning of May till November, from Nine in the Morning till Six o'Clock in the Evening.

Subscriptions for the Season, 10s. 6d.—Non-Subscribers per Glass, 6d.—Non-Subscribers per Bottle, 6d.

Besides the Public Assembly Rooms and Theatre, there are also in Brighthelmston, PUBLIC GARDENS, that open at the beginning of JUNE, and close about the End of OCTOBER.

Terms of Admission:—Family Subscriptions, 10s. 6d.—Single Subscription, 5s. 6d.—Non-Subscribers, 6d. each.

The BRIGHTHELMSTON RACES, perhaps the best in England, with the Exception of Newmarket and York, are fixed by the Steward, Sir Thomas Charles Bunbury, Bart., with Lord Egremont, and other the principal Nobility of the County, at the close of JULY or the Commencement of AUGUST.

The RACE STAND, which completely commands the Course, and a most excellent View of Beachy-Head, and the intermediate Sea and Country, was built by Subscription in 1788. It stands 385 feet above the Level of the Sea at low Water, and the distance you command from it on the Sea, is nearly 25 miles. The Admission to the Stand, or to the Betting Ground, is 2s. 6d. each Race Day.

PLEASURE BOATS.—These (with Attendants) may be had at Wallis's, at the Rising Sun, in East-street, at One Guinea each per Day; or Half-a-Guinea for a short Excursion.

☞ The nearest Watering Place to London, BRIGHTHELMSTON, has long been the most frequented, and is now without Exception, one of the most fashionable Towns in the Kingdom. The Improvements IN IT, have kept pace with the Patronage OF IT; uniting in itself the Retirement of a Country Village, with the Gaiety of the Metropolis; and possessing every Advantage of Situation; it may dispute with any Town in England, the Credit of best accommodating its Visitors in every Thing ›ch can contribute to their Health, their Comfort, and their Amusement. quiet without dulness, busy without noise, and fashionable without a

INTRODUCTION. v.

PRINCIPAL RESIDENTS.

His Royal Highness the PRINCE of WALES.

His Grace the Duke of Marlborough, Lord Viscount Torrington, Lord Carrington, Lady Caroline Hervey, Lady Emily Hervey, Sir Godfrey Webster, Bart., Sir Robert Batson Harvey, Bart., Lady Shelley, Sir John Bridget, Knight.

W. Wade, Esq., Master of the Ceremonies, No. 53, East-street.

MAGISTRATES ACTING FOR THE COUNTY OF SUSSEX:
Sir Godfrey Webster, Bart.   Charles Scrase Dickens, Esq.
Mr. William Attree, their Clerk.

Lieut.-Colonel Samuel Moore, Barrack-Master.
Peter Simon, Esq., Principal Coast Officer.
Andrew Sproule, Esq., Commander of the Sea Fencibles on this Coast.
James Charles Michell, Deputy-Judge Advocate for the County of Sussex.
&c., &c., &c.

PRINCIPAL INHABITANTS.

(A) Alder, Walter Kettilby, Esq., New Steyne.

(B) Barnes, Reverend William, Margaret-street; Batchelor, James, Esq., Ship-street; Bray, Reverend Bartholomey, East-street.

(C) Chapman, John, Ship-street.

(D) Dring, Reverend John, Parsonage.

(H) Hamilton, Reverend Frederick, Air-street; Hanson, Francis, Esq., Bellevue; Heath, Charles, Esq., Bellevue; Hudson, Reverend Thomas, Parsonage.

(M) Mighell, Philip, Ship-street: Mitten, Thomas, Ship-street.

(N) Nodes, William, Broad-street.

(R) Read, James, Russel-street; Rice, Reverend John, East-street.

(T) Tilt, Reverend William, East-street.

(W) Welsford, Roger, Esq., North-street.

PROFESSIONS.

(A) Attree, William, Attorney, 8, Ship-street; Attree, John, Attorney, 8, Ship-street; Austin, William, Artist, 20, Russel-street.

(B) Brook, William, Academician, 1, West-street; Brooker, Henry, Attorney and Notary Public, 97, North-street.

(D) Dix, Robert, Surgeon, 31, East-street.

(G) Guy, Thomas, Surgeon, East Cliff.

(H) Henderson, Richard, M.D.; Hall, John, Surgeon, 105, North-street; Hargraves, John, Surgeon, 32, North-street; Hughes, Joseph, Attorney, 84, North-street.

(K) Kennedy, James, Academician, Duke-street; Kipping, Pankhurst, and Barrett, Surgeons, 28, West-street.

(M) Michell, James Charles, Attorney, 58, East-street, and 7, Steyne.

(N) Newnham, Richard, Surgeon, 4, Steyne Lane; Newton, John, Surgeon, 35, North-street.

(P) Paine, Cornelius, Academician, North-street.

(R) Rickman, Wigney, and Co., Bankers (New Bank), 2, Steyne Lane.

(S) Scott, Edmund, Portrait Painter, &c., &c., 6, Craven Buildings; Shergold, Michell, Rice, Rice, and Mills, Bankers (Bank), 103, North-street; Smith, Nathan, Inventor, Patentee and Operator of an Air Pump for extracting the Gout, &c., 3, Artillery Place.

PARISH OFFICERS, &c.

HIGH CONSTABLE—Cornelius Paine, North-street.

HEADBOROUGHS—*Old:* Thomas Paine, John Martin, Philip Morling, Thomas Mascall. *New:* Simon Wisden, Jonathan Grenville, Thomas Penticost, John Gilburd.

CHURCHWARDENS—Stephen Poune, John Baulcomb, William Chapman.

OVERSEERS—*Old:* Benjamin Pierce, Thos. Newington. *New:* Jonathan Steele, Adam Maiben.

ASSESSORS OF TAXES—Charles Rudhall, William Gates.

COLLECTOR OF ASSESSED TAXES—William Gates, 16, Ship-street.

SURVEYORS OF THE TOWN AND COLLECTORS OF THE TOWN RATE—Four Commissioners of the Town.

SURVEYORS OF THE HIGHWAYS—*Old:* John Stone, Three Tunn Square; Philip Vallance, West-street. *New:* Daniel Hack, East-street; James Patching, Russel-street.

COLLECTORS OF THE HIGHWAY TAX—Daniel Hack, James Patching.

MASTER OF THE WORKHOUSE—John Sickelmore.

TOWN CRYER AND BEADLE—Thomas Waring, 3, East-street.

TRADESMEN.

(A) Ackerson, John, jun., Builder, North-street; Ackerson, Robert, Builder, 11, Duke-street; Akehurst, Thomas, Tailor, 14, South Parade; Akehurst, Samuel, Baker, 14, Little Russel-street; Alderton, William, Cabinet-Maker and Upholder, 6, Little East-street; Allen, William, Innholder (White Horse), 65, East-street; Allen, Richard, Grocer and Blacksmith, 83, North-street; Arnold, William, Baker and Grocer, 45, King-street; Attree, Harry, Wine-Merchant, Draper, and Upholder, 15, Ship-street; Attree, Robinson, Auctioneer, 15, Ship-street; Atheral, Isaac, Victualler (Cricketters), 13, Black Lion-street; Austin, William, Drawing 'er, 20, Russel-street.

Baker and Co., Hatters, 37, North-street; Baker, John, Cord- 19, Little East-street; Baldey, John, Toyman, 11, Ship-street,

Baldey, Alexander, Grocer, 14, Ship-street; Barnard, Mary, Victualler (Blacksmiths' Arms), 85, North-street; Barnard, Henry, Cordwainer, 28, Middle-street; Barnard and Co., Smiths and Farriers, 3, King-street; Batho, Aaron, Victualler (Chimney), 1, Market-street; Batho, Matthew, Tailor, 55, Middle-street; Batho, Elizabeth, Mantua-Maker, 55, Middle-street; Bartlett, Robert, Blacksmith, 3, Margaret-street, and Grocer, 5, New Steyne-street; Baulcomb, John, Innkeeper (New Ship), 5, Ship-street; Bayley, Thomas, Victualler (Horse and Groom), 47, North-street; Bean, Thomas, Cordwainer, 28, York-street; Bedding, Matthew, Butcher, 19, East-cliffe; Bennett, Thomas, Hair-Dresser, 17, East-cliffe; Bradford, William, London Stage Waggoner, 47, East-street, and Miller, 7, Little Castle-square; Bradford, Nathaniel, Fish Merchant, 8, Church-street; Bridgman, William, Cordwainer, 43, West-street; Brooker, Richard, Hair-Dresser, 51, Ship-street; Brooker, Joyce, Milliner and Mantua-Maker, 51, Ship-street; Brook, William, School-Master, 30, West-street; Brown, Joseph, Turner, 5, Market-street; Buckwell, James, Baker, 9, Prospect-row; Budd, Charles, Cricket-Bat and Cabinet-Maker, 5, West Street-lane; Bull, Elizabeth, Stamp-Distributor and Stationer, 9, Ship-street; Burfield, John, Linen-Draper, 26, North-street; Burt, William, Plumber and Glazier, 1, Nile-street; Bushnell, Charles, Cordwainer, 7, West-cliffe; Butler, Richard, Woollen-Draper, 19, Black Lion-street; Burtenshaw, Henry, Stationer and Librarian, 23, Ship-street.

(C) Carden, Mary, Grocer, 1, Little Castle-street; Carter, James, Baker, 14, Little East-street; Carter, Elizabeth, Fruiterer, 4, South-row; Case, William, Tea-Dealer and Tallow-Chandler, 36, Brighton-place; Chapman, William, Brewer, 38, Ship-street; Chapman, Sarah, Fruiterer, 13, Castle-square; Chapman, John, Gardener, 36, West-street; Cheesman, John, Calico Glazer, 20, West-street; Chittenden, Joseph, Draper, &c., 54, North-street; Clark, Edward, Cordwainer, 29, Middle-street; Clark, John, Turner and Chair-Maker, 20, Duke-street; Cobby, Edward, Hatter, Hosier, and Undertaker, 2, Prince's-place; Cobby, Ruth, Mantua-Maker, 5, Castle-square; Colbron, George, Baker, 61, East-street; Colbron, James, Hair-Dresser, 30, New-street; Colbron and Saunders, Builders, 10, New-street; Colbron, William, Upholder, 10, New-street; Collard, John, Chemist and Druggist, 31, North-street; Comber, Michael, Grocer, 10, Boyce's-lane; Cook, William, Grocer, 43, East-street; Cook, Nathaniel, Poulterer, 18, New-street; Colchin, Thomas, Victualler (Star and Garter), 16, East-cliffe; Corbyn, Messieurs, Dancing-Masters, 35, New-street; Crawford, Andrew, Post-Master, Steyne; Cornford, Edward, Baker, 9, Market-street; Coupland, Mary, Farrier and Grocer, 1, Church-street; Cripps, Robert, Grocer, 9, Middle-street; Cripps, William, Coach and Sign Painter, 27, North-street; Cripps, Thomas, Painter, 16, West-cliffe; Cripps, Ann, Milliner, 16, West-cliffe.

(D) Dadswell, Robert, Draper and Slopseller, 8, Boyce's-lane; Daniel, William, Poulterer, 15, Meeting-house-lane: Davis, John, London Stage Waggoner, 52, Middle-street; Davison, Joseph, Victualler (Unicorn), Cowkeeper, and Milkman, 78, North-street; Deacon and Co., Drapers and Haberdashers, 1, Prince's-place; Dean, Thomas, Victualler (King's Head), 8, West-street; Delasson, Peter, Straw Manufacturer, 37, East-street; Dine, John, Shoe-Maker and Leather Cutter, 6, Market-street; Dingle, Mesdames, Milliners, 4, Castle-square; Dodd, Henry, Wheel-wright, 4, Kent's-buildings; Donaldson and Wilkes, Librarians (Marine Library), 7, Marine-parade; Dring, William, Grocer, Tea Dealer, and Oilman, 12, North-street.

(E) Edwards, Thomas, Victualler (Spotted Dog), 35, Middle-street;

Elmore, George, Horse Dealer and Livery Stable Keeper, North-street, and 24, Church-street; Elphick, N. and J., Lewes Carriers, 3, Nile-street; Elphick, John, Butcher, 87, North-street; Erridge, William, Hair-Dresser, 82, North-street.

(F) Farliy, Thomas, Plumber and Glazier, 24, Ship-street; Fegan, Thomas, Gardener, 23, Brighton-place; Feldwicke, James, Cordwainer and Salesman, 27, Brighton-place; Fisher, Frederick (late Crawford), Librarian, Steyne; Flemming, William, Hat-Manufacturer and Hatter, 50, Middle-street; Foster, David, Hair-Dresser, 14, East-street; Francis, Thomas, Victualler (Three Tuns), 3, Three Tuns Court; Fricker, Mark, Plumber and Glazier, 7, Prince's-place; Furner, Elizabeth, Victualler (Gun), 15, Little Castle-square; Furner, John and Thomas, Gardeners, 96, North-street.

(G) Gafney, Mary, Victualler, 21, East-street; Gates, Ambrose, Cordwainer, 3, Middle-street; Gibbs, Thomas, Salesman, 41, North-street; Gilburd, John, Hair Dresser and Toyman, 38 and 39, North-street; Gillett, Henry, Victualler (King's Arms), 1, George-street; Glaisyer, John, Baker, 16, Black Lion-street; Glaisyer, John, Chemist and Druggist, 11, North-street; Glassbrook, John, Hair Dresser, 49, East-street; Goddard, John, Turner and Chair-Maker, 45, Middle-street; Goldsmith, Mary, Grocer, 53, North-street; Gorringe, Richard, Tailor, 1, West-cliffe; Gourd, Boulton, Tilt, Hicks, Baulcomb, and Co., London Coach Proprietors, 1, North-street, and 47, Ship-street; Graham, George, Basket Maker, 34, New-street; Greening, George, Victualler (George), 1, West-street; Gregory, James, Librarian, Steyne,—Medicine Warehouse and Toy Shop, 2, North-street,—Coal Merchant, Middle-street; Grenville, Jonathan, Watchmaker and Goldsmith, 9, North-street; Grenville and Prince, Music Sellers, 9, North-street; Grenville, Isaac, Milkman and Poulterer, 14, Brighton-place.

(H) Hack, Daniel, Linen-Draper, 36, East-street; Harben and Wayte, School-Mistresses, 6, German-place; Hargraves, Brown, and Lashmar, Coal Merchants, Ship-street, Middle-street, and West-street; Harman, Thomas, Wire-Worker, Grocer, and Auctioneer, 43, North-street; Hart, John, Milkman, 3, Market-street; Haymes, Susan, Milliner, Fancy and Fashionable Dress Maker, 38, East-street; Heather, Thomas, Victualler (Sloop), 3, Steine-street; Heithersay, Matthew, Stay Maker, 28, Brighton-place; Henwood, Crosweller, Cuddington, Pockney, Harding, and Co., London Coach Proprietors, 44, East-street, and 24, North-street; Henwood, William Henry, Innholder (New Inn), 24, North-street; Hicks, John, Innholder (Old Ship), 46, Ship-street, and 28, East-cliffe; Hicks, Thomas, Corn-Chandler and Livery Stable Keeper, 2, Stable-lane, North-street; Hyde, John, Pastry-Cook, 44, Middle-street; Hill, Edward, Upholder and Cabinet-Maker, 8, Middle-street; Hilton, John, Baker, 10, West-street; Hind, William, Grocer, 4, Market-street; Hobden, Henry, Miller, Church-street; Hobden, Richard, Victualler (Bell), 30, Russel-street; Howell, Thomas, Builder, 6, East-cliffe; Howell, John, Cordwainer, 14, Castle-square; Howell, Hannah, Mantua-Maker, 20, Brighton-place; Hughes, John, Poulterer, 30, Brighton-place; Hughes, Robert, Porkman, 37, Brighton-place; Humber, Richard, Schoolmaster, 41, Middle-street; Humphrey, Richard, Tailor, 8, Brighton-place.

Ide, Thomas, Victualler (Thatched House), 28, Black Lion-street; Irish, James, Watchmaker and Silversmith, 5, North-street; Isted, William, Cordwainer, 13, South-parade.

TRADESMEN.

(J) Jackson, John, Cabinet-Maker, 2, Middle Street-lane; Jenkins, George, Whitesmith and Bell-Hanger, 11, East-street; Johnson, Nicholas, Builder, 5, Steyne-street; Jordan, John, Hair-Dresser, 10, Castle-square.

(K) Kellett, Thomas, Grocer, 46, King-street; Kendal and Co., Hatters, 99, North-street; Kennedy, James, Schoolmaster, 17, Duke-street; Kennett, Henry, Baker, 1, Little Castle-street; Kent, Thomas, Builder, 1, Kent's-buildings; Kent, Messieurs, Builders and Lime Merchants, 59, West-street; Kent, Sarah, Mantua-Maker, 6, Boyce's-lane; Keys, Susannah, Green Grocer, 14, Meeting House-lane; Killick, James, Sail-Maker, 7, Kent's-buildings; King, John, Grocer, 15, Russel-street; Kirby, John, Bottle Porter, Beer, Perry, and Cyder Vaults, Prince's-place; Knapp, Thomas, Builder, 18, Duke-street; Knight, Henry, Pastry-Cook, 98, North-street.

(L) Lacon, Mrs., Milliner, 18, Castle-square; Laffan and Shee, Tailors, Steyne; Lambert and Chapman, Stone-Masons, 4, Portland-yard; Lansdell and Moppett, Cabinet-Makers and Upholders, 6, East-street; Lashmar, Richard, Grocer and Draper, 15, Middle-street; Lashmar, John, Baker, 20, Ship-street; Lashmar, John, Grocer, 10, Little East-street; Last, John, Victualler (Little Castle), 3, Little Castle Square; Law, Henry, Hosier, 9, Castle-square; Law, Crossweller, and Co., London Carriers, 22, Little East-street; Leach, James, Victualler (Ship in Distress), 1, Middle-street; Leach, John, Builder, 6, Little Castle-street; Lee, William and Arthur, Printers, 44, North-street; Lee, William, Grocer, 17, New-street; Leffen, Thomas, Victualler (Catherine Wheel), 6, Pool-lane; Lennen, Charles, Tailor, 97, North-street; Looms, George, Grocer, 17, Church-street; Lucas, Richard, Tailor, 26, Ship-street; Lucas, John, Brewer, 56, Middle-street; Lynch and Tayler, Linen Drapers, 3, North-street.

(M) Maiben, Adam, Sadler and Harness-Maker, 93, North-street; Marchant, John, Schoolmaster, 2, Brighton-place; Marchant, Mary, Mantua-Maker, 2, Brighton-place; Marshall, James, Butcher, 25, Ship-street; Martin, Francis, Pastry-Cook and Confectioner, 33, East-street; Martin, John, Man's Mercer, &c., 30, North-street; Martin, Edward, Linen-Draper and Tailor, 91, North-street; Martin, Thomas, Cordwainer, 13, North-street; Martin, Lucy, Haberdasher, 22, North-street; Mascall, Thomas, Cooper, 19, Ship-street; May, James, Boat-Builder, 11, Margaret-street; Measor, Harry, Cordwainer, 25, Brighton-place; Measor, George, Hair-Dresser, 40, Ship-street; Measor, Thomas, Cordwainer, 41, Ship-street; Measor, Thomas, Cordwainer, 8, King-street; M'Kelvie, Hugh, Pastry Cook and Victualler, 8, Black Lion-street; Merle, Joseph, Victualler (One Tun), 52, Ship-street; Mighell, William, Grocer, 80, North-street; Moon, Francis, Grocer, 11, Little Castle-street; Moore, Elizabeth, Fruiterer, 8, East-cliffe; Moppett, Richard, Victualler (Greyhound), 64, East-street; Morling, Philip, Spruce Beer Brewer, North-street; Morling, John, Victualler (Coach and Horses), 23, North-street; Morris, John, Fruiterer and Green Grocer, 35, Brighton-place; Morris, Mesdames, Mantua and Fashionable Dress Makers, 35, Brighton-place; Morris, John, Tailor, 34, East-street; Myrtle, William, Butcher, 10, Little Castle-square; Myrtle, William, Tailor and Hatter, 11, Castle-square; Myrtle, John, Butcher, 12, West-street.

(N) Nevell, William, Baker, 20, Middle-street; Newbold, William, Linen-Draper, 15, North-street; Newington, Thomas, Tailor, 1, Portland-yard; Nightingale, Thomas, Glover and Breeches Maker, 3, North-street;

TRADESMEN.

Norris, John, Fruiterer and Green Grocer, 32, Brighton-place; Nye, George, Plumber and Glazier, 3, Brighton-place.

(O) Owen, Hugh, Baker, 3, Portland-yard.

(P) Paine, Cornelius, School-Master, 92, North-street; Paine, Richard, Drawing-Master and Stationer, 8, North-street; Paine, William, Porkman, 52, West-street; Pain, Richard, Victualler (Half Moon), 51, West-street; Paine, Thomas, Builder, 16, Brighton-place; Paine, John, Builder, 17, Brighton-place; Palmer, Thomas, Farrier and Blacksmith, 4, Mulberry-square; Palmer, George, Hatter, 20, East-street; Palmer, Richard, Tailor, 40, West-street; Palmer, John, Whitesmith and Bell-hanger, 21, New-street; Palmer, Edward, Whitesmith and Bell-hanger, 88, North-street; Pankhurst, William, Grocer, 13, West-street; Parker and Co., Cordwainers, 18, East-street; Peck, William, Victualler (Dolphin), 3, East-cliffe; Pelling, Thomas, Cordwainer, 14, West-street; Penfold, William, Grocer, 19, Duke-street; Penfold, William, Victualler (King and Queen), 1, North-row; Penticost, Thomas, Plumber and Glazier, 14, North-street; Philcox, John, Builder, 7, New Steyne-street, and Wheelwright, 4, Town-parade; Pickering, Mesdames, School-Mistresses, 41, West-street; Philps, Richard, Breeches Maker and Glover, 30, East-street; Philips, Thomas, Builder, 2, Margaret-street; Peircy, Henry, Liquor Merchant, 1, Duke-street; Piggott and Ustonson, Grocers, Tea Dealers, and Oilmen, 2, Castle-square; Pike, Philip, Cordwainer, 34, Brighton-place; Pilfold, William, Builder, 47, King-street; Pimm, William, Grocer and Green Grocer, 3, East-street; Piper, John, Fish-Monger and Merchant, 15, East-street; Pocock, John, Victualler (Hen and Chickens), 20, King-street; Pocock and Co., Boat-Builders, Russel-street; Pocock, Sarah, Mantua-Maker, 16, West-street; Pocock, Thomas, Builder, 33, Russel-street; Pollard, John, Corn-Chandler and Stable Keeper, 3, Town-parade; Pollard, Francis, Grocer, 26, Brighton-place; Postle, William, Hair-Dresser, 3, East-street; Poune, Stephen, Builder, 60, West-street; Poune, James, Builder, 17, Russel-street; Prior, Jeremiah, Baker, 1, Prospect-row; Prince, William, Organist and Music Master, 4, Prince's-place; Pullen, Isabella, School Mistress, 5, New-steyne.

(Q) Quartermain, William, Cordwainer, 9, Prince's-place.

(R) Richardson, George, Linen-Draper, 12, Castle-square; Rickworth, Barbara, School-Mistress, 48, West-street; Roberts, Beach, Tinman, &c., 3, Ship Street-lane; Roberts, George Foster, Earthen-ware Man, 11, West-street; Roberts, Henry, Fruiterer and Seedsman, 46, East-street; Robinson, Charles, Stay-Maker, 27, East-street; Roach, Thomas, Grocer, 38, West-street; Rolfe, John, Butcher, 4, East-street; Rudhall and Dudlow, Ironmongers and Braziers, 20, North-street; Russel, Richard, Butcher, 15, Brighton-place; Ruxton, Thomas, Sadler and Harness-Maker, 13, Castle-square.

(S) Salmon, Thomas, Gardener, 89, North-street; Samuel, Israel, Silversmith and Toyman, 22, East-street; Sanders, Samuel, School-Master, 45, West-street; Saunders, Edward, Victualler (Black Lion), 23, Black Lion-street; Saunders, Henry, Cooper, 49, Middle-street; Saunders, Hugh, Hair-Dresser, 2, Ship-street; Sayers, James, Muffin Manufacturer, 3, Castle-square; Shackleford, Thomas, Baker, 22, Black Lion-street; Shaw, Benjamin, Farrier, 5, George-street; Shoubridge, John, Corn-Chandler, 74, North-street; Short, Peter, Tailor, 48, Ship-street; Short, James, Tailor, 1, Castle-square; Shrivell, Thomas, Grocer, 27, King-street; Shrivell, Cornelius, Tailor, 5, Church-street; Sickelmore, Richard, Hair Dresser, 34, Ship-street; Sickelmore, John, Baker, 33,

New-street; Sickelmore, James, Grocer, 33, North-street; Simpson, Thomas, Cordwainer and Leather Cutter, 48, North-street; Skinner, Henry, Victualler (Spread Eagle), 28, East-street; Smith, Richard, Haberdasher, 53, West-street; Smith, Edward, Grocer, 12, East-street; Smith, John, Pastry-Cook and Confectioner, 4, North-street; Snelling, William, Collar and Harness-Maker, 6, Ship-street; Spencer, Christopher, Tea-Dealer and Basket-Maker, 16, East-street; Stent, William, Gardener, 8, Market-street; Stent, Hannah, Mantua-Maker, 16, Market-street; Stepney, George, Pastry-Cook and Baker, 24, Middle-street; Stepney, William, Cordwainer, 3, Boyce's-lane; Stevens, Michael, Porter, &c., 12, Market-street; Stone, John, Cordwainer, 24, East-street; Streeter, Richard, Baker, 50, West-street; Streeter, Edward, Baker, 57, North-street; Stiles, Harry, Surveyor and Auctioneer, 2, Prince's-street; Stiles, Hezekiah, Grocer and Cheese-Monger, 8, West-cliffe.

(T) Terry, Mark, Grocer, 1, Craven-buildings; Thompson, Jedediah, Blacksmith and Green Grocer, 21, North-street; Thompson, Jedediah John, Whitesmith and Bell-Hanger, 1, Poplar-row; Thompson and Patchen, Mantua-Makers, 4, West Street-lane; Thunder, Edward, Builder, 2, Poplar-row; Tierney and Co., Tailors, 10, Ship-street; Tilt, Thomas, Innholder (Castle), 19, Castle-square; Tolhurst, Mary, Mantua-Maker, 12, Middle-street; Townley and Adean, School-Mistresses, 62, West-street; Tugwell, William, Cordwainer, 51, Middle street; Tulley, William, Victualler (Seven Stars), 21, Ship-street; Tuppen, Henry, Butcher and Tallow Chandler, 11, Middle-street; Tuppen, William, Builder, 35, East-street; Tuppen, William, Builder, 29, Brighton-place.

(V) Vallance, Messieurs, Brewers, 6, West-street; Venner, Ambrose, Grocer, 31, Middle-street; Vine, John, Grocer, 9, New-street; Vine, Thomas, Grocer, 28, Ship-street; Viner, Joseph, Coach and Harness-Maker, 63, North-street; Verrall, William, Upholder and Tallow Chandler, 9, Nile-street.

(W) Wayte and Harben, School-Mistresses, 6, German-place; Walker, George, Broker and Appraiser, 29, North-street; Walker, Frances, Mantua-Maker, 29, North-street; Walker and Wheeler, Hair-Dressers, 48, Ship-street; Wallis, William, Victualler (Rising Sun), 68, East-street; Wallis, John, Victualler (White Lion), 75, North-street; Walls, Joseph, Blacksmith, 61, North-street; Washington, Lydia, Mantua-Maker, 45, North-street; Webb, Thomas, Victualler (Crown and Anchor), 4, Margaret-street; Westgate, Thomas, Victualler (Gardeners' Arms), 9, Church-street; Wheeler, James, Perfumer and Toy-Seller, 2, West-cliffe; Wheeler, Frances, Milliner, 1, Three Tuns-square; Whichelo, Elgate, Wine Merchant, 21, Middle-street; Whichelo, John, Brewer and Porter-Merchant, 39, Middle-street; Wigram, William, Plumber and Glazier, 2, Boyce's-lane; Wilmot, Richard, Cutler, 1, Ship-street-lane; Wilmshurst, Thomas, Watch-Maker and Silversmith, 7, North-street, and Leather Cutter, 19, Middle-street; Wingham, Baruch, Cordwainer, 21, West-street; Wisden, Simon, Blacksmith, 60, North-street; Williams, Richard, Tinman and Cutler, 31, Brighton-place; Williams, William, Stone-Mason, 25, East-cliffe; Williams, John, Tailor, 48, East-street; Witch, Henry, Victualler (Golden Cross), 2, Cross-street; Wolescraft, Mary, China and Glass Warehouse, 1, Brighton-place; Wood, Henry, Victualler (Carpenters' Arms), 46, West-street; Wood, Stephen, Builder, 13, Charles-street; Wood, James, Watch-Maker, 36, North street; Wright, John, Hair-Dresser, 13, Middle-street; Wymark, John, Baker, 2, Marlborough-row.

(Y) Yeates, John, Victualler (Wheat Sheaf), 19, New-street.

LODGING-HOUSES.

STEYNE.

No.	Proprietor.	Dg. Rm.	Parlors.	Bet. Bds.	Ser. Bds.
1	William Tuppen,	—		2	2	2
2	William Tuppen,	—		2	2	2

BLUE AND BUFF.

1	Richard Lashmar,	—		2	4	5
2	George Hemsley,	—		2	4	4
3	William Colbron,	—		2	4	4
4	Stephen Gourd,	—		2	4	4

NORTH PARADE.

3	Nicholas Johnson,	—	1	2	3	1
4	Nicholas Johnson,	—	1	1	3	3
5	William Leppard,	—		2	3	4
6	Elizabeth Downs,	—		2	3	4
7	Thomas Coates,	—		2	3	4
8	Ally Hillman,	—		2	3	4
9	William Lee,		1	2	4	4
10	George Wille,	—		2	4	4
11	Henry Piercy,	—		2	4	3
12	Ann Piercy,	—	1	2	4	4
13	Daniel Stableford,	—	1	2	4	4
14	William Wood,	..		2	3	4
15	Stephen Wood,	—	1	1	4	4

SOUTH PARADE.

1	Charles Wiick	—	1	2	4	5
2	Deborah Mighell,	—	1	2	4	5
3	James Poune,	—	1	2	4	5
4	Thomas Howell,	—	1	2	3	5
5	Henry Bathy,	—	1	2	5	5
6	Henry Piercy,	—	1	2	3	3
7	Thomas Knapp,	—	1	2	4	5
8	Thomas Panton,	—	1	2	4	4
9	William Reynolds,	—	1	2	4	4
10	Benjamin Pearce,	—	1	2	5	6
11	Stephen Wood,	—	1	2	5	6
12	Edward Thunder,	..	1	2	5	6
15	Nicholas Johnson,	—	1	2	3	5
16	Nicholas Johnson,	—	1	2	3	5

SOUTH ROW.

| 1 | James Gregory, | — | 1 | 1 | 6 | 6 |
| 3 | Richard Franks, | — | 1 | | 3 | 4 |

MARINE PARADE.

1	Richard Lashmar,	..	1	1	4	3
2	John Gallard,	—	1	1	4	3
3	John Pollard,	—	1	1	4	4
4	James Gregory,	—	1	1	4	3
6	Daniel Scully,	—	1	2	4	5
7	Donaldson & Wilkes,	—	1	2	4	6
8	Thomas Howell,	—	1	2	3	2
9	George Doncaster,	—	1	1	3	3
10	William Tuppen,	—	1	1	3	3

MARINE PARADE—(continued).

No.	Proprietor.	Dg. Rm.	Parlors.	Bet. Bds.	Ser. Bds.
11	Thomas Phillips Willis	1	2	4	4
12	Richard Spearing,	—	1	2	4	4
13	Isabella Pullen,	—	1	2	4	4
14	William Tuppen,	—	1	2	4	4
15	James Gregory,	—	1	2	4	4
16	Elizabeth Likeman,	—	1	1	3	3
17	Stephen Wood,	—	1	1	3	3
18	William Nodes,	—	1	2	4	4
19	Matthew Walker,	—	1	2	5	5
20	Matthew Walker,	—	1	2	5	5
21	Edward Thunder,	—	1	2	3	4
22	Edward Thunder,	—	1	2	3	4

ROCK BUILDINGS.

1	John Smith,	—		2	2	3
2	John Smith,	—		2	2	3
3	John Smith,	—		2	2	3
4	John Smith,	—		2	3	6

ROCK HOUSE.

| John Smith, | — | 1 | 3 | 3 | 6 |

NEW STEYNE.

1	Matthew Walker,	—	1	1	2	2
3	Sophia Belcher,	—	1	2	4	4
4	Isabella Pullen,	—	1	2	4	4
6	Matthew Walker,	—	1	2	4	4
7	Matthew Walker,	—	1	2	4	4
8	George Wood,	—	1	2	4	4
9	Christopher Ford,	—	1	2	3	3
10	Samuel Burton,	—	1	2	3	3
13	Elizabeth Downs,	—	1	2	3	4
15	Thomas Vine,	—	1	2	3	4
16	William Pilfold,	—	1	2	3	3

NEW STEYNE-STREET.

| 11 | Ann Stephens, | — | 1 | 2 | 2 | 2 |

YORK-STREET.

1	James Gregory,	—	1	1	3	3
4	Isaac Walter,	—		1	2	1
35	Ann Howard,	—		1	2	2
36	William Gallard,	—	1	2	2	2
37	James Gregory,	—	1	2	4	4

GERMAN-PLACE.

1	John Cunningham,	—		1	2	1
2	John Cunningham,	—		1	2	1
5	Isabella Pullen,	—		2	2	1
7	John Cunningham,	—	1	2	4	4

BROAD-STREET.

| 1 | Thomas Howell, | — | 1 | 2 | 9 | 6 |

LODGING-HOUSES.

BROAD-STREET—(continued).

No.	Proprietor.	Dg. Rm.	Parlors.	Bst. Bds.	Ser. Bds.
2	Thomas Howell,	—	1	2	3	2
3	James Greenfield,	—	1	1	3	3
4	William Alderton,	—	1	1	3	2
5	William Gallard,	—	1	1	3	2
6	James Greenfield,	—	1	1	3	2
7	William Russell,	—	1	1	3	2
8	Nicholas Johnson,	—	1	2	3	2
9	Abraham Leany,	—	1	1	3	2
10	John Garrett,	—	1	1	2	2
12	Frances Tuppen,		1	2	2
13	Richard Leggatt,	—		1	2	2
14	Thomas Andrews,	—		1	2	2
15	William Nodes,			2	2	4

CHARLES-STREET.

1	Henry Washer,	—	1	1	3	2
10	George Slade,	—	1	1	3	2
11	George Slade,	—	1	1	3	2

PROSPECT ROW.

2	Maria Chismer,	—		1	2	1
7	Isabella Pullen,	—	1	1	3	2
9	James Buckwell,	—		1	3	3
10	Thomas Vine,	—	1	1	3	3

CRAVEN BUILDINGS.

2	William Izard,	—	1	1	3	3
3	Thomas Webb,	—	1	1	3	3
5	Mary Eckley,	—	1	1	4	3

STEYNE-STREET.

| 1 | James White, | — | | 2 | 2 | 3 |

PRINCE's-STREET.

| 3 | Adam Maiben, | — | | 1 | 2 | 1 |

PAVILION PARADE.

1	Henry Winter,	—		2	4	3
2	Benjamin Pierce,	—	1	2	6	8
3	Thomas Knapp,	—	1	2	4	5
4	Peter Delasson,	—	1	2	3	6
5	Elizabeth Furner,	—	1	2	4	5
6	Colbron and Saunders		1	2	4	5
7	Anthony Lawson,	—	1	2	4	5
8	Colbron and Saunders	1	2	4	5

TOWN PARADE.

| 2 | John Pollard, | — | 1 | 2 | 3 | 3 |

NORTH BUILDINGS.

1	William Michell,	-	1	2	3	3
2	Charles Wick,	--	1	2	3	3
3	Thomas Bevis,	—	1	2	3	3
4	Thomas Bevis,	—	1	2	3	3
5	Jonathan Steele,	-	1	3	4	4

NORTH ROW.

| 12 | Elizabeth May, | — | | 1 | 2 | 2 |

NORTH ROW—(continued).

No.	Proprietor.	Dg. Rm.	Parlors.	Bst. Bds.	Ser. Bds.
13	Elizabeth May,	--		2	2	2
14	Edward Bevis,			1	2	1

MARLBOROUGH ROW.

1	Eleanor Sayers,	—	1	1	4	2
3	Richard Burton,	—	1	2	3	3
4	Ann Chisman,	—	1	2	3	3
5	John Stone,	-		2	4	6
6	John Stone,	—	1	3	6	6

EAST-STREET.

1	Thomas Howell,	—	1	2	4	3
39	James Jermyn,	--	1	1	4	4
40	John Hall,	—	1	1	2	1
41	Stephen Gourd,	—	1	1	3	3
52	Daniel Scully,	—	1	2	6	6
53	James Jermyn,	—	1	2	4	4
54	Thomas Beard,	—	1	1	3	2
56	Beach, Roberts,	—		2	3	4
59	Charles Lashmar,	—	1	2	4	5
60	Joanna Davis,	—	1	2	4	5
69	Kelsey and Comfort,	—		2	2	3

WARDEN's BUILDINGS.

| 2 | Martha Gresham, | — | 1 | 1 | 2 | 2 |
| 3 | Martha Gresham, | - | 1 | 1 | 2 | 4 |

BRIGHTON PLACE.

| 18 | Ann Paine, | — | | 1 | 2 | 2 |

MARKET-STREET.

| 7 | Thomas Paine, | — | | 1 | 2 | |

NILE-STREET.

4	Nicholas Elphick,	—		2	3	2
5	John Priest,	—		2	2	1
6	Frances West,	—		1	2	1
8	Mary Priest,	—		1	1	1

BLACK-LION-STREET.

| 24 | John Pankhurst, | — | 1 | 2 | 3 | 3 |
| 29 | ——— Townsend, | — | 1 | 1 | 4 | 2 |

NORTH-STREET.

10	John Glaisyer,	—	1	1	3	3
55	Joseph Chittenden,	—		1	1	1
58	Edward Streeter,	—		1	2	1
63	Joseph Viner,	-	1	1	3	2
94	George Grantham,	—	1	1	2	4
95	Daniel Holder,	—	1	2	4	2
104	Mary Moron,	—		2	4	2

SHIP-STREET.

| 3 | Sarah Daniel, | — | | 1 | 2 | 3 |
| 43 | Mary Davis, | — | | 3 | 5 | 4 |

MEASOR's GARDENS.

| 39 | John Rothwell, | — | | 1 | 2 | 2 |

LODGING-HOUSES.

MIDDLE-STREET.

No.	Proprietor.	Dg. Rm.	Parlors.	Bst. Bds.	Ser. Bds.
5	Charles Lind,	—	2	2	2
7	Edward Hill,	—	2	3	1
22	Henry Batley,	—	1	2	4	4
52	John Davis,	—	1	2	4	3
53	Mary Davis,	—		3	5	2

WEST-STREET.

No.	Proprietor.				
2	Thomas Bridger,	—		1	2	3
9	John Hilton,	—	1	1	4	3
19	Baruch Wingham,	—		2	3	3
25	Susannah Patching,	—		2	4	2
26	Elizabeth Kent,	—		2	4	4
44	Sarah Buckoll,	—		2	2	3
49	Richard Poune,	—	1	2	3	4
62	Stephen Poune,	—		2	5	7
63	James Gregory,	—	1	3	8	6
64	Esther Thrale,	—		2	3	6
67	Charles Budd,	—	1	1	3	3

WEST-STREET LANE.

No.	Proprietor.				
7	James Pledge,	—		1	2	2

RUSSEL-STREET.

14	Stephen Poune,	—	1	2	3	3
18	John Thomas,	—		2	3	2
21	James Patching,	—		1	2	2
35	Thomas Pocock,	—	1	2	3	3

ARTILLERY PLACE.

1	Nathan Smith,	—	1	2	3	4
2	Nathan Smith,	—	1	2	3	4
4	Nathan Smith,	—	1	1	3	4

ARTILLERY PLACE—(continued).

No.	Proprietor.	Dg. Rm.	Parlors.	Bst. Bds.	Ser. Bds.
5	Thomas Pocock,	—	1	2	4	4
7	Nathan Smith,	—	1	1	3	4

WEST BUILDINGS.

1	Ann Walls,	—		2	2	3
2	Joseph Walls,	—		2	2	3
3	Thomas Kent,	—		2	2	3
4	Mary Goldsmith,	—		2	2	3
5	Henry Wood,	—	1	2	3	3

WEST CLIFFE.

4	Joanna Davis,	—		2	3	2
11	James Leach,	—		2	3	5
13	William Pain,	—	1	2	4	3
17	Henry Winter,	—		2	2	3
22	Sarah May,	—		1	2	2
23	Sarah May,	—		1	2	2
24	Sarah May,	—	1	1	4	3
25	James Patching,	—	1	2	3	3
26	Isaac Levy,	—	1	2	3	3

EAST CLIFFE.

4	Thomas Howell,	—		2	2	3
5	Thomas Howell,	—		2	2	3
13	George Jenkins,	—		1	2	2
19	Matthew Bedding,	—		1	4	1
21	Tho. Phillips Willis,	—		5	3	3
22	Josiah Hawkins,	—		2	3	4
23	George Richardson,	—		1	2	1
25	Elizabeth Williams,	—	1	1	4	3
26	Ann Mansell,	—	1	1	1	2
27	John Hicks,	—		3	5	3

BOARDING-HOUSES.

Casey, Mary, 18, East-cliff.
Clifford, Daniel, 29, East-cliff.
Dennett, Sarah, 3, Steyne.
Kirby, Mary, 12, Charles-street.
Scrace, Sarah, 15, East-cliff.
Scully, Daniel, 1, North-parade.
Taylor, Willoughby William, 57, East-street.

LODGINGS.

STEYNE-LANE.

No.	Proprietor.	Dg. Rm.	Parlors.	Bst. Bds.	Ser. Bds.
1	Martha Cobby,	—		1	2

NORTH PARADE.

| 2 | Thomas Glaisyer, | — | 1 | 1 | 1 |

CROSS-STREET.

| 1 | James Vandergutch, | — | | 1 | 1 |

NEW-STEYNE STREET.

| 4 | Matthew Walker, | — | 1 | 1 | 5 |

MARGARET-STREET.

8	Edward Boxall,	—		1	1	1
9	Charles Gardiner,	—		1	1	1
10	Thomas Mockford,	—		1	1	1
12	George Edwards,	—		1	1	2

CHARLES-STREET.

2	Jonathan Beaumont,		1	2	1
3	James Newman,	—	1	2	1
4	Thomas Harman,	—	1	2	1
5	John Elam,	—	1	2	1
6	Mary Wille,	—	1	2	1
8	James Durrant,	—	1	2	1
9	George Slade,	—	1	1	1

PROSPECT ROW.

1	Jeremiah Prior,	—	2	3	2
3	John Saunders,	—	1	1	1
5	Elizabeth Parsons,	—	2	2	3

CRAVEN BUILDINGS.

1	Mark Terry,	—	1	3	2
6	Edmund Scott,	—	1	1	1
7	Susannah Stiles,	—	2	2	2
8	George Raggett,	—	2	2	2

MANCHESTER-STREET.

1	William Wood,	—	2	2	2
2	Ann Cord,	—	1	1	1
3	Daniel Scully,	—	2	3	4

STEYNE-STREET.

| 2 | George Wood, | — | 2 | 2 | 1 |
| 4 | Benjamin Pierce, | — | 1 | 3 | 3 |

PRINCE's-STREET.

1	William Tuppen, jun.		1	2	2
4	Richard Sayers,	—	1	1	1
5	Thomas Knapp,	—	1	2	1

TOWN PARADE.

| 1 | Ann Chisman, | — | 1 | 2 | 2 |

CHURCH-STREET.

No.	Proprietor.	Dg. Rm.	Parlors.	Bst. Bds.	Ser. Bds.
32	William Leppard,	—		1	1	1

MARLBOROUGH ROW.

| 2 | John Wymark, | — | | 1 | 1 | 1 |

EAST-STREET.

4	John Rolfe,	—		1	2	1
13	Edward Smith,	—		1	2	2
14	David Foster,	—		1	1	1
16	Christopher Spencer,	—	1	1	1
17	Mary Smith,	—		1	1	2
22	Israel Samuel,	—		1	2	2
24	John Stone,	—			1	
27	Charles Robinson,	—		1	1	
30	Richard Philps,	—		1	1	1
31	Robert Dix,	—		1	2	2
33	Francis Martin,	—		1	1	1
34	John Morris, jun.	—	1	1	1
36	Daniel Hack,	—		1	2	2
37	Peter Delassen,	—		1	1	1
43	William Cook,	—		1	1	1
44	Samuel Case,	—		1	2	4
45	William Henwood,	—	1	4	2
55	William Skinner,	—		1	2	1
62	Elizabeth Short,	—		1	2	
66	Edward Henwood,	—		1	1	1

CASTLE-SQUARE.

1	James Short,	—		1	1	
11	William Myrtle,	—			1	
12	George Richardson,	—	2	6	3
13	Thomas Ruxton	—		1	2	1

LITTLE EAST-STREET.

2	Thomas Bridger,	—		1	1	1
3	John Dumbrell,	—		1	2	
8	Ann Philcox,	—		1	2	1

BRIGHTON PLACE.

1	Mary Woolescraft,	—	1	1	1
2	John Marchant,	—	1	2	1
3	George Nye,	—	1	1	1
23	Thomas Fagan,	—	2	3	2
24	Daniel Stableford,	—	1	1	1
26	Francis Pollard,	—	1	1	1
27	James Feldwicke,	—		1	1
30	John Hughes,	—		1	1	1
31	Richard Williams,	—	1	1	1
33	Mary Roberts,	—	2	3	2
34	Philip Pike,	—		1	2	1
35	John Morris, sen.	—	1	3	3
36	Samuel Case,	—		1	3	2

MARKET-STREET.

| 2 | Mary Leach, | — | | 1 | 2 | |

LODGINGS.

MARKET-STREET (Continued).

No.	Proprietor	Dg. Rm.	Parlors	Bd. Bds.	Ser. Bds.
4	William Hind,	—	1	1	1
5	Joseph Brown,	—	1	1	1
6	John Dine,	—	1	1	1
13	Richard Venner,	—		1	1
14	Sarah Watts,	—	2	3	3

NILE-STREET.

| 1 | William Burt, | — | 1 | 3 | 1 |

BLACK-LION-STREET.

1	George Richardson,	—	1	2	3	5
2	Susannah Humphrey,	1	1	5	1
3	Samuel Brown,	—		1	1
8	Mary M'Kelvie,	—	1	3	1
14	Sarah Brapple,	—	2	3	2
30	Leah Hicks,	—	1	4	4
31	Thomas Nutley,	—	2	2	1
32	John Pollard,	—	2	2	1
33	William Carol,	—	2	2	1

NORTH-STREET.

5	James Irish,	—	1	3	1
6	Ann Tillstone,	—	2	2	6	6
7	Thomas Wilmshurst,	—	2	3	3
8	Richard Pain,	—	2	3	2
19	Jonathan Grenville,	—	1	3	4
12	William Dring,	—	3	3	3
13	Thomas Martin,	—	1	1	
23	Lucy Martin,	—	1	1	1
26	John Burfield,	—	1	3	3
29	George Walker,	—	1	2	2
30	John Martin,	—	1	2	1
31	John Collard,	—		1	1
32	John Hargraves,	—	1	3	2
35	John Newton,	—	.1	1	1
36	James Wood,	—	1	1	
38	John Gilburd,	—	1	3	1
43	Thomas Harmar,	—	1	2	1
60	Simon Wisden,	—	1	1	1
61	Joseph Walls,	—	1	2	1
62	George Hemsley,	—	1	1	1
74	Ann Greenaway,	—	1	3	1
79	William Mighell,	—	2	2	4
89	Thomas Salmon,	—	1	1	1

PORTLAND YARD.

| 1 | Thomas Newington, | — | 1 | 2 | 2 |

NEW-STREET.

1	Adam Maiben,	—	2	4	4
2	Thomas Tilt, jun.,	—	3	4	3
5	William Yeates,	—	1	2	4
13	Thomas Furner,	—	1	2	1
14	John Furner,	—	1	1	1
15	John Dawes,	—	1	1	1

KING-STREET.

| 29 | William Westgate, | — | 1 | 1 | 1 |
| 30 | William Piper, | — | 1 | 1 | 1 |

SHIP-STREET.

No.	Proprietor.	Dg. Rm.	Parlors	Bd. Bds.	Ser. Bds.
1	Mary Wells,	—	1	3	2
2	Hugh Sanders,	—	1	1	
9	Elizabeth Bull,	—	2	5	2
14	Alexander Baldey,	—	1	1	1
15	Harry Attree,	—	3	12	10
19	Thomas Mascal,	—	2	2	
23	Henry Burtanshaw,	—	1	1	2
25	James Marshall,	—	1	1	
26	Richard Lucas,	—	1	1	1
28	Thomas Vine,	—		1	
33	Mary Grover,	—	2	3	2
34	Richard Sicklemore,	—	1	3	1
35	Susanna Pollard,	—		2	
36	John Blease,	—	1	3	3
37	Emanuel Hyman Cohen,		1	2	1
39	John Walker,	—	1	2	1
40	George Measor,	—	1		
42	Ann Piercy,	—	2	2	2
44	Thomas Farmer,	—	2	4	3
51	Richard Brooker,	—	1	4	2

DUKE-STREET.

1	Henry Piercy,	—	1	3	2
3	Ambrose Venner,	—	1	2	1
8	Edward Thorpe,	—	1	2	
10	Thomas Wigram,	—	1	2	2
18	Thomas Knapp,	—	1	2	1
20	John Clarke,	—	1	1	1
22	Richard Burton,	—	1	2	1
23	Sarah Best,	—	1	3	1

MIDDLE-STREET.

6	Elizabeth Jones,	—	1	1	1
8	Edward Hill,	—	2	6	4
12	Mary Tolhurst,	—	1	2	1
14	Daniel Haylar,	—	1	1	
31	Ambrose Venner,	—	1	1	
34	John Buckman,	—	1	1	
41	Richard Humber,	—	1	2	2
44	John Hyde,	—	1	1	1
45	John Goddard,	--	1	2	2
46	Henry Blaber,	—	1	1	
47	Richard Hollands,	—	1	1	
55	Matthew Batho,	—	1	2	
57	John Lucas,	—	1	2	1

BOYCE's-LANE.

| 2 | William Wigram, | — | 1 | 2 | 2 |
| 10 | Michael Comber, | — | 1 | 1 | |

WEST-STREET.

11	George Foster Roberts,		1	2	1
12	John Myrtle,	—	1	2	1
13	William Pankhurst,	—	1	2	1
15	Richard Allen,	—	1	1	1
16	John Pocock,	—	2	2	3
17	William Reynolds,	—	1	2	2
23	Thomas Coates,	—	2	2	2
24	Robert Killick,	—	1	2	2
34	Mary Piper,		1	1	

LODGINGS.

WEST-STREET (Continued).

No.	Proprietor.	Dg. Rm.	Parlors.	Bst. Bds.	Ser. Bds.
52	Richard Smith,	—	1	1	1
55	Sarah Cousins,	—	1	1	1
59	Samuel Burton,	—	1	1	
60	Richard Kent,	—	1	1	1
61	Stephen Poune,	—	1	2	2
66	——— Cook,	—	1	4	4

RUSSEL-STREET.

1	Abraham Benjamin,	—	2	3	1
11	John Walder,	—	2	3	1
15	John King,	—	2	2	2
16	Cordelia Jones	—	1	1	1
17	James Poune	—	1	2	2
19	Mary Moron,	—	1	3	2
20	William Austen,	—	2	3	2
32	Allen Salvage,	—	2	3	1

KENT's-BUILDINGS.

5	Isabella Jackson,	—	1	1	1
6	Thomas Hillman,	—	1	1	1
7	James Killick,	—	2	1	1
8	Peter Davis,	—	2	1	1

ARTILLERY PLACE.

| 3 | Nathan Smith, | — | 1 | 2 | 1 |
| 6 | Henry James, | — | 1 | 2 | 1 |

WEST CLIFFE.

No.	Proprietor.	Dg. Rm.	Parlors.	Bst. Bds.	Ser. Bds.
1	Richard Gorringe,	—	2	2	2
5	Joanna Davis,	—	1	2	1
18	Mary Webber,	—	1	1	1
20	Hannah Smith,	—		1	
21	Thomas Dine,	—		1	1

EAST CLIFFE.

2	Ruth Curley,	—	2	2	1
17	Elizabeth Furner,	--	1	1	1
20	Matthew Bedding,	—	1	1	1

LITTLE-CASTLE-SQUARE.

| 2 | Moses Jacob Cohen, | — | 1 | 2 | 1 |
| 6 | Joseph Hughes, | — | 1 | 1 | |

POOLE LANE.

| 1 | Samuel Carden, | — | 1 | 1 | 1 |
| 2 | Mary Carden, | — | 1 | 1 | 1 |

THREE TUNS SQUARE.

1	Frances Wheeler,	—	1	3	
4	Michael Comfort	··	1	2	2
5	John Stone,	—	1	2	2

C

(18)

LIST of the *POSTS, POST-COACHES, STAGE-WAGGONS, CARRIERS*, and other *CARTS, &c., &c., &c.,* from BRIGHTHELMSTON to LONDON, &c., &c., &c.

—:o:—

POSTS.

POST-OFFICE on the STEYNE.

The LONDON MAIL is made up every Monday, Tuesday, Wednesday, Thursday, Friday *(not Saturday)*, and Sunday, at *Six*, and Letters are received until *Seven* o'Clock in the Evening.

The LEWES MAIL is made up every Evening (without exception) at *Six*, and Letters received until *Seven* o'Clock.

> The Towns of EAST-BOURNE, SEAFORD, HAILSHAM, and UCKFIELD, &c., and the Places adjacent, are from the Delivery of LEWES, and the Letters are sent daily.

> DITCHLING is also from the same Delivery, but the Letters are dispatched from LEWES only on Sundays, Wednesdays, and Fridays in the Morning.

The EAST-GRINSTEAD MAIL is made up every Evening (*Saturday* excepted) at *Six*, and Letters are received until *Seven* o'Clock.

> The Towns of CROYDON, BLETCHINGLY, GODSTONE, &c., are from the Delivery of EAST-GRINSTEAD, and the Letters sent daily.

> CUCKFIELD, CRAWLEY, LINDFIELD, and other Places immediately in that Neighbourhood, are also from the Delivery of EAST-GRINSTEAD, but only three days in the Week.

The SHOREHAM MAIL is made up every Evening before *Seven* o'Clock, and sets out early every Morning with Letters for SHOREHAM and WORTHING.

The STEYNING MAIL, on to ARUNDEL, CHICHESTER, PORTSMOUTH, GOSPORT, &c., &c., &c., is made up every Evening before *Seven* o'Clock, sets out early every Morning, and contains also Letters for STORRINGTON, MIDHURST, EMSWORTH, PETWORTH, BOGNOR, GODALMIN, GUILDFORD, PORTSEA, &c., and their immediate Neighbourhoods.

> HENFIELD, is from the Delivery of STEYNING, but only three Days in the Week.

The HURST MAIL is made up every Tuesday, Thursday, and Saturday Evening before *Seven* o'Clock, and is dispatched early every Wednesday, Friday, and Sunday Morning.

> ROTTINGDEAN, is from the Delivery of our Post-Master, who sends the Letters there daily.

☞ Letters for *Horsham* and the *North West* Extremity of the County, and for *Battle*, *Hastings*, and other Towns in the *Eastern* Extremity, pass through London.

COACHES.

LONDON POST-COACHES, by Messieurs Henwood, Crossweller, Cuddington, Pockney, and Harding, from the Coach-Office, No. 44, in the East-street, to the Blossoms-Inn, Lawrence-lane, Cheapside; and Hatchett's White Horse Cellar, Piccadilly; passing through *Preston, Patcham, Cuckfield, Crawley, Reigate, Sutton, Mitcham, Tooting, Clapham*, &c., &c., &c., set out in the Summer Season every Morning at Eight and Nine o'Clock, and arrive in London about Six o'Clock in the Evening.

LONDON POST-COACHES, by Boulton, Tilt, Hicks, Baulcomb, and Co., from the General Coach-Office, No. 1, in the North-street, for the Golden Gross, Charing-Cross; the Old White Horse Cellar, and Gloucester Coffee-House, Piccadilly; and Swan with Two Necks, Lad-lane; passing through the same Towns and Villages, set out in same Season, at the same Hours, and arrive in London about the same Time.

LONDON POST COACHES, by Boulton, Tilt, Hicks, Baulcomb, and Co., from the General Coach-Office, No. 1, in North-street, and for the same Inns, passing through *Lewes, Uckfield, Maresfield, East Grinstead, Godstone, Croydon,* and *Streatham*, set out in the Season every Morning, at Seven o'Clock, and arrive in London, about Five o'Clock in the Evening.

LONDON POST NIGHT-COACH, alternately from the Office, No. 44, in East-street, and No. 1, in North-street, by the *Cuckfield* Road, sets out every Evening in the Season at Ten o'Clock, and arrives in London about Seven o'Clock next Morning.

BATH, BRISTOL, CHICHESTER, and PORTSMOUTH POST-COACH, from the Old Ship in Ship-street, sets out every Tuesday, Thursday, and Saturday Morning, at Eight o'Clock, passing through *Shoreham, Arundel, Southampton, Salisbury, &c., &c.,* and returns on Mondays, Wednesdays, and Fridays.

LONDON COACH, from the Gun Inn, on the East Cliffe, sets out in the Season every Monday, Wednesday, and Friday Morning, at Seven o'Clock, for the Spread Eagle, in Gracechurch-street, passing through *Henfield, Horsham, Dorking, Leatherhead, Epsom,* &c., from whence it returns every Tuesday, Thursday, and Saturday Evening, at Six o'Clock.

WAGGONS.

LONDON STAGE WAGGON, by Bradford, through *Cuckfield, &c.,* sets out every Monday Evening from the Waggon Office, No. 47, East-street, and arrives at the Nags-Head Inn, in the Borough, every Wednesday Noon, from whence it immediately returns and arrives at the Brighton Office, every Friday Evening.

LONDON STAGE WAGGONS, by Law, Crosweller, and Co., through *Cuckfield,* &c., set out every Monday and Thursday Evening, from the General Waggon Office, No. 22, in Little East-street, for Hatchett's New White Horse Cellar, Piccadilly; Swan Inn, Holborn Bridge; and George Inn, in the Borough; and return from the New White Horse Cellar, Piccadilly; and the Swan Inn, Holborn Bridge, every Wednesday; and from the George Inn, in the Borough, every Saturday Evening.

LONDON STAGE WAGGONS, by Davis, through *Cuckfield*, &c., set out early every Tuesday and Saturday Evening, from the General Waggon Office, No. 52, in Middle-street, arrive at the Talbot Inn, in the Borough, and Harrison's Old White Horse Cellar, Piccadilly, every Monday and Wednesday Noon; return from Harrison's every Monday and Wednesday Noon; and from the Talbot Inn, every Tuesday and Thursday Morning early, and arrive at Brighton every Wednesday and Friday Evening.

LEWES WAGGON, by Messieurs Nicholas and John Elphick, sets out every Tuesday, Thursday, and Saturday Morning, at Seven o'Clock, from No. 3, in Nile-street, and returns the same Evening.

CARTS.

LEWES CART, by Edwards, sets out every Day about Three o'clock from the Greyhound, in East-street, and returns the next Morning about Twelve o'clock.

SHOREHAM CART, by Moorey, sets out every Day about Three o'Clock from the King's Head, in West-street, and returns the next Morning, about Twelve o'clock.

EASTBOURNE CART, by Erridge, through *Rottingdean, Newhaven, Seaford,* &c., sets out every Tuesday Morning, from the Gun Inn, on the East Cliffe, about Eight o'clock, and returns every Monday Evening about Six.

ROADS.

FROM BRIGHTHELMSTON TO LONDON,

BY LEWES.

	MILES.		MILES.
Falmer, ...	4¼	Fell Bridge, ...	2
Lewes, ...	3¾	New Chapel, ...	2
Uckfield, ...	8¼	Godstone, ...	6
Maresfield	2	Croydon, ...	9½
Nutley, ...	3¾	Streatham, ...	4½
Witch Cross, ...	3	London, ...	5
Forest-Row, ...	2½		
East-Grinstead, ...	2½		59

BY CUCKFIELD.

Preston, ...	1¾	Sutton, ...	10
Patcham, ...	1½	Mitcham, ...	3
Clayton, ...	3¾	Lower Tooting, ...	2
Cuckfield, ...	7	Upper Tooting, ...	½
Hand-Cross, ...	4½	Ballam, ...	1
Crawley, ...	4½	London, ...	4½
Horley, ...	4		
Ryegate, ...	6		54

FROM BRIGHTHELMSTON TO LONDON,

BY HORSHAM.

Henfield, ...	10	Epsom, ...	2½
Cowfold, ...	5	Ewell, ...	1½
Horsham, ...	6	Morden, ...	3¾
Capel, ...	7	Merton Abbey, ...	2¼
Dorking, ...	6	London, ...	7
Mickleham, ...	2½		
Leatherhead, ...	2		57
Ashsted, ...	1½		

FROM BRIGHTHELMSTON TO TUNBRIDGE WELLS,

BY LEWES.

Falmer, ...	5	Crowborough Beacon, ...	7
Lewes, ...	3	Tunbridge-Wells, ...	7
Uckfield, ...	8		30

OR ;

Lewes, ...	8	Tunbridge-Wells, ...	2
Maresfield, ...	10¼		
Groombridge, ...	13		33¼

FROM BRIGHTHELMSTON TO MARGATE,

ALONG THE COAST OF

KENT AND SUSSEX.

	MILES.
Rottingdean,	4
Newhaven,	5
Bishopstone,	2
Bletchington,	¾
Seaford,	¾
Eastdean,	5½
East-Bourn,	2½
Pevensey,	5½
Bexhill,	8
Hastings,	6
Gestling,	4
Winchelsea,	4
Rye,	3
Lydd,	12
Romney,	3
Hythe,	9
Sandgate Castle,	2
Folkstone,	2½
Dover,	8½
Ringswold,	6
Walme,	1½
Deal,	1½
Sandwich,	5
Ebb's Fleet,	2
Cliff's End,	1¼
St. Lawrence,	1½
Ramsgate,	¾
St. Peter's,	3
Margate,	3
	113½

FROM BRIGHTHELMSTON TO SOUTHAMPTON,

CONTINUED TO

BATH AND BRISTOL.

Hove,	2
New Shoreham,	4
Lancing Pad,	1
Arundel,	14
Chichester,	10
Portsmouth,	18
Southwick,	8
Wickham,	4
Southampton,	14
Rumsey,	7
Salisbury,	15
Deptford Inn,	11
Warminster,	11
Bath,	18
Bristol,	12
	149

FINIS.

A Peep into the Past, &c.

E BRIGHTHELMSTON DIRECTORY FOR 1800.

A Peep into the Past, &c.

THE BRIGHTHELMSTON DIRECTORY FOR 1800.

INTRODUCTION.

AN OCTOGENARIAN has not often an opportunity of seeing a portrait of himself in childhood. If such should occur, he would doubtless be astonished at his presentment: so diminutive, so quaintly dressed, and with surroundings which, if once familiar and pleasing, he has long affected to despise. As with an individual portrait, so with that of a town. Contemporaneous descriptions of a town, so long back as three-quarters of a century, do not often come to light, and, when they do, one may well feel astonished at the details presented—at the many and almost inconceivable changes between past and present—and especially in a town of such rapid and vigorous growth as Brighton.

It was with some such feeling that we saw a rare local work —"THE BRIGHTHELMSTON DIRECTORY FOR 1800. By Edward Cobby. Brighton: Printed by W. and A. Lee. Price, 2s. 6d." The work is printed in demy 8vo., and contains, in all, with the Roads, &c., 52 pp. There are in it, however, so many interesting particulars respecting the old town, the inhabitants, their pursuits, amusements, &c., in conjunction with other local facts, that we shall make no apology for giving our readers an idea of its contents, coupled with such additional information as may be gleaned from early historical publications and from other sources.

First, of the town itself. It is well known that at the period when the Directory was issued, and for a long time previously, the opinions of visitors were freely expressed respecting Brighton, and, though contradictory in some instances, many are the reverse of flattering. One, so early as 1736, says, he "lived almost underground." Another, in Dr. Russell's time, 1747-59, describes Brighton houses as "consisting of one or more stories, and with the doorways so low that you must stoop to enter, and then, probably, stumble down a step or two into the sitting room."* In 1766, one Dr. Coe calls Brighton a "small, ill-built town," resorted to "by the gay and polite on account of the company which frequent it. * * * Through the recommendation of Dr. Russell, it has become one of the principal places in the kingdom." (It had, then, six streets!) "A Diary" of an

---

* Some few specimens of old Brighton houses still exist: There are two or three in Marlborough-place (formerly North-row), and another just below the *Brighton Examiner* office; but all are somewhat modernised. In addition to having to go down a step or two into these houses, the doors almost invariably open into the front-room, subjecting one, as a lady once remarked,

Excursionist to Brighton in 1778 says:—"This town is built on spots, in patches, and for want of regularity does not appear to advantage; every man, as to building, seems to have done what appeared right in his own eyes. * * * Brighthelmston was only a small obscure village, occupied by fishermen, till silken folly and bloated disease, under the auspices of a Dr. Russell, deemed it necessary to crowd the shore and fill the inhabitants with contempt for their visitors." Dunvan (author of the "History of Lewes and Brighthelmston") says, so lately as 1795:—"In summer, Brighthelmston too frequently becomes the chief receptacle of the vice and dissipation which the sickening metropolis disgorges into our watering-places at this season;" and he then laments "the inadequacy of the High Constable and two headboroughs "to preserve the order and safety of the town amidst such a medley!"

We might multiply such quotations *ad nauseam*. But away with them! Let us hear the *true* character of the town from "One of Ours." Let us call "Edward Cobby," the Compiler of the "BRIGHTHELMSTON DIRECTORY FOR 1800," into Court, and hear *his* evidence. *Ex. gr.*:—

"☞ The nearest Watering-place to London, BRIGHTHELMSTON, has long been the most frequented, and it is now, without Exception, one of the most fashionable Towns in the Kingdom. The Improvements IN IT have kept pace with the Patronage OF IT; uniting in itself the Retirement of a Country Village with the Gaiety of the Metropolis; and, possessing every advantage of situation, it may dispute with any Town in England the Credit of best accommodating its Visitors in every Thing which can contribute to their Health, their Comfort, and their Amusement. It is quiet without dulness, busy without noise, and fashionable without a Court."

The last sentence is worthy of Dr. Johnson himself; and may possibly have been found among the waste-paper of that lover of antithesis after a visit at Mrs. Thrale's, in West-street! One cannot, however, help smiling at the description of Brighton in 1800, by its latest trumpeter, Mr. Cobby, and especially when one reflects what it really must have been, with its 17 or 18 irregularly-built streets, intersected by lanes, twittens, &c.; its 1,500 houses, not a few of which were built in old Brighton style; its two hotels and half-a-dozen boarding-houses; its small dimensions; and without a continuous carriage-road along its sea-frontage, even between streets so near to each other as East-street and West-street, where, if a carriage was required to pass from the former to the latter, it must needs go up Middle-street, and through what is now called South-street,—then West-street-lane.

But we will not be hard upon our friend Cobby. We have too much to thank him for in other respects. He was only, in the above passage, doing what hundreds of his fellow-townsmen have done since,—and what we do now,—namely, offering our

---

to the "inconvenience of not being 'out' to any visitor." There are some "originals," with over-hanging stories, in Black Lion-lane. But more interesting to the archæologist is the old gabled house, with over-hanging storey on corbelled support, situated in Meeting-house-lane; an unique illustration of "Old Brighton."

wares to our customers to the best advantage: *his* merchandize being the town itself. His facts, however, have more interest for us; and, with the one exception just quoted, his book is wholly made up of interesting facts. Here are a few which he gives, illustrative of the growth of the town :—

"Previous to the year 1770, the town consisted of only Seven principal streets, and of less than 600 houses. The number of inhabitants was then about 2,500. In 1794 there were fifteen streets, the number of Houses was upwards of 1200, and the number of inhabitants 5,600. (The actual number was 5699.) The present Town (in 1800) consists of Eighteen streets, containing about 1,500 houses, and the number of inhabitants is estimated at 7,000 and upwards." (The Census of 1801 gives it 7,339.)

Rapid, however, as was the growth of the little town in the 24 years (1770-94) above-mentioned, during which the population more than doubled, it was far outstripped by the next 27 years (1794-1821), when it was more than quadrupled! increasing from 5,669 to 24,429. What would have been the Compiler's wonderment if he could have looked "adown the stream of time" to the Year of Grace 1879—a little more than three-quarters of a century from the date of his Directory,—and have foreseen that the town (excluding Hove and Preston) would contain 100,000 inhabitants; that the houses, inhabited and uninhabited, numbered no less than 15,809, with an estimated rental of over half-a-million sterling; that the streets were between 600 and 700 in number, one alone (Western-road, non-existent in his day,) containing 286 houses; the places for Divine Worship 80; and the various Charitable Institutions 69. That Hove and Preston (out-lying villages in the year 1800, nearly two miles distant from Brighton,) had each in 1879 become so closely united to it by "bricks and mortar," that it is difficult to tell where the one ends or the other begins; that Preston had, for Local Government and School Board purposes, become absorbed into it; and that the three now formed one Parliamentary, as they should one Municipal, borough.*

---

* With the view of affording a clear idea of the growth of Brighton, both in population and in houses and the rateable value of the latter, we append the following table :—

BRIGHTON.	1761	1770	1794	1801	1811	1821	1831	1841	1851	1861	1871	1879
Population	2000	About 2550	5699	7339	12012	24429	40634	46661	65569	77693	90011	Approximate 99522
Houses	..	..	600	1233	1282	2077	3947	7700	8137	10943	13339	15376	15809
House Assessment	..	In 1784 £2304	In 1791 £3740	..	In 1814 £5790	..	..	£ 280050	£ 292113	£ 341249	£ 414067	£ 528899

As showing also the increase in value of property in Brighton "past and present," it may be mentioned that the highest house assessment in Brighton in 1757 was forty shillings; in 1879 the highest is £3,280, nearly as much as that of the whole town in 1791.

[The return for 1881 is—Population, 99,049; assessments, 18,465; rateable value, £605,412 5s. For 1891—Population, 102,699; assessments, 19,903; rateable value, £627,940 15s.]

Let us now glance at some of the details of what may be deemed the "Directory" proper. Their classification is intelligible, though not very clear in definition. For instance, a list is given of the "Principal Residents" and of the "Principal Inhabitants." These terms are generally regarded as synonymous; but here "Residents" must be understood as applying to those who had houses in the town, in which they resided during the season; and "Inhabitants" to those who were permanent residents. The season in Brighton was, formerly, from June to September; ending, in fact, where it now begins; and though the "Directory" bears no date, we should infer that it was published *out of the season*, as the "Residents," or those whom we should now call Visitors, are (if we except official gentlemen) exactly *ten* in number. They include H.R.H. the Prince of Wales, the Duke of Marlborough, Lord Viscount Torrington, Lord Carrington, the Ladies Caroline and Emily Harvey, Sir Godfrey Webster (who lived at the Wick), Sir Robert Batson Harvey, Lady Shelley, and Sir John Bridget. Amongst the official gentlemen named, precedence is given to the "Master of the Ceremonies," W. Wade, Esq.; following whom are the Magistrates acting for the County, Sir Godfrey Webster and Charles S. Dickens, Esq., with Mr. Wm. Attree, "their Clerk." *
The Deputy Judge Advocate was James Charles Michell, Esq. †
The Barrack Master was Lieut.-Colonel Moore (who used to Drill the Volunteers on the ground behind the Old Battery House, Artillery-place, the men using faggot-sticks !) The principal Coast Officer was Peter Simon, Esq.; Andrew Sproule, Esq., being Commander of the Sea Fencibles (Volunteers), who were accustomed to exercise with boarding-pikes in Belle Vue Field, now Regency-square.

The "Principal Inhabitants" given are *seventeen* in number. Of these, seven were Clergymen, including the Vicar, the Rev. Thomas Hudson, who was appointed in 1789, and who was instrumental in building the Chapel Royal, in Prince's-place, the first Chapel-of-Ease in the town. The others were the Rev. John Dring, the Curate (who ministered at the military execution of Cooke and Parish, of the Oxford Militia, in Goldstone Bottom, in 1795, and who never afterwards recovered the shock to his nerves); the Rev. W. Barnes, the Rev. B. Bray, the Rev. F. Hamilton, the Rev. T. Rice, and the Rev. W. Tilt. The last (the son, we believe, of Mr. Tilt, of the Castle Tavern,) happened to be in France when war was declared, and was

---

* Mr. Attree (one of the founders of the firm now known as Clarke, Howlett, and Turner) was also Vestry Clerk, receiving the appointment at a Vestry Meeting held at the Old Ship, Jan. 13, 1790; the salary being 10 guineas per annum, increased, in 1805, to 30 guineas. Mr. Somers Clarke, who, on his partner's death in 1830, was elected to succeed him in the office, still holds it, returning thanks for the appointment at the last Easter Vestry Meeting for the 50th time.
[At Easter, 1891, Mr. Clarke was elected as Vestry Clerk for the 61st time. He entered upon his 90th year on the 21st July following.]

† Mr. Michell, who resided for many years at 58 (now 63), East-street, re-edited, in 1829, Dr. Relhan's *Short History of Brighthelmstone*, adding many valuable and interesting notes. Dr. Relhan's second wife, Lady Hart (the widow of Sir William Hart, a London banker), built, we believe, 58, East-street, for her summer residence; and there the Doctor and Lady Hart annually passed some months until his death in 1776.

MRS. THRALE'S HOUSE IN WEST STREET.
(Formerly opposite "The King's Head.")

for some time a French *détenu*, but, being small and delicate looking, he subsequently escaped in woman's clothes. The lay "Inhabitants" include several more or less known, as W. K. Alder, Esq., J. Batchelor, Esq., John Chapman, Francis Hanson, Esq., Charles Heath, Esq., Philip Mighell, Thomas Mitten, William Nodes, James Read, and Roger Welsford, Esq.

The list of "Professions," as it is called, is, like the "Inhabitants," not a very lengthy one. It contains five attorneys, three academicians, one artist, one portrait painter, one physician, nine surgeons, and two banking firms; in all 22. The banking firms were Shergold, Michell, Rice, Rice, and Mills, who kept the Old Bank, at 103, North-street (now the Royal Library); and Rickman, Wigney, and Co., who kept the New Bank, at 2, Steine-lane, an entrance to which was also in Castle-square. Both Banks have for some years ceased to exist; the former in Feb., 1826, and the latter (then in East-street, where the Avenue now is,) in 1842. The attorneys included Messrs. William and John Attree, of 8, Ship-street; Mr. Henry Brooker, who for a long period carried on his profession in the office where the *Brighton Herald* is now published (and where until lately one of the oldest windows bore his name, scratched on with a diamond); Mr. Joseph Hughes; and Mr. James Charles Michell, of 58, East-street. The one physician was Dr. Richard Henderson, a very popular gentleman, who, at a Vestry Meeting, held at the Unicorn Inn, February 10, 1794, was presented with a pint silver cup, for his care and attention to the parish. Among the surgeons were several who were well-known up to a comparatively recent date, as Mr. Richard Newnham, of Steine-lane; Mr. Robert Dix, of East-street; Mr. John Hall (head of the subsequent firm of Hall, Bond, Brewster, and Seabrook), of 105, North-street (where the Capital and Counties Bank now is); and Mr. John Hargraves (latterly of West-street, occupying the house once belonging to Mrs. Thrale, pulled down prior to the erection of the Grand Concert Hall). The others were Mr. Thomas Guy, East Cliff; and Messrs. Kipping, Pankhurst,[*] and Barrett, of West-street. The academicians were Mr. William Brook (West-street) and Mr. Cornelius Paine (North-street). The one local artist, Mr. W. Austin,

---

[*] Mr Pankhurst was one of the four medical men who, when the town (in 1786) was ravaged with the small-pox, assisted at the general inoculation ordered at a Vestry Meeting. The 1,887 persons who escaped the disease were inoculated, the charges being :—the poor, servants, and day labourers, 2s. 6d. each ; other persons, 7s. 6d. It was a common practice at that period, and for some years previously, for persons to be inoculated and "conducted through the distemper" at the houses of medical men. One Dr. Cooper Sampson, of Ditchling, was among the earliest of such practitioners whom we read of. In 1758 and several subsequent years he made known to the world through the *Sussex Weekly Advertiser* his success as an inoculator—"not one of his patients having any bad symptoms, which are usual in the natural small-pox." His fee was 4gs., he "finding all manner of necessaries, or if patients chuse to find their own *wine, tea, and sugar*, 3½gs." He was "to be spoke with every Saturday at the White Horse and Verral's Coffee House in Lewes;" at the Inns of various places in the County; and at those in "Brighthelmston every Thursday, where Messages are taken in." The old Doctor must have done well out of inoculation; for he tells us that in two seasons (1760-61) he inoculated, in 33 different places in the County, 92 persons (in Brighthelmston, 8, the highest but two in the list). A Mr. Dennet, of Storrington, advertised in 1774 that "his house is constantly open for the

resided in Russell-street—then a fashionable locality! and the one portrait painter,* Mr. E. Scott, at 6, Craven-buildings, a locality which does not now exist,—at least, in name. The "professional" list concludes with a calling so peculiar that we must give it in its entirety :—

"Smith, Nathan, Inventor, Patentee, and Operator of an Air Pump for Extracting the Gout, &c., 3, Artillery-place."

As we have never heard of a successor to this worthy benefactor of the human race, possibly his invention was known only to himself, and that, when he died, his pump was probably buried with him!

Following next in order, the "Directory" gives a list of the Parish Officers in 1800, a list interesting, in more respects than one, to old Brightonians :—

HIGH CONSTABLE—Cornelius Paine, North-street.
HEADBOROUGHS—*Old:* Thomas Paine, John Martin, Philip Morling, Thomas Mascall. *New:* Simon Wisden, Jonathan Grenville, Thomas Pentecost, John Gilburd.
CHURCHWARDENS—Stephen Poune, John Baulcomb, William Chapman.
OVERSEERS—*Old:* Benjamin Pierce, Thos. Newington. *New:* Jonathan Steele, Adam Maiben.
ASSESSORS OF TAXES—Charles Rudhall, William Gates.
COLLECTOR OF ASSESSED TAXES—William Gates, 16, Ship-street.
SURVEYORS OF THE TOWN AND COLLECTORS OF THE TOWN RATE—Four Commissioners of the Town.
SURVEYORS OF THE HIGHWAYS—*Old:* John Stone, Three Tunnsquare ; Philip Vallance, West-street. *New:* Daniel Hack, East-street ; James Patching, Russel-street.
COLLECTORS OF THE HIGHWAY TAX—Daniel Hack, James Patching.
MASTER OF THE WORKHOUSE—John Sicklemore.
TOWN CRYER AND BEADLE—Thomas Waring, 3, East-street.

---

reception of patients; who are safely conducted through the distemper, and accommodated with all necessaries for three weeks, *tea and sugar included*, for two guineas." There was "competition," it appears, in the olden time, even in inoculation ; as Messrs. Saunders and Sutton, of Framfield, charged 5gs., 4gs., and 3gs., respectively (*tea, sugar, and wine excepted*). Certainly, patients of the latter were treated according to the "SUTTONIAN SYSTEM," whatever that might have been, and were conducted through the distemper with "chearfulness, ease, and safety."

* What the distinction is between an artist and a portrait painter, we are at a loss to conceive. Perhaps Mr. Cobby meant to convey that Mr. Austin was a landscape painter. Poor Austin! His career experienced a sad close. He was a pupil of Bickham, and practised in London about the middle of the 18th century ; exhibiting at the Academy in 1776. Subsequently he resided in Brighton, where he died in 1820, in extreme poverty, in his 80th year. We have seen a letter sent by him, dated 1817, from "Oxford-place, on ye Levell, No 10, Brighton, Sussex," and addressed "To ye Gentleman, ye Name lost, who Belongs to ye Itallion, French, and English Print Warehouse, near Pall Mall, Chairing Cross, London." In this letter he says he has kept his room above 30 weeks, has lost his sight, is sadly distressed for want of assistance to keep him alive, &c., and thus touchingly concludes :—" Now, my good Blessed Freindly Man, Pray assist me a little, to help me to live a little longer, as I have lost By Death a good many Friends, and whatt is left are gone to France and Itally. Pray strech a Point to help me ; for I never thought to be so Poor. But great losses and long illness, and fammily ; and God blessing for your Charity and my Prayers I hope will make you amends."

It will, perhaps, provoke a smile among modern Brightonians—familiar with the elaborate machinery of Municipal government in all its multiplicity of detail—the various officials and their departments—rate collectors, police, &c., &c.—to see on what limited a scale their forefathers managed town affairs: four of the Commissioners acting as Town Surveyors and collecting the town-rate; the Surveyors of the Highways being also the collectors of the highway-tax; and the collector of the assessed taxes being one of the Assessors! It is not shown whether or no the Overseers collected the poor-rate; but it is probable that each filled his office, and all performed their duties, gratuitously,—at all events, down to 1808, when Mr. Jonathan Grenville (Headborough in 1800) was formally appointed poor-rate collector "at a compensation of 3d. in the £ on all monies collected; the appointment to be discretionary in the 'Breast' of the Parish Officers." The inhabitants were ignorant of police, watch, and other such like rates, which present Brightonians may be supposed to luxuriate in. The supervision of the town was then chiefly performed by the High Constable and his Headboroughs; the duties at night being carried out by one or two watchmen—"Old Charlies,"—one of whom, in winter time, acted as bell-man, perambulating the town and proclaiming hourly in most lugubrious tones the time of night or morning and the state of the weather, a custom which did not fall into desuetude till near 1830.* Not the least important individual in the list of Parish Officers is the last—the Town Crier and Beadle, † who, when fully attired *en règle*—in cocked hat and other insignia of office—doubtless considered himself, and was considered, the concentrated embodiment of parochial authority. By an entry in the Parish Vestry Book, under date March 31st, 1800, his appointment and duties are thus set forth :—

"That Mr. Thomas Waring be appointed Beadle and Cryer at a salary of Twenty Pounds and Cloathes. It is understood that his duty is to make the Poor Books, the Church Books, the Surveyor's Book, and the Town Book. He is also to attend the North and West Galleries of the Church on Sundays. He is to go round the town with the Officers to make the Militia List, and is likewise to officiate as Headborough in the town; but not elsewhere, and to be sworn for the purpose."

---

* "Poss" Lynn, a fisherman, for many years officiated as the local Dogberry; and, without taxing the memory of the "oldest inhabitant," many, doubtless, recollect his matutinal cry of "Past four o'clock and a cloudy morning" (or "fine," as the case might be). "Poor old Poss Lynn!" In the latter years of his official life his custom was to make a Christmas call on the principal inhabitants for a "remembrancer." At such times he wore a tall black shiny leather hat, around which was tied a piece of paper, bearing some such doggerel as the following : -

"Men and maids arise,
Make your puddings and your pies,
A merry Christmas and happy New Year,
And when you die to heaven to steer.
Remember poor old Poss Lynn."

† The office of Town Crier fell into desuetude in Brighton in 1877, on the death of Giles, junior.

With such a salary and such multifarious and onerous duties, Mr. Thomas Waring's office was no sinecure *; but, probably, the Parish Officers were not unmindful of the "Order of Vestry," passed two or three years previously, in 1796 :—

"All vagrants and beggars are to be apprehended by the Crier, who is to receive a shilling a head for their capture."

A substantial addition this to his salary, possibly; and, as beggar-hunting was profitable, doubtless the town enjoyed considerable immunity from vagrants. Perhaps the local Charity Organization Society will take a hint.†

THE TOWN IN 1800.

The old "Directory" tells us that,—

"In 1800, Brighton consisted of Eighteen Streets, containing about 1,500 Houses, and the number of Inhabitants is estimated at 7,000 and upwards."

Those familiar with Brighton at the present time—with its nearly three miles of sea frontage, and its streets and houses stretching east, west, and north to districts which, even some 40 or 50 years ago, would have been scarcely conceivable—will perhaps smile at the Compiler's summary of its extent, &c., in 1800,—so brief, yet comprehensive. Eighteen streets! He does not count as such the

---

* It appears to have been a failing with our forefathers to make their officials earn their salaries. Erredge gives a quotation from the Vestry Book in 1707, which is as follows:--"John Mockford appointed Clerk at Church; part of his duty is to *wash the Church linen* and scour the Church plate."

† What punishment was accorded to beggars, when apprehended, deponent sayeth not. Like "Poor Tom," they may have been "whipped from tything to tything;" or "stocked, punished, or imprisoned," according to ancient law; for, by 1st James I., a beggar was to be "stripped naked, from the middle upwards, and to be whipped until his body was bloody, and to be sent from parish to parish, the next straight way to the place of his birth." Certain it is that this cruel Statute was put in force in Brighton so lately as July, 1819, when *(vide Brighton Herald)* the judicial business commenced by three vagrants being brought up and ordered, by the sitting Magistrates, "*to be flogged until their backs were bloody.*" The sentence (it is added) was put into execution next day; but, from the Beadle's deficiency of practice in such exercise (not, we suppose, from any desire on the part of the Magistrates to mitigate the sentence) the flagellation was comparatively light. The excuse, however, given for the punishment is, to say the least, very singular:—"This mode of punishing these beggars was adopted, *because symptoms of fever displayed themselves in the House of Correction! and which have rendered it necessary to enlarge all the vagrants confined therein.*" In Lewes the same punishment had been inflicted from an early period; for, in 1617, says Dunvan, "John Taylor, a native of Halden, in Kent, was whipped at Lewes, *according to law,* for begging in the town, and sent home with a written testimonial of his hospitable reception, though the deep characters of *tyrannizing legislation,* not *justice,* on the poor fellow's back, might have saved the writer's trouble;" and in January, 1782, one J. O'Brien, for "repeated acts of vagrancy," was sentenced to three months in the House of Correction, and "at the expiration *to be publicly whipped at the Market-place,* and then discharged."

lanes, &c., or the localities where the old pioneers in building had begun their work; still, contrasted with the town of some 20 or 30 years before (in 1779), Brighton had more than doubled its houses

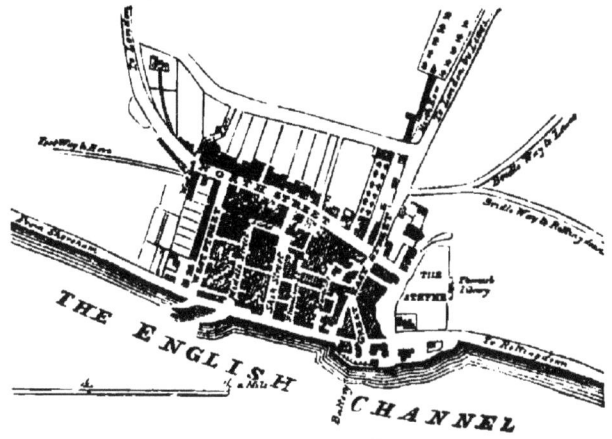

BRIGHTON—1779.

and its population. Within that period the "small obscure village" had undergone a complete transformation, and had come to be regarded as one of the "most fashionable towns in the Kingdom." Granted that in the older parts of the town the houses were meanly and irregularly built, in several places, particularly in the neighbourhood of the Steine and eastward (on the Marine-parade), houses of a better class and more pretentious architectural character had begun to be erected; consequently (apart from its having become the resort of Fashion *par excellence*), Brighton in 1800 could not have been deemed an unattractive place of residence. It was, in fact, a large country village by the sea; and a rural or marine walk or drive was equally open to the visitor, as choice dictated. If rural, where, within such easy access, was such a glorious and apparently limitless sweep of Downs open to him, over which he could roam at will without let or hindrance? Certainly, the central piece of sea-frontage in 1800 did not afford such an opportunity as now for a carriage-drive: its extent was only about ten furlongs!—from what is now Markwell's Hotel to the bottom of Middle-street; but, once through Middle-street-lane, and beyond West-street, there was little cause for complaint. The visitor, too, could wander where he listed by beach or cliff, east or west, having, in either direction, an uninterrupted sea view open to him, as well as more particularly to the west, a pleasing and diversified landscape of almost unlimited extent. Even from some parts of North-street a wide expanse of the Downs was visible; for, standing above Ship-street, the Race Stand could be easily seen. Then, what a glorious view of sea and land was presented from the old Parish Churchyard! the old town, with its sea front and rural surroundings, lying within its narrow limits at your feet.

A more detailed glance at the dimensions of the town in 1800, as pictured in the Map which forms the frontispiece to the old "Directory," will not be without interest, if only for the opportunity it affords of comparison with Brighton in 1879, and showing as it does the rapidity with which the town has grown and the immense area which has been covered with buildings in three-quarters of a century.

Beginning at the West. In 1800 Russell-street formed the western boundary of the town. There were no buildings beyond, except Artillery-place (in front of the West Battery, on which eight guns are indicated,) and the few mansions along the sea-frontage, the more westerly being "Belle Vue." There was not a single building west of St. Nicholas Church, between the western and north-western boundaries of the parish (we might also add, up to Hove); the only place indicated on the Map is a road "To Wick" (the Chalybeate). Old St. Nicholas is away from the town, on the hill, with the old chalk-pit,—filled in when the present Upper North-street was formed, —immediately to the south-west of it. What is now Western-road (the road "To Wick") was then little more than a foot-path to Hove; and there were then no roads between this foot-path and the Sea. The only carriage road from North-street, by the Church, was that "To Henfield" (and Steyning, to London); the present Dyke-road, which forms a junction with this road beyond Hove Place (formerly the residence of the late Mr. Bright Smith), did not exist.

Turning to the North. From Air-street (now Queen's-road) to East-street (the road now running through the Pavilion Grounds) the old Map shows only two thoroughfares leading from North-street to Church-street, namely, King-street and New-street (now Bond-street). All below Air-street to King-street is blank, except that "Hick's Garden" is shown as being at the back of the White Lion; but, between King-street and New-street, Mulberry-square and Jew-street —each a *cul-de-sac*—are indicated. To the east of New-street is Furner's Garden (now New-road), and abutting on to it eastward is "Promenade Grove," near which are the Quakers' Meeting House, the Chapel Royal, and Prince's Place; and to the north-east is the "Riding School." On the eastern side of East-street, the only places named are the Castle Tavern (and Castle-square), the Pavilion, and the Duke of Marlborough's. Beyond Church-street, northward,—from North-row at the bottom, to the "Road to Henfield" at the top,—all is nameless but two places; Hick's Garden, opposite that at the back of the White Lion, and Elmore's Stables, opposite King-street.

In the centre of the town, the old Map affords no indication of the Enclosures. Where Marlborough-place now is, there are some houses (including the "King and Queen") designated as North-row; and the few others beyond this (facing south and in a line with the present North-road) were then the extremity of the town northward! There are no other buildings in this direction, except two or three opposite the "King and Queen," on what is now the Grand-parade, but then known as the "Town Parade." The only buildings in 1800 running from what is now Edward-street (then the "bridle way to Rottendean") into St. James's-street, are those of George-street, which only extend about half way up. Just above these, looking into German-place, is a block of buildings called Prospect-row; but no other buildings are indicated in this direction. St. James's-street itself was unformed; but the bottom, from Gregory's Library on the Steine to Manchester-street, was known as Craven-buildings. The Steine had, in 1800, a continuous row of houses on its eastern side: those south of Gregory's Library being known as South Parade, and those north of it North Parade. Beyond these latter was only one other continuous block of houses, namely, those known as the "Blue and Buffs" (Charles Fox's colours), and those of Prince's-street and the Pavilion-parade; the last abutting on the " bridle way to Rottendean."

The tide of building, however, in 1800, ran eastwardly; and up the Marine-parade at that period a large area was in the course of being covered with "bricks and mortar." Broad-street and German-place are indicated on the old Map. German-place (some houses in which had been erected previous to 1790) is shown to be at the top of Broad-street; its subsequent continuation down to the Marine-parade depriving Board-street of that characteristic to which, originally, it owed its name. Between Broad-street and the Steine, Charles-street and Manchester-street appear to be completed; and Steine-street, with its "Meuse" (Mews), is in course of formation. Three new streets are being completed between German-place and the New-steine, namely,—York-street, Margaret-street (in front of which, on the cliff, is the East Battery, mounting four guns), and New Steine-street. The New Steine itself is being laid out; and houses extend as far eastward as Rock-buildings (now Rock-gardens). "Rock House," which stands at the south-western corner, was, indeed, the first house erected on the East Cliff, and was so named from being opposite some huge rocks formerly seen high above the sand at low water, but which have been covered now for some years —owing to more efficient groyning. Upon the theme of Rock-buildings, a writer in 1809 grows quite eloquent. He says,—they "command extensive and diversified land and sea views. The enclosed pleasure ground, including a verdant walk and flower-gardens. * * * The houses in their construction, combining elegance with simplicity, are much admired. The situation may justly be designated *Rus in Urbe*, from its rural beauties, and close approximation to a bustling town!" Rock-buildings have long been shut in, as it were, by the growth of the town; but when the houses were originally erected there, at the close of last century, by Mr. John Smith, he was looked upon as mad, by the "knowing ones," for building so far out of the town! *

---

* Rock-gardens has this year (1879) undergone another cycle of change. The Corporation, with the view of obtaining a new drive from the Marine-parade to the Downs, obliterated the old "enclosed pleasure ground" in the centre of the Gardens, as well as the boundary wall at the top, in making a carriage-road, with pavement on each side. At the same time several important alterations were carried out in Upper Rock-gardens, by the removal of Neville

Possibly, they had poor Otto in their minds. He, in 1798, built three houses at each end of the Royal Crescent; but dismayed, we suppose, at his own temerity, he, to quote a local chronicler, "bolted, leaving his creditors in the lurch." As another instance of the rapid growth of the town, later on, in another direction—northward—it may be mentioned that when, in 1821, the late Mr. John Hilton built his grocery warehouse at the south-west corner of Gardner-street, it was deemed by his friends an act of arrant folly to attempt to establish a business in such an outside locality. When Mr. Hilton died, in 1865, houses extended in continuous streets nearly a mile northward of Gardner-street, and still further to the east and west of it.

By the old Map it appears that the situations of three public buildings in 1800 were different to what they are now, namely, the Post Office was then at the south of the Steine; the Theatre was in Duke-street; and the Quakers' Meeting House was in North-street.

While treating of the old town, a peculiarity may be alluded to which seemed to prevail here—as in many other old towns—among the earlier builders, and which their successors for many years did their best to imitate, namely, the formation, in every available place in the principal streets, of courts, yards, blind alleys, &c. It would astonish not a few modern Brightonians to know the number of these even now, their entrances being frequently but little unobtrusive passages, which give no indication that they lead to batches of houses beyond. Modern improvements have materially lessened the number of these courts, &c., particularly in North-street (where two small ones only now remain): Salmon-court, Unicorn-yard, Durham, Petty France, &c., having disappeared some years ago. But in Middle-street, West-street, Russell-street, &c., there are yet several of these courts. For instance, in Middle-street, there are at least half-a-dozen such; and there are more, probably, in West-street and Russell-street. Indeed, till the erection of St. Paul's Church and the Schools behind it effected a clearance, there was, between West-street and Russell-street, a complete nest of courts, &c., running somewhat after the fashion of the Lanes between North-street and Ship-street, but in a much more filthy condition. Ship-street can still boast of a court; and in Black Lion-street, within a few yards of the King's-road, another yet exists in almost a primitive state.* Why such a system

---

House (once the residence of the late Earl of Egremont) and adjacent buildings, and making the new road through the pretty paddock once devoted to the Noble Earl's racing stud. The paddock, &c., is now being laid out for the erection of houses, some three or four of which will face into Edward-street.

* It is probable that, until Nov., 1875, when Messrs. Parsons and Son announced a sale of "half-a-dozen tenements, known as Saunders's-buildings, situate at the bottom of Black Lion-street," not one Brightonian in ten knew of such a locality, much less that such a nest of wretched, age-begrimed, and ill-constructed habitations lay in close proximity to the King's-road, the gayest and most fashionable thoroughfare of the Queen of Watering Places. Yet there they were, and there they have been for generations. Who was their builder,—whether he came in with the Conquerer, or, more probably, with the Flemings,—it is useless to enquire. Whoever he was, he must have been endowed with a large share of ingenuity, or he never could have constructed within the space at

OLD ROCKS—BRIGHTON, 1809,

(Formerly opposite Rock-gardens,) with the Marine-parade and Undercliff, Russell House, &c.

of building dwelling houses should have prevailed in Brighton to the extent it once did—there being no want of "elbow room"—is astonishing, seeing the many inconveniences it entailed, irrespective of the difficulty of access, &c. It was probably, "the fashion," and it would seem to have been an enduring one; for, even after the town extended beyond its old boundaries, as in Church-street, North-road, and roads northward, the same fashion was persisted in, though not quite to the same extent as formerly.

THE PROFESSIONAL AND TRADING COMMUNITY IN 1800.

One of the most interesting portions of the old "Directory" is that devoted to "Professions" and "Tradesmen,"—in fact, to what may be called the Directory proper. The details are not so methodically arranged or so conveniently classified as we have been accustomed to in more recent Directories. We have, therefore, been at some pains to put the particulars into "ship-shape," so that a tolerably

---

his command—a square of barely 40ft.—half a dozen houses (three on the east side and three on the west) of such dimensions as these, each with a front entrance and outlook, though the latter is limited to the fore-court (about 13ft. across), whilst the only objects to be seen are the dingy houses, or, it may be, their dingier interiors opposite. The builder, probably, studied "appearances," the fronts of the houses being made presentable at the expense of their backs, for not one of them has either back-yard or back-door; they are all built up flush with the boundary walls, the space thus saved being thrown into the fore-court, which, being open to all the houses, appears much larger than it really is. This forecourt, however, subserves a variety of purposes. It is a recreation ground for the juveniles; a drying-ground; and there was once a well in the centre; but, thanks to sanitary inspection, this has been removed, though its erstwhile companion,—a nameless erection, of huge proportions,—still stands at the northern end of the court, close to the dwellings. These dwellings are true types of primitive Brighton erections: with flint-and-brick fronts, and red-tiled roofs; flat small-framed windows; and the front doors opening direct into brick-paved and low-pitched rooms. The ground-floors lead into still darker rooms behind, described as "washhouses;" but one we saw seemed barely large enough to hold a tub. It was not 4ft. across! What the two bed-rooms and attic—the "parlour next the sky"—were like, we did not care to note. Yet the occupants seemed contented enough; of course, as one remarked, "they would like the place done up a bit." One occupant said he had lived there for 20 years; and he looked none the worse for it! How "Saunders's-buildings" came to be so named, we cannot say with certainty. The family of Saunders would appear to have been located in Black Lion-street from time immemorial. In 1784, the long-since defunct old "Black Lion"—the original inn of the street, and whence its name is derived—was kept by a Mrs. Saunders, and even after 1800 a Saunders was still in possession. It is, therefore, probable that some member of the family was concerned in their erection; and, like another Cheops, built for immortality! Certain it is, the old "Black Lion" is gone; but Saunders's-buildings still exist, though, thanks to their present owner, in a better condition in every way than they have been for many a long year. The whole batch realised, at the sale above mentioned, £920; Mr. R. Bacon, of the Old Ship, being the purchaser.

correct idea may be formed of the professional and trading community of the town in 1800.*

The professional gentlemen—legal and medical, artists, &c.—do not number much more than a score. The "attorneys" can be counted on one's four fingers and thumb. Fortunate old town! There was not even a Magistrates' Court held in Brighton. (The first Petty Sessions was held in 1812.) If parties had an affray, they had to take an eight miles' journey to Lewes to have it settled! Then, with respect to the medical profession, Brighton in 1800 could not have been a very hopeful field for the followers of Esculapius : there were but 13 medical gentlemen in the town,—chemists, and Mr. Nathan Smith, the "gout pump" inventor, included in the list. In these "degenerate days," 1879, we have 220 doctors, &c., with some 27 undertakers in their train! Brighton in 1800 had but *one* undertaker,—and scarcely that. People, of course, *did* then die in Brighton, as the Old Church-yard testifies ; but the one undertaker appears to have had so little encouragement that funerals formed only the secondary part of his business; hosiery being the primary one. The individual (we are very well pleased to make his acquaintance *now*) who in 1800 performed this melancholy office for his fellow-townsmen, when they *did* "shuffle off this mortal coil," was no other than Edward Cobby himself, of 2, Prince's-place,—the compiler of the "Directory for 1800." † But, returning to the "Professions," the list is concluded by an artist, a portrait painter, and three "academicians." What occult qualification these last possessed to secure them a passport into the hallowed precincts of "professionalism" it is impossible now to determine. It was something special, no doubt; for "out in the cold," among the "tradesmen," are six schoolmasters, ten schoolmistresses, two drawing-masters, two dancing masters, and an organist and music master.‡

---

* At this period, too, these communities had become of a settled character. In earlier times, both the professional and tradesman only visited the town "in the season." Thus, in a bookseller's advertisement, in 1759, we learn that a work may be had of "E. Verral, Lewes, and also at their shop in East-street, Brighthelmston, during the season." In 1776, one John Chatfield, of Lewes, announces that he has "opened a shop on the Cliffe, near Ship-street, Brighthelmston," where he purposes "to attend every Thursday, and oftener, if it shall be found necessary, with a good choice of Hatts of all sorts." Prince's-place was a favourite rendezvous of the migratory tradesmen between 1790 and 1800 : it had then a colonnade round its entire circuit ; and there was an opening at the upper part into the Promenade Grove (subsequently absorbed into the Pavilion Grounds).

† Mr. Cobby was, we believe, the father of Mr. Ed. Cobby, for many years Clerk to the old Commissioners.

‡ What a contrast, in point of numbers, with schools and schoolmasters, professors, &c., at the present time ! In the Directory for 1878, the local professors, teachers, &c., are 154 in number ; the boarding-schools 143, and the day schools (independently of some of the Board Schools), 49. No town at the present day has probably more schools in proportion to its size than Brighton. The earliest boarding-school in Brighton which we read of was opened in 1757, by Richard Marchant (late of Truley, in Edburton). His curriculum *was* comprehensive. It included "Writing, Arithmetic, Algebra, Geometry in its several Branches of Planimetry, Altimetry, Longimetry, Stereometry, Trigonometry, and Navigation ; Heraldry, or the Art of Armoury and Blazoning ; Bookkeeping and Merchants' Accompts ; Surveying, and making Draughts and Maps

THE BRIGHTHELMSTON DIRECTORY FOR 1800.

But let us now look a little more into the details of what may truly be regarded as the trading community of Brighton in 1800. We have alluded to the healthiness of the old town; and something, in this respect, may probably be set down to good living; for there appear to have been no less than 137 tradesmen, or about one-third of the entire trade of the town, who ministered to the eating and drinking requirements of the inhabitants. As to the eating: there were 19 bakers; 1 miller; 5 pastry cooks; 7 butchers; 2 porkmen; 4 poulterers; 36 grocers, &c.; besides, 2 fish merchants; 8 fruiterers; and half-a-dozen gardeners. Then, as to the drinking: there were 41 victuallers, innkeepers, &c.; 5 brewers; 3 wine and liquor merchants; 2 porter, &c., merchants, and one spruce beer brewer. There is one other trade in this category which seems singularly restricted,—that of milkman. There were 1,200 houses in the town, with some 7,000 inhabitants; and yet there was only one *bond fide* milkman! Two other individuals, certainly, supplemented other businesses by doing a milk-trade; but how the trio contrived to supply the wants of such a community, so that each one "might have a little," we do not venture to conjecture. It may, however, be stated that one lived at the Unicorn Inn, close to which was the time-honoured town-well; the other two in Brighton-place and Market-street respectively, each being in the neighbourhood of an old town-pump!

Knowing how largely the old town was patronised by visitors, it is only natural to suppose that there would be plenty of tradesmen to supply their wants in the matter of dress, &c. For instance, the hairdressers and perfumers are 17 in number; the tailors, 16; haberdashers, drapers, &c., 15; mantua makers, dressmakers, milliners, &c., 15; stay-makers, 2; glove and breeches makers, 2; calico-glazer, 1; straw manufacturer, 1; and muslin manufacturer, 1. To this list might be added 5 watchmakers, goldsmiths, &c. There

---

of Land, &c., with proper Decorations and Coats of Arms; Chronological or Ecclesiastical Calculations of Time, &c." Free Schools also had an early growth in Brighton: Springet's about 1725; Grimmett's in 1769; Girls' School of Industry, 1788; and the Union School (Lancasterian) in 1807. Mr. Sharp—a man of sterling worth—was first master of this last School. He was, however, a strict disciplinarian; and some of his modes of punishment were decidedly original. In addition to the orthodox "strap" and "birch;" the "dunce's cap"; and the "red tongue" for talkers; there was for the incorrigibles a "wooden collar,"—an unpleasant necklet; and for the truant, a "log"—this latter a veritable log of wood, some 3ft. long, which, chained to the leg, had to be dragged by the truant several times round the school, amid the ill-concealed jeers and scoffs of his fellows. Then there was the "basket"—about a four bushel one—which used to hang, with a long rope attached, *in terrorem*, from one of the beams in the school, and when used for punishment was lowered to receive the urchin in disgrace, who, being placed in it, was drawn up a certain height, and then for some time spun round or swung to and fro by other boys! Verily, school-boys now-a-days have advantages over their predecessors in modes of punishment! One of Mr. Sharp's methods of teaching the alphabet to the more juvenile aborigines was "racy of the soil," namely, by a "sand-class." A wooden trough, filled with sand, was placed before the youngsters, and when suitably smoothed with a board, the monitor drew some letters in the sand with his finger, or taught the little ones to do so, and when they had become familiar with these, the smoothing-board was again passed over the sand and other letters made, and so on until the whole alphabet was mastered.

were in the town 9 librarians, music sellers, &c., 2 printers, and some 3 or 4 toymen.

The building trade, considering the rapid rate at which the town increased, was, doubtless, a thriving one. No less than 21 master builders are down in the list; 6 plumbers, painters, and glaziers; 9 cabinet makers, upholders, &c.; 2 ironmongers; 2 blacksmiths; 2 tinmen; 3 stonemasons; and 4 whitesmiths and bell-hangers. In the furnishing way are 1 earthenware man; 1 china and glass man; 2 cutlers; 2 coopers; and 1 basket maker. Three auctioneers were ready to do duty for the community in the way of disposal of goods, &c.; but if a more quiet way were preferred, 1 broker and appraiser was at their service, who might, if occasion arose, be supplemented by 1 porter.

The conveyance of visitors, &c., to and from the town, was, as might be supposed, an important business. There were no less than 12 London coach-proprietors; 2 London stage-waggoners; 3 London carriers; 2 Lewes carriers; 3 corn chandlers; 1 horse dealer; 3 livery stable keepers; 5 farriers; 4 saddlers and harness-makers; 2 coachmakers; 1 coach painter; and 1 wheelwright.

The miscellaneous trades may be summarised as follows :—3 coal merchants; 1 sign painter; 1 wire worker; 3 boat builders; 1 sail maker; and 1 cricket bat maker. Altogether, the trading community numbered 422 persons, irrespective of lodging-house-keepers, whose calling was not then, as it is now, followed as a business.

In going through the list of the "tradesmen" of the town in 1800, we cannot help noticing the extraordinary junction of trades carried on by various individuals. For instance, Mr. James Gregory, who was Librarian on the Steine, had a medicine and toy-warehouse at 2, North-street, and also carried on a coal-merchant's business in Middle-street; Mr. Wilmshurst, a watchmaker, at 7, North-street, had also a leather-cutting business at 19, Middle-street; Mr. Thomas Harmer, at 43, North-street, combined the businesses of wire-worker, grocer, and auctioneer; Mr. Cobby, of 2, Prince's-place, hosier and undertaker; Mr. Verrall, 9, Nile-street, upholder and tallow chandler; Mr. Harry Attree, 15, Ship-street, wine-merchant, draper, and upholder; four individuals were both blacksmiths and grocers; another did business as tea dealer and basket maker; another as pastry-cook and victualler, and another as silversmith and toyman.*

---

* The practice of individuals carrying on two or more trades in conjunction would seem to have been a primitive one; for as early as 1758 Thomas Lulham, at Brighthelmston, advertised for an apprentice to an "upholder, tallow chandler, and soap boiler." Surely the Mr. Verrall above-mentioned, who carried on the same trades in 1800, did not learn his art and practice under Thomas Lulham! In 1764, Wm. English, of Lewes, and Ship-street, Brighton, sold gold and silver goods, cutlery, and iron and tin ware; Bibles, Testaments, and Common Prayers; Books and Almanacs; likewise trusses for ruptures!

LODGING HOUSES AND LODGING LETTING IN 1800.

An especial feature of the "Directory" is the information it affords respecting "Lodging Houses" and "Lodgings" in Brighthelmston at the date of its publication, 1800. More than one-third of the book is devoted to such particulars, which are set forth with a clearness and minuteness of detail that is most commendable, and must have saved both lodging-letters and lodging-seekers much correspondence and many enquiries. The Brightonians of 1800 were, undoubtedly, a practical-minded people, having also a keen eye to business. They had an intuitive perception, fostered by experience and tradition, that visitors must needs be housed and tended; and that, among those who came to the Royal-favoured "Village by the Sea," money was, practically, no object, if only accommodation could be obtained.

What "Fashion" paid, in 1800, for this accommodation it would be difficult to guess; it was not quite so cheap, probably, as in 1736, when a clergyman and his family had two parlours, two bedchambers, pantry, &c., for 5s. a week! A quarter of a century later on, "terms" had doubtless increased. Valetudinarianism, thanks to Dr. Russell, had in the interval induced numbers to come to Brighton (the visitors, with their children and servants, were estimated, in 1761, at 400); and, this being subsequently supplemented by the votaries of Fashion, such an impetus was given to lodging-letting that for fifty years and more it knew "no retiring ebb." [*] Lodging-houses had, in fact, come to be regarded as a kind of El Dorado; and in 1800,—and for several years previously, it might be truly said,—there was scarcely a well-to-do tradesman who did not own one or more, while not a few of the better class, without any sacrifice apparently of their dignity or importance, received lodgers at their own houses. Even noblemen did not disdain to let their houses to visitors! for we are told that (in 1779) "the Duke of Marlborough, though his income is immense, letts his house out, even to different families at the same time."

---

[*] The townsfolk in the interval did their best to provide the much-desired accommodation. Between 1753-60, says Dr. Relhan, "the inhabitants, encouraged by the late great resort of company, seem disposed to expend the whole of what they acquire in the erecting of new buildings, or making the old ones convenient;" and, he adds, "should the increase of these in the next seven years be equal to what it has been in the last, it is probable there will be but few towns in England that will excel this in commodious buildings"! The increase *did* take place, and for many another seven years after; and still the supply was not equal to the demand. It would seem that the erection of German-place was owing to the lodging-house mania; for in the *Lewes and Brighthelmston Pacquet* of Oct. 15, 1789, is the following:—" Sunday, died here, Mr. John Daniel Richards, a German, proprietor of a range of lodging-houses near the Steine, known by the name of German-place."

But this by the way. Among the well-to-do tradesmen who owned lodging-houses in 1800 were Mr. Thomas Howell, lucky man ! who had no less than seven * ; John Smith, James Gregory, Matthew Walker, and Nicholas Johnson each had five ; Nathan Smith and William Tuppen, four ; and, among others who had more or less, John and William Gallard, John Cunningham, Stephen, William, and George Wood, and Edward Thunder. The "lodging-letters" are too numerous to mention ; they comprised, in fact, everybody who was able to convert any portion of his house into apartments ; the most successful in this respect being Mr. Harry Attree, wine merchant, draper, and upholder, of 15, Ship-street, who had no less than "three parlours, twelve best beds, and ten servants' beds." It must have been a mammoth establishment, for Mr. Robinson Attree also carried on his auctioneer's business on the same premises. Brighton at the period in question was, in reality, neither more nor less than a huge lodging-house, the proprietor of every house laying himself out to provide the utmost possible accommodation. †

To afford, however, some more definite idea of the extent to which this branch of business was carried, we may state that in 1800 there were altogether about 1,500 houses in Brighton, of which no less than 211 were let solely as "lodging-houses," and another 208 in which "lodgings" were to be obtained, so that nearly one-third of the houses of the town may be said to have been devoted to the lodging business ! We have had the curiosity to count the "accommodation," and it appears that the lodging-houses afforded 679 "best beds" and 687 "servants' beds ;" and the lodgings 403 "best beds" and 294 "servants' beds ;" altogether 1,953 beds, besides drawing-rooms and parlours. Enough, it would be thought, and to spare, for any demand likely at that time of day to be made. It was not so, however; for it is on record that on more than one occasion,— and notably in August, 1809, and even (in the season) up to 1816,— "there was neither house nor lodgings to be got in Brighton for love or money !" And it had been the same in the season for several years previously. In 1791, a writer says—"There is not now a house on the Steine or on the Bank to be let ;" and in August, 1793, another states—"Every house brimfull ; many who could not

---

* Mr. Thomas Howell was the father of the late Mr. Charles Howell, of Dial House, Hove, who founded "Howell's Almshouses," in George-street, for the benefit of reduced inhabitants of Brighton and Hove. Mr. Thos Howell, besides being the largest local lodging-house keeper, owned a stage-coach, running between Brighton and London. Whilst on the road to town, in 1804, he had a fit of apoplexy, and died in the inn at Handcross.

† Matters had, doubtless, improved in 1800; but the experiences of "A Diarist," in 1778, did not say much for the "accommodation" at that period. He lodged, he says, in "a poor man's house in Ship-street (Mr. Mercer, shoemaker), who has a large family ; took a small bed-room the sooner on that account, though the music is rather too powerful, *for the cherubims and seraphims continually do cry*. This, added to the spiritual songs and hymns which some females (attendants at Lady Huntingdon's Chapel) in the next house are continually chaunting, make up something like a concert"! And yet the Diarist's landlord had informed him "that his bed had been lain upon by not only lords and knights, but also esquires"!

get beds were happy in being accommodated with the first floor in a post-chaise, or to repose on carpets."

We have said that the Brighton lodging-house keepers of the olden time saved many enquiries by the details which were published in the "Directory;" and here is an example of how they did it, being a portion of the Marine-parade list of "Lodging-houses":—

No.	Proprietor.	Drawing Room.	Parlours.	Best Beds.	Servants' Beds.
1.	Richard Lashmar	1	2	4	3
2.	John Gallard	1	1	4	3
3.	John Pollard	1	1	4	4
4.	James Gregory	1	1	4	3
6.	Daniel Scully	1	2	4	3
7.	Donaldson and Wilkes	1	2	4	6
8.	Thomas Howell	1	2	3	2
9.	George Doncaster	1	1	3	3
10.	William Tuppen	1	1	3¹	3
11.	Thos. Phillips Willis	1	2	4	4
12.	Richard Spearing	1	2	4	4

A similar plan was adopted with respect to "Lodgings." It would astonish many modern Brightonians to know the streets and other like places in which there were "lodging-houses." Nile-street and Warden's-buildings (East-street), for instance, would scarcely be thought desirable localities for such at the present day; yet in the former place there were no less than four lodging-houses, and in the latter two, each of these having, besides other accommodation, a drawing-room! Russell-street, again, had four "lodging-houses," two with drawing-rooms; and some eight or more houses in that street had "lodgings" to let. There was even a "lodging-house" in West-street-lane (now South-street). Nothing shows more clearly the rapid rise of the middle-classes in England than the contrast of the accommodation which suited the citizens of London 70 or 80 years ago, and that which is now demanded by their sons and grandsons. Middle-street and Russell-street sufficed for the one, Brunswick-square and terrace, Palmeira-square, and the palatial mansions of West Brighton can scarcely suffice for the other! Parts of Brighton long handed over to the humblest classes were once favourite places of resort for our visitors. Thus, in the "Topography of Brighton" (1809) we are told of Devonshire-street (surely Devonshire-place must have been meant?) that "The situation of this street is unexceptionable; for it is unconfined, salubrious, and fashionable!" Dorset-gardens, we are assured, "is an elegant range of buildings, which are constructed in a uniform, light, and elegant manner!" In the same work we are told that "the southern part of Russell-street is principally composed of small tenements, but, higher up, the houses are larger, and which, during the summer, are occupied by our fashionable visitants!" Air-street (now Queen's-road) was at this period a desirable locality, and contained a few good houses. It was then, probably, innocent of those peculiarly-shaped erections, the frontispieces of slaughter-houses, &c., which in after periods so long disgusted both the inhabitants of the town and its visitors; and those filthy nests of hovels, once situated at its southern end, and known as "Durham" and "Petty France," were, probably, in 1800, in their pristine beauty!

Fashionable and Popular Amusements.

INTRODUCTION.

THE fashionable amusements of Brighton in the olden time grew, as it were, out of the "situation." The earlier visitors to the "pretty fishing village" were content to bathe; to "buy fish," "sun themselves upon the beach," and "count the ships in the road"; to stroll on "the plain adjacent to the town" or upon the lovely Downs in the neighbourhood. Later on, when, under the auspices of Dr. Russell, the valetudinarian resorted hither, and was visited by family, friends, or acquaintances, the "old order changed." He might study the "Dissertation on the Use of Sea Bathing," descant upon its virtues or act upon its rules, enjoy the fresh air in his sedan chair, &c. But for them, in the full flow of health and spirits,—"cooped within a narrow O" and all but shut out from intercourse with the world,—the only amusement or recreation open was—a walk on the Steine and beach, or on the beach and Steine. Such pastime as this became irksome and monotonous; hence, the opening of a Library, the engagement of a band, the occasional organisation of a ball at Shergold's new tavern,—each simple enough in itself,—was, in the then condition of things, hailed as a positive delight; and such was the encouragement given to these amusements that increased efforts to provide others promptly followed. And none too soon. Brighton, at this period, was fast rising into popularity as a marine resort *par excellence;* there being none other so near to the Metropolis or so easy of access; and ere long pleasant spots, dear to the invalid, his family, &c., were invaded by the high born and the wealthy, the idler, the man of fashion, the prosperous "Cit.," the artist and the professor, the adventurer and the man of the world; each and all seeking either health or pastime, profit or excitement, according to his bent. The Steine now became the great rendezvous—the centre to which all converged. Another Library was opened; the Assembly and tea rooms were enlarged; and gossip and scandal—balls and card parties—gambling for heavy stakes as well as for trifles—pic-nics and private concerts, each in turn ruled the hour. A few years more and another revolution was given to this social kaleidoscope. The orthodox round of fashionable amusements still held their own, but there was, in addition, an unconquerable impulse in an undesirable direction—namely, towards frivolity and excitement. The Heir Apparent—George, Prince of Wales—chose Brighton for his marine residence; and with him, or in his wake,—especially in the earlier years of his visitation,—came the gay and the dissolute. the sporting-man and the "black-leg, and a throng of hangers-on, whose chief pastimes and pursuits were alike unseemly and disreputable. The Prince's residence was near the Steine; and the Steine accordingly became the most favoured spot for reckless folly and vulgar taste to display itself. The Heir Apparent was an apt student,—in fact, a master,—in the school of frivolity; one of his afternoon diversions being dove-shooting on the Steine, finishing by lowering the chimney pots of his uncle's residence. His associates were quite on a par with him; for whilst one nobleman would race a waiter,* another would emulate a professional acrobat; and the taste of a third lay in senseless freaks.† Though contemporaneous with, these frivolities lie outside those staple fashionable amusements of which we propose to treat; and which, if not altogether harmless or indicating a very high standard of social taste, were, at least, indulged in with an outward semblance of propriety and decorum. First, of

THE ASSEMBLY ROOMS, &c.—THE "M.C." DYNASTY.

"M.C." I. (W. WADE, Esq.)

Card assemblies, balls, tea parties, &c., were among the earliest of the amusements indulged in by fashionable and other visitors in the olden time; and the inns more especially associated with them were "The Old Ship" (still one of the principal hotels in the town) and "The Castle" (pulled down in 1823); the proprietor of the former being (in 1735-65) Mr. William Hicks, and of the latter (when first opened, in 1755,) Mr. Samuel Shergold. Excepting these, there was scarcely a decent inn in the town in the middle of last century; and, certainly, none at which the class of visitors who had then begun to frequent Brighton would assemble. It was no wonder, therefore, that each proprietor, with true professional instinct, seeing that a public room was so urgently needed, should do his best to

---

* After the Races, in August, 1784, when the Prince of Wales and the Duc de Chartres were on the Steine with their friends, a French Nobleman (a companion of the Duke's), wagered Sir Thomas Bunbury 20 guineas that he would run half the length of the Steine backwards in less time than any man Sir Thomas might produce could run the entire distance forward. Sir Thomas sent for a waiter from "The Castle," and the start took place; but somebody halloaing, the Nobleman, thinking himself beaten, stopped—and lost his stake! Sir Thomas, however, refused to take the money.

† On Oct. 27, 1788, Earl Barrymore's brother ("Cripplegate") rode a horse up the stairs to the topmost room of Mrs. Fitzherbert's house. The horse could not be induced to make the return journey; and two blacksmiths were at last called in to get the animal down by main force, the reward for their pains being a bowl of punch at "The Castle."

provide it. Indeed, this was Mr. Shergold's first object when he purchased the private house which was subsequently converted into "The Castle;" and Mr. Hicks, about 1761, built a room which, for splendour, was said "not to be excelled, perhaps, by any in England, that of York excepted." The present unique assembly room at "The Old Ship" was erected about 1767;* also, the dining room (now known as the "Telemachus Room," the wainscot originally exhibiting part of the story of Telemachus, painted in bronze on a blue ground), an elegant card room (by Golden, of London), tea rooms, &c.; the ground floor having been for some years earlier devoted to a handsome coffee and other rooms. Altogether, the house was said to be "commodious," and in "every respect calculated for the reception of company." "The Castle" underwent important alterations in 1766. Mr. Shergold then took Messrs. Tilt and Best into partnership; and, in addition to a noble coffee room, &c., four handsome assembly rooms were constructed by Mr. Crunden, of London; the more important being the card room and ball room. The latter was a rectangle (80ft. by 40ft.), with recesses at each end and side (16ft. by 4ft.). The walls were most tastefully decorated with paintings; those placed over the entablature at each end being "Aurora" and "Nox." In many respects this ball room was, at the time, considered one of the largest and most elegantly covered rooms in the kingdom.

With the accommodation thus afforded by the above-named hostelries,—and with every disposition on the part of visitors to avail themselves of it,—balls, assemblies, &c., soon became consolidated into regular institutions; and at "The Castle" a ball was held every Monday, with card assemblies on Wednesdays and Fridays; whilst at "The Old Ship" the ball took place every Thursday, with card assemblies on Tuesdays and Saturdays. These amusements were varied by concerts; and English and foreign artists † having thus early discovered where Fashion most did congregate, our visitors even at this primitive period had no lack of excitement or gaiety. That these were then in full flow is shewn by the following lines from "A LAMENT," on leaving the Steine, published in the *Lewes Journal*, October 10th, 1774:—

> "Exchang'd, alas! the splendid scene,
> The frequent walk, the cheerful STEINE,
> Her verdant honours gone;
> Deserted now the brilliant room,
> Where lately in their native bloom
> Unrivall'd beauties shone.

* * * * *

---

* Mr. Wm. Hicks did not live to see this assembly room completed (he died in 1765, "very rich," it was said). Whilst the work was in progress, and just forward enough to be healed in on one side, "it was blown to the ground by a hurricane," some £200 or £300 damage being done.

† In August, 1768, a Mr. Noel (assisted by Mrs. March) gave a concert at Shergold's. He performed on the violin and on the pantaleone and salterione (an instrument 11ft. long, fitted with 276 strings.)

"Who now, while critic Fops admire,
And Belles with envy round expire,
　　Shall teach the *Tone* of France!
Pass'd, to our grief, those happy days,
When, with superior grace and ease,
　　The H—rl—nds led the Dance.

"What private set in *Shergold's Bow*,
At *Winney*, *Twenty-one*, or Loo,
　　Shall pass the weary hour?
E'en mighty Pam his subject line,
Kings and Plebeians, all resign,
　　And abdicate their power.

"Save where, perhaps, one table spread,
Some superannuated maid
　　Commands a scanty Pool;
And (heav'nly preparations o'er)
Finds in the darling Matadore
　　A comfort to her soul.

"Ye Cards, whom fairer hands have pressed,
Whom beauties with their touch have blest,
　　How pitiable your lot!
Victims reduc'd to snuff and spleen;
Transform'd to brown your snow-white mien,
　　Your better fates forgot.

"No more the ready chairmen's ply,
Or pond'rous coaches rolling by,
　　Disturb a people's rest;
One gen'ral stillness reigns throughout,
No noisy servants' rabble rout
　　These peaceful scenes infest."

One of the earliest public balls given in Brighton took place at "The Castle," August 19th, 1758; and it is thus spoken of in the *Sussex Weekly Advertiser*:—

"The news of the taking of Cape Breton was received at Brighton with all those transports of joy which must naturally rise in the Breast of every true Englishman, upon so great and interesting an event. In the Evening, the Company, who do so much honour to this place, assembled to the number of 200 in Mr. Shergold's Room. The Ball was exceeding splendid, and was finished before eleven. Then the Company sat down to an elegant Supper; and concluded by drinking the Healths of His Majesty and Royal Family, Admiral Boscawen and General Amherst, and success to their further operations, &c. The Dragoons quartered in Brighton were drawn up on the Steine and went through their firings. Near this was a Bonfire, where the Populace drank out three Hogsheads of Ale in loyal Healths. The Cannon also upon the Cliffe were fired. The whole expense was defrayed by a Subscription, raised by the Gentlemen for this purpose. And tho' everything was Joy and Gladness, it was conducted with all the good order and decency imaginable."

As showing how early these assemblies, &c., had become recognized fashionable institutions, it may be mentioned that, in 1758 and subsequent years, they were regularly announced in the *Sussex Weekly Advertiser* as follows:—

"THIS is to acquaint the Nobility and Gentry that the BALLS at BRIGHTHELMSTON for the present Season will be on MONDAYS and TUESDAYS."

Then it is recorded that the Duke of Gloucester, who was in Brighton in July, 1765, went "in the evening to the Public Rooms." Two days after the Royal Duke gave a ball at Shergold's Rooms : "the company being very brilliant; there being present upwards of 250 gentlemen and ladies." The same evening " Admiral Swanton dropt down as he was going from Mrs. Hicks's ball, and died soon after." In the following month, August, 1765, there was "the largest and most brilliant ball at Shergold's that ever was there; near 400 gentlemen and ladies, some of the first rank, were present, who declared they never saw so numerous and splendid assembly before." The next year, August, 1766, the Duke of York was in Brighton, and "was present at the Ball at the Castle." In 1768, at a ball at Shergold's, there were upwards of 450 present, "the greatest meeting ever known in Brighton." One wonders where the guests came from, or, rather, where they resided; for most certainly they could not all have found accommodation in the "obscure fishing village."

Balls, &c., having become established institutions, an "M.C." was of course necessary for their proper regulation and enjoyment, as well as to ensure that the guests were worthy to enter the charmed circle. *When* this important personage was first installed into all the "pride, pomp, and circumstance" of his great office,—who installed him, whence he came, and what were his emoluments—history is silent!* That there *was* an acknowledged "M.C." in Brighton in 1767, who attended, alternately, the Balls at "The Castle" and "The Ship," is evident from the fact that at each house there was a grand ball in the season "for the Master of the Ceremonies." In 1768 these balls were again given, but in that year they were stated to be "for the *benefit* of the Master of the Ceremonies." Two years later, 1770, the announcements of the same Balls took the following form:—

"For the Master of the Ceremonies at Brighton. At Mr. Shergold's Room, a Ball. Tickets of Capt. Wade, at his house in Black Lyon-street."

Thus, for the first time, we learn the name of the "M.C."; and it is reasonable to suppose, as the gallant Captain (he did not long use the prefix) whom the Nobility and Gentry had installed as guardian of the portals of Fashionable Society resided in *Black Lyon-street*, that that locality was at the period an aristocratic one ! Perhaps he was, as yet, desirous of holding his honours meekly; for he was then "yours most obediently." But the man was mortal! Who, in such a position, exposed to such temptations as he was; courted, flattered,

---

[* We have since learnt that Captain Wade came from Bath, where he was appointed as "M.C." in 1769, but was compelled to resign in 1777.]

deferred to, on every occasion,—could have "flung away ambition?" Really and truly, by virtue of the peculiar powers with which he was invested, the "M.C." was absolute. Fashionable society,—that is, in its habits and some of its amusements,—was then in a state of transition; and the Master of the Ceremonies became Dictator; he promulgated laws, and all willingly yielded obedience. Hence the first duty of visitors to Brighton was to pay their respects to him. Mothers, with marriageable daughters, were anxious to stand in his good graces; the unprotected maiden of uncertain age, the lone dowager, reluctant to relinquish her waning opportunities of shining in society, each sheltered herself under his ægis; portionless sons, or, it may be, needy adventurers, seeking prizes in the matrimonial market, assiduously sought his favour; the proprietors of the respective assembly rooms were content to do him homage; and as for the town authorities, such as they were at the period, they neither interfered, nor sought to interfere, in the domain over which the sway of the "M.C." extended. And so for several years he reigned—supreme. What wonder was it, then, that the man changed? Who would not have done so? under such circumstances—under the weight of such an office—master of such a "situation." His announcements, therefore, assumed a new form. The old obsequiousness became obsolete; and "orders" were in force. *Ex. gratia:—*

"Brighthelmstone, July 1, 1778.

"THESE are to acquaint the Nobility and Gentry that the BALLS and other Amusements for the Season will begin on Monday, the 13th inst.

"By order of W. WADE, Esq., Master of the Ceremonies.

"S. SHERGOLD & Co.,
"J. HICKS, } Proprietors of Public Rooms."

At the present day, when fashionable and other amusements take place under altogether different arrangements from those of the olden time, it is difficult to understand what was in reality an honorary office, should have arrogated to himself so much authority as the "M.C." then did, and without apparent question. The town authorities might exercise supervision over the town and town affairs, but the Steine, and all that was associated with the comfort, convenience, or the amusements of the World of Fashion, was evidently regarded by him as being exclusively under his personal control and subject to his arrangements. No stronger proof of this could be adduced than the following "Notice," issued from "The Castle," we suppose, "under his hand and seal," and dated July 23, 1787:—

"THE STEINE, BRIGHTHELMSTONE.

"NOTICE IS HEREBY GIVEN, that if any Person or Persons run any Foot, or other Race, on this Place, or *Fight*, Play at Cricket, Trap, or Ball, or any other Game or Games thereon, or in any manner disturb the Company resorting thereto, *he and they will be prosecuted.*

"The STEINE is enclosed, there is a FINE TURF, which is kept constantly mowed and swept every day, where Ladies and Gentlemen and their Children may walk with the greatest Safety and Pleasure; and care is taken to keep off all Beggars and Disorderly Persons.

"There will be BALLS at the Public Rooms during the Races at Brighthelmstone.

"WM. WADE, Master of the Ceremonies."

Passing by the thrift of making the "Notice" serve the double purpose of warning to offenders and affording information as to the Race Balls, the most singular fact in connection with it is, that, within a week after (on July 30th), arrangements were made for a grand Foot Race on the Steine, for one hundred guineas, between Flint of Surrey and a Man from Kent!* attracting thither thousands of spectators, including the Duke of Cumberland and numbers of the nobility and gentry. The Prince of Wales had arranged to be present, but arrived when the race was just over.

The most serious invasion, however, upon the domain of the "M.C." was made in the following year by Mr. Fox, the lessee of the Theatre, who, on seeking a renewal of his license, obtained permission to open his house on Tuesdays, Thursdays (of all days of the week, when there was regularly a Ball at the Old Ship!), and Saturdays. This invasion was a serious one, and the more so, that it was wholly unexpected. (Mr. Fox had up to this period subordinated his nights of performing to those of the "M.C.," and was in subsequent years compelled to do so again.) What distress of mind was undergone by the heretofore absolute Potentate of Fashion at such a direct blow to his authority—at such an unparalleled interference with his season's arrangements—is unknown. Whether or no he "fulmined over the Steine and shook the Pavilion," is not written in local chronicles. All that has come down to us is simply the following :—

"Brighthelmstone, Saturday, July 19, 1788.

"IN consequence of the Justices at Quarter Sessions, holden at Lewes on Friday last, having been pleased to grant Mr. James Fox a license to perform Plays, &c., three times a week *(and no more)* on TUESDAYS, THURSDAYS, and SATURDAYS during the Season,

"The Master of the Ceremonies is under the necessity of Regulating the Amusements at the Public Rooms for the Season as follows :—

"*Sunday* ... ... Public Tea and Promenade ... at Shergold's.
Monday, ... A BALL ... ... at Shergold's.
Tuesday ... ... A Card Assembly ... ... at Hicks's.
Wednesday ... A Card Assembly ... ... at Shergold's.
Thursday ... ... A Card Assembly ... ... at Hicks's.
Friday ... ... A BALL ... ... at Hicks's.
Saturday ... ... A Card Assembly ... ... at Shergold's.

"WILLIAM WADE, Master of the Ceremonies."

---

* This race, which occasioned much excitement in the town—sums to the amount of £8,000 being bet on it—was won easily by the Kentish man, whose mother, by-the-bye, on the morning of the race, *sent him an empty purse!* (He took it home full.) The race was run on each side a rope, stretched tight in the middle of the ground, "to prevent jockeying or foul play." The stakes were deposited in the hands of Mr. John Hicks, of "The Old Ship"—a stroke of policy, perhaps, seeing his influence and intimacy with the "M.C."

These new "Regulations" of the "M.C." were speedily conformed to, and the Card Assembly, instead of the Ball as heretofore on the Thursday, doubtless afforded as much pleasure as it did on the Friday. Was not the Ball on the latter day in anticipation! It is astonishing, however, to what extent card-playing was indulged in in the olden time—some 200 or 300 people, oftentimes more, frequenting one or the other of the Assembly Rooms four times a week to play at cards! These assemblies, of course, afforded opportunities for the meeting of friends, for conversation, for *tête-à-têtes*, &c., but the chief occupation of the guests was cards. Card-playing was, in fact, a favourite social pastime of the period; and not a few of the nobility, following a fashion which "came in with the Germans," played cards regularly on Sunday evenings. At Carlton House, the London residence of the Prince of Wales, Sunday evening card playing, &c., was the "order of the day."

To many, the Sunday public amusements in Brighton at the close of last century would not, perhaps, be regarded as orthodox. Yet the tea and promenade at "The Castle"—the one amusement in which, if not all the rank and fashion, all the respectable portion of the community participated,—was as innocent *per se* as it was, doubtless, enjoyable. It should be borne in mind that, if the public could not have resorted to the Steine and "The Castle" to spend their Sunday evenings pleasantly, other sources of amusement, far more objectionable, might have cropped up; for the old Parish Church (up to 1793 the only church in the town) was but rarely opened on Sunday evenings. There were, certainly, the two or three Dissenting Chapels open; but they, excepting among the Nonconformists, were far less popular than now. All things considered, therefore, the Sunday tea and promenade had in it much which should exempt it from sweeping condemnation. The inhabitants and visitors must needs be abroad; and what more sociable, or, indeed, more harmless, than to meet friends and acquaintances (and very numerous they were when the weather was fine)—to indulge in agreeable conversation—to promenade the Steine—to listen to the Band—and then, at about nine o'clock, to repair to the noble Ball room of "The Castle" (which on Sunday evenings was open for promenade)? The entrance-money was paid at the door, and this included tea, toast, and gossip *à volonté*. People walked and talked; at the ringing of a bell, they divided into parties as inclination dictated, and sat down to tea; and thus finished the evening.[*]

The "M.C." had, probably, little to do personally with the Sunday tea and promenade, farther than they were subjected to his

---

[*] The terms of admission to the balls, &c., were as follows:—To Subscribers (the subscription for the season was 10s. 6d.), for each ball, 3s.; Sunday tea and promenade, 1s.; card assemblies, *free*. Non-Subscribers—for each ball, 6s.; Sunday tea and promenade, 2s.; card assemblies, 1s. Some of the "M.C.'s" announcements are difficult to understand. In 1800, on one occasion there was to be on the Monday "An *Undressed* Ball" at Tilt's! What this implied, or what difference there was between it and the "Undress Ball" at Hicks's, on the Thursday, wiser heads than ours must determine.

arrangements. He, doubtless, when in Brighton,* honoured them with his presence; bowed patronizingly upon the assembled throng; and they, in their turn, most likely regarded him with deferential awe. That he looked with no disfavour on the Sunday assemblies may be inferred from the fact that his announcements of the arrangements for the week were not unfrequently dated on Sunday!

But this by the way. The duties of "M.C." must have been in the closing years of last century somewhat onerous, though not unprofitable,—that is, if every new arrival (who entered his name in a book) deposited a guinea, as was the custom in later times. The town was then in the season thronged with fashionable company; and to supervise the various amusements, to make calls, to receive visitors, to perform the ever-recurring ceremony of introductions, to do homage to Royal and Noble, to confer with the proprietors of "The Castle" and "The Old Ship," to attend night after night either the assembly or the ball at their respective houses, &c., must have needed a "giant's strength." To have regularly attended even the balls alone must have tasked the strongest. In 1792-3, and for years later on, there was a ball every night during the Brighton and Lewes Race week; then there was a dress ball on the following Monday; and dress and undress balls every succeeding Monday throughout the season. In addition, the special balls required his presence, such as the Prince of Wales's Birth-day Ball —the Terpsichorean "event" of the season for many a year—Rose balls, masked balls, &c. These multifarious duties appear to have been performed satisfactorily; of course,—despite tact, courtesy, and patience,—disputes would sometimes arise; but, notwithstanding this, in the closing years of Mr. Wade's reign there was a sensible diminution of the "M.C.'s" power and authority. Other forms of amusement were coming into favour; the Libraries especially, with their manifold attractions; concerts, picnics, &c. Royal and fashionable tastes were, with regard to the assemblies, &c., undergoing a change. Visitors, too, were more numerous; but the "M.C.'s" influence and introduction—though still respected and acknowledged —had not that supreme importance which once attached to them.

Mr. Wade continued, however, to exercise the duties of his office almost to the close of his life—though in 1806-7 his duties were wholly devoted to "The Castle." But even there only in the height of the season; for out of season in 1806 Mr. Tilt announced and superintended the Balls himself. The "M.C.'s" influence was evidently waning; and it must, indeed, have been a source of grief to the veteran to have been absent from the grand ball given by the Prince of Wales at "The Castle," on December 8, 1806, the Heir Apparent himself being present, and the "whole of the fashionables of the district." The closing year of the first "M.C.'s" reign was

---

* Mr. Wade only resided in Brighton "in the season," when duty called him hither; and it used to be formally announced in the Lewes journal after this fashion :—" On Thursday last, arrived at Brighton for the season, Wm. Wade, Esq., Master of the Ceremonies."

1807. He arrived in Brighton so early as June that year; but the announcements, for some reason, were long deferred. On the first night of the season only "about 10 couple danced!" If, however,

"he had cause
To wail the dimming of his shining star,"

its expiring rays were especially brilliant. The Race Ball was attended by all the "rank and elegance of the place"; but *the* Ball of the season was the Birth-day Ball of the Prince of Wales—one of the grandest ever given at "The Castle," at which the Prince and his Royal brothers and over 700 guests were present. The "M.C.'s" Ball,—his last, as it proved to be,—was given at the Castle on August 22, 1807; 200 fashionables attended, including the Duchess of Marlborough, Lord and Lady Huntingfield, Earl Craven, Mrs. Fitzherbert, and others; and henceforth he, who for 30 years and more had exercised sway over the World of Fashion in Brighton, is heard of no more! Even his death,—which took place, it is believed, in May, 1808,—is unrecorded!

"M.C." II. (WM. FORTH, ESQ.)

On the death of Mr. Wade there was, naturally, much speculation in fashionable circles as to who was to be his successor. Who appointed the first "M.C." (probably he appointed himself!) none will ever know; and the same obscurity exists respecting the self-constituted "Committee of Election" who appointed "M.C." II. All that the world knew respecting it appeared in the *Brighton Herald* of June 18, 1808:—

"On Wednesday last, the appointment of W. Forth, Esq., to succeed Mr. Wade, as Master of the Ceremonies, was confirmed at the Castle."

And a fortnight later the same journal stated:—

"The new Master of the Ceremonies resumed *(sic)* his office here, on Tuesday last, and paid his respects to the Nobility in public."

And henceforth "M.C." II. was installed in his office. But how different was his status from that of his predecessor! Mr. Wade appeared simply to have *entered* upon his office; exercised, apparently, unquestioned power and authority; issued orders; laid down regulations; was, in fact, controller of all that concerned the fashionable amusements of the town. But with Mr. Forth this was all changed. He was indeed "M.C.;" the acknowledged medium through whom the units of fashionable society were brought together at assemblies, balls, &c.; but, in other respects, the duties of his office had become simply passive—he had merely "entered into another man's labours." There were many reasons for this, the more important being the rapid increase in the number of residents and visitors, and the change in the manners and customs of society. Disunion likewise prevailed—his "kingdom was divided." Mr. Hicks, of "The

Old Ship," as with his predecessor of late years, would have none of him; and it was solely at "The Castle" that the more public functions of the "M.C.'s" office were exercised.* Yet his first announcement of the opening of the ball season would appear to indicate, by its courteous terms, that he did not desire to emulate the style of his predecessor in days gone by:—

"THE Nobility and Gentry are most respectfully acquainted that the Balls for the Season will commence on Monday, the 25th instant, at Tilt's Rooms.
"W. S. FORTH, Master of the Ceremonies.
"July 14th, 1808."

The first public ball under his auspices was well attended; as were his own assemblies, two of which were now given in each season. But it is needless to recapitulate these, or the Race and other Balls, which recurred each season with varying success. To attend these Balls would seem to have been the "M.C.'s" principal duty;—a simple and pleasant matter, it would have been thought. But no! Calumny was abroad; malice pointed its shafts; rivalry uttered its taunts; and with a section of the fashionable community Mr. Forth was evidently out of favour. With another section he was all in all. Pæans by the latter were sung in his praise. One of these was as follows:—

> "Hail! to the Chief who delights in protecting
> The roses of beauty from calumny's thorn;
> Youth and age all confiding around him collecting,
> Regret not the moments which ne'er shall return.
> Heaven grant him happiness,
> Earth lend him every bliss,
> Joyous to dwell in the circles of mirth;
> While ev'ry Brighton Belle,
> Joining to wish him well,
> Hasten to the gay dance, protected by FORTH.
>
> "And hail! to the maid, who her parent obeying,
> Ne'er seeks for amusement where vice has a share;
> The circle she joins in, with caution surveying,
> And alike of the wit and the coxcomb takes care.
> Widow, or Brighton maid,
> Never shall be betray'd,

---

* The "reason why" does not appear, but there was, at this time, a spirit of rivalry, which continued for some years, between "The Castle" and "The Old Ship,"—assemblies being held at each on the same evening. In Sept., 1808, the ball at "The Castle" was opposed by a divertisement at "The Old Ship"—about 140 attended the former, and over 500 the latter. This rivalry entered also into other departments of business besides assemblies, judging by the following paragraph, which appeared in a contemporary publication:—"The Castle, fronting the Steyne, and almost adjoining the Prince's Palace, has in no other point of view whatever the advantage of situation of the Old Ship, which inn is more centrally seated in the town, in Ship-street, and though the rays of Royalty but seldom irradiate the premises, the first families of Nobility resort thither."

> Fearless shall tread in the footsteps of mirth;
> Lightly skim o'er the ground,
> While ev'ry voice shall sound,
> Long may the dance be directed by FORTH.
>
> "Joy to the maids, who the pride are of Brighton,
> And gaily all innocent pleasure pursue;
> May the sun of prosperity shine with fresh light on
> Each fair one who seeks to give merit its due.
> Join all your voices then;
> Let our shores sound again;
> Weave the fresh laurels for honour and worth;
> Loud let the echoes ring,
> While ev'ry maid shall sing
> Long may our Balls be directed by FORTH."

The " M.C.'s " office, therefore, was not a "bed of roses." On the death of Mr. Tilt, "The Castle" changed hands. His successors, Messrs. Gilburd and Haryett, did their best to render the rooms all that could be desired; but the public taste drifted in other directions,—towards concerts, entertainments, &c., which were numerous in Brighton during the season. The weekly assemblies were at a discount; so much so that, in August, 1815, Messrs. Gilburd and Haryett closed the rooms for want of support, returning the money to subscribers, who did not exceed 20! Then came a "difference," between the "M.C." and the proprietors of "The Castle," "difficult to adjust;" and, in consequence, the Assembly Rooms remained closed with, it was said, no prospect of re-opening. While the difference was being adjusted, a Mr. Wilson announced that "he had been appointed 'M.C.' of the new Assembly Rooms on the West Cliff;" that "he would give his first Ball there on October 12;" and further, that he would give instruction in "waltzing, cotillons, French dances, English country dancing, Irish and Scotch reels," &c. This rivalry soon healed the breach at "The Castle;" it being forthwith announced that "lovers of dance will no longer be deprived of their weekly amusements." So things went on pleasantly for a year or more. The "M.C." rose with the occasion; for, in 1817, he actually showed a spice of his great predecessor's quality, making the following announcement:—

"The introduction of TEA into the Ball room at 'The Castle' having been the last season much objected to by the Company, the Master of the Ceremonies has been induced *to alter it*, and in future Tea will, on any one ordering it, be served in an adjoining Tea room, at 1s per head."

The anti-tea drinkers *must* have been satisfied with this grand exhibition of the M.C.'s power! The remaining ten years of Mr. Forth's official life were, however, not of the brightest. There were balls and balls. But Mr. Shuckard (Mr. Hicks's successor), of "The Old Ship," engaged his own "M.C." Then the assemblies at "The Castle" once more failed for the want of support;—subsequently, the proprietors made their own announcements of assemblies, &c. The fortunes of "The Castle"—so long the centre of fashionable

LIEUT.-COLONEL ELD

(The last "M.C." of Brighton).

gaiety—apparently waned fast; for the Race Ball in 1819, as well the Regent's Birth-day Ball, were given at "The Old Ship," Mr. Forth officiating there (his rival " M.C. " had departed) for the first time. A year or two later "The Castle" ceased to exist; and all public assemblies, &c., were for the future at "The Old Ship." The " M.C.'s " balls continued there, with more or less patronage; but his health was giving way, and he was held of less account than ever in connection with the fashionable and public assemblies. Hints were thrown out of *resignation.* Shade of William Wade! "to this complexion had it come at last!" But resignation was a serious matter; the emoluments of the " M.C.'s " office, in spite of its diminished importance, being, at this period, over £1,000 a year! Candidates for the expected vacancy were soon in the field; notably Captain Maher and Lieut.-Colonel Eld. The latter, in February, 1827, issued the following :—

"A CARD. — TO THE RESIDENTS AND VISITORS OF BRIGHTON.

"LADIES AND GENTLEMEN,—Having received a promise from Mr. Forth that he will resign the situation of Master of the Ceremonies to me, *upon certain pecuniary conditions*, which are not yet arranged, I beg leave to offer myself as a CANDIDATE whenever a vacancy may take place: and if you think me sufficiently worthy of your confidence to honour me with your support, I will do all in my power to deserve it.
"I have the honour to remain, Ladies and Gentlemen,
"Your obedient, humble Servant,
"JOHN ELD."

Another year passed; and still Mr. Forth was " M.C." In spite of hints to the contrary, he showed great reluctance to relinquish office; but finally ABDICATED in March, 1828; when "a meeting of fashionables took place at 'The Old Ship,'—Sir W. Inglis, C.B., in the chair," and, being elected " without a dissentient voice,"

"M.C." III. (LIEUT.-COLONEL JOHN ELD)

Reigned in his stead! The new Potentate of Fashion subsequently published the following address :—

"TO THE RESIDENTS AND VISITORS OF BRIGHTON.

"LADIES AND GENTLEMEN,— I return you my sincere thanks for the favour you have conferred upon me this day in appointing me to the situation of MASTER OF THE CEREMONIES. It shall be my chief study to merit your confidence and support by exerting myself to the utmost to promote and regulate those amusements which you may be pleased to place under my direction.
"I have the honour to remain,
"Your obliged and obedient humble Servant,
"JOHN ELD."
"Old Ship, March, 1828."

None who knew Lieut.-Colonel Eld—an English gentleman in the best sense of the word: his public and private character irreproachable; his demeanour, never exacting, but at all times forbearing and considerate—doubted that he would do his utmost to fulfil the promise of his address and faithfully carry out the duties of "M.C." of Brighton according to the latest fashion. But how changed was this fashion to that of times gone by—when the first "M.C." held sway! One wholly regulated and supervised the early assemblies, &c.; the other was only too pleased to act *under direction*.

The difference in the official position of the respective "M.C.'s" was, however, merely the reflex of the great changes which, socially and otherwise, had taken place in the town during the interval when the first "M.C." entered upon his office, as controller of the gaieties of a village resorted to by "company," and when the last " M.C." was appointed to promote and regulate, as directed, the amusements of a large and populous fashionable town. During the interval of 50 years the population of Brighton had increased from about 3,000 to nearly 40,000; and the growth of the town had been in a corresponding ratio. It could now boast of being the favourite marine residence of Royalty and Fashion; for several years large numbers of the wealthier middle class had resorted to it either for health or pleasure; whilst within the town itself commercial activity was rife in every direction.

With such changes, the fashionable amusements were almost imperceptibly adapted to surrounding circumstances, and were given under different auspices. In earlier times the higher class of assemblies, &c., were confined to a comparatively small circle; but 50 years later the area was largely extended. Many of those who had hitherto been kept without the narrow confines now sought to be admitted; for the World of Fashion—though it had long since broken its own leading-strings with regard to balls, &c.,—erected self-devised barriers against encroachments from without. Lady patronesses, with "vouchers," were brought into vogue; and the old forms of introduction, &c., through the "M.C." became more and more obsolete. An ancient matron or an antiquated beau, who possibly in their youthful days underwent the then imperative introduction to the "M.C.," might still deem it orthodox to enter their names in his book, or impress their younger charges with its necessity or importance. The "meeting of fashionables" in 1828 had, doubtless, a leaven of the "old school," and hence were unwilling wholly to discontinue a time-honoured office, which, if latterly unsatisfactorily filled, yet served a purpose so far as it went. The conditions, however, under which Lieut.-Colonel Eld accepted office indicated its ultimate extinction. He attended the fashionable balls, made introductions, &c.; but this duty gradually became more and more a matter of form than of necessity; for the ancient glory of the office had departed, and what remained was but the semblance of its former dignity and importance.

The death-blow, however, to the expiring office of "M.C." came from an unexpected quarter. While coaches brought visitors to Brighton by hundreds only, the "M.C." might take cognizance of the votaries of Fashion; but when the "iron horse" supplanted coaches and brought visitors by thousands and tens of thousands—the major portion of whom knew little, and cared less, for old usages and ceremonies—the "M.C.'s" occupation was virtually gone. The office was, in fact, behind the age. Lieut.-Colonel Eld ceased soon after, we believe, to have a book at the Libraries ; and shorn of this source of income, the emoluments of his office in its closing days must have been of the scantiest. Still the gallant old Lieut.-Colonel, like a true soldier, held to his post, and, though past three score years and ten, bated no jot of his old style or dignity. However, by reason of death, absence, or other causes, the interest in, and attendance at, the "M.C.'s" Ball yearly became less; yet, singularly enough, one of his last Balls—if not the last—on November 20, 1854—was a brilliant success. Over 500 were present, including the Russian officers taken prisoners in the Crimean war (on *parole*, at Lewes), the officers of the Regiment then in Brighton, &c. ; but a little over a year later—on the 22nd December, 1855, in his 76th year—Lieut.-Colonel Eld passed to his long home, and at his death the "M.C." Dynasty in Brighton ended.

The last "M.C." of Brighton is more remembered by his personal characteristics than by his office. He was *sui generis*. When abroad, he was always on foot, and rarely with company. But those who ever saw him, and noted his erect form, his dancing gait, his singularity of dress, eccentricity of action, and his altogether quaint appearance —felt involuntarily that he was "somebody." The peculiarities, however, of the late "M.C." have been so faithfully limned by the late Rev. Sydney Smith, that a notice of the last local representative of a defunct institution could not be more fittingly closed than by transcribing it :—" *Who* he is, I know not; but I am certain *what* he is. It is that distinguished functionary, the Master of the Ceremonies. It could be no one else. It was a gentleman attired *point device*, walking down the Parade, like Agag, ' delicately.' He pointed out his toes like a dancing-master; but carried his head like a potentate. As he passed the stand of flys, he nodded approval, as if he owned them all. As he approached the little goat carriages, he looked askance over the edge of his starched neckcloth and blandly smiled encouragement. Sure that in following him, I was treading in the steps of greatness, I went on to the Pier, and there I was confirmed in my conviction of his eminence ; for I observed him look first over the right side and then over the left, with an expression of serene satisfaction spreading over his countenance, which said, as plainly as if he had spoken to the sea aloud, ' That is right. You are low-tide at present ; but never mind, in a couple of hours, I shall make you high-tide again.' "

THE OLD THEATRES.

"Near the Stein."

The first Temple devoted to Thalia and Melpomene in Brighton was of the humblest character. It was simply a barn; situate "near the Stein,"—on the very spot, we believe, where was subsequently reared and devoted to other deities,—to Bacchus and to Circe,—the Brighton Pavilion! The honour of opening the first Theatre (temporary as it proved to be) in Brighton is due to Mr. Johnson, then the Proprietor of the Salisbury, Chichester, and Portsmouth Theatres, and, seeing the difficulties to be surmounted, it is marvellous that he should have undertaken the task.* He doubtless had heard—who had not?—of the fashionable company who were wont to visit Brighton in the season,—of the glories of the Steine, of the assemblies and balls, tea parties and promenades, and other gaieties indulged in,—and deemed a well-conducted Theatre would be no unworthy supplement to them. But *where* was it to be opened? One or other of the Assembly Rooms,—at "The Castle" or at "The Old Ship"—as the scenery and accessories would have interfered little with the ordinary amusements there, would naturally be first thought of. Seeing, however, that such was not the case, and having regard to the singular but unavoidable obligations to which the Proprietor was subjected, it must be conjectured that the visit of Mr. Johnson's company was not regarded with favour by that all-powerful Potentate of Fashion, the then "M.C." of Brighton! Was it not an intrusion on his domain?—would it not detract from the splendour of his Assembly Nights?† Whether or no this was the case, Mr. Johnson had no alternative but to open, as stated, in a barn and under contract to quit "as soon as convenient to bring the Harvest Home." However, he set to work with great energy, and "no expense was spared to make the Theatre commodious." The ground-

---

* From what is known of Mr. Johnson, he would seem to have been a pioneer in provincial theatrical catering. His Theatre at Chichester (opened in 1764) was originally a malthouse; and that of Southampton (opened 1766) was converted from a silk-mill, by a subscription from the inhabitants. Seeing, too, that Mr. Johnson had a Theatre at Chichester in 1764, it is most probable that it was he (though his name is not mentioned) who brought the "Chichester Company of Comedians" in Nov., 1764, to Brighton, when they performed the *Busy Body* and the *Mock Doctor* in the Barn which abutted on to the north-western corner of Castle-square (near where the County Bank is now), which, when not in use for corn, did duty as a repository of the Fine Arts, learned pig exhibitions, &c. The "company of comedians" included Mr., Mrs., and Miss Bruton, Mr. and Mrs. Peto, Mr. Peto, jun., Mr. and Mrs. Salmon, Mr. Irish, Mr. Adams, and Mrs. Cuthbert. The prices of admission to this primitive entertainment were: Pit, 2s.; First Gallery, 1s.; Upper Gallery, 6d.

† That the Master of the Ceremonies exercised a powerful influence for and against the Theatres in Brighton is certain, by the fact that, for nearly half a century later, the nights of performance, with few exceptions, had to be subordinated to the ball nights at "The Castle" and "The Old Ship." So lately as Jan. 13th, 1823, when the "M.C.'s" ball took place at "The Old Ship," the Theatre was closed!

floor was dug out to form the "Pit;" the "Boxes" and "Stalls" were probably ranged round the sides; the loft being devoted to "the gods." The stage, scenery, &c., were provided for at one end; while, to disguise the character of the interior, the sides were covered with canvas stretched upon poles; and, altogether, says a chronicler of the period, the Theatre "is fitted up in an elegant manner." It being past the middle of July, the enterprising Proprietor had only to lift up his eyes to the harvest fields,—which then stretched from what is now the Marine-parade (where there were three mills!)—to far beyond what is now Edward-street,—to see that they were already "whitening," which rendered his hope for "speedy commands" justifiable. The "house," it may be explained, was first opened in the day-time; but here is the Proprietor's preliminary advertisement:—

"Thursday, July 19, 1770.

"MR. JOHNSON, Proprietor of the Salisbury, Chichester, and Portsmouth Theatres, presents his compliments to the Nobility, Gentry, &c., now at Brighthelmstone, and begs leave to acquaint them that he is fitting up a temporary Theatre near the Stein, in which his Company will exert their utmost abilities to perform such Pieces as shall be advertised, *with the utmost decency.* As they merit, only hope for encouragement. The Company are obliged to resign the Theatre, as soon as convenient to bring the Harvest Home, by which their Stay will be SHORT, and their Expenses GREAT; therefore humbly hope for the speedy Commands of such Ladies and Gentlemen who intend favouring them.

"MR. JOHNSON proposes to perform the celebrated Mr. FOOTE'S Comedies once a Week, *in the Day-time,* the better to enable him not to intrude upon the regular Assembly Nights; to begin precisely at One o'Clock, and conclude at Half-an-hour after Two. *Any Morning so wet as to prevent the Gentry riding out, they will begin at Twelve, and furnish proper Amusement till Two.*

"The Company will begin to perform on WEDNESDAY NEXT.

"*⁎*⁎* No expense will be spared to make the Theatre commodious."

The day was subsequently altered to *Tuesday,* and so, on July, 24, 1770, a Theatre was first opened in Brighton; and, it is pleasant to note, to a "numerous and polite audience." What piece or pieces were performed, who were the actors, or how they acquitted themselves in their respective parts, is unrecorded; but the following is

THE PROLOGUE,

Spoken by Mr. JOHNSON, at the Opening of his Theatre at Brighthelmstone.
[*Behind the Scenes.*
PRAY let me go;—now do, good brother Tom,
Let's see our Barn before the Players come.
Enters in the Character of a Farmer.

Zooks! what a change!—I vow I shouldn't know it;
The droll contriver surely was a *Poet,*
Or some *Improver,*—(both alike their brains!)
Who else would change plain Nature with such pains!

But all is *hocus-pocus'd* with such art,
The damn'd *fire-eater* must have had a part.
   Where! all our skins, that hung on yonder beam?
Vanish'd they are, like visions of a dream!
In gloves the fair, on whiter skins now wear 'em,
Unless, perhaps (I'd tell if I were near 'em)——
Here dwell'd some lambs,—and still, I trust, they're found,
Sitting transform'd, in innocence, around.
The late black cobwebs, by some witch's paws,
Are conjur'd all—to lady's lace and gauze.
Our oats, no more! but, if the truth were known,
Here, in their stead, a few *wild oats* are sown.
Our chaff and straw are also stole, or fled!
Yet soon return,—in *Players*, poorly fed!
But, *short* their stay,—I must 'em friendly warn—
For Harvest's near—and I shall—sweep the Barn.
Zounds! now I think; in this same Barn, I'm told,
They've dug a Pit—that can a *hundred* hold:
Who knows, the Play'rs (the surer way to thrive)
Mean to inter their Landlord, here, alive?
Be *that* their game?—then, by the setting sun,
My worthy friends, 'tis time for me to run.
But you'll sit still, and listen to their play;
To pay our rent, nay, come here ev'ry day.
                                    [*Going.*

Soft! ere I go;—I hope I've not offended;
                                    [*Returns.*
A Peasant, I;—my manners must be mended.
With aught I said I meant not to offend;
For, *each to please*, is every being's end;
That point in view, why speak not as we can?
To man, *free-born*, a man is but a man.

On the following Tuesday, *at Six in the Evening*, the comic opera of *The Maid of the Mill* was performed, by desire of the Right Hon. the Countess of Pembroke. Then came the Lewes Race week, and the Proprietor, with a shrewd eye to business,—having ascertained *where* all the Fashionables would be in the afternoon—gave performances "*every morning at eleven of the clock.*" The Right Hon. Lady Masham gave her patronage on the 14th August, the comedy of *The Clandestine Marriage* being performed. But the "inevitable" was at hand: the reapers had done their work—the Harvest was coming Home; and the Proprietor's next announcement was as follows:—

"N.B. The Company will perform on Wednesday, Friday, and Saturday; and, as they are *obliged to quit the Theatre in a short time*, they humbly hope for the speedy encouragement of the Ladies and Gentlemen in and about Brighthelmstone."

There were, however, a few more performances, one of *The Wonder*, by desire of the Hon. Mrs. Brudenel, on which occasion there was "a polite and crowded audience; and the play was conducted with *regularity* and *decorum*." The last play performed in the original Theatre was *The Merry Wives of Windsor*, on Tuesday,

August 30th, by desire of Master and Miss Bathurst. In announcing it, the Proprietor adds :—

"N.B. The Company beg leave to return their thanks in the most respectful manner to the Nobility, Gentry, &c., who have hitherto been pleased to honour them with their countenance, and take this method of informing them that, as they have been *obliged by contract to quit the place of performing*, they have fitted up another Barn on the Steine, where (as they have spared no expense to render it as commodious as possible) they humbly hope for a continuance of their favours, which they will endeavour to meet by a close attention to their business during the short remainder of their stay here."

No record—no tradition—exists as to where the "company of comedians" opened their new "house," or when they quitted it, or what they performed ; and it may be said of their sojourn here, as of the apparitions evoked by the witches in *Macbeth*—they

"Come like shadows, so depart."

The Theatre in North Street.

About four years elapsed (August, 1774,) before another Theatre was opened in Brighton. This time it was of a more permanent character. Its situation was in North-street (the entrance being that of the present No. 53), and it was built by "Mr. Samuel Paine, a bricklayer," the Manager being Mr. Roger Johnstone (formerly the property-man at Covent-garden). The following is the first "bill of the play" :—

At the NEW THEATRE in BRIGHTHELMSTON.

On TUESDAY, Aug. 30, 1774, will be performed, a COMEDY, call'd

THE JEALOUS WIFE.

Oakley - by Mr. HAGUE. Major Oakley - by Mr. GRAHAM.
Charles Oakley - - by Mr. G. GRAHAM.
Rupert - - by Mr. WEST. Lord Trinket - - by Mr. HUTTON.
Sir Henry Beagle - - - by Mr. WILKS.
Captain O'Cutter - by Mr. HOLLAND. Paris - by Mr. HAWKINS.
Tom - by Mr. BROWN. William - by Mr. MILWARD.
Mrs. Oakley - - by Mrs. GRAHAM.
Lady Freelove - by Mrs. ROBBINS. Harriet - by Mrs. WILKS.
Toilet - by Mrs. HARRISON. Chambermaid - by Mrs. HAGUE.

A HORNPIPE - - by Mr. WILKINSON.

To which will be added, a FARCE, call'd

LETHE, OR ÆSOP IN THE SHADES.

Æsop - - by Mr. HAGUE. Charon - - by Mr. HAWKINS.
Old Man and Fine Gentleman - by Mr. HUTTON.
Drunken Man - by Mr. HOLLAND. Frenchman - by Mr. GRAHAM.
Fine Lady - - by Mrs. GRAHAM.

What attendance there was on the opening night of the new Theatre is not recorded; or what were the prices of admission. Later on they were as follows:—Boxes, 3s. 6d.; Pit, 2s.; Gallery, 1s. There was no "half price" at this period; and "doors opened at 6; to commence at 7." The season lasted till November 7, the "bill of fare" being of a high standard both in comedy and tragedy. For the benefit of Mr. Samuel Paine, "the only Proprietor of the New Theatre," *Richard III.* was performed, "with Entertainments." On the "last night of the season" there was

AN EPILOGUE,

Written by a GENTLEMAN at BRIGHTHELMSTON, and spoke there by one of the ACTORS.

OUR diff'rent PLAY'RS to diff'rent PARTS we suit,
Hague plays *King Richard*, I'll perform *Sir Brute*.
Wilks struts *Mercutio*, *Capulet's* by *Fryar*,
Graham and *West* in turns have play'd the *Lyar*.
Some FEMALES, too, increase our little scene,
One *creeps a Chambermaid*, one *storms a Queen*.
Thus to *some purpose* are *our Wives* converted,
Nor *we* displeas'd to think *they've you diverted*.
But in our motley set (the case is hard)
Not one among us all can play a BARD;
Hence, to our grief, between the *piece* and *farce*
Dull Country Music fills the place of Verse;
No welcome EPILOGUE to charm the ear,
How very awkward must that hour appear;
While, tir'd with tragic rant and fond caressing,
Some weary *Queen* for *second part* is dressing.
Now, to remove this long-prevailing evil,
Some *Stranger* here (and sure 'tis wond'rous civil)
Has sent this EPILOGUE!—Can we refuse
The timely present of so free a muse?
Besides, his future lines proclaim our meanings
And speak in pleasant verse our sep'rate feelings;
As bound in duty ere this season's o'er,
And headier billows beat this sea-girt shore;
Ere (as our children say) "*for good and all*,"
No hearers left to please, our curtain fall,
'Tis sure but right to thank you for the favours
So kindly shewn to our theatric labours.
But for those favours shewn, perhaps our stage
Had felt the fullness of its *Builder's rage*,
And *heav'n born Gods* and *Kings* (how hard their fate)
Thro' the close lattice of some dimly grate,
To *subjects vile* had stretch'd the suppliant palm,
And e'en from passing *clowns* implor'd an alm;
From day to day had led a life precarious,
With date *obolum* like *Belisarius*;
While *pitying Queens* had pledg'd the *camblet stole*,
The *glass-set coronet*, and *tragic bowl*;
Nay, *perhaps more*, had truck'd their own sweet charms
To buy their dearer husbands to their arms.
In other places sure such things have been,
And dimm'd the lustre of the *trav'lling scene*;

But thro' your aid, distresses such as these
Ne'er damp'd our poor accomplishments to please.
Free from th' unfeeling Dun's relentless claw,
The Bailiff's cunning, and the prison's law,
Secure we've liv'd—our lives to *you* we owe,
And to your smiles these grateful numbers flow.

The Theatre was opened subsequently for an occasional night or two; on December 19, with *Barbarossa*, when for the first time "stars" appeared,—Mr. Williams (from Drury-lane) and Miss Stede (from Covent-garden); the latter, it being announced, will "dance a hornpipe at the end of the play"!

In the next season (which began in June) there was an excellent company both for tragedy and comedy; the celebrated dancer, Mons. Rollet (from Drury-lane) being also engaged. *The Wonder* was performed on the opening night. Shakespeare was duly honoured during the season (for Mr. Paine's benefit, *King Lear*); varied by sterling comedies and some capital farces. Nor was there lack of novelty; for the last new tragedy, *Matilda; or the Rival Brothers* (by the Rev. W. Franklin) was produced; also the then new musical farce, *The Waterman* (with music by Dibdin). Pantomime was in this season (but not at Christmas) first introduced to Brighton audiences, the entertainment being entitled *Harlequin from the Moon; or a Trip to the Regatta*, with "new Scenes (one an exact representation of the Thames Regatta), Cloaths, Machinery, Decorations, &c."

The following season there was equal liberality in catering, with a fresh company, which included Messrs. West, Stretton, Slaney, Everard, Painter, Lyons, Waylett, and Creswick, and Mesdames Johnston, Painter, Dunn, Snook, and Sharpe. But whether successful or not, or whether or no the general supervision and responsibility were more than Mr. Paine cared for, is now unknown; certain it is, that in 1777 he let the Theatre for a term of 15 years, at the annual rent of 60 guineas, to Mr. Fox, of Covent-garden Theatre.*

With the new management, the Theatre was re-decorated and had new machinery; the scenes were re-painted by Mr. Carver, of Covent-garden Theatre; and on Tuesday, July 1, 1777, was duly opened, "By His Majesty's Servants from the Theatre Royal in London," with *Jane Shore*. On the play-bill was the following N.B.: "No person whatever admitted behind the scenes, nor any money returned after the curtain is drawn up." The company included some of the best dramatic talent of the day, including Mr. and Mrs. Ward, Mr. and

---

* Mr. Fox, by the covenants of the lease, appears to have "stolen a march" upon Mr. Paine. The latter stipulated for the *net receipts* of one night each season, and for his family to have the free use of the Theatre at all times to witness the performances; but when the lease was afterwards referred to, it read *net profits*, and Mr. Paine was called upon to defray the expenses of his benefit night! He, however, soon "turned the tables." The right of gratuitous admission to the Theatre to himself and family, or to the places they might occupy, was never disputed; and he, therefore, with them, entered the Theatre for a succession of nights, and resolutely occupied the best seats in the boxes. Thus opposed, Mr. Fox speedily consented to ratify his first agreement.

Mrs. Farren (the parents of "old" Farren of a later time), Messrs. Dighton and Creswick, and the celebrated Mrs. Baddeley, a versatile and most accomplished actress, to whom no character seemed to come amiss, either in the higher walks of tragedy or comedy.*

Without enumerating the pieces performed during this or the following seasons, it may suffice to say that the catering, for a provincial Theatre, was in every way excellent. "A Diarist" in 1778, speaking of Brighton Theatre, says he was "pleasingly disappointed, because the company performed a great deal better than from information (surely, not tea-table detraction at the "Castle"?) I had been taught to expect; the ladies also were, what all stage-ladies not always are, extremely *decent*." Among the "events" of Mr. Fox's opening season was (in August, 1777,) the first recorded grand concert in Brighton, the *prima donna* being the celebrated Signorina Storace. The boxes and pit were put together at 10s. 6d.; gallery, 5s. A speciality of the following season was the performance of *four* pieces in one evening, on the occasion of the Manager's benefit; and he assured the public "they are for a few hours' pleasantry, and *will be all over by ten o'clock, and hopes for their kind protection"* ! There must have been this season—shall we say it? a "smell of tallow" in the house; the Manager announcing that for the future he should use only the "best spermacetti oil and wax candles." †

---

* Mrs. Baddeley was endowed with a lovely face, a handsome figure, and with numberless personal graces; but her habits of life were most discreditable. She was the daughter of a serjeant-trumpeter to Geo. II., and was born in 1745. At 18 she eloped with an actor, named Baddeley, and shortly after made her *début* at Drury-lane, playing Cordelia. She subsequently proved to be a most versatile actress. The King was so pleased with her as Fanny, in *The Clandestine Marriage*, that he commissioned Zoffany to paint her portrait in that character. If gifted as an actress, she was a most depraved woman. She wept penitently one day to her mother (who sent for her, when dying,) and the next (says a biographer) "started off to Paris to meet a paramour. She plunged into all the gaieties of the French metropolis, and returned to London more confirmed in her vicious inclinations than ever." When she was at Brighton, Mrs. Baddeley's beauty and charming manners were the theme of all tongues, and persons passing her, when promenading on the Steine, would exclaim, "There is that divine face!" "What a sweet woman!" &c. Her extravagance and depraved life eventually led to sad embarrassment. A public subscription procured for her temporary relief; but, relapsing into her old courses, she died, under the most deplorable circumstances, in Edinburgh, in July, 1801.

† Gas has been used so long for lighting Theatres, &c., that the inconveniences of the "oil, wax, and tallow era" are practically unknown to the present generation. In the olden time, in Theatres, &c., the Candle-Snuffer was an "institution"; the duties being performed when the Act-drop or curtain was down, or when the scenes were shifted. Have we not the authority of the immortal Gil Blas on the point! Who can forget his visit to the green-room (Book vii, ch. 8), where he says:—"I was not let off with the kisses of the actors and actresses only: I was compelled to endure the polite attentions of the scene-painters, of the fiddlers, of the prompter, of the candle-snuffer, and the under-candle-snuffer," &c.? In the *Rejected Addresses*, too, in the imitation of Crabbe, occur the opening lines:—

"'Tis sweet to view, from half-past five to six,
Our long wax candles with short cotton wicks."

This was written in 1812, and refers to the fact that Drury Lane Theatre was at that time lighted with candles. There were, however, Candle-Snuffers and Candle-Snuffers! One worthy "to write M.A. after his name" would, with polished weapon and pliant hand, take off the "wick" deftly; while another of the craft, less skilful, "would'nt know were to have it;" and, consequently, smoky wick and inevitable "gutter" dispensed unsavoury odours through the house.

FASHIONABLE AND POPULAR AMUSEMENTS—THE OLD THEATRES. 47

"Royalty," in the persons of the Duke and Duchess of Cumberland, accompanied by Lady Ferrers, the Hon. Miss Luttrell, and Sir Thomas Fowke, paid, in August, 1779, its first visit to the Brighton Theatre, a box being specially fitted up for the Royal party and ornamented with the Ducal Arms. The house was "crowded, the company putting forth their fullest strength." *The School for Scandal* and *Three Weeks after Marriage* were performed; and, adds a chronicler, "every body was delighted by the affability shown by the apparently happy pair."

In the season, too, of 1779, the celebrated Mrs. Robinson first appeared in Brighton, and whilst here, performed, in addition to other important characters, Perdita, with which her name was ever after indissolubly associated.* In subsequent years, there seemed to be on the part of the Management no efforts spared to deserve success. Not only did Shakespeare and the legitimate drama have the pre-eminence, but there was scarcely an actor or actress of note at the period who did not appear to Brighton audiences.† Digges (who played Douglas on the first night of the production of that tragedy in Edinburgh), and the veteran comedian, Ryder, each did a round of Shakespearean characters, and with them was Booth and Wilson from Covent-garden. Mrs. Baddeley again appeared, with Mrs. Sharp and Mrs. Wilson from Drury-lane. Quick, too (in August, 1787,) made his bow at the "Village by the Sea;" and in the *Duenna* (in his celebrated character of Isaac Mendoza), *Barnaby Brittle*, and other comic operas achieved immense success.‡ After the

---

* Poor Perdita! She was of surpassing beauty; and such, we are told, was the early ripeness of her charms, that she received an offer of marriage before she was thirteen years of age; at which time she went to a school in London kept by Hannah More and her sisters. Mrs. Robinson's maiden name was Darby. She was born at Bristol in 1758. She was clandestinely married in her 16th year; and separated from her husband (whom she accompanied to prison, when he was arrested for debt, and who proved to be a heartless profligate), in her 19th year. Thrown upon her own resources, Garrick (who himself became her instructor) and Sheridan encouraged her to adopt the stage as a means of subsistence. Her *début* at Old Drury, as Juliet, was eminently successful; and subsequently she took the "lead" there both in tragedy and comedy. The Prince of Wales became enamoured of her, on seeing her as Perdita, in *A Winter's Tale*, after a performance by Royal command, and wrote to her under the name of "Florizel." He was then in his 19th year; she was in her 21st. The Prince of Wales's association with, and subsequent conduct towards, this gifted actress were among the most discreditable episodes of his early career. Previously to her first interview with the Prince of Wales, he had enclosed her a bond for £20,000, to be paid on his coming of age; but, on the very day of his majority, she received a cold letter from him, saying, "We must meet no more." But enough of such details. She later on resided alternately in England and France, and in 1787 fixed her residence in Brighton; and it was here she wrote the celebrated lines "To him (the Prince of Wales) who will understand them," and "The Haunted Beach." Mrs. Robinson was the authoress of several works, including two volumes of poems. In 1797 she undertook the poetical department of the *Morning Post;* but it was only for a brief period, her death taking place Dec. 26th, 1800.

† "Tradition" says Garrick appeared at the old house; but there is no record of it. A Mr. Kean did, in 1786, in "Attic Entertainments," consisting of readings, recitations, and music.

‡ Quick was a "Whitechapel boy," who joined a theatrical company at the early age of 14, and at once "leaped into success." He was a great favourite with Geo. III., and, indeed, with all the Royal Family. As an actor, he was humorous

regular season had closed, he even "tried his fortune in a second fight," by opening the house again for a few evenings longer, "at the instance of a Personage whose commands he holds himself honoured in obliging;" the Prince of Wales and the Duke of York being frequently present to witness the performances.

Royalty, evidently, was not chary of its patronage to the old Theatre. Not only did the Prince of Wales honour it with his presence on his first visit to Brighton (the captivating dames of Cytherea—one a self-styled Duchess—vieing with each other to attract the eye of the Royal youth, and public curiosity being so great that there was an overflow of two hundred persons), but, subsequently, whenever the Prince or any of the Royal Family were in Brighton, the Manager invariably had the honour of a bespeak. In September, 1788, the Prince of Wales, the Duke of Gloucester, Mrs. Fitzherbert, and all the rank and fashion in Brighton, were present three times in one week; the notorious Earl Barrymore ("Hellgate") essaying his skill as an amateur actor.* If he failed to achieve success (His Lordship, it is said, was "under the influence of timidity,"—surely, for the first time in his life!) he was the means of bringing many golden guineas into the Managerial exchequer, by reason of the house being fully attended on each occasion. (Into the Mrs. Hill episode,—in October, 1786, that lady being induced to play Scrub in the *Beaux's Stratagem*, and then ridiculed for her pains!—of which Royalty, or some one closely associated with Royalty, was said to have been the chief instigator, we need not enter; as, though creating much sensation at the time, it was more or less a personal matter.)

---

in spite of himself. He once essayed to play Richard III. at Covent-garden; but so ludicrous was the effort that, the audience "could not choose but laugh;" and he, thereupon, gave a complete burlesque of the character, "fooling" them to the top of their bent.

* Earl Barrymore was one of the "fastest" of the Prince's earlier companions. When he appeared at the Brighton Theatre he was not 21. On coming of age he inherited £24,000 a year, and evidently did his best to spend it. He built at Wargrave, his country seat, a theatre for amateur performances and concerts, bringing the actresses and vocalists from London and elsewhere; kept a pack of hounds; had a stock of red deer for hunting; started a phaeton with four greys, and exhibited his skill as a coachman by racing on the Bath road one of the stage coaches. He graduated on the "turf," at Newmarket, in 1789, —the Races at which the Prince of Wales's Traveller beat the Duke of Bedford's Grey Diomed, and on which race alone £200,000 depended. But the Noble Lord was such a heavy loser at Newmarket,—not only of considerable sums in betting, but every horse which he ran lost,—that he publicly declared after the meeting he would entirely give it up. He appears to have forgotten this declaration very soon! for he ran several horses at Brighton Races in 1790-1-2, and probably for years after. About 1791 he was evidently in the hey-day of that "fun and frolic" for which he was so distinguished. Twice during a fortnight did he get into "hot water" on the Steine; and a lawyer had to settle the business. When he went to the Theatre, he must needs create a sensation by going in a "vehicle called *Punch's coach!*" Then in September of that year he and his companions played the "MERRY MOURNERS" in Brighton—engaging a person to walk on all-fours with a coffin on his back at night-time; standing a coffin, with a mock corpse in it, upright against a door, so as to fall upon the person opening it after a knock, &c., and so frightening females or the unwary. A tradesman's wife was so much frightened by the falling of the mock corpse upon her, that premature labour was brought on, and the child died.

Despite, however, of Royal and other bespeaks, the patronage generally accorded to the Theatre would not seem to have been encouraging to the Lessee. The season of 1787—with Ryder and Quick as "stars"—was closed abruptly in August, for want of support; Mr. Buckle, the Manager, who "deserved better success than his reign experienced, retiring from the theatrical throne," and, it is added, "many of the infatuated followers of the sock and buskin will have to trudge numberless miles for fresh engagements!" Sorry encouragement this; and it would seem to have improved but little in the subsequent seasons. Half-prices were introduced in 1789; it being announced that after the first three acts "latter accompts will be taken: boxes, 2s.; pit, 1s.; gallery, 6d." No efforts appear to have been wanting to render the Theatre attractive. In 1786 the house was newly fitted up in an elegant manner,—the staircases widened, and the scenery repainted by artists from Covent-garden; and again in 1788 it was newly painted and beautified. The complete way in which many of the pieces were put upon the stage was marvellous. On one occasion (Mr. Fox's benefit) the *Tempest*—not as Shakespeare wrote it, but as Dryden and Davenant altered it!—was produced, "with Music, Machinery, Decorations, and other Incidents proper to the Play, with the Representation of a Ship in Distress, and afterwards Wrecked." In Pantomime, too,—" new speaking Pantomime," as it was then called,—the achievements would appear to have rivalled modern efforts in this direction. In October, 1782 (Pantomime was not then a Christmas treat*),—when Bates, from Covent-garden, was Harlequin,—*Touchstone, or Harlequin Traveller*, was produced. There was a representation of an Irish Giant, 8ft. 2in. in height; and Bates "jumped down his own throat;" the Pantomime concluding with "views of the Stein, the Libraries, Orchestra, &c., and a dance by the characters." The Manager also did his best to attract patronage by florid descriptive announcements. Thus, when *Macbeth* was performed, he says:—

"MACBETH. Written by Shakespear, and universally allowed to be the greatest Production of that immortal Bard. The Grandeur and Fire of the Language, the Flights of Fancy in the Scenes of the Witches (where the Poet has really soared above the Reach of Mortal Imagination), the beautiful Pathos of the Story (which is founded on FACT and recorded in the History of Scotland), and the inchanting Harmony of the Airs and Choruses, cannot fail producing the most delightful Effect and Entertainment."

Apart from the supposition that the influence of the reigning "M.C." was prejudicial to the patronage of the Theatre by the townsfolk and visitors, a possible reason for the scant encouragement afforded may have been the dislike of late hours in such an outside and ill-lighted locality as North-street then was, and seeing the little

---

* The first time that a Pantomime associated with Christmas was produced in Brighton was January 6, 1823. It was entitled *Harlequin* versus *Shakespeare; or Christmas Gambols;* and terminated with the defeat of the former and his associates.

protection afforded by the authorities,—for, in the announcements, the Manager was ever harping upon "early closing"—"The Prompter has orders to ring up the curtain exactly at the time advertised;" "The audience shall not be delayed long between the acts;" "The performances shall be over by 10.30 at farthest;" and on one special occasion he requested "punctually at the time of opening, that country visitors may not be detained (especially as it is moonlight) longer than 10.15."

The closing performances at the Theatre in North-street were in 1789. There was "no sign" that such was to be the case; the lease having two more years to run. But Mr. Fox, the Lessee, seems to have desired to have a Theatre of his own (one adequate to the accommodation of the increased population of the town), which was opened in Duke-street during the following year, when the house in North-street was closed till the lease had expired. It was subsequently—the Proprietor failing to obtain a license after the Duke-street Theatre was opened—converted into a printing office; was afterwards occupied for many years by a wine merchant; and, when he vacated it, again did duty as a printing-office.

The Theatre in Duke Street.

This Theatre, which was opened July 13, 1790, must have risen "like an exhalation," having been built by Mr. Fox in a few months. The license of the North-street Theatre was transferred to that of Duke-street, without the sanction or knowledge of Mr. Paine, the Lessor of the former building. On the face of it, Mr. Fox's conduct in the matter does not appear to have been altogether honourable, as it involved Mr. Paine in a pecuniary loss of several hundreds of pounds per annum, the North-street Theatre being useless without a license. As a *solatium*, we suppose, for this loss, Mr. Paine had a "benefit" at the Duke-street Theatre about six weeks after it was opened!

The new Theatre (which cost little short of £2,500) was constructed principally of wood; the front entirely so, though marked out in oblong squares to resemble stone. It had a plain tiled roof. It was built by Mr. Poune, of Brighton; Mr. Stills being the surveyor. As a reference to the annexed *plate* will give some idea of it, a description of the exterior is unnecessary. The interior was square; and, in the elegant way in which it was planned and fitted, it was said to have been little inferior to the Haymarket at that period; whilst the scenery, &c., by Williams, was entirely new. There was little or no ceremony on the opening night; not even an "address" being spoken; and the first "bill of fare" was *The West Indian* and *Barnaby Brittle*.

Mr. Fox's catering, during the opening season, deserved success: a constant succession of novelties was kept up, ranging from Shakespeare down to the latest "spectacle;" in fact, such was the high

character of the entertainments that, before the season closed, he received "marks of approbation from H.R.H. the Prince of Wales." Among the specialities were the production of *Cymbeline*; the "grand tragic-comic pantomime" of *Don Juan*, with a "beautiful display of the Fiery Abyss"; and the opera of *Marian*. This last, it was said, "would not be repeated," as the Proprietor of Covent-garden Theatre had lent the music and accompaniments with the stipulation that they "must be returned the day after the performance!" A great success was the *Life, Death, and Renovation of Tom Thumb the Great; or, the Fatal Effects of Misguided Love;* the "sensation" scene being "the Emancipation of Tom Thumb from his Confinement in the Abdomen of the Red Cow." Mr. Fox was evidently great in spectacular effects; for early in the season he displayed "The Review of the Grand Fleet," so as to afford a "just idea of our present naval preparations." The grandest achievement, however, in this direction was in October, 1790, when he produced *The Triumph of Liberty*. The announcement was as follows:—

An entirely new and splendid Entertainment, founded on the French Revolution, call'd,

The Triumph of Liberty; or, the Destruction of the Bastille.

In the course of the piece the following display of new Scenery, painted on purpose, including

A VIEW of the OUTSIDE of the BASTILLE, the GOVERNOR'S HOUSE, DRAWBRIDGE, MOAT, &c.

A Picturesque View of

THE INSIDE VIEW OF THE BASTILLE, WITH THE VARIOUS INSTRUMENTS OF TORTURE.

The different Gratings, Dungeons, and Cells from which the Miserable Objects made their Emancipation.

IN PART I. THE ATTACK, STORMING, AND DEMOLITION OF THE BASTILLE.

IN PART II. THE RELEASE OF THE PRISONERS; THE PROCESSION OF THE GOVERNOR TO EXECUTION.

The Procession that followed on the memorable occasion of the French Revolution attended by "BRITANNIA," who congratulates the Sons of France on the Establishment of "FREEDOM."

To conclude with a Full Chorus.

The *Triumph* was got up in capital style, and exhibited with unbounded applause; and, in consequence of its success, was repeated again and again.

Mr. Fox's company in the opening season included Messrs. Darley, Barrett, Kelly, jun., and Waylett; Mesdames Westray,

Waylett, Illiff, and Rivers, and Miss Fontenelle.* Among the "stars" who appeared were Bannister, jun., and Mr. Palmer, from "Old Drury." But the "bright particular star" was Mrs. Crouch, † who appeared as Polly in the *Beggars' Opera* (with Mr. Kelly, as Captain Macheath), for Kelly, jun.'s benefit.

In his second season Mr. Fox was again most liberal and energetic in his catering. Sterling comedy, opera, farce, and pantomime followed in quick succession. He had an entirely new company, but, though a writer says the "spirit of the public appears willing to reward the Proprietor for his endeavours to merit their protection and favour," he was in serious pecuniary difficulties. The Duke of Marlborough gave his patronage for his first benefit in August; and the Prince of Wales and Mrs. Fitzherbert were frequent visitors. Mr. Fox took a second benefit in September, the special attraction being the elder Bannister and Miss Fontenelle, who appeared in the *Beggars' Opera ;* but, strange to say, there was but a poor audience to welcome the veteran actor and his charming associate. One of the most amusing productions of the season was Cibber's burlesque tragedy of *Alexander the Little; or the Rival Queans*, the inscribed banners of the "Mock Triumphal Procession of Alexander into

---

* Miss Fontenelle was a charming and most vivacious actress. Of her Moggy, in *The Highland Reel*, it was said, "the matchless girl is equal to Mrs. Mostyn." She subsequently performed the character at Lewes; and an impressible youth of that ancient town, under the pseudonym of "Edgar," addressed to her on her departure

"AN HUMBLE TRIBUTARY LAY."

"Where'er you play, may taste attend, | May all admire your worth, like me;
And every critic be your friend. | An Edgar each spectator be;
Success be your's where'er you go; | Each say of favourite FONTENELLE,
Each benefit an overflow. | ' *Qui rive la* MOGGY *sans pareil.*'"

The popular actress, who was much esteemed both in public and private life, subsequently went to America, and died there from an attack of yellow fever in July or August, 1800.

† Mrs. Anna Maria Crouch was one of the most charming vocalists and actresses of her day. To Brightonians a special interest attaches to her, from the fact of her last days being spent in the town; and that her mortal remains lie in the churchyard of St. Nicholas, beneath a storied monument, surmounted by a classic urn, erected to her memory by Mr. Kelly, who was associated with her by the closest ties. She was the daughter of Mr. Phillips, an attorney, and was born in Gray's Inn, London, in 1763. Such, however, was the precocity of her musical talent, that, when only 10 years of age, Lady Lewes (wife of Sir Watkin Lewes, Lord Mayor of London,) had her almost constantly at her house, and introduced her to visitors as a songstress of great promise. At 16, she was articled to Mr. Linley, of Drury-lane, at a rising salary of from £6 to £12 a week; and her *début* as Mandane was a general triumph. She went to Dublin in 1783, where her beauty and talents excited the greatest sensation. Of her charms it is said, that so sweet a countenance, elegant person, and ravishing voice were not to be found united in one individual twice in a century. John Kemble fell desperately in love with her; but was refused. On her second visit to Dublin, a gentleman threatened to shoot her, if she would not receive his addresses! Soon after, she eloped with the son of a nobleman, but was brought back by her parents. She subsequently married Lieut. Crouch, R.N.; but the marriage proving unhappy, a separation took place by mutual consent. The marriage not being *legally* dissolved, she entered into a solemn *contract* with Mr. Kelly, a distinguished vocalist, with whom she was ever after associated in vocal and other engagements. When in the full perfection of song and beauty, Mrs. Crouch was seriously injured by a carriage accident; and the original strength and sweetness of her voice was lost for ever. Her health afterwards gave way. A change at Brighton was recommended; but it was without avail, as she died here, Oct. 2, 1804, breathing her last in the arms of her ardent admirer, Mr Kelly.

Babylon" being peculiarly appropriate and amusing; that of "Alexander's Fruiterer" preceding a "Jack Ass, Panniers, and Driver."

On the death of Mr. Fox, in 1792, Mr. J. Palmer (of Drury-lane, who had in the previous seasons appeared with much success) officiated as probationary Manager. He showed a most commendable energy in his new vocation; he had the house re-decorated; engaged a capital company (acknowledged to be "the completest out of London"), the *prima donna* being Mrs. Esten; and performed himself alternately at Brighton and at the Haymarket during the season! an instance of professional industry, it is said, " which has never been exceeded, if we except Mr. Elliston's alternate exhibitions at Bath and London, which procured him the title of the 'Telegraphic Actor.'"* Nor was there lack of "stars." In addition to Captain Wathen, there were Bannister, jun. (who appeared as Jerry Sneak), Mr. R. Palmer, and Mr. W. Parsons, from Drury-lane; the last was the best Sir Fretful of his day.† Late in the season of 1792, there was brought out a local interlude, entitled *Smoaker's Invitation to a Revel on the Beach*, in which doubtless the idiosyncrasies of the noted Brighton bather furnished ample food for mirth. The "great" night, however, was the last, when, by the desire of Mrs. Fitzherbert, there was an amateur performance, for " the benefit of those persons who unluckily failed in their former attempts." The tragedy of *The Orphan* was the piece selected, the performers being " principally young persons of the town." Of this first local amateur effort a critic says :—" The amateurs acquitted themselves in a manner that *must* have pleased the audience ; for they were in bursts of laughter throughout the tragedy. The Prince, we thought, *would have cracked his sides*." Of the lady who essayed the heroine, he adds (ungenerous man !) " the motion of her arms would better qualify her for a laundry than the stage ! "

Mr. Palmer, on the close of the season, seceded from the management of the Brighton Theatre, though his engagement had been made for two years longer. ‡

[* Mrs. Siddons rivalled Elliston later on. *The Times* of October 3rd, 1798, records:—"Among the wonders of the present day Mrs. Siddons' late achievements at Brighton, Bath, and London should not be forgotten. She positively performed at each of these places within the incredible short space of 96 hours!"]

† Mr. Parsons died in 1795. His widow (the daughter of the Hon. James Stewart) took his death so little to heart that she married her son's tutor four days after, and, it was said, had in the house for some days a dead and a living husband at the same time !

‡ Mr. John Palmer had a pleasing countenance, was of commanding stature, and of dignified bearing. His career as an actor was not altogether successful ; though he evidently strove hard to attain eminence in his profession. One of his best parts was Joseph Surface. His private character, however, militated somewhat against his success on the stage; for, though a delightful companion, he was both unprincipled and profligate ; and his treatment of his wife—who had sacrificed friends and fortune for him—was that of a ruffian. Yet the manner of his death showed that he was not without strong domestic feelings ; for being engaged to play the Stranger at Liverpool, the play was compelled to be put off by reason of his distress on hearing of the death of his son. A day or two later he made an effort to go through the part, but in the 4th Act, where the Stranger relates to Steinfort the cause of his domestic afflictions, he became visibly agitated, and had no sooner uttered the words, "There is another and a better world !" than he fell lifeless on the stage !

54   A PEEP INTO THE PAST.

Mr. Wild (erst Prompter at Covent-garden) succeeded Palmer in the management of the Brighton Theatre in 1793, "deputed by the widow and trustees of Joseph Fox, deceased." The season, though the company was said to be "very superior to last year," was not a successful one. This was in a great measure attributable to the formation of the Brighton Camp, which possessed strong counter attractions to both sexes. The Manager did his best to stem the current in that direction by the production of military spectacles, &c., such as *Richard Cœur de Lion* * (played upwards of 300 nights at Drury-lane). *The Siege of Valenciennes*, &c. A new interlude was also brought out, entitled *Old England's Glory*, one of the scenes in in which represented the march of the troops from Waterdown to the Brighton Camp. But "imitations" failed: for was not the real thing within easy distance ? The chronicles of the "house" state that Charles James Fox and Mrs. Armstead visited the Theatre this season. † Incledon made his first appearance in Brighton on August 6, 1793, but to a poor house, though on his benefit night the receipts amounted to £70.‡

The "sensation" of the season was the appearance, early in September, of the celebrated fencer, "Chevalier" D'Eon, or "Mdlle." D'Eon; for *he* or *she* appeared under both titles. "All the world wondered," no one appearing to know, whether the fencer was *man* or *woman!* "Mdlle." chiefly favoured female attire; and at the Brighton Theatre exhibited her skill opposed by an Officer of the Regiment then in Brighton. Curiosity to see the "*lady*" was wrought up to the highest pitch; and never was there such excitement at the Theatre since it had been opened. The Pit was wholly laid out into boxes; and, in less than half-an-hour after opening the

---

* The closing scene of this Entertainment is thus described :- "The outward walls of the Castle (in which Richard was confined on his return from Palestine) assaulted by Matilda's troops; after a most obstinate resistance a Breach is made; and Richard leaps from the fortress ! The piece concludes with a Grand Battle, and Richard is restored to his faithful Matilda !"

† Edmund Burke was also in Brighton later on, staying "at a house at the end of the Steine." He, in company with Lord Thurlow, visited the Brighton Camp, and out of compliment to them there was a partial field-day on the occasion."

‡ Incledon was well-known to old Brightonians; for, after his retirement from the stage, he passed his latter days in the town. He early developed remarkable powers of voice, and at the age of eight, under the celebrated Jackson's tuition, was entered a chorister of Exeter Cathedral. He continued there until his 15th year, when, unknown to his friends, he entered as a sailor on board the Formidable. During the four years he was in the Navy he was in several actions. He subsequently went upon the stage, making his *début* as Alphonso, at Southampton. Later on he appeared at Bath, &c.; and in 1790 at Covent-garden, and was not long in becoming an established favourite with the public. He was but a poor actor. He preferred to appear in Macheath to any other character; and would, it was said, have arisen from his bed at midnight to play it. Incledon's voice was of rare power, both in the natural and the falsetto. His great forte was ballad, of the best English school; and, in his prime, in the singing of such songs as "Black Eyed Susan," "The Storm," or in a pretty love ditty of Shield, he was unsurpassed. Such was the power of his voice, an old inhabitant of Brighton relates that, when singing "The Storm," at the New-road Theatre, he could be easily heard by those outside. Incledon was a frequent attendant at the old Brighton Glee Club, held at "The Sea House," and subsequently at "The Golden Cross" [now the "Marlboro',"] Pavilion-street. He died of paralysis, at Worcester, in February, 1826.

doors, there was not a vacant seat in the house. In fact, numbers were unable to obtain admittance; and Duke-street was thronged with the disappointed. The "fencing" was preceded by *The Irish Widow*, &c.; but Mrs. Bateman's Widow Brady, though played with rare vivacity, could scarcely command a hand.* All interest was centred in the appearance of the "Chevalier" *or* "Mdlle." D'Eon, who seemingly had on a new dress for the occasion, partly *male* and partly *female*, which made curiosity more rife. This dress consisted of a blue satin shape, a white satin petticoat, and a large helmet, decorated with a plume of white feathers, which gave *her* or *him* a formidable, but somewhat droll aspect. The Officer was in a close-fitting white dress, but masked. Some admirable fencing was displayed by both; but this, though enthusiastically applauded, was looked upon as a minor matter; that which was regarded of the greatest importance was to determine, if possible, the *sex* of the "Chevalier" or "Mdlle." But the curious went home unsatisfied! †

The following year (1794) the Theatre was opened under new auspices; Mr. Cobb, an attorney, of Clement's Inn, London, having since the last season become the proprietor.‡ Mr. Cobb's first manager was Mr. Powell, whose company (Mr. and Mrs. Ward, Mr. Townshend, Mr. Maddocks, &c.) chiefly "hailed" from "Old Drury." The season opened with *Wild Oats;* a new local sketch, by Dibdin, called *A Loyal Effusion*, concluding with a representation of "Lord Howe's Fleet and the French Prizes taken by him on that ever-memorable day, the 1st of June"; and *The Agreeable Surprise*. In this last Mrs. Powell appeared as Mrs. Cheshire, playing, it is said, "with a degree of chastity which but seldom accompanies that character in the country." The company later on was reinforced by other London actors. Both Quick and Palmer shone as "stars;" for two or three nights Mrs. Bateman and the

---

* Mrs. Bateman herself was a skilled fencer; and, in 1793, had actually fenced with Mdlle. D'Eon, whom she had invited for the purpose to a grand *déjeûner*, which she gave at her house in Soho-square, London, to a distinguished company.

† This personage, who was really of the male sex, passed and dressed as a woman for the greater portion of his life. He died in London, May 21, 1810.

‡ Mr. Cobb's proprietorship of the Brighton Theatre came about in a curious way. He happened to be in Brighton in 1793, for the Races; when a "good natured friend" (who knew Mrs. Fox) asked him to endeavour to procure a purchaser for the Theatre, as the creditors (Mr. Fox dying £2,700 in debt) had resolved to sell it. He did not succeed, owing to the incumbrances connected with the purchase; but, eventually, having taken an interest in the affair, he consented to advance £1,600 himself by way of mortgage. Poor Mr. Cobb! He knew as much about a Theatre as he did of the other side of the moon; but, like the "triple pillar" of old Rome, woman's tears (Miss Nelly Fox joined her mother in entreaties) were too much for him; and, unable to resist, he took an "old man" on his back, which he never wholly shook off. He first compounded with the creditors; then he paid (under arbitration) £150 to Mr. Paine; but was still refused a license to the Theatre, unless he paid off Mr. Fox's mortgage! He first agreed; then refused, thinking it an extortion; an action was the consequence, and the verdict was against him. The next year he allowed Mrs. Fox a benefit and £100; but, finding himself at the close of the season £200 behind, he reduced Mrs. Fox's annuity to £75 for the future. Some time after Mrs. Fox's death (at Bath, July, 1798), the annuity being continued to the family, he bought it up, and the Theatre then became his own property.

"Chevalier" D'Eon again appeared; and Master Standen (aged 5) enacted Tom Thumb.* Fox, jun. (son of the original proprietor), was among the company; and one of the greatest attractions of the season was announced for his benefit, namely, a "new Grand Musical, Historical, Pantomimical Entertainment called *Mary Queen of Scots*." A description of one of the scenes adds a new fact to the history of that terrible instrument, the Guillotine:—"Execution of Bothwell on 'THE MAIDEN,' which was used in that period in Scotland; and now in France, under the appellation of the Guillotine." But the season was unsuccessful. It closed with *The Jew*, to the representation of which " all the performers paid great attention;" a writer adding, "had they been equally assiduous on former occasions, they would doubtless have been better attended, and the Proprietor, of course, better rewarded than he has been."

Mr. Cobb *must* have congratulated himself on his association with "the players"! His first Manager "went into exile;" and the Theatre was let to a Mr. Bernard, who fell ill, when Mr. Hull, of Covent-garden, officiated as deputy. The company included, in the earlier part of the season, Messrs. Holman,† Emery,‡ Wilde, Holland, and Sedgwick; Misses Hopkins and Phelps; Mesdames Follett, Hargrave, and Bridgeman (the last, on her benefit night, played Douglas!); and Madame St. Amand, "who introduced a style of dancing quite novel in this country." This clever *danseuse*, in the next month, appeared as Columbine in a new Pantomime which the

---

* Master Standen was very diminutive, and, though the *smallest* actor, it was prognosticated that he would be the *greatest* performer on the English boards. Alas, for the precocity of genius! we hear no more of him.

† Mr. Holman was a native of Oxford, and entered, when a young man, Queen's College, with the view of taking Holy Orders. But the applause he met with in some amateur dramatic performances, gave him a strong desire to take to the stage as a profession; and he made his *début* as Romeo at Covent-garden, in 1784, establishing a theatrical reputation on the first night of his appearance. He performed for three seasons at Covent-garden; then in Dublin and Edinburgh, &c., winning the highest encomiums. He was for a long time the powerful rival of John Kemble, and was said to have excelled that great actor in the character of Lord Townley. He subsequently went to America; and, receiving so much applause, was induced to take the Theatre at Charlestown. It proved a sad venture; and in the midst of his difficulties, he (with several of his company) was struck down by the autumnal fever. His wife first succumbed to the direful malady; and he died two days after, August 24th, 1817.

‡ To Brightonians, Mr. Emery's dramatic career has a special interest, for his first appearance was made upon the Brighton boards. Intended for the musical profession, he was, when quite a lad (about 1791—2), engaged in the local orchestra; but his predilection for the stage developing itself, he was encouraged to go behind the curtain; and his first appearance, as Old Crazy, the bellman, in *Peeping Tom*, was a great success. During the next year or two he "strolled" through Kent and Sussex, and at 15 joined Tate Wilkinson's York company, with which his reputation, as an "old man," was established, drawing the attention of London managers towards him. His first appearance in the metropolis was in 1798, at Covent-garden, as Frank Oatlands, in *A Cure for the Heart Ache*, and Lovegold, in *The Miser*, in each of which he was well received. His great character—one in which he has never been surpassed—was Tyke, in *The School of Reform*. His Caliban, too, was a marvellous impersonation. In his favourite parts, this great actor was unrivalled. Mr. Emery's private character was most exemplary; and both as an actor and as a man he was one of whom the stage may justly feel proud. He died when he was in the zenith of his fame and powers, from the rupture of a blood-vessel, July 25, 1822, in his 45th year.

Management brought out, and which was evidently most amusing. To afford an idea of the character of Pantomimes at the close of the last century, we give the details in their entirety from the playbill on the occasion of Mrs. Follett's benefit, September 8th, 1795 :—

A NEW PANTOMIME, CALL'D
HARLEQUIN'S MEDLEY ; OR, THE CLOWN IN DISGRACE.
Principal Pantomime Characters :
Harlequin - by Mr. BROWN.   Sir Gregory Whimsey - by Mr. EMERY.
Captain O'Leary - by Mr. HOLLAND. Paddy Rooney O'Gaffey - by Mr. ROCH.
And, Timothy Hardhead (the Clown) - - by Mr. FOLLETT.
Mother - - - - by Mrs. GREEN.
And, Columbine - - - - - - by Madame ST. AMAND.
Musical Characters by
Mr. BERNARD, Mr. FREEMAN, Mr. SUCHBALD, and Miss HOPKINS.

In the course of the Pantomime (for that night only)
THE CLOWN WILL JUMP THROUGH A HOGSHEAD OF FIRE.

THE STORY.

HARLEQUIN, being for some Time in Disgrace with his good Genius, PHILIDEL, is transform'd and fix'd as Servant to *Sir Gregory Whimsey*, a superannuated old Knight ; during his penance, he falls in love with COLUMBINE (Daughter to *Sir Gregory*) ; PHILIDEL releases him from his State of Servitude ; permits him again to re-assume the well-known Patchwork Locket ; assists him against the machinations of *Sir Gregory, Clown, &c.*, and, at last, happily unites him to COLUMBINE.

The PIECE commences with Harlequin in the Farm-Yard. Any Thing better than Drowning. After Sorrow comes Joy.
SCENE II. - None can Love like an Irishman. The Lover in amaze. Who Father's the Child ?
SCENE III. - Breakfast Chamber - Harlequin in the Tea-Pot. The Devil in the Candlesticks and the animated Chair.
SCENE IV. - The Bottom out of the Green Basket. And the Clown taking Care of his Man.
SCENE V.—Harlequin in the Dog Kennel ; and then in the Pidgeon House. The Clown stealing the Pidgeons ; and the old Woman's Revenge.
SCENE VI.—All at the Ship Launch. The Mariners' Glee.
SCENE VII. - A Public House. Harlequin's Magic Pitcher. A Dispute, to decide who's Black or who's White.
SCENE VIII.—Hermit's Cave. Harlequin Hermit. None the Wiser.
SCENE IX.—The Waiter's Ballad. All pleased. Shower of Rain creates Confusion ; by which Harlequin loses Columbine.
SCENE X.—The Stray Sheep Found. Safe bind Safe find. Love will break through Stone Walls. How to empty a Hamper.
SCENE XI. - The Lawyers are Met. The Chimney-Sweep's Pranks. Wine warm'd if Fire can make it so.
SCENE XII. - All in the Dark. The whimsical Battle. The favorite Ballad of the Watchman.
SCENE XIII.—The Painter, Dog, Cat, Goose, and Kitten. Harlequin in the Chest. How to take off Boots. Clown good at a Jump.

SCENE XIV.—Killing, no Murder—exemplified in Paddy's Quarrel with Himself.
SCENE XV. Harlequin and Father reconciled. Lover in the dumps. Philidel approves the Match. This Life is like a Country Dance, proved in a Song by Mr. BERNARD.

The PROCESSION of the TROOPS as they passed WATERDOWN on their March to BRIGHTON CAMP.

The Whole to Conclude with the Song of " RULE BRITANNIA."

During the season there appeared Mr. and Miss Betterton, Mrs. Clendining, Bannister, junior (in *New Hay at the Old Market*), and Mr. Bland. The pieces, too, were up to average. Prospects, however, were not of the brightest, though there had been no lack of Royal patronage; the ill-fated Princess Caroline attending the house at every opportunity. On one night in August (it was, certainly, Lewes Race night,) the receipts of the house were only two guineas! and the Theatre had, it may be stated, throughout the season, strong opposition in the fireworks and other attractions at the Promenade Grove, then in the full tide of prosperity.

The theatrical campaign of 1796 was expected to have been a brilliant one. The frequent visits of the Princess Caroline in the previous year induced the Proprietor to hope that these would be repeated; accordingly, during the recess, the interior of the Theatre was remodelled (its original square form being converted into that of a horse-shoe) and re-decorated, a Royal box newly fitted, &c., the alterations involving an expenditure of nearly £600. But, alas for Mr. Cobb's hopes—and his pocket! the Princess never visited Brighton again. The improvements effected, however, rendered the Theatre, in the opinion of connoisseurs, "the completest provincial Theatre in the kingdom." The scenery, by Holland (whose services were retained for some two months after the opening), was deemed equal to that of Covent-garden.

Mr. Diddear was Lessee in 1796; and his company included Messrs. Archer, Williamson, and Keys, Mr. and Mrs. Emery, Mrs. Kendal, &c., and, also, Miss Diddear (the Lessee's daughter), a child under seven, whose histrionic abilities in several parts were most extraordinary, and who spoke the Prologue on the opening night. Before Holland left he gave Brightonians a "spice of his quality" in a Pantomimical Ballet, which was admitted to be "the grandest spectacle ever exhibited on the Brighton stage." The scenery included "Views of the Streets of Brighton, the Pavilion, the Steine," &c.; but the most beautiful effect was said to have been "the Dispersion of the Clouds before the Chariot of the Gods, which displayed in lively characters the popular sentence, 'LONG LIVE THE PRINCE!'"

Another speciality of the season was the production of a new play by a local author—Mr. Sicklemore. It was entitled *A Dream*, and had two excellent comic scenes "by a 'spouter,' who is reclaimed from the vice of drunkenness by making him believe he is dead, and in a place of torment, for his crimes."

The play-bills this season included a *poetical* one, issued by Mr. Findlay, the oldest "standard" of the Theatre. It was not a work of genius; but a portion of it, relating to *The Rivals*, was as follows:—

> " He takes, we're informed, a much-favoured Play,
> Call'd THE RIVALS. ('Tis written by Sheridan they say.)
> 'Twill be done very decently—none can dispute;
> Emery's name's first in bill for the old Absolute;
> Young Walcot's the Captain; Squire Acres is Mate;
> Morton, Irish Sir Lucius—he'll very well play't;
> Wheeler's Country David; Mr. Fag is by Field;
> And Archer plays Falkland—who to jealousies yield.
> Mrs. Malaprop, the wife, by Mrs. Fullam is done;
> Mrs. Archer's the Lucy—'we'll go see the fun.'
> Mrs. Kendal plays Julia, a part full of anguish;
> Mrs. Field's the romantic Lydia Languish."

Mr. Diddear's second season (1797) opened on June 7, with *Speculation*, the company including Mr. and Mrs. Pritchard, Mr. and Mrs. King, and Miss Arnold. Still greater actors appeared by and by. Quick led the way, drawing capital houses, departing, it was said, "with a free purse, his terms being very high;" then came Incledon, —" The Storm," sung on his last night, drawing tears from a brilliant audience,—Elliston, and Munden.* The last played in one night three characters—Sir Francis Gripe in *The Busy Body;* Nipperton, in *Sprigs of Laurel;* and Lazarillo, in *Two Strings to your Bow;* singing a song to boot —"Oh, what a country for people to marry in!" In this season was produced a new opera, by a local composer

---

* This sterling comedian was perhaps more familiar with Brighton play-goers in the olden time than any other of the great actors of his day. His connection with Brighton extended from 1797 down to 1823, there being scarcely a season during that period that he did not appear some two or three times; and he invariably drew good houses. He was, originally, an apothecary's shop-boy; then a writing clerk to an attorney. His *penchant* for the stage was excited by his frequent attendance at the Theatre to witness the acting of Garrick. He made his *début* at Liverpool; but *very* humbly—as a banner-bearer, &c., at 1s. per night! ekeing out his subsistence in the office of the Town Clerk. During the next year or two he resumed the quill; but the theatrical mania was occasionally strong upon him; and subsequently, when out of employment, he went on to the stage, playing at Windsor, &c., with tolerable success, at 10s. 3d. a week! By and by he became first low comedian at the Manchester Theatre with a good salary; and on the death of Edwin, in 1790, was engaged at Covent-garden. His first appearances there were as Sir Francis Gripe and Jemmy Jumps, and his success in these characters—coming after such actors as Parsons and Edwin—was deemed little short of a miracle. His reputation was at once established; and he most worthily sustained it, for over 20 years at the same house, in a variety of characters, not a few of which he was the original representative. In 1813, he left Covent-garden for Drury-lane, where he remained until May 31, 1824, when he took leave of the stage,—his last characters being Sir Robert Bramble and Old Dozey. Of this great actor's facial peculiarities, Charles Lamb thus discourses:—"What a mutable face was his! a countenance ever shifting, ever new—his globular, liquid eye, glistening and rolling alternately, illuming every corner of his laughing face; then the eternal tortuosities of his nose, and the alarming descent of his chin, contrasted, as it eternally was, with the portentous rise of his eyebrows. He lavished more contortions of countenance on a single part than other actors can afford to do on a range of characters. His face was a visual kaleidoscope, and its changes were unlimited." Notwithstanding his comic powers, Munden, like Grimaldi, was of sombre disposition off the stage.

(Mr. Prince, organist to the Chapel Royal). It was entitled *The Disagreeable Surprise; or Saltinbanco;* and a critic says: "The music did the composer credit for the taste, harmony, and chastity it displays; in many parts it does not fall far short of the beautiful simplicity so conspicuous in Shield's compositions." It was performed again and again,—a proof of its merit.

The season of 1798 may be regarded as among the most memorable in the annals of the local stage; for, on September 4, the great tragic actress, Mrs. Sarah Siddons, appeared in Brighton for the first time. She was then in the zenith of her fame—the most brilliant luminary in the then theatrical sphere—and was, of course, not to be had "for the asking." To recoup himself for the heavy expenses of the engagement, the Manager raised the prices to all parts of the house. Mrs. Siddons elected to appear on her first night as Calista (in *The Fair Penitent*), one of her most successful characters. The announcement of the performances was as follows:—

NEW THEATRE, BRIGHTON.

The Manager of the Theatre most respectfully informs the Nobility, Gentry, and Public in general, that he has engaged that celebrated Actress,

MRS. SIDDONS,

Who is to perform on Tuesday and Wednesday.

On TUESDAY, September 4th, 1798, will be presented a Favourite Tragedy, called

THE FAIR PENITENT.

THE PART OF CALISTA BY Mrs. SIDDONS.

From the great Expense attending the above Engagement, the Manager flatters himself a grateful Public will not think him intruding when he informs them the PRICES the Nights Mrs. SIDDONS performs must be as follows:—

Boxes, 5s.   Pit, 3s.   Gallery, 1s. 6d.

☞ Those Ladies and Gentlemen who take places for the Boxes are respectfully informed that unless they take Tickets, and send Servants to keep their places, they cannot be secured.

Strange to relate, the great actress drew good, but not crowded, houses (increased prices might have militated against the attendance), and on her second appearance (in *Douglas*) the audience was chiefly composed of ladies,—three to one gentleman. On her benefit night, in the following week, when she appeared in *Isabella; or, the Fatal Marriage*, there was not, even then, a full house, the receipts (with higher prices) only reaching to between £70 and £80.*

The respective Managers of Duke-street Theatre had on several occasions shown a marked ability in spectacular representations of popular historical events; notably "The Fall of the Bastille;" "The Brighton Camp;" "Lord Howe's Victory;" &c; but these were all

---

* Mrs Siddons appeared again at the Duke-street Theatre, in September, 1800, when there were crowded houses at each performance; the receipts on the first night reaching to nearly £100.

surpassed by that of Nelson's "Victory of the Nile." As this great naval engagement only took place in August, 1798, to have produced a representation of it in October says much for the energy and enterprise of the Management. It was announced as follows:—

An Entire New Entertainment, consisting of Dialogue and Songs, in commemoration of the Gallant Admiral Nelson's Victory over the French Fleet in Abouker Bay, called

THE GLORIOUS FIRST OF AUGUST;
OR, BRITISH TARS TRIUMPHANT.

The Dialogue and Songs written by a Gentleman of Brighton. The Music entirely new, and composed by Mr. Jouve, of the King's Theatre. In addition to the Orchestra that night the Steine Band is engaged.

A SHORT DESCRIPTION OF THE SCENERY.

The Piece opens with a view of the Mountainous part of the Country near Alexandria.

A VIEW OF ALEXANDRIA.

The French Fleet at anchor, landing Troops, &c.

AN ARABIAN CAMP.

An EXACT REPRESENTATION of the FRENCH FLEET IN ABOUKER BAY,

As making preparations to receive the English, who are first discovered at a distance bearing down upon them under a crowd of sail; soon after the attack commences the English pass through and break their line. After an obstinate contest the French Admiral's ship is blown up, one ship is sunk, and two only out of the whole effect an escape. The remainder strike their colours, and are captured by the British Fleet.

The Battle over, a grand Transparency of the noble Admiral descends gradually; Britannia enters in a triumphal car, drawn by sea horses, bearing in one hand a wreath of laurel, with which she graces the brow of the British Conqueror; English Sailors, &c., follow in procession with trophies which they drop at her feet.

The whole to conclude with an appropriate Song and Chorus to the tune of
"BRITONS NEVER WILL BE SLAVES."

The season of 1799 opened under new Lesseeship—that of Messrs. Blogg and Archer—with *The Wonder*. The company on the first night included Mr. and Mrs. Archer, Mr. and Mrs. Swendall, Mr. and Mrs. Dormer, Mr. Waddy, Mr. Emery, Mr. Haymes, Miss De Camp (of Venetian parentage; a charming vocalist and actress, who later on became Mrs. Charles Kemble), &c. The performances during the season were of average character. There were, however, in September, a whole galaxy of "stars." On the 6th, Charles Kemble first made his bow on the Brighton stage (had the pretty Venetian, Miss De Camp, aught to do with this visit?) as Rolla in *Pisarro*. He performed it again on two successive nights; and on each occasion there was an overflowing house. For his benefit he appeared as Hamlet, and, strange to say, "to a very slender audience." On the 18th—Mr. Sedgwick's benefit night—there was a strong contingent from "Old Drury," including Barrymore, Dignum,

Wathen, Suett,* and Miss De Camp; and there was an overflowing house long before the curtain was drawn up. In the following week, Munden and Charles Bannister appeared for one night; and on another (for Mr. Holland's benefit) there were other celebrated actors down from Drury-lane, namely, Dowton, C. Kemble, R. Palmer, Mrs. Walcot, Miss Biggs, and —one, whose first appearance on the Brighton stage is, locally, of more interest than all—Miss Mellon, who subsequently became Mrs. Coutts (in her widowhood the richest woman in Europe), and eventually Duchess of St. Alban's; and as such, in after years, was a centre round which, season after season, all the world of gaiety and fashion in Brighton revolved! †

The "records" of the house in 1800 are most scanty; mention merely being made of the appearance, during the season, of Mrs. Siddons (in the second week of September), of Incledon, Bannister, jun., and Emery. The Lessees had a "difference;" Archer seceded; and Mr. Swendall (a member of the company in the previous season) was appointed Manager during the remainder of the Lessees' term. The elder Brunton, destined a few years later to take a prominent part

---

* "Dickey" Suett—whom "Elia" has immortalised—appeared, we believe, only on this occasion in Brighton. "He was known," says dear Charles Lamb, "like Puck, by his note, ' Ha! ha! ha!' sometimes deepening to 'Ho! ho! ho!' with an irresistible accession, derived, perhaps remotely, from his ecclesiastical education, foreign to his prototype, of 'O la!' He drolled upon the stock of these latter two syllables richer than the cuckoo." He may be said to have died with them on his lips; for when he received the last stroke of death at a public-house, in Clare Market, July, 1805—he exclaimed to Robert Palmer, who was with him, "O la! O la! Bobby!" Another account of his death relates, that it was preceded by the rattles in the throat, and Palmer, going to the window to conceal his tears, heard Suett exclaim, "Bobby, my boy, the watchmen are coming—I hear the rattles!" Suett was an inveterate punster, and never, says a biographer, performed Endless without saying, as he emerged from the sack, to the infinite enjoyment of the gods, "Flour and suet make excellent pudding."

† Miss Mellon's metropolitan dramatic career extended over some 20 years. When a child she appeared in "small parts" in provincial theatres in the North; but her original engagement at Drury-lane, in 1794 (at 30s. a week), was obtained through the influence of Sheridan. Her leave-taking of the stage at "Old Drury," was on February 7th, 1815, as Audrey, in *As You Like It*. She was to have retired as Mrs. Candour, considered as one of her best characters; but was deterred probably by an ill-natured newspaper paragraph, which (foreshadowing in future Mrs. Coutts intimated that "she would cease to play Mrs. Candour in public, and commence playing Lady Teazle in private life." Miss Mellon was married to Mr. Coutts in March, 1815, he being in his 86th year. A more loving and devoted wife than she proved to be to the aged banker could not have been found the wide world over. In fact, it was said, that Tom Coutts had in his wife what a French adage regards as the three scarcest things in the world —"A good melon (Mellon), a good woman, and a good friend." He himself regarded her as "the greatest blessing of his life." Mr. and Mrs. Coutts visited Brighton in 1817, staying at the house at the corner of the Steine some two or three months. Mr. Coutts died March 2, 1822, leaving the whole of his immense fortune to his widow. She was subsequently married to the Duke of St. Alban's; and it was more as the Duchess of St Alban's than as Mrs. Coutts that she was best known to Brightonians. Her visits to the town each season, for several years, up to 1837, diffused general joy among all classes; to the higher, for the never-ending succession of gaieties at St. Alban's House; to the tradesmen, as one of the most liberal of purchasers; to the poor, for her charity, which was absolutely boundless. This estimable lady, whose whole career was a veritable romance, died August 6, 1837, leaving the bulk of her large fortune, estimated at £1,800,000, to Miss Angela Burdett-Coutts, now the Baroness Burdett-Coutts, who in "devoted charitable deeds" most praiseworthily emulates the noble lady from whom she received the munificent bequest.

in theatrical management in Brighton, was one of the company on the opening night. Mrs. Glover appeared on the 29th August, as Susan in *The Follies of a Day*. A local chronicler, speaking of the performance, says :—"She played with great spirit; but the part was spoilt by her *dress*, which ill-became the waiting-maid, as, in its elegance, it eclipsed that of the Countess." A still more celebrated lady—Mrs. Jordan*—performed in September, and appeared as Amaranthis, Lady Racket, Lady Teazle, Roxalana, and Letitia Hardy. The chronicler just quoted (not the most flattering, apparently, to stage ladies) says of the first night's performance, " The house was fashionable, but not crowded;" of the second, "The audience was less in number and less fashionable;" and of the third, "There were not enough present to constitute a *middling* house." The writer was evidently bent on playing the "descending scale." He must, however, have been sadly disconcerted on the great actress's benefit night, when she appeared as Peggy, in *The Country Girl;* the house being full, and the receipts amounting to £100! (Mrs. Jordan was in Brighton in 1794; but she did not visit the Theatre.)

In 1802 there was yet one more Manager—Mr. Haymes, whose reputation, in more than one respect, was not of the best. Early in the season, the local playgoers were treated to a novelty, namely, Moritz's "Phantasmagoria." The announcement respecting this stated—

"M. MORITZ will produce the PHANTOMS or APPARITIONS of the DEAD or ABSENT. * * * To give a proper idea of his skill, he will produce the figures and most perfect resemblance of MARTHA GUNN, OLD SMOAKER, and several well-known characters. To render the performance more interesting, *the various apparitions will be evoked during the progress of a tremendous thunder-storm*."

It *would* have been interesting to have heard Old Smoaker's "opinion," when enjoying his evening pipe at "The Dolphin," if any one had told him that he had just seen his "apparition" in a thunder-storm at the Theatre.

The great "event," however, of Mr. Haymes's first season was the appearance of Braham (the "Sweet Singer of Israel") and Madame Storace, who proved to be to the exchequer "magnets of the first

---

* This charming actress's real name was Dorothy Bland. She made her *début*, in the name of Miss Francis, at Dublin, in 1777, and did not assume the name of Jordan till some years after. She first appeared at Drury-lane in 1785, as Peggy, and played the piece with such consummate art, that the applause of the house was boundless. She eventually became a great favourite with the public, both in London and the provinces. Hazlitt says of her—"Nature had formed her in her most prodigal humour. Her face, her tones, her manner, were irresistible. She was all gaiety, success, and good nature." Yet, though the most amiable of women, she was sadly ill-fated. She was never married. Her association with the Duke of Clarence, his subsequent abrupt separation from her, and, finally, her pecuniary distress, doubtless brought her private affairs more prominently before the public than they otherwise would have been. To trench on these is beyond our province; but it may be mentioned, that, under sad embarrassments, she returned in 1815 to Paris, and died at St. Cloud, under the weight of her afflictions, in June, 1816.

strength."* The house each night was filled beyond all precedent; and on more than one occasion the Prince of Wales, with the Russian Princess Galitzen, the Countess Sarebtzoff, and Mrs. Fitzherbert were present. In Mr. Haymes's second season there was a succession of great actors, including Dowton, Munden, Bannister, Raymond, Quick, &c. During Quick's visit there was performed the farce of *Barataria; or, Sancho turned Governor*, the popular actor taking the part of Sancho, "mounted on his favourite Dapple." There was a strong contingent of London performers on the Manager's benefit night, which was honoured with the patronage and presence of the Prince of Wales.

The Management of the house was in 1804 and subsequent seasons undertaken by Mr. Brunton, with, subsequently, his brother for *aide-de-camp*. There was a capital company, but the "chronicles" are barren of interest. It may be mentioned that the prices of admission to the boxes and pit were now raised respectively to 5s. and 2s. 6d. This was, doubtless, owing to the advanced rent which Mr. Cobb now required—£500 a year, clear and unincumbered (it had previously ranged from £200 to £450, he paying all outgoings). The house held, at the increased prices, when quite full, from £100 to £110; no half-price was taken. The next season (1805) was a short one. Miss Brunton was leading lady; and among the company were Mr. and Mrs. Egan, Mrs. St. Leger, Miss Marriott, Mr. Klanat, Mr. Marshall, &c. The Prince of Wales gave his patronage for Miss Brunton's benefit (August 19), ensuring her an overflowing house. In the previous week he had visited it, with the Duke of Orleans and the Prince of Condé; Mrs. Fitzherbert being also present. In September there was a fresh company from the Haymarket; and Munden and Blanchard were down for a night or two. The Theatre closed November 2nd, the last night's performance being under the patronage of the Royal Clarence Lodge of Freemasons.

The closing season of the Duke-street Theatre was in 1806. It opened with *The Honeymoon;* Juliana by Miss Brunton.† During its career the house had, with all its changes of managers, worthily upheld the character of the stage; both with regard to the pieces performed and the actors who had appeared in it—the latter among the best of the day. The "stars" who illumined its dying glories included Munden and Emery, each in their respective lines unsurpassed; Roe and G. F. Cooke; Incledon, &c. There was, however, this season, for the first time, some tight-rope performances by the celebrated Richer; Bologna, of subsequent pantomime celebrity,

---

* Mr. Haymes was Manager of the New-road Theatre in 1810, when Braham performed several times in October. There also appeared during the season Bannister, the elder Matthews, Incledon, and Emery; and "Romeo" Coates played Othello; but the house was closed in November, Mr. Haymes's management proving a "financial failure."

† Miss Brunton, the daughter of the elder Brunton, was of elegant appearance and charming manners; an actress also of consummate ability in a high range of characters. She invariably commanded a fashionable house, and not unfrequently Royal patronage, whenever the Prince of Wales happened to be in Brighton. Miss Brunton subsequently became the Countess Craven, having been married to Earl Craven, September 12th, 1807.

officiating as Clown. The last performance in the house took place on November 1, 1806, for Mr. Waldegrave's benefit, the pieces being—*A Cure for the Heart Ache* and *Raising the Wind*. A significant pantomime sketch, entitled *Harlequin Skeleton*, followed; then the curtain fell and, without a parting word, the "eventful historie" of the Duke-street Theatre ended. But, no! "beneath the lowest deep, a lower deep." There was one phase more the old house had to pass through—its demolition under that potent instrument, the auctioneer's hammer! *Ex. gratia:*—

TO CARPENTERS, BUILDERS, &c.

TO BE SOLD BY AUCTION, by Mr. ATTREE (on the Premises), on TUESDAY, the 21st April, 1807, in lots, the whole of the BUILDING MATERIALS of the OLD THEATRE, in Duke-street, Brighton; consisting of a large quantity of capital Timber, Joists, Scantling, of various dimensions, Boards, Pantiles, Slates, Lead, &c.

Catalogues to be had six days previous to the Sale, of Mr. Attree, at his General Agency and Lottery Offices, Middle-street.

The Sale to begin at Eleven o'clock in the Forenoon.

A few weeks later, the Duke-street Theatre was no more! and

"Like an insubstantial pageant faded,
Left not a rack behind."

The Theatre in New Road.

If not beyond our purpose, we should have been pleased to follow the varied fortunes of the new house,—to tell of "all one feels, and all one knows," respecting the great and the gifted who have "fretted their hour" upon its old familiar stage in the days gone by. But we forbear. The first stone of the new Theatre, it may be stated, was laid by Mr. Brunton, sen. (one of the last Managers at Duke-street), on September 10th, 1806; and the house was subsequently opened on Saturday, June 27th, 1807. The original decorations, by Luppino, were in the highest degree superb. The scenery, too, was entirely new, the artists being Phillips and Luppino, of Covent-garden; Greenwood, Smith, Luppino, jun., and Timmins, of Drury-lane, &c. The opening performances were as follows:—

NEW THEATRE, BRIGHTON.
Under the Patronage of His Royal Highness the Prince of Wales.
WILL OPEN, on SATURDAY, June 27th, 1807, with the Tragedy of
HAMLET.
Hamlet, Mr. C. KEMBLE.   Ophelia, Mrs. C. KEMBLE.
Laertes, Mr. T. BRUNTON.   The Ghost, Mr. MURRAY.
A New Ballet Dance.
And the Farce of
THE WEATHERCOCK.
Variella - - - Mrs. C. KEMBLE.

Without venturing too far upon new ground, it may be mentioned that, among the more interesting of the early memorials of the Theatre in the New-road were the appearances of Mrs. Siddons, the "great Sarah" Siddons, in August and September, 1809. The universally acknowledged "Queen of Tragedy" appeared there no less than nine times. Her opening performance was, on August 8th, as Mrs. Beverley, in *The Gamester*. The boxes were so crowded on the occasion that, we are told, "many persons of fashion and consequence were nearly the whole evening without seats, being content to bear the fatigues of an erect position for several hours, rather than give up the intellectual treat which they had there assembled to enjoy;" the writer adding, "Mrs. Siddons was received with a burst of applause; but the finest compliment which could be paid to her talent was the universal silence which succeeded—not a whisper, nor a murmur, was heard—so anxious appeared every one that not an accent which escaped her should be lost; and this profound attention was paid by the auditory almost from the first to the last scene of the drama." The receipts of the house amounted to £134 19s. Mrs. Siddons's next performance was as Lady Randolph, in *Douglas*, when there was another crowded house. But the appearance which occasioned the greatest excitement was on August 15th, when the great actress performed Lady Macbeth, the receipts of the house amounting to no less than £176 16s.; those of the boxes alone reaching £117. Mrs. Siddons subsequently appeared as Isabella in the tragedy of that name; also as Elvira in *Pizarro*; the receipts, when the latter was performed, amounting to £146. In the following week she appeared as Margaret of Anjou, in *The Earl of Warwick*, for the benefit of the veteran Murray, when the receipts were £150 5s.; the Theatre, it is stated, "being honoured by the presence of almost all the rank and beauty of the place, the boxes exhibiting such a fascinating display of lovely women as, within similar limits, perhaps, was not to be equalled in any other part of the world." Mrs. Siddons's performances in September were as Alicia, in *Jane Shore*, and as Belvidera, in *Venice Preserved*. Mr. Charles Kemble, who happened to be in Brighton, took the part of the Jaffier; and, consequently, there was, in this conjunction, a histrionic treat of the highest order. On the 9th September, she appeared as Mrs. Haller, in *The Stranger;* and on the 12th—her last performance on the Brighton boards—the great tragic actress again impersonated Lady Macbeth, for the benefit of Mr. Creswell, on which occasion the receipts amounted to £100, and would, it is said, have been much higher, but, from some cause or other, the fact that she was to perform "was not announced." These extraordinary receipts were, however, exceeded in October, 1814, when Edmund Kean appeared as Richard, above £200 being taken; and in October, 1815, when Miss O'Neill took her benefit—the highly-gifted actress impersonating Isabella and drawing upwards of £230, the highest amount which the records of the house show up to this date. It may be stated, however, that the admission to the boxes was 7s.; to the pit, 3s. 6d.

We must here take our leave of the "Old Theatres."

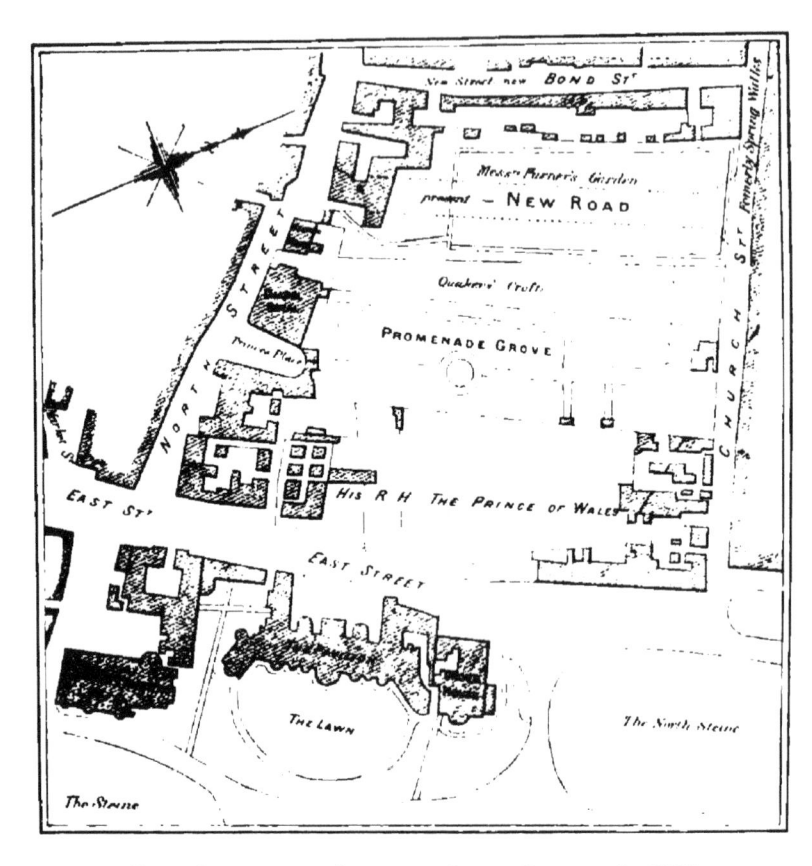

PLAN SHOWING THE PROMENADE GROVE, PAVILION, &c., 1803

THE PROMENADE GROVE.

The Promenade Grove,—a portion of which was subsequently converted into the western portion of the Pavilion Grounds by H.R.H. George Prince of Wales,—was the first public Pleasure Gardens opened in Brighton. The idea was a happy one; and, whilst it supplied an acknowledged want, the excellence of the general arrangements, as well as the liberality of the Management, conduced greatly to its success as a place of fashionable resort *par excellence*. Whether it realised, in a pecuniary sense, the expectations of its promoters, is not recorded. The Promenade Grove, with its amusements, &c., may not be inaptly described as a *locale* for "Pic-Nics" on a grand scale; for it combined within the precincts of the town the beauties of the country, with the multifarious adjuncts necessary to *al fresco* enjoyments, and without any of the inconveniences or disagreeable concomitants sometimes associated with a rural excursion.

If there was one out-door amusement more than another needed by the fashionable visitors to Brighton at the close of the last century, it was that of a rural kind, and of a select character; for the one promenade,—the Steine,—was treeless,[*] monotonous, open to all. Hence, in the season, by way of change, country parties and "picnics" were daily arranged to various districts—some going to the Preston Tea Gardens or the Grove; some to the quiet retirement of Rottingdean; whilst others went to Copperas Gap or Southwick,—the latter a favourite resort of the Princess Caroline of Brunswick during her residence in Brighton.

In the Promenade Grove, as we have said, the desiderata essential to the enjoyment of the truly rural "pic-nic" were all to be found, in a greater or less degree. Once within its gates, the town, and all associated with it, was almost lost to view. The only side open to peering eyes from without was the East,—from the present road through the Pavilion Grounds (then known as East-street); but even here, along its extent, there was an enclosed meadow, with doubtless a hedge-row. The green sward of the Grove, as soft and velvetty as the pile of a Turkey carpet, was always kept nicely mown and smooth; the ground, too, was perfectly level, the undulations of the present Western Lawn of the Pavilion Grounds being an after-formation. Some portion of the Grove was originally a farm meadow, known as the "Dairy Field;" and it extended (from North to South) almost from the Spring Walks (now Church-street) to Prince's-place, and included the ground now covered by the western portion of the Pavilion

---

[*] As illustrating how much the lack of trees was felt at Brighton by our visitors, even from an early period, we quote from "The New Brighthelmstone Directory" (1770) the following lines, which occur in a song descriptive of a visit to Lewes Castle by a party from Brighton:—

"For now, the feast ending, the ladies all rose,
And to dance on the green did challenge their beaux;
Then, dancing in circle, they worship'd a tree,
Because trees at Brighton so seldom you see."

Dormitories. On the West, the Grove was bounded by an enclosed meadow belonging to the Society of Friends, and known as "The Quakers' Croft," through a part of which the New-road was subsequently formed.

The grounds of the Grove were tastefully, though not profusely, laid out with choice flowering and other shrubs. But its chief attractions were the avenues of noble elms; for in addition to those now forming "The Rookery," there appears to have been a parallel double-row lower down, running straight across the centre of the present Lawn from North to South, and known, we believe, as "The Rutland Walk." The wide-spreading, umbrageous branches of these finely-grown trees afforded a cool and an agreeable shelter in summer-time, as beneath them visitors could walk or rest, as inclination dictated. There was much, besides, that rendered the Grove delightful. A good band was always in attendance; and, not unfrequently during the opening season, an additional one was engaged from the Brighton Camp, then formed at Hove. For the information and edification of others, newspapers, &c., were liberally supplied; there being an elegant Saloon, "fitted up in a stile entirely new," and in and around it comfortable seats were ranged. The Public Breakfasts—sometimes partaken of "under the elms," at others in the Saloon—were, however, regarded as the more prominent of the morning attractions to the Grove; and the admirable way in which these were served left little to be desired. All, too, appears to have been conducted with the utmost order and decorum. The majority of the morning company of the Grove consisted of the Prince of Wales and his more immediate associates; of the nobility and gentry, &c., either residents or visitors to the town; and all being more or less familiar with each other, these gatherings opened up an opportunity—divested of ceremonial or conventional State etiquette—for pleasant intercourse and a charming mingling of the higher classes of society. Thus, not only the Public Breakfasts, but the other morning amusements of the Grove, were entered into with all the zest of a new-found pleasure.

Whether the projectors of the Promenade Grove were a company, or whether it owed its existence to the enterprise of a private individual, we know not; for its records are very scanty. But enough has come down to us to afford some idea of the ten years' doings at this much-favoured fashionable resort of Brighton in the Olden Time. The original Prospectus published was as follows:—

Under the Patronage of
HIS ROYAL HIGHNESS THE PRINCE OF WALES.
THE BRIGHTHELMSTON PROMENADE GROVE,
FOR THE AMUSEMENT OF THE NOBILITY AND GENTRY,
Will be opened on the following terms, viz.:—

Each Subscriber, on paying half a guinea, will be entitled to the perusal of the papers, and the use of the Promenade; which will be opened every day, Sunday evening excepted, during the Season. The admission of Non-Subscribers will be by being introduced by Subscribers, that is to say, Gentlemen may introduce Gentlemen, and Ladies, Ladies. Tickets for each Non-Subscriber will be one shilling for the day.

PUBLIC BREAKFASTS are intended to be given, but the admission to them will be the same both to Subscribers and Non-Subscribers. In the Saloon refreshments of various sorts suitable to the place will always be in readiness on the usual terms, for such of the company as may be disposed to call for them.

Mr. BAILY, under whose sole direction and management the Promenade Grove will be opened, humbly hopes the plan and terms which he has thus the honour of procuring, will meet the encouraging approbation of a generous and discerning Public. He most sincerely assures them that his endeavours to deserve success shall be unabating; his care to exclude improper company most particular; and his attention to give general satisfaction, unremitting.

N.B.—The Gardens will Open on Saturday next, the 13th instant.

July, 1793.

The first Public Breakfast took place on Saturday, July 13, 1793, as announced, and was an unqualified success. The guests were served with "tea, coffee, or chocolate,"; whilst the tables were dressed with various kinds of fruits, cold meats, jellies, and other articles suitable for a morning repast. Among those present were the Duke and Duchess of Marlborough, the Earl and Countess Cardigan, the Countess of Ailesbury, Mr. Douglas and Lady Catherine Douglas, Sir Richard and Lady Heron, General Dalrymple, Mr. Metcalf, Mr. Wade, M.C., and family, &c. The weather, too, was all that could be desired. The sun shone brilliantly; and when the company promenaded after their matutinal meal "the delightful shade afforded by the fine row of elms elicited entire approbation."* On the 24th July, H.R.H. the Prince of Wales honoured the Public Breakfast with his presence; and there was a grand gathering of the nobility and gentry on the occasion, including Lieut.-General Sir William and Lady Smith, Mrs. Fitzherbert, Sir Richard and Lady Heron, &c. The Prince was profuse in his praises of the Grove, expressing not only his highest approval of the new species of entertainment, but his determination to give it his support; and His Royal Highness, on leaving, announced his intention of being present on the following Wednesday. This gratifying announcement induced the Manager of the Grove to request those of his patrons who intended to be present "to send for their tickets on the Tuesday, that they might be properly accommodated." The charge for Breakfast tickets to Subscribers was, it may be stated, 2s. 6d.; but Non-Subscribers were admitted to the Grove at 1s. for the day, "which entitles them to refreshments!"

One of the grandest Public Breakfasts of the opening season was on August 7th, at which the Prince of Wales and 400 guests were present. It was, a writer says, "most elegantly attended by all that is noble, fashionable, or respectable at Brighton." Lord and Lady Jersey and Sir John and Lady Lade were among the guests! He adds:—"There has rarely been such an assembly of beauty and

---

* The summer of 1793 was most tardy; but when it did set in the heat was intense—a quaint writer of the period characterised it as "infernally hot!" Such a fine time for harvesting was never remembered: the rakers were constantly at the heels of the mowers; in short, it is recorded "that the harvesters had nothing more to do than to cut and carry."

fashion, who all expressed their approbation of this novel species of entertainment, and seemed unwilling to quit the enchanting place, and many staid till near four o'clock." The band of the Surrey Militia played in different parts of the garden during the day, and it is related, "The effect of the music in the Grove was most enchanting."

The Public Breakfasts were continued during the remainder of the season on Tuesdays and Fridays; and with unceasing favour, if the number of nobility and gentry who attended them is to be the guide to a decision on the point. Towards the close of the season the Management introduced an addition to the amusements, namely, dancing on the green;—it being announced that a "Band will be provided for such of the company as may choose to dance." One wonders whether dear old Sir Richard and Lady Heron or pursy old General Dalrymple,—who were among the more frequent patrons of the Grove,—danced "Sir Roger de Coverley"!

Stimulated by the success of the opening season, the Management made strenuous efforts to deserve increased patronage for that which was to follow. During the recess, a very tasty entrance to the Grove was erected (on the site of the old Head Quarters of the 1st Sussex Rifle Volunteers, Prince's-place, removed October, 1891);* and internal improvements were carried out. Arrangements were also made or a series of Summer Subscription Concerts (10s. 6d. admission to the series of three, or 5s. for each), under the direction of Messrs. Barthelemon and Attwood. The Public Breakfasts were to take place on Wednesdays, and the admission for Non-Subscribers was raised to 1s. 6d., to include tea and coffee. Nothing, however, was said about "Refreshments;" possibly the experience of the first season (when they were included in the 1s. admission) did not warrant a continuance of that practice. The company could, however, be accommodated with breakfast, jellies, fruit, and, if desired, "afternoon tea."

The first of the Summer Concerts was given on the evening of July 22nd, 1794, and was honoured with the presence of the Prince of Wales and a most distinguished company; half the profits being given to the widows and orphans of the gallant soldiers and sailors who fell in Lord Howe's victory, on the "glorious First of June." The concert was a vocal and instrumental one. Among the artists who appeared were Mrs. Barthelemon and Master Welsh, Misses Barthelemon, Bridgetower, Harrington, Mahon, and F. Attwood.

The Grove on the occasion was, for the first time, illuminated by "new patent lamps;" the effect of which was very pleasing. A local chronicler, who was present at the concert, says—"No place can be better adapted for Summer Concerts—ladies of rank having dispensed with the parade of dress; and after their walk on the Steine in the open air, they retire to this delightful spot, where they either walk under the sheltering branches of the trees and flowering shrubs, or rest themselves in and around the Saloon, and are content

---

* At the same period (1794) several new and handsome shops (for the period) were erected on the Eastern side of Prince's-place, a colonnade being erected on each side from North-street.

with a concord of sweet sounds." The writer adds—"The singing of Master Welsh far excelled in taste, pathos, and sweetness of tone, any singing we have ever heard."

With the Prince of Wales the Grove was in high favour. All the amusements there were "By command" of His Royal Highness, or under his patronage. It was only fitting, therefore, that on his birthday, August 12, the Management should do its best to celebrate the event. And this it did by a brilliant illumination of the Gardens in the evening; and, martial music being discoursed by the Dorset and other bands, the Festival was the grandest yet given in the Promenade Grove. Brighton, we are told, "has never had to boast of such an assemblage of beauty and fashion. They exceeded 1,200 in number; and every one contributed to the general mirth and good humour of the occasion. The gardens were light with new-invented reflecting lamps between the trees; the Saloon, Cottage, and other buildings were tastefully ornamented with festoons and musical devices in various coloured lamps. At the end of the Rutland Walk was a transparent painting of His Royal Highness's coronet and crest, adorned with red roses, and 'LONG LIVE THE PRINCE.' At the end of the cross walk, the Garter Star, decorated with woodbines and lilies; and at the end of the Lawn His Royal Highness's initials, beautifully wrote in flowers, crowned with a wreath of laurel; the whole encircled with the British oak and acorns—the motto, 'BRIGHTON'S SUPPORT.' They were all much admired and did great credit to Cripps, who painted them. Although the scene was entirely new at Brighton, and the company so numerous and mixed, everything was conducted with pleasing regularity and decorum." The Prince did not attend; but among those present were the Countess of Guildford and Albemarle; Lady C. Greville, Lady K. Douglas, Ladies A. and C. North, the Hon. Mr. and Mrs. Bridgeman, the Earl of Mornington, Sir R. and Lady Heron, Sir G. and Lady Ellison Winn, Sir Wm. and Lady Young, Sir W. and Lady Lawson; Generals Bruce and Dalrymple; Rev. Mr. and Mrs. Ashburnham, Mrs. Cowel, the Misses Cooper, Mrs. Somers Cocks, Mrs. Horsley, the Misses Auguish, Mr. and Mrs. Ingram, Colonel and Mrs. Newton, Mr. Shelley and family, the Misses Thrale, Mr. and Mrs. Cooper, Mrs. Lawes, Colonel Pelham, Colonel Cartwright, Sir Robert Harland and most of the Officers from the Camp, Mr. Tyrwhitt, Mr. Metcalf, Mr. Boothby Clopton, &c.

On the Duke of York's birthday, the following week, the illumination was repeated with an additional transparency, extra devices of different coloured lamps, &c. New "boxes" were erected on the occasion "for such of the company as may choose to sup." Both the Prince of Wales and the Duke of Clarence were present; and the general company numbered 900. The last illumination of of the season was "by command" of the Prince; the price of admission being raised to 2s.

There was, as already stated, dancing on the green at the close of the first season; and at the close of the second season there was again dancing; but with a difference—"a platform 50ft. long was laid down before the Cottage"! What a boon for the votaries of Terpsichore in high life! The "platform," however, appears, to have been appreciated; for dancing was kept up till four o'clock in the afternoon. The company—it is not stated who among them danced—included the Duchess of Marlborough, the Ladies Spencer, the Countess of Albemarle, the Earl of Mornington, the Earl and Countess Euston, Lord Torrington, &c.

The season of 1795 opened auspiciously for the Grove. The Prince of Wales and his newly-wedded wife, the Princess Caroline of Brunswick, were residing in Brighton at the time; and Their Royal Highnesses' patronage was obtained for the Public Breakfasts and other entertainments; but whether or no the Royal Pair honoured them in company is not recorded. Most probably they did; as they were frequently seen together in public—at the Theatre, on the Steine, and in the Camp. The management of the Grove evidently did its best to show an appreciation of the Royal patronage; for, in addition to the Breakfasts, &c., special amusements were announced in honour of the Prince's birthday (August 12); including a grand display of fireworks. The gardens were decorated and illuminated; there was also a vocal and instrumental concert; and, verily, under such an aggregation of attractions, the public gaieties of the old town were growing apace! This great fête was, as stated, "in honour of," for it did not take place *on*, the natal day of His Royal Highness. In order, probably, that it might not interfere with the birthday festivities of the Steine,—which always took place on the 12th, or, with what was much more important, the ball of the "M.C." at the Castle!—the fete took place on the 14th; and, with the view of showing the character of the fireworks at that period, a copy of the announcement of the display is appended:—

In Honour of His Royal Highness The PRINCE of WALES'S Birthday.

PROMENADE GROVE, BRIGHTON.

On FRIDAY EVENING NEXT, the 14th of August, 1795, will be

A MAGNIFICENT DISPLAY OF FIREWORKS.

Under the direction of Signors ROSSI and TESSIER.

ORDER OF FIRING.

1. A Salute of Maroons.
2. A Horizontal Wheel in Brilliant Fire, adorned with Roman Candles and Pot de Brins.
3. A Bomb Shell Illuminated.
4. A Cascade of Wheels in Brilliant Fire.
5. A Discharge of Pot de Brins.
6. Two Transparencies adorned with Rayonant Fire and Maroons.
7. A Bomb Shell Illuminated.
8. A Gillocke in Brilliant Fire.
9. A Regulated Piece of four Mutations of different changes.
10. A discharge of Pot de Grades.
11. The Initials of His Royal Highness the Prince of Wales adorned with Rayonant and Brilliant Fire.
12. A Grand Display of Roman Candles.

13. Six Wheels in Brilliant Fire, with a Reprize in Chinese Fire with Maroons.
14. To conclude with a discharge of Pot de Grades and Bomb Shells.

The GARDENS will be splendidly decorated and ILLUMINATED, and the Dorset Band will (by permission) perform martial music, interspersed with glees.

The doors to be opened at Eight o'clock. Admission, 2s. each person.

The PUBLIC BREAKFAST will be on Tuesday, at eleven o'clock, with music. Admission, 1s. 6d. each person, Tea and Coffee included.

The exhibition, which attracted no less that 1,400 spectators to the Grove, was described as "truly magnificent" and as having elicited "universal approbation." (The pyrotechnists were, it appears, from the once celebrated Ranelagh Gardens.) The novelty of such fireworks must have "astonished the natives;" and, doubtless, there was on that occasion, as on many subsequently, a grand gathering of aborigines on "the Knab" (Brighton-place), whence a fine view of the display could be obtained, inasmuch as the lower part of North-street, from just above the present Union Bank to Pritchard's Library, was then open garden ground. There was a second display of fireworks on September 22nd, at which over 1,000 spectators were present; and it "exceeded in variety of fanciful design and splendour of exhibition all previous efforts." The last piece in the "order of firing" was a graceful tribute to the Princess Caroline, and consisted of—

"Three Pedestals, supporting the initials of H.R.H. the Princess of Wales, in Slow Fire; a Grand Reprize of Nine Fans, or Chinese Fire, with a discharge of Maroons; to conclude with two Bombshells Illuminated, and a Flight of Rockets."

"Two Bombshells *Illuminated*" must have been a pyrotechnic curiosity! In the following season (1796) there were more "summer concerts"—the Band performing in a very pretty new Orchestra, designed and painted by Mariani—and more fireworks; the latter "under the patronage of the Prince and Princess of Wales." The Prince himself was present on the occasion; as were also all the fashionable visitors in Brighton. When there was a repetition on His Royal Highness's birthday, there was a splendid company; the fireworks "exceeding the most sanguine expectations." The great "event" of the season, however, was the "Original Poney Races." Pony Races in such a circumscribed area as the Promenade Grove! and in the evening, too, of all times of the day! The Course was lighted "in various devices with different coloured lamps;" and was laid out in "the Amphitheatre of the Grove;" but it would be difficult, at this time of day, to describe how matters were arranged. The announcement was as follows:—

FOR ONE NIGHT ONLY.

ORIGINAL PONEY RACES.

Under the Patronage of their Royal Highnesses the PRINCE and PRINCESS OF WALES.

PROMENADE GROVE, BRIGHTON.

On WEDNESDAY EVENING NEXT, August 17th, 1796, in the Amphitheatre of the Grove, will be run

A GRAND MATCH

By those five celebrated Poneys of Messrs. Jones's, of the Royal Circus, St. George's Fields, as originally exhibited before Their Majesties at the Frogmore Fête, and upwards of 60 Nights successively at the Royal Circus.

Names of the Poneys and Colours of the Riders :—

BLACK AND ALL BLACK	Green Striped.
HIGH FLYER	Blue and Scarlet.
LITTLE GIPSEY	Pink.
ROCKINGHAM	Striped.
POT 8 O'S	Yellow.

FIRST HEAT—Three Poneys will start; the winner will be drawn.
SECOND HEAT   ditto   ditto   ditto.
THIRD HEAT   ditto   ditto   ditto.

FINALE—"The three winning Poneys to start for the GRAND SWEEPSTAKES."

The Course will be Lighted in various devices with different coloured lamps; a Band of Music will perform in the new Orchestra before and between the heats.

The doors to be Opened at Seven o'clock, and the Poneys to Start at Half-past Eight o'clock.

Admission, 2s. each person.

Nearly 600 persons were present at the Races, the success of which induced repetitions in the following week: once after the Public Breakfast and once in the evening.

There was another grand day at the Grove on September 5th, the Officers of the Royal Horse Guards (Blue) giving a Fête to a select party of the Nobility and Gentry of Brighton. The guests numbered 300, and a spacious tent and "temporary boxes" were erected for their accommodation. The breakfast took place at noon; the tables were covered with every delicacy; after breakfast the company danced in the Saloon and on the Lawn—no less than three Bands being present: that of the Regiment and those of the West Kent and West Essex Militia;—and, we are told, "the whole was conducted with the nicest order and decorum."

With each recurring season the Public Breakfasts were continued. But in 1797 there was a new attraction, the Management announcing "There will be a PUBLIC TEA DRINKING, with Music;" the terms of admission to the Grove being " 1s. 6d., Tea included!" With such liberal terms, no wonder the Grove became popular, more especially as the evening concerts were really of a high-class character; for among the vocalists at the opening concerts were Mr. Cooke, from Drury-lane, and Mr. Sleigh, from Covent-garden. The fireworks, however, still held their own as the premier attraction of the Grove; the first display of the season being honoured with the presence of the Prince of Wales (in company with the Duke of Bedford and Lord

Egremont) and about 600 fashionables. But, later on, a new entertainment "became quite the rage." This was "The Fantoccini"—a decided novelty, the fame of which had preceded it in Brighton; it had "made so much noise at Ranelagh." The following is a copy of one of the announcements:—

Under the Patronage of Their Royal Highnesses The PRINCE and PRINCESS OF WALES.
PROMENADE GROVE, NORTH STREET, BRIGHTON.
The Nobility, Gentry, &c., are respectfully informed that on Wednesday, August 23rd, 1797, will be presented by
THE NEW FANTOCCINI,
A Musical Entertainment, entitled, LES TROIS RECETTES; to which will be added the favourite petite piece of L'ERREUR DU MOMENT, with Dancing and other Entertainments between the Acts.
New Scenery, Dresses, Machinery, and Decorations. The Scenes by Mr. Lupius, Jun., Mr. Pugh, and Assistants; the Dresses by Signior Cisterini; and Machinery by Signior Rebecqui.
The whole under the direction of Mr. WHITE.
N.B.—The Fantoccini will be performed on Saturday Evening, August 26th, instead of Friday, *on account of Mr. Wade's Ball.**
By permission, the Monmouth and Brecon Band will perform.
Songs between the Acts.
The doors to be opened at half after Seven o'clock, the Fantoccini to begin precisely at half after Eight. Admission, 2s. each.

The fashionable company at Brighton appear to have been greatly delighted with "The Fantoccini;" and they expressed, in the most flattering terms, their admiration at "the flying performers." The dancing, in particular, was said to be "a perfect imitation of the first characters in the profession;" and, speaking of it as a whole, it was "not known which merits the greatest praise, the ingenuity of the mechanist, the taste of the taylor, or the pencil of the painter." The points of the dialogue, it may be added, were received with repeated bursts of laughter. "The Fantoccini" were exceedingly popular, and their stay at the Grove was prolonged for some weeks. The season was closed with a firework display, and a concert, sustained by several vocalists from the Ranelagh Gardens;—in fact, the Grove was now regarded as the "Ranelagh of the South."

The concerts and fireworks had become the staple amusements at the Grove; and, notwithstanding their frequency, were as popular as when they were first instituted. The Prince of Wales was evidently fond of the fireworks. He was present at the first display in 1798, accompanied by the Prince of Orange, Prince Ernest, the Duke of Bedford, the Earl of Egremont, &c.; and on his birthday there was a

---

* The "M.C.," as previously explained in the history of that functionary, evidently exercised his authority respecting amusements in a very absolute manner; for, on the 6th of September, 1798, when a private display was to have taken place, it was postponed by the "M.C." on account of his Ball at "The Old Ship"!—a great disappointment, it was said, both to the Managers of the Grove and to the Public, the night being beautifully fine.

magnificent display, attended by over 800 persons; the grand concert which followed being led by Lavenu (a pupil of Cramer). But *the* display of the season was at the Grand Gala on the 24th August, in honour of the birthdays of the Dukes of York and Clarence. It was given under the direction of Signor Hengler, "Artist and Engineer in Fireworks to H.R.H. the Prince of Wales and the Duke of Clarence,"—an addition, this, to the Royal office-bearers hitherto unknown to the world. The skill of the Signor, however, appears to have fully qualified him for his high position; for, if description can convey any idea of his display, it must have been truly superb. Two closing pieces are thus described:—

"A REPRESENTATION OF TWO SHIPS IN ACTION AT SEA,
The same as was performed in honour of Lord Viscount Duncan at Hampton Court, where the Royal Family were present, and other persons of distinction, with a beautiful transparency of RULE BRITANNIA in a glory of brilliant fire.

"A superb piece of mechanism, solely invented and executed by Signor Hengler, representing TWO RATTLE SNAKES in PURSUIT of a BUTTERFLY, whose beautiful colours will be represented by blue, yellow, green, and other diversified fireworks; at the same time two splendid Mosaicks will be set on fire by a flying Pidgeon."

It were needless to detail the amusements of the Grove during the next season or two; there were breakfasts and concerts, and concerts and breakfasts; fireworks and illuminations, and illuminations and fireworks. One morning, after breakfast, there was a "lottery," which, from its novelty, was said to have afforded the company "much amusement, and every one seemed anxious for a prize." In August, 1800, a "Grand Masqued Ball," under the patronage of the Prince of Wales, was announced; but nothing further respecting it is recorded.* Perhaps it had to "follow suit" with that of the "M.C.," which was put off on account of Lewes Races, "he having obtained the permission of H.R.H. the Prince of Wales to do so." Among the various artists who appeared at the concerts were Mrs. Kliff and Dighton, from Covent-garden; and one of the best concerts ever given at the Grove was in August, 1801, when a Grand Gala took place in honour of the Prince of Wales's birthday. Mrs. Kliff and Dighton were among the vocalists, and the instrumentalists included some of the best performers of the day; but the special feature of the concert was a performance of an ODE in honour of the day, written by Mr. Sickelmore, of Brighton, and composed by Mr. Prince, Organist to the Chapel Royal. It was a great success, and was repeated by "particular desire" at Mrs. Kliff's benefit, later in the season. The fireworks in 1801 were by Mr. Mortram, who introduced Chinese fireworks of superb design; the much-admired " Palm Tree;" and, shade of Halley! a "representa-

---

* "Masquerading" at the Grove was not popular. "A Grand Masquerade," with numerous attractions, took place in the following year. It proved a sad failure. It was put off for a night "on account of the rain," and, adds a local chronicler, "as it turned out, it would have been more to the interest of the Directors to have put it off SINE DIE."

tion of the Wonderful Comet that appeared in the year 1758." The "novelty" of the season was, however, the "Rural Fête, Dutch Fair," &c., on September 10th and 11th, "by command of the Prince of Wales." Surely, this was not the September Fair of the aborigines transferred, from "under the Cliff" and " on the Bank," to the domain of Royalty and Fashion! History is altogether silent as to the "doings" at the Fête, &c., whether fair and noble dames presided at the stalls, or whether the well-known itinerant vendors of toys, gilt gingerbread, &c., did duty on the occasion. Doubtless, there was much excitement in the town, as the attractions were of a character which appealed to all sections of the community. The announcement of the Fête was as follows :—

By Command of His Royal Highness THE PRINCE of WALES.
PROMENADE GROVE, BRIGHTON.

The Nobility, Gentry, and Public in general are most respectfully informed that on THURSDAY and FRIDAY NEXT, September 10 and 11, 1801, there will be

A Rural Fete, a Dutch Fair, and a Public Breakfast,
At the PROMENADE GROVE,

The Breakfast to commence at Twelve o'clock, and continue till Two, after which time what Refreshments are had must be paid for.

Proper Musicians are engaged for COUNTRY DANCES, &c.

In the evening the GARDENS will be ILLUMINATED, and the Saloon lighted up for Dances till Twelve o'clock, after which time no Dance will be called.

Admittance, Five Shillings each evening. Tickets to be had at the Grove.

Doors to be opened at Twelve.

What proved to be the closing season of the original Proprietary of the Grove (1802) showed no falling off either in novelty or in attractiveness. It opened, August 1st, with a firework display, and on the following Wednesday, after the Public Breakfast, there was a "new sensation"—a Balloon ascent! at two o'clock. The announcement stated that a "GOLDEN AIR BALLOON" would ascend "under the direction of Mr. Mortram, who has had the honour of conducting three balloons. The process of filling the Balloon may be seen by the company in the morning." The ascent of what was described as the "little balloon" took place at a quarter to three ; the machine going away in an easterly direction. Subsequently, it was reported that "it was picked up by a poor boy, about seven o'clock the same evening, in a field belonging to Mr. Hawes, of Frant, about two and a half miles from Tunbridge Wells, and conveyed to Brighton by coach, where it arrived on the following Friday in rather a mangled state;" it being added, "but it is to be repaired for another expedition on some future day ;" and in the following week another ascent was made.

But the "knell" is sounding! The end of the Grove and its amusements is at hand! This doom is foreshadowed in four lines of

The Lewes Journal, of August 16th, 1802 :—"The Prince has purchased the Promenade Grove, on a part of which His Royal Highness intends to have erected a spacious tennis-court." *

But the end is not yet. Hilarity rules the hour! On September 2nd, there was a Grand Gala, with TIGHT-ROPE DANCING—the "celebrated Signor Saxoni (just arrived from Paris) will shew his favourite Tambourine Dance and Hornpipe, also the Russian Manual and Platoon Exercise on the Rope, concluding with the celebrated Flag Dance." As a matter of course, there were fireworks in the evening; and the Prince of Wales's Band discoursed delightful music during the display.

It might be said of the Proprietor of the Grove, that, in the closing days of his management, "nothing became him like the leaving it." Not only did he do his best to make a pleasant ending, but he availed himself of the opportunity to give substantial proof of his appreciation of the patronage bestowed upon him during his career. He accordingly announced a grand entertainment at the Grove, coupled with Pony Races on the Race Course, sending far and wide bills headed "A DAY AT BRIGHTON." This heading is generally supposed to have come in with the Railway era; but a "Day at Brighton" is in reality "old style." *Ex. gratia :—*

A DAY AT BRIGHTON.

Under the Patronage of His Royal Highness the PRINCE OF WALES.

PROMENADE GROVE.

The Nobility, Gentry, and Public in General, are most respectfully informed there will be a

PUBLIC BREAKFAST AND CONCERT

At the above place, on THURSDAY NEXT, September 9, 1802.

A SILVER CUP, given as a testimony of gratitude by the Proprietor of the Grove, will be afterwards run for by Ponies. (See Advertisement which follows.)

In the Evening the Gardens will be Magnificently Illuminated, and SAXONI will again exhibit his skill on the Tight Rope.

The whole to conclude with an unexampled display of CHINESE FIREWORKS, in which will be exhibited THE GRAND SPECTACLE OF MOUNT VESUVIUS AFTER AN ERUPTION,

under the direction of Mr. Mortram.

Subscription for the day, 5s.; Breakfast only, 2s. 6d.; Fireworks only, 3s. 6d.

RACING.

To be Run for, an elegant FIFTEEN GUINEA CUP, given by the Proprietor of the Promenade Grove, Brighton, on Thursday, the 9th

---

* The Prince had been the Lessee of the Dairy Field, east of the Grove, since 1795; and in December, 1803, purchased it from Nathaniel Kemp, Esq., for £4,200. In September, 1803, His Royal Highness leased of Mr. Philip Mighell a large piece of land adjoining the Dairy Field, on the north-west, at the yearly rent of £50; and, under a clause in the lease, purchased it in 1819, for £1,000. The "Quakers' Croft," immediately to the west of the Grove, was assigned to the Prince in May, 1806, for £800.

of September, by Ponies not to exceed thirteen hands high (catch weights). To be shewn in the Promenade Grove, and approved by the Clerk of the Course at 12 o'clock of the same day, and to pay one guinea entrance. To start at half-past two o'clock. Heats. The New Course, about a mile and three-quarters.

"The Day at Brighton"—though the weather in the morning was most unpropitious—proved a great success; attracting a very large number of visitors. The Public Breakfast was well attended; but the great interest of the midday proceedings centred in the Pony Race. All the rank and fashion of the town assembled on the hill, their numbers being swelled by some thousands of the inhabitants and visitors from the country districts. His Royal Highness the Prince of Wales was present; also, the Russian Princess Galitzen, the Earl and Countess of Clermont, the Earl of Peterborough, Sir John and Lady Lade, Mrs. Fitzherbert, Col. Montgomery, Mr. Day, Mr. Travers, Mr. Allen, Mr. Howarth, Mr. Mortram, Mr. Goldsmid, Capt. Harvey, &c. The Race, in which five ponies ran, proved an exciting one; and Bobtail, which won the first heat, and was also victorious in the second, secured the Silver Cup for his owner, a Mr. Newton. The amusements of the "Day at Brighton" finished up at the Grove, where there was a grand gathering in the evening to witness Saxoni's tight-rope dancing and the brilliant display of fireworks.

What would appear to have been the last public Gala at the Grove, under the original Management, took place on Thursday, September 16th, 1802, which was thus announced:—

Under the Patronage of His Royal Highness the PRINCE OF WALES.

PROMENADE GROVE.

The Nobility, Gentry, and Public in general are respectfully informed that on THURSDAY NEXT, September 16th, 1802, there will be

A GALA AT THE ABOVE PLACE.

In the course of the Concert will be introduced a Concerto for the Horn and Bassoon, by L. Maloch and — Rhea, Jun.

The whole to conclude with a Grand Display of CHINESE FIREWORKS, in which will be introduced

THE GRAND SPECTACLE OF MOUNT VESUVIUS

At the time of its greatest Eruption (for the last time) in 1737, under the direction of Mr. Mortram.

Doors to be opened at Seven. Concert to begin at Half-past Seven.

Fireworks at Nine o'clock. Admittance, 3s. 6d., Tea included.

The last Grand Gala closed with the "Eruption of Mount Vesuvius;" and, like this, the Promenade Grove may be said to have "ended in smoke"!

There would seem to have been a feeling of regret that such a fashionable and popular place of amusement as the Promenade Grove should cease to exist; and, in compliance with a request made to him early in the following year, we learn that H.R.H. the Prince of Wales was graciously pleased "to permit Mr. Quartermain to use his recently-purchased estate, the Promenade Grove at Brighton, during the present season, for the reception of company, as heretofore, he undertaking to pay the accustomed rent for the same into the hands of the Parish Officers for the benefit of the poor."

The existence of the Grove as a place of public amusement was therefore prolonged, under new auspices, for one more season; and this, as regards attraction, was scarcely less brilliant than any which had preceded it. A Gala on August 12th, in honour of the Prince of Wales's birthday, when there was a vocal and instrumental concert, tea, fireworks, &c., was honoured by the presence of His Royal Highness and the Duke of Clarence, the Earl of Egremont, the Earl and Countess Berkeley, Lord George Cavendish, Mrs. Fitzherbert, Lady Lade, several foreign Noblemen, and by nearly all the company in Brighton. In fact, such was the success of the Gala, that it was repeated the Thursday after, "by particular desire." In the following month, on September 22nd, there was another Gala still more brilliant, when, in addition to the fireworks, &c., the Grove was illuminated. This Gala was given "by command of H.R.H. the Prince of Wales," who, doubtless, was desirous that this, the closing Fête at the Grove, should be a brilliant one. The great fashionable and popular gathering on the occasion showed how much the Gala was appreciated. A day or two later, the last recorded public breakfast took place. It was given on the invitation of Lady Charlotte Lennox, a splendid company being present. A feature of the concert was the performances on the pedal harp, by Mdlle. Mereille, an artist who had made such a sensation at the Prince of Wales's Gala. Henceforth amusements at the Promenade Grove ceased; and, ere long, William Porden, Esq., was hard at work upon the Rotunda (now the Dome), the Riding House, &c., and "Capability" Brown's pupils were actively engaged in transforming the Grove into the pretty piece of miniature landscape now known as the Western Lawn of the Pavilion Grounds.

POPULAR AMUSEMENTS.

The popular amusements of Brighton in the olden time appear to have been comparatively few,—at all events, only brief particulars respecting them have come down to us. Neither record nor tradition states whether or no our aborigines availed themselves of the "declaration" of James I., drawn up by one of the Bishops, setting forth that, "for his good people's recreation, his pleasure was, that on the Sabbath, after the end of Divine Service, they should not be disturbed, letted, or discouraged from any lawful recreations, such as dancing, either of men or women, archery for men, leaping, vaulting, or any such harmless recreations; nor having May-games, Whitsun ales, or Morrice-dances, setting up of May-poles, or other sports therewith used."

It is doubtful whether the "declaration" reached so far "down

South." If it did, it would probably have been of no effect; for it is scarcely to be conceived that a genuine Brighton fisherman of the olden time ever footed it featly in a Morris-dance, or indulged in that essentially rural pleasure of "bringing in the Maypole,"* and on Sunday, too, when, of all days, it was a time-honoured custom to walk "on the Bank." No; his habits and his tastes lay in another direction. Blunt, honest, and industrious, wholly absorbed in his occupation, he had from time immemorial "hugged the sea." He might, indeed, associate with the landsmen in some national festival; the celebration of a victory, &c., when a bonfire blazed, or an ox was roasted, and ale ran freely; but as regards other popular amusements—such as cricket, foot races, and sports "of that ilk,"—the fisher population took little or no part in them, except as spectators. The sports enumerated were indulged in at Brighton in earlier times, but chiefly by the agricultural population on its outskirts, their competitors coming from the neighbouring rural districts. Judging, too, by the frequency which Brighton appeared in the cricket field, and the number of men who at various times were associated in matches with those of other districts, even so early as the middle of last century, it would seem that the local team of cricketers had then no mean reputation for prowess, that, in fact, it could boast of "giants in those days." But of this, more by and by. For convenience of description, the popular amusements may be broadly classified thus—"Loyal Festivities," "Horse Racing," "Cricket," "Cock-fighting," "Bull-baiting," &c.

Loyal Festivities, Sports, &c.

The earliest form in which loyal or national festivities were wont to be celebrated in Brighton and neighbourhood was of a very simple character; and, considering the characteristics, habits, and comparitively low social position of the rural population—and of many of the artisan class, even in towns, in primitive times—it is probable that the form in vogue was a very happy arrangement It had one great element in its favour—there was no restriction as to the number who might join in it. It feasted the eye, gladdened the heart, and afforded scope for unbounded hilarity—all important essentials in a popular festivity.

We have alluded (page 28) to one of the earliest local celebrations, in 1758, on the occasion of Admiral Boscawen's victory; and in October, 1761, when George III. and Queen Charlotte were crowned,

---

* May-day would appear to have been observed in Brighton from an early period; for when the Prince of Mecklenburg-Strelitz was staying for the benefit of his health at "The Castle," in 1771, on the 1st of May several little girls went to the inn to show their garlands, and the Prince gave to each of them half a guinea.

there were, no doubt, at Brighton, as at Lewes,* grand festivities with the customary accessories. The most important, however, of the local rejoicings recorded was on the 12th August, 1789, the birthday of His Royal Highness the Prince of Wales, when, it was said, there was such "mirth and festivity as were heretofore unknown in this country." The Heir Apparent had at this period chosen Brighton for his marine residence; had identified himself with the welfare of the inhabitants; and on the occasion of the first local celebration of his birthday, he, accompanied by his Royal brothers, Mrs. Fitzherbert, Mr. Fox, and a great number of the nobility, "appointed the diversions." "The weather," says a chronicler of the scene, "was heavenly. Grandeur and Elegance shook hands with Good Humour and Familiarity, and furnished out a treat surpassing description for its blandishment and brilliancy." The morning was ushered in with the ringing of bells. The "diversions" commenced at noon, and consisted of "Jack-ass racing; foot-races by ladies for gowns; men running in sacks," &c.; the ludicrous situations in which several of the competitors were placed causing much amusement. There were no less than five marquees on the ground for the accommodation of the Prince and his friends. At a convenient distance from these an ox was roasted, and, when ready, was carved by Mr. Mercer (His Royal Highness's butcher) with a huge broadsword, and then handed in slices to the crowd on a large fork, this latter serving the additional purpose of "keeping the guests in subjection." Mercer effected his task with admirable address, much humour being excited by his grotesque appearance. As an accompaniment to the roast beef, 1,000 loaves were distributed, and twenty hogsheads of strong beer were set in the open field and broached for the populace, who were exceedingly numerous. Then in the afternoon, for the especial behoof of the fishermen, there was a sailing match by the fishing-boats, for a suit of sails, given by the Right Hon. Colonel Pelham. The whole town was splendidly illuminated in the evening.

A week after, on August 19th, the birthdays of the Dukes of York and Clarence were celebrated in nearly the same manner as that of the Prince of Wales; but in addition to the rustic sports of the 12th, there was "dancing by young men and women" and a "game at football." The Duke of York played during the day a game of cricket for 100 guineas with Colonel Tarleton, and lost. *Two* oxen were roasted on this latter occasion. They were set down to the fire between five and six a.m., and were served out at three; Mercer carving one and "Butcher" Russell the other. Mercer, as we suppose he was in the previous week, was dressed in full "canonicals,"—that is, in a milk white coat and night-cap, this latter decked out with two blue and buff favours. Across his

---

* Lewes had from an early period been noted for its loyal festivities. In October, 1746, at the "Thanksgiving for the happy defeat of the Rebels by the Duke of Cumberland," there was ringing of bells, sermons in the Churches, drinking healths to the Duke of Cumberland and the Duke of Newcastle, illuminations, bonfires, fireworks, and other demonstrations of joy.

THE CELEBRATION OF A ROYAL BIRTHDAY
(From a rare Print of the period

DAY IN BRIGHTHELMSTON, 12TH AUGUST, 1789.

riod, in the possession of Mr. FIELD).

breast was a broad sash of Royal purple; a tremendous broadsword being pendant at his side. The guests seemed to group themselves in three divisions, one being desirous of obtaining bread, another beer, and a third beef; but an eye witness says, "judging by the hands held up to catch the loaves canted in the air, the majority were in favour of bread." He then summarises the distribution thus—

> "Of oceans of strong beer and mountains of bread;
> With carcass on which some like cannibals fed:
> HALF ROASTED or RAW, 'twas the same just at last,
> Ere THE SKELETONS finished this novel repast."

The vast quantities of strong beer, however, given to the populace produced, we are told, "various feats in the art of pugilism." In the afternoon there was a race between the vessels of Capt. Chapman and Capt. Burton for 25 guineas (given by the Prince of Wales), which was won by the former. At night there were grand illuminations, and between "one and two o'clock in the morning, superb fireworks." *

These details will suffice to show the character of the early loyal festivities. The "sports" usually associated with them were mostly simple "diversions," arranged, not so much for sport as for amusement to the lookers-on, such as might be afforded in the falls of the competitors in the "jumping in sacks"; or in the stumbling of the "blind-'uns," or their falling foul of each other, in the "jingling matches;" or, as in the "Jack-ass racing," might be got out of a stubborn or impulsive animal, and in this last case, to meet either contingency, the prizes were usually awarded to the "first" or the "last" donkey passing the winning-post. The "feats in the art of pugilism" were supplementary diversions, and varied according to circumstances, —that is, according to the effect of the "strong beer" imbibed by those who had a *penchant* for the practice of the "noble art."†

In 1790—on the 20th August—there was a double celebration in honour of the Prince of Wales's and the Duke of York's birthdays, which was of much the same character as that of 1789, two oxen being roasted and bread and beer distributed, followed by rustic sports, which, however, included the novelty of a "jingling match." For some reason or other, now unknown, the roasting of oxen, &c., and the

---

* On the 21st August, the Duke of Clarence's 25th birthday, Shoreham emulated Brighton in the matter of a firework display. We are told "The Siege of Gibraltar was most strikingly represented, and the red-hot balls from the garrison had a most striking effect. The whole was under the direction of Captain Robarts of that place." So pleased was the Royal Duke with the compliment, that he called the next day on Captain Robarts, and afterwards went on board his packet, "amidst the acclamations of a vast concourse of the sons of Neptune." This Captain Robarts, it may be added, had twice circumnavigated the world with Captain Cook; and in October, 1790, it was arranged that there should be another expedition to the South Seas for fresh discoveries, and of this he was to have the sole command.

† Both the Prince of Wales and his Royal brothers were, as was the fashion then, great patrons of pugilism; and few encounters took place in the neighbourhood in the latter part of the century, and even later on, at which one or the other of them was not present. At a "set-to" in September, 1790, between a butcher and an ostler, on the Level, the Prince of Wales, the Duke of Cumberland, and many of the Nobility and Gentry of Brighton were among the spectators.

more hilarious popular festivities, on the Royal birthdays, and occasions of national rejoicings, ceased for several years after this. There were, however, the ringing of the Church bells, and illuminations, Royal salutes, and, later on, military displays, *feux-de-joie*, &c. In October, 1801, on the Ratification of Peace, "which was announced to the Town by the *Gazette* being read by the Cryer, amidst the acclamations of the people," there was a very joyful celebration. "The bells (we are told) were rung *from six in the morning till twelve at night*. Young and old wore ribbons emblematic on the occasion— *Peace and Plenty!* The Sea Fencibles fired a *feu-de-joie*; then marched to the Prince's house, and gave him three loud huzzas. He ordered them two hogsheads of beer." The town was in the evening brilliantly illuminated; the Prince of Wales had flambeaux burning round his house, and every window lighted.

But in 1806 the "old style" was revived; and after a grand review, which afforded gratification to thousands of spectators, there was an adjournment to the Level to witness manœuvres of a different kind, namely, the carving of two roasted oxen, and the distribution of beef, with bread and beer, under the direction of "Butcher" Russell, as Commander-in-Chief. But the scene was one of great noise and confusion; which was rendered "worse confounded" by the unseemly conduct of the Nottinghamshire Militia, who happened to be encamped on the Level at the time.

It is possible that the Prince of Wales, in ordering oxen to be roasted, and bread and beer to be distributed, on festive occasions, deemed it to be a boon to the poorer classes. It may have been in 1789; but twenty years later—in 1809, during which the population of the town had more than doubled—it had become very questionable. On August 12th in the latter year two oxen were roasted in the hollow to the left of the Prince's Cricket-ground (now Parkcrescent), whither, after a grand military and naval review, the populace (some 5,000 in number) adjourned. They were subsequently joined by the Nottinghamshire Militia, &c. About eight o'clock there was a general scrambling for the roast beef, which "flew about in every direction." Bread, also, was distributed to the multitude. But the hogsheads of ale on the ground did not, probably, mend matters; for at ten o'clock, we are told, the Militia and townspeople were each striving to obtain the remainder of the carcases of the oxen. The Militia triumphed, and "carried them off to their camp, spits and all."

Of what may be deemed the "sports" proper at these celebrations, foot-racing by men and by "ladies" was the most ancient. At what date it had been an acknowledged sport in the neighbourhood it would be needless to enquire; but so early as 1746 it could boast of a local champion; for in that year it is recorded that Woods, the "famous runner," was beat by "one Verral, at Lewes, for £40, the said Woods carrying a 2lb. weight in each hand." Walking-matches and running-matches were, in fact, every-day matters at the period, among all classes and both sexes. In November, 1746, at Steyning, Mr. Jno. Wheeler, "the old gouty Alderman of that place," walked from Steyning to

Findon, for a considerable wager. He was allowed 1½ hours to do it in; but did it in 1 hour 5 min., and "astonished everybody"—except, perhaps, his backers! Women would seem to have early participated in the "sport" of running, though the practice was apparently not then in high favour with "the country people," jndging by the following advertisement, which appeared in the *Lewes Journal* of June, 1759:—

NOTICE IS HEREBY GIVEN, that, on THURSDAY NEXT, the 21st instant, 1759, WILL BE RUN FOR, at Mr. Clare's, at Rottingdean. a HOLLAND SMOCK, with Ribbon, value 30s., by SIX or MORE YOUNG WOMEN; the best of three Heats. The Winner to have the Smock; the Second to have a Pair of Cotton Stockings, Value 5s.; the Third, a Pair of Pumps; and the Fourth, a Flannel Petticoat, Value 4s. To be at Mr. Clare's at or before Twelve o'clock, and to start exactly at One.

N.B.--The Young Women may depend on a Protection from any Insults from the Country People, as proper Care is and will be taken by hiring Persons for that Purpose.

After this, "foot-racing by ladies" at the Prince's birth-day celebration could have excited no wonder. It was a thing of custom,* though it would have been more "honoured in the breach than in the observance." But this *en passant*. Of foot-racers of the hardier sex "Brighton in 1800" could boast of some two or three "redoubtables." One noted pedestrian was the "Brighton Shepherd;" then there was one Grinley, or Grinning, the "Brighton Boot-closer," and he was the more famous of the two. In November, 1806, in a 100 yards race, Grinning beat the Horsham champion, Potter, on the Race Down, by 3 yards. Over 3,000 spectators were present, including several ladies in carriages. Large sums were won and lost on the match. The "Boot-closer" was less successful in the following April, when he ran 140 yards in Hyde Park with a military gentleman, losing by 1¼ yards. The pace in the latter race may be judged by the fact that it was run in 13 seconds! But still more celebrated in local sporting circles than either of the former was Abraham Wood, a "Lancashire lad." He performed a great match against time in September, 1806, on the Race Course. He was to run 20 miles in 2¼ hours, but did it in 2 hours 5½ minutes. At starting, 100 guineas to 60 guineas was laid against him; but after the first 10 miles it was 3 to 1 in his favour. The first four miles were run in 22¾ minutes; the 2nd, in 23½; the 3rd, in 24¾; the 4th, in 26¾; and the last in 27¾. So little fatigued was he after his task, that he offered to start again and run 10 miles within the hour for any sum that should be mentioned. His offer was not accepted. What brought Wood more particularly to the fore was his great match for 200 guineas

---

* In August, 1786, after some pedestrian races on the Steine by gentlemen, a lady present challenged a gentleman to run for 10 guineas, which was at once accepted. The lady, we are told, "went home to breech and otherwise equip herself for the conflict." The company waited some time in expectation of her return, but she failed to appear—probably thinking better of it!

with the celebrated pedestrian, Captain Barclay (who was staying in Brighton in 1807)*: each was to do his best in 24 hours, the Captain to have 20 miles start. For months the race was the talk of sporting circles throughout the kingdom. Each being free to choose his own ground, Wood named the Brighton Race Course. The Captain at first was undecided; but, eventually, both agreed, and the race was run at Newmarket. It proved, after all, a great disappointment, Wood having given up, after running 40 miles in six hours. It was declared by some "unfair play" (as he had done the distance previously in five hours, and 100 miles in a short time). This, however, was proved to the contrary, the pedestrian being, shortly after starting, evidently ill. The Captain did 36 miles in his six hours; his opponent having gained four miles upon him in the time. It would not, perhaps, be out of place to state that the Captain, at Newmarket, in June and July, 1809, successfully accomplished the great feat (for the first time on record) of walking 1,000 miles in 1,000 consecutive hours.

Foot-racing "events" at the period might be multiplied *ad infinitum*; but one or two of those which occasioned most excitement must suffice. Lieut. Hooper, of the South Gloucester Militia, when encamped in Brighton, in February, 1807, undertook to pick up 100 stones a yard apart, and to deposit them separately in a basket at the starting point within an hour. The distance traversed was about 5¾ miles; and the task was accomplished in 47½ minutes. This was surpassed in the following month, on the same ground (the Prince's Cricket Ground), by Lieut. Hollis, of the same Militia, who undertook to pick up 100 stones a yard apart in 45 minutes. He did it, with two seconds to spare; a chronicler adding, "much money being won and lost." There was a singular "event" at Finchley Common in November, 1807, which made no little sensation,—namely, a sporting gentleman undertaking to hop half a mile in 12 minutes, on the right leg, without touching the ground with his left; which he lost by one minute, to the "no small disappointment of the knowing ones."

Horse Racing—Brighton Races.

Horse Racing early took root on Sussex soil. It may be that the incomparable greensward and apparently limitless extent of the glorious South Downs afforded strong inducements for the sport. It was, doubtless, mainly promoted and supported by the higher-classes; but so generally patronised was it by the community at large that Racing may be fairly characterised as a "popular amusement." The establishment of a permanent Race Meeting at Lewes dates a long way back into the last century; and emulous, probably, of that of the old County town, other places less happily situated must needs have their

---

* The Captain, whilst here, did a little "sparring" with Gully, at "The White Swan," in High-street, "affording much sport. At the close each party had received blows which caused the blood to flow very copiously."

BRIGHTON RACE COURSE AND STAND, 1790.

little " Meets." Eastbourne was early to the fore ; and Steyning "followed suit." Even Shoreham, in 1763, had a two days' " open meeting," entries to be made at " The Ship :" a silver cup was run for on the 1st day, in heats—a heat being " three times round the Sheep Field." The earliest horse racing at Brighton we know of was a four-mile heat on the Downs, on March 5th, 1770, between the horses of Mr. Shergold (of " The Castle ") and of Dr. Kipping, for 10 guineas a side, the stakes being won by the Doctor's horse.*

It was only natural that Brighton, when it became the " resort of company," should patronise Lewes Races, they being so near at hand ; and from about 1760-65 there was on the days of the Meeting a grand exodus, not only of the nobility and gentry staying here, but of numbers of the townsfolk. In fact, such was the local interest in Lewes Races that, in 1774, a " Brighthelmstone Plate of £50 " was raised by subscription and run for on Saturday, August 6th, the last day of the Meet. The race was " free for horses, of all ages," under certain conditions as to weight, &c.; and the first Brighton Plate was won by Sir John Shelley's bay horse, Fantail, beating five others.

The " Plate " was the last " event " on the card; but the pleasure which the race afforded was marred by a sad accident, which, at the time, was thought to be fatal. The Duke of Richmond's horse, Antiphas, in running the last mile, fell, throwing his rider, whose neck, it was said, was dislocated; but, immediate assistance being at hand, he was eventually pronounced out of danger. The horse received no hurt.

The " Brighthelmstone Plate of £50 " was given to Lewes each subsequent year down to 1783, when it seemed to have occurred to the subscribers that they should have Races at Brighton. There was in close proximity to the town the finest spot imaginable for a Course, and the use of the ground could be obtained on the easiest terms. Among the visitors were many noblemen and gentlemen who took a lively interest in racing, notably, the Duke of Cumberland, the Duke of Queensbury, Lord Egremont, Lord Geo. Cavendish, Sir C. Bunbury, Sir H. Featherstone, and others ; † and the idea, once mooted, was soon carried out. The Course was made, and on Tuesday and Wednesday, August 26th and 27th, 1783, the first Brighton Races took place ; the announcement respecting them being as follows :—

BRIGHTHELMSTON RACES, 1783.

On TUESDAY, the 26th of August, will be run for, over the new Course of Brighthelmston,

---

* The Doctor, though a worthy disciple of Galen, was an ardent sportsman and an expert swordsman. Fighting once an impromptu duel in West-street, where he resided, with an Officer who had insulted him, he took in the encounter the Officer's sword ; keeping it for over a week, much to the latter's chagrin. A descendant of Dr. Kipping, the late Captain Kipping, of Vernon-terrace, emulated his sporting proclivities ; his sad sudden death after a day's hunting [1879] will doubtless be fresh in the remembrance of many, and also his funeral, when his dogs followed the mournful procession to the grave.

† The Earl of Chatham and Lord Stowell matched their hunters on the Brighton Downs, in August, 1781, for 200 guineas ; the Duke of Cumberland and many of the nobility being present.

A PLATE of FIFTY POUNDS, by four years old Colts, carrying 8st. 2lbs. Fillies, 8st. The best of three two-mile Heats.

Same day, a SWEEPSTAKES of FIVE GUINEAS each, to which will be added a PURSE of THIRTY GUINEAS, given by the Town of Brighthelmston, by PONIES, not exceeding 13 Hands, carrying 7st.; all under 13 Hands to be allowed at the rate of 7lb. for an inch. The best of three four-mile Heats.

Mr. Dymock, Mr. Williams, Mr. Bannister, and Mr. Broadhurst are Subscribers to these Stakes.

And on WEDNESDAY, the 27th, will be run for

A PLATE OF FIFTY POUNDS, by any horse, &c. Four year olds, 7st. 4lb.; five year olds, 8st. 4lb.; six year olds, 8st. 11lb.; and aged, 9st. The best of three four-mile Heats. Mares to be allowed 3lb. for the above Plates. Winners of a Plate since 1st of March, 1783, to carry 3lb.; of two, 5lb.; and of more than two, 7lb. extra.

The horses, &c., to be shown and entered at the Castle at Brighthelmston, on TUESDAY, the 19th of August, before the hour of seven in the afternoon, paying three guineas entrance, or double at the Post. Not less than three reputed running horses to start for either of these Plates, unless by permission of the subscribers present; and if only one horse, &c., is entered, he shall not start, but shall receive ten guineas and his entrance money returned; or if two horses, &c., fifteen guineas between them. Post entrance to be made before five in the afternoon on the day previous to the day of running.

Certificates of the age and qualifications of each horse, &c., to be produced at the time of entrance, and to run according to the King's Plate Articles.

Winners to pay a guinea for weights, scales, &c. To start each day at one o'clock precisely.

Seeing the grand proportions to which Brighton Races have grown in 1879,—the Meet extending over three days; the races altogether being 22 in number; and the amount of money given (including a Cup value £300) exceeding £3,600,—one is tempted to smile at their humble beginning, when there were but three races in *two* days, and one of these was for ponies!

The Duke and Duchess of Cumberland, and a "deal of company," were present at the Races. One and all were pleased with the new Course; and, doubtless, when the Prince of Wales came down to Brighton for the first time, some ten days after (September 7th, 1783), the old Duke expatiated in glowing terms to "Taffy," as he was wont familarly to call the Prince, on the first Brighton Races. The results of the opening Meet were as follows:—

TUESDAY.

The £50 PLATE, for four year olds:—

Mr. Adams's grey colt Puff	2	1	1
Major O'Kelly's bay colt Adjutant	1	2	2
Duke of Richmond's ch. colt by Trentham	3	dr.	

A sporting chronicler says—"The odds being in favour of Adjutant, the 'knowing ones' were taken in."

A SWEEPSTAKES of Five Guineas each, to which a Purse of Thirty Guineas was added, for PONIES, the best of three four-mile Heats :—

Mr. Williams's grey mare	1	1
Mr. Broadhurst's bay gelding	2	3
Mr. Dymock's brown gelding	3	4
Mr. Bannister's brown mare	4	2

WEDNESDAY.

The £50 PLATE, for Horses of all ages, the best of three four-mile Heats :—

Sir C. Bunbury's bay mare Eliza	4	1	1
Sir Ferdinande Poole's bay horse Diadem	1	2	2
Mr. Henwood's bay horse Willy	2	3	dr.
Mr. Eccles's bay mare, by Herod	3	4	dr.
Major O'Kelly's ch. horse Ticklepitcher	5	5	3

The chronicler above-mentioned adds—"The 'knowing ones' were again worsted; the odds being in favour of Diadem."

At this period (and for some two or three years later) there was no permanent Race-Stand; and the only advantage of view which the Royal and noble frequenters of the Meet had over the crowd was from their carriages, or from being on horseback.

In the following year, 1784, the Races also took place on Tuesday and Wednesday (August 2nd and 3rd). On the first day there was run for a Plate of £50 (won by Mr. Twycross's Grasshopper beating the Duke of Queensbury's Regent and Mr. Bowler's Venture), and Sweepstakes of 50 guineas and 30 guineas respectively; on the second day, a Sweepstakes of 30 guineas, a Plate of £50 (won by Lord Egremont's Trentham, beating the horses of Sir C. Bunbury and Sir F. Evelyn), and a match for £50 between the horses of Sir Harry Featherstone and Mr. Vegierski. There was but very poor running, the favourite horses for the most part being easily beaten. In 1784 the Prince of Wales (who was accompanied by the Duc de Chartres, Philip l'Egalité) honoured the Races with his presence; and from that time forth he took a lively interest in the Meet.*

In 1785 Brighton Races assumed greater proportions; and in consequence it became necessary to make the Regulations for entering horses a little more stringent. There was, too, this addition to them—"All horses to be plated by a subscribing smith of one guinea." With better Races, there was also a much larger attendance; and here, again, there were new Regulations respecting the erection of booths, &c. The most important of these were the following :—

"*No one to erect a Booth on the Course who has not subscribed one guinea towards the Plates and who resides more than five miles from Brighthelmston;* nor shall any Tub or Tubs of Beer (without a Booth or Stall) be sold unless the owner of each pays 10s. 6d. to the Plates."

The Prince had, at this period, a splendid racing stud of his own, acknowledged to be the most complete in the kingdom, and Brighton-

---

* The Prince was at this period a splendid horseman; it was only in the previous week that he did his famous ride from Brighton to London and back in the same day, doing the double journey in 10 hours.

ians hoped to have had an opportunity of judging of their quality, the Prince entering horses for several stakes; as did also the Duc de Chartres. They were, however, doomed to disappointment; for both paid forfeit.

As the Races had now obtained Royal and distinguished patronage, and were evidently growing into popularity, the "M.C." felt desirous of "going with the tide"; and under his auspices, in 1785, the first of what was destined to be a long series of Race Balls took place. His announcement was as follows :—

SEVERAL Ladies and Gentlemen having expressed a Desire that there should be a BALL each Night during the Races at this place, Mr. WADE, who is ever desirous to obey their commands, begs leave to acquaint the Public that there will be on,—

Aug. 1st, a DRESS BALL at Shergold's;	Aug. 3rd, a COTILLON BALL at Shergold's;
" 2nd, a COTILLON BALL at Hicks's :	" 4th, a DRESS BALL at Hicks's.

In 1786 there were four days' Races, on August 1, 2, 3, 4, and on each day some capital sport. The Prince of Wales and the Duke of Orleans (Philip l'Egalité) again entered horses; and both again paid forfeit.* The attendance each day on the hill was very large. Besides the Prince of Wales and the French Duke, there were the Marquis of Conflans, the Duke of Queensbury, Lord George Lennox, Mr. Fox and Mrs. Armstead, and many persons of distinction. The great Whig Statesman no doubt retained a lively recollection of this Meet, it being stated that "Mr. Fox was a heavy loser by several races."

Both in 1787 and 1788, the Races extended over four days. In 1790, and also in 1791, the ill-fated Duke of Orleans gave a Stakes of 50 guineas to be run for. In 1788 the new Stand, which had been erected by subscription, was occupied for the first time. The *Lewes Journal* thus describes it :— "For convenience and elegance, the new Stand challenges any in the Kingdom. The inside is so happily contrived for the accommodation of company, that, by means of regular ascending platforms, it commands a full and equal view of the whole Course, at every part of it beyond even the possibility of obstruction, however crowded, which is not the case in others that have their floors on a level." When it is known what the Stand was which succeeded

---

* How it was that horses were entered by the Prince at Brighton Races in 1786 we cannot say ;—probably they were what are known in the present day as "nominations"; for it was only in the previous May that, with the view of curtailing his establishment, his magnificent racing-stud, carriage horses, &c., had been sold by auction. His love of racing, however, soon revived; for in the next two or three years he possessed another fine stud; several of his horses running in 1790-91 at Brighton, Lewes, and Newmarket. At the Lewes Meet of 1791 the Prince was very fortunate. His well-known horse Smoaker carried off a Sweepstakes ; Pegasus walked over for the King's Plate ; and Scota won the Ladies' Plate. After the "Escape" affair, in October, 1791, which resulted in his expulsion from the Jockey Club, the Prince's stud was again sold, and once more he retired from the Turf. He returned to it again in the early part of the present century, and ran horses for some years at Brighton Races; in fact, his love for racing continued to the end of his days.

this building, and which, it is but reasonable to suppose, was an improvement upon it, one is apt to think that its "convenience and elegance" were somewhat exaggerated.*

It would be beyond our purpose to follow the varied fortunes of Brighton Races each succeeding year. How they rose and waned, and rose again; of the support accorded to them by the Prince of Wales; of his splendid "turn out" whenever he went on the hill;† of the distinguished company that followed in his wake; of the doings of the Noble and more influential sporting men of the day; of the achievements of "Smoaker" and "Pegasus," and many another famous horse; of the great match between "Sancho" and "Pavilion"; of the "beautiful display of E.O. tables," &c.; of pocket-picking and pugilism;‡ and other undesirable adjuncts then invariably associated with Racing. Is it not all "written in local chronicles?" An episode of the Races in 1793, given in *Minutes on a Tour to Brighton*, is, however, worth quoting. The writer says—"Went to the Races on the Downs—race between Sir John Lade and the Hon. Mr. Butler, who rode their own horses—the latter won—another heat between Butler and Bowes, riding-master to the Prince; rode their own horses—Butler won (Bowes went on the wrong side of the post)—another heat between Sir John Lade and Butler; the latter won hollow—agreed it was a humbug of Sir John's (Butler being a young man) to take him in for something more capital. The Prince and all the great characters of the town were there."

---

* Some idea of the original Race Stand and Course—which latter was understood to have been about two miles in length, and ran, as at present, in a horse-shoe shape on the ridge of the hill—may be gathered from a quaint old print—or, rather, caricature—which was published in "June 1, 1790, by Messrs. Robinsons, Paternoster-row." The most prominent object in the print is the old wooden Stand on the right, the occupants of which are some 24 in number! Architecturally speaking, the Stand could not have been more plainly built. It was oblong in shape, and the only relief to its uniform plainness were the partitions which supported the front, sides, and roof. There were no windows in it; the spectators obtained their view of the Races from the front, between the five partitions; the openings being from about two-thirds up the front to the roof. The Stand appears to have been enclosed in front by wooden railings, the space thus secured, being, probably, the "Betting Ground." The Course itself was quite open; at all events, no rails are observable in the print, and it would appear to have been between the two lines of spectators and the horses and carriages. Neither booths nor refreshment stalls are shown anywhere. On the opposite side of the Course to the "Grand Stand" was the Judge's Stand: this was entirely open, and was reached by outside steps. At a little distance from it to the northward was a post and cross-beam, shaped like a gallows. The extremity of the beam bears a hook; but for what purpose it was used we cannot say, unless it was for weighing the jockeys!

† In 1790 the Prince was on the hill in an open landau, drawn by six black horses; Sir John Lade driving. The Prince was magnificently dressed in the uniform of the 10th Light Dragoons.

‡ In connection with the Meet of 1788, the "fancy" had arranged for the delectation of the company no less than *six* fights! Owing, however, to some great "event" in the sporting world they did not come to Brighton until the day *after* the Races. The gentlemen, however, still determined to have their sport, which took place on a stage erected in front of the Race Stand. Two fights were "satisfactorily" finished; but, the third resulting in the death of one of the combatants (Earl, a shoemaker), the "sport" was brought to an abrupt close. The Prince of Wales, on hearing next day of the matter, and learning that Earl was the only support of a widowed mother, generously settled upon the poor woman an annuity for life.

One year (1798, we believe,) however, the Races had a very narrow escape from being abruptly extinguished. The farmer who rented the race ground was accustomed to receive each season a quarter of a pipe of wine for permitting the Races. Not having received his wine as usual, the farmer waited on the Jockey Club (then sitting at "The Castle" inn), and peremptorily told the members that unless they immediately paid him 100 guineas he should begin another sort of race—with his plough! An ambiguous answer being given him, he repeated his demand the next morning; and, again receiving an unsatisfactory answer, immediately set his plough to work. The Club were, however, more than a match for him; for before a few ridges were finished, a *press-gang* made its appearance, when the clodhoppers abandoned their charge and made a precipitate retreat! The Races subsequently took place without further interruption.

In earlier times, the fixture of Brighton Races was very uncertain; sometimes it would be in July and at others in August; and there was equal uncertainty both with regard to the days of the week on which they would take place, and the number of days over which they would extend. In 1785-86 they were on Monday, Tuesday. Wednesday, and Thursday; in 1788-89-90, on Friday, Saturday, Monday, and Tuesday; in 1794-95, on Friday, Saturday, and and Monday; in 1798, on Wednesday, Thursday, and Friday; and in 1800, on Tuesday, Wednesday, Thursday, and Friday. Later on the same variations occurred; but, generally, the arrangements were such that Sunday divided the days of the Meet, on which day there was held "White Hawk Fair," on the White Hawk Down, to the south-east of the Stand. In the first few years of the present century, this Fair used to be much frequented by the fashionable visitors to Brighton; but by and bye its patrons became of a less exalted character, and about the year 1821 or 1822 it was abolished, though the farce of keeping it up in a small way did not die out for several years later.

The original Race Stand was destroyed by fire in 1803; owing to the carelessness of a pauper, who had obtained permission to reside in it when the Racing season was over. The Stand erected in its place—a "shabby wooden building." as a local chronicler styles it—stood till 1851, when the present handsome and commodious structure was built, at a cost of £6,000. Since then two wings have been added, and other important improvements made, making the total cost over £15,000.

The modern improvements of the Race Stand are entirely due to the Race Stand Trustees, in whom the property became vested, after overcoming almost insuperable difficulties, in 1849-50. To their energy, also, it is owing that the Races have attained their present high position; being held twice a year (three days in Summer and three in Autumn [altered to Spring in 1890]); and are wholly self-supporting, and rank among the most important Meets of the Kingdom. [In March 1891, the then Trustees—Aldermen Abbey, Brigden, and Ridley, and Mr. W. Seymour Burrows—generously presented the Corporation with the East End Park, at a cost to them of £12,000.]

Cricket.

Why and wherefore the title of "cricket" was given to this now world-known game, we do not pretend to say; but there can be no question that "cricket" is a purely English game, and that Sussex in the olden time was not the least amongst those Counties wherein "bat and ball" was played with the greatest skill. Without entering into a dissertation upon the history of the game *per se*, or following out the several changes which have taken place in the shape of the implements used in playing it, there is no doubt that the earliest players defended their "wickets" solely by a stout cudgel, such as the greatest of our national poets alludes to when, in his "A Lover's Complaint," he says, "So slides he down upon his grained bat;" a term still used by country people for a stout stick.

Cricket was a recognised game in Sussex in the earlier part of the last century; and was known and played in it for some years anterior; but the records of the prowess of its ancient champions are very scanty. Brighthelmston, however, is among the earlier places mentioned where bowls* and cricket were played, and whence players went forth, sometimes alone, and at other times associated with those of Lewes and Rottingdean, to uphold the supremacy of the "dwellers by the Sea."

Nearly a century ago the County Ground may be said to have been at Brighton; and here, as at many a subsequent period, in some of the grandest matches ever played, the most celebrated local cricketers have exhibited their skill, and held their own against all comers. The County Ground is still at Brighton (west); but the County cricketers have been for some few years past "under a cloud"—the achievements of the Elevens have not been as of yore; their old supremacy has sustained some rude shocks, and (must it be said!) for the time is lost. But we cannot believe—while so many noblemen and gentlemen still maintain the greatest interest in the game, while every town and village in the County boasts of its Club and the love of cricket is stronger than ever—that the ancient glory of Sussex "has departed from her." No; properly marshalled, and with persistent and systematic practice on the part of the players; with tact, judicious supervision, and liberality on the part of the management, Sussex, there is good reason to hope, will ere long, as in days gone by, once more take front rank among the cricketing Counties of England.†

---

* In *Goodwyn's Rental* (1665) frequent mention is made of a "Bowling Green" on the Steine, at Brighton. "A Bowling Green" was opened at Lewes, by Charles Boore, May 4th, 1753; "when and where all Gentlemen who are lovers of that diversion are entreated to subscribe their names to a Club," the conditions being "to pay five shillings for the season, *and to spend sixpence when present*. No penalty for being absent."

[† It is pleasing to note that, during the past two or three seasons up to 1891, there have been welcome indications of a revival of the County's old skill and prowess, which, it is hoped, will long continue.]

The earliest records of cricket show that the game was played in most of the villages of the County in 1747; and matches by Lewes and Chailey, Mayfield and Warbleton, Hastings, and other places are frequently alluded to in newspapers of that period; and, singular to relate, Sussex women as well as men were then proficient at "bat and ball," as will be seen from the following extract from the *Lewes Journal* of July 13, 1747:—

"On Monday next there will certainly be played in the Artillery Ground, London, the match at Cricket that has been so long talk'd of between the Women of Charlton and Singleton, in Sussex, against the Women of West Dean and Chalgrove, of the same County."

The same journal records in June, 1747, a match of stool-ball by women under somewhat novel circumstances :—

"On Whitson Monday a Match of Cricket was played on Rushlake Green at Warbleton, 14 of a side, by the Inhabitants of the place, which gave great satisfaction to the neighbourhood. The evening concluded with a Ball, and the next morning usher'd in by four o'clock a fine Match at Stool Ball, played by the Maidens on the same Green."

Women, therefore, in those days did not disdain the bat. Returning, however, to cricket, one of the earliest great matches was in June, 1749, between Hastings and Pevensey, for 100 guineas, 20 guineas a man being deposited, play or pay. West Sussex, too, seemed to be as fond of cricket as the East; for, in September, 1749, a match was played by the Duke of Richmond's sons and the Halnaker boys, the umpire being "Thomas Wymark, whom the Duke formerly kept to play at Cricket,"—a proof this of how early the game had a root-hold in the County. The earliest County match we know of was that in which Sussex played with Surrey, on Longdown, in October, 1752. No details are given either of the players or of their respective scores; but the result is thus recorded—"Surrey beat by about 4 score notches."

The first mention of Brighthelmston players is in 1758. As the announcement contains also the names of early players from other County localities, we give it in its entirety :—

THIS is to acquaint the Public that on Wednesday, June 28, 1758, will be play'd at Rottingdean, near Lewes, a great Match at CRICKET for a Guinea a Man; Newick, Chailey, Lindfield, and Hamsey, against Lewes, Brighthelmston, and Rottingdean. The Wickets to be pitched at Twelve o'clock, and the Game to be played out. The Gamesters to be chosen out of the undermentioned : -

    NEWICK: James Burt, Henry Kennard. CHAILEY: Thomas Hoather, John Turle. LINDFIELD: Richard Harland, Francis Blaker, Edward Fain, John Tabb, George Haynes, Thomas Blaker, Thomas Finch. HAMSEY: William Howell, Henry Smith.

LEWES: Nicholas Groves, Richard Winter, John Postle, Thomas Goldsmith, Stephen Eager. BRIGHTHELMSTON: George Barnham, John Howell, Thomas Baker. ROTTINGDEAN: John Newington, Stenning Beard, Thomas Clare, Phillip Emery.

The result of the match is not recorded; nor that of the return match, which was played at Cooksbridge, on the 10th of the following month, the Stakes being then " For a Crown a Man.". Often, however, as the "Gamesters" of Lewes, Brighthelmston, and Rottingdean united for defensive purposes, they had occasionally friendly contests against each other, as the following announcement shows:—

ON Monday next, May 14, 1759, will be played on Basden (Balsdean) Flats a great Cricket Match, for Five Pounds a side, between Brighthelmston and Rottingdean. The Wickets to be pitched at Twelve o'clock.

In the following month, there was on Basden Flats a "Great Game at Cricket: St. Michael's Parish, in Lewes, and Ringmer, against Rottingdean and others from Brighthelmston, for a considerable Sum"; another, "on the Broil," for Half-a-Guinea a Man: Ringmer and St. Michael's against Rottingdean, Brighthelmston, and one from Isfield; and, "on our Hill" (Lewes), a "third Great Match": Rottingdean and four from Brighthelmston against St. Michael's and Ringmer, "for a considerable Sum." In July, 1759, the local teams went further afield—to Eastbourne Sands, where was played a "Great Match at Cricket by the Gamesters of Battle and Eastbourne against Brighthelmston and Rottingdean, for a Guinea a Man"; the announcement adding—"N.B. A great many Wagers are already depending."

These matches were played in "old style" (the Rules, which subsequently formed the groundwork of the present game were not framed till 1774). "The wickets" (stumps), we are told,[*] "were only two in number,[†] one foot high and two feet asunder, with one bail, and a ball passing between them did not make the batsman out; whilst the block-hole was not, as now, in front of the wickets, but midway between them, into which the batsman had to 'ground' his bat before the bowler 'popped' (*unde* 'popping crease') the ball into it. The old bat was curved somewhat like a butter-knife and made to the height of the elbow. Defensive batting was unknown. The best batsmen were all hard hitters, and had, therefore, generally, a short and merry life of it; while the early bowlers were very swift, all along or near the ground, and, of course, under-hand."

No result of the before-mentioned matches have come down to us. "Scores" were rarely, if ever, published. The "notches" were probably made on a stick, which, when the game was over, was

---

[*] "Sussex Cricket: Past and Present," by an "Old Sussex Cricketer." Lewes: Alex. Rivington, 1879.

[†] The third stump was introduced in 1775, after a memorial match in the Artillery Ground, Finsbury, between five of the Hambledon Club and five of All England.—*The Cricket-bat; and How to Use It.*

perhaps broken, the "Gamesters" wending their respective ways, one to his farm and another to his merchandise, each content with his own prowess and the applause of the hour.

It is needless to recount the many subsequent games which took place in the latter half of the last century. But, as showing how early "The White Lion," Brighton, was a cricketers' house—which it continued to be for over 50 years later—it may be mentioned that when, in 1765, a great match was played here :—Brighthelmston and one man from Lewes against Angmering, the "ordinary" was at Lulham's, "The White Lion."

The Duke of Richmond, with his team, twice manfully did battle with the Hambledon Club in 1768; losing the first match, but winning the second and "near £1,000" besides. But what may be termed the Royal era of local cricket began about 1788-89. Both the Prince of Wales and his brother (the Duke of York) were exceedingly fond of cricket. There are no records of the Prince's exploits in the field; but, it is said, "he would be often engaged in this manly game, with the noblemen and gentlemen of his suite, and was esteemed a very excellent player." He was, however, frequently on the ground as a spectator; and when the great match, between Brighton and Wadhurst, took place on the Level, in August, 1790, he was present both days. This was, we believe, the first match in which the celebrated Hammond—acknowledged to be the greatest cricketer of his time—played for Brighton; and on the same side were Mr. Borrer, Messrs. J. and P. Vallance, Streeter (the miller), and Jutten (of "The Cricketers.") Brighton lost by three wickets. In the return match, however, played in the following week on Woodburn Down, Brighton won by five wickets. The Duke of York was a frequent player; and, doubtless, at his birth-day celebration on August 19, 1789, when he played a single-wicket match with Colonel Tarleton, "amazed the wond'ring rustics ranged around" to see a *rale* live Duke at cricket ! In the previous week, however, he had played a grand match—one innings—"on the flat, near Brighton," with the Colonel, each to choose eleven men. The game was not played out, for want of time. The Colonel was evidently overmatched; for in the return match—for 100 guineas—he was to have Streeter, the miller.

In September, 1790, was played on the Level what we suppose was the first match between Sussex and Kent—Brighton and Tunbridge Wells. It was a hollow affair; the Brighton men proving so formidable, that the Kentish men "gave up the game." In the return match, at Tunbridge Wells, the Brightonians were again the victors.

The Prince's Cricket Ground was formed in the following year, 1791. It extended from the northern part of the present Level to the north of Park-crescent—the road now running between the Level and the south wall of the Crescent almost equally dividing it. One of the first matches played on the Prince's Ground was in September, 1791, between Brighton and Marylebone, but the result would appear to be unobtainable. In 1792, the local players right worthily maintained their reputation. On August 7 and 8, in the great match, Brighton v. Hampshire, played on the Prince's Ground, Brighton won by six wickets. The local team made 155 runs in their first innings, to which Marchant contributed 44, Mr. Borrer 33, and Mr. P. Vallance 33. The Brighton Club (with Boxall given) also came off victorious a fortnight later on the same Ground in a match with nine Gentlemen of the Marylebone Club, with Collins and Purchase given. The match occupied *four* days, and terminated in favour of Brighton by three wickets. As the score is interesting in more than one respect, we give it in full :—

MARY-LE-BONE.

FIRST INNINGS.		SECOND INNINGS.	
G. Monson, Esq., b Boxall	0	b Boxall	4
H. Ashton, Esq., b Hammond	0	not out	2
— Hussey, Esq , c ditto	0	b Hammond	4
— Leicester, Esq., b ditto	0	b ditto	15
Mr. Purchase, not out	38	c Boxall	7
Earl Winchelsea, b Boxall	4	run out	8
Hon. E. Bligh, c Hammond	4	b Boxall	0
G. Louch, Esq , b Boxall	8	c G. Vallance	8
Hon. H. Fitzroy, b Hammond	2	c Boxall	0
Mr. Couldham, c Capron	0	run out	6
Mr. Collins, b Boxall	11	run out	6
Byes	1	Byes	2
	68		62

BRIGHTON.

FIRST INNINGS.		SECOND INNINGS.	
Mr. Capron, c Purchase	1	not out	21
Mr. Jutton, run out	2		
Mr. Boxall, b Purchase	3	not out	10
Mr. Leffen, b ditto	2	b Purchase	1
Mr. Hammond, b ditto	11	c G. Monson, Esq.	24
Mr. Marchant, b Collins	4	b Collins	4
Mr. Borrer, c G. Monson, Esq.	0	c G. Monson, Esq.	13
Sir J. Shelley, c Hon. E. Bligh	8		
Mr. P. Vallance, c Earl Winchelsea	14	c ditto	1
Mr. Gregory, b Collins	2	b Collins	1
Mr. J. Vallance, not out	4	b Purchase	2
Byes	0	Byes	3
	51		80

After this grand match was finished, the Earl of Winchelsea and Harvey Aston, Esq.,—two of the most ardent lovers of cricket at the period—made up another match for 1,000 guineas. The Earl's team consisted of six gentlemen from Marylebone and five from Hampshire ; and that marshalled by H. Aston, Esq., of four Surrey players, one from Kent, and six from Brighton. It was won by the latter gentleman's side in one innings and 44 runs to spare. *The* local match of the season, however, took place on the 6th, 7th, and 8th September, —Middlesex, with T. Walker and Fennex, against the Brighton Club, with Purchase, for 500 guineas. The Brighton Club won by five wickets ; the Middlesex gentlemen being, it was said, "handsomely taken in, as, after the first innings, they betted freely five and six to one." The score was as follows:—

MIDDLESEX.

FIRST INNINGS.		SECOND INNINGS.	
Lord Winchelsea, hit out	6	— b Hammond	8
E. Bligh, Esq., c J. Vallance	2	— b Purchase	0
— Louch, Esq., b J. Vallance	31	— b Hammond	3
H. Ashton, Esq,, b Hammond	0	— run out	3
— Fitzroy, Esq., c Jutton	1	— not out	4
Mr. T. Walker, not out	24	— c Leffen	5
Mr Grange, c Hammond	5	— b Hammond	12
Mr. Lord, b Purchase	0	— b Hammond	0
Mr. Shackell, c Purchase	1	— b Hammond	0
Mr. Fennex, b Purchase	2	— b Hammond	6
Mr. Raye, b Hammond	2	— b Purchase	4
Byes	0	Byes	0
Total	74	Total	45

BRIGHTON.

FIRST INNINGS.		SECOND INNINGS.	
Sir J. Shelley, c Grange	2	— c Fennex	8
Mr. Jutton, b Lord	3		
Mr. Leffen, c T. Walker	6	— b T. Walker	8
Mr. Borrer, run out	0	— c Lord	8
Mr. P. Vallance, ditto	1	— c Fennex	18
Mr. J. Vallance, c Shackell	0	— not out	11
Mr. Purchase, run out	2	— not out	24
Mr. Hammond, not out	11	— b Lord	10
Mr. Bedster, c Shackell	8		
Mr. Gregory, c Lord Winchelsea	0		
Mr. Hudson, b T. Walker	0		
Byes	1	Byes	0
Total	34	Total	87

The match derived additional interest from the fact that Mrs. Fitzherbert, the Duchess de Noailles (a French refugee), and many other ladies of distinction were present and dined in a marquee, which had been pitched on the ground for their special use. The Prince's band attended, and performed the whole time the ladies were at dinner. In the evening Mrs. Fitzherbert walked round the ground with the Duchess, Lady Clermont, and Miss Pigott, seemingly to afford gratification to the spectators, who appeared very desirous of getting a view of the French lady. The writer adds—"The Duchess, who appears to be about 21 or 22 years of age, is very handsome, and her figure and deportment are remarkably interesting."*

During the next five years there is little of special interest to record. There was a match in 1793 between the Brighton Colts and the Gentlemen residing between the Shoreham and Arundel Rivers; matches were played in the Camp in 1793; and in 1794 a match took place between the Brighton Club and the Camp, in which the military were the victors. In July, 1802, a grand match was arranged. between the Eastern and Western Divisions of the County, by General Lennox and Colonel Porter; and each side had "given men." The Western

---

* The Duchess de Noailles had only a few days previous escaped from France, dressed in male attire; and during the sea voyage of fourteen hours had "in the coil of a cable!"

had the Hon. Arthur Upton (who made two "duck's eggs"!); and the Eastern, who had T. Smith, Esq., and T. Walker (who made more than half the score between them), were the victors, by six wickets. To show the players of the period, we give the score:—

WESTERN.

FIRST INNINGS.		SECOND INNINGS.	
Paine, c Cooper	3	c Walker	0
Dyer, b ditto	17	b Cooper	3
Soane, b ditto	3	b Cooper	5
Hammond, c Sayers	12	b Walker	10
Hon. A. Upton, c T. Smith, Esq.	0	b Walker	0
Haynes, c Marchant	0	b Walker	5
Lamport, b Cooper	4	not out	2
Stedman, run out	4	st. out	3
General Lennox, b Cooper	1	run out	6
J. Musten, Esq., c S. Smith, Esq.	0	c Budd	1
Shepherd, not out	0	b Walker	13
Byes	0	Byes	5
	44		53

EASTERN.

FIRST INNINGS.		SECOND INNINGS.	
Budd, c Soane	2	c Shepherd	7
Sayers, b Dyer	1	run out	0
T. Walker, b Dyer	5	not out	30
T. Smith, Esq., b Lamport	24	c Paine	7
Marchant, c General Lennox	3		
Baldwin, c Haynes	0		
Smith, b Dyer	0		
Flint, l.b.w.	9		
Francis, b Lamport	0		
Lord Milsington, b Hammond	0	not out	2
Cooper, not out	0	b Dyer	8
Byes	0	Byes	0
	44		54

In 1807 the Brighton Club were getting "saucy"; and, under the auspices of Pollard—a worthy successor to Lulham—of "The White Lion," they published the following advertisement in the *Brighton Herald* of the 13th of August in that year:—

A CHALLENGE.—It being understood that the COWFOLD and TWINE-HAM CLUB would try their skill in a game of CRICKET with the County of Sussex, the Brighton Club, including Rottingdean and Preston, will be happy to meet them out and home any day they chuse, the first match to be played at Brighton. If the Cowfold and Twineham Club are of the same mind to play with the County, they may take any three picked men in England upon allowing the County Messrs. J. Wills and Hammond. —Apply to Mr. POLLARD, White Lion Inn, Brighton.

The latter portion of the challenge was accepted, the picked men chosen by Cowfold and Twineham being Lambert, Beldam, and Lord F. Beauclerk.[*] The match was played in the Prince's Cricket Ground, but Lord Beauclerk, for some reason, took no part in it. It was, how-

---

[*] His Lordship was a splendid "bat," and was very rarely bowled out. He used frequently, as if in defiance of the bowlers, to hang his gold watch on the bails! W. Slater, the well-known old County wicket-keeper, once bowled him out the first ball, when His Lordship, to show his appreciation of the bowler's skill, immediately presented him with a sovereign.

ever, won by the Cowfold and Twineham eleven by six wickets; Beldam, one of the picked men, making 38 and 15—one fourth of the total score. Lambert only made 4 in his two innings. For the County, Hammond made 16 and 36. The "return match" was also won by Cowfold and Twineham, Hammond again making a fine first innings, carrying out his bat for 33; and Budd scored 21. Lambert, for his side, also made in his first innings 33.

We hear of no more challenges from Brighton after this! A few years later, in July, 1811, the Brighton Gentlemen tried *their* strength with Cowfold and Twineham, for 50 guineas,—and lost them! being beaten by 21 runs.

In 1812, G. Osbaldeston, Esq., a well-known sporting gentleman of the period, first played in a local match; and in the same match W. Slater's name first appears. Both took part in a match, for 100 guineas a side, played in July, on Highdown Hill, between the Gentlemen of the Weald and the Gentlemen of the Sea Coast, with six given players each. The match was very closely contested, some fine play being shown on both sides; no less than 11 of the Wealden players being put out in the two innings by Mr. Osbaldeston; and, on the other side, nine by Bennett and four by Hammond. The Wealden team were the victors by seven runs only. The score was as follows :—

WEALD.

FIRST INNINGS.		SECOND INNINGS.	
E. H. Budd, b Osbaldeston	36	b Bentley	38
Bennett, b Lambert	2	b Osbaldeston	19
Hammond, b Osbaldeston	21	b Bentley	0
Walker, b Penfold	6	b Osbaldeston	25
Paine, b Lambert	10	st. Osbaldeston	0
Blunden, b Lambert	12	b Bentley	3
Blaker, b Osbaldeston	1	not out	1
Lee, b Osbaldeston	2	b Lambert	1
Challen, b Osbaldeston	0	b Osbaldeston	3
Wilkson, not out	3	b Osbaldeston	3
Sayers, c Osbaldeston	0	b Slater	6
Byes	1	Byes	7
	94		106

SEA COAST.

FIRST INNINGS.		SECOND INNINGS.	
Lambert, b Bennett	11	c Bennett	17
Osbaldeston, b Hammond	10	c Bennett	28
Robinson, b Hammond	21	c Budd	1
Bentley, b Bennett	23	b Bennett	28
Slater, b Bennett	15	b Budd	19
Penfold, run out	2	b Budd	4
Badcock, b Hammond	4	b Bennett	0
G. Grant, b Bennett	0	b Blunden	0
J. Grant, not out	0	not out	0
Halstead, b Bennett	0	c Blunden	4
Edmunds, b Hammond	0	b Budd	0
Byes	4	Byes	2
	90		103

A match which excited much interest in cricketing circles, though the amount played for was but 40 guineas, took place in the Prince's

Cricket Ground, in July, 1813,—the County v. Wadhurst. The odds at starting were in favour of the County, which was considered to possess a host in Hammond. That celebrated player, however, only obtained *four* runs in his two innings! The two scores of the County only reached 76, to which W. Slater and Marchant contributed exactly one-half,—38. Wadhurst won by nine wickets.

One of the grandest matches which took place on the Level was that arranged by Mr. Osbaldeston, in August, 1815, between Sussex and the Epsom Club, for 1,000 guineas, which was won by the County. It was in this celebrated match that "Jim" Broadbridge, fresh from his father's farm, "won his spurs;"* and that in which Mr. Aislabie—once a well-known player of cricket—first played in Brighton. The score is worth recording:—

COUNTY.

FIRST INNINGS.		SECOND INNINGS.	
Sturt, b Lambert	17	st. Vigne	11
Mellish, c Vigne	34	c Lord Beauclerk	12
Martin, c Tanner	20	b Lambert	0
Hammond, st. Vigne	29	b Tanner	1
Slater, c Woodbridge	4	c Lambert	13
Andrews, c Borradaile	39	b Tanner	4
Osbaldeston, c Lambert	0	c Lord Beauclerk	8
Morley, st. Vigne	4	c Lambert	1
Woodbridge, c Vigne	1	not out	0
Cooper, not out	3	c Lord Beauclerk	2
Broadbridge, not out	0	b Lord Beauclerk	1
Byes	1	Byes	1
	152		54

EPSOM CLUB.

FIRST INNINGS.		SECOND INNINGS.	
Borradaile, b Broadbridge	6	run out	1
Schabner, b Osbaldeston	4	c Hammond	3
Slingsby, b Osbaldeston	0	b Osbaldeston	0
Tanner, b Hammond	0	b Osbaldeston	6
Ward, b Broadbridge	3	run out	0
Lambert, c Andrews	15	c Sturt	50
Lord Beauclerk, not out	30	b Osbaldeston	4
Woodbridge, st. Martin	0	not out	14
Ladbrook, b Osbaldeston	2	b Osbaldeston	6
Vigne, b Broadbridge	0	c Broadbridge	3
Aislabie, b Osbaldeston	0	b Osbaldeston	1
Byes	15	Byes	22
	75		110

The last grand match which took place on the Level—Ireland's Gardens were at this period being projected—was in August, 1822, between Brighton and Dorking, in which all the "dons" on both sides took part; the Brighton team including the Slaters, Meads, Dale, Lanaway, Morley, Pierpoint, and Bowley; and that of Dorking including Lambert, Bothell, Jupp, and Peters. The match could not,

---

* It was a "toss up" previous to the match whether Broadbridge should play or not. His appearance was against him; for he had, probably,—as was his custom in aftertime,—walked in from Duncton that morning, and did not *dress* for the occasion. As he stood apart, with his hands in his pockets, attired in farm labourer's fashion, with his bright red waistcoat, &c., some of the gentlemen eyed him askance, and doubted the desirability of having him on their side; but it was eventually decided that he *should* play; and Jim was not long in showing his mettle, although he made no particular score in either innings.

however, be played out at Brighton (Sunday intervening), and it was subsequently finished at Dorking! Brighton proving victorious by seven runs.

In 1823 Ireland's Gardens (now supplanted by Park-crescent, &c.) were opened; and the splendid cricket ground formed there—it was said to have been the finest piece of turf in England—was henceforth used for all grand matches. The first of these took place on June 28, between Sussex and Marylebone, which was won by Sussex in a fine single innings, with 45 runs to spare. Of the 182 which Sussex made, Saunders contributed 89; Slater, 24; Hooker, 21; and Morley, 14. (The two elevens had contested previously, on June 9th, at Lord's, where Sussex won by ten wickets, having only 4 runs to get in their second innings. They scored 250; Hooker contributing 92; J. Broadbridge, 48; Saunders, 34.) But to tell of the achievements on the Brighton Ground—unquestionably among the grandest in the annals of cricket—would far exceed our limits. Here it was that the Broadbridges and the Slaters; Brown and Lillywhite; Dean the "plough-boy;" Hawkins and the Picknells; Morley, Millyard, Lanaway, Box, and Meads; and, among the gentlemen, Messrs. Charles Taylor and Langdon, and many another Sussex cricketer, measured their strength,—and most successfully, too—against some of the finest players that England could produce: Fuller Pilch, the Mynns, Wenman, Hillier, Wanostrocht ("Felix"), Martingell, Cobbett, Redgate, George Parr, and others.

Cock-fighting, Bull-baiting, &c.

Of these *sports*, there is not much to be said. Happily they have long since been struck out of the catalogue of our national pastimes. Yet each would seem to have been in vogue as such from time immemorial. Of the two, cock-fighting is the more ancient, for it may be said to have "come in with the Romans." In the 12th century, it was on Shrove Tuesday a customary school-boy sport; in the 14th, it was a "fashionable pastime." Edward III. endeavoured to prohibit it by public proclamation; but, in spite of discountenance and opposition, the sport maintained its popularity. Bluff Harry built a "pitt" at Whitehall; and the "sapient" James I. regularly enjoyed the diversion twice a week! In the last century "pits" were legion, and there was scarcely a town of any importance where cock-fighting did not prevail. When the pastime was first indulged in Brighthelmston is now past finding out; but so early as 1746—and most probably long before—cock-fighting took place at "The Old Ship," and in that year was thus announced in the *Lewes Journal*:—

EASTER MONDAY AND TUESDAY, 1746.

THIS IS TO GIVE NOTICE, that on Easter Monday and Tuesday, WILL BE FOUGHT A MAIN OF COCKS, at William Hicks's, at the Old Ship in Brighthelmston, between the Gentlemen of the East and those of the West.

IRELAND'S BRIGHTON ROYAL PLEASURE AND CRICKET GROUNDS.

This was most probably a County match, judging by one of a similar character announced to take place in the following year :—

THIS IS TO GIVE NOTICE, that on Monday and Tuesday, April 27 and 28, 1747, will be fought a FAMOUS COCK MATCH at William Hicks's, at the Old Ship in Brighthelmston, between the Gentlemen of Petworth and those of East Sussex.

Cock-fighting was evidently in "full feather" throughout the County at the period. At "The White Hart," Buxted, on July 3 and 4, 1746, there was a great cock-match, between the Gentlemen of Sussex and Surrey; "to Show *forty-two* Cocks, besides, byebattles." In May, 1749, the "Gentlemen of the East and the Gentlemen of the West" had their match at "The Oak Inn," Hurstpierpoint, "each side to show ten Stags and eleven Cocks, for 2 guineas a battle and 10 guineas the main." Later on, there were other great matches at Preston, Rottingdean, Lewes, and Horsham; one at Lewes, in 1772, being for "5 guineas a battle and 50 guineas the odd battle," and "to show 31 Cocks each side." It did not appear to be, however, all cock-fighting on those occasions; the sport being invariably supplemented by a good dinner! For instance, to the Lewes match announcement, there was the following N.B. : "To go to the Pit at 12, and Dinner to be on table at 3 each day." Seeing how "fashionable" the sport had become, it was only natural that such an aristocratic resort as "The Castle," at Brighthelmston, should have its cock-matches, and there, under the auspices of Mr. Shergold, some of the greatest battles of the day were fought, and many a "day's play," as it was then styled, was indulged in. On July, 1, 2, 3. 1772, a "Main of Cocks" took place there, between the Gentlemen of Horsham and Lewes; "to show 31 cocks each side, and to fight for five guineas a battle and fifty guineas the odd battle; dinner to be on table at 3 o'clock each day." Later in the month, there was a famous cock-match there between the Gentlemen of Horsham and the Gentlemen of Brighton, the former being the victors, winning nine battles out of fifteen. The greatest "event," however, in the cock-fighting annals of "The Castle" took place in December, 1772. It was thus announced :—

TO BE FOUGHT, at the CASTLE, in BRIGHTHELMSTON, on MONDAY, the 28th December, 1772, a WELCH MAIN,* for a Silver Tankard, value 8 guineas, by 16 Cocks. No Cock to exceed 4lb. 4oz. To begin weighing at 8 o'clock, and the Money to be paid at the Scale. The Cock that kills most to have the Tankard ; the 2nd Best to have a Guinea as Stakes ; and the 3rd Best to have Half-a-Guinea. Eight Battles before Dinner, *and Dinner to be ready at One o'clock.*

---

* The Welch Main—a later addition to the "fashionable divertisement" of cock-fighting—was a sad business. Strutt says :—"The Welch Main consists of a given number of pairs of cocks, suppose 16 a side, which fight with each other until one-half of them are killed; the 16 conquerors are pitted a second time in like manner, and half are slain; the 8 survivors a third time; the 4, a fourth time; and the remaining 2 a fifth time; so that *thirty-one cocks are sure to be inhumanly murdered for the sport and pleasure of the spectators.*"

These cock-matches were much frequented both by gentlemen and professional sporting-men; and betting at the "pit" was exceedingly rife, many very heavy sums being won and lost. The "pits," in fact, were among the most fertile haunts of the "knowing-ones." A local censor (in 1784) writing against the gambling associated with the cruel sport of the "pits," says:—"As the tax on race-horses affords so much pleasure and satisfaction, what a pity it is that its full brother in gambling should have escaped notice, viz., Cock-fighting. Would not a license for a Cock-pit be proper, and a Stamp-duty on a ticket for every admission? The license might be from ten to fifty pounds, and the stamp for admission half-a-crown to five shillings. The Blacklegs can afford to pay it."

On the 15th March, 1776, there was a Cock-match at "The Crown and Anchor," Preston, for a silver tankard, value 8 guineas, by 16 cocks, the highest weight not to exceed 4 lb. 10 oz., and to pay half-a-guinea each. Another condition was "The putter-up and winner to spend half-a-guinea each." In March, 1777, a Main of Cocks was fought at Preston by the Gentlemen of Brighthelmston and the Gentlemen of Henfield. But the greatest cock-match at Preston, a "Welch Main," was fought in 1780 :—

COCKING.—A WELCH MAIN, TO BE FOUGHT, at PRESTON, on THURSDAY, April 27th, 1780, by 16 Cocks, for a BAY MARE. The highest weight not to exceed 4lb. 8oz.—To pay fifteen shillings each Cock; the second Cock to have two guineas. Dinner to be on table at one o'clock.

Without, however, following the history of the "sport" in detail, we may state that "The White Lion" had in the early part of the present century become the head-centre in Brighton for cock-fighting as well as for cricket; in fact, was the "sporting house" of the period. Host Pollard was an authority on cock-fighting, and ranked "A 1" as a "feeder," and it was most probably he who built the cock-pit (which was in a room at the back of the house) at "The White Lion." There was a great cock-match there in 1807; and many another subsequently, notably that on June 19, 1810, Brighton against Marden, in Kent. One of the most important cock-fights at "The White Lion" was that on the 18th April, 1811—Gentlemen of the Isle of Wight *v.* Gentlemen of Sussex; Pollard being "feeder" for the Island, and Holden for the County, the stakes being put at "20 guineas a battle and 50 guineas the main." There was a County fight for still greater stakes, superintended by Pollard, on May 14th, 1811, the King's birthday. This took place at Henfield, the advertisement in the *Brighton Herald* stating that it would be a "double day's play;" that the cocks would fight with silver spurs; 10 guineas the battle; 100 guineas the main. This cock-fight was got up chiefly for the diversion of the "amateurs," who on that day would be holiday keeping. In the following month, Pollard arranged for another match at "The White Lion," for 10 guineas the battle. There were, no doubt, other matches in Brighton after this date; but this seems to have been among the last publicly announced.

The practice of "Throwing at Cocks" seems to have been in olden times quite as popular a national pastime as "Cock-fighting." The poor cock was tied to a stake, and thrown at with a stick or cudgel till the bird was wholly disabled or killed. In some places (*vide* Strutt) it was the custom to place a cock in an earthen vessel, and to suspend it about 12ft. or 14ft. from the ground, across the street, to be thrown at by such as chose to make a trial of their skill. Twopence was paid for four throws, and he who broke the pot and delivered the cock from his confinement had him for a reward. Cock-throwing after the old fashion was a popular pastime on Shrove Tuesday at Lewes and other places in the County, down to about 1780, when it appears to have fallen into desuetude; for a paragraph in the *Lewes Journal* of 1778 states,—

" It is with great pleasure we can inform the public that the barbarous practice of throwing at cocks is now so universally exploded in these parts, that last Tuesday (Shrove Tuesday) did not produce a single instance of those acts of riot and cruelty by which this day was long and shamefully characterised, in open defiance of humanity and all civil authority."

We know of no record of cock-throwing in Brighton; but, taking the cue from Lewes, it probably was indulged in in a limited way; and the custom of "*cock-shying*," as it was called,—that is, putting up a heap of beach stones on a groyne-pile, &c., to *shy* at,—by boys, some 40 or 50 years since, would seem to have been a remnant of the original practice. Hone, in his *Every Day Book* (page 254) says, the practice of boys pitching with leaden dumps at leaden capons took its rise from the throwing at cocks. This game, again, was formerly much in vogue with Brighton boys at certain seasons: the "cockaroo" was thinly moulded of lead and made to stand on a thick heavy base, to prevent its being toppled over too easily. But whether the game was "introduced" to Brighton, or was of "native growth," following upon the tradition of an old barbarous sport, we cannot say.

Bull-baiting, though not such an ancient sport as cock-fighting, early became prevalent in Sussex. The fact that it was a legalized sport no doubt tended to confirm it the more; and at one time there was scarcely a town—and especially a market town—without its bull-ring, that is, a ring strongly fastened to the ground, with a chain attached for holding in the animal. The unfortunate beast, therefore, had only a restricted area, while its tormentors, the dogs, had full liberty. A notion used also to prevail at one time (and even by such a practical man as William Cobbett) that the flesh of the bull was much better after baiting! Be that as it may, there was bull-baiting near Brighton—if not in Brighton—so long since as the middle of last century. For instance:—

THIS is to acquaint the Public that, on FRIDAY NEXT, the 26th May, 1758, at the House of Thomas Clare, the sign of the King of Prussia, at Rottingdean, Sussex, will be BULL-BAITING. To begin at Nine o'clock in the morning.

The announcement adds,—

"Likewise whosoever pleases to bring any Cocks to fight may depend upon having them matched for Five Shillings a Battle.—A good Twelve-penny Ordinary at One o'clock."

Rottingdean at the period must have been a lively place! What with "ladies running for smocks," cricket, bull-baiting and cock-fighting, and sports "of that ilk," it must have sadly lacked that "quiet retirement" which some years later was, and still is, its great recommendation with visitors to Brighton.

Preston, in the matter of bull-baiting, was not a whit behind Rottingdean, as the following extract from the *Sussex Weekly Advertiser* for November, 1759, shows:—

"On Wednesday, the 14th instant, there will be a Bull baited, at Aaron Winton's, at the Ship at Preston, where there will be a number of good Dogs and a fine Bull for the Sport."

Lewes, too, had its bull-baiting; for in December, 1781, we learn,— "A Bull will be baited in the Coombe Bottom, behind the Wheat Sheaf, Malling, on the 17th instant;" it being added, "As an encouragement to Gentlemen to bring their Dogs, there will be given "to the first Dog that pins the Bull, 20s.; to the second, 15s.; to the third, 10s.; and to the fourth, 5s."

Coming nearer home, Hove would seem to have been the bull-baiting arena for Brighton; and on such occasions—chiefly Hove Fair day—there was a grand congregation of spectators—not a few of whom were of the most idle and dissolute class of the town and neighbourhood. At the Hove Fair of December, 1807, a bull-bait was announced; but for some reason or another did not come off. A chronicler adds—"There was the usual proportion of idlers from Brighton. * * * Towards evening the folks at the Fair seemed to be a little displeased with each other, and eventually black eyes and bloody noses, among the male part of the assemblage, were pretty equally distributed!" One of the last bull-baits at Hove was on Easter Tuesday, 1810; but the bull broke loose, charged through the crowd of sight-seers, and ran up the gap into a field, where the Blockade-houses now are, and hid itself under a vehicle. It was, however, by means of ropes, dragged out; again fastened to the bull-ring, and, we suppose, baited in orthodox fashion until it succumbed. Owing, however, to the partial failure of Easter Tuesday, another "bait" was arranged for the following June. After this, bull-baiting ended at Hove; but up to within the last 30 or 40 years the "bull-ring" might be seen in the lower road to Shoreham, a little to the south-west of Old Hove-street, showing where in former times some of the most disgraceful scenes connected with bull-baiting in this locality were enacted.

The Steine and its Associations.

The Steine and its Associations.

HE STEINE has from time immemorial been associated with Brighton; and in the olden time much more closely than now, when, by reason of the enormous growth of the town and the mutations which modern requirements have necessitated, its early individuality has to a great extent been lost. The changes which both the town and the Steine have undergone during the last century have been such that each has now altogether different characteristics from heretofore; and the contrast between the modern Steine and that of days gone by is scarcely less marked than that of the ancient "fisher village," with its four or five irregularly-built streets, dotted with squalid habitations, and the present Queen of Watering Places, which rears its "gay and fantastic front" of noble houses to the Sea. One might not inaptly say, as in the sweet song of Ariel,

"There's nothing of them that doth fade,
But hath suffer'd a sea change."

The Steine, neat and attractive as it is, has in its present state nothing,—except, perhaps, the nameless statue* of the erst adored patron of Brighton, George IV.,—to recall its former glories, when Royal and noble personages graced it with their presence; when it was "all the world" to Brighton; and when gay and courtly throngs, and visitors seeking health or pleasure, for many years regarded it as a fashionable resort *par excellence*. By the *beau monde* the Steine is now wholly deserted as a promenade; it is, in fact, given over to the sylvan deities, the dryads and the naïads; and by most visitors—even by many a modern Brightonian—it is merely looked upon as

"An enclosure by the salt sea's brim:
A railed enclosure 'tis to him,
And it is nothing more."

But to those familiar with its past history, and of many a notable spot in its vicinity, a thousand pleasant memories,—chequered, it may be, with some regrets,—involuntarily rise up; and these are so closely interwoven with the fortunes of the town in earlier times that they should not willingly be let die. Like the Steine itself, however, its surroundings have undergone many mutations. The old Manor

---

[* This statue—erected in 1828—was without an inscription until about 1884.]

House—probably one of the earliest houses erected on the south part of the Steine—is gone, and "its place is known no more." Grove House, the Duke of Marlborough's late residence, has long since been absorbed into the Pavilion; while•his earlier and more famous house is now devoted to the offices of the School Board! The Albion Hotel occupies the site of Russell House. All the old Libraries—where once fair ladies and their companions of the sterner sex staked their chances on the throw of a die, and indulged in gossip and scandal—have passed to other uses. "The Castle"—three-quarters of a century ago "The Grand Hotel of Brighton"—has ceased to exist; and of all its former splendour—its grand assemblies and balls, its charming social card and tea parties, &c., each and all mingled with many pleasant associations of the past—nothing has survived, except its name, given to a square to which it was once in close proximity. "Raggett's" Subscription-house, where high play was indulged in and "dice rattled to a merry tune," is now a house of *mourning* (*i.e.*, a mourning warehouse) ;* Mrs. Fitzherbert's is "silent and tenantless"; and "Ichabod" might be inscribed on the old "Blue and Buffs"—the houses enclosing the Steine to the North—for, verily, beneath white paint and stucco, "their glory is departed."

Returning, however, to the early history of the Steine itself, it is unnecessary to go back to that primitive epoch when it was ordered "that no hog go unringed on the Stein, where nets lie, under a penalty of eightpence *toties quoties;*" or, when—as in the fields at Hove—no "foreigner" was allowed to graze his horse upon it. But, coming later down, the convenient formation of the Steine—for the most part a comparatively level piece of greensward, of considerable extent, in close proximity to the sea and to the old town,—doubtless led to its earliest use by the fishermen and others for net-drying, boat-building, the depositing of timber, coals, &c. It was of greater extent seaward, and especially to the westward, than now; and in the latter direction, previous to 1665, it extended a considerable way beyond the lower end of East-street. In "Goodwyn's Rental of Brighthelmston Manor,"† the common pound of the Manor, together with a cottage and garden adjoining to the said pound, are mentioned as being "situated on the Stein, on the *west* side of East-street." A little to the south-east of these, in the early part of last century, there was another cottage, with rope walks, &c., which was subse-

---

[* Now occupied by Lloyd's Art Repository; whilst Mrs. Fitzherbert's mansion—once the resort of Royalty and Fashion—is now devoted to the uses of the Young Men's Christian Association!]

† This interesting document (says Dunvan, in his *History of Lewes*) was made, in 1665, by Charles Goodwyn, Gent., who had been many years Steward of the "Manor of Brithelmston." It was engrossed on vellum, at a considerable expense, for which Mr. Goodwyn "never received the least consideration from the contemporary Lord and Lady of the Manor; but, on the contrary, was dismissed from the Stewardship, after more than 20 years' diligent and faithful attention to that office, without any complaint or cause alledged." The original affidavit of Mr. Goodwyn's wrongs was attached to the last page of the "Rental," which, in 1793, was in the possession of Charles Gilbert, Esq., of Lewes.

quently swept away during a terrific storm. But even after these devastations there was a considerable area, a portion of the early Steine, west of East-street, which was utilized when the Battery was formed there in 1761.* Immediately, too, to the south of the Steine, there were several houses, stretching eastward to what is now the Aquarium end of the Madeira-road. These were in existence long before Dr. Russell "set-up house" in the neighbourhood; and were, it is supposed, destroyed by the storm of 1760, though some wells formerly attached to them were to be seen still open on the beach so late as 1778.

Visitors to Brighton in the middle of last century were, probably, less fastidious than now; for, in 1761, Dr. Relhan characterises the Steine as "the most delightful spot" in Brighton, though promenading there was then comparatively restricted, and, at times, subject to inconvenience. To the north, beyond "The Castle," agricultural roads intersected it; a large ditch also ran along its whole western side; and into this, when the springs overflowed, the Pool, which formerly stretched along the whole front of what became subsequently the Pavilion Lawn, discharged itself, the water running past "The Castle" down to the Pool Valley, and thence into the sea. Then, in the winter time, the southern part of the Steine was not unfrequently flooded; and, if the water became frozen, skating there was common. As "company" increased, however, and houses began to be built round it, the Steine was enclosed; but the finishing stroke to·its earlier improvement was given in 1792, when, conjointly by the Prince of Wales and the Duke of Marlborough, it was drained and levelled and the "Pool" wholly obliterated.

We endeavoured to show (p. 27) how the early visitors to Brighton, —who, more or less, came hither for the advice of Dr. Russell, seabathing, &c.,—grew into a little fashionable community. They so increased and multiplied that, before the Doctor had been gathered to his fathers (1759), the Steine had become the centre of a new World of Fashion, and amusements were specially improvised after "Ye manners and customs of ye Englishe" at that period; Shergold's appearing to be the chief resort for card parties, assemblies, balls, &c.,

---

* The west front wall of this Battery was gradually undermined by the sea, and being so much damaged by the storm of August 7, 1786, fell down on the 3rd November following, with a noise like the report of a cannon. Six of its guns were washed into the sea; and the front of the house that belonged to the Battery was swept away. Several other houses "on the Bank," particularly "The Crown and Anchor" and "The Dolphin" public-houses, were not left in much better situation, the greater part of their foundations being entirely washed away. The extreme western extent of the Battery reached to just beyond where Markwell's Royal Hotel is now; in fact, when digging out to form the foundations of the Hotel, a portion of massive wall, some 4ft. thick, was uncovered, and, by dint of great labour, was cut through, to form an entrance to the Hotel cellars. The remainder of the wall, on account of its solidity, was suffered to remain, and now forms some of the foundations of the building. The massive magazine, with shelves, for storing powder, &c., was also discovered at the same time; but this was again covered in, comparatively undisturbed, as, from the immense thickness of the walls, neither its ut:lization nor removal would have repaid the cost. It may be added, so effectually was the Battery wall undermined by the sea, that, when it fell, "more than a foot in thickness of the main rock came away cemented to the foundation of the brick work."

whilst, for out-door amusements, there were, in addition to promenading on the Steine and bathing, equestrian parties, &c. Brighton had, too, in 1758, a regular pack of hounds; and visitors, if so minded, could "hunt the bounding deer," to which they were occasionally invited by advertisement. The following appeared in the *Lewes Journal*, in March, 1759:—

NOTICE IS HEREBY GIVEN,—to all Gentlemen Sportsmen,—that there is to be a HIND turn'd out at STANMER, on FRIDAY, the 9th of this instant March, at Nine o'clock in the morning, by their humble servant,

Brighthelmston, March 5, 1759.　　　　　　JOHN MOCKFORD.

N.B.—The Hind is to be hunted by Brighthelmston and Henfield Hounds.

There were, of course, times and seasons when "company" could not participate in out-door amusements, and hence the newspaper and the library book became desiderata for home enjoyment. With the need came the supply. The pioneer in vending literature on the Steine at Brighton was Mr. E. Baker (Baker and Co., of Tunbridge Wells), and he it was who built the first Library in Brighton—a little place, with piazza in front, on the East side of the Steine (now the south-west corner of St. James's-street). It was under Mr. Baker's auspices that "James Lambert, painter, Lewes," published his well-known "View of Brighthelmston"* (see p. 40). After Mr. Baker's death the Library was carried on by Mr. Thomas, whose name was for many years identified with it;† and subsequently by Dulot, Gregory,

---

* This clever work was painted (5ft. by 3ft.) in 1765, and an engraving of it published in 1766; the price to subscribers being 5s.; subscribers of £1 1s. to have a chance for the painting, in any way determined on; but the "whole subscription falling greatly short of the expense of engraving and publishing the Print," Mr. Lambert eventually begged to be excused disposing of it. From *Dunran* we learn that Lambert, "indebted to education for no more than the humble advantages of a common writing-school, applied himself to music and painting with the persevering enthusiasm of unassisted genius. As he advanced towards maturity, he received some instruction from a music-master; but in painting he had still to trust solely to his own taste and application; and, with such means, his proficiency in landscape became truly admirable. He was not more respectable for his talents as an artist, than estimable for his candour and benignity as a man. His natural modesty, and his early habits of taciturnity in the cultivation of his favourite art, gave a slowness and hesitation to his language, that, in the company of strangers, bordered on embarrassment. In the unvaried course of a sedentary life, he gradually and imperceptibly contracted bodily infirmities, which accelerated and embittered the close of an useful and unsullied life. He died on the 7th day of December, 1781, in the sixty-third year of his age, and was interred at St. John's, in Lewes." As a painter, his greatest effort was a landscape which he presented to the Society of Art and Sciences about the year 1770, who honoured him with their highest premium for that kind of painting.

† Mr. Thomas's first advertisement, published May 30, 1774, was as follows:—

AT THE BRIGHTHELMSTON CIRCULATING LIBRARY, by R. THOMAS, Bookseller, Stationer, and Bookbinder (late Mr. Baker's), BOOKS ARE LENT TO READ at 10s. 6d. per Year; or 3s. per Quarter. Persons living remote from the Library may be supplied by paying the expense of Carriage. All new and entertaining Books will be added to the Library as soon as published. Stationary and Perfumery of every kind.

The full value given for Libraries and Parcels of Books, and Books exchanged.

N.B.—The Library will be kept open regularly all the year, and all monthly publications taken in.

LAMBERT'S PERSPECTIVE VIEW OF BRIGHTHELMSTON, 1765.

Donaldson, &c.*   Mr. Baker opened his Library—it must at first have been a very temporary one—in 1760, announcing that he would sell books "till the end of October." He doubtless had had a hint to do so by some visitors at the Wells who had been to Brighton. His Library was opened again in the summers of 1761-2-3, when, for the delectation of visitors, he erected in close proximity to it a Rotunda—a wooden building enclosed by railings, for the "musick to perform in when the weather will permit"—another "importation," doubtless, from the Wells. At this time, a writer says, "several shops, with piazzas and benches therein, were erected on the Stean." There was, too,—thanks to Tubb and Davis's and Batchelor's coaches and "machines,"†—no lack of company at this time at Brighton, nor of gaiety and social pleasure; and Lord Chief Justice Wilmot says (in 1763), "Of all the public places I have been at, I like none so well as Brighthelmston."

THE FIRST ROYAL VISIT TO BRIGHTON.

But we must clear the stage. "Royalty is coming—buzz, buzz." It was rumoured—"The Duke of Gloucester will be here in July"! There was bustle and preparation at Shergold's; Mrs. Hicks (of "The Old Ship") and her charming daughters were in a flutter of excitement; the news spread from Baker's to Woodgate's; from Woodgate's to Baker's; from the "benches" to the bathing machines; and thence to the denizens of the old town. *The news was true!* and on Thursday, July 11th, 1765, Brighton received its first Royal visitor. The Duke lost no time whilst here. He went to the Public Rooms in the evening. The next day he breakfasted at Stanmer, the seat of Thomas Pelham, Esq., who gave his guest a right Royal reception. "Whilst His Royal Highness was walking in the Groves of that delightful place, he was most agreeably surprised with the harmony of an excellent Band of Music, artfully stationed, who, unseen, saluted the Prince at each avenue." On his return to Brighton, he gave at Shergold's in the evening a grand ball to a brilliant company of upwards of 250 gentlemen and ladies. On Saturday he breakfasted with Sir Henry Poole, at Lewes, after which Sir Henry returned to

---

* Mr. Woodgate's Library (to the South of the Steine), afterwards carried on by Miss Widgett ("the milliner and library-woman," as Fanny Burney styles her), Mr. Bowen, Mr. Crawford, Mr. Fisher, and others, is not mentioned as such, so far as we know, until 1767; but it was probably established some two or three years earlier.

† "Machines," which came into fashion some time prior to 1750, were considered to be a great improvement on the old conveyances. A friend, writing to us respecting them, says,—"I have before me at this moment a print of the Alton and Farnham 'Machine,' of the date 1750, and it certainly bears a very strong resemblance to a Brighton bathing-machine of our day. It is a clumsy-looking vehicle, carrying no passengers on the roof, but it has a large basket—literally a basket -swung behind for half-price passengers. The coachman has four stout horses in hand, and a postillion rides a pair of leaders. The seat of the coachman is like that of the driver of a Hansom cab, only that it is in the front instead of behind." He adds—"It is noteworthy that the horses used in these machines were called 'machiners,'—a term not quite extinct in the sale bills of horse repository auctioneers of the present day."

dine with him at Brighton. His Royal Highness came in an open phaeton, and "showed so great a condescension as to drive quite gently through the town, that all the spectators might have an opportunity of seeing him. There were six young fellows who met him a little distance from the town, and run before him, whom he paid very handsomely." Whilst here—Hampton and Windsor, "hide your blushing glories"!—the Duke went *twice* to "Rottendean,"—which had even thus early become a fashionable suburb to the modern Baiæ!

In Aug., 1766, Brighton had another Royal visitor in the Duke of York; but his stay was brief. The town, however, was at this period growing more than ever into popularity as a fashionable summer resort; and a writer, in June, 1769, says, "The company flock to Brighton at a great pace; there being, we are informed, but few lodgings to be had in the whole place."* With the increase of company, came an increase of amusements. "The Castle" (though "The Old Ship" to some extent "shared honours" with it) was more and more the great centre for public assemblies, &c.; an "M.C." was installed; and the large numbers who attended balls, &c., showed how eagerly this species of amusement was sought after. The balls, too, must have been gay enough, though the guests showed no want of decorum. The ladies seem to have entered into the amusements of the old town with an especial zest, judging from *The New Brighthelmston Directory*, 1769, the writer of which gives a lively account of their doings in the Libraries, and on the "benches" outside, picking up food for gossip, &c.,

"For whilst you discourse, to each word that is said,
Attentive they listen, and *seem* but to read."

He tells us also of their little raffling exploits, by themselves or with their gentlemen friends; and—*O tempora, O mores!* of their skill at billiards. He says:—

"I saw them, this morn, as I walked on the Stene,
To the billiard-room trip it;—I followed them in;
I was curious to see if a little fair hand
Could handle the mace or the kew at command:
But when I beheld them, oh! how I did stare:—
They handled the sticks with a grace! and an air!"

---

* There was scarcely a person of note in the kingdom who did not come to Brighton. Even Lord Bute ("jackboot," as he was called, one of the most unpopular of Ministers) was here in December, 1769: and, though when riding out he partially concealed himself by the curtains of his carriage, he was recognised by a gentleman. No demonstration, however, took place. It was somewhat different when His Lordship's most bitter assailant, John Wilkes, the Editor of the *North Briton*, came in August, 1770; the bells being rung and other marks of pleasure shown on the occasion. But the champion of "liberty" affected privacy; though every mark of esteem was shown him by the inhabitants that could in such circumstances be expressed to a gentleman so highly deserving the public regard." Mr Wilkes (who was accompanied by Miss Wilkes) remained in Brighton about a week. He again visited Brighton in August, 1773, whilst on a tour of the Coast of Sussex. He was also here in September, 1774. and dined at Mr. Mercer's, surgeon,—where there was "much drinking of healths," &c.; and he came again more than once in subsequent years.

There was a "Club" formed at "The Castle," with the Earl of Tyrconnel at its head, so early as 1769; there were public concerts and private evening parties; there was boating and bathing; deer and "wild fox" hunting* and riding out; picnics; and many another "diversion," showing that "life at Brighton," even in 1769, lacked neither variety nor excitement. The author above quoted grows quite enthusiastic over his country excursions, which it had already become the fashion for visitors to indulge in. He went to Shoreham, where he regaled himself, after the "heated card rooms," with the "scent of the shore and a *spicy cool-tankard;*" to "Rottendean," to "drink tea with fair ladies under the tent;" but Preston was in his highest favour; for he says,—

"But oft'ner I trip it, with some laughing maid,
To Preston's green grove; there partake, in cool shade,
Of the coolest refreshment I ever shall see,—
A sweet frothy syllabub under the tree!
O sweet syllabub under the tree!
Coffee;—tea, green or bohea,
Compared with thee, taste nauseously,
As *saline draughts* from the boisterous sea."

But let us look at the Steine itself at the period—

"Our great public walk,
Where the ladies assemble to giggle and talk;"

for promenading by ladies in public places—following a stupid French fashion—was then deemed "quite vulgar"; they, therefore, for the most part when visiting the Steine sat in parties or sets upon the "benches" under the piazzas, to view the men lounging or walking *à la mode: i.e.*, with "their hands crossed behind them"! The Steine, however, was as yet but a poor promenade for ladies. It was in many parts rough and unkempt, and—true indication that it still retained its primitive characteristics—mushroom "rings" were to be seen here and there; the Pool to the north-west still held its own; and the fishermen, making the most of their "auncient custom," continued to appropriate, without let or hindrance, in season or out of season, such parts as they chose for drying their nets, &c. Then if ladies desired to walk near the Rotunda, to listen to the band, it was not unfrequently the pursuit of pleasure under difficulties, by reason of accompaniments such as at the present day would scarcely be conceived to be in proximity to a fashionable resort. But here are

---

* In October, 1768, a stag was turned out "for the diversion of the gentry who frequent Brighthelmston." At this period, the neighbourhood had a "mighty hunter" in the Rev. Mr. Wenham, of Hamsey. He kept up, at his own expense, a fine pack of hounds; and the gentry were indebted to him for many a splendid day's sport. In March, 1770, for their "diversion," he had a deer turned out at Stanmer; and, in the following May, a second one, which ran no less than 30 miles.

the before-mentioned writer's experiences of "musick," &c., at Baker's Rotunda, on the Steine, in 1769:—

"So, shunning the nets, I went round to a stand,
Or high wooden stage which the green did command.

. . . . . .

Bassoons, clarinets, with flute, hautboy, and horn –
(Their like have not pleased me since e'er I was born),
Played a march, – that did make me to strut on the green
With the air and the step of a theatrical queen.

. . . . . .

Those hogs, replied I, grunting loud in the corn
Round the stand, I suppose, are to aid the French horn !
Those pigs and those children, all trotting before us,
Assist with their squeaking to fill up the chorus."

Allowing something for poetical license, it would seem that long after the "invasion" of Fashion, the primitive maritime and agricultural associations of the Steine still asserted themselves. Notwithstanding this, the Steine was thronged in the season, "with the best of all good company." The great influx of visitors commenced about the middle of June ; and could a week's " latest arrivals " be chronicled in full, it would appear marvellous, as regards rank and numbers, considering the size of the town. For instance, there were, amongst other arrivals in the week ending June 17, 1771, Prince Ernest of Mecklenburg, the Duke and Duchess of Marlborough, Lady Mary Blandford, Rev. Mr. Ashburnham, the Dean of Bristol, Sir Charles and Lady Bingham, the Earl of Egremont, Lady Evelyn, the Hon. Mr. Luttrell (whose sister subsequently became the Duchess of Cumberland), the Countess Pembroke, the Ladies Caroline and Elizabeth Spencer, the Earl of Stamford, Lady and Miss Cust, the Hon. Mr. and Miss Dawnay, Dr. Pepys, Dr. Awsiter, the Hon. Mrs. Yorke, and Rev. Gentlemen and untitled people out of number. Those of a week in June, 1772, were equally numerous, for, in addition to many of the above, the arrivals up to the 20th of the month included Lady Ashley, Sir John and Lady Bridger, the Earl and Countess Donegal, Lady Masham, the Earl of Peterborough, the Earl and Countess Powis, Lord and Lady Ravensworth, Lord Romney, and the Countess of Shaftesbury.

With such an influx of company, "accommodation" must have been scarce ; for as yet there were available—with the exception of a few new houses—only the earlier built houses in the five or six streets which then constituted Brighton. Yet, with all its sundry inconveniences, the popularity of the town as a summer resort increased more and more with the *beau monde*. In September, 1771, the Duke of Marlborough secured a residence in Brighton, purchasing a new house built by Mr. Shergold on the Steine (now devoted to the School Board, &c.) In the same month H.R.H. the Duke of Cumberland paid his first visit here, and expressed himself "highly delighted with the situation of the place, and the conveniences attending it." Fortunate Brighton! It was more than repaid for the reception it gave the Duke; the bells being rung and the guns at the Fort fired, which were answered by a discharge from on board the packets that lay off the town; and grand illuminations took place. The Duke stayed a week, and gave during his stay a public breakfast and a ball. The ladies were delighted with the Duke; as was, in fact, "the whole place in general" with the honour of His Royal Highness's visit. The Duke spent another week in Brighton in June of the following year.

It were needless to recount the doings of the summer visitants to Brighton, which, for some 10 years or more, 1770-80, had little variation. The amusements grew apace. There was now a Theatre; and in addition to the balls, &c., subscription and other concerts were given, at which the best artists of the day appeared. There was hunting and riding out; horse-racing and cock-matches; and country drives were, weather permitting, with numbers a daily practice. But, in the words of a ballad of the period—

"Though in pleasing excursions you spend the long day,
And to Lewes, or Shoreham, or Rottingdean stray;
Or to drink tea at Preston, to vary the scene,
At eve with new raptures you'll fly to the Steine."

Here all seemed to concentrate; and not only in the evening; for to those who did not care to ride or drive; to many of the fair sex, to the lounger, or to the invalid, the Steine seemed to have an especial fascination in the opportunities it afforded for friendly meetings and greetings; for social converse, gossip, &c.

About 1776 the Steine was enclosed by posts and rails and the turf somewhat improved; and when thronged of an evening with "company," dressed in the quaint and varied costumes of the period; some promenading; others in groups; the scene must have been most picturesque. The view, too, from the Steine itself was charming. There was no building save the Library on the east side, and hence there was to be seen a wide expanse of sea to the southeast; whilst to the north and north-east the glorious Downs stretched in bold proportions "free and open" into apparently measureless distance, until they seemed to mingle with the sky above them. For a view of the Steine in 1778 (taken from the south end), see *plate* annexed.

But let us briefly glance at some of the surroundings of the Steine—look into the shops and Libraries—where, as a variation from out-door amusement, not a few of the early visitors to Brighton were wont to spend their idle hours. The shops, which were of small dimensions and contiguous to the Libraries, were, we are told, the chief resort of "fops, women, and children." They seem to have contained as many varieties of merchandise as Autolycus's basket: toys of all descriptions; rare china; lace and millinery, ribbons and muslin, "chintz and cambricks;" tea, and other articles! all of which were, more or less, enhanced in value from the fact that they were *supposed* to have been "smuggled!"* Hence, these goods were not disposed of in the ordinary way of purchase,

"But were set up to sale, by the rattling of dice."

Books and baubles, every article of convenience, every trinket of luxury, was disposed of by this uncertain, quick mode of transfer. There was not a shop without the indispensable "rattle-trap." The amount of business done must have been enormous; for it was rattle, rattle, rattle, from "morn to noon, from noon to dewy eve." The Libraries—which after 1774 were kept open "regularly all the year"—were subscribed to by all the fashionable visitors, and, it might be said, by all the unfashionable visitors, as the fact of a name being entered into the subscription-book afforded a convenient passport into the hallowed precincts of "Society."† The Libraries, like the shops, had their "rattle-traps;" but though indispensable for carrying on business, were regarded only as minor adjuncts to it. A somewhat higher and more exciting game was pursued there. This was the great god "Pam,"‡ who for many a year was the supreme fashionable deity; its devotees including the young and old of both sexes. "Pam" attained early popularity by reason of its affording a convenient opportunity for pastime, for small wit, and flirtation. But by some visitors it soon began to be voted "slow": and a "fair correspondent," in 1777, writing from Brighton, says—"What are called the polite amusements are making such rapid progress that she is under great apprehensions for her old friend and favourite PAM,

---

* Smuggling was a prevalent fashion at the period. It was considered a "fair game" to cheat the revenue officers. In 1776 a chaise was brought to Brighton from Dieppe, and over £1,000 worth of lace was found stuffed in the cushions! A Frenchman was also caught on the Steine carrying some loaves, and, on his attempting to dispose of them at fancy prices, suspicion was excited. When the loaves were opened by the revenue officers, they were found to have "lace" interiors!

† There was a sort of rivalry between Mr. Thomas and Mr. Bowen, the two librarians of the Steine, as to whose subscription-book should most justly deserve the title of the "Book of Numbers"—"names," rather than character or position in society, being regarded as of primary importance. This rivalry induced a constant struggle between the Librarians as to which should be the most courteous, and the effects were those usually consequent upon opposition. Mr. Thomas was from the first regarded as the "fashionable bookseller;" but Miss Widgett's successor, Mr. Bowen, who bowed *à la Noverre* or *Gallini*, soon seemed to carry away most of the custom and company from Thomas's. Fanny Burney says Mr. Bowen was "extremely civil, attentive to watch opportunities of obliging, and assiduous to make use of them—skilful in discovering the taste or turn of mind of his customers, and adroit in putting in their way just such temptations as they are least able to withstand. Mrs. Thrale, at the same time that she sees his management and contrivance, so much admires his sagacity and dexterity, that, though open-eyed, she is as easily wrought upon to part with her money as any of the many dupes in this place, whom he persuades to require indispensably whatever he shows them."

‡ "Pam," or "Loo," was simply a sweepstakes, played for by cards. The subscribers were limited to eight, each staking one shilling. The chances were taken under a fictitious name, as "The Enchantress," "Poor Peter," "Civil Beau," "Prudence," &c., and the full number being obtained, a certain quantity of cards, among which was the Knave of Clubs, or "PAM," were shuffled, cut, and separately dealt and turned; the numbers and fictitious names of the subscribers being called in rotation during the process, and that number against which "PAM" appeared was declared the winner.

whom, it is thought, the ensuing winter will be greatly deserted, and, in despight of all good order and decorum, will be treated with contempt and ridicule by the more polished admirers of *pastille* and *manille, sans prendre, &c.*, though a few years back PAM presided in the best companies there during the winter season with great credit and respect."

The fact is, " Pam " and such "small deer" as were played at the Libraries, and the other games played at the card assemblies at "The Castle" and "The Old Ship," gradually and almost imperceptibly induced a taste for private gaming, where higher stakes and more exciting play were indulged in. So much was this the case, that it early became a reproach to the town. In August, 1779, the *Monthly Chronologer* says it was attempted to turn high play at Brighthelmston to good account; but the paragraph in that journal which relates to this circumstance afford such an idea of fashionable card-playing at the period—not so much by gentlemen as by ladies—that we give it in its entirety:—

" Some ladies of fashion here have proposed that the profits of the card-table shall be devoted to the relief of their country. The plan is, as far as at present digested, that a Committee of twelve ladies shall be appointed as receivers of the public money, who are to settle their accounts every night, and remit the amount once a week to a banker in London ; no card-table is to be allowed without one of the Committee being of the party, or attending during the course of the play; the winners, at breaking up of the night, are to deliver their games to the Committee lady, who is immediately to enter the same in the subscription book, which lies open in the rooms for publick inspection ; and it has been determined *nem. con.* that if any lady or gentleman shall presume to play at cards or dice out of the Assembly Room, they shall be excommunicated, and no lady allowed to speak to the delinquent, or answer any question, under pain of the like punishment. If a large sum may not be expected from such a project, it will eventually put a stop to private and high gaming, which has for some years disgraced this place ; and it will convince the world that our ladies are as ready as their husbands to show their loyalty to their King and their love to their country."

One fine evening in September, 1777, there was a little romantic excitement among the frequenters of the Libraries, &c., and the gay promenaders of the Steine, by reason of the arrival of Miss Max, an Irish heiress, who some time previously had been forcibly carried off by Samuel Phillips, of Froyle, co. Kilkenny (assisted by his father, a Magistrate of that county, his brother and sister, and other persons), and who, in company with two ladies and two gentlemen, embarked in hot haste from Brighton on board a vessel for France. Before the packet in which the party sailed was out of sight, two of Sir John Fielding's men arrived here in pursuit; and offered any of the fishermen a large reward,—it was said as much as £1,300,—who would give chase to the packet and prevail upon the Captain to steer her back to Brighthelmston. But the aborigines stood firm ; not one of them would attempt it, though they admitted (pleasing consolation !) that the packet might have been overtaken. The young lady was only 13 years of age ; and as the runaways first made their route to

Scotland, it was imagined that the lady was there married to young Phillips.

The season of 1777 was a most successful one. The whole summer through the weather had been delightful; and the town was never previously known to have been thronged with so numerous and splendid a company. Alluding to the fact, a contemporary public journal said, "Brighthelmston may now be justly deemed, without boast, the first Watering Place in the Kingdom." Verily, the "fisher-village" was progressing! It had at the time about seven or eight streets; and of these Ship-street and Black Lion-street were deemed fashionable localities, and West-street (Russell-street was as yet undeveloped) was the "Court end of the town!" In each succeeding season—from 1778-82, the "company" was more or less numerous, and included not only members of the Royal Family but those of many of the first families in the kingdom; in addition to many notable personages, both English and foreign; statesmen and men of the world; artists* and authors; and we know not who besides. "All the world," in fact, then came to Brighton; and during the four or five years mentioned the town had reached its highest position as a fashionable watering-place, in the era which immediately preceded that in which it entered upon a new and still more brilliant career, namely, when George Prince of Wales did it the high honour of choosing it for his marine residence.

It would be impossible to enumerate in full the "arrivals" in each of the above years; for visitors then began to come early and stay late; and the season, which formerly lasted only during the three summer months, was now indefinitely prolonged. In June, 1778, there were here, in addition to many another person of rank and influence, the Duke and Duchess of Argyle, Lord Lyttleton, Lady Derby, Lady Augusta Campbell, the Bishop of Worcester, the Hon. Mrs. North, the Ladies Caroline and Emily Hervey, the Countess of Powis, Lady Harriet Herbert, Sir John and Lady Shelley, Lady Mary Coke, the Countess Rothes, and Dr. Pepys. Miss Burney, who was staying in Brighton in 1779 with Mr. and Mrs. Thrale (the latter, she says, "lived on the Steine, for the pleasure of viewing, all day long, who walked with who"), gives in her "Diary" a graphic picture of some of the "company" in May of that year, and who, though the season had not yet commenced, had already arrived: of Lord Mordaunt, a "pretty, languid, tonish young man"; of Dr. Delap, "snug and reserved"; of the "gaily sociable" Bishop of Peterborough; of the beautiful Miss Streatfield; of Sir Philip Clerke; of the "wit and libertine," the Hon. Mr. Beauclerk; of Lord Sefton; of Mr. Gerald Hamilton, "intelligent, dry, sarcastic, and clever"; of Cumberland, the dramatist, and his wife, son, and daughters, at whom "everybody laughs for their airs, affectations, and tonish graces

---

* Among the members of the musical profession in Brighton in August, 1779, were Giardini, Cramer, Lamotte, Tacet, Dance, Baumgarten, Simpson, and Waterhouse. Mrs. Abingdon (the celebrated actress, whom Sir Joshua Reynolds painted as "Thalia") was also residing here at the same time.

1. The Church. | 4. Mr. Philcox's. | 7. The Ball Room. | 10. Hollingbury Castle.
2. Mr. Scrase's. | 5. Mr. Willard's. | 8. The Orchestra. | 11. Lewes Hill.
3. Duke of Marlborough's. | 6. The Castle Tavern. | 9. Thomas's Circulating Library. | 12. North Row.

A PERSPECTIVE VIEW OF THE STEINE AT BRIGHTHELMSTON, 1778.

and impertinences;"* of Lady Pembroke and Lady Di Beauclerk, "both of whom have still very pleasing remains of beauty;" of pretty Mrs. Musters, "the reigning toast of the season;"† of Captain Fuller; of Messrs. Murphy and Selwin, &c., &c. In October, 1782, the "Authoress of *Evelina*" tells us Dr. Johnson was in Brighton; and, doubtless, after tea, "when the Steine hours began," the great lexicographer promenaded with his host and hostess and his "dear little Fanny;" during the day doing his gallop over the Downs, &c. The Doctor appears to have been but little asked out in company whilst here; his *protegé* telling us his "love of victory and superiority" in argument made him "dreaded by all, and by many abhorred." Poor Dr. Pepys, the husband of Lady Rothes, was one evening so roughly confuted in an argument with the Doctor respecting Pope's definition of wit, that he at once bade good night to Mrs. Thrale and abruptly left the house.‡ But this by the way. One incident of the

---

* Oliver Goldsmith styled Cumberland, "The Terence of England; the mender of hearts;" but if Miss Burney's picture of his character be true, his own would appear to have been a little neglected, as well as those of some members of his family.

† This lady was one of the ten "BRIGHTON BEAUTIES IN 1785," whose charms and graces were pourtrayed in as many couplets by a "LITTLE MOUSE," and published in a contemporary journal:—

LADY SEFTON.
In every step there's so much grace,
She seems a Goddess of superior race.

LADY BEAUCHAMP.
As the bright star that first at eve appears,
So lovely Beauchamp this gay circle cheers.

LADY LISLE.
Without commanding, she commands respect,
And seems distinguished with a mild effect.

LADY MARY BLIGH.
Like the fair Spring when first the sunbeams cheer,
But soon will brighten the meridian sphere.

MRS. MUSTERS.
The look of Angels so much beams in you,
You have their graces and their goodness too.

MRS. LAWREL.
So much she's envied of her happy fate,
She is herself a queen in middle state.

MISS BINGHAM.
So much at ease, she seems to be
From every tint of affectation free.

MISS MOLESWORTH.
The Gods their choicest gifts bestow'd,
And form'd her gentle, fair, and good.

MISS SHAKESPEAR.
As many dies as the carnation shows,
So many charms on your fair form disclose.

MISS WOODLY.
An easy grace, a happy smile adorns,
That, without meaning it, she charms.

‡ In Mr. Shergold's "Recollections of Brighton in the Olden Time," published in the *Brighton Herald* some few years since, we have an amusing description of one of the Doctor's feats of logomachy. He says:—"The Thrales went to the Rooms, and Dr. Johnson went there also. The weather was cold, and Michell and Johnson, meeting in an ante-room, they sat down near a fire to warm themselves and converse. For a time their conversation was amicably and peacefully exchanged; but, at last, some knotty and difficult question arose, and not being able to adjust the matter, Michell seized the poker, and Johnson the tongs, with which they enforced their arguments by thumping the grate violently and vociferating. The ladies, who most unscientifically were dancing, became alarmed; the country dance was interrupted; nor was it resumed until Wade, the Master of the Ceremonies, and the politest man in the world, pacified the wranglers."

Doctor's visit to Brighton is worth noting. He went to a ball! "to the universal amazement of all who saw him there." It is not stated whether the "Leviathan" danced; but it appears that he had been so dull the preceding evening, when he was at home alone, that he said a ball "cannot be worse!" Whilst here the Doctor also did a little hunting: "Thrale, who was the kindest creature upon earth to Johnson, and wishing, perhaps, to fortify his health by the pure air of the South Downs, or to present his friends with the view of an anomaly, viz., a poet on horseback, took him with him hare hunting. The hounds threw off, upstarted a hare, and the sportsmen galloped, helter-skelter, ding-dong, after it. Johnson was not the last. Somebody rode up to Thrale, and said—'I am astonished! Johnson rides like a young sportsman of twenty.' The philosopher told Thrale 'that he was better pleased with that compliment than any he had ever received.'"

Among other notable visitors in 1782 was Mr. John Wilkes, who came in June; in August, the Swedish Ambassador arrived; and in the following month, the Right Hon. Lord Clive—son of the victor of Plassy and the saviour of the Indian Empire—was in the neighbourhood, and sojourned for the second time that season at Rottingdean. It is not recorded that he resided at Brighton. On leaving Rottingdean, Lord Clive left £10 to be distributed to the poor.*

Of Royal visitors at the period there were the Duke and Duchess of Cumberland in August, 1779. His Royal Highness arrived a little after four o'clock in the afternoon, which was announced by the ringing of bells and a Royal salute of 21 cannon from the Fort. About two hours after Her Royal Highness the Duchess arrived, "preceded by six running footmen, who went properly dressed from the town for that purpose." In the evening the Castle Tavern and shops on and near the Steine were illuminated, "which, added to the throng of company on the Steine till between nine and ten o'clock, made a very brilliant and splendid appearance." Their Royal Highnesses were attended by the Countess of Ferrars, the Hon. Miss Luttrell, and the Hon. James Luttrell, Sir Thomas Fowke, Colonel Deaken, and other persons of distinction.† The Duke and Duchess

---

[* In the original edition of this work, this gentleman was erroneously deemed to have been the great Lord Clive, whose death took place in 1774.]

† Whilst here His Royal Highness had the opportunity of doing a kindly act, which highly exalted him in favour of the fishing population. After the fashion of the period, the "King's Navee" was recruited by press-gangs making raids upon the young fishermen; and two men having been "pressed," it was so strongly resented by the whole body of fishermen, that the consequences would have been fatal had it not been for the interference of the Duke. He went into the midst of the multitude and, by promising to interpose in behalf of the men, induced the mob to desist from further violence; and on the Regulating Captain assuring them that not one should be impressed without a fresh order, and, even in that case, that they should have twenty-four hours' notice, they repaired cheerfully to their boats. The next evening upwards of 40 sail appeared ready for sea, thus furnishing employment to a great number of men who had been shut up in idleness upwards of eleven weeks through fear of being impressed. Some few years after this (in 1787) there was another attempt at a press-gang raid on the local fishermen, but it proved abortive; this time, not by the action of the men, but by that of their wives and sweethearts; and is thus related in the *Lewes Journal*:—"Capt. B—ll, who lately put the Brighthelmston fishermen

THE STEINE AND ITS ASSOCIATIONS.

were evidently partial to Brighton; for they annually came here in the season during the next four or five years. Each time they arrived in the town similar loyal demonstrations to the above-mentioned took place; and, in 1780, we are told, "a number of young fellows dressed themselves in white and went and met Her Highness on the road, and, running before her carriage into the town, made a very decent appearance"! In August, 1782, the sister of George III., the Princess Amelia, came to Brighton from Stanmer, where she had been staying with Lord and Lady Pelham. Her Royal Highness was delighted with the sea and the Steine; she subscribed to the two Rooms, the Libraries, &c. An unfortunate accident somewhat marred the pleasure of the Princess's visit, the head gunner of the Battery, in superintending the firing of the Royal salute, having his hand so terribly shattered that it had to be amputated.*

Though the visitors to the town more and more increased, there was little alteration in the staple amusements. There were the Public Rooms, with their balls and card assemblies; the Libraries, &c.; bathing and boating; riding and driving; the Steine and promenading. Yet each and all appeared to be enjoyed, and were returned to each succeeding season with undiminished pleasure. Hunting (with occasional racing) seemed, however, to grow more in favour than ever; the sportsmen in the neighbourhood showing a commendable courtesy in affording opportunities for the pleasures of the chase. Foremost among these was Sir John Lade, who, independently of

---

under so much fear of being impressed, in consequence of having hired a number of armed men and given them the air of a press-gang, was on Monday evening last put fairly to the rout by the fishermen's wives and daughters, who assembled in a considerable body, armed with mops, brooms, fire-pans, &c., &c., and therewith pursued the Captain so closely that he was obliged to make his escape out of the windows of several houses in which he had taken shelter, and by means thereof reached a post-chaise and four that was provided for him, and thus escaped the fury of the *Victorious Amazons*, who then returned peaceably to their respective homes to congratulate their husbands and sweethearts on their happy deliverance."

[* In his *The Royal Dukes and Princesses of the Family of George III.*, Mr. Percy Fitzgerald gives the following graphic, though not very flattering, picture of the Princess Amelia, who died in October, 1786:—"Her loss was little felt by the Royal Family of Great Britain, to none of whom did she leave the smallest legacy out of her large property; the bulk of which passed, by her request, to the Prince of Hesse Cassel, who was mean enough to refuse giving mourning to her domestics. The habits of the deceased Princess were very peculiar. Every morning she regularly paid a visit to her stables, for the purpose of examining the state of the horses; and she never got into or out of her carriage at the front of the house, but always in the back yard. Her dress was such, that at first view she might have been taken for one of the masculine gender. She took snuff immoderately, and was no less addicted to cards. Her deportment, however, was exceedingly repulsive, even when engaged at her favourite amusement. One evening in the rooms at Bath, which fashionable place of resort she regularly visited, the Princess addressed her partner in the technical language of the game, 'We are eight, love.' The other jocosely answered, 'Yes, my dear;' on which she got up indignantly, threw the cards in his face, and retired. At another time, a general officer, who was standing by the table where the party were playing, perceiving the snuff-box of the Princess standing open, incautiously took a pinch; which, when Her Royal Highness observed, she ordered the servant in waiting to throw the remainder of the contents into the fire."]

L

his horse-racing proclivities, was an ardent sportsman, keeping his own pack of hounds, and doing much to encourage hunting. In February, 1779, he turned out a hind on Newmarket Hill, "for the diversion of the gentlemen of the neighbourhood." Unfortunately, though numbers attended, the "diversion" was small; for the stag took to the sea at Newhaven and swam out a mile; and though, by the assistance of a vessel, it was brought back alive, the sport collapsed.

But the greatest sensation in local stag-hunting was on October 6, 1780, when the Duke of Cumberland had a stag turned out upon the Steine. There was an immense concourse of spectators, and sportsmen innumerable. The sport, however, proved indifferent; for the stag, after running a few miles over the hills, "jumped off the cliff near Rottingdean, and killed himself on the spot," his carcase being eventually distributed amongst the poor of that place.* A few days after the Duke essayed another local stag-hunt. But this time, to prevent a recurrence of the previous catastrophe, he went further afield, to beyond Withdean. The second stag, unlike its predecessor, gave the sportsmen more running than they bargained for; but as the incidents in connection with this hunt are so extraordinary, we give a description of them from the *Lewes Journal* of October 16th, 1780:—

"The deer turned out before the Duke of Cumberland's hounds on Thursday morning last, between Patcham and Withdean, near Brighthelmston, bent her course towards this place (Lewes), and was seen a small distance from the town in a little better than half an hour after she was turned out, when it evidently appeared to many here that she was by far too fleet and subtle in her movements to afford much sport to her followers, who, by the time they came in sight, were near an hour behind. These, however, in their pursuit, produced a pleasing effect to a great number of spectators from the Castle Banks and Mount, who appeared highly diverted at seeing several of the sportsmen that were in rather late galloping hard different ways on a wrong scent, and the dogs at the same time at fault, twining and winding about as if they were lost in a labyrinth, while the timid animal was pursuing her intricate and deceptive course with equal speed and advantage across the brooks some miles on the other side of the town. The manner in which she effected this advantage without crossing the town was admirable; having first crossed the river near Serjeant Kempe's Bridge, she immediately after made to a sewer a little to the north of Lewes Bridge, and from thence waded a common sewer that runs under

---

* The tragic event was "done into verse" shortly after in the *Lady's Magazine*, from which we quote the following:—

"A noble duke of high renown,
　Residing at gay Brighton's town,
　Where all the fair resort;
　Such num'rous beauties there was
　　seen,
　His Grace resolved upon the Stein,
　To treat them with some sport.

"A stag for hunting was decreed,
　And that the sport might well succeed,
　Was let out on the Stein;
　But, leaving all the beauties gay,
　He from the concourse flees away,
　And hastes to Rottingdean.

"The huntsmen quickly him pursue;
　The hounds behold their prize in view;
　　With joy the stag is seen!
　Who, while pursu'd with numerous
　　foes,
　Soon sees an end of all his woes,
　And dies at Rottingdean.

"For being chac'd on ev'ry way,
　Too near the cliffs he chanc'd to stray,
　And instant down he fell.
　His sudden death the huntsmen mourn,
　And back in doleful dumps return,
　The dismal news to tell."

GEORGE PRINCE OF WALES.

(Reproduced from a scarce mezzotint by Bartolozzi; after a painting by P. Violet. 1791.)

the street of the Cliffe into the river, a great distance to the south of Lewes Bridge, where she again swam across and took to the brooks as above mentioned ; but, notwithstanding all this instinctive caution, she was discovered, and information thereof being immediately carried to the hunt, every advantage was in consequence given to the hounds. But to no purpose; for they never came up with her, till some of the horse people had taken her up near Chinton, where she was found lying down, having run till her feet were entirely worn out, and till she was no longer able to stand. She was put into a barn hard by, and every means used to save her life ; but without effect, as she died the next day."

This was, we believe, the last stag-hunt which the Duke of Cumberland arranged at Brighton.

THE FIRST VISIT OF THE PRINCE OF WALES.

This auspicious event, which was destined to have such an important influence upon the after fortunes of Brighton, took place on Sunday, September 7th, 1783, the Prince having been invited hither by his uncle, the Duke of Cumberland. The arrival of such an illustrious personage as the Heir Apparent to the Throne excited much commotion in the town, not only among the fashionable residents and visitors but the inhabitants generally. Nearly the whole population assembled on the Level (then immediately to the north of the Steine) to welcome His Royal Highness ; and as he approached Grove House, the Duke's residence (subsequently incorporated into the northern portion of the Pavilion), exulting acclamations rent the air, and these being subsequently responded to by the booming of cannon from the Fort and the merry pealing of the bells of St. Nicholas, testified to the general joy. Later in the day, in company with the Duke, the Prince promenaded the Steine, much to the gratification of the many groups assembled. Despite the sanctity of the day, there was a grand illumination of the town and Steine at night, together with a brilliant display of fireworks in the open space (now occupied by the Pavilion-parade, Prince's-street, the " Blue and Buff " houses, &c.,) opposite Grove House, from the windows of which the Prince and the Duke had an excellent view. The Prince stayed eleven days, during which the Duke did his best to render the visit a happy one. The Heir Apparent went to the Theatre ; to a ball at the Castle; he hunted; he bathed ; in fact, he enjoyed himself to his heart's content ; and, on his departure, expressed himself so much pleased with the town that there was every reason to hope for a second visit.*

---

* Both the Prince and the Duke were evidently in high spirits during the visit. On the Tuesday after the Prince's arrival they indulged in a little frivolity, and paid for it! The Hon. Thomas Onslow (a gentleman well-known to the Prince) was, we are told, "driving his gig in at one of the gates of the palisades before the Duke of Cumberland's house at Brighthelmston, when he ran foul of the fence, which occasioned the Prince of Wales and the Duke of Cumberland, who were at the same time looking out of a window, jocularly to arraign his charioteering skill. This induced Mr. Onslow to offer their Royal Highnesses a bet of ten guineas each, that he drove four horses in his phaeton, the leaders galloping, through both the gateways twenty successive times without touching; the bets being accepted by their Royal Highnesses, the horses were immediately

The hopes of the inhabitants as to a second visit of the Prince were not disappointed. He came in July, 1784, occupying Mr. Kemp's house (situated on a spot immediately south of the present Saloon of the Pavilion).* He had been expected on the Thursday evening; and the town and Steine were in a blaze of illuminations in honour of the event. A large concourse of people assembled on the Steine to welcome the Royal visitor. Numbers waited till their patience was exhausted, and every light was out; and, even then, in vain, for he did not arrive until between three and four o'clock on Friday morning! The coming of the Prince, however, diffused universal delight. The Steine, it is said, had previously been "desolate;" but when the fact of the second Royal visit became known "company" daily increased. Among those who visited the Prince during his stay were the Duke de Chartres (M. l'Egalité), the Duc de Lauzan, the Marquis of Conflans, and the Russian Ambassador; and the presence of the Prince and his distinguished visitors upon the Steine, together with the throng of company, made up a scene of life and animation such as perhaps the place had never known before. His Royal Highness had, however, in his wake during this visit some undesirable associates, as Major Hanger, the Hon. Mr. Onslow, Sir John Lade, &c.; but as yet, beyond horse racing and riding, there was little heard of their exploits.

Among the notabilities of the season of 1784 were Lord Chief Justice Mansfield and William Pitt, the latter arriving in September, and staying for some weeks. Charles James Fox was here the same day as Pitt. It was rumoured that a "coalition" was being arranged; and it seemed as if the Prince was desirous of not being in any way connected with such an important matter, for he left the town the day previous.

In the following year the Prince's first visit (in June) was an "early morning" one; and again the illuminations of the previous evening were extinct long before his arrival! This mattered little to the townsfolk; for he was expected to stay all the summer. At all events, he seemed determined to make himself happy in his new marine villa, "50 dozen of wine being laid in for the use of His Royal Highness." Again was the town thronged with fashionable and distinguished visitors; and all the new houses on the East side of the Steine ready for occupation were full. The "company" on the Steine must, however, have been astonished at some of the Prince's out-of-door pastimes. (See p. 26.) His cricket on the Level with many noblemen and gentlemen was to another tune. He played, we are told, "with great condescension and affability," the spectators of both

---

put to, when Mr. Onslow mounted his phaeton and won his bets by performing the task with great ease and dexterity." Of Mr. Onslow's driving—possibly his *only* accomplishment—a rhymester of the period says:—

"What can Tommy Onslow do?
He can drive a chaise and two.
Tommy Onslow can do more—
He can drive a chaise and *four*!"

* The poet Rogers, when staying in Brighton some years ago, told a lady that when a boy he had dined at Mr. Kemp's house, which he characterised as a "respectable farm house."

sexes present expressing "great satisfaction at the engaging deportment of the Prince"! Major Hanger,—the irrepressible Hanger, the inseparable companion of the Prince at the time, much to George III.'s chagrin,—had in September a "field day" on the Steine; namely, a foot-race between his black servant and Scutt, the Horsham carrier. The news got abroad, and a "great part of the company at Brighton assembled round the Steine" in expectation of witnessing the race. They were disappointed; for the Horsham man, after much time had been spent in measuring the ground, determined to pay forfeit (10. 6d.). Hanger, we suppose, was equal to the occasion, for the assemblage had the felicity shortly afterwards of "seeing a race between five girls for a new smock, which afforded most excellent diversion, as did another female race for a hat." The Right Hon. William Pitt was sojourning on the Steine at the time. One wonders what he thought of the "diversion," and of the Prince's associates.*

During the next year or so, there is little to tell of the Steine, except the "old, old story" of the round of fashionable amusements. The Prince came and went; but debts, &c., at this period weighed somewhat heavily upon him. He chiefly occupied himself with the alteration of the Pavilion, and, except promenading the Steine with Mrs. Fitzherbert or a few friends, did not mingle much in society. But the world moved on. Visitors flocked hither. The Steine, the Rooms, and the Libraries were daily thronged with company; and "diversions" on the Steine were not unfrequent. One, however, was so extraordinary that we quote it as it appeared in a contemporary journal in August, 1786:—

"Last Thursday evening a very uncommon race was run at Brighthelmston. A military gentleman, ridden by a jockey, weighing 7st. 5lb., booted and spurred, ran with a fat bullock, unmounted, across the Steine for one hundred guineas, which was won easily by the former. A hat full of money might have been won: three, four, and five to one being offered on the loser, till at last nobody would take it. A great concourse of people were assembled to see this uncommon race, and to whom it afforded most excellent diversion."

A pretty exploit, truly, for a "military gentleman." "Frivolity" could not go much further.

In the following year visitors increased and multiplied. The "inhabitants were in high spirits from the flattering prospects of the ensuing season; and outvied each other in decorating their houses

---

* Pitt, during his journey to Brighton, in the previous week, had some experience of popular feeling in respect of the obnoxious Window Tax. Whilst horses were being changed at Horsham, he ordered *lights* for his carriage; and the persons assembled, learning who was within, indulged pretty freely in ironical remarks on *light* and *darkness*. The only effect upon the Minister was, that "he often laughed heartily." Whilst in Brighton, a country glove-maker hung about the door of his house on the Steine; and when the Minister came out, showed him a *hedger's cuff*, which he held in one hand, and a *bush* in the other, to explain the use of it, and asked him if the former, being an article he made and sold, was subject to a *Stamp Duty?* Mr. Pitt appeared rather struck with the oddity and bluntness of the man's question, and, mounting his horse, waived a satisfactory answer, by referring him to the *Stamp Office* for information!

outside and in." Other watering-places were now growing jealous of the " fishing village "; Margate and Lymington being in some of the London journals held up in competition with Brighthelmston; but (says the *Lewes Advertiser*) " of all the watering-places in the kingdom, the latter has, without dispute, by far the pre-eminence." The Prince of Wales had chosen it for his marine residence; and Fashion "followed suit." His Royal Highness came in July; and there were illuminations and the usual loyal demonstrations. Then followed the Duke and Duchess of Cumberland and suite; and later on a host of brilliant company. The Prince himself still affected "to share his social hours with a select few"; but the Steine was all life and gaiety, and the balls and assemblies, the libraries, the theatre, concerts, &c., were crowded with guests. Never before, probably, had the Steine been more thronged than on the morning of the Races in 1787, to see "the start" to the hill. There were, either on horseback or in their various equipages, the Prince and Mrs. Fitzherbert, the Duke and Duchess of Cumberland, the Princess de Lamballe,[*] Madame La Princesse Couronne, the Duke and Duchess of Richmond, the Duke of Bedford, the Duke of Queensbury, the Duchess of Aucaster, Lord George and Lady Lenox,[†] Lord Grosvenor, Lord Egremont, Lord Abergavenny, Lord Foley, Mr. Fox, &c. The Duke of York, with Prince William, came to Brighton in September. Though the season was waning, yet many visitors still came; and as a proof of the increase of company this year, it may be mentioned that Mr. Crawford's published list of names in his Library-book was "nearly 2,000 in number," and no previous list had ever contained more than 1,000.

It was stated in the *Lewes Journal* that the "company at Brighthelmston was never more respectable, nor more numerous"; but there must have been mingled with it some "choice spirits"; whether Hanger or others "of that ilk," deponent sayeth not. Practical joking on the Steine was rife. The great green-painted chair, well-known for its peculiar make, at Crawford's Library, was one night taken away bodily, and thrown into the sea, a part of it being subsequently picked up off Shoreham Harbour. On another night, the iron work which supported the painting of the P.W. feathers at the

---

[*] This charming but ill-fated lady, the widow of Louis of Savoy and mistress of the household to the Queen of France, was, in 1792, during the worst throes of the French Revolution, after a mock trial, savagely murdered, her beautiful form mangled and mutilated, and portions of it were trailed through the streets of Paris. Her head—with the fair auburn tresses, which once adorned it, besmeared with blood and dirt—was mounted on a pike amid a shout of triumph, and planted under the very windows of M. l'Egalité (Duke of Orleans), and thence carried to the Temple, where the Queen was confined, that she might also see it!

[†] So this name was originally spelt; but it is now and has been for many years spelt Lennox. Whether true or not, the alteration in the spelling is attributed to a witticism of the Prince of Wales. George III., when Prince of Wales, fell ardently in love with Lady Sarah Lenox; and only with the strongest reluctance consented to break off the connection for fear of breaking his mother's heart! When the Prince of Wales heard that his father, George III., while perambulating one of his farms near Windsor, had been pursued by one of the oxen grazing in the fields, "I am sorry for it," said the Prince, "but it is not the first time that my father has been in danger from a *Lean ox*."

front of Dulot's (late Thomas's) Library was wantonly torn down and thrown into a well. My Lord Barrymore, had he been in Brighton, would assuredly have been credited with these exploits; but the advent of that interesting young member of the Irish Peerage did not take place till August in the following year, 1788. He was then 18 years of age; his tastes being chiefly equestrian. He had not yet developed those "more rarer" accomplishments, when he was,

> "In the course of one revolving moon,
> Jockey, actor, coachman, and buffoon."

Sir John Lade must surely have "seen him coming"; for in less than a week after his arrival the worthy Baronet did a stroke of business with him—selling him a phaeton and eight greys for upwards of £1,000! Under Sir John's tuition His Lordship appeared to improve rapidly. The Baronet, doubtless, discoursed of stag-hunting; for Barrymore must needs have *his* stag-hunt. But His Lordship's first attempt, though it was a "sensation" and attracted a large number of sportsmen and spectators to the Race Ground, was a failure; as the stag, after running a few miles, directed his course seaward, and, jumping over the cliff, was killed. Another stag was subsequently turned out; but it did not seem to realise the "situation," and, instead of running, fell coolly to grazing! On being whipped, he ran full butt into the crowd, "putting to rout the *affrighted cockneys* who were formidably assembled to *figure away* in the chace, to the no small diversion of the more experienced sportsmen. The stag, then, as if resolved to throw them out before they had time to recover themselves and rally, set out over the hill, where he knocked down a shepherd that stood in his way, and, directing his course to Patcham, ran into the house of Mr. Paine there, where, after knocking down a maid-servant that attempted to stop him, he sought shelter in the pantry, and was there taken."*

Whilst His Lordship was indulging his equestrian tastes, one of his brothers seemed bent on "playing the fool." We noticed (page 26) this gentleman's freak of riding a horse up to Mrs. Fitzherbert's attic storey. The week after this, it appears, he indulged in another "sally of youth," officiating as *postillion* about the streets of the town to Mrs. Fitzherbert, "whose amiable condescension and great good humour during the performance seemed to give a zest to his capricious levities. Mr. Barrymore had a dress made for the purpose; his jacket was of *pink silk*, and otherwise well adapted to the elegance of the equipage, which made a grand and beautiful appearance." During their first visit to Brighton, two of the Barrymores (His Lordship and the gentleman just mentioned, who was subsequently known by the sobriquet of "Cripplegate," from his having a club-foot) had a horse race on the Downs, which attracted much company. His Lordship proved to be the better jockey of the

---

* "Stag-hunting" must have been "catching" at this time: for some two or three weeks later the Prince of Wales had a young deer turned out on the Steine, "for his and Mrs. Fitzherbert's diversion." They were, however, content to be spectators merely; being present in their carriages, which "did not follow chace."

two and won the stakes; "Cripplegate," however, after dismounting, looked at his misshapen foot, and said, "If I had put my spur on at the *toe*, instead of the heel, I should have won"!

The next three or four years, 1789-93, were perhaps the gayest and most brilliant epoch in the history of the Steine. It was the heyday of the Prince of Wales's pre-nuptial era, when, in the prime of early manhood, surrounded by gay companions, and with as yet no domestic infelicity, life passed pleasantly. Brighton was now his favourite resort; and his presence here attracted not only the nobility and gentry from all parts of the kingdom, but distinguished foreign visitors without number. From its proximity to the Pavilion, the Steine was daily the resort of the *beau monde*. Visitors to Brighton during the years above mentioned were "legion"; and among those who more frequently came were the Duke of Orleans and others of the French nobility, Prince Ferdinand Duke of Wurtemburg, the Duke and Duchess of Cumberland, the Duke and Duchess of Marlborough, the Dukes of Bedford, Grafton, Richmond, and Norfolk; Lords Egremont, Clermont, Egerton, Foley, Cavendish, Eardley, Grosvenor, and St. Asaph; the Wyndhams, the Pelhams, and the Leslies; the Lord Chief Baron Eyre; Ladies Long, Maitland, and Galway; Mrs. Fitzherbert, and other well-known ladies; Sir Ferdinand Poole; Sir Richard and Lady Heron, General Dalrymple and Colonel Tarleton; Mr. Fox, Mr. Addington, Mr. Gerald Hamilton, and many another notability of the time. Then there were the Jerseys, the Lades, and the Barrymores; Hanger and Lord Coleraine; and other "familiars" of the Prince. His Royal Highness and his Royal brothers, the Dukes of York and Clarence, with their more immediate associates, or it may have been with visitors at the Pavilion, invariably, "during the hours," walked on the Steine without restraint among the company, and accosted those whom they knew with politeness and good nature. The Steine at this period must have been gay enough; the balls, assemblies, &c., gayer still; and these varied social pleasures being supplemented by such ever-recurring attractions, as loyal demonstrations, field-days and reviews, races, &c., one may perhaps realize in some degree the truth of the following "Extempore Lines on Brighton," written in 1791 :—

> "Now for Brighton all repair,
> To taste the pleasures that flow there;
> Sure no place was e'er like this :
> All is pleasure, joy, and bliss."

Among the military displays of the period was a field day in May, 1791, in compliment to the Duke of Wurtemberg; but this was outshone by a review of the 10th Light Dragoons in May of the following year, the Prince of Wales being present, and over 5,000 spectators.* A few days after the Review the Duke of York came to

---

* These military displays served to divert His Royal Highness, who was smarting under the "Escape" affair. A moralist, writing from Brighton at the period, says : "Brighton is almost as gay and pleasant as it is in the middle of June. H.R.H. the Prince of Wales, Mrs. Fitzherbert, and many of the nobility graced the Steine. How much better this than to waste property and reputation with the *Jockey Club* at Newmarket?"

see the Prince; and there was a grand field day in his honour. The Duchess, from illness, was unable to come down, and this, adds a chronicler, was a "disappointment to the curiosity of many who had promised themselves a sight of Her Royal Highness's *foot*"! She, however, came down in August, when the Prince gave the Duchess a truly Royal welcome; and, in addition to many special amusements, there was a grand fête "on the Brighton Level; no fewer than four thousand persons were supposed to have attended, the majority to feast their eyes, while the others feasted more substantially on a fine ox, with a proportionable quantity of bread and strong beer prepared for the occasion. The ox was taken from the fire about three o'clock, and very skilfully dissected by Mr. Russell, at the bottom of a large pit, while the spectators and expectants stood in theatric gradation on its sloping sides. The day proved very favourable to this rustic festivity. His Royal Highness's guests were very accommodating and good humoured to each other until the strong beer began to operate. The Prince and Mrs. Fitzherbert looked on for a considerable time with great good humour, and had the satisfaction of hearing that no accident or injury occurred in so large a concourse except a few black eyes and bloody noses at the close of the evening."

There were, however, at this period, "amusements" and "field days," or rather "nights," of less questionable character; in which the notorious Barrymores were the chief actors, and of whose exploits we have previously spoken (pages 26 and 48). It is needless to recapitulate these frivolities, which, however, were evidently regarded by many of the townsfolk and others as very venial matters. For instance, one writer, speaking of the Noble Lord's departure, says:— "His fun and frolic has this season given life and *emolument* to Brighton"; and another, in 1792, coupling him with his equestrian mentor, says:—"Lord Barrymore and Sir John Lade, whose phaetonic exploits have given life and spirit to the Steine circle, have left Brighton for the season."* His Lordship, we might add, was not without imitators in the school of frivolity; for a chronicler, in 1790, tells us that, after the Races, "two gentlemen of rank and fashion at Brighton,

---

* This was, we believe, the last time Lord Barrymore was in Brighton; for, on March 5th, 1793, when only in his 24th year, a shocking accident terminated his existence. It appeared that, as a Captain in the Berkshire Militia, he was ordered with his Company to convey some French prisoners to gaol. He had with him his fusee, loaded with two balls, when near Folkestone, in Kent, by some accident, the piece went off, shattering part of his skull so fearfully that he expired immediately. It was very unusual for an officer commanding a party on the above service to march with his fusee loaded, but, considering the many eccentricities which marked the character of Lord Barrymore, it was not surprising that he should have improperly departed from the customary forms. He was seventh Earl of Barrymore, Viscount Buttevant, and Baron Barry of the Kingdom of Ireland. He was born August 14th, 1769, and succeeded his father August 14th, 1773. He had only some two or three months previous to his death married a niece of Lady Lade; and, there being no male issue. he was succeeded in his titles by Henry Barry, his eldest brother. Considerable property was, it appears, bequeathed by His Lordship's family to the lady whom he might marry, and to his heir. It was so left that he could not during his life receive any part of it; and this of course went to the Countess. Despite His Lordship's idiosyncrasies, juvenile follies, and extravagancies, he had some good qualities; among these, generosity was not the least, which led him into many of those expenses that in the end ruined his fortune.

to vary the scene of amusement, engaged in an *aquatic race*, and, dashing into the sea with all their clothes on, ran till the water reached their chins; but which beat we have not been able to learn."

But enough of this. Returning to the "company" who were accustomed to resort to the Steine in the seasons above mentioned, a visitor computed that there were there one evening in 1793 "in all about 3,000 persons"! He adds—"There was the most beautiful assemblage of ladies, dressed in all the ease and elegance that fancy can inspire; the ladies generally wore white, with single feathers in their hats or bonnets, and many of them in the shape of the Prince's helmet" (plume). The writer does not mention the *style* of hat worn; but in 1791-3, the merits and demerits of the "Gipsey" hat (worn then chiefly by ladies of an *uncertain* age) excited much talk. In spite of disparagement, the "Gipsey" triumphed; for a year later we learn "The rage for the Gipsey Hat is got to be very great among our fashionable BELLES"; the writer adding, "we cannot help expressing our surprize, seeing that it *Disfigures* so many more than it *Becomes*."*

The "heads" of the gentlemen, as well as those of the ladies, were at the time of equal concern to the votaries of Fashion. Following the military, the old-fashioned queues or "tails" were gradually being discarded by gentlemen; and the appearance on the Steine of those who were the first to discard the hirsute addition provoked endless comment and small wit among those who still clung to the original orthodox appendage. A contemporary publication thus alludes to the discontinuance of the "tail":—

"The hair dressers are in great trepidation about the new fashion of gentlemen having their heads sheer'd. The ladies, too, declare they never can admire any man who does not wear a tail. Many gentlemen who have adopted the *cropping* fashion, in order to shew their readiness to follow the *ton*, have the collars of their coats made to fall back and thus let all the world see what an elegant figure a gentleman is without a tail. A correspondent observes that it seems as if both the ladies and gentlemen who move in the fashionable circles had not only read the writings of that old-fashioned author, *St. Paul*, but also had reduced them to practice, for he says, 'If a man have long hair it is a shame to him, but if a woman have long hair it is a glory to her'; for the gentlemen, by the rapid progress of the docking mode, seem as if they were ashamed of their long tails; and, on the other hand, the ladies, by displaying such a profusion of long hair,

---

* A rhymester of the period,—a disappointed old bachelor, surely,—published the following in the *Lewes Journal*:—

THE ORIGIN OF VEILS AND GIPSEY HATS.

Miss Bridget, at fifty, a wrinkle found out.
  Won't paint hide ye? she cry'd in a passion;
Cunning Abigail answered: Dear ma'am, what a rout,
  Why I'd hide it by *setting a fashion*.
A *Veil* and *large Hat* well your Ladyship knows,
  Will cure this vile ravage of Time, *Mem*.
The pale yellow tints won't be known from the rose,
  Nor stale virgins from girls in the prime, *Mem*.
Array'd *à la mode* courtly Bridget was seen,
  Youthful damsels, like birds unfledg'd, taken
In *veils* and *slouch hats* ev'ry day fill the Steine,
  And Bridget a-while saves her bacon!

appear to glory in it. The gentlemen who submit to have their tails cut off evidently show their wisdom, and especially at this warm season of the year, for it must, without doubt, tend to keep their heads *cool*, which is of no small importance when we consider what a *hot-headed* age we live in."*

It should be mentioned that at this period, the Steine—thanks to the Prince of Wales and the Duke of Marlborough—underwent a great improvement. An arched sewer was constructed as a "receptacle" for the stream (or Wellsbourn) which flowed, at times, from the north level and Patcham well, into the Pool north of the Steine, and thence by the "Valley" to the sea. The pool being subsequently filled up, a long-standing cause of reproach by those frequenting the Steine was removed; and, as a considerable portion of the Steine was re-turfed and regularly mown and swept,—no games being allowed which would in any manner disturb the company resorting thereto, and care being taken to keep off all beggars and disorderly persons,—ladies and gentlemen and their children could walk there with the greatest safety and pleasure. So ran the "Regulations." These were, however, very often infringed; but, notwithstanding, the Steine had never previously been in such fine condition for the purposes of a fashionable promenade. Houses now ran along the whole of its eastern side, by the completion of what were then known as the North and South Parades (divided by St. James's-street). The house at the St. James's-street corner of the North Parade was the famous Subscription House of Raggett's. This was really a Club-House in the modern sense of the term; and, though the records referring to it are but scanty, there is little doubt that more than usually high play, even for Brighton, was indulged in. The *Topography of Brighton* (1808) says—"The dice here are often rattled to some tune, and bank notes transferred from one hand to another with as little ceremony as *bills* of the play, or quack doctors' *draughts* to their patients. †

Apropos of "Raggett's," Erredge's *History of Brighthelmston* gives a choice extract from a private diary, which, as illustrating certain sections of Brighton society in the olden time, is worth quoting:—

"August 2nd, 1792.—But little company stirred out to-day, on account of the intense heat of the weather. Sporting men of fashion, dashers, and blacklegs certainly assembled on the Steine, to make their bets for to-morrow's Lewes Races, where much excellent sport is expected. The other part of the day was spent mostly in Raggett's Subscription House, at billiards, dice, &c. *On dit* Lady Lade is returning from Brighton in

---

* Ladies, too, must have affected the fashion of "tails." The *Lewes Journal* of September 22nd, 1794, contains the following paragraph:—"Last Wednesday a hair-dresser was taken up at Brighton and brought before the Magistrates at Lewes, charged by Miss Monro with having stolen her TAIL, which she valued at *twenty-two shillings*. The lady having made good her charge to the satisfaction of the Magistrate, the prisoner's *mittimus* was made out; but being indulged with a little time before he was committed to the custody of the jailor, he sent to Brighton and procured bail, whereby he avoided the disgrace of a prison. But he is bound over to appear at our next Quarter Sessions to take his trial for this curious robbery."

† Raggett's ceased to exist some time prior to 1815. Its successor was a Club House, originally kept by Mr. Bedford in Steine-place, and thence removed to the South-parade, on the Steine, where it was for several years carried on by Mr. Wiick, formerly in the establishment of the Prince of Wales.

much dudgeon, because, forsooth, Lady Jersey, she says, made *wulgar* mouths at her yesterday on the race-ground!"

Late in the year 1792 the Steine was the scene of unwonted excitement, the occasion being the first assembling of the members of a Society, established at Brighthelmston, "for the Protection of Liberty and Property against REPUBLICANS and Levellers." The Society had its rise in the patriotic feeling of the time, which revolted against the horrible excesses that, in the name of Liberty, were then being perpetrated in France. It was, in fact, the beginning of the Volunteer movement, which afterwards was so spontaneously developed, not only in Brighton and the County, but in all parts of the kingdom. The movement was warmly taken up in Brighton, and cordially supported by the neighbouring gentry; and among those who, at a meeting at "The Castle Tavern," formed themselves into a Committee to "carry into effect the ends and purposes of this Society," were Sir John Bridger, Knt., the Rev. Thos. Hudson, the Rt. Hon. Sir R. Heron, Bart., W. Wade, Esq., the Rev. John Mossop, Mr. Wm. Attree, Samuel Shergold, Esq., H. Courthope Campion, Esq., W. S. Campion, Esq., Nathaniel Kemp, Esq., the Rev. J. Dodson, D.D., Charles Scrase Dickins, Esq., Mr. John Hicks, Mr. Thomas Tilt, Mr. John Rice, Mr. Nathaniel Hall, Mr. Nathaniel Blaker, Mr. Philip Mighell, Mr. Harry Attree, Mr. Ed. Cobby, Mr. Cornelius Paine, Mr. Bartholomew Smithers, Mr. James Vallance, Mr. John Vallance, Mr. James Charles Michell, &c. There was subsequently, it would appear, another meeting, on the 13th December, 1792, for the "purpose of entering into an Association"—in reality, for the embodiment of those who may be regarded as the "1ST BRIGHTON VOLUNTEERS"—which is thus described by a local chronicler:—

"A great number of gentlemen and others of this town and neighbourhood assembled here in the morning, and about ten o'clock set out in cavalcade to attend and support the meeting. A large body of yeomen from Hurst, Henfield, and places adjacent joined them on the road, and at the Prince's Cricket Ground they were met and headed by all the principal inhabitants of Brighton, with blue cockades and other emblems of loyalty. The whole formed a very grand and extensive procession, which, accompanied by a band of music, playing '*God save the King*,' paraded the principal streets of the town, admired and applauded, not only by the surrounding populace, but also by a large show of female beauty, whose pretty faces graced the open windows of almost every house, and among whom were some French ladies not the least conspicuous. In short, it was for Brighton the proudest day ever witnessed by the oldest inhabitant in that town, and such as its Royal Patron the *Heir Apparent* must see recorded with heartfelt satisfaction." *

---

* Another popular local Volunteer Corps, the "Sea Fencibles," were raised in March, 1798, Captain Sproule and Captain Brisbane visiting Brighton for that purpose. About 50 mariners immediately enrolled themselves, and there were subsequently numerous additions. The Brighton Sea Fencibles were trained to the use of the cannon and the pike, so as to be ready for the protection of the coast in case of any emergency: the extent of coast under the supervision of the Corps extended from Beachy Head to Selsey Bill. The Hon. Captain Berkeley was the first Commander-in-Chief of the Fencibles; the second in command being Lieutenant Bayden, Conductor of the Signal Tower at Seaford.

During the next two or three years there were wars and rumours of wars; camps were formed at Brighton; and, the Prince of Wales taking a lively interest in the military spirit of the time, there is little of special interest to recount respecting the Steine. It was, however, still the fashionable resort, though the Promenade Grove proved a strong counter-attraction; and the increase of the town itself tended to make it perhaps less exclusive than hitherto. A small camp was formed "near the Steine" in July, 1794. The West Suffolk regiment furnished the first day's guard; the Sussex followed; and the other regiments of Militia in daily rotation. The establishment of the above guard occasioned a ridiculous report, viz., that a project had been formed in France for getting possession of the person of the Prince of Wales by means of a smuggling boat, the proprietors of which were said to have been bribed for that purpose!

One of the most alarming events in connection with the Steine was "The Flood of January, 1795," which in its disastrous effects would appear to have greatly resembled the Pool Valley Flood of 1850. The winter of 1795 was exceedingly severe. During the whole of January there had been a hard frost; the thermometer on one day registering 1½ degrees below zero. There had, too, been heavy falls of snow; and the circumjacent hills were covered. During the night of Monday, the 26th, a rapid thaw with rain took place; when the water, running in torrents from the hills, completely deluged the Level, Castle-square, the Pool, and the whole of the Steine to the depth of several feet. The ground floors and cellars of many of the houses in Castle-square were filled, and furniture was all afloat. The wine vaults of "The Castle" were flooded; and it was only by the continuous use of pumps that Mr. Tilt was enabled to save his valuable stock. The immense body of water flowed seawards by its natural channel, the Pool Valley; and here it accumulated to a depth of seven and a half feet! Pouring into Sir John Bridger's stables (situated between "The Cat and Wheel"—St. Catherine's Wheel, subsequently "The Duke of Wellington"—and the old Baths), three valuable horses were drowned in their stalls. The rush of water from the Steine into the Pool Valley was by the open spaces on each side of Mr. Crawford's Library, which was soon partly undermined; and, "in attempting to turn the course of the water from his house, Mr. Crawford and his shopman were swept away by the force of the current. But for the assistance of Mr. Wigney, the Constable, they must inevitably have been lost, as it was with the utmost difficulty he prevented their being carried out to sea."

But we must change the theme. In the following May Brighton was on the *qui vive*, in expectation of the visit of the Prince of Wales and his newly-wedded wife, the Princess Caroline of Brunswick. The "happy pair" arrived on the 18th June, staying at Mr. Gerald Hamilton's house on the Steine, the Pavilion not being ready for their reception. There were the usual demonstrations of joy; but the weather was wretched, the rain in the evening putting out the illuminations. The news of the arrival of the Prince and Princess at Brighton soon attracted visitors hitherward; and in July, it was said, they were never more numerous. At the Races there was a brilliant gathering, which included H.R.H. the Prince of Wales; Prince Ernest, the Stadtholder; the Dukes of Marlborough, Beaufort, and Bedford; Lords Egremont, Clermont, Gage, Abergavenny, Pelham, Sackville, G. H. Cavendish, F. Spencer, Villiers, and Sheffield; Sir William Ashburnham, Sir C. Bunbury, Sir J. Shelley, Sir F. Poole, Sir H. Featherston, Sir C. Burrell, Sir F. Evelyn, Sir Godfrey Webster, the Right Hon. M. Pelham, with a long *et cetera* and a brilliant display of beauty.* The "M.C." gave in September a grand ball in honour of the Royal visitors. The Steine, of an evening, was literally thronged and gay enough; the Theatre, too, was crowded whenever they attended; and there were field-days and other Royal amusements. The Stadtholder, whilst in Brighton, was as "happy as a Prince": he promenaded the Steine and went to the balls; he accompanied the Prince to a masquerade in the Promenade Grove; he went to the Camp and reviewed the 10th, &c. He also went to the Theatre; but whilst there he appeared to be under the "influence of some *somniferous potion, for he slept during the whole evening*"! Later in the year the Duke and Duchess of York came down, when there was another grand review, so that during the four or five months of the Prince and Princess's stay the town and the Steine were all life and gaiety; though it would appear the Princess did not enter into it with much zest, but rather seemed to prefer retirement. Their Royal Highnesses left Brighton in November, and the Princess never again returned. She was, however, expected in the following year. But the Prince came alone, and the Jerseys—bitter enemies of the Princess—were not long after him; Her Ladyhip staying at the house formerly occupied by Mrs. Fitzherbert, on the Pavilion-parade, "which overlooked the Pavilion," and My Lord finding quarters at the house of Mr. Weltjie!

During the next year or two the Prince's domestic troubles were rife; his military tastes, too, were now in the ascendant; and he did not mingle in the pleasures of the Steine so much as heretofore. But, nevertheless, visitors came to Brighton in larger numbers than ever; and, in spite of continuous building, "accommodation" was at a premium. There is, however, little of interest to record in connection with the Steine and its associations. To speak of the Rooms, with their card assemblies, balls, &c., would be to repeat an oft-told tale. We might, perhaps, allude to an edict issued by the Dictator, the "M.C." at this period, which would lead to the inference that the regions of Fashion were being invaded by some persons ignorant of the usages of "polite assemblies":—

"The Master of the Ceremonies requests that gentlemen will have the goodness not to neglect themselves by appearing with strings in their shoes and round hats, particularly of a ball night, as that MODE of dress is totally abolished in all polite assemblies."

The Libraries, it may be added, were still largely patronized. Dulot's (late Thomas's) had changed hands; the proprietor now

---

* It is not recorded that the Princess accompanied the Prince to the Races. Most probably she did, as she went with him to Lewes Races a day or two after.

being Mr. James Gregory, who was assisted by his brother, Mr. Richard Lemmon Gregory.*

On the last day of November, 1798, the Princess Amelia, the amiable and affectionate youngest daughter of George III., paid her first visit to Brighton. She was then in her 15th year, and is described "as rather tall and very handsome; and was dressed in a light-coloured riding-habit and a close cap tied under the chin with broad lace." This estimable young lady had been staying at Worthing for some months—a veritable martyr to that baneful hereditary disease of her family which subsequently hurried her to her tomb. The Prince of Wales went more than once to see her whilst at Worthing; and doubtless he spoke of the Pavilion and the Steine, which gave rise to her wish to see Brighton, though scarcely able to endure the journey. Her Royal Highness came in one of His Majesty's coaches, drawn by four horses, and was accompanied by Lady A. Cumberland and a gentleman. The Royal carriage, preceded by General and Miss Goldsworthy in a curricle, and attended by General Cuyler on horseback, was drawn very slowly round the Pavilion and Steine, up North-street and down West-street, where it halted for a few minutes at the house of General Cuyler, whose lady waited on the Princess at the carriage door and politely invited Her Royal Highness to alight or to take some refreshment in the coach, both which she with great affability declined, and, taking leave of Mrs. Cuyler, proceeded with her retinue by the lower road on her return to Worthing.

In the first few years of the present century the Steine reached its highest point as the resort of "company"; and, though frequented by far greater numbers, in these years, it in many respects resembled those of 1790-93—the previous most brilliant epoch in its history. Never before had there been within its circumference such a throng of high-born and wealthy and more or less distinguished visitors; and, day after day, evening after evening. during the fashionable hours, it was all animation—all gaiety. In the autumn of 1802, though visitors had previously been "legion," the cry was, "still

---

* Mr. Richard Lemmon Gregory, like one or two other of the Steine Librarians, was a "local character," and known to every visitor. He was subsequently associated with the Libraries in North-street; first at Choat's and then at Loder's. He died in 1851, and the following valedictory notice of him appeared in the *Brighton Herald*: —" Very many of the old inhabitants of the Town will remember a smart, dapper, active, brisk little old man, who dressed in corduroy knee-breeches, speckled worsted stockings, tie-low shoes, a dark-figured swansdown waistcoat, a dark brown single-breasted coat, cut like a Quaker's, and who for many years catered to their literary wants in the Libraries. This was the veritable 'Dick Gregory,' who has just shuffled off this mortal coil in his 84th year. He was remarkably clean in his person; though any thing certainly but a fop. His thin grey hairs he smoothed over his brow, and his face was always radiant with smiles. He had a sharp, ready answer for every one, and every one used to like a gossip with 'Dick Gregory.' He thought for himself; no man more so. He possessed a sturdy mode of reasoning, with gentle or simple—no matter which—and which he never disguised; yet he could say sharp and distasteful things to high-flown Tories, but in a style that amused and rarely, if ever, offended; for all the frequenters of the Library knew what sort of answers—if they put questions—they were likely to get from Dick. He was full of anecdotes, and told them with a gusto that kept the attention of the

they come"; for, says a chronicler, the "attraction is irresistible, and the town was never known to be so full in the middle of October"; and another states, "the Steine was lively even in November." This must surely have been the "Golden Age" of lodging-house keeping in Brighton! Over 100 houses had been built in the previous ten years, yet "accommodation" was insufficient. In the next year or two, the want was still felt; in 1804, perhaps more so. So early as in May of this latter year it was said, "the Steine is increasing in gaiety and fashion." In July, such was the desire to reach Brighton, that, irrespective of visitors brought daily by the numerous coaches, "at Cuckfield and Crawley, in one day, no less than 50 pairs of horses were in requisition for conveyances to that distinguished place of public resort." During race-time, by reason of the influx of sporting men, &c., matters in the way of accommodation reached a climax. Every available place—regardless, in many cases, of very scant convenience—was occupied; and the disappointed, though willing to pay any price, had to go elsewhere—to Hove, Rottingdean, or wherever it was thought they could obtain a night or two's accommodation. The French "invasion" scare was at its height in 1804; and Brighton—from its being the favourite residence of the Prince of Wales—was regarded as *the* spot for Napoleon to land his troops! But this did not deter visitors from coming hither. The *Lewes Weekly Advertiser*, in September of that year, says:—" Brighton still retains a very considerable portion of its company; and, regardless of Master Boney's threats of invasion, the Steine is daily promenaded by crowds of beauty, elegance, and fashion." For several succeeding years, the influx of visitors "knew no retiring ebb"; but to chronicle details would be needless repetition.

One reason, probably, for the rapidly-increasing popularity of Brighton at this period was the fact that the Prince of Wales was more frequently here than heretofore, and his visits were more or less prolonged. He mingled more in society; the entertainments at the Pavilion resumed their former brilliancy; and that gaiety and hilarity in which he delighted,—and which his domestic troubles of the last few years had somewhat clouded,—was again in the ascendant. The Prince, in fact, had now wholly "emancipated" himself from his wife;

---

listener wide awake. Poor Dick! We believe that every soul that knew him liked him. He possessed some property—it has been said that he had claims to much more; at any rate, when years induced him to retire from a vocation he had long followed—librarian—he had enough and to spare, and no man of late enjoyed his *otium* more than Dick. It was quite joyous to see the capers he cut when above eighty, to show that he was as agile as ever; that he could play cricket, of which he was very fond, as well as any boy; and he would challenge any man at half his age to run a mile. He had formed his reasoning for himself, and all the eloquence or logic in the world had no effect whatever on Dick. He knew every body that came to Brighton, and most of them, from the 'man in green' to Macnamara, knew him. He could tell numberless tales off-hand about the American war, when he was a boy; about the first Revolution in France, and how he had seen the priests who came over in a hurry and landed in shoals at Newhaven. His laugh was a sort of crowing—so sharp, clear, cheering, we doubt if he ever knew what the 'blues' are. He was never 'hipped' an hour; but sunshine and smiles always dwelt on his small but handsome features. He died in the 84th year of his age, and will always rank as one of the *characters* of the town. Peace to his manes!"

Colonel Dalrymple. Mr. Trevor, sen. Mr. Day. Earl Craven. Earl Berkeley. Prince of Wales. Duke of Grafton.
Lord Sefton. Sir John Lade. Bp. of St. Asaph. Major Blomfield.
Earl Clermont. Mr. Mellish.
Martha Gunn. Mr. Wilberforce.

THE STEINE AT BRIGHTON IN 1805.

(WITH "THE CASTLE TAVERN," THE ROYAL PAVILION, AND DONALDSON'S LIBRARY.)

THE STEINE AND ITS ASSOCIATIONS.

Mrs. Fitzherbert had renewed her old attachment to him; and Parliament, in 1803, having added £60,000 to his yearly income, he did his best to render himself happy and content. It was no wonder, therefore, that visitors came hither; that the Steine, which His Royal Highness and his associates daily frequented, was thronged. Possibly, during the years mentioned (1800—1807), Brighton was honoured with the presence of more distinguished visitors than at any former period. In addition to the Prince of Wales and his Royal Brothers,—the Dukes of York, Clarence, Kent, Sussex, and Cambridge,—there were the Russian Princess Galitzen and the Countess Garebtzoff; the Stadtholder; the Duke of Orleans and his brother, Count Beaujolais; the Imperial and Spanish Ambassadors; General Dumourier;* the Duke of Argyle, the Duke and Duchess de Caistres, the Duke and Duchess of Marlborough, and the Duke of Richmond; the Marchioness of Clanricarde, the Marquis and Marchioness of Devonshire, and the Marquis of Headfort; the Earl of Egremont, the Earl and Countess of Berkeley, the Earl Craven, the Earl of Darlington, the Earl and Countess of Kenmare, the Earl of Clermont, the Countess Lauderdale, the Countess of Sefton, and Viscount and Viscountess Gage; Lord Thurlow, Lord Erskine, and Lord Arthur Somerset; General Dalrymple, General Hulse, and General Lee; General and Lady Charlotte Lennox, Lady Fortesque, Lady Anne Murray, and Lord and Lady Pelham; Sir C. Burrell, Sir Thomas Bridges, and Sir Robert and Lady Baker; Mrs. Fitzherbert and her interesting ward, the Hon. Miss Seymour, and many another of rank and title. Then there were Pitt and Sheridan; and the Prince's more intimate associates, the Barrymores, the Jerseys, and the Lades. To the list of visitors might be added a host of sporting men of the period, including Captain Barclay, Captain Crampton, Mr. Mellish, Mr. Burke, Mr. Derby, Mr. Clark, Mr. Dalton, &c.; and some few "characters," as Mr. Day ("Gloomy" Day) and Mr. Cope (the "Green Man"). Upon the latter's harmless eccentricities and subsequently sad end, we need not dilate; "are they not fully written in local chronicles?"

The Steine was, at this period, the one spot to which all resorted and where all commingled: Royal and noble, the titled and wealthy, and others of small repute; adventurers and hangers-on; sporting men, "dashers," prize-fighters, and others "of that ilk." The many groups promenading in every variety of costume, and the splendid equipages and numerous equestrians lining the roads outside the Steine, must altogether have made up a charming *coup d'œil*. The ladies' costumes were, for the most part, very elegant. The summer costume was, generally, a white dress; but the head-dresses were varied: some wearing a gold *bandeau*, from which was suspended a

---

* General Dumourier was made much of by the Prince of Wales whilst in Brighton He dined at the Pavilion, and a field-day was held in his honour. As a matter of course, the General promenaded the Steine; and a contemporary journal, alluding to his visit, says—" On the Steine, General Dumourier appears the very centre of attraction, the notice and attention which he commands in the higher circles leave no doubt of his having for ever abandoned to his destiny the ambitious Corsican Usurper."

beautiful veil; others preferring a gipsy hat, and pink, lilac, or white mantles; the parasols were brown, trimmed with white lace; and "some of the first rate *élégantes* wore dove-coloured stockings and shoes." We give, however, in full, the "Fashions" for August, 1807:—

MORNING WALKING DRESS FOR LADIES.—A plain white cambric robe; a short train, made high, so as to wrap straight over the bosom to the left side, and continue open to the bottom; the back of the dress is cut square from the shoulders, and is drawn in the waist to a narrow point; long full sleeves; the bottom of the robe is inlet with two rows of rich point lace, about half a quarter distance from each other; a small French cloak, composed of white silk floss net, lined throughout with rich lilac sarsnet; it is pulled into a narrow band of lilac sarsnet, laced square across the back, fastened on the left shoulder, and is brought over the right with a long strip of sarsnet and tassel, covered with net. A double diamond straw jockey bonnet, trimmed with a quilting of white lace over the right eye, and a small wreath of lilac roses across the front of the bonnet, tied with a lilac silk handkerchief.

AN EVENING FULL DRESS FOR LADIES.—A beautiful pink blossom Italian crape, body and train made with an apron front, which descends to the bend of the knee, trimmed with a broad Brussels lace, worn over a soft white satin slip, ornamented round the border with a magnificent border of hearts-ease, worked with pearls; white satin sleeves made plain and short and worked at the edge with a small wreath of hearts-ease to correspond with the dress; the back made very low and square, inlet in the middle with rich point lace; the bosom easily full, drawn very low down at each corner of the neck, with a crooked pearl slide to separate the bosom; a rich pink girdle, with large full tassels, intermixed with pearls, fastens the waist, and reaches nearly to the extremity of the dress; the hair bound straight across the top of the head, combed smooth on the right side of the head, and lies flat on the face, in an irregular form; long ringlets from the left eye, and from behind the right ear; a rich tiara of pearls in front. Earrings and necklace of *dead* gold. Gloves and shoes of pale pink silk.

MORNING FULL DRESS FOR GENTLEMEN.—An olive-green double-breasted coat, white waistcoat and trousers. UNDRESSES for MORNING are composed of light green mixtures; the latter is called the parsley mixture, which is beginning to usurp the preference—these coats are worn single-breasted, with collars of the same cloth, and almost universally a plaited button; they are also shorter than the evening coats, made without pocket flaps, and rendered as light as possible. Printed striped quilting waistcoats, single breasted, and without binding. Light coloured kerseymere pantaloons and gaiters, or breeches and gaiters; white or Nankin trousers, with or without gaiters, and some few striped trousers.

EVENING DRESS.—Dark blues, with flat gilt buttons, and in general with collars of the same; and forest green, with collars of the same cloth, or of black velvet, according to the fancy of the wearer. The buttons on green coats are guided by fancy. White waistcoats are universal. Breeches are generally of Nankin or light drabs and pearl-coloured kerseymeres.

Company invariably "did" the Steine at the prescribed "hours;" and there was no lack of amusements. In addition to the usual round at the libraries, at the assemblies, &c., there were not unfrequently "bands of Savoyards, with hand organs, tambourines, &c."

There was, too, scarcely a day which did not produce a horse-race or an interesting cricket-match in close proximity to the town; and sometimes matches so ridiculous that it is difficult to characterize them; though they failed not to attract hundreds of lookers-on. The character of these matches may be judged of from the following extract from the *Annual Register*, of 20th August, 1803:—

"A whimsical exhibition took place on the race ground at Brighton. Captain Otto, of the Sussex Militia, booted and mounted by a grenadier of 18 stone weight, was matched to run 50 yards against a pony carrying a feather to run 150; but Captain Otto's rider tumbled over his neck, which he was very near cracking, and consequently he lost the bet. The next match was the same gentleman mounted by the same grenadier, to run 50 yards against a noble lord carrying a feather who was to run 100. He was considerably distanced by the latter."

"Company" in those days must have been easily amused! In 1805, we are told, "to vary the amusements, donkey races were introduced (on the Level) which created much mirth and laughter, in a large and *elegant* assemblage of spectators," who subsequently adjourned to the Steine to see the conclusion of the programme, namely, jingling matches and jumping in sacks.

The Royal Princes and their companions occasionally indulged in "pastimes"—or frivolities—on the Steine, which appeared to afford much diversion. On one day, we are told, Messrs. Mellish, Burke, Derby, and Crampton—well-known sporting-men of the day and associates of the Prince of Wales—laid bets on leaping over handkerchiefs, rails, &c.; Mr. Crampton carrying off the honours. This was followed by a running match between Mr. Mellish and Mr. Hawke; and, though 5yds. were given him, Mr. Mellish came off second best. Then "Young Brighton,"—of whom there was, doubtless, on such occasions, a numerous gathering,—was put on its mettle; match after match being run by boys, the gentlemen betting on their respective favourites. The week following, Mr. Crampton did some extraordinary acrobatic feats on the Steine for the diversion of the Prince and his companions, Earl Barrymore, Sir John Lade, and others. Mr. Crampton first jumped over the rails of the Steine; then over the Earl of Barrymore's horse; and finished by turning a somersault! After such public exhibitions as these, under the auspices of the Prince of Wales, one is somewhat astonished at the following paragraph in the *Lewes Journal* relating to Brighton —"The higher circles here are waiting with impatience the arrival of the Prince, to whose elegance of deportment and amiableness of disposition may be attributed the pre-eminent attractions of the fashionable amusements of Brighton." When His Royal Highness did arrive, we learn from a paragraph in a metropolitan journal (September, 1805):—" The return of the Prince to this place has given new life to its collective population. Hilarity predominates in the circles of Fashion, and the rays of cheerfulness extend to the most humble purlieus of the town." Both Royal and Noble would, however, seem to have been easily amused, judging by the same writer's description of a "morning on the Steine":—"The

Prince was an equestrian this morning for some time, and afterwards appeared as a pedestrian on the Steine. Earl and Countess Craven amused themselves in passing round and round this elegant walk, in their phaeton, followed by out-riders in crimson liveries. The Duke and Duchess of Marlborough occasionally were on the lawn in front of Marlborough House. Lady Amelia Spencer paid her usual wholesome morning visit to the Downs in her chariot; Lord and Lady F. Spencer took a similar course in their phaeton. The equipages of the Marchioness of Downshire, Lord Thurlow, Lady Alvanley, Lady James, &c., were also in motion."

On the Prince of Wales's birthday, August 12th, 1807, there was a walking-match against time on the Steine; a man aged 65 engaging to go 18 times round the inner railing—6 miles—within one hour and five minutes. The match attracted a large concourse of the nobility and gentry; and betting was lively. It was done within the time.

"Events," however, of a less attractive character sometimes took place on the Steine; for in the early part of the century it was ill-lighted* and, under the scant surveillance of the old watchmen ("Charlies"), ill-protected,—and, after dark, would seem to have needed wary walking. An advertisement in the *Brighton Herald*, of June 30, 1810, respecting an occurrence there, tells its own tale:—

"WHEREAS, some sanguinary Villain, in some sort of undress uniform and white trousers, armed with a sword and dirk, attacked the Subscriber on the Steine, between the hours of nine and ten o'clock on Wednesday night, supposed with an intent to assassinate him; the Subscriber will be much obliged to any gentleman to inform him of the Villain—as it was dark when he made his escape from the assault, and he could not see his features. WILLIAM FINLASON."

Whether or no the "sanguinary villain" was discovered, is not recorded. We hope he was, and fitting punishment meted out to him!

The "Associations" of the Steine would be incomplete without some allusion to the "donkeys." These patient animals seemed in the early part of the century to have become a "fashionable" institution. Originally used by children for taking airings, they were subsequently not only requisitioned by ladies, but valetudinarians of the hardier sex seemed to think it no degradation to ride abroad on the patient quadrupeds. In the season, therefore, "donkey tours" to Rottingdean, Preston, &c., were of daily occurrence; the animals being caparisoned *à la mode de Steine*, whatever this might mean; and we are told "It is no uncommon sight to behold a *Jerusalem pony* compelled to groan and sweat beneath a weight of double its own ponderance; for dowagers of twenty stone at least conceive that they are equally entitled to the fashionable donkey mode of killing time, with the slender miss who has but just made an encroachment in her teens." The reign of "donkeydom" as a fashionable institu-

---

* It was lit simply by old-fashioned oil-lamps, placed round it at intervals; it was first lit by gas on May 3rd, 1824.

tion—that is, in their use by adults—was but of a few years' duration; for in 1807 we learn that they were gradually getting into disuse, being superseded by neat little ponies, which were deemed "far more elegant, and were generally preferred by the belles." The poor animal was thenceforth abandoned to the use of children; and has ever since performed its duty as patiently as if its predecessors had never tasted the sweets of an exalted occupation!

In concluding the notice of the Steine, we may briefly summarize some of the more important changes which it underwent after 1800. Early in the year 1806 it was improved by the addition of a spacious brick path all round, within the rails, and for the better preservation of the turf in the centre a neat fence was put up, to prevent traffic over it in the winter, by leaving only the intended circular walk and the bricked road across open. The new fence was intended to be taken away during the summer season, and replaced on the approach of every succeeding winter. The expence of the undertaking was defrayed by voluntary subscription.

In December, 1805, the original Library, on the East side of the Steine, at the corner of St. James's-street, built by Mr. Baker in 1760, was pulled down by Mr. Donaldson, the then proprietor; it being too dwarfish to admit of suitable improvement by additions. The new edifice, of noble elevation and dimensions (as we now see it, though the lower portion of it has since been much altered), was opened in June, 1806, the Prince of Wales graciously paying Mr. Donaldson the compliment of appointing him bookseller and librarian to His Royal Highness. In connection with the Libraries, it may be mentioned that *raffling* was done away with after the passing of an Act of Parliament familiarly known as Mr. Vansittart's "Little-go Bill." This proved at first a sad drawback to the profits of the Librarians, as the dice-box had been the chief means of disposing of the multifarious kinds of ware which, in addition to books, &c., they were accustomed to keep. To remedy the deficiency, *trinket auctions* were had recourse to; the "Auction Lounge" becoming associated with the Library; and of an evening, when the respective Librarians practised "knock-down-blows" with their "magnetic hammers," there were crowded assemblages of the *beau monde*. One enterprising Librarian, Mr. Wilks (some time associated with Mr. Donaldson) had a "Pic-nic Auction" on the Steine itself, which, we are told, "exhibited a blaze of rank and beauty." The novelty, however, of these trinket auctions soon wore off; and the Librarians disposed of their wares in the ordinary way. To provide a substitute for raffling, "Pam," or "Loo," was revived, and, being supplemented by "lively and enchanting music, vocal and instrumental," it maintained its attractive influence for some years more. The position of "Loo," as a fashionable pastime, was, however, rudely assailed in 1810, by an attempt being made to constitute it an illegal game. For that purpose, information was lodged against Messrs. Donaldson and Walker, the proprietors of the Steine and Marine Libraries, and the case was heard at Lewes before a full Bench of Magistrates. It being pointed out that the Magistrates really had no jurisdiction in the matter, the case was dismissed; and the Librarians returned home rejoicing, and " Pam " was, for the time, more popular than ever.

The general characteristics of the Steine at this period (about 1807-8) would seem scarcely recognizable to a modern Brightonian, though there were some general points of correspondence. The Steine was then unquestionably the prettiest part of Brighton ; and very picturesque, with the sea in front ; the Marine-parade (with gaps at intervals) stretching eastward, with wooden posts and rails running along the broken edge of the cliff, itself often shelving down to the beach ; while to the north, beyond the line of handsome houses skirting each side of the broad green-sward, a glimpse was obtainable of grand old Hollingbury-hill. The Steine itself was of greater extent than now, especially to the south and east. It was undivided, except by a footpath across its centre, from Castle-square to St. James's-street. It was, too, for the most part, skirted by a foot-path; and the only pieces of carriage-road in connection with it were on the east and west sides, and to the south-east. If, therefore, it were desired to drive a vehicle from Castle-square to the "Blue and Buff" houses (to the north of the Steine) it was necessary to proceed southward, along the west side of the Steine, into Pool-valley ; round the back of Steine-place (now occupied by the York Hotel), and across the south end of the Steine (in front of Russell House); thence along the east side, round the back of Donaldson's Library (now the Railway booking-office, &c.), and down St. James's-street, whence, passing along the east side of the north part of the Steine, the destination was reached. A pretty circuit, truly, to get from one place to another not fifty yards distant !

This inconvenience was endured for nearly twenty years ; down, in fact, to the year 1826. The delay, probably, arose from the desire of some of the townspeople to preserve the Steine intact as a promenade. But this was no longer possible in the face of modern requirements and the changes taking place on every hand. The Steine was not now the only fashionable promenade; for the sea-front to the west was being opened up, and visitors could and did resort thither. On the Steine itself a new order of things was apparent. In 1822-3 it had been enclosed with iron fencing ; George IV. giving £500 and the Town Commissioners £500 towards the improvement.* The York Hotel had supplanted Steine-

---

* The local fishermen strongly opposed this improvement. They had, says a contemporary journal, "from time immemorial enjoyed the privilege of drying their nets on the Steine, and removing their boats thither in tempestuous weather, paying for these privileges to the Lords of the Manor or their Reeve, a roeve, consisting of six mackerel for every boat, as often as such boats, severally, had landed to the number of one hundred long tale, six score and twelve, but not otherwise. The Commissioners contended that this rent proved the fishermen to be but tenants at will. It was not proposed to shut them out of the privilege of drying their nets on the Steine ; but the aborigines demanded a gate in connection with the new fencing of sufficient width to admit their boats in case of necessity. They further alleged there existed a document, dating from the reign of Elizabeth, in which a grant was made of the Steine to the fishers and to their heirs for ever. The existence of the document was, however, regarded as apocryphal, especially as rent had been regularly paid

place; "The Castle" Tavern, after sinking into decadence, was absorbed into the Royal domain; and the Albion Hotel was being erected on the site of Russell House. Accordingly, in 1826, the town authorities formed, simultaneously with the Western Esplanade (beyond the Battery to Regency-square and westward), the carriage road round the southern portion of the Steine in front of the York Hotel; and this may be regarded as the first substantial effort to adapt the Steine to the growing necessities of modern Brighton.

But even with this improvement, the adaptation was incomplete; for, during nearly another ten years, the foot-path across the Steine was the only direct communication between Castle-square and St. James's-street, and the only carriage entrance into the town from the north was by the present New-road! The inconvenience occasioned by the want of a carriage road in each of these directions is indescribable; but their formation met with strong opposition, chiefly from parties interested in property on the Steine, which they thought would be affected by this diversion of the traffic. The Commissioners, however, resolved that it should be done; but the Steine being vested in certain Trusts, decreeing that it should be kept as a public promenade for ever, and an injunction from Chancery being threatened, a Vestry Meeting on this subject was convened, the result showing that the majority of the inhabitants were in favour of the respective roads being made. Fortified by this result, the Commissioners lost no time in the matter. Early on the following Monday morning a great number of men were set to work, and in a few hours the pavements round and between both the Steine enclosures, with the iron fencing, posts, rails, &c., were removed; the mould and coomb rock were taken up, chalk and flints laid down, and some time before the day was over the new roads were made and vehicles passed to and fro! The first coach which passed from St. James's-street was the "Defiance" (how appropriate the name!), and the first that left Castle-square by the new exit northward for London was the "Extra Times." A chronicler adds—"The change which has been effected is so great that visitors will hardly recollect the Brighton Old Steine again."

At this point we will take our leave of "The Steine and its Associations."

---

from time immemorial. The demand of the fishermen not being complied with, they opposed the progress of the work, and dragged two large boats on to the Steine, leaving them, one at the southern, and the other at the western, boundary. The works were consequently suspended, and a meeting was called at the Old Ship, at which Committees were appointed to discuss the matter *pro* and *con*, their decision to be final. The opposition to the works was deemed to be futile, and the enclosure of the Steine by the curb and iron fencing was completed."

Notable Houses on the Steine.

THE MANOR HOUSE—THE YORK HOTEL.

THE Royal York Hotel is somewhat happy in its associations with the past. Few Brightonians are, probably, aware of the fact that the house which formerly occupied the site of the present Hotel, "Stein House," was the Manor House of the Manor of Brighthelmston. Over 100 years since it was occupied by Mr. Scrase, who, in 1771, purchased of Mr. Henry Sparrow a moiety of the Manor of Brighton.*

In 1779 the Manor House was of very modest proportions; and there were then but three private houses it its vicinity. It was two stories in height; was built of red brick, and had a slate roof; the windows, &c., being of a very primitive character. The land round the house to the north and east, which was enclosed by plain wooden palings, was "formerly part of the Tenantry Down, and enclosed with the consent of the tenant." The back of the house was literally "on the beach,"—no road along the sea-front then existed,—and at

---

* This Mr. Richard Scrase (a descendant of "Richard Scras, of Blatchington," who would appear to have had some connection with the Manor of Brighton in the time of James I.) was born at Seaford, in 1709. He was Town Clerk of Seaford in 1733; and most probably removed thence to Brighton in 1771. He died in 1792, bequeathing his moiety of the Manor to his grandson, Charles Dickins, on condition of his taking the name and arms of Scrase in conjunction with those of his own family. It was to Mr. Richard Scrase, there is little doubt, that we indirectly owe the coming of the Thrales to Brighton and subsequently taking up their residence in the town. Mrs. Masson, in an interesting paper (*Mrs. Thrale: the friend of Dr. Johnson*) contributed to *Macmillan* in April, 1876, tells us that, owing to a fruitless speculation in which Mr. Thrale had been induced to embark in 1771-2, "their distresses" set in. "A sudden run menaced the house, and death hovered over the head of its principal. Dr. Johnson scarcely left Thrale a moment, and 'tried every artifice to amuse, as well as every argument to console him.' But money, in round thousands, was after all the only effectual medicine for the broken-hearted brewer. In their distress they applied to their surest friends first. Down at Brighton there lived an old gouty solicitor, retired from business, the friend and contemporary of old Ralph Thrale. He had money; but how should they get at him, and at his heart, with this long troublesome story? 'Well,' says Mrs. Thrale, 'first we made free with our mother's money, her little savings, about £3,000.—'twas all she had; and big as I was with child, I drove down to Brighthelmstone to beg of Mr. Scrase £6,000 more—he gave it us—and Perkins, the head clerk, had never done repeating my short letter to our master, which only said; 'I have done my errand, and you soon shall see returned, *whole*, as I hope, your heavy but faithful messenger. H. L. T.'"

very high tides the sea invariably set its mark there; the fishing-boats, during the off-season, being "laid-up" immediately behind the house.

At the close of the last century the house would appear to have been considerably enlarged, and stabling, coach houses, &c., were erected on the west side; for, in 1801, when the "Stein House" was leased to Dr. Hall, that gentleman built three houses on the site of the stables, &c.; the row being thenceforth known as Steine-place. The green-sward of the Steine ran down to the forecourts, which were adorned with pretty garden plots and enclosed by posts and rails; and, from their exceedingly pleasant situation, the houses in Steine-place were always occupied by the more distinguished visitors, especially by military notabilities. When the South Gloucestershire Militia was in Brighton, in the early part of the century, Colonel Earl Berkeley, its Commander, resided in Steine-place; and, as scarcely an evening passed during the season without the band of the regiment performing in front of the house, the scene, with its ever-varying crowd of aristocratic visitors and townsfolk, was a most enlivening one.

So matters went on at Steine-place till the year 1819, when two of the houses were put to another use—that of an Hotel. This was chiefly brought about by the Royal patron of Brighton, George IV., being desirous of converting the ball-room of the old "Castle" Tavern into a Chapel, and attaching it to the Pavilion. As his desire was law, steps were soon taken to carry it into effect; and Dr. Hall—who, in addition to his high professional abilities, was a keen, far-seeing man in business matters, and especially in respect of propery—saw his opportunity. He at once set to work to transform some of the Steine-place houses into an hotel, and (having secured for a tenant Mr. C. Sheppard, the then respected proprietor of "The Star and Garter" Inn) the Hotel was opened under Royal auspices, being named, after Frederick, Duke of York, by special sanction, on September 27, 1819.

The Hotel, when opened, at once leapt, as it were, into popularity; and for several years after it was the resort of the most illustrious of the many visitors to Brighton. It was "constantly thronged with *tonish* guests "—in fact, it was *the* fashionable hotel of Brighton. Its "Visitors' Books" are crowded with illustrious names—" Princes, Dukes, and a' that," Among them, the Dukes of Clarence, York, and Cambridge, and the "Iron Duke"; those of the heads of the great County families; that of Prince Polignac, the Marquis de Custin, Count and Countess de Lieven (the Russian Ambassador and his wife), Prince William of Bentheim (Austria), and a "long line of such."

As the only place were fashionable visitors at this period could or did resort was the Steine, the Royal York Hotel had it all to itself. Its noble front windows commanded a full view of the Steine. All that passed there the guests could see; and if the midnight revels, the vulgar daily sports, and other unseemly scenes which not unfrequently took place there in days gone by, had to a great extent there was still no lack of "life." The views, too, from the upper windows of the Hotel, were of the most picturesque character. Despite the "Blue and Buffs," which shut in the Steine to some extent on the north, the eye took in a wide sweep of the valley between the Downs, as well as the Downs themselves, while to the eastward, far as the eye could scan, there was, as now, an almost unbroken view of land and sea, and of the white cliffs which, fencing the shore, stretch into the far distance.

At the time the Royal York Hotel was opened, and during the next few years, Brighton was at the acme of its pre-Railway prosperity; upwards of forty coaches being on the road between Brighton and London alone. The visitors to the town during the years 1821-22 were little short of 20,000; hotel and lodging-house accommodation commanded fancy prices, but, notwithstanding, by reason of its charming situation, the new hotel was throughout the season invariably full of guests. Occasionally, too, concerts and readings were given in the Saloon of the Hotel; a favourite reader there being the late Mr. B. H. Smart, one of the best Shakespearean readers of his day. The first Brighton Tradesmen's Ball, it may be stated, was given at the Royal York Hotel in 1823.

On Mr. Sheppard's retirement, he was succeeded by Mr. George Parsons, of the Sea House Hotel, Worthing (brother to the late Mr. Joseph Parsons, auctioneer, of Brighton), who occupied it for some three or four years. In 1827, the Hotel was in the hands of Mr. Harry Pegg, who came to Brighton from High Wickham. Important additions were made to the Hotel by Mr. Pegg; two houses to the westward and the house to the eastward being taken in, forming the Hotel into one block, as it now stands. The Hotel formerly possessed some very quaint old furniture, articles of vertu, &c., which had once done duty in the Royal Pavilion, but these, together with its stock of wine, were disposed of by public auction when the present proprietor, Mr. Alfred Hoadly, formerly of the Palace Hotel, Buxton, took possession, in June, 1874;[*] the sale occupying no less than seven days, and the catalogue containing no less than 1,752 lots. The Hotel was then closed for a short time, whilst several thousands of pounds were laid out in renovating, redecorating, and refurnishing. It has most extensive accommodation, making up nearly 100 beds; and whilst some of the rooms are of large proportions, all the principal apartments are distinguished by Royal and other names, such as the "Regent," "Clarence," "York,' "Otway," "Spenser," "Pope," "Gay," "Swift," "Byron," "Garrick," and the "Newton" rooms.[†]

[* On the death of Mr. Hoadly, in 1885, the Hotel was carried on by his widow up to January, 1890, when Mr. J. Foster Woosman became the proprietor.]

† An amusing anecdote is related in connection with the "names" of these rooms. A visitor, on being shown the rooms, was told by his attendant that the rooms were so designated because the various personages whose names were on the doors had at one time or another occupied them! When in the "Garrick" room, the attendant blandly said to him, "You have heard of Garrick; he was a great actor, you know. Well, he occupied this room for a long time!" *When*, thought the visitor (seeing that Garrick died many years before the Hotel was built), and passed on.

One of the grandest days in the history of the York Hotel was on Saturday, October 15th, 1820, when the Duke and Duchess of Clarence (afterwards King William IV. and Queen Adelaide) stayed there on their return from Dieppe. Their Royal Highnesses landed on the Chain Pier from the Admiralty yacht, a Royal salute on its approach being fired by the Hyperion frigate, which was in attendance. There was an immense crowd on the Pier, and such was the desire to see the Royal pair, that numbers climbed upon the iron suspension chains and other available places. The Pier was partially illuminated, and sky-rockets were sent up and blue lights were shown by the Hyperion's tender. At 6.50 p.m. the Duke and Duchess were received on the ladder at the eastern side of the Pier by Lieut. Williams, R.N., with sidemen and lanterns. When upon the deck of the Pier, Their Royal Highnesses were saluted by a guard of honour of the Marines; the band of the frigate stationed on the Pier, playing "God save the King" and "Rule Britannia." The Royal party then proceeded on foot to the York Hotel escorted by Marines, where they were received by the Dowager Marchioness of Downshire, Lady Mary Hill, and Mrs. Fitzherbert, the Band of the 15th Hussars playing the above National airs. The Duke and Duchess of Clarence almost immediately after appeared in the balcony, and were loudly cheered again and again by an immense assemblage in front of the Hotel.

Russell House—The Albion Hotel, &c.

To Brightonians a special interest attaches to Russell House, from the fact of its having been built by the celebrated physician, Dr. Richard Russell,* to whom unquestionably is chiefly due the early

---

* Dr. Richard Russell was born in 1687, in the parish of St. Michael, Lewes; his father being Mr. Nathaniel Russell, a respectable surgeon and apothecary practising in that place. Young Russell received his early education at the Free Grammar School of St. Anne's, Lewes, and subsequently was under his father's instruction with the view of becoming a medical practitioner. While resident in his father's house, he had occasion to visit frequently the family of Wm. Kempe, Esq., of South Malling, between whose only daughter and himself sprung up a secret but sincere affection, which resulted in a clandestine marriage. Subsequent to a reconciliation with his wife's father being brought about, Mr. Russell went to Leyden and studied under the learned Boerhaave. On his return, he appears to have resided in London; was elected a F.R.S.; and he afterwards practised at Lewes, and, on the death of his father-in-law, succeeded to Malling Deanery, of which he had become possessed. Still continuing his vocation, he published several works, in addition to his two more important works originally printed in Latin. To Dr. Russell Brighton owes the preservation of the valuable mineral spring at the Chalybeate, which he caused to be enclosed within a basin, a convenient house being afterwards built over it. The Doctor died in London December 19th, 1759, while on a visit to a friend, and his death is thus recorded in the Sussex Weekly Advertiser of December 24, 1759:— "On Wednesday last, died in London Richard Russell, of Malling, near Lewes, M.D., a Gentleman greatly esteemed in his Profession in these Parts." His remains were deposited in the family vault at South

RUSSELL HOUSE, BRIGHTON, 1786.

One of the grandest days in the history of the York Hotel was on Saturday, October 15th, 1829, when the Duke and Duchess of Clarence (afterwards King William IV. and Queen Adelaide) stayed there on their return from Dieppe. Their Royal Highnesses landed on the Chain Pier from the Admiralty yacht, a Royal salute on its approach being fired by the Hyperion frigate, which was in attendance. There was an immense crowd on the Pier; and such was the desire to see the Royal pair, that numbers climbed upon the iron suspension chains and other available places. The Pier was partially illuminated, and sky-rockets were sent up and blue lights were shown by the Hyperion's tender. At 6.50 p.m. the Duke and Duchess were received on the ladder at the eastern side of the Pier by Lieut. Williams, R.N., with sidemen and lanterns. When upon the deck of the Pier, Their Royal Highnesses were saluted by a guard of honour of the Marines; the band of the frigate, stationed on the Pier, playing "God save the King" and "Rule Britannia." The Royal party then proceeded on foot to the York Hotel escorted by Marines, where they were received by the Dowager Marchioness of Downshire, Lady Mary Hill, and Mrs. Fitzherbert, the Band of the 15th Hussars playing the above National airs. The Duke and Duchess of Clarence almost immediately after appeared in the balcony, and were loudly cheered again and again by an immense assemblage in front of the Hotel.

Russell House—The Albion Hotel, &c.

To Brightonians a special interest attaches to Russell House, from the fact of its having been built by the celebrated physician, Dr. Richard Russell,* to whom unquestionably is chiefly due the early

---

* Dr. Richard Russell was born in 1687, in the parish of St. Michael, Lewes; his father being Mr. Nathaniel Russell, a respectable surgeon and apothecary, practising in that place. Young Russell received his early education at the Free Grammar School of St. Anne's, Lewes; and subsequently was under his father's instruction with the view of becoming a medical practitioner. While assistant to his father, he had occasion to visit frequently the family of Wm. Kempe, Esq., of South Malling, between whose only daughter and himself sprung up a secret but sincere affection, which resulted in a clandestine marriage. Subsequently, a reconciliation with his wife's father being brought about, Mr. Russell went to Leyden and studied under the learned Boerhaave. On his return, he appears to have resided in London; was elected a F.R.S.; and received an appointment as one of the Physicians of St. Thomas's Hospital. He afterwards practised at Lewes, and, on the death of his father-in-law, resided at Malling Deanery, of which he had become possessed. Still continuing his studies, he published several works, in addition to his two more important works, originally printed in Latin. To Dr. Russell Brighton owes the conservation of the valuable mineral spring at the Chalybeate, which he caused to be enclosed within a basin; a convenient little building being afterwards built over it. The Doctor died in London December 19th, 1759, while on a visit to a friend, and his death is thus recorded in the *Sussex Weekly Advertiser* of December 24, 1759:—" On Wednesday last, died in London, Richard Russell, of Malling, near Lewes, M.D., a Gentleman greatly esteemed in his Profession in these Parts." His remains were deposited in the family vault at South

RUSSELL HOUSE, BRIGHTON, 1786.

prosperity of the town. We will not say wholly so; for previous to the Doctor's taking up his residence in Brighton, visitors had begun to resort thither for sea-bathing, &c. But they were few in comparison with those who afterwards came under the learned Doctor's auspices, or for his advice. His great work, published in 1750, entitled "A Dissertation on the Use of Sea Water in The Diseases of The Glands," excited much attention among the Faculty; and deservedly so, judging by the number of remarkable "Cases" (cures) it contains; and patients came to Dr. Russell, not only from the metropolis, but from all parts of the kingdom. At this period he was practising at Lewes, residing at Malling Deanery; but in 1754, his patients becoming so numerous, the Doctor removed to Brighton for the purpose of affording them practical treatment under his immediate personal care and attention. Dr. Russell had, doubtless, previously been many a time and oft to Brighton, and, possibly, at the period there was no spot more suitable for the great sea-water Physician's residence than that which he selected, to the south of the Steine, "lying near to the Pool bank," and, of course, close to the Sea. In 1755 the Doctor, who then resided in Brighton, published another work, entitled "The Economy of Nature," at the end of which, in an epistle to his friend, Dr. Frewen, he gives his *beau ideal* of what a sea-bathing place should be, and which would seem to afford a picture of Brighton itself at the period:—

"It should be (he says) clean and neat, at some distance from the opening of a river, that the water may be as highly loaded with sea-salt and the other riches of the ocean as possible, and not overcharged by the mixing of fresh water with its waves. In the next place, one would choose the shore to be sandy and flat, for the convenience of going into the sea in a bathing-chariot. And, lastly, that the sea-shore should be bounded by lovely cliffs and downs to add to the cheerfulness of the place, and give the person that has bathed an opportunity of mounting on horseback dry and clean, to pursue such exercises as may be advised by his physician after he comes out of the bath."

Malling. Dr. Russell was succeeded in his estates by his eldest son, William, a barrister, who subsequently took his mother's maiden name, and was long after known as witty Serjeant Kempe, of Malling. [The following abstract of the Doctor's Will, supplied to me by my much-esteemed friend, the late Mr. T. C. Noble, author of *Memorials of Temple Bar*, will be perused with interest:— "This is the last Will and testament of Richard Russell, of South Malling, in the County of Sussex, Doctor in Physic. In the first place, I give to my beloved wife, Mary Russell, my three houses, with their out-houses, gardens, and appurtenances thereunto belonging, bounded by Market-lane to the east and to Mr. William Michell's garden to the west, and now in the occupation of Mr. Henry Mannings, Mr. Bennet, and Mrs. Mathews, and lying and being in the Parish of St. Michael's, in Lewes, in the County of Sussex; as also my house at Brighthelmstone, in Sussex, with all its furniture, with stable, coach-house, chariot, and the pair of coach horses: to have and to hold by the said Mary Russell for her and her heirs for ever." He then bequeaths to his said wife £1,000. "I also give to my son, Richard Russell, the next presentation of Broadwater, after the present incumbent, the Rev. Dr. Terrick." The Will is dated 8th May, 1759; and a proviso states that sundry bequests are left "upon the understanding that his said wife and children give up and quit claim to the possession of my Pedinghoe farm, in the occupation now of Thomas Smith, and also to the farms at Pyecomb, or any other, whether freehold or copyhold, and leaving to my son William in quiet possession the real and personal estate of her father, late William Kempe, Esquire."

Returning, however, to Russell House. It would appear to have been built on the site of sundry small tenements, a shop, &c., lying to the east of the Pool Valley, and which, with other small property, must have skirted the shore and shut in the Steine to the south from an early period. There appears also to have been an old road, coming from under the cliff eastward, running in front of this small property to the Pool Valley, and thence westward to the original Fish Market (supplanted by Lamprell's Baths, on the site of which "The Clarendon" now stands). At what period these tenements, &c., were erected, we cannot say; but, in reference to those on the site of Russell House, it would appear by a deed, dated April 27, 1739, that they were in existence for some considerable time prior to that date. This deed states that at a "Court of the Mannor of Brighthelmston, held at the special instance and request of Richard Gillam and Anne his wife," before Richard Newdegate, Esquire, Steward, "came, in her proper person, Mary, the wife of Richard Tuppen the younger, only daughter and heir of Martha Smith, deceased, and prayed to be admitted *(inter alia)* to a shop situate upon the Steene, near the Pool, in Brighthelmston, heretofore erected upon other parcel of the Wast of this Mannor, lying to the Pool bank, and also to land now or late of Thomas Mighell towards the West, containing in length 40ft. and in breadth 30ft.," which prayer was granted, "according to the Custom of the Mannor," on her paying a fine of 6d., and "doing fealty therefore to the Lords." This property was in 1747 mortgaged by the husband, Richard Tuppen, carpenter, to James Brooker, mariner, for £16.

On the 2nd July, 1753, Dr. Russell bought the above property—described as "all that Customary Cottage or Tenement, with the Shop, Ground, and other Appurtenances thereto belonging, on the Steane at Brighthelmston, and paying yearly to the Lords tenpence,"—for Forty Pounds; the money being paid "by the hand of Wm. Grover." The price paid was just £1 per foot. What would the same site be worth per foot now? A week or two prior to this transaction, Dr. Russell had purchased other property, connected with the preceding, of Richard Tuppen, for which he also paid him Forty Pounds. The original receipt of this the earliest purchase of Dr. Russell in Brighton was as follows:—

"June 11, 1753.

"Be it remembered yt. in consideration of One Guinea in hand paid—as part of Forty Pounds to be paid at the time of admission that Richard Tuppen, of Brighthelmstone, has sold to Dr. Rd. Russell, of Southmalling, in the County of Sussex, one house, standing upon the Steen at Brighthelmstone, with all that ground, shed, and other appurtenances thereunto belonging, for the sum of Forty Pounds, the remaining Thirty-eight Pounds Nineteen Shillings to be paid to the said Rd. Tuppen on the time he conveys this estate to the said Dr. Rd. Russell—and that the said Dr. Rd. Russell is to pay nothing more—except for the coppy of his admission. I do acknowledge the receipt of the above sd. Guinea and confirm this bargain. Witness my hand,

RICHARD TUPPEN.

"JOHN TUPPEN,
"WM. RUSSELL."

"June 25, 1753.
"Recd. of Dr. Russell, one Guinea more, as part of the Thirty Eight Pounds Nineteen Shillings remaining to compleat the payment of the within written contract. Witness my hand,
"RICHARD TUPPEN."

Dr. Russell subsequently purchased four tenements, and, likewise, for 26s., a small parcel of ground adjoining one of them, formerly part of the "Waste," and on which said customary tenements and "Waste" we learn, from the Court Rolls of 15th July, 1760, when Mary the widow of Richard Russell was admitted, "the said Richard Russell had late erected a large messuage or dwelling house, situate and being on the south end or part of the Stean."

Russell House, when first completed, must have "astonished the natives," for there was then no other house of its size in the town. They must have been still more astonished—and also delighted—to see the numerous visitors resorting thither to see the celebrated Doctor, and who, not unfrequently, with their families or friends, took up their residence, for a more or less lengthened period, in one or other of the few indifferent inns of the "fisher village," or in such of its houses as afforded the necesssary accommodation. The house, which, with grounds, &c., covered a large area (extending from the eastern front of the present Albion Hotel to the western front of the present Lion Mansion), occupied, without doubt, the finest site along the then sea-front of the town. It was, too, of handsome elevation, and the charming views from its windows, both seaward and landward,—

"Far as the ocean pales or sky inclips",—

were wholly uninterrupted. The Doctor's patients, in addition to the use of the enclosed lawn on the Steine front of the house, had originally, we believe, ready access to the Beach for bathing, &c., from its sea front; but later on it became necessary to erect there an enclosing wall to resist the encroachments of the sea, which, to the East of the House, had destroyed to a very great extent the "Waste." (See *plate*.)

The Doctor occupied Russell House up to the time of his death, in 1759. It then passed into the possession of his widow, but it is uncertain whether or no she continued to reside there, or whether it was occupied "by strangers."* Most probably the latter was the case; for,

---

* Several gentlemen were anxious to secure Dr. Russell's professional practice, which was, doubtless, very lucrative. Within three months of his death, the *Sussex Weekly Advertiser*, of March 3rd, 1760, says:—"We hear that Dr. Poole, some years resident Physician in this place (who, on the death of the late Dr. Russell has met with great encouragement from many of the principal Families in the neighbourhood), will attend at Brighthelmstone during the ensuing season, and has taken a house for that purpose"; and in the following July the same journal states, "We are assured that Dr. Schomberg, son of Dr. Schomberg, of London, is settled at Brighthelmstone, to succeed the late Dr. Russell there." But the Doctor's most eminent successor was, undoubtedly, Dr. Relhan, the author of *A Short History of Brighthelmstone in 1761*. Dunvan says of him—"It is, however, but justice to the memory of Dr. Relhan, who succeeded Dr. Russell at Brighthelmstone, to observe that, by his abilities and exertions, he considerably advanced a work so auspiciously begun. His natural history of that town, published about the year 1760, is a lasting proof of his ample qualifications even as a successor to so eminent a physician as Dr. Russell."

in subsequent years, we learn that distinguished visitors occupied "the house to the south of the Steine." H.R.H. the Duke of Cumberland resided there in 1786, and, for some two or three following years, during the season; and other fashionable visitors succeeded him. But years were telling on the famous house, and many another house of more modern character was built in close proximity. Russell House in the early part of the present century would seem to have more or less declined in favour as a fashionable family mansion; for in June, 1807, it was opened by a Mrs. Hill as a boarding house; and continued for awhile as such. By and by, in 1812, there was a "bathing-house" built, and subsequently a toy repository located, under its east wall; and in August, 1816, the enclosure in front of the House was occupied by a mechanical theatre, "with animated objects," which had been removed from the Grand-parade, where it "had been complained of as a nuisance." Then one of its apartments was devoted to a camera obscura. Later on, the "art and practice" of copper-plate printing was carried on in a part of the house; and in 1822 its largest room was secured by an Indian juggler wherein to exhibit his wonders! It had at this period a ruinous appearance; and a year or so afterwards Russell House, with which the early fortunes of Brighton had been so intimately associated, was razed to the ground. Previous to its removal, the town contemplated the purchase of the house, with the view of keeping open the southern extremity of the Steine. The owner, Mr. J. Colbatch, asked £6,000 for it, and this the Commissioners assented to give; but, after numerous delays, the bargain went off. On the removal of the old house, the fine effect of the opening was apparent, and general regret was expressed that the purchase had not been made. The Albion Hotel soon after rose upon its site; and a noble opening to the Sea south of the Steine was lost, most probably for ever.

The handsome new Hotel was opened,—without any formal ceremony, we believe,—on August 5th, 1826; and its charming and then unrivalled situation on the sea-front induced many distinguished visitors to reside there. It is needless to give a list of these; but it may be mentioned that members of the Royal Family did not disdain to honour the Albion by occupying its apartments; neither did many of the first nobility in the kingdom, as well as other more or less distinguished personages. As an Hotel. the Albion has, under its successive proprietors or managers, for many a year ranked, and still ranks, among the best conducted Hotels of the town. So far as events of public interest are concerned, there appears to be little to record—with one important exception—in connection with the Albion, the Hotel from the first having been almost exclusively devoted to its original purpose, the accommodation of visitors. The exception to which we allude was the establishment—in the large room on the ground floor on its western side—of the Literary and Scientific Institution. As this Institution was destined to exercise an important influence on the literary character of the town,—in fact, the formation of the present Free Public Library, Museum, &c., may be said to be entirely due to those connected with it,—it will not, perhaps, be deemed uninteresting if we briefly glance at

THE EARLY LITERARY GROWTH OF BRIGHTON, THE ALBION ROOMS INSTITUTION, AND THE FREE PUBLIC LIBRARY.

It was not till the present century had entered upon its second decade that we hear of any important movement being made in Brighton to furnish solid food for the mind of either inhabitants or visitors, and this was when the late Mr. John Colbatch, Mr. Charles Howell, and Mr. George Wagner (brother to the Rev. Henry Michell Wagner, the late Vicar), met occasionally during the winter to read or discuss. And that is all we know about them. At a later period a Mechanics' Institution, with library, was established in the large house in West-street, facing Duke-street, where lectures were delivered by Dr. King, Mr. Moses Ricardo (brother to the well-known writer on Political Economy), Mr. Henry Phillips, the botanist, projector first of the Oriental Gardens and next of the Anthæum, the prototypes of the Crystal Palace ; and, we believe, also by Mr. Vallance, the ingenious inventor of an Atmospheric Railway for conveying passengers from Brighton to London by pneumatic pressure. The Mechanics' Institution, having run its course, passed away, and a "Literary Society" arose from its ashes, but confined its earlier efforts solely to the maintenance of a Library and Reading Room. Its "local habitation" was a room at the back of a plumassier's establishment (Gillman's) a short distance up the north side of St. James's-street ; the only circumstance indicating the existence of such a Temple of the Muses being the Doric columns on each side of the doorway. For some years this small Society pursued its modest course quietly, though pleasantly and usefully enough. But the town was growing apace ; new people located themselves in it, bringing with them new ideas. Some forty years ago two young men, starting on their careers in life, settled themselves in Brighton : one, as a general practitioner in medicine ; the other, as Head Master of the Proprietary School for boys that was just then established in Ship-street, where it has flourished like a green bay tree to this day.[*] These enterprising strangers,—"foreigners," the aborigines would have called them,—were John Cordy Burrows and Henry Stein Turrell, both of whom gained high distinction in later years ; the former being Knighted and the latter becoming an LL.D. (*Legum Doctor*), or "Doctor of Laws." They joined the old Literary Institution and strove to infuse fresh vigour and life into that somewhat somnolent body. They suggested the desirability of extending its sphere of action, and proposed that some public lectures should be given, of which there had been so long a dearth that they were not only a want but a novelty. The first, we believe, was delivered by Dr. Turrell himself, on the then projected fortifications of Paris. Another was given in the Town Hall by the late Mr. Busby, the architect, upon Astronomy, illustrated by means of an ingenious orrery of his own construction, set in motion by water flowing through a number of circular vessels. Another lecture was given by Mr. Henry Phillips (after his blindness) on the Grasses found in Hove Fields. The bold innovators even ventured to invite Dr. Lardner to deliver some lectures on the Steam Engine. For these he was paid, and a charge was made for admission. The experiment was so successful that a proposal was made to re-construct the Society altogether. At this period (1834) Dr. Mantell, the celebrated

---

[* The School ceased to exist in 1890. *Sic transit gloria mundi.*]

Geologist, came from Lewes (of which town he was a native), and then another Society, called the Mantellian Institution, was formed, holding occasional evening meetings at a house on the Old-steine (now No. 20.) Dr. Mantell himself lectured there on Geology ; Mr. Horace Smith upon Railways ; Mr. Ricardo assisted with occasional scientific discourses ; and Mr. G. F. Richardson, who had been appointed Curator of the Mantellian Museum, followed in their wake. The Society received influential support for a short time ; but it was too exclusive for so small a place as Brighton then was, and when Dr. Mantell, disappointed in his hope of medical practice, removed to London, it came to an end.

But *revenons à nos moutons;* hoping that this little digression has not been without interest. The proposal for remodelling the old Literary Society not having met with a favourable reception among the members, it was thought best to found an entirely new one. Accordingly a meeting, convened by private circular, was held at the Town Hall, when it was resolved unanimously that it would be highly beneficial to establish a Literary and Scientific Institution in Brighton worthy of the growing importance of the town. Sir Cordy, then "Mr." Burrows, and "Dr.," then Mr. Turrell, were appointed Honorary Secretaries, and may fairly be considered to have been the founders of the Society so long known as the Brighton Royal Literary and Scientific Institution, of which Prince Albert became Patron. This was in 1841. The new Society flourished beyond expectation, and the old Society quietly died out of existence, and sold its books ; but the Mantellian very handsomely, through the late Judge Furner and Mr. E. N. Hall, presented the greater part of their library (in 1842) to its successor. Other books rapidly accumulated, and the Committee of Management organised a series of Essays for discussion and Lectures on Literary and Scientific subjects, which were continued at regular intervals down to the time of its final dissolution ; having existed for a longer period - 28 years—than any other Society of a kindred character had lived in Brighton before. It had found more commodious, cheerful, and congenial quarters than any of its predecessors had been able to obtain. When Russell House was pulled down and the Albion Hotel erected in its stead, the whole southern portion of the ground floor was planned and arranged as a Bazaar ; but, this speculation proving a failure, the Brighton Literary and Scientific Institution, when it was founded, rented the place for their Library and Reading Rooms ; and here, for the above-mentioned period of 28 years, it was, perhaps, better known as the "Albion Rooms Institution," than by its proper title.*

The first lecture was delivered on the 14th September, 1841, by Mr.

---

* We may, perhaps, without impropriety, allude to the romantic history of one of the "constant readers" at the Albion Rooms in its latter days, the late Spencer Rogers, Esq. This gentleman was for many years the proprietor of the Dale Hall Pottery Works, Staffordshire, where was manufactured the celebrated "Willow Pattern and Broseley Ware," which had in its composition that particular tint of "blue" deemed so choice amongst connoisseurs. He amassed great wealth from his manufactures ; had large estates in Staffordshire ; kept his pack of harriers ; and, in fact, lived in the style of an "Old English Gentleman—one of the Olden Time." Some time between 1830—40 he happened, at an evening party, to be seated next a lady whose glowing accounts of the profits of the "Tea Speculation," so rife at the time, induced him to embark largely in it. The venture was fatal ; and, as a friend writes, "almost in one night the whole of his splendid fortune went to the winds"! Mr. Rogers could not brook to bear this reverse of fortune in his own district, and henceforth he became almost a wanderer. His few last years were passed at Brighton ; he spending his time almost wholly in reading at the Albion Rooms, where his sad aspect and habitual reserve made him "noted" by the frequenters of that Institution ; but none of whom, save one, knew his "eventful historie." He died at Brighton in 1863 ; and his remains lie in the Extra-Mural Cemetery.

Donovan, upon that *quasi*-science so popular just then –Phrenology. The principle adopted was, that the lectures should be gratuitously given, and admission be free, each member of the Society having the privilege of introducing three friends. The consequence was, the lectures were chiefly delivered by the members themselves. Among the lecturers were Sir J. C. Burrows, Mr. Redknap, Mr. Capon, Mr. J. Merrifield, Mr. W. Seymour, Captain James, Mr. Peto, Mr. Ricardo, Mr. J. O. N. Rutter, Mr. E. Evershed, Rev. Dr. Butler, Rev. G. H. Stoddart, Mr. J. Colbatch, Mr. D. Black, Mr. J. Ellis, Dr. Turrell, Mr. M. L. Phillips and Mr. B. Phillips (sons of the botanist), Mr. E. Maitland, the Rev. J. Sortain, Dr. Rugé, Mr. Penley, Mr. G. de Paris, Sir E. Creasy, Dr. Kebbell, Mr. T. W. Wonfor, Mr. J. Andrews, and many others, some of whom, we are pleased to say, are still living. The Committee, so far as their means allowed, endeavoured to form a Museum, and collected many objects of interest subsequently removed to the Pavilion. They also originated in Brighton those popular assemblies called Soirées, which have since so frequently been held at the Pavilion. At first these Soirées were exceedingly profitable and enabled the Committee to add largely to the library; but they were given too frequently: other parties imitated them, and, at last, Soirées were given for nothing; and so the Literary Institution was compelled to discontinue them.

A variety of circumstances combined to reduce the revenue of the Institution and thereby tend to close its useful career; notably amongst them was the abolition of the taxes upon newspapers, which reduced their price from the almost prohibitive charge of sevenpence to the universal penny. To this Society, with all its imperfections, Brighton is deeply indebted. Besides the many services rendered by it already described, it was in this Society that the College of Preceptors was originated, the Charter having been granted to Dr. Turrell and others named therein, and Dr. Turrell to the day of his death had the custody of it. It was at a Committee of this Society also, in 1858, that the subject of the Oxford and Cambridge Local Examinations, then about to be established, was brought under notice by Dr. Turrell; and steps were taken for introducing them into Brighton. A special meeting of members of the Society and others was convened by Dr. Turrell at his house, and Mr. Barclay Phillips was requested to officiate as Honorary Secretary. This office he accepted with diffidence, for upon him devolved all the preliminary correspondence and arrangements, which ultimately led to the establishment, by a Town Meeting, of the Sussex Board for Local Examinations. Under their auspices, and with Mr. Phillips as their Secretary and Local Secretary for the two Universities, these Examinations have ever since been conducted with such encouraging success. It was by members of the Literary and Scientific Society, namely, Dr. Turrell, Dr. King, Mr. Arthur Wallis, Mr. B. Phillips, Mr. Horne, and Mr. G. Lowdell, that the Brighton and Sussex Natural History Society was founded, the latter three having been selected to draw up its rules.

When the Brighton Literary and Scientific Institution closed its doors, the proprietors,- -for it was a proprietary institution,—liberally gave up their shares, and, raising a subscription among themselves and their friends to pay off their debt, finally presented the whole of their books, to the number of some thousands, together with their Museum, to the Corporation of Brighton, " to have and to hold " for the free use and enjoyment of the public for ever. Whatever may have been its defects, the Society never swerved,—that is, its founders and staunch supporters never lost sight of their great object, the founding of a Public Library, which purpose has now been accomplished.

The idea grew. The late Mr. Wakeford Attree bequeathed a collection of books to the town for the purpose; the late Mr. G. Ballard presented a number; the families of the late Dr. Turrell and Dr. King, each some hundreds of volumes; and upon the lamentable death of the Rev. Julius Elliott, by falling down a precipice in Switzerland, his surviving brother and sisters presented to the town the whole of the library of their father, the Rev. H. V. Elliott, consisting of 3,000 volumes. Again the idea grew. A premature attempt to force upon the town the adoption of the Public Libraries' Act met with a disastrous defeat, the causes of which need not here be explained; but people slowly reconsidered the question, and the proposal to establish a Library being submitted in a less objectionable form, and with better promise of success, the Town Council at last agreed almost unanimously to found one under the powers granted them by the Pavilion Purchase Act. Rooms had already been fitted up in the Pavilion itself (1862) for the formation of a Museum, to which the collection from the Literary Institution was transferred. Dr. Turrell generously presented his cases of minerals; Mr. H. Willett lent his collection of chalk fossils; Sir Charles Dick his collection of old armour; and other inhabitants contributed various specimens of natural history and other curiosities. Though very imperfect, and arranged most unsystematically, the "Town Museum," as it was then called, was an advance upon what had previously existed; but the collection grew so rapidly, and the books accumulated so fast, that, in 1871, the Town Council resolved, almost unanimously, to convert the old coach-house and stabling to the east of the Dome into a Public Library, Museum, and Picture Gallery; and in June the same year the project was submitted to a Vestry Meeting, when it received almost unanimous sanction. The Picture Gallery was formally opened on the 20th January, 1873; and the new Museum and Library were opened on the 12th September following. The proceedings in connection with the latter were of an interesting character, an inaugural address being delivered by Dr. Carpenter, President of the British Association. In the evening, the Mayor (Alderman James Ireland) gave a grand Soirée, invitations being issued to and accepted by upwards of 2,000 of the visiting and resident gentry and principal inhabitants. The entrance to the beautiful Institution which the public now possess is beneath a Moorish archway in Church-street, leading to a noble Central Hall, 112 feet in length, 30 in breadth, and some 40 feet in height, lighted from the top. This forms the Picture Gallery. To the left are two large rooms, looking into the Pavilion gardens, devoted to the Library; to the right, a set of rooms devoted to Archæology; above these are the rooms allotted to Geology, Zoology, and Botany, but communicating by cross galleries, one at each end of the Hall, so that visitors may, as the French say, "circulate" uninterruptedly through all the building, ascending and descending by a handsome stone staircase on each side of the entrance to the Central Hall.

Since this building has been constructed, further presents of books have been made to the town. The late Professor George Long, previously to his death, gave the whole of his valuable classical library; the Rev. Dr. Griffith has been a generous donor; Mr. H. Willett has given a collection of pamphlets and works made by the late Richard Cobden; the late Dr. Ormerod presented a complete set of Transactions of the Royal Society, whilst, since his death, the whole of his medical library has been added by his widow; Mr. James White gave 400 volumes; and, recently, Mr. J. O. Halliwell-Phillipps has generously given a most valuable collection of Shakespearean and early English literature.

[It is satisfactory to add here that both the Library and Museum have, during the past 10 years, attained marked success. As regards the LIBRARY, it was hoped that a Public Free Lending Library might be established in Her Majesty's Jubilee Year (1887), but the scheme for ·ring it into effect failed. In July, 1888, however, the Library Sub-

Committee issued a report showing how a Lending Library could be engrafted on the existing Library, which was subsequently confirmed by the Town Council. To facilitate the arrangements, some official changes were made; the Curator (Mr. Lomax) was given the care only of the Museum and Picture Gallery; whilst a new Librarian (Mr. F. W. Madden) was appointed, with the sole custody and management of the Library, under the control of the Sub-Committee. The Victoria Lending Library was opened on the 16th October, 1889, by the Mayor of Brighton (Alderman Sendall), when Mr. H. J. Mathews (the indefatigable Chairman of the Library Sub-Committee), in giving a brief sketch of its formation, stated that about £2,100, including the munificent subscription of £1,000 from Mr. Daniel Hack, had been publicly subscribed for the Victoria Lending Library during the Mayoralty of Alderman Reeves in 1887 (the Jubilee Year). How successful the Free Library has been may be learnt from the results published in the latest Report (September 30th, 1891). At that date the Reference Library contained 11,778 volumes; and since the opening (16th October, 1889) 69,111 books had been issued to 50,250 readers. The Lending Library also showed most gratifying results. The Library contained on September 30th, 1891, 23,359 volumes. The number of tickets issued (including 1 800 to residents in Hove) since the opening were 9,785; and the books lent during the same period amounted to 236,364. THE PUBLIC MUSEUM, since its opening in September, 1873, has grown apace, under the intelligent and untiring supervision of its respective Chairmen of Sub-Committees, the late Dr. Thomas Davidson, F.R.S., and Mr. Edward Crane, F.G.S. Mr. Henry Willett, F.G.S., Mr. James Ashbury, the late Sir Cordy Burrows, Dr. Davidson, and Count A. Clericetti have contributed largely by gifts and loans of inestimable value to its material progress.* The marble portrait medallion, by Mr. T. Brock, R.A., of Dr. Davidson, which hangs over the South door of the room devoted to British Geology, was presented to the town in 1888 as a memorial of his scientific services. The Museum has been fortunate in having associated with it from time to time several other gentlemen who have taken considerable interest in its systematic development, among whom we may mention the late Dr. Ormerod, F.R.S., Dr. A. Seymour, Mr. Simonds, Dr. E. J. Miles, Mr. B. Lomax, F.L.S., Dr Ainslie Hollis, Mr. E. A. Pankhurst, Mr. A. F. Griffith, Dr. E. Tulk-Hart, and the Rev. T. Calvert, M.A. We must add also the following ladies:—The late Mrs. M. P. Merrifield, who contributed a number of beautiful drawings of invertebrate animals; Mrs. Branwell; and Miss Agnes Crane, who arranged the Paris Basin collection of Tertiary Fossils and the recent Brachiopoda, the Bryozoa or moss-animals, and the Tunicata or "sea squirts." Among the most valued treasures of the Museum may be named "The Willett Collection of Chalk Fossils;" a series of minerals from the chalk; a fine collection of fossils from the Cambridge Greensands, named and presented by Mr. A. F. Griffith; the Davidson collections of the "Rocks and Fossils of the Paris Basin," and of "Volcanic Products," and "The Holmes" collection of Sussex Wealden Fossils, purchased by the Corporation in 1887, through the instrumentality of Mr. E. Crane, who named and classified this fine local series. The Geological Department is very complete, embracing an extensive and fairly representative selection of British Fossils, chiefly named and entirely arranged by Mr. E. Crane, in geological and zoological sequence. Indeed, so far as palæontology is concerned, the Museum may not unworthily rank with some of the more important provincial Museums

---

* Count Clericetti in 1888 bequeathed £500 to the Museum and the Library; £250 was spent in purchasing specimens for the former, and £250 in purchasing books for the latter.

of the Kingdom. It further contains elementary educational series in mineralogy, botany, invertebrate and vertebrate zoology, and a number of archæological and ethnological specimens illustrating the life of pre-historic man and modern savages. All these collections are at present much cramped for want of space. THE PICTURE GALLERY still holds its own with varying fortunes, two exhibitions being held yearly,—one of oil paintings and one of drawings in water colours. Hopes are strongly entertained that provision will ere long be made by the Corporation for a permanent Art Gallery, a nucleus of which may be said to have been formed by the presentation of numerous pictures by Mr. W. J. Wilson (through Mr. G. de Paris, Chairman of the Fine Arts Sub-Committee) and by other gentlemen. The town, too, is to be congratulated upon the transference to it in November, 1890, by Mr. G. de Paris, of the unique collection of prints and books relating to the early history of Brighton, which, thanks mainly to the public-spirited exertions of Mr. de Paris himself, had been purchased by public subscription for £407, from the valuable artistic treasures amassed by the late Mr. Crawford J. Pocock. These prints have been mounted and framed, together with others of the Furner collection (which Mr. de Paris also secured for the town), and hung in the Supplementary Museum of the Pavilion, proving a most valuable and attractive contribution to the history and archæology of the town. It may be added that, in November, 1891, a new Committee was formed, under an Act recently acquired by the Corporation, to manage, regulate, and control the Public Library, Museum, and Art Gallery. This Committee consists of the Mayor, nine members of the Council, and nine other gentlemen, and the new arrangement is expected to be productive of excellent results.]

Marlborough House—"Single Speech" Hamilton's—Lady Anne Murray's.

This house—situated on the West side of the Steine—has in its history many interesting associations with the Past, both with respect to its various owners and to the illustrious visitors to whom its doors were freely opened. It is not only the oldest existing of the notable houses, but is *the* oldest house on the Steine; having been built in 1769, by Mr. Samuel Shergold, of "The Castle Tavern," who with practical foresight thus early sought to afford suitable accommodation for the distinguished visitors who had then begun to resort to the town.* Excepting Russell House, it was also the largest private residence on the Steine, and, moreover, charmingly situated; the

---

* From the Court Rolls of the Manor, it appears that Mr. Samuel Shergold was admitted on the 25th September, 1757, to property described as "two cottages and small piece of land," on Surrender of Swan Downer [who resided at 62 or 63, Ship-street, and whose noble benefactions to the aged poor and to the poor children of the town are still in force to this day], who had been previously admitted as the only son and customary heir of Francis Downer and Ann his wife; the property was then "late Usborne's, and formerly Gunn's." Mr. Shergold was also admitted 4th June, 1765, to some portion of the land on surrender of Richard Tidy. Mr. Tidy also surrendered to Thomas Fuller, and the latter sold to Samel Shergold "All that his Customary Barn, &c., in East-street." In January, 1770, Mr. Shergold also acquired a piece of land from Samuel Dean.

VIEW OF WEST SIDE OF THE STEINE.
(Showing Lady Anne Murray's and Mrs. Fitzherbert's Mansions.)

front windows commanding an extensive view of sea and land. It was not surprising that Mr. Shergold soon found a purchaser for the premises, in the Duke of Marlborough, who had for two years previously (1767-68) been a regular visitor to Brighton, and towards which he had always evinced the greatest partiality. The Duke entered into possession in September, 1771; and the fact diffused general joy throughout the town, His Grace's retinue consisting of upwards of 40 persons. Alluding to the Duke's visit to Brighton, the *Lewes Journal* of that period says—"'Tis incredible to think what a deal of money His Grace expends there, and the help he is to the poor. We are well assured that he buys half a bullock at a time, a whole calf, and his mutton by the carcase, so that, by the over-abundance of his tables the poor have joints given them hardly touch'd, which is a prodigious relief to numbers who at this dear time cannot afford to purchase butcher's meat; a noble example and worthy of imitation."

The house was thenceforth known as "Marlborough House." Externally, its appearance was different to what it is now: it was then brick-fronted, and had a sloping tiled roof. His Grace resided at Marlborough House till 1786, when he removed to Grove House, immediately to the north of the Pavilion. Marlborough House was then put up to auction, the Court Rolls recording that it was "bought by W. G. Hamilton, part from the Duke of Marlborough and part from Cornelius Boon"; but no consideration is stated. The "W. G. Hamilton" referred to was the Right Hon. W. Gerald Hamilton, M.P. for Haslemere, and who, in 1779, was Chancellor of Exchequer of Ireland.[*] This gentleman made considerable alterations to the house, both to the interior and exterior, the latter being re-fronted with what was then known as Adams' artificial stone, giving to its present appearance. The elegant central hall of the house was 20ft. by 18ft., the ceiling was domically coved, the points of intersection being richly moulded with ribs, with an enriched Doric cornice at the base. On the right of the hall was a superb dining room (34ft. by 20ft.), one end of which was apsidal and alcoved, and having a niched ceiling with radiating ribbings; the other portion being rectangular, with recessed sides and moulded pilasters, whence sprung a graceful dome-shaped ceiling, the angles of intersection being festooned; enriched medallions encircling graceful vases adorned the spandrils of the walls. To the left of the hall was a large and lofty drawing room (34ft. by 24ft. 6in.), the doorways

---

[*] Mr. Hamilton (once reputed to be the author of *Junius*) was among the earliest visitors to Brighton. He nearly lost his life on the Downs in 1775; from his horse "cannoning" against Sir Ferdinando Poole's, whilst hunting. He was rendered insensible; but was eventually restored by Dr. Kipping, who happened to be one of the field. Mr. Hamilton was familiarly called "Single-Speech" Hamilton, from having made one remarkable speech in the House of Commons against the Government, and receiving some douceur to be silent ever after! Miss Burney, in her *Diary and Letters*, says—"This Mr. Hamilton is extremely tall and handsome; has an air of haughty and fashionable superiority; is intelligent, dry, sarcastic, and clever. I should have received much pleasure from his conversational powers, had I not previously been prejudiced against him, by hearing that he is infinitely artful, double, and crafty."

having Corinthian pilastres and entablature of a composite type; the ceiling was square, with a beautiful cornice. This room contained an exquisite Sicilian marble chimney-piece, the pilastres being moulded and enriched with medallions, with delicately carved Cupids riding on dolphins; the frieze being adorned with an exquisitely carved representation of "Venus seated in a Car drawn by Cupids." The Library, entered both from the hall and drawing room, was rectangular in form, the ceiling being ribbed out in panels deeply recessed and ornamented.* The house when completed was said to have been "justly admired for its elegance of architecture, as uniting simplicity with true grandeur." It was long after considered, even in "point of exterior beauty, the first house in Brighton"; the enclosed green plat and garden in front with trees at each side, doubtless tending to add to its then elegant appearance.

On the 20th April, 1789, the house, which was appropriately furnished, received its first Royal visitor: His Royal Highness the Prince of Wales coming to Brighton on a visit to Mr. W. Gerald Hamilton, and staying with him from Thursday to Saturday. Though only the bare fact of the visit is recorded, there is no doubt that Mr. Hamilton did his best to entertain the Prince right Royally; for it is probably due to the pleasant recollections of this visit that His Royal Highness was induced a second time to accept the hospitality of Mr. Hamilton. In June, 1795, when the Prince came to Brighton with his newly-wedded wife, the Princess Caroline of Brunswick, the Royal pair with their suite stayed at Mr. Gerald Hamilton's for nearly three weeks, which were among the happiest that the Princess spent whilst in Brighton; for shortly after their removal thence to the Pavilion, the earliest of those sad domestic troubles which eventually clouded her life had begun to set in.†

The Right Hon. Gerald Hamilton died in 1796; and his house, &c., at Brighton, were put up to auction. As the advertisement relating to the sale affords some particulars of the value of East-street and other property at the period, we give it at full length:—

A CAPITAL RESIDENCE AND ESTATES AT BRIGHTON.

TO BE SOLD BY AUCTION, by MESSRS. SKINNER, DYKE, and SKINNER, on SATURDAY, the 10th of September, 1796, at Twelve o'clock, on the Premises, by order of the Executors, in Three Lots.

LOT 1.—An elegant and spacious DWELLING HOUSE and OFFICES, STABLING for six horses, with fore and back court, situate on that delightful and much admired spot, the STEINE, at Brighton, and extending to East-street, commanding an extensive view of the Sea and Cliffs, late the Residence and Property of

The Right Hon. WILLIAM GERALD HAMILTON, Deceased.

* These respective rooms retain at the present time many of their original characteristics.

† In 1817 Prince Leopold negotiated for the purchase of this house (then owned by Lady Anne Murray) in order that the Princess Charlotte might spend a short time there after her *accouchement*. The purchase was, probably, suggested by the fact that the Princess knew that her Royal mother had resided in the house. The lamented death of the Princess, however, put an end ⸺ ⸺tions, and the house was given up.

The Premises are substantially erected on a judicious plan and elevation, and contain two capital suites of lofty and well-proportioned apartments, fitted up in a style of superior taste in which elegance and convenience have been properly blended. Suitable servants' chambers and numerous domestic offices well-arranged and connected, the whole forming a desirable Residence for a Nobleman or Man of Fashion.

LOT 2.—A DWELLING HOUSE and TWO SHOPS in EAST STREET, and adjoining the above Lot, in the possession of MR. GLASSBROOK and MR. BUXTON, at a very low rent of Twenty-eight Pounds per annum.

LOT 3.—ABOUT HALF-AN-ACRE OF PASTURE GROUND, with BUILDINGS thereon, encompassed by a stone wall, situate in CHURCH STREET, let to MR. WITTEN, at £12 per annum.

Half the Purchase Money may remain on Mortgage for three years.

The Estates are Copyhold of Inheritance, but equal in value to Freehold, being subject only to quit rents of a few pence and trifling fines certain.

To be viewed by applying to MR. CRAWFORD, at the Library on the Steine, of whom printed Particulars may be had ; also of the Printers of the *Lewes Journal* ; Dolphin, Chichester ; Sussex Tavern, Tunbridge Wells ; and of Messrs. SKINNER, DYKE, and SKINNER, Aldersgate-street, London.

The property realized at the sale 4,000 guineas ; but the name of the purchaser did not transpire. This purchase must have been subject to a mortgage upon the house ; for the property, by one or other of the previous owners, had been mortgaged for £7,575 13s. 8d. to David Pitcairn, and the mortgage not being paid off, the property, after Mr. W. Gerald Hamilton's death, was released by the Trustees of his will, and they sold it (but no consideration is stated) on the 16th June, 1801, to Lady Anne Murray (sister of Chief Justice Mansfield*), who had previously, in the season, frequently visited Brighton. Her Ladyship was one of the most popular of the then fashionable residents ; for she not only kept up a large establishment, but her hand was "open as the day to melting charity" ; consequently, for several years, whenever she returned to Brighton for the season, it was customary to ring a joyous peal at old St. Nicholas in honour of the event. Lady Anne was, in her tastes, evidently one of the "old school" ; clinging to old customs to the last, even to, when riding out, being seated behind her groom, on a pillion,—that is, on a cushioned seat attached to the saddle. Her Ladyship occupied the house until her death, in her 90th year, in 1818, when it passed by her will (dated September 22, 1804)† to her niece, Lady

---

* Like his sister, the Right Hon. David Murray, the Earl of Mansfield, LL.D., was very partial to Brighton. He died here in 1796, at the age of 69 years.

† An extract from a summary of Lady Anne Murray's will is interesting, as showing her benevolent disposition towards those who had faithfully served her :—"To her housekeeper, who had been nearly 33 years in her service, she has given £3,500, and her wardrobe ; to her butler, who had been 24 years, £1,200 ; to her cook, who had been 19 years, £700 ; to her laundress, who had been 11 years, £600 ; to her two housemaids, one of whom had been 18 years, and the other 9 years in her service, £600 each ; and to her footman, who had been 9 years, £600."

Elizabeth Mary Finch Hatton, who subsequently disposed of it to Thomas Harrington, Esq., for £9,300. Mr. Harrington resided there (with occasional intervals) till his death in 1843; when, leaving it "upon trust for sale," it was purchased by his widow, Martha Harrington, for £6,900. This lady, in 1849, bequeathed the property to her nephew, Charles George Taylor, Esq. (the best Sussex gentleman cricketer of his day, who died suddenly in September, 1869, when only in his 52nd year). From the year 1850 down to 1863 the house was occupied by Captain Thelluson, a gentleman well-known and esteemed in local fashionable circles. He was a descendant of Peter Isaac Thelluson, whose eccentric will at one time excited so much comment and fruitless litigation. Captain Thelluson had for some years previously, we suppose, resided in Brighton, but whether or no the heir to the enormous wealth bequeathed in the will was born here we are uncertain. In a *Series of Letters*, by a German Prince, who visited Brighton in 1828, the author says,—"I saw Mr. Thelluson, a man of forty, who has very little property, and his son, a pretty boy of eight, who is probably destined in his 28th year to be master of twelve millions sterling. I could not help heartily wishing good luck to the little fellow and his splendid hopes." * In January, 1868, Mr. Taylor sold the property to Mr. Francis Henry Breidenbach, perfumer, of Old Bond-street, for £9,500, and who for some time resided in it. He and his family were, in fact, the last private residents in this once-famous house; for, after his death, it remained for some time tenantless. The property was eventually purchased by Mr. John Beal, the well-known stationer, &c., of East-street, by whom the rooms in the basement have been adapted to the increasing requirements of his business, whilst the elegant suite on the ground floor, together with the upper portion of the house,—wherein Royal and noble personages have dwelt, and which have been honoured by the presence of many high-born and distinguished guests in times gone by,—are devoted to the Offices of the School Board, &c. Such are the mutations of Time!

[Mr. Beal sold the Mansion to the School Board on September 29th, 1891, for £7,000.]

---

* Peter Isaac Thelluson was a native of Geneva. He settled as a merchant in London, where he acquired by his industry an enormous fortune. He died at his country seat, in Kent, on the 21st July, 1797, leaving three sons and three daughters. To his wife and children he bequeathed about £100,000; but his large estates, of the value of upwards of £500,000, he left to trustees to accumulate, to be laid out in the purchase of estates in England, *till the male children of his sons and grandsons were dead.* This period might extend to 120 years, in which case the property would amount to *one hundred and forty millions*, when, if there should be no lineal descendant, the property was to go for the use of the country, to the benefit of the Sinking Fund, under the direction of Parliament. This extraordinary will was disputed by the family of the testator, but it was affirmed by a solemn decree of Chancery, though an Act was afterwards passed, by means of Lord Chancellor Rosslyn, to prevent the recurrence of such absurd bequests for the future.

MRS. FITZHERBERT.

(After Cosway.)

The Mansion of Mrs. Fitzherbert.

The most modern of the houses connected with the ancient and departed glories of the Steine is that which, till within a very few years, was generally known as "Mrs. Fitzherbert's," having been built by that lady in 1804. Previous to that date there was on the site a small cottage and garden, occupied by a rope-maker named Male, who removed thither on his previous abode and "walk" being washed away from the sea-front. On the 6th September, 1803, the Lords of the Manor *granted* nearly all the garden of this house to Maria Fitzherbert; and on the 12th December, 1809, they *granted* the piece fronting the Steine, and east of the former piece, both being parts of the "Waste." When originally built, the view to the north-east from the balcony of Mrs. Fitzherbert's Mansion was less interrupted than now; there being then but two houses between it and the "Castle" tavern—one occupied by Dr. Gibney and the other by Mr. Kentfield, father of Mr. Edwin Kentfield, the famous billiard player of his day, who was better known as "Jonathan" Kentfield.* The south-eastern look out is, however, as charming and almost as unobstructed as ever over the Steine to the Marine-parade, the Chain Pier, and the Sea. The Mansion of Mrs. Fitzherbert was built by Mr. Porden, the architect and builder of the once magnificent range of stabling, &c. (now known as the Dome), in the Pavilion Grounds. Orignally it was brick-fronted, with a colonnade, finished in the Egyptian style; but this was blown down during a violent storm in the winter of 1805, when it was rebuilt in the Italian villa style—which now remains almost unaltered—with a spacious verandah and balcony on the upper story; whilst, on the lower, there is a broad flight of steps descending to the forecourt abutting on the Steine; the entrance being on its north side. But the interior has undergone a marked change since the days of Mrs. Fitzherbert, when, within its walls there were oftener more illustrious personages than were ever assembled in any other building in the town—the Pavilion excepted. Princes and noblemen, statesmen and warriors, artists and men of letters, the gifted and the great, high-born dames and ladies of fashion; each and all thronged thither—the guests of the beautiful woman who owned it, and whose natural grace and charm of manner fascinated all with whom she was brought into contact. Many a time and oft

---

* As an illustration of Mr. Edwin Kentfield's skill as a billiard player, we give the following well-authenticated anecdote:—When once in London, he strolled into a billiard-room where he was unknown to the marker; and was "induced" to play a game. The marker, knowing his own skill, but ignorant of that of his opponent, commenced by giving points. He lost! He reduced the odds; and was again beaten! He accepted odds; but again lost! and, alluding to a portion of his adversary's play which gave him the *coup de grace* in the final game, exclaimed, "None but Jonathan or the Devil could make such a stroke as that;" and Mr. Edwin Kentfield, denying that he was one of the "Gentlemen" alluded to, admitted that he *was* "Jonathan."

had the young FitzClarences spent a pleasant hour there, at the juvenile parties given in honour of the Hon. Miss Seymour, the orphan ward of Mrs. Fitzherbert, whom she took at her dying mother's request, and to whom she was devotedly attached. And there, too, eccentricity once had a place; for Mr. Cope, the "Green Man," had the honour of visiting, and, we are told, "amused the guests exceedingly!"

Even if the look-out from the balcony of Mrs. Fitzherbert's Mansion had not been interfered with by the surroundings which time and modern requirements have necessitated, the scenes which were once viewed from it would no longer meet the eye. When the Steine was in its pristine glory, what a spot that balcony must have been from whence to gaze upon the motley throng below! Upon Royal Princes mingling, without restraint, *en promenade* with the world of fashion resorting thither; or, it may be, indulging with their less Courtly associates in a little frivolity—racing and leaping over rails or handkerchiefs, &c. Upon the ever-varying streams of equestrians and carriage-folk, or promenaders, passing and re-passing! Upon ladies in the quaint and *outré* costumes of the period. Thence could also be watched the frequenters to the Libraries or Subscription Rooms, surging in and out; the excited knots of ladies and gentlemen gathered at Race-time at outside impromptu betting rings; the fun of the pic-nic auctions; the rustic sports; or the Fifth of November orgies. And what an animated scene was it, when Colonel Moore, who resided at the house below ("Single-Speech" Hamilton's), drilled the Sea Fencibles, or Colonel Berkeley the Militia, on the green sward opposite, with bands playing and surrounded by admiring crowds!

Many as had been the gay and festive scenes within the Mansion in earlier times, all were surpassed by the grand fancy dress ball which Mrs. Fitzherbert gave there in the season of 1828, and at which there was a brilliant gathering of more than 200 of the leading gentry in the town and neighbourhood. The ball was deemed one of the most splendid ever given in Brighton at a private residence. "No magnificence (we are told) can be conceived greater than that displayed in the various dresses;" and the fine rooms of the noble mansion, brilliantly lighted, presented a dazzling appearance. Mrs. Fitzherbert was attired in a rich dress of white satin, with white dress hat, and, though in her 73rd year, she appeared in excellent health and spirits, and "played the hostess" with that rare grace for which she was so pre-eminently distinguished, winning all hearts. Among the guests were Lords Granville, Shaftesbury, and Templedown; the Marchioness of Bristol and the Ladies Hervey, the Countess of Lindsay, Ladies C. Baring, Stewart, and Porchester, the Hon. Mrs. Dawson, &c. The more important fancy dresses were those of Lady Charlotte Bertie (Turkish dress), the Hon. Miss St. Clare (Dido), Lady Ellenborough (Queen Elizabeth), Lady Emily Butler and the Hon. Miss Law (each as Mary Queen of Scots), Lady Scott (Court Lady, Elizabethan period), Miss Scott (Polish dress), Lady Falkner (Turkish dress), Lord Beresford (Turkish dress), Lady Beresford (a

Sultana), the Countess St. Antonio (Goddess of Music), Lady Gibbs (Parisian costume), Lady Susan Hotham (Swiss costume), and Lady Coutts (Spanish costume). Besides those mentioned there were many tastefully attired as Circassians, Swiss, Poles, Spaniards, Greeks, and Turks; and a great number of the Officers of the Life Guards, Blues, and other regiments; and Naval Officers and others in fancy dresses and uniforms.

A few years more (March 27, 1837), and in that splendid room, in which had been crowded that gay and noble throng, lay all that was mortal of Maria Fitzherbert—the unacknowledged wife of George Prince of Wales, who owned that she was "the only woman he had ever loved"—the walls draped with black, and huge tapers burning round the rich crimson velvet-covered coffin that contained her remains. And possibly there never had before been seen such a crowd on the Steine, as when, a few days later, these were borne "with all the trappings and the suits of woe" to their last resting-place, the Roman Catholic Church of St. John the Baptist, Bristol-road; and where a handsome marble monument by Carew has been erected to Mrs. Fitzherbert's memory.* This monument was erected by the Hon. Mrs. Lionel Dawson Damer (formerly the Hon. Miss Seymour), the following words being inscribed on its base:—" One, to whom she was more than a parent, has placed this monument to her revered and beloved memory, as a humble tribute of her gratitude and affection."

In January, 1838, Mrs. Fitzherbert's noble Mansion was "brought to the hammer," by the celebrated auctioneer, Mr. George Robins. As was his custom, Mr. Robins delivered an admirable address on the occasion, giving a "glowing description of the advantages both natural and artificial of the estate." The first bidding was £3,000, offered by Colonel Webster. This was followed by others, until the highest real bidding, £5,900 was reached. It was ultimately bought in by Mr. Harris, of Covent Garden Theatre, for £6,400. The Trustees of Mrs. Fitzherbert eventually sold the house and lands for £1,000 (£100 of which was the portion for the copyhold) to the Honourable George Lionel Dawson Damer.

The mansion was subsequently occupied, we believe, by the Hon. Mr. Damer, and more recently by the late Wm. Furner, Esq., the much-respected Judge of the County Court, who resided there for several years. The last tenants of the Mansion were the proprietors of the Civil and United Service Club, by whom very extensive interior

---

* The will and codicil of Mrs. Fitzherbert were proved at Doctors' Commons by Sir John Francis Seymour, Knt., and John Gurwood and S. Forster, Esqrs., the executors. The amount of personal property was sworn under £35,000. She bequeathed several legacies, among which were two to her nieces, Mrs. Smythe and Lady Bathurst, of £1,000 each, and a like sum to Mrs. Craven. By a codicil, in her own handwriting, annuities were bequeathed to her servants, varying in amount from £50 to £200. The residue of her property was left, we believe, to the Hon. Mrs. Dawson Damer and Mrs. Jerningham. Among the property bequeathed was the Club House, at the corner of Steine-lane, opposite to Mrs. Fitzherbert's; and the property which originally stood on the site of this house was bought, we are told, with the last sum that Mrs. Fitzherbert received from George IV., namely £4,000, wholly in Bank of England notes.

alterations were made to adapt it to the new requirements. Hitherto, it had been left almost intact by the respective occupants ; and, in fact, for a private fashionable residence, the original arrangements of the Mansion could not well have been improved upon. There was a handsome double entrance hall, with a double staircase of elegant and unequal design, leading to a spacious suite of rooms on the principal floor, including an elegant and lofty saloon, the octagon boudoir opening upon the spacious paved front balcony, a noble drawing room, &c. ; on the ground floor was an elegant dining room opening upon the handsome Doric colonnade, with a flight of steps to the lawn in front ; whilst the other parts of the Mansion were in all respects most complete.

During the alterations of the basement made by the Club, there was a discovery which, for the moment, made quite a "sensation," namely, a stone-trap, just outside the kitchen wall, opening to a vault or subterranean passage, but so choked up with filth and rubbish that the workmen did not care to explore it. The news spread, and it was at once asserted that this was a vault or subterranean passage from Mrs. Fitzherbert's to the Pavilion ! Another discovery, made a day or two later, helped to confirm the assertion ; and this was a secret staircase in close proximity to the vault or passage, but which, at some time or other, had been built in. Some half-a-dozen or more of the steps were to be seen at the left-hand side of a cupboard at the northwest corner of the kitchen—the nearest point to the Pavilion ; and but for such a purpose,—connection with the discovered vault or passage,—there could not be, in that situation, any necessity for their existence. Alas ! for the tongue of scandal and wild surmise. The steps simply led to a *dry area round the front base of the Mansion*, which Judge Furner assured us he had traversed a score of times !

The Mansion of Mrs. Fitzherbert is now unoccupied ; and who is to be its next tenant time alone will show.

[Messrs. Wilkinson and Son disposed of the Mansion, in December, 1883, for £4,250, to the promoters of the Young Men's Christian Association, who made sundry internal alterations to meet their requirements, and reconstructed and brought forward the front of the Mansion as it is at present.]

The Inns of Brighton in 1800 and their Associations.

MRS. FITZHERBERT.

(After Cosway.)

The Inns of Brighton in 1800 and their Associations.

WHATEVER may have been the shortcomings of Brighton in 1800 in other respects, the want of inns and public-houses at the period could not fairly be laid to its charge. Never, surely, was town so blessed! There were no less than 41 inns and public-houses, which, as there were about 1,200 private houses, would give one inn to about every 30 of these latter! As the greater number, however, were old-established inns, and had existed, we might almost say, from time immemorial, there would seem to have been a period in the history of the old town when, the number of private houses being smaller, there was one inn to every twenty houses, or even to a less number than that.

This encouragement of public-houses among our aborigines would appear to have been an hereditary practice, and, probably, the last return, showing that in December, 1879, there were 44 hotels, and 424 public-houses and beershops in the town, may induce some persons to think that it has not yet died out!* So far back even as 1618 the "demand for beer" had become among the inhabitants of the town almost a mania, beer in a large majority of the houses being indiscriminately sold without permit or license. To such proportions, in fact, had the abuse of supplying it grown that, on the revision of "the Auncient Customs heretofore used among and between the Fishermen and Landsmen," it was declared that,—

"For as much as the said inhabitants of the said town of *Brighthelmston*, hath of long time been over-charged and suppressed by the multitude of poor people, which daily are thought to increase by means of many ale-house keepers and victuallers, which do harbour and receive all comers and goers, to the great hurt and hindrance of the said inhabitants, and doth still sell and keep ale and beer without license, and against the said inhabitants' consent, it is now ordered by the said inhabitants, for the suppressing of the said number of ale-houses and victualling-houses, that from henceforth for ever hereafter none of the said inhabitants whatsoever shall at any time hereafter, draw, sell. or keep any victualling or ale-house within the said town without a letter or testimonial of the said inhabitants, in writing, first had and obtained, by and with the consent of the constable, vicar, and curate, and six other substantial men of the said inhabitants, whereof four to be of the seamen, and two of the landsmen in their behalf, to be made unto the Justices of the King's Majesty's Peace   *   *   *   *   and that none other

---

* In March, 1892, the total number of hotels, public-houses, and beershops in Brighton was 572.

of the said inhabitants may use or occupy the same trade of victualling or ale-house keeping in the said town, but so many of them as shall be lawfully licensed as is aforesaid, upon pain and peril of every one so doing contrary to the true meaning of this present order, to forfeit for every barrel of beer so drawn six shillings and eight pence."

The above is pretty conclusive evidence of the " hereditary practice." Much, however, as the " great disorder of the tippling houses " may be attributable to the " lodging and harbouring of strangers," we are inclined to think that the *bonâ fide* inns of the old town were supported chiefly by the aborigines themselves. The number of inns in special localities goes far to prove this. For instance, in the neighbourhood of the old Fish-Market (about where the Clarendon Hotel now stands) there were, in 1800, no less than nine public-houses, counting from " The Gun " (now Harrison's Hotel) in Little Castle-square to " The Catherine Wheel " (supplanted by Brill's Baths) in Pool Valley; running almost in continuous line, and not a dozen yards apart! In every street, also, leading from a " gap " from the beach there was a greater proportion of inns than elsewhere. Our aborigines, therefore, if fond of salt water, certainly showed little partiality for *aqua pura*. Four inns, as if in opposition, were erected close to four of the old town pumps: " The Catherine Wheel " (subsequently " The Duke of Wellington "), in Pool Valley; " The Little Castle," in Little Castle-square; " The Spread Eagle " (subsequently " The Sussex Arms "), in East-street; and " The Unicorn," in North-street; and there is little doubt, considering how prevalent was the ancient local malady, which, for want of a better name, we may call *hydrophobia Brightoniensis*, that the inns were the more patronised of the two! * Two of the inns have certainly outlived the town pumps; and as regards one of those now extinct—" The Little Castle "—an inn and three beershops do duty in its stead in the same neighbourhood!

The inns in the other parts of the town would appear to have been proportioned more according to what would be considered the public requirements than those in the streets running to and along the sea-front. As the town grew, large rooms became necessary for meetings, the old Town Hall being useless for the purpose; and such rooms most of the newly-built houses possessed. The Vestry Meetings in the olden time were invariably held at public-houses. The more important at " The Old Ship "; but other houses at times enjoyed the honour. It has been suggested that these meetings might

* As affording some proof of the amount of business done at the old inns, it may be mentioned that in September, 1819, licenses were deemed to be worth from £600 to £1,000, according to locality; and it is on record that in 1818 or 1819 the High Constable was offered £500 if he would procure a license for a certain house! In July, 1822, there were no less than 34 applications for the opening of new public-houses; but only nine were granted. The new Beer Act of 1830 must have been regarded as a special boon by " tipplers," for in October that year more than 100 additional beer licenses were granted in one week! The *Brighton Herald* of that date, in alluding to this matter, says "Monday, the new Beer Act came into operation, and a high day it proved for the beer-loving and drinking tribes. Many of the landlords of the new beershops gave away beef and beer on the occasion, and in some instances bands of music enlivened the street from temporary orchestras."

THE BLOCK HOUSE, BRIGHTON, 1761.

THE BLOCK HOUSE, BRIGHTON, 1761.

not have been *all* "talking," and that the change of house was on the principle of "giving them all a turn!" Once (we learn from the Vestry Book, May, 1797,) the Churchwardens and Overseers held a meeting at "The Hen and Chickens" (now "The Running Horse"), King-street; but in this case the reason was obvious: the house being kept by the Parish Clerk!

The "auncients" did not seem to be at all particular as to where they opened house. Even the remains of the old "Block House"* were, so lately as 1749, utilised as a place for the sale of spirits! The following advertisement, proclaiming this fact to all the world, appeared in the *Lewes Journal* of September of that year:—

MARY SAUNDERS, WIDOW, at the BLOCK HOUSE, BRIGHT-HELMSTON, Sells fine genuine FRENCH BRANDY, at Nine Shillings per Gallon.

Purchasers ought not to have complained of the price; for nowa-days it is nearer 30s. per gallon.

But let bygones be bygones. Our present business is not so much with the habits and practices of our forefathers in connection with inns and public-houses, as with the inns themselves and their associations. In 1800 there were 41 inns and public-houses in Brighton. They may be grouped as — 1st, those more or less exclusively used by the "fishermen"; 2nd, those which carried on hotel business; and 3rd, those used for the ordinary purposes of supplying beer to the general public.

We have before said that where the fishermen "most did congregate,"—in the neighbourhood of the old Fish Market,— the inns and public-houses were very numerous. There were, in fact, nine, and the two outermost ones were scarcely a stone's throw from each other. The most westerly house of the group was "THE GUN" (now Harrison's Hotel), at the corner of Little

---

* The Blockhouse was built, for the defence of the coast, at the expense of the mariners of the town, about 1558-59, and was situated upon the Cliff between Ship-street and Black Lion-street. It was circular in form, and some 50ft. in diameter; the walls being about 8ft. in thickness and 18ft. in height. Several arched apartments in the walls were used as repositories for powder and ammunition. To the front of the Blockhouse, seawards, was a little battery, called the Gun-garden, on which were mounted four pieces of large iron ordnance. Adjoining the Blockhouse on the east was the Townhouse, surmounted by a turret, in which the town clock was fixed; there was a dungeon beneath for the confinement of malefactors. At the same time with the Blockhouse there were erected, partly if not wholly at the expense of the Government, four gates of freestone; three of which being arched and leading from the Cliff to the lower part of the town, then lying under it, viz., the East Gate (and Portal), at the south end of East-street; the Middle Gate (commonly called the Gate of All Nations) opposite the end of Middle-street; and the West Gate, opposite the end of West-street. From the East Gate, westward, there was built a wall some 15ft. high and 400ft. long; and from the termination of this wall, a parapet, 3ft high, was continued on the verge of the Cliff to the West Gate, with embrasures for cannon. The continued encroachments of the sea, and especially during the storms of 1703 and 1705, which finally swept away the town under the Cliff, gradually undermined the Gun-garden and the wall in front of the town, also the four gates; utterly destroying them. The sea afterwards sapped the foundations of the Blockhouse itself, so much so that part of the inner tower fell, and in 1761 the ruins were lying under the Cliff. *(See plate)*. The remainder was subsequently removed to make the carriage road at the spot more convenient.

Castle square, kept by Mrs. Elizabeth Furner. The house in 1800 had not the fine proportions the present Hotel now possesses; but was a small building of low elevation, with a forecourt enclosed by a dwarf wall, this latter being well adapted for a "lop" for the fishermen and 'long-shoremen, when pursuing their time-out-of-mind habitual daily "Studies of the Ocean." In the early coaching days, at the close of the last century, Wessen's coaches and Tucker's "Dilligence" used to set out from "The Gun"; to which they also returned, and, when convenient, passengers were accommodated with apartments.* In connection with "The Gun," we may quote a curious advertisement issued by the Parish Officers in 1797:—

TOWN OF BRIGHTON.—THIS IS TO GIVE NOTICE, that the Parish Officers of Brighthelmston will (at their next meeting, to be holden at "The Gun Inn," on MONDAY, the 25th day of this instant September, 1797, at Six o'clock in the evening), receive proposals from any Medical Gentlemen (within the said Parish of Brighthelmston) for MEDICALLY FARMING THE POOR OF THE SAID PARISH, from the 29th day of September instant, to Christmas, 1798.

The particulars may be known by applying to Mr. ATTREE, Attorney, Brighthelmston, Vestry Clerk.

On the opposite side of Little Castle-square (No. 3) was "THE LITTLE CASTLE" itself, kept by Mr. John Last; and almost immediately to the north of this latter inn was "THE THREE TUNS," at the top of Three Tun-court, Mr. Thomas Francis being "mine Host." But there is little of interest to record in connection with them. Not far from the "Three Tuns" was "THE STAR AND GARTER" (kept by Mr. Thomas Colchin). When "The Star and Garter" was erected, we do not know. It dates back prior to 1785, for in August of that year a "Giant Exhibition" was held there. The advertisement of the Exhibition was as follows:—

IRISH GIANTS.— The most surprising GIGANTIC TWIN BROTHERS are just arrived in Brighthelmston, and to be seen at the STAR and GARTER, on the Cliffe, every day, Sundays excepted, from Eleven in the Morning to Nine at Night. These truly amazing phœnomena are indisputably the most astonishing productions of the human species ever beheld since the days of Goliah. These modern Colossuses are but twenty-four years of age and very near EIGHT FEET HIGH. Admittance: Ladies and Gentlemen, 1s.; Servants, 6d.

What success attended the Exhibition is not recorded.

---

* Concerning accommodation at "The Gun," and also of the town generally at the period, we extract the following from a "Private Diary" written in 1792 by the Clerk of Arraigns at the Old Bailey, London: — "We were taken in at 'The Gun,' but the driver was obliged to take himself and the horses several miles into the country. Our only accommodation at 'The Gun' was a chamber wherein were two beds, and at night we had scarce swallowed our supper before we were informed that the gentlemen who slept there were desirous to go to bed, which obliged us to decamp to the nightly quarters that had been provided for us at the house of an old woman in the neighbourhood. In the room I slept were two beds, but luckily I had no chum. On my saying that when I was tired of one bed I should get into the other, the old woman very seriously observed that she allowed a person only one bed of a night. She entertained the ladies by giving us the only lighted candles she had, and leaving herself in the dark, eventually disappeared in a manner of walking peculiar to herself and crabfish. The beds were b⸺ ⸺ great plenty."

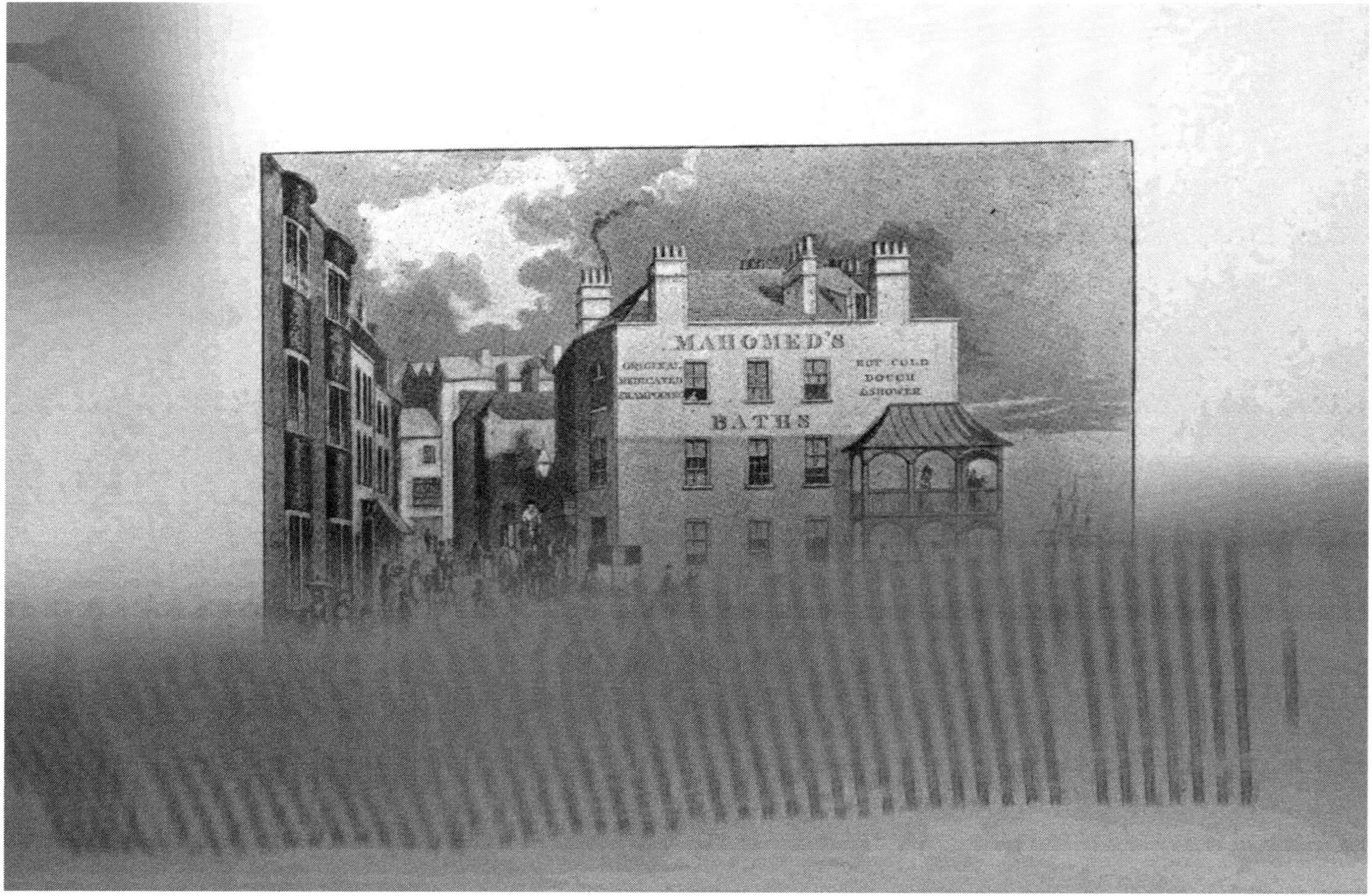
MAHOMED'S
ORIGINAL
MEDICATED
HOT COLD
DOUCH
&SHOWER
BATHS

THE WHITE HORSE HOTEL. "Rising Sun."
Supplanted by Brill's Baths, &c., in 1869.

MAHOMED'S BATHS.

Supplanted by Markwell's Royal Hotel, 1869-70.

The neighbourhood of "The Star and Garter," with fine property in close contiguity, and a broad roadway between it and the rails, has vastly changed since the close of the last century; in fact, there is a marked change between it now and what it was even in 1825. The houses below the Hotel, leading towards East-street, were without shops, the windows of the lower one—about where Dash's is now— being decidedly primitive. The house on the opposite corner of Three Tun-square (now Mr. Dixey's) was in 1825 a coach office. There was then only a very narrow roadway between "The Star and Garter" and the beach, a flight of wooden steps, entirely unprotected, leading directly from the road to the beach, and the sea washed up them at high tide. The width of the road at the point may be judged by the fact that the top of the steps was parallel with the western side of Mahomed's Baths, or about where the steps of the entrance to Markwell's Royal Hotel now are. Close to Mahomed's Baths, in the road, was a capstan; and there was another right in the centre of the road in front of "The Star and Garter," the bar of which, when used, almost went through its window! On the removal of this capstan, in 1827, when that grand improvement, the Junction-road, was being effected (which rendered the road continuous along the sea front from the Marine-parade to the King's-road),[*] and the sea-wall round Mahomed's Baths was formed, the last of the many fights between "landsmen" and "fishermen" took place; the former being victorious! One "Buck" Marchant, the champion of the fishermen, who with his *confrères* used the said capstan, armed himself with an iron crowbar to defend it; but he eventually fell back on the more familiar aboriginal weapon, *clamor nauticus, i.e.*, swearing and bluster, making much noise but doing little harm![†] Another "champion," on the Junction-road being made, appeared. Whilst the workmen were filling in behind "The Dolphin" (to which—and to the tan-yards and herring-dees close by—there had been previously ready access from the beach), he jumped into the gap where the stones, &c., were being thrown, and said that, sooner than let them do it, they should bury him! As neither tablet nor record tells of

---

[*] The "Grand Junction Parade," as it was originally named, was opened December 10th, 1829, by a procession. The cavalcade started from the Old Ship Hotel, headed by the band of the 15th Hussars, mounted, followed by three of the Magistrates, T. R. Kemp, Esq., M.P., S. F. Mitford, Esq., and W. Seymour, Esq., and several of the Commissioners and other persons in vehicles. After passing over the road, the temporary barriers of which were, on the approach of the procession, removed, it returned, round the Steine and up North-street, to "The Old Ship," where, after an excellent dinner, a "great number of speeches were made, laudatory, complimentary, and congratulatory to the persons then and there present."

[†] The affair, however, threatened at one time to be very serious; in fact, such was the aspect of affairs, that Sir David Scott, one of the Magistrates, accompanied the High Constable to North-street and swore in as many as 93 special constables. In the meantime, Mr. G. Vallance, who appeared to have much influence with the fishermen, induced them to put aside their weapons and meet the Commissioners at the Town Hall, with the view of settling the dispute amicably. At the meeting, and after much argument,—the fishermen asserting their legal right to the ground, &c.,—it was eventually decided that the fishermen had no legal status, the roads and ways being vested by Act of Parliament in the Commissioners. The difference was ultimately settled by new capstans being erected by the Commissioners *on the beach.*

the ultimate fate of this would-be aboriginal martyr, it is probable that he thought better of his resolve and—walked away! "The Star and Garter" was at one time kept by Mr. Paul Hewitt, a gentleman who took an active part in local affairs; also by Mr. Boxall, builder. Of late years, Mr. Thos. Smith was "mine Host," who was succeeded by his sons, in the proprietorship. [Mr. T. Grevatt, who succeeded them in 1885, sold the business at Christmas, 1891, to the present proprietor, Mr. Wormald.]

Just below "The Star and Garter," on the opposite side of the road, was "THE DOLPHIN," kept in 1800 by Mr. William Peck. The house (which was removed in 1846, when the Queen's Hotel was built) was in existence previous to the destruction of the old Battery (1786); and was evidently a popular house with the fishermen; probably with the soldiers, too, for the guard-house of the cavalry was for several years within a door or two of it. It was originally little more than a double-fronted cottage (its whole frontage was about 30ft.) with a tan-house behind; but, after it was opened as a public-house, its situation commanded a "trade"; and this may be estimated by the fact that, when sold by auction in 1792, it realised £650.* The only incident of public interest in association with "The Dolphin" was the fact that a dinner, in connection with the 5th November riots in 1817, when Sergeant Rowles was killed, took place there, which occasioned the publication of a once-famous but now little known local satire, entitled "The Battle of the Tar-Tub."

Not far from "The Dolphin," at the north-western corner of Pool-lane (now Pool-valley) was "THE GREYHOUND," the host in 1800 being Mr. Richard Moppett (father of the late Mr. Moppett, tailor, of 41, West-street). The house was originally known by the more nautical name of "The Anchor," and, from a deed in the possession of Mr. Taylor (who owns the adjoining house), the property was in existence prior to August, 1658, the land behind it being described as an "open garden to the easternmost wall in the Poole." When "The Anchor" was changed to "The Greyhound," there is no record.

Opposite "The Greyhound," 65, East-street, was "THE WHITE HORSE," kept in 1800 by Mr. William Allen (father-in-law of the subsequent popular proprietor, Mr. Stephen Hodd). At the time when Mr. Allen kept "The White Horse," it was of less proportions than it afterwards became, prior to its removal for the erection of the noble Baths which now occupy its site. There was, in fact, a private house (occupied by Mr. Willis, a fisherman,) between it and "The Rising Sun"; and this house, when the Hotel was altered by Mr. John Gallard in 1825, was thrown into it. Where the front door of the late Hotel was, a covered carriage road formerly ran through to the extensive stables behind; for the house for some time prior to the close of the last century was a well-known posting-house. The

---

* The purchaser was Mr. Bartholomew Smithers, of Preston, grandfather of Mr. (late Alderman) Smithers, to whom it subsequently passed. As showing, however, the rapid increase in the value of property in the neighbourhood, it may be mentioned that, some years later, in 1829, Mr. Creasy sold some old premises between "The Dolphin" and Mahomed's Baths (about 26ft. frontage), which realised £2,026 10s., or nearly £80 per foot.

THE WHITE HORSE HOTEL. "Rising Sun."
Supplanted by Brill's Baths, &c., in 1869.

landlord in 1789 was Mr. Henwood, subsequently of "The New Inn," and who then, and for several years after, was actively associated with "posting" and coaching. Under his auspices "The White Horse" further developed its business, and especially as a "commercial" house. It was at "The White Horse" that, on Wednesday, August 26, 1789, the first Lodge of "the Ancient and Honourable Society of Free and Accepted Masons of England," H.R.H. the Duke of Cumberland, G.M., was opened in Brighton, by virtue of a warrant from the R.W. Samuel Hulse, Esq., P.G.M. for the County of Sussex, the Lodge being denominated the Royal Clarence, and bearing the No. 534. The Lodge (of which the Rev. J. Mossop was Chaplain) soon "increased and multiplied"; and in the following October received the sanction of Royalty, the Duke of Clarence, in due form, approving the title.*

"The White Horse" was also the Brighton head-quarters during the old County elections. Party feeling then ran higher than it does now; and at an election, some forty or fifty years ago, when Mr. Curteis (whose Committee sat at the Hotel) was one of the candidates, the counter-election cries outside so exasperated the cook at "The White Horse," that she threw a bowl of scalding water from the window upon the crowd beneath.† "Barber" Harmer, a local character of the period, and keeper of the old "Black Hole" (the then temporary "lock-up" for prisoners, situated immediately to the north-east of the present Market), unfortunately chanced to receive the contents of the bowl; and, as he was already lame from gout and other ailments, the poor fellow limped home to his "Hole" in a pitiable condition—silenced, at all events, for that election!

Mr. William Allen, who, as before mentioned, kept "The White Horse" in 1800, was a fine old character, who feared no man, and did not hesitate to speak his mind freely. At a previous election to the above, when Sir Godfrey Webster was "chaired," after winning one of the most expensive County elections that ever took place in Sussex, costing no less than £75,000,—in Chichester alone the "open houses" cost £1,200 per day,—his carriage stopped opposite "The White Horse" (the Committee room of the opposing Candidate), whereupon William Allen came out, and, taking his watch from his "fob," said, holding it up, "Look, here, Sir Godfrey, *this* is paid for, *paid for!*" Sir Godfrey bowed, and the procession moved on.‡

---

* The Royal Clarence Lodge was subsequently removed to Brother Hicks's, at "The Old Ship," where, on December 31, 1800, the "Festival of St. John the Evangelist" was duly celebrated.

† The cry, we are told, was "No red herring soup!" which arose from a report that Mr. Curteis had said that red herrings were good enough food for the poor. During the election, red herrings were suspended from the trees at various places along the road between Brighton and Chichester! When his opponent, Sir Godfrey Webster, paraded the eastern part of the County during the election, his carriage was decorated with red herrings.

‡ The point of Mr. Allen s remark was this: An absurd rumour had been set afloat by Sir Godfrey's supporters that Mr. Curteis had not paid a tavern election bill of some £3,000, which was untrue. The "unpaid bill" cry was revived; but it was effectually silenced by the production of the receipt at one of the election meetings.

Among the "events" associated with "The White Horse" may be mentioned the inquest held there on April 12, 1822, on Mr. Briggs, hatter, of Brighton, and Mr. Knowles, of Cowfold, who, on the 9th April, were returning from Newhaven in a light chaise cart, and who, when about half-way between Rottingdean and Brighton, at a point near Roedean gap, were thrown over the cliff and killed on the spot. It was supposed that, the night being very dark, the unfortunate men lost the track of the road, and in endeavouring to regain it by turning the horse in a contrary direction from the Cliff, the animal ran backwards—he was known to be guilty of that vice— and, owing to their close proximity to the edge of the Cliff (the road where the accident occurred was not more than three yards distant therefrom), they were precipitated a depth of at least 100ft. The horse was also killed, and the cart, with the exception of the wheels, was literally dashed to pieces.

Just below "The White Horse," at No. 68, was "THE RISING SUN," kept in 1800 by Mr. William Wallis, who had been landlord since the 15th November, 1786. He had cause to remember the date; for two days after entering upon the house the great storm occurred which washed away the Battery then at the bottom of East-street. The house was one of the oldest in the town; and was famous in earlier times from being the haunt of the ghost of "Old Strike-a-Light." More beer, in spite of the ghost, was probably drunk at "The Rising Sun" than at any other house in the town. That it was well frequented may be inferred from the fact that the original Brighton Fish Market was held on the beach just below it; and early in the present century,—before Mr. Lamprell dug out the beach for his Baths (subsequently known as "the Bunion") and adjacent buildings,—a large pair of scales used to stand by the side of the house, in the narrow roadway between the Clarendon Hotel and the present Baths, to which the fishermen used to bring their fish from the beach below to be weighed. At the time Mr. Wallis took the house, the rental was £9 a-year; but when he left it some years afterwards, to keep "The St. Catherine's Wheel," so lucrative had business become, that the rent had been raised to £45 a-year.*

Both "The White Horse" and "The Rising Sun" were removed in 1869,† when Brill's Baths Company, who had purchased the site,

---

* The increase of trade at the house was also attributed to the discovery, at the period in question, of the celebrated "Diamond Fishing Ground" off Hastings, which turned out so valuable (hence its name) that our aborigines,— out of sheer gratitude, we suppose,—were wont, after a voyage there, to drink "to its everlasting continuance," in copious draughts of John Barleycorn drawn from the cellars of "The Rising Sun"! The house was then supplied by Messrs. Tidy and Whichelo (whose brewery was in Ship-street, and was subsequently occupied by Mr. William Wigney, the accounts being kept by "tally" (notches on a stick); and when the number of hogsheads amounted to twenty—which, we are told, was at not very long intervals—one hogshead was given in! This surely must have been the "golden age" of brewers and publicans.

† The removal, by Mr. Oliver Weston (a well-known Auctioneer, of Brighton,) of these respective properties, which were somewhat extensive and covered a very large area, was a truly marvellous work. It occupied only 12 days; 105 men being employed night and day (excepting Sundays). The properties seemed to disappear as if under the spell of a magician's wand. One or

erected their large swimming and other baths. Being familiar with the tradition associated with the old house, we made an "exploration" of the cellars while in their primitive state ; and it may not be deemed uninteresting to relate the details of our visit to

Ye Haunte of Olde Strike-a-Light.

It may be premised that "Old Strike-a-Light," or "Jack Strike-a-Light," as he was more frequently called, was but one of several kindred superstitions current a hundred years ago among our aboriginal population, most of which, except the "White Hawk Lady," of the Race Hill, are now buried beneath bricks and mortar, or have died out with time, or disappeared before growing intelligence Few now know aught of " Betsy Bedlam," who, when Belle Vue Fields (now Regency-square) had a capstan and archway in their centre, was the terror of the juveniles of the period ; or of the " Wick 'oman," who " haunted " the gap which formerly ran down to the beach from what is now Lansdowne-place, and whose memory still lingered long after in the echo which the boys of a later day were wont to wake unfailingly, as they crossed the fields before you came to the old Lower Wick Pond (formerly in Western-road, to the north-west of Lansdowne-place), on their way to "the Post" to bathe.

But to " Old Strike-a-Light's " haunt, " The Rising Sun." The original house (the upper portion of the late " Sun " Hotel was of modern erection) was, as already stated, among the earliest inns opened in Brighton. As to the date of its establishment, history is silent. It is sought for in vain in '· The Book of all the Auncient Customs," or in any other well-reputed local chronicle. Of its first host, who he was, when he lived, or when he died,

"By whom lamented, or by whom forgot,"

nothing is known. The only authentic information respecting the house in the early part of the last century is, that it was kept by " Host " Mockford (the grandfather of the late Mr. Mockford, tailor, of the King's-road). The house was then called " The Naked Boy " ; and on the sign over the front door was painted a naked child, having a roll of cloth under his left arm, and a pair of shears in his right hand. Beneath the figure (in accordance with the custom of the time) were the following lines:—

"So fickle is our English nation,
I would be clothed if I knew the fashion." *

Some time after the death of Host Mockford, his widow married a Mr. Thomas, and they together kept the house for many years. When firmly installed (which must have been about the year 1755 or 1760), Host Thomas altered the sign of the house to " The Rising Sun." The old house was of very humble architectural pretensions : its front facing the

---

two "discoveries" were made, namely, a part of the old Battery wall, some 4ft. thick (immediately to the north of "The Rising Sun"), and an old cellar—the existence of which was previously unknown, but it was apparently connected with " The White Horse "—completely filled with empty wine bottles. Van loads of them were removed ; leading to the inference that, if the consumption of beer was enormous at "The Rising Sun," that of wine at " The White Horse " was not a whit behind it.

* These lines were a modern paraphrase of those of old Andrew Borde, in his *Introduction to Knowledge*, ridiculing the eccentricities of the English of his day in copying the ever-varying fashions of the French and other continental people. His lines are :—

"I am an Englishman, and naked I stand here,
Musing in my mynde what rayment I shall were ;
For now I will were this, and now I will were that,
Now I will were I cannot tell what."

old battery ground, and its side windows facing the sea. Being in existence prior to modern improvements as to roadways and groynes (though the old Pump-house-groyne stood a little to the eastward of it), "The Rising Sun," with two other houses on the beach somewhat to the westward of it, was frequently washed, and particularly on the East-street side, by the sea. During very high tides, the waves rolled up the gap at that side, by a portion of the old Battery wall, without let or hindrance; and within the memory of many persons now living, the sea has been seen on several occasions to wash past both the old "Rising Sun" and the "White Horse Hotel," and flow down Pool-lane into the valley.

From the fact of the old "Rising Sun" being situated close to the beach, and its affording a convenient place for smugglers to deposit their unlawful gains in, it has been thought by some that "Old Strike-a-Light's" appearances were "invented," as in many another spot similarly situated, to prevent prying persons from exploring the cellars below. This must remain an open question; but, visiting these old cellars prior to their removal, their massive walls, black and begrimed with age, were sufficient to convince one that, amongst an ignorant and superstitious people, a colour of truth might easily have been given to such supernatural horrors as were said to be connected with them. On the east side of the cellar proper of "The Rising Sun" a ponderous door opened into the wine cellar about six feet in length by about three or four wide—which, as seen by the dim light therein, with the fungi growing plentifully from its blackened roof over the bins, presented anything but an inviting appearance. But, beyond this first cellar, was another recess, to which the light had failed to penetrate, and of much smaller proportions (apparently about 3ft. by 2ft.), intensifying, by deeper gloom and by its greater apparent age, all the repulsive characteristics of the preceding. Lighting a scrap of paper, to get a better glimpse at the interior, we were amazed at the mass of fungi which had been generated there. It hung over and in the bins in huge pendants of nearly a foot in length, in form like the stalactites in a grotto, but covered with filth and festooned with long lines of web, the growth of numberless years. One could not resist glancing at the floor—which consisted apparently of a single stone slab—whence, said tradition, a large amount of money was dug, and whence "Old Strike-a-Light" used to emerge in a miller's dress to perform his nightly mission,—now pointing to the cellar below, and now striking his flint and steel, and making at every stroke an unearthly light to stream from the windows; and beneath which said floor, more substantial authority asserts, a number of human bones were found (subsequently interred by direction of the then Vicar, the Rev. Mr. Michell, in the churchyard of old St. Nicholas), together with a sword, now in the possession of an old townsman, the point of which, it is said, never can be made bright, from the rust caused by the blood on it when it was buried!

Whether or no any deed of blood gave rise to the popular belief in the supernatural appearance of "Old Strike-a-Light" at "The Rising Sun," it is impossible to say; certain it is that he was early "in possession" of the premises—at the time the Thomas's had the house—and was not effectually "laid" till the close of the last century. Mr. Erredge, in his "History of Brighthelmston," gives an interesting legend connecting "Old Strike-a-Light" with a member of the Jervoise family (one of the oldest Brighton families, their vault, the most ancient in the old Churchyard, bearing date 1517), and assigning the credit of "extinguishing" him to a monk of St. Bartholomew. The legend is as follows:—

"OLD STRIKE-A-LIGHT.

"A tremendous gale had ceased, but still the mountainous swelling of the sea beat violently on the shore, when the boat of Swan Jervoise came into the

Brighton roadstead, having weathered the storm. The night was pitchy dark; scarcely could the outline of the horizon be perceived, and not a light illumined the blank. The surprise of Jervoise and his crew was therefore great when they beheld a stream of meteor-like splendour burst from every window of 'The Rising Sun' Inn, and as suddenly all was again involved in utter darkness. This terrific appearance was repeated many times. Swan Jervoise was one of those men who never conjecture, but proceed at once to ascertain a cause. He, therefore, with two of his men, went ashore; but proceeded alone to 'The Rising Sun,' expecting to find the people up. After knocking and bawling loud enough to rouse all the dead in the Bartholomews' Chapel, without wakening the landlord, he was about to force the door, when the light again burst from the windows, and he distinctly heard a ticking as of a person striking a light with a flint and steel, each stroke producing this supernatural blaze of light. In a moment afterwards the door was open, and a being seven feet high, wrapped in a large black cloak, with a high conical white hat, issued forth. He noticed not the poor drenched fisherman, but he strode on until he disappeared in the darkness. Jervoise's hair stood stiff on his head; his limbs trembled with fear; and he shrieked aloud with terror. The landlord heard his cry, and came down with his torch. Seeing his neighbour in such a plight, he bade him come in, roused up a fire, made him take a seat in the capacious chimney, and—having comforted him with good words—placed a rushlight on the table, and then retired to procure a jug of ale. Jervoise, scarcely recovered from his fright, was thus again left alone. As he sat musing by the crackling fire, the dim rush throwing a fitful light around the room, he chanced to turn his head; when, from over the back of the settle, he beheld the deathlike features—pallid as a sear cloth—of the tall man in the conical hat. His countenance was most ghastly, and he fixed his grey glazed eyes full on Jervoise, and poined to the hearth. This was more than he could bear,—he uttered one loud scream, and fell senseless to the ground. He was thus found by the landlord, who conveyed him to bed; and the next day Jervoise related the particulars to Father Anselm, of St. Bartholomew, and then expired. But the Blessed Virgin and Saint Nicholas oft-times bring good out of evil; for, on examining the hearth to which 'Old Strike-a-Light' (as the apparition has since been called—pointed, a vast treasure was found, which is still safely deposited with the Principal of this Order in Normandy; nor has 'The Rising Sun' since been haunted by the unholy spirit of 'Old Strike-a-Light.'"

This interesting old legend, though identical in some particulars, does not altogether accord with the popular tradition respecting "Old Strike-a-Light's" appearances and his "laying" current among our aborigines some 70 or 80 years ago. It may have been that "Swan Jervoise" was too mythical a personage; that the "Father" was a papist a sect of which they had a wholesome horror, and that Normandy was a little too far off to deposit the treasure for such a matter-of-fact people. As to "Old Strike-a-Light's" dress, *white* was decidedly the popular colour; but as to the way in which he appeared, there is a discrepancy in the evidence: some said he used to seat himself astride a barrel in the cellar, chinking a piece of money in a pewter dish; others that he used to appear dressed as a miller, striking a flint and steel, the fitful flashes from which used to stream from every window of the house, and could be seen far out at sea! But, whatever doubts there may have been as to "Old Strike-a-Light's" actual appearances, there was none among our aborigines as to how and by whom he was "laid." They did not want to go to Normandy to learn that. They believed they had unimpeachable evidence nearer home: the personages who accomplished this marvellous feat being no other than the host and hostess of "The Rising Sun,"—Mr. Bradford and his wife, popularly known as "Shaky Bradford" and "Nanny Shaky." It was implicitly believed that, by searching beneath the spot to which "Old Strike-a-Light's" shadowy finger invariably pointed, it had fallen to their lot to discover the crock of gold which had been buried there! the non-discovery of which had for so many years caused "Old Strike-a-Light" to

"Revisit the glimpses of the moon,
Making the night hideous."

In proof of the fact, it used to be said that, when the Bradfords took "The Rising Sun" of the Thomases above-mentioned, they had not the whole of the money necessary to pay for their incoming; and so, because the worthy couple managed to retire from the business in a few years after, and as the appearances of "Old Strike-a-Light" had ceased during their occupancy (more enlightenment being probably abroad), they had the credit of finding the long-hidden and much-envied crock of gold!

The old couple, on their retirement, lived for many years after at the house now known as "The Waggon and Horses," at the corner of Jubilee-street, and, though they were much respected, "Shaky Bradford" and his wife, "Nanny Shàky," never ceased among old Brightonians to have the credit of "laying" the ghost of "Old Strike-a-Light" at "The Rising Sun"!

Behind "The White Horse" stables, in Pool-valley, was, in 1800, "THE ST. CATHERINE'S WHEEL," popularly called "The Cat and Wheel." The sign of the house was most probably derived from the legend of St. Catherine (one of the patron saints of fishermen), who was said to have suffered martyrdom by being broken on a wheel. The Saint's shrine, doubtless, had no lack of devotees, as the colliers at this period chiefly ran in to unload at the old Pump-house groyne on the beach; and "The Cat and Wheel" was the nearest house to it. The house was subsequently known as "The Duke of Wellington." When originally opened, we know not; but the house on the occasion of the Great Storm of July, 1850, had a very narrow escape from total destruction. As this storm (and consequent flood in Pool Valley*) was the most remarkable which had occurred in Brighton within living memory, a few particulars concerning it, summarised from the "Narrative" which appeared in the *Brighton Herald*, may not, perhaps, here be deemed out of place.

THE GREAT STORM OF JULY 17TH, 1850.

This remarkable storm may be said to have commenced about half-past six in the evening of the above day. For several days previously the heat had been most excessive; and on the day previous to the storm a dense sea-fog rolled up from the south-west and covered the whole town. On Wednesday the day of the storm - the weather was very hot and close. Towards evening there rose up, heavy and threatening in the east, an immense "thunder-loft"; while in the west there was a vast blue-black curtain. About half-past six the wind suddenly shifted to the north-west; then worked more to the west, and at times seemed to blow from the south-west, bringing with it in its sweep immense masses of clouds, which appeared to join immediately over the town. No sooner did these masses meet than the town was enveloped in a lurid mist, which concealed every object from sight. Then came—suddenly, as like the explosion of a bomb-shell—one terrific clap of thunder, which seemed to shake the town to its foundations; and immediately after the whole atmosphere seemed to descend in vast sheets of water, which fell with such force on the roofs

---

* Floods, we may state, were in the early part of the century no strangers to the Valley; but they came from the sea, not the land. Visitations of the sea at certain seasons were looked upon as a matter of course in the locality, and there were, we are told, formerly in the parlour of "The Cat and Wheel" the wall registering the various heights to which the water had

VIEW OF POOL VALLEY DURING THE STORM OF JULY 17th, 1850.

of the houses that it bounded up again in a fine mist,—so fine, yet so thick, that it resembled smoke. The rain, too, was so dense, that it seemed to fill the air, so much so, that nothing could be distinctly seen on the other side of the street. Whilst the deluge of rain swept down the hillsides, the streets, and every open space, with such extreme violence as to fill every under-ground drain and sewer,—indeed, the basement of almost every house in the lower part of the town,—the lightning was incessant, now in vivid blue and pink flashes almost immediately overhead, and now playing apparently upon the ground like lurid blue smoke - the thunder burst in continuous volleys on every side, now so close, as if it would shatter every thing around, and now rumbling in the distance, and then, as if having gathered all its energy to make one mighty effort, it returned and broke forth in a clap that made the ear crack, and the very floors of the strongest house shake.* The storm lasted without interruption for nearly an hour, and then went muttering off, like dropping musketry, towards the same quarter whence it had come the west.

Our limits will not permit us to recount the disastrous effects of the storm, which seemed to be almost exclusively confined to Brighton. Suffice it to say that there was scarcely a house in the lower part of the town which did not experience its disastrous effects, either by the bursting of drains or damage to its basement, furniture, &c. When the violence of the storm had somewhat abated, the state of the streets in some parts was as if the town had been submerged. To the north the Level was like a lake, with large sheets of water on each side. The large space between St. Peter's Church Enclosure and the Northern Enclosure was all but impassable. That between the Northern Enclosures themselves was wholly so; and there was no passage along their east side by the Grand-parade: the water reaching from the coping of the railings almost to the areas of the houses, and in some cases poured down them. The Pavilion Grounds were completely swamped. The Steine presented a most extraordinary spectacle. The roads and pavements by which it is surrounded and divided were covered with a wide sheet of water, which also overspread nearly the whole of the green, leaving the Statue of George IV. and the Fountain standing out like landmarks. But the point to which all the currents from the hills and valley swept was Pool-valley, the natural embouchure for water flowing from the north to the sea. There the extent of the deluge and its destructiveness were most apparent. The Valley may be compared to an irregularly-shaped basin. Standing at the bottom of its south-western side was a range of buildings (removed some few years since) - a remnant of old Brighton—consisting of Wood's Original Baths (kept by Mrs. Creak), two workshops, two small tenements, and "The Duke of Wellington" Inn. These buildings, from their situation, speedily felt the full force of the torrents which poured in by the openings each side of the York Hotel and that at the north-western side of the Albion Hotel. The gratings on each side of the Baths being unequal to the task of carrying off the water, a "pool" was speedily formed, which soon flowed over the pavement and into the

---

* The esteemed contributor to the *Brighton Herald*, "REVILO," in considering the causes of the storm, wrote as follows in reference to the lightning and thunder :—"To say that the lightning unceasingly *flashed* would be a preversion of such a mild term, for it literally *blazed*, and to such an extent as I believe appalled the manliest heart; in two instances it descended in a shower of sparks. The lightning was generally of a pale roseate hue, and, contrary to law, struck the lower buildings and spared the higher; and the thunder instead of making a report as from a gun, in many instances really made a noise like the hissing of water when red hot iron is plunged into it, combined with the cracking produced by rending a piece of timber, and a crashing noise, such as might be supposed would take place from the decrepitation of a multitude of electric sparks, close at hand."

front door of the Baths. The door was at once shut; but the pressure of water soon burst it open, and, pouring in, soon filled all the rooms in the basement—20 in number. All resistance to the invading element was out of the question: Mrs. Creak and her assistants immediately ran to the upper rooms, leaving to the mercy of the torrent all below. Tables, sofas, chairs, &c., were soon afloat; the water rising in the reading room to about 5ft., and, on its subsidence, leaving its mark on the walls by a line of mud. Mr. Strong's painter's shop (some 30ft. in length), next the Baths, was soon filled, to the height of 5ft. 6in., and paints, brushes, and every other implement of the trade were soon floating about. It was the same with the carpenter's shop next door.* The cottage adjoining this latter shop was completely gutted (the occupant making his escape out of the window by swimming); and so was Mrs. Ransom's little grocer shop next this; all the stock being destroyed. "The Duke of Wellington"—the end house of the range fared very badly; for so rapid was the inrush of water that Mr. Peters, the "host," had only time to save his cash box and account books. The flood, after filling the beer and wine cellars, throwing every cask from its stollage and spoiling their contents, rose to 5ft. in the bar, and reached to the seventh step of the staircase to the upper rooms. The houses on the west side of the Valley also suffered considerably.

Efforts were made during the storm by Mr. Cordy Burrows and Mr. Strong to clear the choked up gratings each side of the Baths; but when they reached the spot, being unprovided with necessary implements, the depth of the water and the strong current made their efforts useless. Soon after two boats were brought by some fishermen, and the attempts to clear the gratings were renewed; but it was nearly half-past eight—about a quarter of an hour after the storm had passed off—before a free passage was given to the water, and it began to subside. Such was the Pool-valley flood of 1850. (*See plate.*)

Resuming our narrative in connection with the old inns, we may state that "The Duke of Wellington" was the ninth house of the group we have alluded to. Should, however, any of the fishermen have happened to stray "out of bounds"—no uncommon practice—there was, a little way up East-street, No. 28, "THE SPREAD EAGLE" (kept by Mr. Henry Skinner), with "open wings" ready to receive them! The name of this house was in 1816 changed to "THE SUSSEX ARMS."

Returning to the Cliff, the first public-house in Black Lion-street, —not very far up, by the bye,—was "THE THATCHED HOUSE," kept in 1800 by Mr. Thomas Ide. Why it was named "The Thatched House,"—whether it was originally *thatched*, or, previous to its conversion into a public-house, used as a barn (the land near it being devoted to hemp gardens),—is a matter of conjecture. Certain it is that, within living memory, the roof of the house was *not* thatched. From time immemorial, Brightonians have been accustomed to a thoroughfare through the house from Little Castle-square, Black Lion-street, &c. By some it is thought that this custom was originally a public right; that the road was once a "bridle way" running by the side of the house, and which "way" was retained when the house was subsequently enlarged. Others believe that the "way" through the house was only by "sufferance;" it being part of an old route, used

---

* These shops were, we believe, originally Sir John Bridger's stables, in which three horses were drowned during the Pool-valley flood of January, 1795.

in rough weather by the fishermen when the sea-front was impassable.* At one time—much more so than at present—the traffic through "The Thatched House" was considerable. Immediately in its rear were the old Pig Market, the old Town Hall, the Workhouse, ' stocks," &c. In fact, long after the old Town Hall was removed, the parish " stocks " stood by the side of the pathway leading from "The Thatched House" to the old Pig Market. Tradition says it was by these very "stocks" that that interesting local colloquy—frequently quoted on occasions, even now, by old Brightonians—took place between Mrs. Elizabeth Marsh (in " fishery" parlance, Betty *Mash*) and her husband :—" They *shan't* put you in the stocks, Jacky ! " "*But 1 be in*, Betty !"† " The Thatched House," notwithstanding the traffic through it, was not,—at least up to 1800,—considered a " paying " house. The rent could not, at least, have hurt the landlord ; for in 1800 the house was let at £16 a year. The original Brighton Market was, down to the middle of the last century, situated at the bottom of Black Lion-street (about 20ft. to the east of the Town House), and this, probably, induced some enterprising individual to open "The Thatched House." This first Market, the charter of which dates back to Edward II., in its closing days (for the old building was, like the Block House, &c., undermined by the sea, and demolished), consisted chiefly of a few butchers' shambles. It was, however, deemed a "centre;" for an "old inhabitant," living in 1830, heard George III. proclaimed in front of it in October, 1760.‡

Opposite "The Thatched House," one Hugh M'Kelvie is named in the " DIRECTORY FOR 1800 " as a "victualler" and pastrycook ; but his house had no sign.

Just above "The Thatched House," on the same side of the street, was, in 1800, the old house known as "THE BLACK LION,"

---

* This route was from Pool-lane, up the twitten in East-street between (Nos. 10 and 11) ; then across Little East-street ; by the south side of the old Market (the site of the present Town Hall) ; then from Little Market-street through the lane leading by the Old Town Hall to the back of "The Thatched House"; across Black Lion-street into " The Old Ship " Yard ; thence by a passage in Ship-street (now closed) through Bashford's once well-known stables (at the rear of the present Jews' Synagogue) into Middle-street, and so on to the west of the town.

[† About 50 or 60 years ago, at the entrance to the inn pathway from Little Market-street, two sisters,—Betty Witney and Sally Witney, "local characters" they might be deemed, kept a crockery-store for many years. The pair always attracted attention by their quaint costume—wearing tall hats, cloth jerseys, and serge petticoats. They came to Brighton, we believe, about 1812-15, from some part of Hampshire, with a tilted waggon laden with crockery. They originally had a long stall outside the old Market, near the back of the " Three Tuns ;" they attended to their stall during the day and slept in the van at night ! What became of them in later years—whether they died, or retired with a fortune—deponent sayeth not.]

‡ This was, doubtless, the usual place in the olden time for such proclamations ; for Erredge, in his " History of Brighthelmston," quotes a Vestry minute of March 19th, 1701, as follows :—" Israel Paine, Constable, being accompanyed with the chief Inhabitants of the town, (after open proclamation made by the Cryer) did in the Mercat Place, about Eleven of the clock in the forenoon, solemnly proclaim our Gratious Soveraign Lady QUEEN ANNE, Queen of England, Scotland, France, and Ireland ; upon which there followed great shoutings and acclamations of all the people. Saying, GOD SAVE QUEEN ANNE."

in rough weather by the fishermen when the sea-front was impassable.* At one time—much more so than at present—the traffic through "The Thatched House" was considerable. Immediately in its rear were the old Pig Market, the old Town Hall, the Workhouse, ' stocks," &c. In fact, long after the old Town Hall was removed, the parish " stocks" stood by the side of the pathway leading from "The Thatched House" to the old Pig Market. Tradition says it was by these very "stocks" that that interesting local colloquy—frequently quoted on occasions, even now, by old Brightonians—took place between Mrs. Elizabeth Marsh (in "fishery" parlance, Betty *Mash*) and her husband:—"They *shan't* put you in the stocks, Jacky!" "*But I be in,* Betty!"† "The Thatched House," notwithstanding the traffic through it, was not,—at least up to 1800,—considered a "paying" house. The rent could not, at least, have hurt the landlord; for in 1800 the house was let at £16 a year. The original Brighton Market was, down to the middle of the last century, situated at the bottom of Black Lion-street (about 20ft. to the east of the Town House), and this, probably, induced some enterprising individual to open "The Thatched House." This first Market, the charter of which dates back to Edward II., in its closing days (for the old building was, like the Block House, &c., undermined by the sea, and demolished), consisted chiefly of a few butchers' shambles. It was, however, deemed a "centre;" for an "old inhabitant," living in 1830, heard George III. proclaimed in front of it in October, 1760.‡

Opposite "The Thatched House," one Hugh M'Kelvie is named in the "DIRECTORY FOR 1800" as a "victualler" and pastrycook; but his house had no sign.

Just above "The Thatched House," on the same side of the street, was, in 1800, the old house known as "THE BLACK LION,"

---

* This route was from Pool-lane, up the twitten in East-street between (Nos. 10 and 11); then across Little East-street; by the south side of the old Markot (the site of the present Town Hall); then from Little Market-street through the lane leading by the Old Town Hall to the back of "The Thatched House"; across Black Lion-street into "The Old Ship" Yard; thence by a passage in Ship-street (now closed) through Bashford's once well-known stables (at the rear of the present Jews' Synagogue) into Middle-street, and so on to the west of the town.

[† About 50 or 60 years ago, at the entrance to the inn pathway from Little Market-street, two sisters,—Betty Witney and Sally Witney, "local characters" they might be deemed, kept a crockery-store for many years. The pair always attracted attention by their quaint costume—wearing tall hats, cloth jerseys, and serge petticoats. They came to Brighton, we believe, about 1812-15, from some part of Hampshire, with a tilted waggon laden with crockery. They originally had a long stall outside the old Market, near the back of the "Three Tuns;" they attended to their stall during the day and slept in the van at night! What became of them in later years—whether they died, or retired with a fortune—deponent sayeth not.]

‡ This was, doubtless, the usual place in the olden time for such proclamations; for Erredge, in his "History of Brighthelmston," quotes a Vestry minute of March 19th, 1701, as follows:—"Israel Paine, Constable, being accompanyed with the chief Inhabitants of the town, (after open proclamation made by the Cryer) did in the Mercat Place, about Eleven of the clock in the forenoon, solemnly proclaim our Gratious Soveraign Lady QUEEN ANNE, Queen of England, Scotland, France, and Ireland; upon which there followed great shoutings and acclamations of all the people. Saying, GOD SAVE QUEEN ANNE."

THE BLACK LION STREET BREWERY.

Founded by Derrick Carver—the oldest business premises in the town after which the street was subsequently named. Of the history of this old house little is known beyond the fact that it was erected more than 300 years ago. During all those years it does not seem to have been associated with any local event worth recording. It was kept in 1800 by Mr. Edward Saunders; but early in the present century it was supplanted by private houses; these latter having been removed when the present Market was built.

Almost opposite the old "Black Lion" was the well-known BLACK LION BREWERY, which was coeval with, if not anterior to, "The Black Lion" itself. It is the oldest Brewery, and, probably, the oldest building (except St. Nicholas) in the town*; the original proprietor of it being Derrick Carver, the proto-martyr of Sussex, who, in the reign of Queen Mary, suffered death by fire, in front of the house known by "the signne of the Starre" in Lewes. July 22nd, 1555.† Carver, like the Whichelos, Mighells, &c., was, it is presumed, of Spanish origin, though he came to Brighton from Flanders (whither, probably, he had originally been driven from Spain by persecution on account of his religion), commencing business here as a brewer about the year 1545. The brave, God-fearing brewer was one of Nature's noblemen;—his blameless life; his unaffected piety; his meekness under persecution and sore trial; and his indomitable courage in holding fast to his religious principles, despite the alternative of the "Stake," render him worthy to stand in the foremost file of the "Noble Army of Martyrs." Foxe says, "he was a man whom the Lorde had blessed as well with temporall ryches as with spiritual treasures; * * * of the which (his ryches) there was such havock, by the greedy raveners of that time, that his poore wyfe and children had little left, save their hope in God." Whether the Brewery was carried on by Carver's family after his death, we know not; but his son's signature in 1580 to the "Auncient Customs," having the prefix

---

* Some of the property in the neighbourhood of the Black Lion Brewery was also built at an early date. Opposite "The Cricketers" was an old house (supplanted by a confectioner's shop, which was itself removed in 1890, when the upper part of Black Lion-street was widened,) which bore on the lintel of its front-door the date 1669. This house at the close of the last century was occupied by one Richard Butler, tailor, whose stock-in-trade, judging by the contents of the sign-board affixed to his house, was of the most comprehensive character, namely:—" Naps, beavers, cloths, narrow and broad serge, flannels, dulys, cuffs, fustians, thicksets, trowsers, long and short, boys' and men's buttons, thread, twist, and silk."

† The day following, John Launder, husbandman, of Godstone, Surrey, suffered the same fate at Steyning. Derrick Carver and Launder were both apprehended in October, 1554, by "Edward Gage, gentleman," as they, with some few others, were at prayers in the house of Carver. Gage sent them up to the Queen's Council, which, after examination, consigned them to Newgate to await the pleasure of Bishop Bonner. Carver was brought before the Bishop on the 10th June, 1555, who asked him whether he would abide by his confession, with the articles and answers? to which Carver answered, says Foxe, that he would; "for your doctrine is poison and sorcery.* * * You say that you can make a god; ye can make a pudding as well. Your ceremonies in the church are beggary and poison. And further I say that auricular confession is contrary to God's Word.' The Bishop, seeing his steadfastness, and finding that neither flattery nor threats could move Carver, pronounced his usual "blessing'; as well upon Derrick Carver as upon John Launder, who, after the like process, manifested the same constancy. They were then both delivered to the Sheriff to be conveyed to their respective places of execution.

THE BLACK LION STREET BREWERY.

Founded by Derrick Carver—the oldest business premises in the town.

ORIGINAL FRONT OF THE OLD SHIP HOTEL IN SHIP STREET.

of "*Mr.*," leads to the inference that he was a man of position in the town. In 1800, and for many years subsequently to that date, the Black Lion Brewery was carried on by Mr. William Chapman, with whose name it became more familiarly associated. It is still known as "Chapman's Brewery."

Separated from the Brewery by the narrow twitten running into Ship-street was "THE CRICKETERS," Mr. Isaac Atherall in 1800 being "mine host." The house originally was known by the not very euphonious name of "THE LAST AND FISH CART;" but was popularly known as "The Last" (10,000 fish). Under the sign, immediately over the door, were the following lines :—

"Long time I've looked for good beer,
And at 'The Last' have found it here."

The house was taken in 1790 by Jutten, one of the local cricketers of the period, who altered its old sign to that of "The Cricketers."

Passing to other inns to the westward, we come to what is now the oldest inn in the town, "THE OLD SHIP," kept in 1800 by Mr. John Hicks, and then described as situate and being at 46, Ship-street, and 27, East-cliffe. No authentic data exists relating to the establishment or the early history of "The Old Ship." For aught we know, the timber used in the original building (as was the case with other old houses in the town) may have been part of an old ship (and hence its name), and the probability of this being the case is strengthened by the fact that a piece of an old ship, apparently part of a stern, rudely carved, may still be seen at the east end of the ceiling of the Ship-street entrance to "The Old Ship" stable-yard. One of the earliest allusions to the existence of the house is in the Court Rolls of the Manor of Brighthelmston, which record an admission, on 23rd August, 1670, "to one cottage or inn, known as the Old Shipp, situate in the Hempshares of Brighthelmston * * in the tenure of George Hackett." The previous owner was Richard Gilham. Little is known concerning "The Old Ship" until the early part of the last century, when the "Town Book" records that a Vestry meeting was held there on October 18, 1727, at which it was agreed that the Churchwardens and Overseers should borrow £100, upon interest, towards building a new Workhouse. When Mr. William Hicks became proprietor (about 1750) it was then *the* inn of the town, posting-house, &c. During the "famine," in the winter of 1756-57— when serious acts of incendiarism were anticipated—the suffering poor of the neighbourhood vented their grievances through the medium of "The Old Ship" post-box, a paper being deposited there, on which the following was written :—

"You covetous and hard-hearted Farmers, that keep your Stacks and Mows of Corn to starve the Poor, if you will not take them in and sell them that we may have some to eat, we will pull them down for you by Night or by Day, from

"JACK POOR,   WILL STARVE,
  WILL NEEDY,   PETER FEARNOT,
              and others."

The week after this (it may be added) nearly 200 poor people people came in a body to the town, complaining of the great price of corn. "They broke open a warehouse belonging to Mr. Cardin, but did not offer to touch anything; upon which Mr. Cardin went to them and promised them as much Wheat as they would have at 5s. 6d. per Bushel, which pleased them so, that they asked his Pardon for the Damage they had done him, and after buying about seven or eight Bushels amongst them they withdrew themselves."*

Mr. William Hicks, during his proprietorship, rebuilt and enlarged "The Old Ship," and, following the example of Mr. Shergold, of "The Castle," built a "public room;" which, says Dr. Relhan, in his *Treatise* (1761) was "convenient;" and a few years later, a writer in *The Gentleman's Magazine*, speaking of the assembly room at "The Old Ship," says the house was kept by Mr. Hicks, "who also keeps a coffee shop."† Mr. Hicks projected the building of the present unique and elegant assembly room; but did not live to see its completion. After his death (in 1765) the house was carried on by his widow, aided by her three daughters; and eventually by his son, Mr. John Hicks, who appears to have inherited all his father's energy and aptitude for business. "The Old Ship," for many subsequent years, must have done a good trade. A "Diarist" (in August, 1779) says :—"Breakfasted at the New Ship; the Old Ship has too much custom." It may be mentioned that the writer, in this instance, "went further and fared worse." He says: "Ordered a small dish of fish at the New

---

* The price of wheat at Lewes at this time was £14 per load.

[† In the original coffee room of "The Old Ship," it is supposed, the interesting and valuable portrait of Dr. Richard Russell, the eminent physician, was first hung. But when the noble Card Room was completed and "in every respect calculated for the reception of company," the portrait of Dr. Russell was doubtless removed thither, as the most honourable place which could be assigned to it, the room being constantly resorted to by the rank and fashion visiting the town, and there for nearly a century and a quarter it remained "the observed of all observers." This earliest historical Art treasure associated with the town was in August, 1887, generously presented to the Corporation by its owners, Mr. Robert Bacon and Alderman Samuel Ridley (formerly joint proprietors of the famous old Hotel), and it has since been placed in the Corporation Picture Gallery. A tablet at the base of the picture frame bears the following inscription :—

"DR. RICHARD RUSSELL,
Born 1687. Died 1759. Aged 72.
Painted by T. ZOFFANY, R.A."

Zoffany was a famous portrait painter in the latter half of the last century and one of the earlier members of the Royal Academy. He painted many well-known portraits, as those of "George III. and his Family," Garrick, Foote, and others; and it was doubtless Zoffany's great reputation which induced the then energetic and enterprising proprietor of the "Old Ship," Mr. William Hicks, to apply to him, with a view to secure for what were then known as his "public rooms" a "true presentment" of the eminent man whom visitors and inhabitants alike justly looked upon as the founder of Brighton's popularity as a fashionable resort for health and pleasure. Without attempting to analyze the artistic merits of this portrait of Dr. Russell—the only contemporary one known to exist—it may be said to have the appearance of being a very characteristic, and, in fact, "speaking likeness." There is the stamp of high intelligence and the calm serenity of self-conscious knowledge in those noble features—in the bright eyes, the large open forehead, the bold aquiline nose, the small lips and massive chin—set off by a wealth of hair, worn after the fashion of the day; nor does the ample white neckerchief, or the collarless coat, with huge sleeve-cuffs and ruffles, detract from its dignity. *See frontispiece.*]

THE OLD SHIP HOTEL, BRIGHTON, ABOUT 1845.
Cuff and Strachan, Proprietors.

Ship, made one good meal pass for dinner and supper.—Memo.—Waiter and master (the former seems the latter) hardly care if they serve a wayfaring passenger or not, *unless he wears a horse or carries a carriage about with him.*"

Mr. John Hicks was evidently a man of energy. He "moved with the times;" and, as Brighton became more and more the resort of the then fashionable world, "Hicks's" shared honours with "The Castle" in the assemblies, undress balls, tea and card parties, concerts, &c., then in vogue; (see "FASHIONABLE AND POPULAR AMUSEMENTS," pp. 26 to 39), but "though the rays of Royalty seldom irradiated the premises ('The Castle' had a monopoly of these), the first families of the Nobility resorted thither." So much was "The Old Ship" resorted to by fashionable visitors, that the proprietor deemed it expedient to obtain an extension of premises on the sea-front. This he succeeded in doing; and in 1794 Mr. Hicks issued the following advertisement:—

HICKS' HOTEL, TAVERN, AND INN, "THE OLD SHIP."

J. HICKS most respectfully begs leave to return his sincere thanks to the Nobility, Gentry, and his friends in general, for the many favors conferred on him, and to inform them that he has purchased TWO LARGE HOUSES, pleasantly situated on the Cliff, between Ship Street and Black Lion Street, which he has added to his other house, having a communication therewith. In the new part he has five very good sitting rooms fronting the sea, with bedrooms near them, therefore will have it in his power to accommodate Families, &c., in the genteelest manner.

⁎ The best old Wines.

Brighthelmston, May 31, 1794.

The more important portion of "The Old Ship," must, however, have been at this period in Ship-street; for in 1802, when, on the death of Mrs. Leah Hicks (widow of Mr. John Hicks) it was put up to auction, the particulars stated that the Tavern in Ship-street contained numerous "dining and sleeping apartments, and made up 60 beds;" while the "brick house, with semi-bow front from the basement to the third floor, situate in the most eligible part of the Cliff, and used as an appendage to the Tavern," had only eight bedrooms.

From an early period "The Old Ship" was the "business" house of the town; the more important Town meetings, property sales, &c., taking place there. Singularly enough, one of the early property sales (in June, 1778,) was "one undivided fourth part of that well-known and elegant Tavern and Assembly Room, call'd the Castle (Shergold and Co.), together with part of the household furniture." At a Vestry Meeting held there in January, 1790, Mr. William Attree was appointed Vestry Clerk, at £10 10s. per annum; which salary was increased 15 years later to £30 per annum.

On the 4th May, 1795, a Court Martial was opened at "The Old Ship," under the presidency of Colonel Sloane, of the North Hants Regiment, for the trial of thirteen men of the Oxford Militia, charged with mutiny at East Blatchington. The trial lasted nine days, the result being that three of the men were condemned to be shot; which sentence was carried out upon two of them (Cook and Parish) in Goldstone Bottom, on the 12th June following, the other (Haddocks) being pardoned, "on condition of being transported to Botany Bay for 10 years." Six others were sentenced to be flogged, one to receive 500 lashes; one 1,500; and the rest 1,000 each. The remaining four were liberated.

The subject of incorporating the town was first mooted at a meeting held at "The Old Ship" in 1806; and there, in 1809, the plan of a harbour for Brighton was also considered. The first meeting of the Town Commissioners, under the new Act, was held at "The Old Ship" in May, 1810; and the first local Petty Sessions of the Brighton Magistrates (under Serjeant Runnington) in 1812. The Brighton Corn Market was originally held there. The Freemasons held their Lodge meetings at "The Old Ship" from the year 1800. We might multiply examples. The first meeting with the view to establish a County Hospital was held at "The Old Ship," in February, 1813; the Earl of Egremont offering to contribute £1,000 towards the building, and other gentlemen £1,000 more. But nothing came of it till December, 1824, when, at another meeting held at "The Old Ship," it was finally determined on; the foundation-stone being laid some 13 months later,—16th March, 1826,—by the Earl of Egremont.* In February, 1821, a meeting at the old house passed a resolution "to construct an iron railway between Brighton and Shoreham," which, however, was never destined to be carried out. It is stated in Erredge's "History" that, on the 19th July, 1821, "The Old Ship"—or rather its stableyard—was used for a very different purpose from any of the above. On that day a party connected with smugglers assembled in the yard —the Custom House Officers being then on the Level enjoying the Coronation sports!—and, at a given signal, about 30 kegs of Hollands, brought from the beach, were "slung" and carried off before the few persons present could comprehend what was going on.

At a Vestry Meeting, held at "The Old Ship" in March, 1823, it was resolved to erect a new Church (St. Peter's) on the Level, to the north part of the town, "being the best site obtainable." At a subsequent meeting, held in June, it was resolved to raise the money necessary to erect the Church during the ensuing five years; His Majesty's Commissioners having offered the money required without interest, provided it was repaid at the expiration of that time. When the Committee met, in August, at "The Old Ship," to select a plan, and to appoint an architect, there were no less than seventy-nine packages, some of them containing several plans and one model, awaiting their selection. The Committee spent five hours on the plans, and eventually selected that of Mr. Barry (afterwards Sir Charles Barry); 30 guineas, for the second best plan, being awarded

---

* The Earl of Egremont subscribed no less than £3,000 towards the building; Thomas Read Kemp, Esq., gave £1,000, and the ground on which the Hospital was erected. A four days' Fancy Fair (December 13, 14, 15, 16, 1827), was held at "The Old Ship" for the benefit of the Hospital, and realised the large sum of £1.315.

THE BRIGHTON ROYAL SUSPENSION PIER (with South of Steine and Marine Parade),—about 1825.

THE BRIGHTON ROYAL SUSPENSION PIER (about 1870).

Projected by Captain Sir Samuel Brown. Commenced in October, 1822, and opened on the 25th November, 1823. Length, 1,150 feet. Cost of building, £30,000.

to Messrs. Wild and Busby. The foundation stone of the Church was laid by Dr. Carr, May 8th, 1824; and the consecration took place on January 25th, 1828.

It was at "The Old Ship" that it was decided, on the 26th February, 1822, to erect the Chain Pier (now, alas! doomed to destruction so soon as the Brighton Marine Palace and Pier is erected). The Chain Pier was designed by Captain Brown (afterwards Sir Samuel Brown), and was eventually built, at a cost of £30,000, in ten months from its commencement, being opened in 1823.

The Brighton Toy Fair was originally held under and along the Cliff in front of "The Old Ship." This Fair was essentially an aboriginal "institution." The fisherwomen monopolized the stalls, and their rattling of dice-boxes, with the unvarying cry of "One in, who makes two? Try your luck! try your luck!" (for nuts or gingerbread) was kept up unceasingly throughout the day. The old women were sheltered under veritable canvas, their stalls being composed of boat sails, &c., shored up by spars and secured by ropes fastened to the cliff rails. A drawing in the Local Museum gives a lively picture of this Fair, with canvas, fixings, &c.; a peep-show occupies the Ship-street corner of "The Old Ship"! The "roundabouts," however, connected with the Fair found accommodation in the open space then at the back of "The Thatched House."*

"The Old Ship" was in the "market" in 1803; and was eventually taken by Mr. Shuckard, a German. He was a very popular "Host," and under his auspices the old inn for many a year increased in favour among visitors. He was succeeded by Messrs. Cuff and Strachan, who, to obtain more accommodation for their patrons, built, in 1838, the western portion of the Hotel, at the corner of Ship-street; in fact, that portion of the Hotel which contains the spacious coffee-room, with the apartments, &c., above and below it; the site occupying an area of about 1,094 superficial feet. This property was sold in 1878,—pursuant to an Order of the High Court of Justice, Chancery Division, made in the matter of the estate of Eliza Michell, deceased, *Farrer* v. *Michell*,—and was stated to be subject to the tenancy (at the rent of £100 per annum) of Mr. Robert Bacon (the present proprietor of the Hotel), which expired on the 25th day of December in that year. Mr. Bacon purchased the property, which realised no less than £8,300.† The Hotel, therefore, now remains intact.

---

* Brighton Fair was subsequently removed landward, when it attained much larger proportions. It was then frequented by itinerant theatres; shows of fat women, dwarfs, learned pigs, &c.; toy and ginger-bread vendors, *et hoc genus omne*. It was, however, shifted from one locality to another—(in Ireland's Gardens, 1825-35, it probably attained its highest prosperity), and may be said to have died ignominiously a few years since in a field near the Race-hill.

† The price realised for the property seems, at first sight, to be enormous; but when it is known that there are single shops on the King s-road, less advantageously situated, and with only restricted accommodation, for which a rental of some £300 a year or more is paid, the purchase will not be regarded as a bad bargain. As showing, however, the vast increase in value of property in the neighbourhood of "The Old Ship" at the present time, as compared with that of the past, we may take an extract from an old "Diary," published in 1779. The writer says:—" Am viewing my worthy friend Mr. Bull's house, or rather

Of the earliest history of "THE NEW SHIP," situated in Ship-street (nearly opposite "The Old Ship,") very little is known. From authentic data it would appear to have been the "original Coach office" in Brighton; for coaches started from it so early as 1741. In 1756, the "Host" was Mr. William Lucas, and during his occupancy the house, like "The Old Ship," was frequently used for the transaction of public business, the disposal of property, &c. A couple of sales, announced in the *Sussex Weekly Advertiser*, may be quoted. The first, in 1756, was as follows:—

TO BE SOLD, at Brighthelmston, in the County of Sussex, a new DWELLING HOUSE, with two large cellars, and three rooms on the first floor, three on the second, and one on the third; situate and lying at the lower end of the Ship-street, now in the occupation of Mr. WILLIAM LUCAS, at "The New Ship." For further particulars enquire of FRANCIS CHEESMAN, at the sign of "The George," in Brighthelmston aforesaid, and he will make them the lowest price and a good title to the same.

The next was:—

TO BE SOLD, TO THE BEST BIDDER, on THURSDAY NEXT, the 28th instant, by EDWARD DAVIS, at Mr. WILLIAM LUCAS'S, the Sign of "The New Ship" in Brighthelmston, a large quantity of FRENCH BRANDY, to be put up in Lots. The Sale to begin at Two o'clock, and the Brandies may be tasted any time in the day before the Sale begins.

August 25, 1760.

Mr. Lucas's successor was Mr. Rickwood, who occupied the house for many years. In September, 1764, Preston Farm (then in the occupation of Mr. Smithers) was sold by auction at "The New Ship." At the same date the first "packet service" between Brighton and France was started; but business at the outset must have been somewhat uncertain; for the announcement stated that "Captain Saunders (of 'the Prince of Wales' packet) was to be heard of at 'The New Ship,' and will sail when desired."

When the Act of 1773, for "holding and regulating a Market," *

---

box, upon the Clift, between Ship-street and Black Lion-street * * * [This house was situated two doors east of the present Old Ship Hotel front.] The ground whereon it stands is copyhold—measuring nearly *eighteen feet square*. The fine is both certain and small. About fifty years ago, this piece of land was sold for *four pounds*. Thirty years since, a purchaser gave eleven; and, about this time two years, the Alderman bought it for one hundred pounds, to build upon." The writer adds—"What an instance of improvement!" What would have been his astonishment if he had lived to know the price which property in close proximity to it realised a century later!

* For some years after the destruction of the old Market on the Cliff, Brighton was wholly without a Market; and (says Dunvan) "the very reduced state of the town, together with the great expense of erecting groynes, put it out of the power of the inhabitants to build a new Market-place, till the unexpected influx of summer visitants began to introduce new wealth and sentiments into Brighthelmston. Not only a new Market-place, but even a daily sale of the necessaries of life there, became peculiarly desirable for the accommodation of strangers who fixed their temporary abode in the town." The new Market was erected in 1774, on the site of the old Bartholomews property. This Market was subsequently removed (in 1829-30) when the erection of the present Town Hall was determined on.

was obtained, the first mortgage of the tolls took place at "The New Ship"; the advertisement, which is interesting in more respects than one, being as follows :—

NOTICE IS HEREBY GIVEN, that the Commissioners appointed for putting an Act (of George the Third) into execution, for holding and regulating a MARKET in the TOWN OF BRIGHTHELMSTON, in the County of Sussex, will meet at the house of STEPHEN RICKWOOD, bearing the Sign of "The New Ship," in Brighthelmston aforesaid, on WEDNESDAY, the 18th day of this instant August, in order to treat with any person or persons who is or are willing to lend any Sum of Money not exceeding FIVE HUNDRED POUNDS on the Credit of the Tolls arising from the said Market.

August 1st, 1773.   WILLIAM ATTREE, Clerk.

In connection with "The New Ship" in the olden time may be mentioned the following mysterious affair :—On Tuesday, the 14th August, 1770, a clergyman, the Rev. Mr. Gwynn, who had only recently been made Principal of Brazenoze College, Oxford, went, with his servant, to "The New Ship." He ordered dinner, and then said he would take a walk whilst it was being prepared. As he did not return, and as nothing was known whither he was gone, several persons went in search of him; but their efforts to find him proved fruitless. On the following Sunday, however, a little girl discovered a body in a field of barley to the west of the town; and it was identified as that of the missing gentleman. Deceased was lying upon his face; his whip by his side; and he was still wearing his gloves, boots, and spurs. How he came by his death was never revealed. There were no marks of violence about him; and a considerable sum of money which he had in his possession,—his pocket-book contained three bank notes of £100 each,—was untouched.

Some 20 years later, on Monday, September 10, 1789, the Chevalier Maupeau, the son of a French nobleman, took apartments at "The New Ship"; and on the evening of the following day shot himself under the hedge of a field to the west of the town. The unfortunate man had, through family differences, left France, and twice attempted to drown himself during his passage to England in "The Princess Royal" (Captain Chapman). The effects which he brought with him to "The New Ship" were of considerable value. They included two gold watches, two diamond crosses of the Order of the Knights of Malta, three miniatures of a lady (all set in gold), &c.; and he had about him a large sum in gold and silver, in addition to letters of credit on different bankers in London. On the outside of the packet containing these was written in pencil, and evidently with a trembling hand, "*Je meurs innocent, J'en atteste le ciel.*"

In October, 1790, the then "Host" (Mr. Baulcomb) had an unusual number of guests, viz., a bevy of elderly nuns, some 37 in number, who, driven from a convent in Lisle, had been brought from France by Captain Burton in the "Prince of Wales" packet. The Prince of Wales and Mrs. Fitzherbert paid these unfortunate ladies a long visit; and, as they had only £30 amongst them when they landed, His Royal Highness set on foot a subscription for their relief, which, in a short time, amounted to upwards of £100. The worthy landlord had great difficulty in finding accommodation for them, inasmuch as they could not be prevailed upon to sleep two in one bed. They subsequently, it is said, went from Brighton to Brussels.

What the extent of the accommodation of "The New Ship" was, in 1790, it would be difficult to ascertain; but, in 1784, the inn—to which was then attached a barn, coach-house, and stables—was rated at only £17 10s.; not a fourth of that of "The Castle," and only a little over a third of that of "The Old Ship" at the same date.

In October, 1805, Mr. Baulcomb experienced a lucky turn of Dame Fortune's wheel, being the holder of a sixteenth share of a lottery ticket (the first drawn, by the bye), entitled to £20,000.* Mr. Baulcomb occupied "The New Ship" for a number of years. One of his sons with his wife and daughters were living at St. Helena at the time Napoleon I. was there, and frequent mention is made of them in O'Meara's *A Voice from St. Helena*. "The New Ship" during Mr. Baulcomb's occupancy, and for years after, was much frequented by the tradesmen of the town, whose custom was to dine together annually on New Year's Day. "The New Ship" was for many years carried on by the late Mr. W. Vaughan, who increased its accommodation considerably by the purchase of contiguous property. He was succeeded in the proprietorship by his son.

Two other inns are mentioned as being in Ship-street in 1800. The first of these, "THE ONE TUN," at No. 53, was kept by Mr. Joseph Merle. This inn has long ceased to exist, and its exact position is now unknown. The other inn was at the top of the street, and known as "THE SEVEN STARS"; the landlord being Mr. William Tulley. When Ship-street was first subject to the "sweet influence of the Pleiades," is difficult to ascertain. The signboard has now inscribed upon it—"ESTABLISHED 1535." There may be authority for this; but we cannot trace an earlier date than November 4, 1692, when it is recorded in the Court Rolls that "Edward Howell and Jane his wife" were admitted to "a cottage and garden in Hemshares-street." The house during the earlier half of the last century passed into various hands; and eventually, on the 29th April, 1767, was purchased of Thomas Pumferry, husbandman, by Isaac Grover, brewer, who enfranchised it in 1785. In the deed of enfranchisement first mention is made of the house as "The Seven Stars"; the inference, therefore, is, that it was opened under that sign after it came into the possession of Mr. Isaac Grover. The house is still owned, we believe, by Mr. Grover's successors, Messrs. Vallance and Catt; and after the death of Mr. Stoneham (who occupied it for many years) it was carried on by Mr. H. Newnham, an old servant of the firm.

"The Seven Stars" may be said to conclude that section of the

---

* In the previous lottery, three sixteenths of £30,000 fell to the lot of persons living in the neighbourhood of Brighton; and a share of a £500 prize was, we are told, also obtained "by a deserving person residing on the Cliff."

inns which in 1800 was more or less patronised by the native population residing in what was then regarded as the eastern part of the town. These eastern residents were, formerly, popularly known as the "East-streeters"; and their boundary line may be said to have terminated at Ship-street. We now purpose to notice those inns patronised more or less exclusively by the "West-streeters," or the residents of the western part of the town, in Middle-street, West-street, &c. These divisions were, probably, produced by the fact that there were in 1800 no "gaps," as now (opposite "The Old Ship"), leading from the beach to the centre of the town; the only approaches from the beach being then situated at the east and west ends.

The first, then, of the public-houses frequented by the "West-streeters" was situated at the bottom of Middle-street (west corner), called "THE SHIP IN DISTRESS," the "Host" in 1800 being Mr. James Leach. It was, at the period, a wretched-looking, miserable old building. The windows of its principal rooms faced the sea; but, like many of the old houses along the sea-front, its entrance was from the eastward. Over the front door was a picture representing "A Ship in Distress," with the following lines beneath:—

"By danger we're encompassed round,
Pray lend a hand, our ship's aground."

Such an appeal as this to "fishery" proclivities,—and especially after a night's cruise,—must have been irresistible; and no wonder the old house did well. If it was "tumble down" in appearance, was there not the traditional nautical motto in its favour—"*any* port in a storm!"

The house subsequently underwent both exterior and interior alterations, to keep pace with the changes and improvements going on in the town. For many a year after Brighton had become the resort of Royalty and Fashion, the sea-front of the town, at least for vehicles, terminated at "The Ship in Distress," and those requiring to go further westward, to West-street, &c., had to turn up Middle-street, and through Middle-street-lane (now South-street). There was, certainly, a causeway, floored with planks, &c., from "The Ship in Distress" to the eastern corner of West-street; but this was passable only in fair weather; it being the custom in rough weather to place a barrier at each end of the causeway with the notice written up "No Thoroughfare."* The inconvenience of this break in the drive along the sea-frontage was so much felt that, in 1821, some influential inhabitants, and others interested in neighbouring property, set to work to secure a carriage drive in its stead. Subscriptions were set on foot: George IV. gave 200gs.; the Town Commissioners, on

---

* There had, originally, been a carriage way there with wooden railings along the edge of the Cliff: but all had been washed away prior to the close of the last century. From the "Diary of a young Quakeress," Elizabeth Grover (in the possession of Mr. Thomas Glaisyer, of the firm of Glaisyer and Kemp), we are told, concerning the Cliff rails, under date, 1726, "In this Year the Railes was Sett upon the Clift."

its completion, promised £300; Mr. Thomas Read Kemp, Mr. W. Wigney, and Mr. W. Izard each gave £100; and the inhabitants generally liberally contributed. The result was, that the carriage road between Middle-street and West-street was completed by January, 1822; and on the 29th of that month, the anniversary of the accession of George IV., His Majesty opened the road in person, amid the acclamation of 10,000 people; the road thenceforth being called the King's-road, which name was subsequently applied to the whole sea-frontage from East-street to Brunswick-terrace. His Majesty was in an open laudau, and was accompanied by the Dukes of York, Wellington, and Dorset; the Duke of Devonshire and other noble personages attending on horseback. When His Majesty's carriage reached the centre of the road, a Royal salute was fired from the 42-pounders at the Battery, which was answered by Royal salutes from the "Linnet" and "Hound" revenue cutters in the roadstead. A somewhat ludicrous incident, which gave rise to much talk at the time, occurred during His Majesty's passage along the road. In accordance with "auncient custom "—even now not unfrequently kept up at the weddings at St. Nicholas—some of the inhabitants bestrewed His Majesty with sugar-plums, &c., "for luck!"* Not being "to the manner born," and not at first recognising the peculiar "shot" fired at him, His Majesty was dumbfounded; but he speedily saw through the matter, and smiled pleasantly as he passed along. (It was reported in the town that His Majesty had been pelted with gravel! a report which occasioned no little commotion among the inhabitants till the matter was satisfactorily explained.) The populace finished up the day on the beach, where several casks of strong beer were distributed (the remainder of the Coronation Day supply), and "rejoicing and dancing groups were to be seen from the base of the cliff to the water's edge."

The opening of the King's-road effected a material improvement in the value of house property alongside it. It would, however, surprise many to know what small sums some of the property fetched even a year or two after the road was opened. For instance, in March 27, 1823, the "Watch House," 19, King's-road (subsequently the old Custom House), was sold by Mr. Shotter, at "The Ship in Distress," for £530! It was bought by Government, who, four years previously, had obtained a lease of the house "for 30 years, at £8 8s. per year"!† The house, No. 53, King's-road (now Mr. Thomas's), was bought about the same time by Mr. Salmon (the owner of Salmon-court, North-street), for £150. His wife was much

---

* In the old "Diary," to which we have frequently alluded, under date of September 13th, 1778, we are told—"A *new* man and wife have just passed me. The town's-people preserve some customs here that smack of great antiquity, and seem peculiar to the County of *Sussex*. At a marriage there are strewers, who strew the way from Church, not only with flowers, but with sugar-plumbs and wheat. Why sugar-plumbs and wheat, I wonder? Many ceremonies have been retained longer than the history of their origin or foundation."

[† In 1891 this property (which is now occupied by the Brighton and South-Coast Aerated Bread Company) was sold, before it was rebuilt, for considerably over £3,000.]

grieved at the purchase, and strongly urged him to get rid of his bad bargain. He was unable to do so,—fortunately, as it afterwards appeared; for, soon after his death, his daughter let the house for 28 years, at a ground rent of £75 a-year. She died just as the lease ran out, when the property was bought by the late Mr. Gregory, hosier, &c., of North-street, for, we believe, £2,300.

"The Ship in Distress" was re-built by Mr. John Gallard for Mr. Wigney, about 1825 or 1826, when probably the old name was changed to "The Sea House." There was then a fine room made in it; both the Magistrates and Town Commissioners for several years holding their sittings there. The "Brewster Sessions" was held at "The Sea House" in September, 1831. The Brighton Tradesmen's Glee Club held its last and its most successful meeting there : the Club was all at once broken up—because the landlord raised his price for "grogs"!

Among the associations of this house may be mentioned that, in September, 1830, the Viscountess Bronté (widow of the immortal Nelson) resided there, and, during her stay, King William IV., called upon her. His Majesty had desired that there might be no ceremony in his reception, and he saw Lady Nelson in the coffee room, remaining in conversation with her three-quarters of an hour. (The "Host" improved the occasion by thenceforth calling the house "The Royal Sea House Hotel.")*

By reason, we suppose, of the increased value of property along the sea-front, "The Sea House" underwent a few years ago considerable alteration, the inn business being restricted to the South-street corner of the house, the southern portion of the property being cut off and subsequently converted into a toy and fancy repository.

The only other public-house in Middle-street in 1800 was "THE SPOTTED DOG, No. 35, the host being Mr. T. Edwards. This house was formerly a popular "soldier's house," being much frequented by the troops quartered in the town, especially by the South Gloucester Militia, some of whom occupied the barracks at the West-street corner of Little Russell-street. The subsequent removal of this and other regiments to different quarters had, doubtless, an effect for the worse upon the fortunes of the house, as "The Spotted Dog" "never joyed after"; and in 1807 the then landlord, Mr. Fairs, obtained permission to remove the license of the house to "The Richmond Arms," Richmond-place, which was then for the first time opened by him as a public-house.

Immediately below "The Spotted Dog" was in 1800 the well-known Brewery of Mr. John Wichelo, which was afterwards carried on for many years by Mr. William Wigney. This Brewery dated back

---

* We might supplement this Royal anecdote by another. In August, 1822, while the Duke of York was taking his usual morning promenade along the Cliff, an oyster-woman, who was standing with her barrow near the bottom of Middle-street, made to His Royal Highness a most profound and graceful courtesy; upon which the Duke good-humouredly gave her a piece of silver, observing, "You have not, I believe, drank my health this year." An eye witness relates that, "in less than a minute, the *lady* was at 'The Ship in Distress," drinking Vallance's porter, and ejaculating sentiments of the most fervent loyalty."

from an early period. The proprietor in 1757 was Mr. Richard Tidy (High Constable in 1761)* with whom Mr. Richard Lemmon Wichelo and his son were subsequently associated in business; and for many years the names of "Tidy and Wichelo," brewers, were known far and wide. The Lemmons and the Wichelos (who appear to have been closely allied) are among the oldest Brighton families, dating back to the middle of the 16th century.† Mr. Richard Lemmon Wichelo formerly occupied the house in Middle-street in which Mr. Charles Catt now resides; and much of the property in the neighbourhood of the old Brewery, in Boyce's-street, &c., is still owned by members of the Wichelo family. A relative, we suppose, of Mr. Wichelo, the brewer, Mr. Elgate Wichelo, in 1800, carried on the business of wine-merchant at No. 21, Middle-street, nearly opposite the Brewery.

At the bottom of Middle-street, No. 58, was another Brewery, owned in 1800 by Mr. John Lucas, whose private residence was situated at the east corner of Middle-street, opposite "The Ship in Distress." Many will remember this little old-fashioned house—the last, probably, of what was once "a long line of such"—which was taken down about 10 or 12 years since, having been previously occupied for many years by the late Mr. Altenacker, perfumer, and on the site of which the present lofty building was erected. Mr. Lucas's Brewery, which covered a large area at the rear of his house, has long ceased to exist; it was altered and for many years used as livery stables, &c. These were removed last year, and on the site were erected the magnificent show-rooms of Messrs. Lewis and Son, goldsmiths, &c., of the King's-road. Whilst the stables were being cleared, several portions of the old Brewery were discovered.

Migrating from this point westward, we come to the old public-houses in West-street. The first inn in the street was the well-known "GEORGE," kept in 1800 by Mr. George Greening. The house is an old one, though erected subsequently to "The King's Head," situated higher up the street. "The George" was a house of good repute among the tradesmen in olden times, and also among the "West-streeters." The fact of its being the first house in sight coming up from the West-street gap may have accounted for this latter predilection. Then the old town "fire-cage"—formerly used to guide fishermen on returning to shore at night—was suspended from the Cliff nearly opposite the house. The well-known "Bank," too, where, previous to the formation of the King's-road, the fishermen were wont to perambulate, was just to the east of it.‡ "The George" was at one

---

* Mr. Tidy married in April, 1758, Miss Richardson, only daughter and heiress of the Rev. Mr. Richardson, Vicar of Cowfold and Rector of Edburton, and niece of the Rev. Dr. Lynch, Dean of Canterbury.

† Captain Richard Lemmon died in June, 1758, aged 90. He was born in the town and always lived here, excepting when at sea. He retained his senses to the last, and had previously experienced but comparatively little decay of health or strength. Several members of the Wichelo family attained a great age.

‡ The "Bank," as this portion of the Cliff was called, was always a favourite spot for promenade with well-known West-end master mariners—the Spicers, Cardens, Humphreys, Allens, &c., men who owned boats, and who were really well-to-do—and especially on fine Sunday afternoons. In the early part of the century, and for years after, they might invariably be seen most Sundays "walk-

period kept for several years by a German, named Hubert, a fine, soldierly-looking man, who had formerly belonged to the German Legion, and had seen much service with his regiment, from which he was drafted into the 10th Hussars. Hubert was very fond of relating incidents of his military career, and also of his personal history. But valiant as may have been Hubert's achievements when engaged against the King's enemies, one thing he certainly had not conquered—the "King's English." "My father," he used to relate, "had twelve children; and when the drums and fifes did play through the village, I thought I would go for one soldier." A wag once made him open his eyes wider, and sit more upright than usual, by remarking, between the puffs of his pipe, "he couldn't well see how he could go for *two!*"*

"The George" was some years after Hubert's occupancy kept by Mr. Long, another of the 10th Hussars, and who removed thence to keep "The King and Queen."†

The next public-house up West-street was "THE KING'S HEAD," so well known in connection with the escape of Charles II. It has long been regarded as one of the oldest inns of the town; but as the more important historical incidents associated with the house occurred at a period long antecedent to 1800, and have been fully related in local "Histories," and repeated *ad nauseam* in "Guides," &c., it is unnecessary to enlarge upon them here, except to state that, up to about 1830, the memory of Charles's visit was commemorated, on the 29th of May, by a huge bough of oak being suspended over the front door of the inn, and where formerly a portrait of His "black-wigged Majesty" served for its sign.‡ We might, perhaps, mention that an

---

ing deck." Their costume, if quaint and picturesque, was at the same time neat and becoming; consisting of dark blue velveteen jacket, with pearl buttons, nankeen breeches, tied below the knee, flock hose, and low shoes with buckles. But fashions have changed; and the last time that probably the old costume was seen was when it was worn by some patriarchal fisherman in the "Old Men's Gallery" at St. Nicholas, previous to the Church being restored.

* In Huish's *Memoirs of H.R.H. Princess Charlotte*, a good anecdote is related of an enforced visit of Prince Leopold to "The George," during his stay in Brighton in March, 1816. His Serene Highness was walking on the Cliff, when, being overtaken by a violent storm, ne sought shelter in the inn. Seating himself, he began to read the newspaper; and the "Host" (it could *not* have been old soldier Hubert; for "the lion knoweth the true Prince"), unaware of the honour which was paid him, eyed his guest, in expectation of something being called for. Considering that a *quid pro quo* was the basis of all trade, he at length accosted the Prince, asking him what he would be pleased to take? The Prince replied, "Nothing." Something of a hint was given by Boniface that he should make but a sorry living if he had all such guests; but two gentlemen, coming in soon after, recognised the Prince. They respectfully saluted him, and, the salute being returned with the greatest condescension, mine Host was soon made acquainted with the rank of his guest. His confusion may be easily imagined, and a string of apologies was stammered out. The house was soon in a bustle; but the tempest being now over, Prince Leopold took his departure, leaving a handsome gratuity for Boniface, who immediately declared he *was* a Prince— every inch of him.

[† The old "George" was pulled down in January, 1892, and the present handsome structure erected on its site."]

‡ "A TALE OF A SHIRT!" contributed to the *Brighton Herald* a year or two since, is worth quoting:—"In the account of the Merrie Monarch's escape from Brighthelmstone in 1651, given by Lower in his *Sussex Worthies*, p. 208, we read that, in order to conceal the real nature of the voyage, 'Tattersal' gave out that

absurd story arose in connection with the house about the year 1840. A window was being put in at the north end, when a small room or cavity was discovered on breaking through the wall, which is very thick; and, as it was given out that it "had been evidently formed for the purpose of concealment," the "Merrie Monarch's" refuge in the house soon became associated with it. Considering, however, that Charles's coming to the house was previously unknown to the landlord, and that he remained but a few hours in the place, there was little probability of the room having been built for *him*. In January, 1844, the foot-posts of the bed upon which it was said Charles II. slept while at "The King's Head" were offered for sale at a furniture warehouse in the Western-road; but what became of them afterwards is unknown. "The King's Head" was in 1800 kept by Mr. Thomas Dean, his successor being Mr. W. Eales; and the house was next occupied for some years by Mr. Brigden (father of Alderman Brigden).*

Close behind "The King's Head" was the well-known Brewery, now known as Vallance, Catt, and Co.'s. This Brewery is one of "the auncients." By whom and when originally established we know not; but in the middle of last century Mr. Isaac Grover was the proprietor, trading as a brewer and coal merchant. At the time of his death, in October, 1789, Mr. Grover was in partnership with Messrs. Killick and Buckoll, and when this partnership was dissolved, in January, 1790, the Brewery was carried on by Mr. Robert Killick and Messrs. John, Phillip, and James Vallance; and subsequently, by the Messrs. Vallance alone. The Brewery was originally of comparatively small dimensions; for in the Town rate-book of 1784 it is assessed at £22 10s., thus:—"Grover and Co., brewhouse, malt-houses, mill-house, store-rooms, vaults, &c." Mr. William Catt afterwards became associated with the firm, which was thenceforth known as Vallance, Catt, and Co.'s, and for the last ten years the business has been wholly in the hands of members of Mr. Catt's family.

---

his ship 'had broken from her moorings, and, having got sufficient crew on board, *went home for a bottle of aqua vitœ*, told his wife the secret, and set sail with his Royal freight at five o'clock the next morning.' There is, however, a story extant among the Cooke family, that an ancestor of theirs lived near West-street, and went, as was probably his wont, to 'The King's Head' to smoke his pipe and hear the news. Whilst talking to the landlady, Tettersell entered in a hurry, and called out, '*Mistress, give me a clean shirt!*' Whereupon 'Mistress' looked up with surprise and hesitancy, as if revolving something in her mind; but at last exclaimed, 'Tettersell! if you want your clean shirt to-night, you're going to see the King!' 'Hush! give me a clean shirt,' was the reply. The shirt was fetched; Tettersell—for so he is yclept on his tombstone—buttoned his rough coat about him, and passed out into the darkness. The next news of him was, that he had safely landed the King on the French coast."

* Alas for tradition! The late Mr. F. E. Sawyer, F.M.S. (whose painstaking researches among old Brighton documents brought many interesting and curious facts to light), in a communication to *Notes and Queries* dispossesses "The King's Head" of all its historical romance. He says:—" I have carefully examined the Court Rolls, but cannot trace that there was any George Inn in West-street before 1754, though there was in 1656,on the east side of Middle-street, "an Inne called the George." It probably occupied the site of No. 44, Middle-street (at present the residence of Mr. Charles Catt), and this, there can be little doubt, was the place actually visited by the King. The present 'King's Head Inn,' West-street, was not even known as the George until 1754, while that now known by that sign is evidently the third house of the name."

Higher up the street, on the opposite side, at the corner of Boyce's-street, was "THE HALF-MOON," No. 51, kept in 1800 by Mr. Richard Pain. Mrs. Pain was, we believe, sister to Mr. Scott, the trainer, who a few years after kept the house himself. The original "Half-Moon" was higher up on the other side of the street. Erredge says, in his "History," this latter was a "low public-house, which stood out prominently and fronted down West-street, immediately below Bunker's Hill." The old house in summer time was thronged with gipsies and beggars; but, on their usual autumn departure in 1790, the owner, Mr. Patching, pulled down the old house, and built another (until recently the "Brighton Sauce Warehouse," now removed), so as to afford them better accommodation. This proved to be a mistake; for the gipsies and others, fearing that a "better house meant higher prices," went to other quarters. In fact, the custom of the house fell off so much that its license was transferred to the present "Half-Moon." In the old house there was occasionally a little "cock-fighting;" and on Easter Monday, 1786 (when Mr. Harwood kept it), a grand Welch main was fought there for high stakes.

Just above "The Half-Moon" was another old house, popularly known as "THE COMPASSES," but being in reality "The Carpenters' Arms." Singularly enough the host's name was Wood, but history is silent as to whether or no he was a "chip of the old block." The house, some years later, was kept by Mr. Charles Shelley; and one evening in 1830 there was no little excitement both outside and *inside* the house, when Cherriman, the well-known portly crier of the period, having to "cry down"* Mary (Mrs. Shelley's Christian name) the wife of Charles *Shirley*, took his station in front of "The Compasses," and, after duly ringing his bell, proceeded to "cry down," in stentorian tones, what the crowd innocently understood to be "Mary, the wife of Charles *Shelley!*" hence the commotion, as a more worthy woman than Mrs. Shelley never lived.†

The only other inn west of West-street, in 1800, was "THE BELL," in Russell-street, kept by Mr. Richard Hobden. On the sign was painted an inverted bell, with the following couplet:

"Good liquor here is to be found;
The Bell for luck's turned upside down."

The house is now known as "The Lord Nelson." The only local

---

* "Crying down" was an ancient local custom used by a husband to warn the public against trusting an unfaithful spouse, or one who was in the habit of running into debt without his knowledge.

[† "The Compasses," about 50 years since, was kept by Mr. John Richard Penderell, a recipient of Charles II.'s bounty, which he inherited as being a direct descendant of Richard Penderell ("Trusty Dick," as he was called by the King), who, with his four brothers, gave home and shelter to Charles after his defeat at Worcester, at "Boscobel," a lone house on the borders of Staffordshire. The host of "The Compasses" was at one time butler to Earl Gage and to Lady Chichester (mother of the present Earl). On retiring from the inn, Mr. Penderell resided for a long period at Rottingdean, whence he removed to 21, Cross-street, Hove, where he died in September, 1883, at the ripe age of 80 years. His eldest son is now, we presume, the recipient of the bounty. The family are said to have in their possession the original portrait of "Trusty Dick."]

"event" of any special interest connected with "The Lord Nelson" was the inquest held there, before G. Gwynne, Esq., one of the Coroners for the County, on the body of one James Smith, whose death was caused by injuries received in a fight (for a sovereign) on the Race Hill, with one Daniel Watts, in the presence of between 3,000 and 4,000 spectators. The jury returned a verdict of "Manslaughter" against Watts, who was committed to Horsham Gaol to await his trial, and where, a few days after, he also died from the injuries which he had received during the contest.

Passing hence to the inns in North-street, we come to "THE WHITE LION," the first inn opened in that street. The earliest Court Rolls available for reference (1675), record that the messuage, &c., which subsequently became "The White Lion," was in the possession of one John Fryland (Freeland); and on his death (October 15, 1685) his youngest son, Cornelius, was admitted into possession, according to the custom of the Manor, "Borough English" (the *youngest* son being heir where it obtains). The property then consisted of a "messuage, barne, and croft of land, lying on the north part of the North-street of Brighthelmston, and one yard and a half of land lying in the common fields of Brightelmston, formerly Goulds." The house was then, in fact, a farm house, and, like others lower down the street (afterwards "The Unicorn" and "The Blacksmith's Arms,") had been built by one of the early owners of what was then known as the "north laines."

One Thomas Tutt was "admitted" to the old house October, 1705, on the surrender of Freeland, the "fine" paid to the then Lord of the Manor on admission being £6 9s.*

The property, to which 30 acres of land were now attached, was surrendered the following year to Richard Masters (High Constable in 1710), who devised it by will to his son, Richard Masters the younger, by the following description:—

"All that my copyhold messuage or tenement, with the garden, barne, close, croft, and two yards and a half of copyhold or customary land, with the appurtenances thereto belonging, situate, lying, and being in Brighton aforesaid, and in the *Comon Laines* there, &c., late Freelands."

On the demise of Richard Masters the younger (High Constable in 1734), the property passed (October, 1757,) to his nephew, Richard Tidy, brewer (High Constable in 1761). There is little doubt that, shortly after Mr. Tidy came into possession, the house was opened for public accommodation; for in his will, dated December 26, 1788, he speaks of it as his "public house, with buildings, yard, and appurtenances." The title deeds do not mention the house, "called or known by the name or sign of the White Lyon," till 1798; but a *Brighton Directory* for 1790 mentions it as being an inn, and states that the keeper of it was Thomas Colchin. There was, in fact, every inducement for the owner to open it as an inn.

---

* When the house was enfranchised by Messrs. Vallance, Catt, and Co., in 1851, the fine paid to the Lord was £315.

THE WHITE LION HOTEL—about 1858.

It was the first house in the town at which the old waggons and coaches, as well as foot passengers, coming by the "London-road, through Steyning," could stop at. Besides, there was opposition lower down! "The Unicorn" was doing business, with James Sicklemore as "Mine Host," in 1790, and Sarah Barnard had accommodation at "The Hammers," as "The Blacksmiths' Arms" was then universally called. Then, too, a "coffee house and tavern" had been erected (1785) on the site of the present Clarence Hotel.

In 1799 "The White Lion" was sold by Mr. Wichelo (the partner of Mr. Tidy, and who afterwards succeeded him in the brewery) to Mr. William Wigney. Singularly enough, it was the first house in Brighton that his brother, Mr. Robert Wigney, known by the sobriquet of "Gipsy Bob," put up at, when he came here as a travelling "pack-man"—the house at one time being much frequented by that class of "commercials." "The White Lion" was subsequently owned by Messrs. Wigney, and from them passed to Messrs. Vallance, Catt, and Co., by whom it was sold to the Corporation in July, 1872, for £8,000. In all the later deeds relating to the house there is specific mention of the "Soldiers' Room" attached to the premises, which was, probably, what was afterwards so well known as the "long room." It was customary at one time to have such rooms attached to public houses. Brighton was a regular billeting place for soldiers when marching through this district; and a "halt" meant a serious loss to local Bonifaces, who were compelled to accommodate as many as 50 men for a very inadequate remuneration.

Mr. Wallis, the "Host" in 1800, did not occupy "The White Lion" many years; and it was he who opened the wine office at No. 44, North street (the premises once associated with "The Theatre in North-street"), afterwards carried on by Mr. James Cordy. The "Host" of the old inn after Mr. Wallis was Mr. Pollard, who seems to have been an enthusiastic lover of old English sports, such as cricket, cock-fighting, &c.; and under his auspices "The White Lion" soon became a "centre." (See pp. 104-5.)

In the early part of the century there was always a set of "loafers" hanging about the old house—the denizens, probably, of the neighbouring slums of "Durham," "Petty France," and "Bunker's Hill"; their favourite spot for lounging being against the side wall of "The White Lion" facing down West-street. (The entrance to the house was originally from the "Yard," by a door facing east.) A singular but well-authenticated anecdote is related of an occurrence at this spot. Jemmy Botting, the hangman, a once well-known Brighton character, was passing by "The White Lion," during the period when he was acting as substitute for Jack Ketch at the Old Bailey and elsewhere, and the "loafers" there assembled taunted him so unmercifully about a man he had recently hung, that a passer-by was prompted to interfere, and suggested retaliation. "No, no," replied Jemmy; "I never quarrel with my *customers!*" One of the most prominent of Jemmy's assailants was a man named Falkiner, who, strange to relate, was hung by Botting, at Horsham, only two or three months afterwards, being executed on the 12th April, 1817, for rape at Hove; whilst a companion, Bowley, was transported for life.

The old "Brighton Society for the Prosecution of Thieves" held its meetings at "The White Lion" in 1809 and later on; but local chronicles fail to record anything of their doings, except an "annual dinner,"—a custom which the Society in the neighbouring parish of Preston, started about the same time, did their best to emulate!

"The White Lion" was, to a great extent, rebuilt in 1821-2; and in the December of the latter year it was occupied by Mr. Vincent, who removed to Brighton at that date from "The Angel Inn," Islington. As showing the increase which has taken place within the last 70 years in the value of property in North-street, "The White Lion," in 1784 was rated (with the coach-houses and stables) at only £8 15s.; it was raised in 1814 to £14 10s.; but in 1872, when Mr. F. Incledon Vincent kept the house (which was again altered after the opening of the Queen's-road), the rateable value was £207! The house was pulled down in May, 1874, by the Corporation, for the purpose of widening that part of North-street; and the present hotel and contiguous shops were subsequently erected on part of the site.

Three or four doors below "The White Lion" was the equally well-known "UNICORN." "The Unicorn" was opened as a public-house in the middle of the last century by an ancestor of Messrs. Bartholomew and Henry Smithers, but it had been for a long time previously used as a farm house.* "The Unicorn" would seem to have retained its connection with farming, &c., long after it did public-house business; for the landlord in 1800, Mr. Joseph Davison, is described in the old "Directory" as "milkman and cowkeeper";—he was, in fact, one of the only two *bonâ fide* milkmen in the town! Doubtless the old house, in the year 1800, was a thriving one, from the fact of there being then a barracks immediately behind it.

"The Unicorn," like other inns, was at times used for Vestry Meetings. In February, 1794, a Vestry Meeting was held there, at which Dr. Henderson was presented with a pint silver cup "for his care and attention to the parish." Mr. Boxall was "Host" about 1811, and for some time afterwards. The "mantle" of his neighbour, Mr. Pollard, of "The White Lion," appears to have fallen upon him as regards cricket (probably cock-fighting occupied all Mr. Pollard's attention); for at the cricket matches about this period Mr. Boxall used to provide booths, &c., and attend matches on the Prince's Ground and other places, to supply refreshments. The house would, however, appear to have been devoted to other matches besides those of cricket; for instance, we are told:—

"His Royal Highness the Duke of Cumberland (accompanied by the Earl of Yarborough and Colonel Blomfield) and a long list of the

---

* As affording, probably, some evidence of its age, when the alterations were made in the present eastern portion some few years since, a shilling of Charles I. was found beneath the ground floor.

THE UNICORN INN, NORTH STREET,—about 1865.

nobility and gentry and admirers of the 'elegant fancy' (*sic*) attended a sparring exhibition, which took place on Tuesday, November 5th, 1811, in a large room behind 'The Unicorn Inn,' North-street, for the benefit of Molineux (a black prize-fighter, who had recently been defeated by Cribb, after a terrific encounter), Burns, Hall, &c. For the delectation of the Royal Duke and his friends, some fine specimens of the art of self-defence were exhibited. The Duke, it is stated, was a very attentive observer, and, in reference to the late sanguinary encounter between Cribb and the black, observed that he should have felt much regret had the laurels of the champion been destined to adorn the brows of a FOREIGNER. On two of the subordinate professors setting-to, in imitation of the old school, His Royal Highness laughed heartily, and said he could do as well himself." The price of admittance was 3s. each, and there were nearly 100 persons present. On the two following days similar exhibitions took place, and on both occasions the room was crowded."

"The Unicorn" was put up to auction at "The Castle Tavern," in May, 1792, being described "as a large messuage and buildings, containing a good cellar, two parlours, kitchen, taproom, washhouse, seven bedchambers, and stabling for six horses, with offices attached and detached, in the occupation of James Sicklemore, a tenant-at-will." (The stabling was subsequently very much extended, being divided into two sections, and covered a large area.) When the property was sold, as stated, in 1792, it realised £840 ; and, as another instance of the increase in the value of property in North-street, it may be mentioned that £2,000 has been asked (but not given) as compensation for setting back the front in a line with the property on each side of it.

Mr. Vollar succeeded Mr. Boxall at "The Unicorn," and during his time (40 or 50 years ago) the house was, like "The White Lion," much used by carriers and hucksters, and especially by the latter on Brighton Market days, Thursdays and Saturdays. On the mornings of these days the scene in the yards of "The Unicorn" and "The White Lion" was a very lively one. The hucksters, having finished their business at the Market early, returned to the inns "to bait" their horses *and* themselves. At such times the kitchens (with their huge fires ablaze) at both inns were crowded with guests impatient for their morning meal ; and "Little Joey Stilwell," who kept a small chandler's shop just opposite "The Unicorn," did a "roaring trade" in supplying provisions. The house, after Mr. Vollar's retirement, was for several years kept by "Charley" Briggs (his son-in-law), a very popular landlord, during whose tenancy the house was much frequented by a section of those tradesmen who took a prominent part in managing the affairs of the town.*

[* The old building—after the existence probably of 300 years or more - was pulled down (March, 1892) with the view of erecting, for Messrs. H. W. Smithers and Son, of the Western-road Brewery, who now own the property, a new inn on its site. The latter (designed by Mr. S. Denman, a Brighton architect) will have a frontage of cement and red brick, treated in the Renaissance style, with flat windows on the ground floor, and bold cant-bow windows to the two storeys above. The frontage to Windsor-street will be treated in the same style. In the centre of the North-street frontage will be a handsome entrance, leading to a corridor paved in mosaics. On the right of this corridor will be a spacious bar, with bar parlour and tenant's parlour in the rear, whilst on the left will be

Nearly opposite "The Unicorn" was "THE HORSE AND GROOM," kept in 1800 by Mr. Thomas Bailey; subsequently changed to "The Bricklayers' Arms," by Mr. Shrivall, a bricklayer by trade, who kept the house for several years. At "The Bricklayers' Arms" were held several of the old Benefit Clubs, once so numerous, but not one of which is now in existence; whilst the inn itself was converted into a private house and shop a few years since.

Lower down the street, on the opposite side of the road, near the corner of King-street, was another public-house, "THE BLACKSMITHS' ARMS," popularly known as "The Hammers," the landlady being, in 1800, Mary Barnard (the widow of the original proprietor of the smithy behind, and which is still in existence and in the hands of a descendant, Mr. Stephen Barnard.) Like "The White Lion" and "The Unicorn," higher up the street, "The Blacksmiths' Arms" was originally part of a farm-house, there being a good-sized farm at one time close to the building, which was separated from it when King-street was formed. The original "Blacksmiths' Arms" was not, however, as now, at the corner of King-street, but at the door above; the house at the corner being a private house subsequently occupied by Mr. Comber, a watchmaker. The two small houses were converted into the present premises about 1822 or 1823, by Masters Bradford, for Mr. Chapman, who was succeeded, in 1833, by Mr. Hugh Saunders.

Higher up King-street, at No. 20, was another small public-house, known, in 1800, as "THE HEN AND CHICKENS;" the landlord being Mr. John Pocock, who occupied it as early as 1790; and, probably, opened it, for it did not exist in 1784. Comparatively obscure as was the situation of the house, the Vestry Book, under date 20th May, 1797, records a meeting there of the Churchwardens and Overseers, at which a resolution was passed—"That Phœbe Hassell's rent be paid from the present time, and that her weekly allowance be discontinued." We take it, that the meeting was held there, not so much on account of the convenience the house afforded, as out of respect to the landlord, who was then one of the ringers at the Old Church, where he subsequently officiated for over 40 years as Parish Clerk. The Brighton Society of Change Ringers held their club-meetings for many years at "The Hen and Chickens," and in one of the rooms there may yet be seen two of the numerous old tablets, bearing record of grand peals (in 1779 and 1823), which formerly hung in the belfry of St. Nicholas.* The major portion of these old tablets have long since passed into the hands of the marine-store dealer;

---

a commercial room, and two smoking rooms behind, with lavatories in the rear. Over the commercial room and smoking rooms will be a Club room, measuring 38 feet by 24 feet, suitable for dinners and gatherings of various descriptions. The rest of the accommodation on this floor and on the second floor will be given up to sitting and bedrooms. Extensive cellarage will be provided, and from the basement there will be a lift communicating with the upper floors. The building, in short, is admirably planned for the purpose it is designed to serve, and, though Brighton will lose one of its most interesting old hostelries, it is clear that in the new "Unicorn" the ancient hostelry will have a worthy successor.]

[* These are now in the possession of Mr. G. F. Attree, with the view to their being shortly replaced in the belfry of St. Nicholas.]

but, from the associations which attached to them, they deserved a better fate. There was one, if not two, dated 1817, which we know were especially interesting to some old Brightonians. On these were inscribed, in the place of the name of one of the ringers, "A VOLUNTEER"—the "Volunteer" being no other than Edward Martin, tailor, a well-known member of the Society of Friends, residing in North-street at that period, who was passionately fond of bell-ringing, but who did not like his name to appear in connection with it. He regularly attended on practice nights, not unfrequently accompanied by one of his workmen, named Jones, of Waldron. On such nights, as soon as the worthy Quaker heard the first bell, he used invariably to call up the stairs of his workshop (then in a yard, opposite "The Clarence Hotel" Yard), "The child's a crying, Jones," and master and man at once went off to the Belfry ! *

About 50 years ago the sign of the house was changed from "The Hen and Chickens" to that of "The Running Horse," by which name it is now known ; but this was long after Mr. Pocock left it. He, in fact, was the "host" of "THE GARDENERS' ARMS" (now "The William the Fourth") as early as 1806 ; for by an advertisement in the *Brighton Herald*, of October 15th, in that year, a sale is announced by "Mr. Verrall, Auctioneer, of the corner of New-road," to be held "at the house of Mr. John Pocock, bearing the sign of 'The Gardeners' Arms,' New-street" (now Bond-street). Mr. Pocock was not, however, the first landlord of the house. It was kept in 1800 by Mr. Thomas Westgate, and, when originally opened, at the close of the last century, was quite "out of the town." The name of "The Gardeners' Arms" was changed to that of "The William the Fourth" on the accession of that Monarch in 1830, by the then Host, Mr. George (who subsequently opened "The Prince Albert Inn," Trafalgar-street), and a finely-painted full-length portrait of His Majesty, in his Coronation robes, was placed over the front door of the house in Church-street, but has since been removed.

Immediately below "The Gardeners' Arms," in New-street, in 1800, was "THE WHEAT SHEAF," kept by Mr. John Yeates. He was succeeded about 1807 by Mr. Mantell. It was afterwards kept by Mr. Wymark (who married the widow of Mr. Mantell) for many years, and then by Mr. William Pope. The house was at one time, and especially during the early occupancy of Mr. Pope, much

---

* It may be interesting to note that the bells of old St. Nicholas—said to be, a century ago, "the best and most compleatest in the County"—were cast in 1777 by Mr. Thomas Rudhall, of the City of Gloucester, brother to Mr. Rudhall, brazier, of Brighthelmston. There were originally eight bells in all, the tenor being F, and weighing 16 cwt. The peal was opened on the 1st January, 1778, by part of the Horsham Society of Cumberland Youths, "with 5040 Holt's Grandsire Triples," which were completed in three hours and six minutes, in order, as follows:—

Thomas Jones ...	... triple.	Harry Weller ...	... 5th.
Thomas Lintott...	... 2nd.	John Foreman ...	... 6th.
Benjamin Hall ...	... 3rd.	Thomas Bristow	... 7th.
Edward Aldridge	... 4th.	James Wilson ...	... tenor.

In 1818 two more bells were added to the peal ; they did not, however, accord with the original eight, and when the clock at St. Peter's was put up they were removed to the tower of that Church for chiming the quarters.

frequented by theatricals during the season; and old visitors to the parlour even now dwell with delight on many an interesting reminiscence of pleasant hours spent there in a bygone time. "The Wheat Sheaf" was also at one time the tailors' "house of call," the trade Society being held there for many years.

Returning to North-street: almost opposite New-street was "THE NEW INN" (now the "Clarence Hotel"). The earliest named occupiers of the house were Messrs. Scott and Owden (in 1793). "The New Inn" was kept in 1800 by Mr. William H. Henwood (previously of "The White Horse"), who was also the leading partner of the firm of London coach proprietors, Henwood, Crosweller, Cuddington, Pockney, Harding, and Co., whose offices were at "The New Inn," and who occupied the extensive range of stabling originally attached to it. The house was erected about 1785, by, we believe, Mr. Wichelo, brewer (members of whose family retained a share in it down to a recent period), and was among the first of those hotels which, as Brighton became more and more crowded with fashionable visitors, were built to afford that accommodation which 80 or 90 years ago was so much sought after, but which it was so difficult to obtain.* "The New Inn" was happily situated; for when the entrance to the town from London by Steyning was down North-street, it was the first place in the street where what could really be called hotel-accommodation was available. When the coach *route* was altered in 1807-8—by Pyecombe, "avoiding all hills"—the house would appear to have been equally favourably situated; for, by an advertisement in the *Brighton Herald* in 1808 (inserted by Mr. Wichelo, of Glynde, on behalf, of the executors of Mrs. Henwood), the situation of "The New Inn" is described as "about the centre of the town, nearly opposite the New-road, lately made by H.R.H. the Prince of Wales, at the entrance from London!" † The house was taken by Mr. Matthew Phillips (one of the original proprietors of the *Brighton Herald*); but his occupancy was not successful.‡ He retired in 1811; and when the lease was put up to auction, in June of that year, it realised £20! For some years previously coaches had ceased to run from "The New Inn"; and this, probably, had something to do with the decline of the house at that period. The house must have been a serious undertaking—the rent being 600 guineas per annum. It was let by tender in the following August, the accommodation being stated as—"Large coffee-room, billiard room, 10 sitting-rooms, 26 bedrooms, two kitchens, and tap attached to the premises; two stable yards, with accommodation for nearly 50 horses and six coaches."

* The *Lewes Journal*,—in 1785,—in alluding to the opening, says :—"A coffee house and tavern has just been opened in North-street,—a thing never before attempted in Brighton." This was scarcely correct; as William Hicks, in 1765, in addition to "The Old Ship," "kept a coffee shop."

† The New-road was made in 1805 by the Prince of Wales; the inhabitants having given up to him the old road running from East-street to Church-street northwards, when, in 1803, he was desirous of enclosing the Pavilion.

‡ Miss Phillips, his daughter, who subsequently became a very popular actress, was born at "The New Inn."

THE NEW INN (now THE CLARENCE HOTEL)—1818.

The house was taken by Mrs. Heather in 1813; and in 1818 it was kept by the relict of Mr. Charles Gilburd, the daughter of Mrs. Heather. "Mine host" in 1822 was Mr. Pattenden, and during his occupancy, and for several years subsequently, Snow and Co.'s van office was carried on in a portion of the basement, a few steps leading down to it, between the east side of the portico-entrance and the "Shades." When Mr. Pattenden's occupancy ceased, the house was closed for a time. The subsequent landlords have been numerous; including Mr. Grove (who named the house "Grove's Family Hotel and Tavern"), Mr. Augustus Osten, Mr. Bull, and Mr. T. Rose.* The house is now, and has been for years past, one of the most popular and most frequented "commercial" houses of the town.

Various alterations and improvements—to meet changed requirements—have taken place in "The New Inn." In 1818, its front was quite plain: all the windows, like the present upper ones, being flat, the portico-entrance only projecting; and beneath the third floor windows were then, in large letters, "LODGINGS AND APARTMENTS FOR GENTLEMEN AND FAMILIES." Subsequently, the "Shades" were opened on the ground floor of the eastern portion of the house, and sundry other alterations have since been made. The name of the house was changed from "The New Inn" to "The Clarence Hotel" about 1830, out of compliment, we suppose, to His late Majesty William IV., then Duke of Clarence.

"The New Inn," from its situation and the accommodation it afforded, has been associated with several important local events. On the 1st November, 1809, a grand dinner was given there to Mr. Philip Mighell, who, at his own expense, at the Jubilee of George III.'s reign, October 25th, 1809, feasted 2,300 of the poorest inhabitants of the town. The enthusiasm of the promoters of the dinner to Mr. Mighell was unbounded; and it was proposed, before breaking-up, to continue the compliment annually; but—like too many after-dinner arrangements—it ended with the proposal, for it was never held again! In 1814 the High Constable's (Mr. R. Ackerson's) "Feast" was held there with great *éclat*. "The New Inn" was the first place in which a local Magistrate's sitting was held. This was in 1808. It will, perhaps, provoke a smile from modern Brightonians to read the announcement of Messrs. Brooker and Colbatch, solicitors, of Brighton, who acted as clerks, with respect to the above Magistrate's sitting:—

"NOTICE IS HEREBY GIVEN, that a Magistrate will attend at The New Inn, every Monday, Wednesday, and Friday, from twelve to one, or until the business that happens to be brought forward shall be completed, then and there to determine all matters that shall be brought before them. * * * And when any matter requires the interference of a second Magistrate, upon notice thereof being given, the attendance of a second Magistrate will be procured, *if possible*"!

[* Mr. Rose retired in 1877, since which time the Hotel has been carried on by his eldest son, Mr. T. Rose, the present esteemed proprietor.]

Notices were issued at the same time to this effect :—

"All vagrants, common beggars, and suspicious persons, who may from time to time appear in this town and its neighbourhood, will be taken into custody."

Constables were allowed a large license in this primeval epoch of Brighton history! All the "body politic" must have been known to him, or else suspicious persons, vagrants, and common beggars (whatever this last designation might mean), must have been scarce, for his powers of "custody" were exceedingly restricted. It may be here stated that it was not till 1814 that the first regular Petty Sessions were held at Brighton. These were held at "The Old Ship" (Mr. Serjeant Runnington being Chairman), whence they were removed to "The New Inn" in 1822; but they did not stay long in their new quarters, as in the following year they migrated to the miserable old Town Hall, where they were held twice a week—Mondays and Thursdays.

Almost the last Court held by the Magistrates at "The New Inn" was on the 4th March, 1823, when there was a special sitting to inquire into the circumstances connected with the death of Mr. Williams, a gentleman of Brighton, whose body had been washed ashore between Rottingdean and Newhaven, and in such a mutilated condition as to leave little doubt that the unfortunate man had been murdered. An inquest was held at Rottingdean, and a verdict of "Accidentally Drowned" was returned. But this was deemed so contrary to evidence—the medical evidence being directly against such a conclusion—that further investigation was deemed necessary, and the Magistrates met as above stated. The result was that a reward of 200 guineas was offered for such information as would lead to the apprehension of the supposed murderers, Mr. Peel (afterwards Sir Robert Peel), the Home Secretary, promising on the part of the Government a free pardon to one accomplice. No information, however, was obtained; and the murder of Mr. Williams was another addition to the catalogue of "undiscovered crimes."

But to return to "The New Inn." No event in earlier times probably gave it more notoriety than the hoax of February 19th, 1810, known as "The Hunter Hoax." Just previously to that day, some individual, for purposes of his own, sent carefully-worded letters to numerous individuals in Brighton, and to a number of others in various parts of the County, requesting their attendance at "The New Inn," North-street, Brighton. The letters,—which offered tempting and substantial advantages, varied according to the business or position of the person addressed,—were all signed "JOHN HUNTER." The baits took, and during the day the numerous applications for "Mr. John Hunter" almost distracted both proprietor and servants of "The New Inn," who were unceasingly occupied in answering enquiries and explaining that no such person as "Mr. John Hunter" was known in the house! With the Brighton applicants this was bad enough; but when the country arrivals began to put in an appearance,—many from distant parts and at considerable expense, and who, finding they had been "sold," were not slow in expressing their chagrin,—the scene may be, in conventional phraseology, "better imagined than described." The miscreant who concocted the hoax was never discovered. He was undoubtedly a local man, with a *penchant* for that species of amusement called "practical joking;" for about a fortnight after (Sunday, March 3) another hoax was perpetrated: "The Clergyman of the Parish Church of St. Nicholas reading the banns of marriage of two couples, who, it was afterwards discovered, were entirely ignorant of the circumstance"! As in the former case, the perpetrator could not be discovered: the only result of inquiries being, that the notices were left with the Parish Clerk on the Saturday evening by a little girl, she having received 6d. from a woman, a stranger to her, for so doing. A few days after (March 13th) the town was startled by another hoax, by the announcement, in a London evening paper, of the "Death of Mr. Beach Roberts," a well-known local character, coupled with many extravagant particulars concerning him; that gentleman being at the time in perfect health! With this last hoax the perpetrator appears to have "rested from his labours;" for we hear no more of him!*

But to proceed. Next door to "The New Inn" was "THE COACH AND HORSES" (No. 23); "Mine Host" in 1800 being Mr. John Morling, whose brother Philip carried on, in the same street, the business of "spruce-beer brewer." Every house is said to have its history. "The Coach and Horses" is probably no exception to this rule; but we have been unable to find it. Nothing that we know of, in earlier times, appears to have disturbed the even tenour of its way. Judging by the following advertisement in the *Lewes Journal*, a little cock-fighting would, however, appear to have been carried on there:—

COCKING.—A WELSH MAIN.—A SILVER CUP, value Four Guineas, will be fought for by EIGHT COCKS, at the house of WM. YEATES, bearing the sign of the "Coach and Horses," North-street, Brighthelmston, on WEDNESDAY, December 28th, 1785.

N B.—No cock to exceed the weight of 4 lbs. 10 oz., and to subscribe HALF-A-GUINEA towards the Cup.—To begin fighting at 11 o'clock.

☞ Two large Cocks to fight for Five Guineas each.

---

* We may add here, though unconnected with "The New Inn," the particulars (extracted from the *Lewes Journal*) of another local hoax, which took place in October, 1804:—" A hoax (suggested probably by an attempt lately made by a person at Margate to walk on the sea) was on Friday se'nnight successfully played off at Brighton. A bill was posted about the town, stating that a man would, at four o'clock in the afternoon of the above day, walk on the water from the eastern to the western groyne, and that he would depend on the voluntary contributions of the spectators for remuneration for his surprising and dangerous exploit. An immense concourse of people were in consequence assembled on the cliff, where they waited, numbers of them till nearly dusk, to behold the miracle; but somewhat like the Bottle Conjuror of old, the professor failed to appear, and the multitude departed without having their appetites for novelty gratified. The next day another bill was posted in North-street, thanking the people for their kind attendance, which had won the advertiser a considerable wager, and inviting every one of them to a COLD COLLATION on the Downs, near the Race Stand, to be provided at his expense, on that day at three o'clock; but certainly without the least expectation that this, his *second attempt* on the credulity of HONEST JOHN, could succeed."

An extraordinary exhibition took place at "The Coach and Horses" in August, 1808. The advertisement in the *Brighton Herald* of that date respecting it was as follows :—

TO BE SEEN, at The Coach and Horses, North-street, Brighton, adjoining The New Inn, a GREAT CURIOSITY OF A MALE CHILD, only two years and five months old, such as was never brought before the public, in this or any other country, and is allowed by the Faculty to be one of the greatest wonders ever seen.—Admission 1s.

In what the "great curiosity" consisted—whether the child was of extraordinary size or very diminutive, we have been unable to discover; but, as an incentive to visitors, the advertisement had the addition—"His stay here will be but short." There was also the N.B.: "Any family wishing to see the child, *will be waited upon at any hour*, by sending information to the above"—rather scant courtesy, it will be thought, to visitors *to* the house.

"The Coach and Horses" was kept in 1822 by Mr. Charles Sharood, who was succeeded, we believe, by Mr. William Fleet (previously of "The Seven Stars"), a well-known "whip," who was accidentally killed whilst driving a coach between Brighton and Maidstone, on which road he drove for many years. His widow continued at the house, and subsequently married Mr. Demmen (butler to Mr. Laurence Peel), who thenceforth assumed the position of "Mine Host" of the old inn. After Mr. Demmen's death the house was carried on for many years by another "whip," Mr. Ambrose Pickett.

The exterior of "The Coach and Horses" was originally very unpretentious and plain; in fact it was North-street "old style." The present front—erected a few years ago—will not, probably, be regarded as an improvement on it.

Among the associations of "The Coach and Horses," mention might, perhaps, be made of the famous "Billy-goat Dinner," which took place there some sixty years ago. This festive gathering was brought about somewhat in this wise. The Magistrates at the period had issued an order that "all dogs found loose in the town were to be shot;" the important office of "executioner" devolving upon William (*alias* "Billy") Catlin, the beadle. "The Castle" stables were then nearly opposite "The Coach and Horses," and occupied the site of the present Royal Colonnade. There was kept at the stables a well-known goat, who, being allowed his "run," would, like many another fine fellow, frequently stray out of bounds. "Billy," one day, unconscious of impending danger, took a walk as far as the corner of Bond-street, when Catlin, gun in hand, and intent on duty, happened to be coming through the street, and (being short-sighted) mistook the goat for a dog! Fatal error! The gun was pointed; the trigger pulled, and "Billy," receiving the charge, was "no more" to the world at large. His body was, however, removed to "The Coach and Horses;" not for an inquest to be held upon it; but to be roasted and eaten! Whether or no Billy Catlin was invited to the feast, we know not. He ought to have been; for he never heard the of his exploit. Years after, when he was appointed beadle on the

Western Esplanade, while he was doing duty in the upper part, small boys would occasionally assemble in the lower, and greet him with cries of "Ba-a-a," and the annoying shout of "Who shot the billy-goat!"

"The Coach and Horses" was, in 1800, as now, the last public-house down North-street. We must needs, therefore, take a long flight to "THE KING AND QUEEN," No. 1, North-row (now the northern portion of Marlbro'-place), the host of which in 1800 was Mr. William Penfold. Mr. John Pollard was the previous landlord, and during his occupancy, in 1795, the house was purchased by Mr. Philip Vallance, merchant, of Mr. Isaac Grenville, who himself kept the house in 1786. The old inn, like many other houses at the then north part of the town, had been originally a farm-house, but was known as "The King and Queen" as early as 1779; for at this period we learn, from a description of the town, that "a few houses, called North-row, with 'the King and Queen,' constituted the whole of the buildings in this direction."

The character of this spot about 1779 was very different from what it is now. The ground now forming the Enclosures was then a barren waste, or rather rough grass-land, and commonly known as "The Level." It was at certain periods of the year more or less covered with water, by reason of the overflowing of the rivulet which ran through it towards the Pool Valley and to the sea from Patcham, and which not unfrequently inundated the whole valley hereabouts, the Steine included. The district in the neighbourhood of "The King and Queen," in 1779, was purely agricultural. A road then ran across the "Level" to what is now Carlton-hill, the hill-slopes to the east and north-east being either corn-land or down. At the bottom of Church-hill (Spring-walks, now Church-street,) was a farm-building with homestead, &c., and all the land on the north side of Church-street, from this building to what was known as the Church Down, by the Old Church, was down-land. At the opposite corner of Church-street, where North-gate House now is, were other farm buildings, and about 30 or 40 yards to the south of these, about where the road is now which leads to the Pavilion entrance to the Dome, was a pretty farm-house, facing eastward, with trees in front, a road leading from it across the Steine to the bridle-road (now Edward-street) to Rottingdean.

Even down to so lately as 1807-10 the ground in front of "The King and Queen" was known as "the Level"; for during the Races in 1807, a Mr. Polito, designated as the "modern Noah," announced the exhibition of his Menagerie "on the Level, near 'the King and Queen.'" In alluding to this wonderful Menagerie, a chronicler says—"The proprietor, highly to his credit, will not suffer any animal or bird to be called by any other than its real name"! A few days after the above Races, there was, we are told, a sparring match between Gully and Cribb, in the presence of the Prince of Wales and his Royal brothers, on "the Level," but whether in front of "The King and Queen," or further north, is uncertain, but it is more likely to have been the former.

One of the most notable events associated with "The King and Queen" was John Fuller being located there, on the 28th March, 1811, previous to undergoing his sentence of "standing in the pillory" at the bottom of North-street. Fuller's offence was the passing of a "2d." note for one of £2. The novelty of the punishment—it was the first time, we believe, that such a sentence had been carried out in Brighton—caused much local excitement; and a vast crowd assembled outside "The King and Queen" to see the culprit escorted to his place of "exhibition," which was in the road at the bottom of North-street, nearly opposite the door of the present County Bank. The pillory was fixed upon a platform about 10ft. or 12ft. from the ground. It was computed that over 5,000 persons witnessed the spectacle, every shop in the neighbourhood being closed. Fuller stood in the pillory for an hour, from twelve o'clock till one, exposed to the gibes and taunts of the unsympathising crowd; to whom

"He, poor wretch, had nought to say;
'Twas not his speechifying day."

No "pelting" took place, public notice having been issued that it was illegal, and would be punished with imprisonment. There was, of course, much excitement (Fuller became almost black in the face before his hour had expired), but no serious disturbance occurred, thanks to the prudent arrangements of the Under-Sheriff, G. Palmer, Esq., who, with his officers, was present, as were also the High Constable of Brighton (Mr. Harry Colbron), the headboroughs, &c., not forgetting old "Billy" Catlin, the beadle, who put Fuller "through his facings."

One can scarcely believe that such an event took place in Brighton—where Royalty dwelt and where the votaries of Fashion were wont to congregate—scarcely "seventy years since." Yet such was the case; and if anything could be offered in excuse, it is the knowledge of the fact that Fuller was an arrant knave. He induced an illiterate countryman to give him 40s. change for the "2d." note, and had actually got off with the money. When apprehended, a "5d." note was found on him. The week previous to the crime for which he suffered punishment, Fuller had obtained of another countryman, for a "2d." note, 32s. worth of potatoes and apples, and 8s. change!

Another important local event associated with "The King and Queen" was the holding there the inquest on the body of Mr. John Rowles, headborough of Brighton, who, during the 5th November riots on the Steine in 1817, when the military were called out, received a bayonet thrust through his side. Mr. Rowles died the next day at his residence on the Grand-parade, and the inquest was held at "The King and Queen," from its being the nearest public-house. The inquest lasted over nine days, the jury returning a verdict of "Wilful Murder" against John Day (the soldier who wounded the unfortunate man), John Williams (High Constable), and James White (stationer). They surrendered to their bail at the

Assizes at Horsham in the following March, when a verdict of " Not Guilty " was returned, and they were discharged, the Judge remarking that, so far from any blame being attached to Messrs. Williams and White, he was fully persuaded that they acted throughout with the greatest prudence, coolness, and discretion.

In the same year, 1817, the Enclosures (in front of "The King and Queen" and that northward) were formed, pauper labour being utilized to a great extent. The place, previously, had been a "shame and reproach" to the town ; and a Committee to carry out the project and to remedy the nuisance was appointed at a meeting held at " The King and Queen." on the 1st February, 1817. The expense was defrayed by public subscription; the Prince Regent giving £500; Mr. Hart 100 guineas; Col. Olney 60 guineas ; other sums being raised among the owners of property in the neighbourhood. The laying out of the grounds was undertaken by Mr. Furner, the Prince's gardener, the trees and shrubs being given by the Earl of Chichester. It was originally intended to call the Southern Enclosure the Regent Steine, and to erect the Prince's statue in it ; but the intention was not carried out. The Southern Enclosure was opened in July, 1818, and the Northern in 1819 ; but both are now known as the North Steine Enclosures.

"The King and Queen" was never a "soldier's house"; but it is probable that, in the early part of the century, it took more money from soldiers than any other house in the town. "Stolen kisses" are said to be the sweetest, and, on the same principle, the connection between the soldiery and "The King and Queen" being a "secret," libations were, probably, the more indulged in. The fact is, there was a small "hole in the wall" which separated the Barracks yard (formerly at the bottom of Church-street) from the back of "The King and Queen"! and through this, on a given signal, liquor used to be passed in any quantity. The hole had been there from time immemorial. It was about 10 inches square, and on "The King and Queen" side was covered by an iron door, and is to be seen, even now, in the present pantry of the Hotel, which was formerly the "tap" cellar. The hole, doubtless, owed its origin to some thirsty inventive genius. There was only a wall between him and his beer ; and, happy thought ! if he could not get the latter *over* the wall, he, at least, might get some *through* it ! But "The best laid schemes o' mice and men, gang aft a gley." Whether the secret was "blown," or other causes militated against it, the "hole in the wall," at least on the Barracks side, was effectually closed some time previous to the Barracks being removed.*

After Mr. Penfold, "The King and Queen" was kept for many years by Mr. Long (formerly of the 10th Hussars), and subsequently

---

* As showing how singularly traditions are confirmed and preserved, we may mention that, a few years ago, when we went into the old Barracks yard, to look for the whereabouts of the " hole in the wall," we encountered there a fine old man, employed by the Corporation, on one of the stone-heaps. He told us that he was formerly in the " Guards " and recollected the hole quite well ; in fact, that he had had many a pot of beer through it !

by his son-in-law, Mr. Reed, and of late years by Mrs. Funnell. The Brighton Corn Market, on its being removed from "The Old Ship," was held for a long time at "The King and Queen," whence it was removed, in October, 1868, to the present Corn Exchange, Royal Pavilion.

Passing hence to the Steine, we come to the *locale* of an inn which has for nearly sixty years ceased to exist; one which to Brightonians of the present generation is little more than a myth: its splendour, its varying fortunes, and its subsequent extinction, being known only by tradition, or by brief chronicle. We allude to "The Castle Tavern," occupied in 1800 by Mr. Thomas Tilt.

Of this fine old building (with its magnificent assembly room), where the first Royal visitor to Brighton (1765) resided; where, subsequently, Royal Princes revelled and feasted; and where a fugitive King (Louis XVIII.) once slept—the place where, of all others, in the olden time, beauty, rank, and fashion visiting Brighton most delighted to assemble and to participate in the amusements of the period—nought now remains; and its place is only known by the name which it gave to the thoroughfare, at the bottom of which it once stood—Castle-square!

"The Castle" occupied the site of the block of buildings now forming the northern side of the eastern end of Castle-square, and had also a considerable frontage to the Old Steine. It was originally a small private house, and was opened as an inn in 1755 by Mr. Samuel Shergold. There had been for some years previously—at all events prior to 1750—a little inn known as "The Fountain" in close proximity to the house which was converted into "The Castle." (The Steine, therefore, had a "Fountain," before that erected by public subscription, through the exertions of Mr. Cordy Burrows.) It is possible that the business of the original inn was transferred to "The Castle"; for it was entirely removed in 1776, when the latter was altered and enlarged and the handsome ball room was built (see page 27). Under the active supervision and management of Mr. Shergold the fortunes of "The Castle" throve apace; its proximity to the Steine,—the only resort of Fashion in those days,—tending much to increase the patronage it received both from residents and visitors. Mr. Shergold, it would appear, retired from the proprietorship of "The Castle" early in 1776; for it was in that year occupied by Mr. Stuckey, but only for a short time (his widow, in the following year, married Mr. Bradford, miller, of Brighthelmston). Mr. Shergold then again became "Mine Host," and so great was the increase of business, that he took Messrs. Tilt and Best into partnership, which continued down to February 14th, 1791, when Mr. Shergold finally retired. The wine-trade of the firm was thenceforth carried on by Mr. Best, and the business of "The Castle Tavern" by Mr. Tilt. During Mr. Tilt's occupancy, which continued till his death, in 1809, "The Castle" experienced little diminution of its earlier prosperity; and "in the extent, elegance, and commodiousness of its accommodations in every respect, it hardly yielded to any tavern in the kingdom." Mrs. Tilt carried on the house after her husband's death for

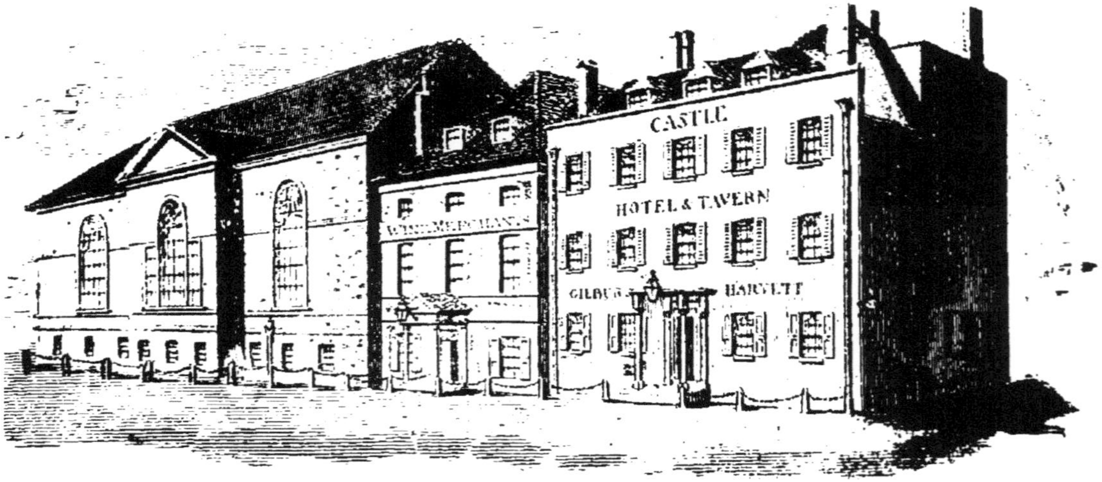

THE CASTLE TAVERN, BRIGHTON, 1814.

a short period, and, on her demise, "The Castle" was put up to auction at Garraway's, London, by Mr. Willock, but was bought in.

In 1814, Messrs. Gilburd and Haryett became the proprietors of "The Castle"; but, in spite of sundry improvements in the house itself, and the erection of a fine organ in the Ball-room, the fortunes of the old inn waned; for at the Opening Ball the subscribers did not exceed 20! Then came a dispute between the proprietors and that great Potentate of Fashion, the "M.C.' of Brighton; and "the rooms were closed"! On the adjustment of the matter, however, the "M.C.'s" Ball (such was the homage paid by the votaries of Fashion to their dictators) had above 500 guests. The proprietors, by promenade concerts, &c., also did their best during their occupancy to keep up the attractiveness of "The Castle," and if the prospects of the house seemed to brighten now and then, it was only for a brief period, and, ultimately, business became the reverse of encouraging. But a more powerful Potentate still, George IV., may be said to have finally decided the fortunes of "The Castle." The greater part of it having become his property, when Regent, by purchase,* with the object of opening the front view of the Pavilion on to the Steine, he, in 1821, converted the noble Ball-room into the Pavilion Chapel,† which was opened with much ceremony on January 1, 1822.

There was, probably, no inn in the town held in higher estimation, either by visitors or townsfolk, than "The Castle" during the greater part of its existence;‡ and, excepting, perhaps, "The Old Ship," there was none more intimately associated with local events. We need not again dilate on the Sunday public tea assemblies, the balls and card parties, &c., held at "The Castle"; or on the "Grand Rose Ball" (in 1805), and the "Masked Ball" (in 1807); or the introduction there, for the first time in Brighton, of the "Waltz," entirely throwing into the shade the old dances, with "up the sides and down the middle;" for much relating to these matters has been alluded to under "FASHIONABLE AND POPULAR AMUSEMENTS" (pp. 25 to 39); "THE STEINE AND ITS ASSOCIATIONS" (pp. 107 to 145), &c.

There are, however, other local matters of interest associated with "The Castle," as with other inns of the town, which may be adverted to. The Parish Officers, in earlier times, transacted much of their

---

* His Royal Highness purchased in July, 1815, ¼ of the Castle Tavern and Assembly Rooms, from Samuel Shergold, son and heir at law of S. Shergold, deceased, for £1,960. The conveyance described it as "late in the occupation of Thomas Tilt, Vintner and Tavern Keeper, deceased." In December, 1816, H.R.H. purchased another ¼ from the surviving Trustees under the will of Thomas Best, for £2,450; and in June, 1822, from James Shergold's representatives, the remaining moiety for £6,800; thus paying for the property a total sum of £11,210.

† This Chapel, when the Pavilion became the property of the town, was pulled down and re-erected in Montpelier-place, and consecrated as St. Stephen's in 1852.

‡ Trivial as it may seem, the visitors throughout the town in 1761, and for a long period after, preferred the water from "The Castle," the townsfolk having theirs from the old well in "The Unicorn" Yard. The town at this period was all to the south of North-street, and the greater number of the wells being near the sea-shore, the water was brackish.

business there; and one of the advertisements, relating to the Parish Contracts for 1790, which appeared in the *Brighthelmston Pacquet* of that year is in many respects worth quoting :—

TO GROCERS, MEALMEN, BUTCHERS, DRAPERS, &c.

SUCH Persons as are willing to supply the POOR HOUSE belonging to the Town and Parish of Brighthelmston, in the County of Sussex, by Contract, for One Year certain, to commence from the 1st of January, 1790, are desired to send in their Proposals, sealed, with their lowest Prices, as no Abatement can be made after the Seal is broke, to the Churchwardens, Overseers, and Committee, who will meet at the CASTLE Tavern, in Brighthelmston, aforesaid, on TUESDAY, the 29th of December instant, between the Hours of Two and Three o'clock in the Afternoon, to receive such proposals.

FIRST CONTRACT—Shoulders and Necks of the best Beef, with 12lbs. of Suet per Week, at per Stone. Legs, Shins, and Heads of Beef, at per Stone. Corn-fed Hogs, not exceeding 30 Stone, or under 27 Stone, at per ditto.

SECOND CONTRACT—Good second Wheaten Flour, at per Bushel.

THIRD CONTRACT—Cheshire, Gloucester, and Derby Cheese, at per Cwt. Best Waterford Butter, at per ditto.

FOURTH CONTRACT—Good Malt, at per Quarter. Ditto Hops, at per lb.

FIFTH CONTRACT—The best Oatmeal, and boiling Peas, at per Bushel.

SIXTH CONTRACT—Good Candles, at per Dozen. The best brown Soap, at per Cwt.

SEVENTH CONTRACT - The best Newcastle Coals, at per Chaldron.

EIGHTH CONTRACT—Linsey-woolsey and Baize for the Women and Girls Cloathing. Check, for Aprons and Handkerchiefs. 7-8th and 3-4th sleek Dowlas, for Shirts and Shifts. Blue Honley for Men's and Boys' Clothes. Blue Yarn Stockings, and Blue Linen for round Frocks. Felt Hats for Men and Boys, Straw Hats for Women and Girls.

Samples of the above Articles to be seen at the Town Hall.

NINTH CONTRACT - Strong Leather Shoes for Men, Women, and Children, at per Pair, according to the different sizes.

TENTH CONTRACT – Making Men's and Boys' Clothes, at per Suit.

N.B. – The Bills for the several contracts to be paid every three months.

WANTED, a GOVERNOR for the POOR HOUSE of the said Town; a single Man, of good Character, about 40 Years of Age, who is every Way qualified for such an Employment: a liberal Salary will be given. For Particulars enquire of the Churchwardens, Overseers, and Committee of the said Town and Parish.

After the establishment of Brighton Races, the old inn was for many a year at Race time in "high feather," as all horses had to be "shown and entered at the Castle," and there was no little excitement there in 1806, when the "Smoaker Stakes" were inaugurated by the Prince Regent, *in memoriam* of "Smoaker" Miles, his bather. The Prince entered his own horse, Albion, which won by "about a neck." The "Stakes" came to grief in the following year. They were "on the card"; but no horses were entered, and thenceforth we hear no more of them!

THE INNS OF BRIGHTON IN 1800 AND THEIR ASSOCIATIONS.

Not the least important of the meetings held at "The Castle" was that, on the 25th August, 1803, when the "landlords, householders, and inhabitants of the town and parish," were called together "pursuant to notice given in the Church, on Sunday, the 21st August," to consider a proposition of the Prince of Wales, to enclose, within the Pavilion grounds, that portion of East-street lying between North-street and Church-street; he stipulating to form the New-road in lieu thereof. The Prince's proposition was unanimously accepted; and when the resolution of the inhabitants was the same day presented to him, he observed "that the town of Brighthelmston should never lose anything by obliging him."

Among the associations of "The Castle" must be mentioned the fête given there in October, 1806, to celebrate the coming of age of Earl Delawarr. It was considered to be one of the grandest ever given in England. The ball-room was superbly decorated, under the superintendence of Mr. Harrison, of the Opera House; and Mr. Ward, of Bond-street, London, supplied the supper, to the taste and magnificence of which, it was said, "it is impossible to do adequate justice." First-rate cooks and table-deckers,* and a numerous train of ornamental decorators were procured from London, "as well as (*mirabile dictu*) fashionable hair dressers and other appendages of the *beau monde* too numerous to mention." The fête, which was attended by between 300 and 400 of the most "distinguished fashionables," was calculated to have cost nearly £2,000. The High Constable and Headboroughs of the town had been solicited by the Earl to attend the fête; but, at the last moment, they were informed that their attendance would be unnecessary, as a company of soldiers had been engaged to preserve order!

In June of the following year there was another great "event" at "The Castle"; not a "celebration" but a "consolation." This was the grand "Consolation dinner," as it was called, given by the "independent freeholders of the County" to Colonel Warden Sergison, of Cuckfield Place. It was one of four or five given at various places in the County, after the gallant Colonel's defeat in the great County election of that year—one of the severest and most expensive of our County elections on record. The candidates were Wyndham, Fuller, and Sergison; the election lasted fifteen days, and though Colonel Sergison was declared the popular candidate, he was lowest on the poll by 57 votes. Such was the excited state of popular feeling at the time that, on its being announced by Mr. Wigney at the above dinner that a fund was about to be raised to petition against Mr. Fuller's return, no less than £579 was at once subscribed by the guests for the purpose!

In August, 1808, a moiety of the New Theatre (including scenery, machinery, wardrobe, &c.), just erected in the New-road, was sold at "The Castle," by Mr. H. Phillips. It was purchased by Sir Thomas

---

* A feature of the table decorations was the "sand work," which was universally admired.

Clarges for 5,250 guineas. Sir Thomas offered a similar sum for the other moiety, which was refused. The standing annual rent of the Theatre at that time, including taxes, was £850.

We have alluded (p. 189) to the Court Martial held at "The Old Ship," in 1795, on the mutineers of the Oxford Militia. A Court Martial was held at "The Castle," in July, 1810, also on an Oxford Militiaman, Corporal Curtis, who was sentenced to receive *one thousand lashes*. He bore 200; the remainder being remitted.

Among the distinguished visitors of "The Castle" in later times may be mentioned the Duc d'Angouleme and the unfortunate Count de Lille (commonly known as Louis XVIII.). They arrived, with a suite of seven persons, at "The Castle," on the 4th July, 1811, whence they departed on the following morning for the Duke of York's seat at Oatlands. Some four years later, in July, 1814, "The Castle" had an "eccentric" visitor in the person of a Mr. Webb, whose prodigality was unbounded; whilst his means. in bank notes and gold, appeared to be inexhaustible. His fame had preceded him; and the news of his arrival spreading, a swarm of men, women, and children quickly beset the doors of "The Castle," in the hope of obtaining a share in a "distribution." They were, however, disappointed; for it appeared that Mr. Webb "only gave money to those who chose to follow him to a distance from their homes." Several had done so; and four emigrants from Tunbridge Wells received between them £50, and £5 to pay their expenses; and others from Lewes £5, £2, and £1 each. Mr. Webb left "The Castle" the following day, on his way to Arundel, followed by several fisherwomen and boys; but, excepting four of the boys, none proceeded further than Shoreham. The four boys hung on behind Mr. Webb's chaise until he reached "The Pad" inn, where, on presenting themselves, he gave to each a £5 note! Mr. Webb, it subsequently appeared, was suffering from mental derangement; and was shortly afterwards placed by his friends in an asylum.

On March 16th, 1818, St. James's Chapel was sold at "The Castle" by Mr. H. R. Attree (father of Mr. George Attree). It realised £3,566; and was bought by a Mr. Tyndell, solicitor.

In October, 1823, the old house,—linked with so many pleasant associations of Brighton in the olden time,—was pulled down by Mr. Boxall, builder, who had purchased it of His Majesty. Surely, "Ichabod" must have been written on its walls; for a local chronicle thus speaks of the event:—"That huge and incongruous mass of building, contiguous to the Pavilion, and known for many years as 'The Castle Tavern,' has, at length, been taken down!" *Sic transit gloria mundi!* By the removal of "The Castle," 15ft. was added to the width of the Castle-square, and 12ft. to the Steine path at that point.

Besides "The Castle" there remain only some two or three other public houses of the town in 1800 to notice. The first of these is "The Chimneys" (now the "Golden Fleece"), No. 1, Market-street, which was kept by Mr. Aaron Batho. The house was, we believe, originally opened by a sweep, and at one time the sign over the door consisted of a rude painting of a stack of chimneys. Then there was "The Golden Cross" (now "The Marlboro' ") 2, Prince's-street (now Pavilion-street), the Host in 1800 being Mr. Henry Witch. This house was subsequently kept by Mr. Maiben (who during his occupancy purchased, in 1818, "The Castle" stables in the New-road); and also by Mr. Ireland, the original proprietor of the Royal Gardens and Cricket Ground (now Park-crescent, &c.). The old Brighton Catch and Glee Club (founded, we believe, by the celebrated Incledon), was for many years held at "The Golden Cross."

East of the Steine in 1800, the public houses were but few and comparatively of recent erection. There was "The King's Arms," in George-street, of which Mr. Henry Gillett was Host. He was succeeded by Mr. Thos. Francis (father of Mr. John Francis, formerly a well-known Brighton printer). Whether or no Host Francis of "The King's Arms" was desirous of emulating Host Pollard of "The White Lion," in the matter of cock-fighting, we know not; but the "sport" was occasionally indulged in there, as an advertisement in the *Brighton Herald* of January 4, 1811, shows:—

COCKING.—A main of Cocks will be fought at the King's Arms Yard, George-street, on Thursday, Jan. 17, 1811, between George Knowles and John Pollard, for 5 guineas the battle and 20 guineas the main. Feeders, F. Holding, of Henfield, and J. Pollard, of Brighton.

N.B.—A Pair of Cocks to be in the Pit at 11 o'clock.

In July, 1816, "The King's Arms" was the "winning post" of a famous "match against time," when Captain Wombwell, of the 1st Life Guards, undertook, for a bet of 500 guineas, to drive a tandem from the Marsh Gate, Westminster Bridge, to "The King's Arms," George-street, Brighton, without changing horses. The Captain started at four a.m., and arrived at "The King's Arms," in fine style, at 8.45, notwithstanding every disadvantage in respect of weather, for rain fell in torrents the whole distance. The horses appeared to be very little distressed on their arrival. The route (52 miles) taken by Captain Wombwell was by Croydon, Reigate, and Hickstead.

"The King's Arms" was at one time much frequented of an evening by a section of the tradesmen of the town; and at one of these meetings the idea was originated of erecting a statue on the Steine to George IV., which was eventually carried out by Chantrey at a stipulated price of 3,000 guineas (it cost the great sculptor no less than 6,000 guineas); but, though the subscription list remained open over eight years, the sum was not realized.

The two other public houses east of the Steine were "The Crown and Anchor," kept by Mr. Thomas Webb; and "The Sloop" (now "The Packet"), kept by Mr. Thomas Heather. With the mention of these we will here close our notice of "THE INNS OF BRIGHTON IN 1800 AND THEIR ASSOCIATIONS."

Sea-Bathing.

SEA-BATHING may justly be said to have laid the foundation of Brighton's prosperity. It was the primary cause which induced so many wealthy visitors to resort to the town,—some for health, others for pleasure,—and ultimately secured for it the honour of being chosen as a Royal residence. In the present day, when other attractions exert their influence—the unrivalled marine drives and promenades, the unlimited accommodation obtainable in the palatial residences and magnificent hotels which adorn the sea frontage, and the fashionable society always to be found here—bathing, though indulged in as much as formerly, has become of secondary importance, or, rather, it has become so merged in the general combination of local attractions, that it has lost that prominence which formerly attached to it. Still, as connected with the "Past," and being intimately associated with the early history of the town, some particulars respecting it will not be without interest.

It will be needless to go back to any primeval epoch to ascertain when Brighton was first resorted to as a bathing-place. Enough for our purpose in this respect is the fact that a visitor here (the Rev. W. Clarke, of Buxted), in a letter, dated July 22nd, 1736, tells a friend, "My morning business is bathing in the sea." But Mr. Clarke was, probably, only one among many who at that period came hither for the same purpose in summer-time, or at a season when the state of the old roads admitted of travelling. The "pretty fisher village" had, doubtless, even then, acquired a reputation, though necessarily a limited one, for its bathing facilities. There is every reason to believe that such was the case. In what other place would be found such a glorious sweep of sea, where the water is always clear, and, as an old writer says, "without any mixture of ooze or of muddy fresh water, which always deposit a quantity of filth." The bottom is sandy, and the "descent is gradual, not rocky; and where the tides do not suddenly rise to make bathing dangerous. Such a shore for sea-bathing is to be preferred, and the perfection of such a shore Brighthelmston can boast."

These natural advantages were undoubtedly strong recommendations to Brighton as a bathing place; but they would, probably, have failed to secure for it that pre-eminence which it ultimately attained had it not been for Dr. Russell. To that justly-esteemed and highly-gifted man Brighton is greatly indebted for its position as the "Baiæ of England." Dr. Russell took up his residence here in 1754, in a house which he built,—subsequently known as "Russell House," standing on the site of the Royal Albion Hotel. He had long before seen the great advantages resulting from sea-bathing and the drinking of sea-water in scrofulous and other diseases, and his work, entitled *A Dissertation on the Use of Sea Water*, in which numerous cures were cited, soon attracted the attention of the Faculty.* Patients were accordingly sent here from all parts of England; and as the scanty accommodation which the town then afforded was soon absorbed, houses began to "increase and multiply," especially in proximity to the sea-front. The worthy Doctor died in 1759; but the good work which he promoted was still carried on by his indefatigable and able successors, Dr. Relhan, Dr. Awsiter, and others.

The great majority of visitors to Brighton at this period,—1760-70, —were probably persons in ill-health, to whom sea-bathing and sea-water drinking was a really serious business. At this time of day, the precautions given as to how to bathe and when to bathe, the recipes for drinking sea-water, &c., may, perhaps, provoke a smile; but it must not be forgotten that sea-water was then a comparatively new panacea for various diseases; and its efficacy in " preventing feverish infections," in " strengthening and bracing the muscular fibres," and in "exciting the skin to throw out any matter which offends the pores," and as a "sovereign preservative from the bad effects of chill nightly dews in hot climates," were not so well known as they are now. Many persons, no doubt, who came here a century ago, bathed injudiciously. As the practice has not yet died out, we will give Dr. Russell's advice on the subject, *minus* the fee :—

"Many persons are apt to hurry into a course of bathing before the body is altered, and sufficiently prepared by drinking sea-water, or by a previous course of other remedies; which hurry is always detrimental to the patient, by protracting his cure."

This may be supplemented by Dr. Awsiter's remarks, in his *Thoughts on Brighthelmston, concerning Sea-Bathing and Drinking Sea-Water* (1768). He says :—

"It is not prudent in our climate to use cold bathing after the body has been heated by exercise. We should use exercise after bathing, and those who cannot, should have their limbs well rubbed, and their bodies warmly, but not hotly, cloathed, to renew a proper degree of perspiration. When we use the cold bath for pleasure, to prevent any injury from it, we should bathe when our stomachs are empty and our spirits calm. To those who use exercise no preparatory physic is required, agreeably to Hippocrates's opinion, but the indolent and sedentary require this, that no future injuries may arise from a Plethora."

---

* There had already grown up a demand for sea-water for places inland and especially in the metropolis. At the old Talbot Inn, Southwark, "Sea-Water from Brighthelmstone" was on sale so early as 1756, the following advertisement appearing in a London journal :—

TO BE SOLD, at the Talbot Inn, Southwark, Sea Water from Brighthelmstone, in Sussex, took off the main Ocean by T. SWAINE.

NOTE.—The Portsmouth, Gosport, and Isle of Wight Waggons go out from the said Inn, where constant attendance is given to take in Goods, &c., by John Rowe.

Then as to sea-water *drinking*, the same writer says, "There are many constitutions too delicate, and stomachs too weak, to bear the nausea and sickness it (sea-water drinking) produces, and even where this inconvenience is overcome by struggles, it makes the party very thirsty for the remainder of the day." To remedy these inconveniences, Dr. Awsiter recommends an admixture of milk. "United with milk (he says) they become a noble medicine; they are correctors to each other; and milk and sea-water, so combined, will agree with the stomach that could not bear either of them separately." If sea-water is required "as a cleanser, a purifier of the blood, and a cooler," the Doctor recommends the following :—

"Take of sea-water and milk, each four ounces, put them over the fire, and when they begin to boil, add a sufficiency of cremor (*sic.*) tartar, to turn it into whey, strain it from the curd, and, when cool, drink it."

But to return to sea-bathing. The accommodation for this, in 1768, was, so far as the number of machines were concerned, somewhat limited; not more, in fact, than *one* set of about half-a-dozen for ladies and another set for gentlemen. What the character of the "originals" were in Dr. Russell's time, we do not know; but a writer (about 1770) says :—

"The bathing-machine is a wooden box, about double the size of those of the sentries in St. James's Park. It is raised on high wooden wheels. The bather ascends into it from the beach, by several wooden steps. The machine is then pushed forward into the sea, whilst the bather is preparing for the ablution. The guide waits on the middle of the steps to receive the bather; who, when dipt, re-ascends the machine, which is then dragged back again upon the beach."[*]

When Dr. Awsiter came hither (in 1768), his professional eye saw that the invalid with respect to his sea-bathing was subject to many disadvantages, and in his *Thoughts* are the following recommendations :—

"One half the number of machines, at least, should be provided with skreens, to extend projectingly from the top of the door to the water, somewhat after the manner of those at Margate; these would keep off the wind and make the machines more private. * * * When the sea is much troubled, the machines should be turned, and pushed backwards a sufficient depth into the sea, that the person bathing may go into the water with his face to the shore, and from this position of the machine will arise two advantages : The waves will be prevented from breaking against the door of the machine, and wetting the party while *undressing* or *dressing*, and the machine by being placed between the person bathing and the sea, will break off the force of the waves, and be a shelter from the wind; and when several are placed near to each other, after this manner, the shelter of them will be very considerable, and consequently the bathing rendered much more comfortable."

---

[*] It would be difficult to say wherein the machine of the present day differs from that of 1770. Like the bathers themselves (in dress, habits, &c.), the old order changeth not—"as they were, so they are." [A few years since there was an "innovation"—some few of Westman's machines, of a new pattern, being introduced to Brighton; but they do not seem to have become popular.]

Whether or no the Doctor's recommendations were acted upon, there is no record. Most probably they were not; for the Doctor, becoming impressed with the insufficiency of accommodation for the necessities of many patients, who used cold baths, expressed his hope that he might see a "set of baths erected for the use of such unhappy persons as stood in need of hot-bathing." No steps were, however, taken to carry so salutary a measure into execution, and the Doctor determined to undertake the troublesome office (so he expressed himself) on an enlarged plan. In October, 1769, the first stone of the building was laid, the architect being Mr. Golden, of London (who designed the Card-room of "The Old Ship Hotel.")* Provision was made on one side of it for six cold baths, and on the other were a hot bath, a sweating-bath, and a showering-bath; the baths being supplied with water from the sea by means of an engine. In his pamphlet, the Doctor says:—

"The utility of these Baths is obvious; they may be used either for hot or cold bathing. There are some individuals to whom cold bathing would be serviceable, could they be able to bear the fatigue of being dipt in the sea, and (what is more material) to be exposed to the cold air. If the weather happens to be stormy, and the sea so rough as not to admit of bathing in it, recourse may be had to the baths: by this means bathing would be made more universal, be unattended with terror, and no cure protracted. Moreover, invalids would have the advantage of this bathing remedy all the year round; whereas, on account of the variability of our

---

[* *The Public Advertiser* of October 10th, 1769, publishes a "Letter from Brighthelmstone, Oct. 4th," which gives the following interesting particulars concerning this event:—"This day Lady Hart and Miss Harriot Cecil, attended by Dr. Awsiter, laid the first Stone for erecting at this Place a Set of hot and cold Sea-Water Baths for the Use of those whose Health may require more constant Bathing than the Sea will naturally admit of, as well as Persons labouring under particular Disorders, for the Suppression of which hot Baths are peculiarly efficacious. I cannot but congratulate the Public on this Event, as all who in future have Occasion to frequent this Place may bathe regularly and constantly, and may also vary that Bathing from Cold to Hot, or otherwise, as their respective Infirmities demand. As these Baths are planned, and to be executed under the immediate Care and Direction of Dr. Awsiter, the Gentleman who some Time since favoured the World with some ingenious Remarks on the general and particular Use of bathing in Salt Water, I have no Doubt that when finished they will give entire Satisfaction, and fully evince how weakly and malevolently are founded those Cavils and Objections that Ignorance and Envy have raised to this truly laudable and salutary Scheme." Mr. James S. Creak (son of Mrs. Creak, who last kept the Baths) in a letter to a local journal some years since, says that Dr. Awsiter's Baths were but an enlargement of a previous building erected in 1738. We know of no contemporary or later record which refers to the existence of this latter building, and as it may be classed among "the things not generally known," we give Mr. Creak's statement respecting it:—"The Baths were built by a Tontine Company, the shareholders in which were chiefly London people. * * * The Tontine Company obtained from the Lord of the Manor a piece of land, or rather as much of the beach as was necessary for the erection of the building, the foundations of which were laid in the solid rock below the beach. After the house was erected, one bath was built (since known as bath 'No. 8,' or the 'Royal Bath'); a groyne was also made some 100 feet or so into the sea, at the base of which the pipes were laid that conveyed the sea-water into a reservoir at the Baths, by means of a Pump House which was erected on the top of the groyne." Mr. Creak further states that No. 8 Bath was called the "Royal Bath," because George III. and other members of the Royal Family bathed in it. Contemporary evidence does not confirm this; for Mr. Shergold, of "The Castle," says—"George III. *never* came to Brighton."]

THE BATHS AT BRIGHTON, 1803.

climate, it is denied them at present, except in the summer months, and then only in calm weather."

These Baths were erected in Pool Valley, and were known (prior to their removal, in 1869, to form the "Ladies' Swimming Bath" of Brill's Baths Company), as "Wood's Original Baths," and were subsequently kept for many years by the late Mrs. Creak. As will be seen (on reference to the annexed *plate*) the Baths, when first erected, were, as their projector intended them to be, "close to the shore and sheltered from the wind." The plate bears date 1803, some 30 years or more after their erection; but even then the present York Hotel did not exist; Steine-place (which it supplanted) had not been erected, and visitors walked direct from the Steine on to the beach to the Baths, which were, as a building, of a very unpretentious character, architecturally speaking; and the nautical surroundings, the hog-boat in front of them, with the capstans and gear, and boats on the shore ready to be drawn up, sufficiently indicate their proximity to the ocean.

For what purpose the barn-like erection of large dimensions south of the Baths was used, we know not,—it may have been a "herring-dees," or a tan-house, or one of the old cottages which formerly stood on the beach near the original Fish Market, which was held close by. The skeleton erection (south of the building and abutting on the groyne), with its four uprights and four cross posts, was probably where the original pump, or engine, was placed; the groyne being subsequently known as the pump-house groyne.

These baths, unquestionably, served a very useful purpose at the time of their erection, and for many subsequent years, down even to the time of their removal. But a large majority of the fashionable visitors at the period bathed for health or pleasure; and, hence, preferred "the open." Dr. Awsiter (who had only been a few days in the town when he wrote his *Thoughts*) says —"I think the shore on the east of the town is allotted to the use of the ladies, without any mixture of gentlemen, and I think a further rule should take place: That no man-servant or inhabitant be permitted to bathe on that side of the town during the season."* The East side of the town was then imme-

---

* Whether or no it had in more primitive times been the custom for both sexes to bathe at the same spot is not on record; but contemporary publications would seem to infer that such was the case. Be that as it may, it would appear to have been a favourite pastime with the sterner sex to watch the ladies bathing; and in 1766 a classic gentleman—fresh, we suppose, from *Alma Mater*—thus expresses himself in the *Lewes Journal* :—

ON THE LADIES BATHING AT BRIGHTHELMSTON.

From foaming waves the Goddess Venus sprung,
How true I know not -thus the poets' sung—
That on its curling waves, the rattling tide
Safe wafted her to shore in all her pride.
Tho' it's false, the tale will always please us,
To read of love, beauty, and a Venus.
But when on Brighton's sands the lovely Fair
Smile at the rocks and hollow surges dare;
When here so many Queens of Love we see
Caress the waves and wanton in the sea,

diately to the east of Russell House (supplanted by the Albion Hotel), the present " Public Bathing Station," immediately south of the front entrance to the Brighton Aquarium. There were, we are told, "experienced women to attend the ladies;" the "two Maries" (Howell and Cobby), Martha Gunn, and other " Mistresses of the Bath," who had adopted the " profession " as early as 1750, probably earlier. The number of machines being limited, the business, for many years wholly in their own hands, was exceedingly profitable in the season.

The gentlemen, we suppose, bathed at the west end or—where they could. The number of machines for their accommodation was *seven*,[*] of which John Miles (*alias* " Smoaker " Miles) was Major Domo. Considering the number of bathers, we do not wonder at learning that the machines were at a premium, and that the difficulties of securing possession often gave rise to some lively scenes. Some idea may be formed of these difficulties by an extract from *A Diary, kept in an Excursion to Littlehampton and Brighton in 1778-9.* The writer (an inveterate bather, for in another part of his Diary he tells us that one afternoon he was so much pleased that he resolved to spend "half my time on, in, and under water,") had been disappointed several times in getting a machine, and, after ruminating on "the Selfishness of the Bathees at Brighthelmston," thus relates his experience :—

" Each man runs to a machine-ladder, as it is dragging out of the sea, and scuffles who shall first set foot thereon : - some send their footmen and contend by proxy ; others go in in boots, or on horseback, to meet the machines :—so that a tolerably modest man, on a busy morning, has generally an hour and a half, perhaps two hours, for contemplation on the sands, to the detriment of his shoes, as well as the diminution of his patience."

Further on, the " Diarist " has an entry, in which he relates, with infinite gusto, " how he matched the bathers and bathees." He says :—

"About 6 a.m. I drew the machine along the sands, of which I had become seized by prescriptive right, by legal possession, having deposited part of my wearing apparel therein, tho' I had requested the assistance of *marine centaur*, the man on horseback, in vain. As the tide was flowing, I soon plunged into the sea, stretched a long way out into the offing, and continued rolling and laughing among my brother *porpuses*, to think what

---

We justly, Brighton, love thy envied shore.
Poets, adieu to fables, lie no more !
From dreams and fancy—*they* their Venus drew ;
Of these we feel the charms, and know it true.
No more, ye rhymers, in romantick strain,
Sing one Venus when here so many reign.

A " Diarist in 1778 viewed the ladies bathing with other eyes ; and thus he moralises :—" Sunday—September 13th.—Took the liberty of surveying all the bathing machines. Fine ladies going—fine ladies coming away. Observe them at the instant of bathing. How humiliating :—They appear more deplorable than so many corpses in shrouds "!

[*] At the present time (1880) there are in front of Brighton alone (irrespective of those at Hove) no less than 250 bathing machines : 150 ladies', and 100 gentlemen's. [The numbers in 1891 were, 120 ladies' ; 122 gentlemen's.]

a loss the company on shore would sustain for want of one machine out of seven, it being a very fine, busy morning. The bathers halloo'd and bawled in vain ; for I could not, indeed, would not, hear. After swimming backwards and forwards along the shore, about four miles in the whole, the tide setting strong to the eastward all the time, I returned about nine ; and *Smoaker*, growling like a bear with a sore head, swore bitterly : he believed I had been to *France* or *Holland*, and, cooling by degrees, desired to know the news ! I told him the *Dieppe* Monsieurs had laughed heartily at the mode of retaliation I had instituted at Brighton ; that they grinned at the account stated, and allowed that the *bathers* ought to behave like *bathers*, and the *bathees* like *gentlemen*."

It is satisfactory to learn that good results followed. In the next day's entry, the " Diarist " says :—

"Yesterday's exploit has produced an amendment. Shame sometimes follows at the heels of reflection. A man may now be accommodated nearly in turn, which was all that was wished."

The large amount of business done by the original bathers—at least among the ladies—induced others to obtain a share of the gains ; and, accordingly, one fine morning, at the end of March, 1780, Martha Gunn and the "Two Maries" were astonished to find located on the beach a set of new machines—painted *red*, as a distinguishing colour —with " five strong women," Mistress Martha Tutt and others, " all used to the sea," ready for business ! History is silent as to what passed between the ladies belonging to the respective opposition machines. It is as well probably that it is so. Nor is there any record of Smoaker's " opinion " of the *interlopers*—a relative of his being among the " originals." The former were, however, determined to make good their foothold on the beach ; for in the *Lewes Journal* of April 3, 1780, they made the following announcement :—

BRIGHTHELMSTON.   SEA BATHING.

THIS is to acquaint the Nobility, Gentry, and others resorting to Brighthelmston, that MARTHA TUTT, MARY GUILDFORD, SUSANNAH GUILDFORD, ELIZABETH WINGHAM, and ANN SMITH, five strong Women, all used to the Sea, have compleatly fitted up a set of NEW MACHINES, with a Careful Man and Horse to conduct them in and out of the Water, for the purpose of BATHING LADIES AND CHILDREN, the Ladies at One Shilling each, and Children Sixpence.—Attendance will be given every morning.

N.B.—Orders received at " THE RISING SUN," near the Battery. March 27th, 1780.

This was carrying matters a little too far. To have "opposition" machines on the beach was bad enough ; but to let all the world know it through the medium of a newspaper called for some corresponding action on the other side. The " originals," therefore, in the next week's paper "appealed to their friends " as follows :—

BRIGHTHELMSTON.   SEA BATHING.
THE OLD BATHERS FOR THE LAST THIRTY YEARS PAST.

THIS is to acquaint the Nobility, Gentry, and others resorting to Brighthelmston, that MARY HOWELL, MARY COBBY, MARTHA

odds.* The Prince, in fact, was desirous to relieve, if not to cure, the complaint from which he, in common with others of his family, suffered, and of which the Princess Amelia was said to have died, viz., glandular swellings. The Prince, it may be assumed, derived benefit from bathing; and this probably induced him to repeat his visit to Brighton in the following year, and afterwards to make it his marine residence.

If sea-bathing had previously been popular among our visitors, and "silken folly and bloated disease deemed it necessary, under the auspices of Dr. Russell, to crowd our shores," it may be supposed that, when it became known that the Heir Apparent to the English Throne purposed making Brighton a Royal residence—and the remedial virtues of salt water came to be acknowledged by Royal authority—the fashionable world would hasten more than ever to the "obscure fishing village," and indulge with still greater zest in what was deemed to be its Royal visitor's most favoured pastime—sea-bathing.

The next fifteen or twenty years may, therefore, be regarded as the "golden era" of sea-bathing at Brighton. The score or two of machines stationed at the bathing-places at the east and west ends of the town were *always* at a premium. To obtain them at all was, in fact, a favour; and it was a common practice with ladies to bespeak them the previous night. Some may be disposed to wonder that there were not more machines brought into use. But the bathees were, in their way, a shrewd set of people. They might be ignorant "o' book-larning;" but they understood (even now, it is supposed, their successors still understand,) one great principle in political economy,—that the price of an article rises in proportion to its scarcity,—as well as Adam Smith himself. Hence, while seeming to condole with the disappointed, they the more readily filled their pockets! They, doubtless, lost a few customers; and, probably, could afford to do so; and it would be interesting to have known Smoaker's freely expressed opinion of the individual who resorted to bathing *minus* a machine. There was, of necessity, at this period a good deal of "open bathing"; but the narrow sea-front of the town was very different from what it is now; and most of the houses situated there faced towards the east, with their sides to the sea. The Cliff had not yet become the fashionable promenade of the town, much less the drive; and the line of unsafe wooden railings, which surmounted the rugged and unkempt slopes leading from the cliff down to the beach, was not attractive to fashionable loungers.

Among the bathing-attendants at this period were some two or three whose idiosyncracies and popularity subsequently so intimately identified them with local sea-bathing that we must make some pass-

---

* The "Diarist" previously quoted says of "Turk": -"The Duke of Cumberland's great TURK, a Newfoundland dog, as big as a middling-sized calf, though he is not above eighteen months old, swims much better than I do." This dog appears to have been most mornings in the sea with the bathers; and the writer adds "Turk hath a political head, not much unlike Lord North's. He hath a familiar way, too, of shutting his eyes, and appearing to be fast asleep, when he is all the time perfectly awake."

ing allusion to them. In a "Directory" of the town, published in 1790, the bathers are given as follows:—

Mary Cobby, dipper.
Mary Howell, dipper.
James Patching, bather.

John Miles, bather.
William Miles, bather.
— Saunders, bather.

The "Directory" gives but six, which is incorrect, for there were nearer 20; and it is curious to note that the "Ladies of the Bath" are called "dippers," whilst it is the men who are called "bathers." Whether or no the former designation arose from any peculiarity of process, we are unable to say. Singularly enough, the name of the most noted Brighton "dipper," Martha Gunn, does not appear in the "Directory" of 1790.

But this by the way. The most noted personage in the above list,—in fact the earliest known local bather,—was John Miles, or, as he was more generally called, "Smoaker." Miles, in his way, was a "character." In his prime, he was a sturdy, thickset man, of about 5ft. 6in. in height; and had the enviable reputation of being able to swim "quite as well as a mackerel." If at times somewhat *brusque* in his manner,—blunt, and apt to speak his mind in not over-choice epithets when provoked,—he was, at others, exceedingly humorous. For ready wit and repartee, Smoaker was a match for all comers, and rarely came off second best in an encounter. When the Prince of Wales came to Brighton, Smoaker was employed to superintend his bathing operations and to teach him swimming. The Prince "took" to him at once; as much, probably, from his originality of character as from the way in which he performed his duties. No better example of the reciprocity of feeling between the Prince and his bather could be afforded than by the following anecdote, given in the "Recollections of Brighton in the Olden Time," written by Mr. Samuel Shergold for the *Brighton Herald:*—

"A very boisterous night was succceded by a very rough sea; the waves broke upon the beach with great violence. The Prince, nevertheless, repaired to his usual bathing-place, where Smoaker was waiting to receive him. 'I shall bathe this morning, Smoaker!' 'No! no! Mr. Prince,' replied Smoaker; 'it's too dangerous.' 'But I will,' said the Prince, and was proceeding towards a machine, when the courageous bather stepped before him, and putting himself in a boxing attitude, -for the fellow could box as well as he could swim,--said good naturedly to His Royal Highness: 'Come! come! this won't do; I'll be d——d if you shall bathe. What do you think your Father would say to me if you were drowned? He would say, this is all owing to you, Smoaker! If you had taken proper care of him, poor George would have been still alive.' The Prince wisely desisted."

In *Erredge* there is another anecdote of the Prince and Smoaker worth quoting:—

"One day, when the Prince of Wales was bathing, he ventured out further than old Smoaker considered prudent. In vain Smoaker called, 'Mr. Prince, Mr. Prince, come back,' his holloas only causing His Royal Highness to dash out further. As the only means to exact obedience, in rushed the old man, swam up to the Prince, and seizing him by the ear, lugged him, *nolens volens*, to the shore. When his young aquatic student remonstrated upon receiving such treatment, Old Smoaker rolled out a round oath or two, adding, 'I ar'nt agoen' to let the King hang me for letten' the Prince of Wales drown hisself; not I, to please nobody, I can tell'e."

Smoaker was a frequent visitor to the Pavilion; and the domestics, knowing the Prince's partiality for him, always "took care" of him. Once, in the winter, Smoaker actually *walked* to London, and called at Carlton House to enquire after the Prince's health! How Smoaker accomplished this feat is a mystery. To say nothing of the length of the journey, our seafaring men, when on land, have an hereditary taste for "hugging the shore." Even so lately as within these 40 or 50 years, if a landsman met a fisherman so far north as "The Hare and Hounds," it was a standing joke to ask the latter "if he had lost his way"! Or, should he by chance have strolled as far as the Chalybeate or the Lovers' Walk, the landsman involuntarily wondered how he would get home! However, Smoaker *did* walk to London, and saw the Prince, who received him kindly, and desired one of his domestics to show "great attention" to the worthy fellow; which great attention resolved itself into Smoaker's being taken into the kitchen, where he was supplied with liquor till he fell under the table! He was then put to bed, and next day sent down to Brighton; whether the better or the worse for his exploit, is not recorded.

Smoaker died "full of years" in February, 1794; and the following valedictory notice of him appeared in the *Sussex Weekly Advertiser*:—

"On Thursday last the remains of John Miles, *alias* Smoaker Miles, who died a few days before, in the 74th year of his age, were interred at Brighthelmston. The above well-known character had been for many years the chief bather at that place. His Royal Highness the Prince of Wales had distinguished him by several marks of his favour. His blunt though unoffending sincerity made him many friends, as his remarks seemed to proceed from a heart which was incapable of injuring any person, and his benevolence of disposition was clearly seen in the use he made of the produce of his honest industry; for he never could refuse his purse to his friends and relations, who are very numerous, and many of them very needy. He died universally regretted not only by them, but also by most of the inhabitants. His portrait, a finished likeness by Russell, was recognised in the Exhibition by many of his friends and customers. The Prince, on being made acquainted with Smoaker's death, and not unmindful of the distresses of his widow, with that goodness of heart which is so peculiar to himself, ordered a sum of money to be given to her, which afforded her great consolation in the hour of her affliction."

Erredge says, "Smoaker is buried near the west boundary-wall of the Old Church Yard, immediately opposite Upper North-street. The spot is marked by a tombstone, but the inscription has been wholly obliterated by time."

Smoaker was succeeded as Royal bather, by his brother William, who was also known by the same cognomen. Smoaker II. was, however, now falling into the "sere and yellow leaf." But he was not

MARTHA GUNN.

forgotten by his Royal Patron, the Prince granting him a pension as long as he lived. In his latter days, Smoaker II. might be frequently seen on the Cliff, attired in a bright scarlet frock coat (most probably a cast-off Royal livery coat), and no one was more proud than he to talk of "the Past." The old man's end was somewhat singular. A vessel, we are told, laden with liquorice-root, was wrecked off the town, and large quantities of the root were washed ashore. Smoaker, like the rest, gathered of the strewn root, and having partaken of it freely, fell ill, and died. A contemporary of the later Smoaker was "Doctor" Tattersall; and his end also was a sad one. It is thus recorded in the *Lewes Journal* of January 13th, 1806:—

"Last Friday the following melancholy circumstance occurred:—As Gabriel Tattersall, better known as the DOCTOR, one of the company of Old Bathers, was hanging across one of the groynes to dip water, he was overpowered by a strong gale of wind from the west, and forced into the sea, where, though an excellent swimmer, he soon sunk, and was drowned in the presence of many spectators on the beach, some of whom soon put off in a boat to his assistance, and in about half-an-hour recovered the body. On its being brought to shore, every means recommended by the Humane Society were tried to restore animation, but in vain, as the vital spark had totally left him. The fatality of the accident is attributed to his great coat having been blown over his head as he was falling, which so entangled him that he was unable to exert his skill in swimming. Verdict, 'Accidental Death.' The deceased was a descendant of the renowned CAPT. NICHOLAS TATTERSAL, who, in the year 1651, favoured the escape of King Charles the II. from these shores, by taking him privately on board his coal brig in the night time and safely landing him at Fescamp in Normandy."

Place aux dames. Of Mrs. Cobby, the original "dipper," and the contemporary of Martha Gunn in the office of "Priestess of the Bath," tradition has left but few memorials. She resided in East-street; was reputed to be a "very good, jolly sort of woman"; and the old "Diary," from which we have quoted previously, credits her with originating the well-known story of "The Three Black Crows." The "Diarist" says:—

"Mrs. Cobby, the bathing woman, of East-street, told me, when I went this morning to bathe. at the bottom of the Steine, that a poor neighbour of hers, who had fretted herself ill on account of her husband having been pressed and sent on board the tender, had, in the night time, vomited up—something *as black as a* CROW"!

This, by repetition, became magnified into *three black crows!*

Of Martha Gunn there are but few reliable records. We know that from about 1750 till the beginning of the present century she was acknowledged the "Queen of the Bath"; and, as if to confirm her title, Smoaker's daughter was her handmaiden. Martha and Smoaker were allied in regal bathing honours; for, as the old song says:—

> "There's plenty of dippers and jokers,
> And salt-water rigs for your fun;
> The king of them all is old Smoaker,
> The queen of 'em old Martha Gunn.

"The ladies walk out in the morn,
To taste of the salt-water breeze;
They ask if the water is warm,
Says Martha—''Tis, Ma'am, if you please.'"

The machines Martha Gunn superintended were always the most in request, for she was immensely popular with bathers. Like Smoaker, Martha was a "character." In "A Donkey Tour to Brighton" (Simpkins and Marshall, 1815,) is a vivid description of Martha and her peculiarities in her latter days:—

"'What, my old friend, Martha,' said I, 'still queen of the ocean, still industrious, and busy as ever; and how do you find yourself'?-'Well and hearty, thank God, Sir,' replied she, 'but rather hobbling. I don't bathe, because I a'nt so strong as I used to be, so I superintend on the beach, for I'm up before any of 'em; you may always find me and my pitcher at one exact spot, every morning by six o'clock.'—'You wear vastly well, my old friend, pray what age may you be'?—'Only eighty-eight, Sir; in fact, eighty-nine come next Christmas pudding; aye, and though I've lost my teeth I can mumble it with as good relish and hearty appetite as anybody.' 'I'm glad to hear it; Brighton would not look like itself without you, Martha,' said I.—'Oh, I don't know, it's like to do without me, some day,' answered she, 'but while I've health and life, I must be bustling amongst my old friends and benefactors; I think I ought to be proud, for I've as many bows from man, woman, and child, as the Prince hisself; aye, I do believe, the very dogs in the town know me.'—'And your son, how is he'? said I.—'Brave and charming, he lives in East-street; if your honour wants any prime pickled salmon, or oysters, there you have 'em.'—I promised her I'd be a customer; she made me a low curtsey, and I left her hobbling to the side of the London coach, to deliver cards from the repository of her poor withered, sea-freckled bosom; for, like a woman of fashion, her bosom was her pocket."

The practice of delivering cards in Castle-square in the old coaching days was a common practice with bathing-women; their quaint costume exciting no little curiosity among strangers.

Martha Gunn was a great favourite with the Prince of Wales; and had, accordingly, acquired a right of entry to the Royal kitchen, the servants being very good to her. There is still current a well-authenticated anecdote of one of these visits:—

"When in the kitchen, one afternoon, Martha was presented with a pound of butter. The Prince at that moment was seen entering the kitchen, and Martha, whispering the servant, quickly deposited the butter in her pocket. This little bit of legerdemain was, doubtless, observed by the Prince; and, being ripe for a joke, he speedily entered into conversation with Martha, getting the 'butter side' of her nearer and nearer to the great kitchen fire. It was a sad dilemma The Prince kept talking, and the butter kept melting! but the venerable dame - whose rueful countenance doubtless betrayed her sensations—was afraid to move. External evidence on the floor, however, soon after showed the Prince that his design was accomplished, and he bade the old lady 'good day.' The internal evidence he was content to leave to Martha herself. What *this* was, may be imagined, but deponent describeth not."

In her last days, Martha was as round as a dumpling. The "old girl" died, after an illness of several months, May 2nd, 1815, being then in her 89th year. She was buried on the following Monday in the Old Church-yard, and the *Brighton Herald*, in alluding to the funeral, says, "The whole town was in motion to witness it. Her remains were followed to the grave by about 40 relatives and friends, chiefly bathers. The ceremony, throughout, was conducted with the greatest order and solemnity."

Resuming our history of bathing, there is little deserving of special mention down to the period of the old "Directory," in 1800. Even from this we learn only the following :—

"The SEA BATHING from the Machines, both at the East and West End of the Town, is particularly safe and pleasant.—The Expense is 1 s."

Of the bathers themselves,—that is, the ministers who daily officiated at Lord Neptune's Levée, as Smoaker II. and his coadjutors,—not one name is recorded. Respecting, however, the Baths, in Pool-valley, there is more information ; and the particulars as to the rates of subscription, &c., are not without interest, as affording a point of comparison with those at the present day. It states :—

"The Subscription to the Hot Bath is, for Three Months, £10 10s.—Two Months, £7 7s.—One Month, £4 4s.

"The Subscription to the Cold Bath is, for Three Months, £3 3s.—One Month, £1 11s. 6d.

"Non-Subscribers pay for Cold Bathing, 1s. 6d., and for Hot Bathing, 4s.

"Subscriptions are not admitted to the Showering Bath—each Person pays for the Use of it 1s. 6d. each Time.

"If any Bath be wanted at a particular Hour, Notice may be given at the Bath House, where Persons are always in waiting."

It is a singular circumstance, seeing the great increase from 1750 to 1800 in the number of visitors who resorted to Brighton for bathing, that there should have been up to the latter date only one set of private baths in the town.* Was there a feeling against them excited by aboriginal prejudice ? Those existing were built by a "furriner" (Dr. Awsiter); and they were in opposition to open-air bathing ! Fancy, then, a bathee,—Smoaker, for instance,—descanting to a visitor, the broad ocean before them, on the relative merits of "The Sea" *v.* "Awsiter's Baths." The latter would be simply—nowhere !

A few years later, 1806-7, the practice of " open " bathing in front of the town became a nuisance. The cliff was much more frequented as a promenade than it had been a few years previously,—and so strong had the feeling against the practice of " open " bathing become

---

* A few years afterwards, in 1803, Mr. Williams opened his baths on the site of what is now the Lion Mansion ; and these were subsequently followed by other private baths, as those of Sake Deen Mahomed ; the Royal Hotel (now New Steine) Baths ; Nathan Smith's " Artillery Baths " ; Lamprell's (the " Bunion," removed March, 1871); Buggins' Brunswick Baths ; and more recently by the grand suite erected by Brill's Baths Company; and, in addition to these, there is the grand Hammam in West-street, built by the Turkish Bath Company.

in the town that a public meeting of the leading inhabitants,—presided over by Mr. Cornelius Paine, churchwarden,—was held, and a series of resolutions passed with a view to repress the practice. Over 100 guineas were subscribed at the meeting (William Wilberforce, Esq., M.P., giving £5 5s.); and further subscriptions being solicited, between £200 and £300 were speedily raised. Under the resolutions, persons were restricted from bathing, except from a machine, "within the limits of the brick-kilns on the West, and eastern part of the Crescent, on the East Cliff;" exception being made in favour of "infirm persons," the Committee being "empowered to grant TICKETS, entitling the bearer to have a machine gratis." During the next year the nuisance was abated; but in 1808 it again cropped up, and so offensively, that the Committee had to resort to stringent measures, prosecuting a notorious offender at the next Assizes. The old ground of defence was set up, that the *sea was free;* but the Judge, in summing up, gave his opinion very strongly that indecency must be restricted. And, as it would appear, not before it was time; for in the *Morning Herald* of August 28, 1806, under "Brighton," we get the following:—

"The greatest novelty, however, that this part of the coast exhibited this morning, was in a gentleman's undressing himself on the beach, for the purpose of a ducking, in front of the town, attended by his lady, who, *sans diffidence*, supplied him with napkins, and even assisted him in wiping the humid effects of his exercise from his brawny limbs, as he returned from the water to dress."

After the above conviction, there was little cause of complaint on the score of open bathing for several years. The heavy penalty (£5 for every such offence) which was imposed exercised probably a wholesome check. "Poor Invalids" were, however, still assisted, the 4th "Bathing Regulation" being as follows:—

"Any person being an invalid, and unable to pay the expense of bathing from a machine, may receive an order, Gratis, by applying every Friday, either by letter or in person, to the Directors and Guardians, at the Town Hall, from the hour of eleven to one o'clock."

Our notice of local sea-bathing would be incomplete did we omit one of the most important episodes in connection with it, viz., the visit, in August, 1851, to the Great Exhibition of some 120 or 130 bathing men and women,—to say nothing of the husbands, sons, and daughters who accompanied them, under the escort of Mr. Lewis Slight, Mr. S. Thorncroft, and Mr. W. Bowdidge. The party assembled at the Town Hall at 6 a.m.,—the women attired in new dark blue bathing dresses and bonnets, the oldest among them being Mrs. Taylor, who, though 68, was as hale and hearty as ever. The men were dressed in blue guernseys and straw hats, the "father" being old George Harman, who had never been to London before, nor even ridden in a railway carriage! Many of them, in fact, had never been farther than Rottingdean; others not farther than Preston; whilst some had never been out of the town at all! We cannot enter fully into the events of this memorable day;

suffice it to say that the party, on reaching London, were mustered at the Terminus, and then marched two and two through the streets on their way to the Exhibition, Mr. Slight taking the lead ; Mr. Bowdidge keeping his eye on the rank and file ; and Mr. Thorncroft acting as whipper-in. The quaint appearance of the party excited no little sensation as they passed along, and also in the Exhibition itself. There were, of course, during the day, some amusing episodes ; parties were "lost," &c. All, however, appeared to enjoy their novel expedition, and got home safely, finishing up by assembling before Mr. Bowdidge's house, between nine and ten, and giving three hearty cheers !

The Coaching Era.

THERE are few things of which old Brightonians have more pleasurable recollections than the "coaching days," linked as they are with so many interesting associations: the visits of distinguished personages; important local events; delightful journeys amid lovely rural districts; the bustle and excitement of the "inns" and "outs" in Castle-square, where hearty welcomes were indulged in, or, it may have been, sad farewells exchanged; and a hundred other cherished memories, which to Brightonians of the present day are in some respects comparatively unknown. In another point of view, too, the "coaching days" had a special interest to our forefathers—that of profit, by reason of the influx of visitors. The "season" of coaches (summer) was the season of lodging-letting and of increased business among tradesmen. Then, too, the public balls were given and the assemblies held; the card, tea, and breakfast parties took place; the Theatre was opened; the Steine enlivened by bands; and other amusements were arranged, imparting life and gaiety to the town which, at other seasons, were to a great extent wanting.

The present generation cannot fully realise the glories of Coaching as it was some 50 or 60 years ago. The iron-horse has so completely superseded those of flesh and blood as a means of conveyance, that the memory of the "road" and its pleasant associations have almost died out. The new order of things evoked new demands— new requirements. Putting aside the impulse given to commercial activity by the introduction of railways, and the manifold blessings they have conferred,—by annihilating, as it were, time and space between centres of manufacture or of produce,—the teeming populations of our large towns are now so accustomed to cheap and rapid transit; the man of business and of pleasure are both so educated up to "facility," that, for all save a pleasant day's outing (and only those who have experienced a day "on the road" can tell how vastly pleasant it is,) the coachman's "occupation's gone"!

It would be difficult to determine the exact date when the Coaching Era commenced in Brighton. We hear little of it until about the middle of the last century, when invalids and visitors began to resort here for the purpose of bathing, &c., or, it may be for pleasure. Of the character, too, of the pre-historic vehicle which first gladdened the eyes of the inhabitants of the "pretty fisher village," there is but little information. The good folk, with an instinct sharpened by self-interest, were, probably, willing to welcome any vehicle which brought them such profitable commodity as visitors, respecting whom "increase of appetite grew with what it fed on." (This old taste, it is said, still exists!) When, however, the original vehicle began to run to and from the old town, the inhabitants had probably risen superior to the prejudices of an individual who, some fifty years previously, had denounced stage-coaches as "the greatest evil that had happened of late years to these kingdoms;" as those who travelled in them "contracted an idle habit of body, became weary and listless when they had rode a few miles, and were then unable to travel on horseback, and not able to endure frost, snow, or rain, or *to lodge in the fields!*"

The old system of "Carrying" preceded the Coaching Era. One Thomas Smith, of Lewes, is among the earliest-mentioned Sussex "carriers," doing duty early in the last century. He died in 1746, and was succeeded in his business by his widow! the good lady's advertisement in the *Lewes Journal* of December 8th, 1746, being as follows:—

THOMAS SMITH, the OLD LEWES CARRIER, being dead, THE BUSINESS IS NOW CONTINUED BY HIS WIDOW, MARY SMITH, who gets into the George Inn, in the Borough, Southwark, EVERY WEDNESDAY in the afternoon, and sets out for Lewes EVERY THURSDAY morning by eight o'clock, and brings Goods and Passengers to Lewes, Fletching, Chayley, Newick, and all places adjacent at reasonable rates. Performed (*if God permit**) by

MARY SMITH.

How long the "dauntless Mary" continued the carrying business, is not recorded. She deserved to have made a rapid fortune for her pluck and energy.

Among the pioneers of the Brighton Coaching Era was James Batchelor,—in fact, an ancestor of his was the first to set up a stage

---

* This "saving clause," which was subsequently in common use, may have been originally adopted by Sussex carriers and coach owners in consequence of the difficulties of travelling at that period by reason of the badness of the roads, the state of which had early become proverbial. In "Extracts from the 'Iter Sussexiense' of Dr. John Burton," read by W. H. Blaauw, Esq., at the Archæological Society's Meeting at Horsham, in July, 1855, there is the following description of Sussex roads in 1751:—"I fell immediately upon all that was most bad, upon a land desolate and muddy, whether inhabited by men or beasts a stranger could not easily distinguish, and upon roads which were, to explain concisely what is most abominable, Sussexian. No one would imagine them to be intended for the people and the public, but rather the by-ways of individuals, or more truly the tracks of cattle drivers; for every where the usual footmarks of oxen appeared, and we, too, who were on horseback, going on zigzag almost like oxen at plough, advanced as if we were turning back, while we followed out all the twists of the roads. Not even now, though in summer time, is the wintry state of the roads got rid of; for the wet even now in this mud is sometimes splashed upwards all of a sudden to the annoyance of travellers. Our horses could not keep on their legs on account of these slippery and rough parts of the road, but sliding and tumbling on their way, and almost on their haunches, with all their haste, got on but slowly." The Doctor's epistle thus concludes:—"Come now, my friend, I will set before you a sort of problem in Aristotle's fashion:—Why is it that the oxen, the swine, the women, and all other animals are so long-legged in Sussex? May it be from the difficulty of pulling the feet out of so much mud by the strength of the ankle, that the muscles get stretched, as it were, and the bones lengthened?"

coach from London to Lewes, in some primitive epoch prior to turnpikes being erected. Among Mr. Batchelor's earliest announcements were the following in the *Sussex Weekly Advertiser* of May, 1756, and May, 1757 :—

NOTICE IS HEREBY GIVEN, that the LEWES ONE DAY STAGE COACH or CHAISE sets out from the Talbot Inn, in the the Borough, on Saturday next, the 19th instant.
When likewise the Brighthelmston Stage begins.

Perform'd (*if God permit*) by
JAMES BATCHELOR.

FOR THE CONVENIENCE OF COUNTRY GENTLEMEN, &c.

THIS IS TO GIVE NOTICE that the Brighthelmston and Lewes TWO DAYS' STAGE COACH will not set out from Brighthelmston till Nine o'clock in the Morning, and from William Verrall's, at the White Hart, in Lewes, till One o'clock at Noon, from

Their very humble servant to command,
JAMES BATCHELOR.

NOTE.—The Lewes and Brighthelmston ONE DAY'S STAGE as usual.

A good FOUR-WHEEL POST CHAISE may be had to any part of the Country, of Mr. Verrall, at the White Hart, aforesaid.

Mr. James Batchelor was, however, not allowed to have the Stage Coach business all to himself. "Competition," even in the primitive coaching days, soon arose; the *Lewes Journal* of July 4th, 1757, containing the following announcement :—

NOTICE IS HEREBY GIVEN, that there is to be Lett, at the Star Inn, Lewes, or of DANIEL AUSTEN, Salesman, a very handsome four-wheel POST CHARIOT, with a Pair of able Horses, and a careful Driver.

NOTE.—The same Chariot, in general, to set out from the Star Inn, on Monday and Friday mornings, at Eight o'clock, for the Castle at Brighthelmston, and return again at Night, for Three Shillings each Passenger. *The Passengers to be at no Expense for Man or Horses there.*

Whether Batchelor levied contributions on the passengers for "Man or Horses" is not recorded. It may have been an "ancient custom" not approved of; and Austen, doubtless, expected to obtain patronage by the introduction of a new system. His "competition" with Batchelor was, however, only of short duration. But a few years later, in May, 1762, Batchelor had a far more powerful rival in the field, namely, "J. Tubb," with whom (in the early part of his career) was associated one "S. Brawne." The introduction, by Mr. Tubb, of a specially constructed new vehicle, called a "FLYING MACHINE," which did the journey in *one* day, rendered his competition the more serious. He, moreover, carried *four* passengers to Batchelor's *two*, or occasionally three ! Mr. Tubb's advertisement was as follows :—

LEWES and BRIGHTHELMSTON new FLYING MACHINE (by Uckfield), hung on steel springs, very neat and commodious, to carry

Four Passengers, sets out from the Golden Cross Inn, Charing Cross, on Monday, the 7th of June, at Six o'Clock in the Morning, and will continue Mondays, Wednesdays, and Fridays to the White Hart, at Lewes, and the Castle, at Brighthelmston, where regular Books are kept for entering passengers and parcels; will return to London Tuesday's, Thursday's, and Saturday's. Each Inside Passenger to Lewes, Thirteen Shillings; to Brighthelmston, Sixteen; to be allowed Fourteen Pound Weight for Luggage, all above to pay one penny per Pound; half the fare to be paid at Booking, the other at entering the Machine. Children in Lap and Outside Passengers to pay half-price.

Performed by { J. TUBB.
S. BRAWNE.

N.B.—The Proprietors will not be answerable for Plate, Jewels, or Writings, unless entered as such and paid for accordingly.

Mr. Batchelor determined, however, not to be out-done. In the following week he started, at the same fares, a "new large FLYING CHARIOT, with a box and four horses (by Chailey), to carry two Passengers only, except three should desire to go together." Batchelor's days of setting out and returning were the same as Tubb's; but he retained his original reservation, "performed *(if God permit).*" So matters went on for a few months between these pioneers of the "Coaching Era." But in December, 1762, a crisis arose: Batchelor, whose custom had probably fallen off, *reduced his fares!* This was more than "J. Tubb" could stand, and he published the following in the *Lewes Journal*, in November, 1762:—

THIS IS TO INFORM THE PUBLIC that, on Monday, the 1st of November instant, the LEWES and BRIGHTHELMSTON FLYING MACHINE began going in *one day*, and continues twice a week during the Winter Season to Lewes only; sets out from the White Hart, at Lewes, Mondays and Thursdays, at Six o'Clock in the Morning, and returns from the Golden Cross, at Charing Cross, Tuesdays and Saturdays, at the same hour. Performed by

J. TUBB.

N.B.—Gentlemen, Ladies, and others, are desired to look narrowly into the Meanness and Design of the other Flying Machine to Lewes and Brighthelmston, in lowering his prices, whether 'tis thro' conscience or an endeavour to suppress me. If the former is the case, think how you have been used for a great number of years, when he engrossed the whole to himself, and kept you two days upon the road, going fifty miles. If the latter, and he should be lucky enough to succeed in it, judge whether he wont return to his old prices, when you cannot help yourselves, and use you as formerly. As I have then been the remover of this obstacle, which you have all granted by your great encouragement to me hitherto, I, therefore, hope for the continuance of your favours, which will entirely frustrate the deep-laid schemes of my great opponent, and lay a lasting obligation on

Your very humble Servant,
J. TUBB.

To this "J. Batchelor" replied in the same journal as follows:—

WHEREAS, Mr. Tubb, by an Advertisement in this paper of Monday last, has thought fit to cast some invidious Reflections upon me, in respect of the lowering my Prices and being two days upon the Road, with other low insinuations, I beg leave to submit the following matters to the calm Consideration of the Gentlemen, Ladies, and other Passengers, of what Degree soever, who have been pleased to favour me, viz. :—

That our Family first set up the Stage Coach from London to Lewes, and have continued it for a long Series of Years, from Father to Son and other Branches of the same Race, and that even before the Turnpikes on the Lewes Road were erected they drove their Stage, in the Summer Season, in one day, and have continued to do ever since, and now in the Winter Season twice in the week. And it is likewise to be considered that many aged and infirm Persons, who did not chuse to rise early in the Morning, were very desirous to be two Days on the Road for their own Ease and Conveniency, therefore there was no Obstacle to be removed. And as to lowering my prices, let every one judge whether, when an old Servant of the Country perceives an Endeavour to suppress and supplant him in his Business, he is not well justified in taking all measures in his Power for his own Security, and even to oppose an unfair Adversary as far as he can. 'Tis, therefore, hoped that the Descendants of your very ancient Servants will still meet with your farther Encouragement, and leave the Schemes of our little Opponent to their proper Deserts.

I am, Your old and present
most obedient Servant,

December 13, 1762.   J. BATCHELOR.

The climax of the great "Tubb and Batchelor Controversy" is buried in oblivion! Both, however, continued on the road. Mr. Batchelor, in 1764, started a "Hearse"; but the objects and character of this vehicle, except that it did regular stages on certain days in the week, are not particularised. Mr. Batchelor died in 1765 or 1766, when, we believe, his widow disposed of her husband's business to Mr. Tubb, who, shortly afterwards, took into partnership with him a Mr. Davis, and these two jointly established a firm which ranked second to none in the coach and waggon business down to the close of the last century. In 1767 Messrs. Tubb and Davis started "The Lewes and Brighthelmstone Flys," to and from London, every day, carrying four passengers.

In 1770 there were two "machines" (one owned by Messrs. Tubb and Davis) and a "waggon" on the road between London and Brighton. Tubb and Davis's "machine" came by way of Chailey and Lewes, on Mondays, Wednesdays, and Fridays, to "The Old Ship" at Brighton; and on Tuesdays, Thursdays, and Saturdays, by way of Uckfield and Lewes, to "The Castle" at Brighton. It left, according to advertisement, "The Golden Cross," Charing Cross, at "five in the morning, and returned at six every morning from Brighthelmstone." (A remarkable feat, this, with *one* "machine.") The fares were:—"Inside passengers pay 14s. to Brighthelmstone, and 12s. to Lewes. Luggage above 14lbs. paid for at 1d. per lb." The other "machine" came from "The Swan with Two Necks," Lad-lane, London, "through Steyning to 'The Old Ship' and 'The New Ship,' in Brighton, on Mondays and Wednesdays, returning on Tuesdays and Saturdays." The fare to Steyning was 11s.; to Brighton, 14s. What time was occupied in the journey—what accommodation there was for the passengers—

how much of the distance the latter "walked," or what was the character of the "machines" themselves, there is no evidence to show. The query suggests itself: Did they resemble the present bathing "machines," which, doubtless, derived their name from the original vehicle?

In 1776 Messrs. Tubb and Davis thus announced the commencement of the season:—

TUBB and DAVIS acquaint the public that the LEWES AND BRIGHTHELMSTON MACHINE will BEGIN TO FLY* on Monday next TO AND FROM LONDON every day during the Summer Season.

Of the "Waggon" accommodation of the period little is known, further than that Mr. Davis's was the only one on the road. It came "from 'The Talbot' Inn, in the Borough, every Thursday morning, returning from Brighthelmstone every Tuesday." No information is afforded of the character of this vehicle or the extent of its accommodation. From what was known of such vehicles at a later period, it may have resembled that in which Roderick Random and Strap rode to London; new comers on the road tumbling into the straw, under the darkness of the tilt, amidst the previous occupants, with whom they got reconciled as best they could!

In April, 1777, Lashmar and Co. ran a common stage waggon from "The King's Head," Southwark, to "The King's Head," Brighton. It left London every Tuesday, at three a.m., and arrived at Brighton on Thursday afternoon. The firm evidently had not much regard for "expedition," seeing that the journey was accomplished in three days and two nights—about a mile an hour! Parcels, it may be added, were carried at the rate of 3s. and 2s. 6d. per cwt.

Early in the season of 1784 Tubb and Davis started a new coach, "insides" only; still running, however, their old vehicles. Their advertisement was as follows:—

LEWES and BRIGHTHELMSTON LIGHT POST COACH, Carrying FOUR inside Passengers ONLY and no Outsides on the top.

Sets out from Brighthelmston every Monday, Wednesday, and Friday Mornings at Half-past Six to the GOLDEN CROSS, Charing Cross, and returns from the said GOLDEN CROSS every Tuesday, Thursday, and Saturday Mornings at Six o'Clock - Mondays and Fridays by Chailey, and Wednesdays by Uckfield.

·N.B.- OLD MACHINE and POST COACH from the above Golden Cross, Charing Cross, every Morning at Six of the Clock, Sundays excepted, from Brighthelmston the same time. Fares as usual.

MACHINE up by Uckfield, Mondays and Fridays; by Chailey, Wednesdays.

OLD POST COACH up by UCKFIELD, Tuesdays and Thursdays; by Chailey, Saturdays; return the same Roads. They all set out from

---

* This "flying" would appear to have had some special significance,—with reference to speed, probably,—which was understood at the period; for the same firm announced in November "that the Lewes and Brighthelmston coaches *ave left off flying*, and continue three times a week only during the Winter to ondon and back.

Lewes a Quarter before Eight. Inside Passengers of the above Coaches allowed 14lbs. of Luggage, all above to pay 1d. per lb.

Performed by
TUBB and DAVIS.

THE LIGHT POST COACH begins this day, May 31st, 1784.

In May, 1791, some mail coaches of novel design were put on the road. Though handsome in appearance, they seemed only available for "summer wear." A local chronicler thus alludes to them :—

"Last Saturday afternoon one of the new coaches designed for the conveyance of the mail from Brighton and Lewes to London arrived here, and this evening it will proceed on its duty from Brighton. These Coaches are elegantly finished and make a very showy appearance, which, added to the expedition they must necessarily observe on the Road, may induce some persons to travel in them during the Summer months, but in the Winter it is impossible they can be made to answer here unless what is at present allowed the Conductors from the Post Office be then considerably augmented."

A few years later, when a visit in the season to the "village by the sea" had come to be fashionable, coaches, &c., increased and multiplied exceedingly; for, in 1788, we learn, by Crawford's *Description of Brighthelmstone*, there were running between Brighton and London three "machines," two coaches, and three light post coaches; and one conveyance, Tucker's "Diligence," ran between Brighton and Chichester. The "machines" were *said* to accomplish the journey in eleven hours; the coaches in nine; while the so-called "Diligence" took an indefinite time, starting each morning at eight and arriving "that evening." At this period Mr. Tubb's name does not appear; but among those mentioned are his partner, Mr. Davis, who "set out" for London from "The Castle" and "The Old Ship"; Ibberson and Co., from "The White Horse"; and Mr. Wessen, from "The Gun Inn, upon the Cliff" (whence the "Diligence" also set out). A "stage coach" was also run in 1788 between Lewes and Brighthelmstone twice daily, by Thomas Smart; his stipulation with passengers being, "The Money to be paid when the Place is taken." Like the coaches, &c., the waggons had also increased, as, in addition to Davis and Co.'s (from his house in Middle-street), Bradford and Co.'s left their warehouse, in East-street. No improvement in waggon speed, however, took place, for in 1788, as in 1777, the time occupied by the journey was three days and two nights.

In 1788, the following "pacquets" are mentioned as sailing (wind and weather permitting) from Brighthelmston to Dieppe :— Three schooners: "The Prince of Wales" (Captain Burton). "The Princess Royal" (Captain Chapman), "The Prince William Henry" (Captain White), and "The Speedwell" cutter (Captain Lind). A "N.B." says—"The pacquets always sail in the evening, about two or three hours after the coaches arrive from London."

Six years later (1794) coaching enterprise was still active. Some of the original proprietors had been supplanted, as Ibberson and Co., by Scott, Henwood, and Co. At this period, Messrs. Davis and Co.

announced, in addition to their original post-coach, "cheap and pleasant travelling by one of those justly-admired patent coaches, which carries twelve insides, at 13s. each." The advertisement stated that "a party engaging the coach may be taken up and set down at their own houses, *if not very inconveniently situated*." Considering the size of the town in 1794 (being mostly within North-street, East-street, and West-street), modern Brightonians will scarcely repress a smile at this announcement. Tucker's "Diligence" to Chichester had, in 1794, been superseded (surely it was not worn-out by over-exertion!) by Kemp and Co.'s coach, from "The Old Ship'; a coach ran to Eastbourne; and an additional waggon (Grenville's) set out from North-row. But as yet coach-offices were not; the starting places being various inns—a profitable arrangement, doubtless, for the landlords, as we now find that, besides those above-named, "The White Lion," "The Golden Cross," and "The New Inn," had each become a starting-place for a coach!

The "patent coach," however, does not appear to have taken, for, after a few years, it was discontinued. It was, nevertheless, a laudable attempt at improvement in the character of the vehicles previously employed on the road. The old four-horse coaches of the period were, at best, but poor affairs—little more, we are told, than "genteel waggons, with a rumble-tumble, or basket behind, in which soldiers, sailors, workmen, &c., travelled; and as the rumble-tumble had no springs, the exercise in it must have been just as delightful as if a person were to employ a man to kick him all the way from Brighton to London."

Some idea of coach travelling between Brighton and London at this period (about 1790) may be gathered from a quotation from Mr. Shergold's *Recollections of Brighton in the Olden Time*. He premises his description by saying that the journey was a "very formidable affair. It was really an event only to be well got through by men of a robust constitution, and women who had been inured to fatigue by early rising and scrubbing and rubbing." He then tells us:—

"There were three roads from Brighton to London. The first and chief passed through Cuckfield and Reigate. This was the Appian way for the high Nobility of England. The other two were vulgar. The ône passed through Lewes; the other, through Horsham. The best method of conveyance on the Cuckfield-road was by the pair-horse coaches. These started at eight o'clock in the morning, and, if nothing intervened, proceeded steadily and boldly as far as Preston, where they stopped at the public-house—it being a prescriptive right of all coachmen in those days never to pass a public-house without calling. Coachmen were also persons of much consideration; a great deal of the business of the country being transacted by them. After quitting Preston, the coach *snailed it on* to Withdean and Patcham, stopping, of course, a little time at each. The next stoppage was at the bottom of Clayton Hill—the formidable Clayton Hill—where the coachman descended from his box and civilly obliged all passengers, outside and in, to walk up, on the plea 'that the roads were very heavy; it being absolutely killing to his horses.' This walk to the top of Clayton Hill took about half-an-hour, and was very fatiguing, especially if a man had the gallantry to offer his arm to a fat widow. From the top of Clayton Hill you had a most delightful view. From

Clayton Hill the coach *snailed it on* towards Cuckfield, the coachman not deeming it proper to ask the passengers to walk above three or four times until he arrived at that little town. At St. John's Common, on the hither side of Cuckfield, was a neat little public-house where the coachman usually took a snack, which consisted of a mouthful of bread and cheese and five or six glasses of gin and bitters, for that was the liqueur *par excellence* of coachmen in that day. When the coach arrived at Cuckfield it was usual for some of the passengers to say to one another, 'Well, as the coach will stop here for some time, we will walk on.' This walking on often consisted of a hard tug, up hill and down, over five or six miles of slimy, slippery road. * * * Before the coach overtook the passengers who had proposed to walk forward, they arrived at Hand Cross, a complete rustic inn, of which the landlord bore the impress of Sussex rusticity. With that kind and benevolent attention to the happiness and comfort of walking travellers which innkeepers by the road-side usually possess, a number of stools and benches were always placed in front of the inn to receive the wearied muscles of the promenaders. Bannister, the publican of Hand Cross, walked forth from his inn, carrying a gallon bottle of gin in one hand and a small wicker basket of slices of gingerbread in the other. 'You must be tired, gentlemen,' said he; 'come! take a glass and a slice.' So we all partook of gin and gingerbread; and I can safely aver that I never heard a gentleman's character disputed, or his reputation blackened, because he took a glass of gin and ate a slice of gingerbread at the rustic hostelerie of Hand Cross. But the coach was soon seen tending towards Hand Cross, and the outside and inside passengers, leaping up, took each person his place, and off we went, at the quiet and everlasting rate of four miles and a-half an hour! As we had a downhill passage from Hand Cross, and not above four or five public-houses to stop at, we soon arrived at Crawley, a miserable place, the sight of which always gave me the stomach-ache. At Crawley we delayed not more than was sufficient just to kick the dust from our feet, which Horace, or some other poet, mentions as a demonstration of contempt. We then bundled on to Reigate, and arrived at the King's Arms, the horses absolutely trotting up to the door as if they took a real pleasure in presenting their passengers in grand style. At the door of this comfortable inn there was always standing (I mean in the days of coaching) a waiter, who, after handing out the passengers, informed them that dinner was ready, and would be on the table in five minutes. Every man felt hungry; for, out of the thirty-two miles which lie between Brighton and Reigate, they had walked twenty. When they entered the room where dinner was to be served, they found some other passengers, who had come by a downward coach, waiting to dine. * * * Here, then, we were, about fifteen ladies and gentlemen of the coach-going community,—and who were not coach-goers in those simple and happy days?—about to sit down to a plain dinner, with two bottles of wine, at two o'clock in the day, at one of the best inns of the sort in the kingdom. The waiter put everything expeditiously on the table, wine and all, and said, very obligingly, ' Ladies and gentlemen, you have just two minutes for dinner! The coachman is putting-to his horses, and he will be round at the door immediately.' [This almost occasioned a "scene"; but the writer says, the coachman was appealed to, "firstly, to the stomach, by a tumbler of sherry; and, secondly, to his brains, by plain and solid argument," and "time was allowed."] After dinner, the coach went on as fast as two horses could carry us. The coachman, after we quitted Reigate, entered into an able soliloquy, addressed to me, to prove that eating dinners at two o'clock, and drinking heavy port wine, was imprudent. I was sitting on the box, and perfectly agreed with him. He did not say anything about drinking sherry, so I did not allude to it; but when he told me that he was quite sure he should lose his place for staying so long at Reigate, we on the outside all gave him a shilling a piece; so that, by delaying ten minutes, he gained seven shillings and a tumbler of sherry. The coachmen of those days were such honest men—not at all cunning! But those were the days of the olden time, before the slippery railroads came into fashion! * * * * When the coach arrived at Reigate Hill, all passengers, inside and outside, were requested to descend. This hill was the most formidable tug on the road. The best and easiest way of arriving at the summit of the hill, was to follow humbly the movements of the coach; but some ladies and gentlemen ventured up a steep which led almost perpendicularly up the hill, and joined the road by a transverse path. Here was the trial of sound lungs, and easy and comfortable lacing. Ladies who looked more to dapper shapes than easy respiration were sure to be brought to a *non-plus* about the middle of the path, and it was necessary sometimes to despatch a deputation of the gentlemen, who were walking near the coach, to aid in dragging the impeded ladies up the path. The fair passengers, however squeamish, were obliged to submit to the pulling and pushing movement; for there was only this method of surmounting the difficulties, unless they preferred to be rolled down the steep like a bundle of goods, and thus rejoin their fellow-passengers below. When we arrived at the top of Reigate Hill, we,—the travellers of the ancient epoch,—considered the journey to London almost as completed; for we were so accustomed to slow travelling, that an hour in a coach was as patiently borne as five minutes are now on the railroad. At 'The Cock,' at Sutton, we delayed a little half-hour, as the French say, and then valiantly proceeded on to the noted 'Elephant and Castle,' where we waited for the completion of many businesses, such as change of coach, if you were going into the City; and other necessary duties. The destination of the Brighton coaches in those days was 'The Golden Cross,' Charing Cross,—a nasty inn, remarkable for filth and apparent misery, whence it was usual to be conveyed to the place to which you were going in one of those large, lumbering hackney coaches, with two jaded, broken-winded, and broken-kneed hacks, which were common in those days, before the introduction of safety cabs and light flys. These vehicles were always damp and dreary, the very epitomes of misery. On arriving at the house you were going to in London, of some friends or relations, the following conversation often occurred: ' Happy to see you: but what brings you so soon?- didn't expect you before nine, and it's now only seven. - 'We have been eleven hours on the road is not that enough'? 'Oh! quite enough; but formerly the Brighton coaches arrived at midnight. Travelling improves every day. I wonder what we shall arrive at next! Only eleven hours from Brighton to London! Wonderful! Almost incredible!'"

In 1800 there was still more activity in coaching; offices devoted exclusively to the business having been opened some three or four years previously; notably those of Henwood, Crosweller, Cuddington, Pockney, and Harding, at 44, East-street (corner of Steine-lane, subsequently "Hine's), and Boulton, Tilt, Hicks, Baulcomb, and Co., at 1, North-street. In addition to the regular "post-coaches," a night post-coach (at 10 p.m.) started alternate days from these offices "in the season." A coach ran three times a week, by way of Chichester and Portsmouth, to Bath and Bristol (what time it took on the road is not stated); and a waggon (Nicholas and

Elphick's) "set out" to Lewes three times a week. About 1800 the "Cart" era was inaugurated,—Edwards's (to Lewes), Moorey's (to Shoreham), and Erridge's (to Eastbourne). The carts took their own time, apparently, on the road, as no information is afforded respecting their journey or arrival. The waggons had actually increased their speed, doing the journey to London in two days and a night! The coaches, presumably, did the journey in "about nine hours"; the "about" being a saving word of great virtue; for, what with stoppages and walking (the passengers doing on foot about half the journey!), it more frequently took 11 or 12 hours. Possibly, by keeping to routine time, the proprietors considered the wishes of the passengers were best consulted; for, it may be mentioned, that Palmer's mail-coaches were at this period running nine, and even ten miles an hour; and the public mind was so much agitated by the knowledge of this rapid travelling, that the gloomiest forebodings were indulged in, for thus "knowingly spurning the ways of Providence." The late Lord Campbell relates that he was frequently warned against travelling in Palmer's coaches, on account of "the fearful rate at which they flew," and instances were supplied to him of passengers who had died suddenly of apoplexy from the rapidity of the motion! *O tempora! O mores!* What would have been said if the Railway express speed could then have been imagined!

A Company, under the title of the Royal Brighton Four-Horse Coach Company, was started in 1802. Who the promoters were, we know not; but there was evidently no fraternization between them and the "old stagers," judging by the following advertisement, which was issued by the Company in July, 1802 :—

THE ROYAL BRIGHTON Four Horse Coach Company beg leave to return their sincere thanks to their Friends and the Public in general for the very liberal support they have experienced since the starting of their Coaches, and assure them it will always be their greatest study to have their Coaches safe, with good Horses and sober careful Coachmen.

They likewise wish to rectify a report in circulation of their Coach having been overturned on Monday last, by which a gentleman's leg was broken, &c., no such thing having ever happened to either of their Coaches. The Fact is it was one of the BLUE COACHES instead of the Royal New Coach.

⁎ As several mistakes have happened, of their friends being BOOKED at other Coach Offices, they are requested to book themselves at the ROYAL NEW COACH OFFICE, CATHERINE'S HEAD, 47, East Street.

As we have given previously the vicissitudes of a journey from Brighton *to* London about the year 1790, it may be interesting to give here some details of a journey *from* London to Brighton some 10 years later :—

"In 1801 two *pair*-horse coaches ran between London and Brighton on alternate days, one up, the other down, and they were driven by Crosweller and Hine.* The progress of these coaches was an amusing one.

---

* There was, probably, no coachman in his day more respected than Mr. Hine, senior. He was the oldest coachman on the road; his connection with Brighton coaches dating as far back as 1801. He was, too, universally liked;

The one from London left 'The Blossoms' Inn, Lawrence-lane, at 7 a.m. ; the passengers breaking their fast at 'The Cock,' at Sutton, at 9. The next stoppage for the purpose of refreshment was at 'The Tangier' (Banstead Downs), a rural little spot famous for its elderberry wine, which used to be brought from the cottage 'roking hot,' and, on a cold wintry morning, few refused to partake of it. George the Fourth invariably stopped here and took a glass from the hand of Miss Jeal as he sat in his carriage. The important business of luncheon took place at Reigate, where sufficient time was allowed the passengers to view the Baron's Cave. Handcross was the next resting-place, celebrated for its 'neat' liquors, the landlord of the Inn standing bottle-in-hand at the door. (He and several other Bonifaces, at Friar's Oak, &c., had the reputation of being on pretty good terms with the smugglers who at this period carried on their operations with such audacity along the Sussex coast.) But the grand halt for dinner was made at Staplefield Common, celebrated for its famous black cherry trees, under the branches of which, when the fruit was ripe, the coaches were allowed to draw up and the passengers to partake of its tempting produce. The hostess of the hostelry here was famed for her rabbit puddings, which were always waiting the arrival of the coach, and to which the travellers never failed to do such ample justice that ordinarily they found it quite impossible to leave at the hour appointed; so grogs, pipes, and ale were ordered in, and, to use the language of the fraternity, 'not a wheel wagged' for two hours. The coach then went on to Clayton Hill, and as the passengers had to walk up this ascent, a cup of tea was sometimes found to be necessary at Patcham, after which Brighton was safely reached by 7 p.m."

Slow or fast, coaching at this period must have been a lucrative business. In the *Brighton Herald* of November 19, 1808, an advertisement appeared offering for sale the good-will of one-twelfth part of the business of No. 1, North-street. It states—"The returns of the trade are now more than £12,000 sterling a year, and it has paid, from Christmas, 1794, to Christmas, 1808, £7 10s. per cent. on the capital employed, besides purchasing shares of four of the partners, viz., Messrs. Samuel Shergold, John Hicks, Richard Wood (of Reigate), and John Davis, &c." The fares at one office (Waldegrave's) in 1808 were 23s. inside, and 13s. outside—an advance of one-third upon those of a dozen years earlier !

The coaching business during its subsequent career rapidly increased. This increase was, doubtless, much facilitated by new routes

---

and whether as regarded skill, caution, good humour, strict integrity, or a desire to promote to the utmost the comfort of his passengers, few could compare with him. It has been computed that he could not have brought less than 100,000 persons into the town, and this without a single accident. Among the celebrities of the day whom Hine was accustomed to bring down were Mathews, in his "prime and bang up," Munden, Russell, and Emery, each of whom used invariably to borrow his huge box-coat of seven capes when appearing on the Brighton stage; Lieutenant or Jack Bannister; Quick, another famous actor; John Thornton, Esq., of Clapham; the Rev. Rowland Hill; and many noblemen of the Court of George IV. Among other persons whom the late Mr. Hine first introduced to Brighton were the late Sir Matthew Tierney and Mr. George Faithfull (the latter one of the two first representatives of Brighton in Parliament). The former rode on the box with Hine and kept the passengers in good humour and on the broad grin, from "morn till noon," &c.; but on entering Brighton he suddenly exclaimed, "Now, Hine, I must put on a long face, for I am come here to make my fortune!" Mr. H. G. Hine, the celebrated artist, is a son of the famous old coachman.

(avoiding hills) and by the improved state of the roads themselves. In 1808 two new "coach concerns," Waldegrave and Co., and Pattenden and Co., were opened.

In 1809, Messrs. Cuddington, Fricker, and Co. ran "elegant light accommodation coaches" from Brighton to Worthing, four times a week, starting at "seven o'clock in the morning"; Crosweller and Co. ran "morning and night coaches" from Brighton to London; and in the same year "Miller" Bradford and some dozen others formed a Company, and ran two four-horse coaches, the increased speed of which revolutionized the trade. In 1810, the Royal Night Mail Coaches commenced running between Brighton and London. They were established (with the acquiescence of H.M. Postmaster-General) by J. Willan, of "The Bull and Mouth," London, and M. Phillips, of "The New Inn," Brighton. These coaches started every night at 10, going "by the new cut to Croydon," and doing the journey in eight hours, "no pretences being permitted to cause a delay in the journey." This improved speed inaugurated improved postal arrangements; letters in Brighton being delivered two hours earlier—at six in the morning. *Apropos* of this, the *Brighton Herald* of May 26, 1810, relates that a well-known tradesman of East-street, being roused two hours earlier than usual by the "postman's knock," and thinking a joke was being played upon him, put his nightcapped head out of the window and threatened to beat the innocent official into a *post*, if he wern't off!

On February 5, 1812, however, there was a coaching episode of a serious character. This was the abstraction from "The Blue Coach" of a parcel containing Brighton Union Bank Notes, of between £3,000 and £4,000 in value. Messrs. Brown, Hall, Lashmar, and West, of the Union Bank, it appears, hired of Messrs. Crosweller and Co. a box beneath the seat of "The Blue," for the purpose of transmitting cash with greater security to and from London. On the day in question, Messrs. Weston, Pinhorn, and Co., of the Borough, Southwark, placed the notes in the said cash-box, to be forwarded, as usual, to Brighton. It was deposited and secured in the customary place; but on the arrival of the coach in East-street in the evening, Mr. John Pocock (Messrs. Brown and Co.'s clerk) discovered, on unlocking the seat of the coach, that the cash-box had been broken open and the whole of the contents abstracted! All the light the coachman could throw on the affair was: That six persons were booked for inside places; two (a gentleman and lady) only appeared at the time the coach started; two gentlemen were taken up on the road, and the others never appeared at all. On the coach reaching Sutton, the lady was taken suddenly ill, and obliged to alight at the inn, where he left her and her husband. On arriving at the inn at Reigate, the two other gentlemen inside left the coach to make enquiry, as they said, after a friend; they, however, quickly returned, and told the unsuspecting coachman that, having ascertained that a gentleman, who they supposed was at Brighton, had returned to town, it was useless for them to proceed further! A reward of £300 was immediately offered for "information so that the aforesaid parcel can be recovered." This was subsequently altered to 100 guineas for "information of the offender," and £300 "upon the recovery of the whole of the above property, or 10 per cent. upon the amount of so much thereof as shall be recovered."

The perpetrators of the robbery, we believe, were never discovered; nor were the notes recovered, though an attempt was made about twelve months after to put them into circulation. Who "paid the piper," we know not; but there was a significant addendum to a coach advertisement in the next week's *Brighton Herald*:—"Not accountable for any parcel above £5, unless entered as such and paid for accordingly."

In September, 1821, "The Union" Brighton Coach was robbed, near Tooting, of a portmanteau belonging to one of George IV.'s footmen, which contained the Royal State liveries, a large stock of linen, &c.

In June, 1811, there were no less then 28 coaches running between Brighton and London, and it was computed that, in the previous five months,—not a favourable period, as many coaches only commenced running in April or May,—between 50,000 and 60,000 persons had been conveyed between the two places.

From about 1811 to about 1819 the coaching business was in a transition state. There was not only competition between the coaches with respect to speed, but also with respect to fares. These latter reached their minimum in 1814, when the fares of "The Regent" were: inside, 10s.; outside, 5s. Increased speed was, of course, a desideratum; but there was a large class of travellers who strongly objected to accommodate themselves to the new order of things—who clung to old habits, and who preferred, in fact, to go upon the "slow and sure" principle. Some of the coach proprietors, it must be admitted, did their best to accommodate each class of customers! Mackerell (Waldegrave's successor) started in 1811 "The Royal Brighton" and "The Telegraph" on "an improved principle, and particularly constructed for SAFETY." Then, three or four years later, there was "The Bellerophon" (driven by William Hine)—a decided concession to the old school of travellers, as it took plenty of time on the road. This vehicle (which was named after Captain Maitland's ship, on board which Napoleon surrendered after Waterloo,) was a huge concern, with two inside compartments, carrying four and six respectively, and with ample accommodation for "outsides." In reality, it was a revival of the old "patent coach." But the "slow coaches," though patronised by a section of the community, had eventually to succumb to the "fast," which daily grew in public favour. The career of the Bellerophon itself was but a short one. Speed had, in fact, now become almost a *sine quâ non* to secure patronage; and in this respect—considering at what rate coaches had previously gone—some extraordinary travelling was performed. Mr. Whitchurch was the first to start a coach (in 1813) to go from Brighton to London and *return the same day*—a feat which excited an immense sensation in the town. His success soon called forth a competitor, in "The Eclipse," from " The Red

Office," in Castle-square, which also did the journey in six hours. A local chronicle, in alluding to the speed of "The Eclipse," says—" A person, after breakfasting in Brighton, may go to London, transact business, and take his dinner, after which, he may, if he pleases, return to this place to supper"! How far the story is true, we cannot say; but it is related that one of these coaches always did the journey *within* the time, as certain Hebrew visitors travelling by it bargained that, unless it did so, they should ride free! * This speed, great as it was thought at the time, was, as is well known, exceeded at a later date. "The Red Rover," on November 2nd, 1830, brought down the King's Speech in four hours and twenty minutes; and the same coach, on June 10th, 1832, did the journey from Brighton to London in four hours and ten minutes. The greatest feat with regard to speed was, however, performed by "The Criterion," which, on February 4th, 1834, brought down King William IV.'s Speech on the assembling of Parliament, doing the journey from London to Brighton in *three hours and forty minutes !* The coach was driven by Charles Harbour. †

But speed was not without its disadvantages. The "old folks" could quote numerous accidents against it, and it gave rise to the objectionable practice of racing. So prevalent had this become that some of the older offices, as "The Blue," used to advertise, as a guarantee of safety to the public, "that the proprietors will not allow RACING, or like folly, with other coaches." The accident at "The Sussex Pad" (between Shoreham and Lancing), a year or two previously, in which a gentleman named Cole, of Worthing, lost his life, was doubtless fresh in the public mind. This accident was solely attributable to the racing of the two Worthing coaches: one of the coachmen admitted at the inquest that he had received orders

---

* This story, probably, had its origin in the fact that, in 1816, some Jews started the Brighton Coach to run from Brighton to London in six hours or pay penalty of carrying passengers for nothing. The horses galloped all the way. On one journey the coachman broke three whips! In one week fifteen horses died! The Coach, however, was never overturned; but continued to run for three months. At last information was laid, in Newington parish, against the drivers for furious driving, and the result was to lengthen the time of reaching Brighton by about an hour.

[† As an interesting contribution to coaching "speed," we give the following particulars of the late Mr. James Selby's remarkable coaching performance from the *London Daily News* of July 14th, 1888 :—" REMARKABLE COACHING PERFORMANCE—TO BRIGHTON AND BACK IN EIGHT HOURS.—The 'Old Times' coach, which runs between the White Horse Cellars in Piccadilly and Brighton, yesterday did the unexampled performance of making the return journey in less than eight hours. The previous best record for the distance was something like eight hours and a half, and in the old coaching days nine hours was considered an exceptional performance. A wager of £1.000 to £500 was made that Mr. James Selby, a well-known 'whip' for the last quarter of a century, and a driver on the Brighton road for the last ten years, would not complete the double journey in eight hours. Yesterday was selected to test his powers. Fortunately the weather was fine, and the roads, despite the recent heavy rains, were in excellent condition. Elaborate arrangements had been made, the four horses being changed sixteen times during the journey. The coach, with a party of six, started from Piccadilly just on the stroke of 10 a.m. The first change was made at the Horse and Groom, Streatham, which was reached in twenty-eight minutes, and where the change of horses and re-starting of the coach occupied only forty-seven seconds. Streatham and Patcham

"*to get in first, though he should lose a horse!*" Then there was the affair between Snow's "Dart" and "The Phœnix"; when "The Dart," in endeavouring to pass "The Phœnix," at Preston, ran foul of it and overturned it. The crash was a fearful one, and the shrieks of the passengers were heartrending. Mr. Taylor, of "The Golden Cross," had his thigh broken, and others of the passengers were seriously injured. So culpable, in fact, was "The Dart" coachman's conduct, that it was determined to prosecute him at the next Assizes.

The Government of the day could not be accused of encouraging fast travelling. In their tender for mails, in the year 1817, all the speed asked for was "seven miles an hour" from London to Croydon, and "six miles an hour" from Croydon to Brighton!

The names of the coaches at this time would seem to indicate that speed was all in all. There were "The Dart," "The Alert," "The Rocket," "The Irresistible,"* "The Vivid," "The Comet," &c.; and, as if emulous of the coaches, a packet to Dieppe was started in 1814, called "The Flying Fish"! (Captain *Partridge*, commander,) which professed to do the journey, in a fair wind, in seven hours! A year later we hear nothing of her—perhaps she overshot the mark, and came to grief, or, what is more likely, failed for lack of custom; for the number of packets at this period was out of all proportion to the passengers, and the Revenue Officers had a strong suspicion that business of another character was carried on by them.

What may be called the golden era of coaching was between 1819 and 1839,† though the coaches on the road were more in number at

eventually divided the honours for first place, both occupying forty-seven seconds, and the longest stop, including necessary attention to the bearings of the coach, was only a little over a minute. Some little delay was experienced at the level railway crossing at Crawley, where the gates were closed, but with this exception there was no unfavourable incident, the traffic in Piccadilly even giving very little trouble, owing to the excellent arrangements which had been made. By the route taken by the coach the distance to the Old Ship at Brighton is calculated at 54 miles from the starting point, and the down journey was completed in 3 hours 56 minutes, 10 seconds. Not more than a second's stay was made in Brighton, the team being immediately turned and proceeding homeward. When it is remembered that 108 miles had to be covered, or an average, inclusive of stoppages, of 13½ miles in the hour, it will be seen that the task was not an easy one. The advantage obtained on the down journey was increased at the various stages on the return, and when the coach drew up at the starting point in Piccadilly it was found that the distance had been covered in exactly 7 hours and 50 minutes. At the White Horse Cellars, there was a large gathering of sportsmen, who heartily congratulated Mr. Selby on his 'record' performance, and the spirited directors of the coach on the success which attended their endeavour."]

* "The Irresistible," which was started in 1817, was a popular coach in its day. We had always regarded its proprietor, Mr. Rugeroh, as a "foreigner"; but, by a tombstone to his memory, nearly opposite the belfry door of St. Nicholas Church, it would appear he had long resided in the town. The stone records that his wife died in Brighton, in 1787; his daughter (who married Mr. Tuppen, of the Marine Library,) in 1824; and he himself in 1846, at the ripe age of 80.

† As showing the amount of business done in the palmy days of coaching, it may be mentioned that, in 1828, it was calculated that the 16 permanent coaches (*i.e.*, running winter and summer) received between them £60,000 a year; and including the amount received by the "butterflies" (summer coaches), not less than £100,000 per annum was spent in coaching between Brighton and London. In one day, on Friday, October 25th, 1833, upwards of 480 persons came

the earlier than in the latter part of the era, when the prospect of a Railway had paralysed to some extent the coaching interest. In September, 1822, there were as many as 62 coaches running daily between Brighton and other places, the larger half of which ran to and from London. The following list gives their number and destination:—

To and from London	39
" " Portsmouth	2
" " Southampton	2
" " Lewes	6
To Hastings	2
To Tunbridge Wells and Maidstone	1
To Oxford	1
To Windsor	1
To and from Worthing	8
Total	62

In 1828 there were some fine coaches on the road, well horsed and driven, and admirably appointed; and among the best of these were "The Times," "The Regent," and "The Union," driven respectively by Goodman, Gray, and Pickett. "Safety Patents" were also in vogue, and "The Patriot" had fitted to it "Cook's Patent Life Preserver"! *

In 1839, the coaches running between Brighton and London had decreased to 23. At this latter date, Castle-square (though there were offices at various other places) was the "head centre" of coaching; six out of the seven principal offices being situated in it. Of the London coaches, five ran from "The Blue" office (Messrs. Strevens and Co.); five from "The Red" (Mr. Goodman's); four from "The

---

into Brighton from London by the stage coaches. [As a pendant to this statement, we quote the following from *The Times* of September 21, 1891:—"At the time when the proposed Railway to Brighton was occupying the attention of Parliamentary Committees, there were 36 coaches running between London and that town. These were unitedly licensed to carry 3,453 passengers per week, and their actual weekly average in the year 1835 was 2,263, or a total of 117,676 per annum. The average fare paid by each passenger was 21s. for inside and 12s. for outside seats, and the average time occupied on the journey was six hours. Two mail coaches ran daily, included in the 36 already named, and these made 14 journeys per week, carrying nine passengers on each journey. There were, however, other distinct services between London and Worthing, Bognor, Horsham, Dorking, and Epsom, as well as regular services between Brighton and Worthing, and between Brighton and Shoreham and Steyning. Finally, there was a special service of two coaches between Windsor and Brighton, which carried, on an average, 144 passengers per week, and occupied eight hours on the journey. The total value of the passenger traffic on these several services, including Brighton and London, was in 1835 about £123,000."]

* In the *Sporting Magazine* (1828), Vol. xxii., p. 409, a good joke is related respecting the "Preserver":—"Just as Pickett was starting with his 'Union' coach out of Holborn, up comes a pursy old citizen, puffing and blowing like a grampus—'Pray, coachman, is this here the Patriotic Life Preserver Safety Coach?' 'Yes, Sir,' says Pickett, not hearing above half of his passenger's question : —'room behind, Sir!—jump up, if you please!—very late this morning!' 'Why, where's the machinery?' cries the old one. 'There, Sir,' replied a passenger (a young Cantab, I suspect), pointing to a heavy trunk of mine that was swung underneath; 'in that box, Sir; that's were the machinery works.'—'Ah!' quoth the old man, climbing up, quite satisfied, 'wonderful inventions now-days, Sir. We shall all get safe to Brighton! no chance of an accident by *this* coach!'"

Spread Eagle" (Messrs. Chaplin and Crunden's); three from "The Age" (Messrs. T. W. Capps and Co.); two from Hine's (in Eaststreet); two from Snow's (of which Mr. T. W. Capps and Mr. W. Chaplin were the proprietors); and two from "The Globe" (Mr. Vaughan's). About 15 or 20 coaches went to and from other places.

The coaches, in their equipment, horses, &c., were, at this period, as near perfection as possible; and there was probably no better representative of the "Era" than "The Age," the property of Mr. Thomas Ward Capps. It was a model coach, and in every respect worthy of the genius of Herring, who has immortalised it in his wellknown painting. "The Age" was always splendidly horsed (in its palmy days by that prince of "whips," Sir St. Vincent Cotton*), and the coach itself and its appurtenances were really superb. No man, in fact, took a greater pride in his coach (indeed in all his coaches), than Thomas Ward Capps. Nothing but the best satisfied him. All the fittings (and even the colouring) of "The Age" were unique: the pole-chains, &c., were of burnished steel. The "ribbons" too, were of the dantiest—Paliser's best make—exciting the envy and admiration of the coaching fraternity. And then the horse-cloths! Who ever saw their match, edged as they were with broad silver lace, and adorned with gold mountings, and having at each corner (embroidered in coloured silk and silver) the Royal Crown and a sprig of laurel? Altogether, though there were many other splendid contemporary coaches, "The Age" may be regarded as the best representative of coaching in its glory. Singularly enough, in later days, it represented it in its decline, being the last coach on the road! †

Let us here revert to Castle-square in the old coaching days, some forty or fifty years ago, and recall some pleasant memories. What a changed aspect does it now present! We allude not so much to the buildings and houses, though these have all been more or less metamorphosed to suit modern requirements. The porter's lodge, outoffices, &c., formerly attached to the Pavilion, and occupying the greater portion of the northern side of the Square, have long since

---

* Sir St. Vincent Cotton was a Cambridgeshire Baronet, and a descendant of the collector of the Cotton MSS. In the early part of his life he is said to have been so much addicted to gambling that he lost two fortunes at the table. A characteristic anecdote is told of his propensity. Some friends and he were one day, after dinner, cracking nuts over their wine, when a race between some maggots from the filberts was suggested. No sooner said than done. The table was cleared, maggots selected, and needles obtained to spur them on. From the first, Sir St. Vincent's *horse* took the lead, and betting and excitement ran high, as each pricked on his maggot to increase his speed. By and by an "outsider" crept up to the leading maggot, giving promise of a brilliant finish, when Sir St. Vincent, who stood to win or lose heavily, in his eagerness to urge on his filbertian steed, pricked it *too deeply*; at once it coiled itself up, and the outsider came in the winner! Sir St. Vincent was said to have lost by the race £30,000. He subsequently came into a third fortune, when he "settled down" at Madingley Hall, near Cambridge, which was occupied by the Prince of Wales when at the University, and where, it was said, the Prince Consort contracted the fever of which he died.

† "The Age" horse-cloths (with other interesting relics of the old coaching days) were last year [1879] presented to the Brighton Museum by Mr. Thomas Ward Capps, the esteemed proprietor, who still dwells among us. [Mr. Capps died at Brighton in September, 1887, in his 87th year.]

Sir St. Vincent Cotton.
THE "AGE" (Stevenson's).—A SKETCH FROM CASTLE SQUARE, BRIGHTON.

SOUTH GATE OF THE PAVILION

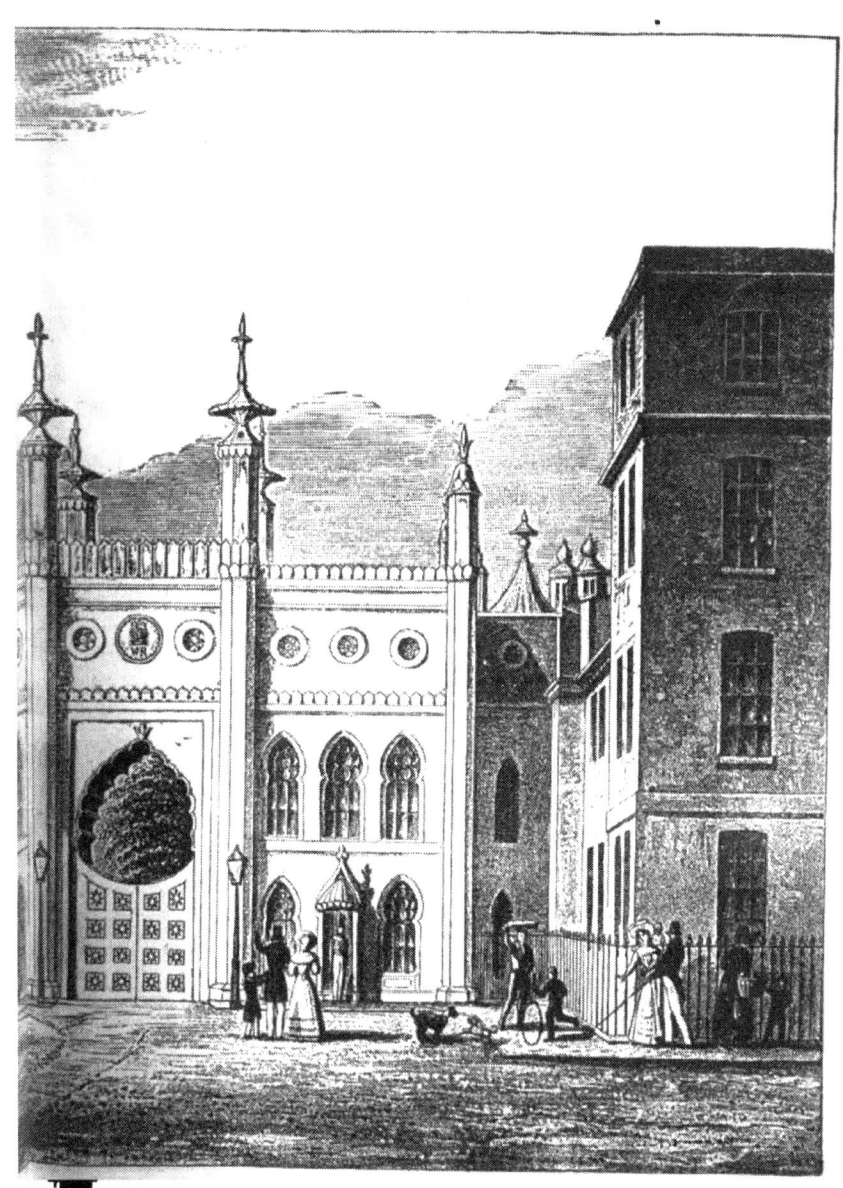

BLUE COACH OFFICE, &c.

made way for the fine row of business premises known as the Pavilion-buildings. The south gate of the Pavilion itself, which, standing in a line with North-street, faced down East-street. The old Blue Coach office (Strevens's, formerly Crosweller's), a genuine piece of old Brighton house architecture, with the familiar old weathercock on the roof, and Reynolds's cigar shop next door, are now supplanted by the premises of Messrs. Treacher. The south side of the Square is also much changed. All the old coach offices, save one, "The Red" (now used as the Railway booking-office), have been swept away, and handsome shops supply their places. These great material changes are, however, nothing to those which have taken place in the life and movement of the Square since the decline and fall of the "Coaching Era." From early morn till late at night—from the bottom of North-street to the Steine—in olden times the Square was crowded with a motley, ever-changing throng of life, and was at times impassable. Bustle and activity, such as may now only be seen at the Railway Station, on the departure of an excursion train, pervaded the whole space. Groups of idlers—*quid nuncs*, anxious to learn the latest news (for coaches in those days, were the earliest purveyors of intelligence*)—were to be seen around the various offices, watching the arrival and departure of the coaches; and, mingled with these, were passengers hurrying to and fro to secure their places, followed by busy porters with luggage, boxes, &c. Cads and touters were here, there, and everywhere, on the look-out for a job. Cabs were constantly going to and from the Square, or busy setting-down or taking-up fares. At the doors of half-a-dozen offices at one time might be seen brightly-coloured coaches, horsed by splendid teams, champing their bits or pawing the ground, as if entering into the excitement of the scene, and eager for the start. On some of the coaches were trimly attired, bright-coated guards, "towering in their pride of place," ever and anon playing their bugles. "Swell" coachmen,—not unfrequently a nobleman or a baronet, and dressed *au rigueur*,—were pacing to and fro the offices, the "observed of all observers." And then, when the start was about to take place, what redoubled excitement was there! when the passengers were at last seated; the luggage piled or stowed away; when the coachman had mounted the box, had tightened the "ribbons," and flourished his whip in conscious pride; and when, at a given signal, as the clock struck the hour from the old Pavilion tower, the horse-cloths were dexterously snatched away by the attendant ostlers, the guard struck up a familiar air on his bugle, and the words issued from many a mouth, "Off she goes!" Altogether, it was a scene which one cannot adequately describe, but which can never be forgotten by those old enough to have witnessed it.

---

* Miss Martineau relates that, during the trial of Queen Caroline, "all along the line of mails, crowds stood waiting in the burning sunshine for the news of the trial, which was shouted out to them as the coach passed." And so during various stages of the Reform Bill the mail coach roads were sprinkled over for miles with people on the *qui vive* for news from London, and the coachmen and the guards on the tops of the coaches shouted out the tidings.

A sense of sadness, however, mingles with these old memories, for, in looking back to the days of coaching in its glory, how many pleasant, well-known faces do we miss! Of the old "whips"—so famous, and so courted in their day—it may almost be said—

"All, all are gone, the old familiar faces."

Bob Pointer, Black Sam, Crosweller, Pattenden, and the Newnhams; Captain Gwynne,* and other members of the old Four-in-Hand Club, —all have long since rested from their labours. And so of those known in later times: the Hines, father and son; the Snows, Charley Lee, Sheel,† Harry Holdsworth, Dick Cooper, Gray, the Picketts, Deere, Butcher, George Clark, George Cross, &c. Then, too, of the gentlemen coachmen; some are dead, some have left us—all, all, are gone, since the old days—as the Marquis of Worcester, Henry Stevenson (the original starter of the "Age"), the Duke of Beaufort, Robert Brackenbury (a descendant of Richard the Third's and Shakespeare's Lieutenant of the Tower), Sir St. Vincent Cotton, &c. Among those associated with coaching in a less exalted sphere were Laker, the "fat porter at Snow's," the Robinsons ("Archie," father and son), Lebright ("German George," an old soldier of the first Napoleonic era), Howell, Varney, Rook, "Sprightly," and many another less known to fame, but not to be over-looked in a retrospect of the "Coaching Era" in Brighton.

Our notice of the "Era" would scarcely be completed without allusion to some of the more important casualties, &c., in connection with it:—

On February 12th, 1808, the coaches to London were unable, for the first time within memory, to proceed on their journey, by reason of the snow, and all had to return after going a short distance. Mr. Pattenden, in driving his post-coach over the Downs, by the Devil's Dyke, experienced the greatest difficulty in proceeding; though full inside and out, the wind was so high, that every moment it was expected the coach would be overturned. Then the frost was so severe, that several passengers declared that they must have perished, had they not returned. An elderly man, named Bursbee, was totally deprived of feeling, and slipt from the top of the coach, unobserved by the other passengers, but missing him on their arrival at the coach office, a search was instituted and he was brought safely back. Had he remained on the hill but a short time longer he must inevitably have perished.

On the 25th June, 1810, an accident happened to Waldegrave's "Accommodation" coach, whilst on its journey to London. The coach was so heavily loaded that the hind wheels were suddenly crushed by the weight they supported, and the coach was overturned near Brixton Causeway. Singular to relate, a farmer's waggon passed the coach at the very instance that the accident occurred, and received the greater part of the outside passengers! As it was, one gentleman had his thigh broken, and contusions and bruises were pretty equally distributed.

---

* The Captain was always attended by two servants in livery, one of whom looked after the horses and the other attended to the passengers.

† For several years Mr. Edward Sheel drove "The Times" coach between Brighton and London, and was highly respected on the road. He died at Brighton in 1819; and his funeral was attended by the principal part of the Prince Regent's domestics, among whom he was much esteemed.

For some days, during the second week of January, 1811, the entrance to Brighton, both by Preston and Lewes roads, was so impassable, by the water which overflowed them, by reason of the "grand arch" of the old sewer (situated a little to the north of the junction of the two roads, and by which the water was conducted underground to the sea), being choked by ice, that the coaches were obliged to come into Brighton by Preston hedges to the Dyke-road, and over Church-hill, to avoid danger.

On the 22nd January, 1814, the severity of the weather again prevented the coaches going to London.

In August, 1819, "The Coburg" coach was overturned at Cuckfield; and of the eleven passengers on the roof, not one escaped unhurt: one gentleman died the next day, and five others had to remain at Cuckfield, being unable to proceed on their journey.

A frightful accident happened to "The Alert" on October 9th, 1829. The coach was taking up passengers on the King's-road, when Mr. Hine, jun., the driver, got down, still holding the reins, to assist the porter to raise a trunk to the coach. He asked a boy, who was passing, to stand at the head of the horses; and it is supposed that the lad, in attempting to catch hold of the reins, caused the animals to start. An effort was made to stop them; but they turned sharply round, ran against the iron fence opposite the Belle Vue Mansion, which broke like glass, and, in an instant, down went horses and coach to a perpendicular depth of 15ft. or 16ft. to the gap below. The horses had, in their fall, by the breaking of the pole, detached themselves from the coach, and, strange to say, escaped unhurt. The body of the coach was shattered almost to pieces; and Mrs. Steward was taken from it bleeding profusely from the head; her collar bone was broken, and she was otherwise seriously hurt. Another coach having been subsequently procured, Mr. Hine, sen., with the same horses, proceeded to town!

On the 25th August, 1832, the Brighton Mail Coach was upset near Reigate, and the coachman was killed on the spot; the guard also being severely hurt.

The coach accident which excited the most consternation probably from its happening in the town—was that of "The Quicksilver," on the morning of July 15th, 1833. The coach was overturned at the south end of Glo'ster-place, the coach in falling just clearing the palisades of the Enclosures, against which all the outside passengers were thrown, the violence of the concussion breaking several railings and dislodging several feet of the stonework. The coach itself was dragged nearly to the Glo'ster Hotel before the horses were stopped. All the outside passengers were more or less injured. A Mr. Lyon, who had been jammed between the coach and the palisades, was picked up in a pitiable condition, with both jaws and four ribs broken and other serious injuries; a Mr. Pearson had two ribs broken; Mrs. Ready, a broken arm; Snow, who drove the coach, was picked up saturated with blood, his clothes cut to ribbons; and Mr. Hayller (the real coachman of "The Quicksilver") and Mr. E. Strevens, were much cut and bruised, though not dangerously.

A serious accident befell "The Criterion" coach in the Borough, London, on Saturday, June 7th, 1834, by which Sir William Cosway, a resident of Brighton, lost his life. The deceased Baronet was in the act of climbing over the roof, when the coach was accidentally overturned by a collision with a dray. Other passengers were injured by the accident, but Sir William Cosway's was the only fatal case.

The "great snow storm" of Christmas, 1836, sadly interfered with coaching. On Christmas Eve, the mail coach from London to Brighton could only reach Clayton, the guard, with a countryman for his guide, bringing in the bags on horseback to the Post Office, which he reached, half-dead, at 1 a.m. Monday. The mail coach from Brighton to London, started, as usual, at 10.30; but got no farther than Patcham, and had to return. The Gloucester Mail, instead of reaching Brighton on Sunday, was not heard of until past one on Monday; and then could not get farther than Shoreham, the bags being sent on by the Worthing mail cart. "Boxing Day" was a blank—not a single coach left or entered the town; and the coach-offices were besieged by anxious enquirers. On Tuesday, the London mail was despatched from Brighton by six men on foot, who got as far as Cuckfield; here they took horses to Crawley, whence they got a post chaise to London. It was not until Wednesday that the regular communication was opened with London.

"The Magnet" came to grief at Patcham, in March, 1836, by reason of the axletree breaking and causing the horse to start; the coachman was thrown, and the coach wheels going over his leg, it was broken.

The last fatal accident in connection with the Brighton coaches was that of the overturning of "The Times" Southampton coach, at Salvington, on the 18th February, 1840; by which poor Upfold, the coachman, lost his life.

The "Coaching Era" may be said virtually to have ended with the opening of the Railway to London (September 21st, 1841). On the principle, we suppose, of "making hay while the sun shines," there was, in May of that year, a simultaneous rise in coach fares to London, the charges being 12s. outside and 21s. inside. But this lasted only until the Railway opened; for a fortnight after this event, in the vain hope of opening up a competing traffic, the coach fares were reduced to 12s. inside and 6s. outside! The "iron horse," however, became "first favourite." Coach after coach ceased to run; and horses might have been had almost for the asking: many a noble animal, which a few years previously would have fetched 60 or 100 guineas, was knocked down for 10 guineas, or even less.

An episode of the period of competition ("Coach v. Railway") claims a passing mention. This was the starting of a new coach, by Messrs. Capps and Co., called "The Rail Road." The hand-bill announcing it was cleverly worded, being as follows:—

THE RAIL ROAD.

Considerable disappointment has been expressed by the public in consequence of the delay and difficulties in deciding on a Line of Rail Road for Brighton, T. W. CAPPS AND CO., anxious to meet the wishes of their friends, have established a "RAIL ROAD" for their accommodation, free from all the objections urged against the other Lines. They have dispensed with the tedious and expensive form of carrying a Bill through the House of Commons; and, the necessary arrangements having been completed, it is now ready for the conveyance of travellers.

The advocates of Sir John Rennie's Line are informed that this is the most Direct that the circumstances will admit of; and those who are opposed to Sir John are assured that Capps's Line is entirely free from tunnels and cuttings; and as the original "Age" Office, No. 5, Castle-square, was formerly associated with the name of Stevenson, it is presumed that no objection will be offered by the supporters of the Shoreham Line; while the opposers of that route will be pleased to hear that no foggy districts or unhealthy marshes will be passed through; that no gentleman's pleasure grounds will be cut up, and that the prosperity of Brighton is not likely to be compromised by a digression to Worthing.

The Curves and Gradients have been reduced as much as possible; and in order to meet the wishes of all parties the Termini will neither be at Nine Elms, London Bridge, Rose Hill, nor the Antheum; the London Terminus is at "The Globe" Tavern, Baker-street, and the Brighton Terminus at "The Age" Office, No. 5, Castle-square, whence "The Rail Road" starts every day, at two o'clock, upon the usual estimated fares.

N.B.—The Passengers will not be troubled with "Smoke," excepting over their tea at Merstham.

Capps's "Rail Road" was, however, soon distanced by Rennie's; and in less than a year after starting the coach ceased to run. A year or so later (1842-43) coaches to London ran only from one office in Brighton, "The Red," Mr. Capps, the proprietor, being the "last man"; his coach, "The Victoria," did not cease to run till November 8, 1845. The old "Blue" office, at the corner of North-street, had been pulled down during the previous month. "The Age," originally the property of Mr. Capps, was, as already stated, the last coach on the direct Brighton road to London. The last Lewes coach ran on July 12, 1846, about a month after the Lewes Line was opened.

Thus ended the original "Coaching Era" in Brighton, and we may here give the following valedictory lines upon it, which appeared at the period in a local journal:—

A FAREWELL TO THE ROAD.
"Ichabod! Ichabod! the mighty are fallen."

Alas! that ever the day should come when Castle-square should be cadless and coachless—when the stroke of twelve at noon should not be the signal for every soul who can see beauties in a perfect four-in-hand to transfer himself to its vicinity—when its ample space should no longer be filled with half-blood teams, covered with rich trappings, prancing and curvetting and showing their rounded limbs and glossy skins in the sun—when the far-reaching whip should cease to be flourished aloft in triumph or cracked in the full exuberant spirit of the road! Alas! that the day should come when four-in-hands should be reckoned amongst the things of the past, and take their place with the broad-wheeled wains of our ancestors - when "The Age" and "The Times" should not be the fastest-going things on the road, but be as much outstripped in the race of time as the laziest carrier's cart that ever crawled along the surface of the earth!

Yet all this is come to pass, and we are not old men. We have seen Castle-square a mere desert at twelve o'clock; we have beheld it stripped of that mighty corps of coachmen, porters, cads, and others, that long exercised in it the sway of power; we have turned the corner of the Blue without having the breath squeezed out of our body; we have passed the narrow straits of the Red without having our corns trodden upon; we have doubled the Spread Eagle without breaking our shins over heaps of luggage. Nay, more—we have not heard one jest, nor seen one practical joke played off, not smiled at one sally of humour or exhibition of character in that most fertile of all places for jests, comicalities, and practical jokes—all has been "dull, flat, and unprofitable."

Thus and therefore is it that, in bidding farewell to the stage, we do it with all kindness and no little sorrow.

Some few years later "The Age" was again on the road between Brighton and London, and continued to run, during the summer, up to about the year 1862, when it closed its career. It was then the property of and driven by Mr. George Clark,* the route being *viâ* Kingston and Dorking (where the "Coach" dined), to Brighton.

In the year 1866 there was a revival of coaching to Brighton, started by Mr. Charles Lawrie, then of Mount Mascal, Bexley, Kent. Chiefly through his exertions a little yellow coach, called "The Old Times," was subscribed for in shares of £10 each, and made its appearance on the Brighton road, the Duke of Beaufort, Mr. Chandos Pole, Mr. Cherry Angell, Lord H. Thynne, and Mr. Lawrie being among the shareholders. The venture proved successful, so much so that in the following year two new coaches were built especially for the work by Holland, and, horsed by the Duke of Beaufort, Mr. Chandos Pole, and Mr. Cherry Angell, ran during the summer. Alfred Tedder and Pratt were the coachmen, and the lunching-place (where the coaches met) was "The Chequers," at Horley, an inn subsequently kept by Tedder. At the end of the season of 1867, Mr. Chandos Pole determined to carry on one coach through the winter, and with the aid of his brother, Mr. Pole-Gell, "doubled" the coach in the succeeding summer. At the close of the season some lovers of the road gave a dinner to "the Squire" (Mr. Chandos Pole) at Hatchett's, Piccadilly, after which he was presented with a silver flagon (value £50), "to commemorate his plucky behaviour and in admiration of his wonderful ability as a whip;" Tedder, at the same time, being presented with a smaller flagon (value £20), as "a token of the appreciation of his friends of his ability on 'the bench,' *i.e.*, the driving-seat." In 1869, Mr. A. G. Scott took the post of Honorary Secretary to the Brighton coach. The year proved the best the coach had known; never once having had a "clean bill" up or down. It ran for some two or three seasons after; and since that period one or more coaches have been on the road during the season, with more or less success, the pleasure as well as the novelty of a journey by coach inducing many to avail themselves of it.

---

* Mr. George Clark was the last professional coachman on the London and Brighton road. He was the son of a Suffolk yeoman, and well connected. He died, after a very long and painful illness, brought on by the entire change of his pursuits, consequent on the close of the coaching era. In his latter days, he was most generously aided by His Grace the Duke of Beaufort.

The Railway and its Growth.

MUCH as Brighton is indebted to its Railway connection, its early efforts towards securing such an important adjunct were of a very lukewarm character, approaching to indifference and seasoned by doubts. So well had the town prospered under the old system of travelling—so confident was it in its superior powers of attraction—that its inhabitants were totally unconscious of the fact, which subsequent statistics have confirmed, but which it would have been treason at one time to hint at, that the population (1831-41) was actually declining, and it was not without difficulty that they were brought to acknowledge that a Railway was really a necessity. Had it not some 40 or 50 splendid coaches, harnessed to some of the finest and fastest teams that the world could produce, and driven by incomparable whips? What more *could* be wanted? Southampton, Bath, and other places might think differently; *they* might need Railways; but Brighton could not understand that coaching was becoming *passé*, or that a Railway would do any thing but degrade and vulgarize her. So early, indeed, as January, 1825,* some people entertained a notion that a Railway between Brighton and London and other places would be advantageous to the former; and the Surrey, Sussex, Hants, Wilts, and Somerset Railway Company was projected, under most influential auspices, with Mr. John Rennie as Engineer. But it was not destined to be carried out. Though much favoured by the landowners of the district, a similar fate attended the Brighton and Shoreham Railway, projected in February of the same year. In

---

* The idea of a Railway "down South" in 1825 most probably arose from the knowledge of what was doing in the "North," where in that year the first public Railway was opened. Some particulars respecting this Railway, with other matters, as given in *Cassell's Technical Educator*, are worth quoting:—
"The 27th of September, 1825, saw the opening of the first public Railway, when, at a given signal, the engine started, at the rate of twelve miles an hour, with 450 passengers, and ninety tons of coals and merchandise, and reached Darlington, a distance of 8¾ miles, in 65 minutes. When the Manchester and Liverpool Railway was before Parliament in the same year, Stephenson, in the face of strong opposition from interested antagonists, gave much valuable information respecting the practicability and safety of trains drawn by locomotives, though, as yet, he had no idea of the speed that exceeded twenty miles an hour; but even this was so greatly doubted that one of the members of the Committee remarked, that 'the engineer who conceived such ideas was only fit for a lunatic asylum'! Opposition crushed, and legal sanction given, the Railway Company set to work, and, with a salary of £1,000 per annum, Stephenson was appointed

1826-27, Mr. Vallance brought before the public an Atmospheric Railway, by which it was said a train could be propelled 100 miles an hour and a collision rendered impossible. Some experiments which the ingenious inventor made seemed to be satisfactory; but much incredulity prevailed respecting it, and eventually it was abandoned.

In 1835, however, the Railway question began to be seriously agitated in Brighton; and a Town Committee was formed to consider the merits of various lines, viz.: Sir John Rennie's (Direct), 47 miles; Mr. Palmer's (South Eastern), 50 miles; and four Western Lines, viz., Mr. Stephenson's, 53 miles; Mr. Vignolle's, 54 miles; Mr. Cundy's, 54 miles; and Mr. Gibbs's, 51 miles to Vauxhall, 58 to London Bridge. The Direct Line of Sir John Rennie (which was to run from Kennington Common to the Hanover Cricket Ground—now Park Crescent) was first considered by the Committee; but it was put aside " by reason of insurmountable difficulties"! They had been told of gradients, cuttings, and embankments; and one portion of it —some 5½ miles—would, it was said, occupy some six or seven years in making! Mr. Stephenson's Line (with the termini of Mr. Gibbs's) was, therefore, declared first favourite; and at a town meeting, held September 22, 1835, a resolution was passed requesting the Borough Members to support its adoption in Parliament. So popular was Mr. Stephenson's Line at this period, that the shares were soon quoted at £16 premium. In the following year, however, this resolution was reversed; at all events, a great revulsion of opinion took place, owing to Mr. Stephenson's terminus being at Shoreham; and the inhabitants were more than ever impressed with the advantages of a Direct Line. A severe Parliamentary contest took place—costing upwards of £100,000, the Committee sitting 80 days*—and, after all,—Line after Line being thrown out,—it seemed that the Session of 1836 would close without any definite decision being arrived at. The town was involved in the *embarras de richesses*; but did not seem to know which Line to choose. At this point the Government stepped in, and appointed a military engineer, Captain Alderson, to report on the

---

their engineer, with instructions that the Line between Manchester and Liverpool was to be kept as straight as possible. In this great undertaking, the first novel series of engineering had to be undergone—viaducts were to be built, hills tunnelled, embankments formed from the *debris* of cuttings, and the four miles of dreary bog known as Chat Moss converted into a hard and firm way ere the Line was completed; and £500 was offered for the best locomotive that could be brought forward for competition in running by a certain day. Stephenson determined to compete; and on the 8th October, 1829, three engines were brought forward: The Rocket' by him, and two others by Hackworth and Messrs. Braithwaite and Ericson. The test assigned was to run a distance of thirty miles at not less than ten miles per hour, along a two-mile level near Rainhill, with a load thrice the weight of the engine. One locomotive was disabled by the failure of the boiler-plate; another attained fifteen miles an hour, but failed to accomplish the distance; and 'The Rocket' alone stood the test, and won the prize, attaining a maximum speed of twenty-nine miles an hour. This day was somewhat of an epoch in engineering, as coke was burned instead of coal, and coke and water were carried in a tender attached to the engine."

* Sir John Rennie was in the witness-box *seven days*; and the report of his examination filled one hundred and thirty-two pages of folio!

merits of the different Lines, and his conclusion was "That the Direct Line (Rennie's) is the best Line between London and Brighton." This Line was accordingly adopted, and on July 15, 1837, the Bill for its formation received the Royal assent.

And so Brighton took its Railway "from that day forward, for better for worse"; the first Chairman of the Company being John Harman, Esq.; and on the 12th July, 1838, ground was first broken at the deepest part of the great cutting on the north of Merstham Tunnel. The formation of the Line and the construction of works connected therewith were carried on with the utmost vigour, under the superintendence of John Urpeth Rastrick, Esq., C.E.; and, by a singular coincidence, the Railway was opened for passenger traffic to Hayward's Heath on July 12th, just three years afterwards. The first permanent rail of the London and Brighton Line was laid at Hassocks Gate on the 4th February, 1839, by Mr. Alfred Morris (the present Clerk to the Guardians), in the presence of Mr. Statham, the Resident Engineer, and Mr. George Thornton, the contractor of that portion of the Line. Meanwhile over a mile of permanent rail had been laid on the Shoreham Branch at Portslade, and other portions of the work completed,—hundreds of men working night and day. On May 27th, 1839, the foundation stone of the New England Viaduct was laid with Masonic honours, by Mr. D. M. Folkard, the W.M. of the Royal Clarence Lodge of Freemasons, the Brethren walking in procession thither from "The Old Ship," with flags, banners, and all the symbols and honours of their craft.[*] Among those present were Lord Monson, P.G.M. for Surrey; Sir A. Cromby, P.G.M. for Aberdeen; the Rev. Dr. Shepherd (wearing the gorgeous Order of a Knight Templar), Sir D. Scott, &c. Mr. Harman, Chairman of Directors, presented Mr. Folkard with a silver trowel wherewith to perform the ceremony, which was followed by three

---

[*] The inscription on the stone was as follows:—

BY THE BLESSING OF ALMIGHTY GOD, IN THE REIGN OF QUEEN VICTORIA, DANIEL MANTHORP FOLKARD, WORSHIPFUL MASTER OF THE ROYAL CLARENCE LODGE OF THE ANCIENT FRATERNITY OF FREEMASONS, LAID THIS FOUNDATION STONE OF THE VIADUCT ON THE LONDON AND BRIGHTON RAILWAY, ON THE 27TH DAY OF MAY, IN THE YEAR OF OUR LORD, 1839, AND OF THE EVE OF MASONRY, 5839, ASSISTED BY HIS BRETHREN AND THE FREEMASONS IN THE PROVINCE, AND UNDER THE AUSPICES OF THE FOLLOWING DIRECTORS OF THE LONDON AND BRIGHTON RAILWAY COMPANY:—

JOHN HARMAN, Chairman.
G. R. BEAUCLERC,
JOHN CATTLEY,
HENRY MORETON DYER,
ISAAC LYON GOLDSMID,
MOSES ASHER GOLDSMID,
JOHN GOULD,
RICHARD HEAVISIDE,
MAJOR-GENERAL HODGSON,
JOHN HODGSON,
DONALD MACLEAN,
LIEUT.-COLONEL MOODY,
JOHN MOXON,
CAPT. JOHN W. PRINGLE,
FRANCIS RICARDO,
THOMAS S. ROBINSON,
JOHN SHEWELL,
NEWMAN SMITH,
ROBERT SUTTON.

JOHN URPETH RASTRICK, Engineer.
THOMAS HENRY STATHAM, Superintendent of Works.
JOHN HALE, GEORGE WYTHES, Contractors.
MAY GOD PROSPER THE WORK.

hearty cheers from the assembled spectators; the Band of the 12th Lancers playing the National Anthem. It was computed that within and without the railed portion of the ground set apart for the ceremony, and on the surrounding eminences commanding a view of it, not less than 10,000 persons were assembled.

The first portion of the Company's system opened for traffic was that running between Brighton and Shoreham, the event taking place on Monday, May 11th, 1840. Most of the Directors were present on the occasion; and there was a very large number of spectators. No one was admitted inside the Station without a ticket; but 1,000 of these having been issued, entitling the bearer to take the trip gratuitously, there was not far short of that number who availed themselves of it. The first train started about three o'clock, amid the strains of the Lancers' Band and the cheers of the spectators, to the majority of whom the Railway train was a "new sensation." The trip occupied 11½ minutes: the return trip taking a trifle longer. The train continued running throughout the afternoon, and the scene down the whole Line was exceedingly animated, crowds of persons assembling at the different points to witness its passing. "Business" commenced next morning at eight from Shoreham, the train returning from Brighton at nine. During the day 1,750 passengers were carried, not a few visiting the Swiss Gardens, where the opening of the Railway was celebrated by a grand fête. To afford a comparison between past and present, we subjoin the Company's first advertisement:—

LONDON AND BRIGHTON RAILWAY.—THE PUBLIC are informed the SHOREHAM RAILWAY is NOW OPEN, and that the Trains of the Company will start as under until further notice:—

From BRIGHTON.	From SHOREHAM.	ON SUNDAYS.	
		From BRIGHTON.	From SHOREHAM.
9 Morning.	10 Morning.	9 Morning.	10 Morning.
11 Morning.	12 Noon.	2 Afternoon.	¼ before 3 Afternoon.
1 Afternoon.	2 Afternoon.	4 Afternoon.	¼ after 5 Afternoon.
3 Afternoon.	4 Afternoon.	6 Evening.	7 Evening.
5 Afternoon.	6 Evening.	8 Evening.	9 Evening.
7 Evening.	8 Evening.		

The Trains will stop at the Intermediate Stations to take up and set down Passengers.

THE FARES WILL BE.- The First Class Carriage, 1s.; Second ditto, 9d.; Third ditto, 6d. In the Coupé of the First Class Carriages, 1s. 4d. The Doors of the Booking Office will be closed precisely at the Hours appointed for Departure, after which no Person will be admitted to go by the Trains.

May 12th, 1840. THOS. WOOD, Secretary.

Business went along pleasantly for the remainder of the week; for day after day hundreds embraced the opportunity of a Railway ride. On the Sunday evening, however, a fatal accident occurred. A young man named Atherell, who was incautiously sitting on the tail-board of a luggage waggon, which had been temporarily used to accommodate the extra traffic at Shoreham, was at Southwick pre-

OPENING OF THE SHOREHAM BRANCH OF THE LONDON AND BRIGHTON RAILWAY. MAY, 1840.

cipitated by a sudden jerk beneath the train and killed on the spot.*

As already stated, on the 12th July, 1841, the London and Brighton Line was opened as far as Hayward's Heath—the passengers being conveyed the intermediate distance to and from Brighton by *coaches*. ("To this complexion had they come at last"!) The journey was thus accomplished in about four hours; four trains running from London and four from Hayward's Heath, daily; and two each way on Sundays. The following is the Company's advertisement:—

LONDON AND BRIGHTON RAILWAY.—Open from LONDON to HAYWARD'S HEATH; from thence PER COACH to BRIGHTON.

Daily Trains down to Brighton: Morning, ½-past 9 and ½-past 11; Afternoon, ½-past 1 and 5 o'clock. Daily Trains up to London: Morning, 7 and 9; Afternoon, ½-past 12 and ½-past 4.

Sunday Trains down to Brighton: Morning, 8; Afternoon, ½-past 5. Sunday Trains up to London: Morning, 7; Afternoon, ¼-past 5. Fares: First Class, 15s.; Second Class, 11s.; Children under ten years of age, half-price. The Train stops at all the intermediate Stations, if required, to set down or take up Passengers. As only a limited number of Passengers can be conveyed throughout from London to Brighton, places must be secured, by booking them the day previous, at the principal Booking Offices.

On the day of departure, places can be secured only at the London Bridge Station, in the event of the limited number not being full.

A daily down Train, at 9 p.m., for Croydon only, and on Sunday a down Train for Croydon only at 8, and ½-past 9 p.m.

Fares to Croydon: First Class, 2s.; Second Class, 1s. 6d.

By Order,
August 18th, 1841.　　　　　THOMAS WOOD, Secretary.

The whole Line was completed between London and Brighton by the middle of September, 1841, and, having been inspected by Sir F. Smith, the Government Inspector, to his satisfaction, there was the following "flourish of trumpets" respecting its opening in a local journal:—"The arrival of the first train, with the Directors and their friends, at noon on Tuesday (September 21st) will be hailed by a triumphal chorus from all the musical force, both vocal and instrumental, available in the town, assembled at the Brighton Terminus, under the direction of M. Oury."

The eventful day at length arrived when the Railway was to be opened; and no event probably had of late years excited so much

---

* The original third-class carriages were of the poorest description: little better than cattle trucks. They were wholly uncovered, and some had not even the accommodation of seats, the divisions of the sections in each carriage being simply an iron rail. Travelling under such circumstances was the reverse of pleasurable: the dust and smoke from the engine were annoying in the extreme; but worse than these was the almost constant descent of fine ashes! and umbrellas were in frequent requisition by passengers to prevent these getting into the eyes and to avoid the chance of a burn. Their condition when these unpleasant concomitants were associated with a high wind or a driving rain may be better imagined than described. By and by "covered carriages" were introduced, but without windows! These latter luxuries, with, in some cases, cushions, &c., are modern improvements, which were altogether unknown to the "Parliamentarians" in the earlier days of Railway travelling.

interest in the town. Old things were passing away and the inhabitants hailed the opening of the Line as the commencement of a new era. The Union Jack was hoisted at St. Nicholas, and the bells from the old tower sent forth a joyous peal. All was bustle and excitement, and numbers flocked to the Terminus to witness the departure of the first train to London ; but this and the two following trains were soon lost to view by reason of a heavy mist which prevailed in the distance. This had, however, cleared away by noon, when the great event of the day—the arrival of the first London train, with the Directors and their friends—was to take place. At this time the Terminus and all the points of vantage in the neighbourhood presented a most animated spectacle. Every road leading to the Terminus was thronged by pedestrians and vehicles. Tickets of admission having been liberally distributed, many hundreds were quickly assembled within the area of the Terminus to await the arrival of the train. Thousands were also assembled on the green slopes west of the Railway, commanding a view of the Line nearly as far as Patcham Tunnel ; and the New England-road and even the London-road (whose glories, alas ! were about to pass away) were skirted by carriages. On every brow, and in every field and meadow, from Preston to Withdean and Patcham, there was a mass of people. On the more elevated points in this direction the approach of the train was first perceived ; when, at about 12.20, a thousand cries of " Here they come" announced the fact to those from whose sight the train was yet hidden by the winding of the hills. The first indication of its coming was the cloud of steam which issued from the mouth of Patcham Tunnel, and the next moment the train was seen gliding swiftly along the Line ; and as it came along towards home, hearty salutations were given from the crowds assembled. The train having reached the Terminus, the National Anthem was played and sung whilst the Directors and their friends alighted. The bands continuing playing for half-an-hour, when the National Anthem was again sung and the company dispersed.

Not in Brighton alone, but in all the villages through which the Line passed, from Hayward's Heath, was its opening hailed with joy and festive signs. " Up to Clayton (we are told) the country poured forth its inhabitants. Hurst and Ditchling sent forth their populations, in holiday array, to meet the train at Hassocks Station ; and Patcham, Withdean, and Preston all lent their quota to make up one general sum of joy."

In the town of Brighton the after-part of the day was devoted to the same purpose. Many of the tradesmen illuminated their houses ; the prices of admission to the *Concerts d'Eté* were lowered to give a wider scope to the attraction of music ; there was a display of fireworks at the Royal Gardens, which drew together a great number of people ; but the point at which the event of the day was more particularly to be celebrated was " The Old Ship," where the Directors were invited by the town to a splendid banquet, Mr. E. H. Creasy, High Constable, presiding.

The first " DEPARTURE AND TIME-TABLE " between Brighton and

SAMUEL LAING, ESQ.,

Chairman of the London, Brighton, and South-Coast Railway Company.

London in 1841 presents a marked contrast with that of the present time, both as to the number of Trains and the various Stations. The Trains were as follows :—

BRIGHTON TO LONDON.—Mixed Train, 6.45 a.m. ; Express Train, 8.30 a.m. ; 1st Class Train, 10.45 a.m. ; Mixed Train, 11.45 a.m. ; 1st Class Train, 2.15 p.m. ; Mixed Train, 4 p.m. ; and a Mixed Train (Croydon to London), 2.45 p.m. SUNDAYS : Mixed Trains, 7.45 a.m., and 4.0 and 7.0 p.m. ; Croydon to London, 7.0 a.m.

LONDON TO BRIGHTON. - Mixed Train, 9.45 a.m. ; 1st Class Train, 10.45 a.m. ; Mixed Trains, 1.45 and 2.45 p.m. ; 1st Class Train, 3.45 p.m. ; Express Train, 4.45 p.m. ; and a Mixed Train (London and Croydon), 7.0 p.m. SUNDAYS : Mixed Trains at 8.0 and 10.45 a.m., and 7.0 p.m. London to Croydon, 10 p.m.

The Stations were :—Brighton, Hassocks Gate, Hayward's Heath, Balcombe, Three Bridges, Horley, Red Hill, Merstham, Stoat's Nest, Godstone Road, Croydon, New Cross, and London.

The time occupied by the respective Trains between London and Brighton and *vice versâ* was as follows :—Express, 1h. 45m. ; 1st Class Trains, 2h. ; Mixed Trains, 2h. 30m. The fares were—1st Class, 14s. 6d. ; 2nd Class, 9s. 6d. ; Children in 2nd Class, 6s. 6d. (No fares are given either for Express or Mixed Trains,—the latter, we suppose, being those with Parliamentary carriages attached.)

With these few brief details concerning the early history of what may now be regarded as the greatest Institution associated with Brighton, we will now proceed to give some particulars respecting it up to the close of 1879—a period of about 40 years. Closely connected as the Railway is with the town, there are probably but few who are aware of its extraordinary growth or the masterly way in which its various ramifications have been developed ; the magnitude of its capital ; the immensity of its resources ; or the marvellous amount of work which it now performs ; and fewer still of the extraordinary influence it has had upon the increase, progress, position, and character of the town. Let us see, first,—

HOW THE RAILWAY HAS GROWN.

The Railway throughout its career has been, for the most part, fortunate in its Direction, and also in having had for many years (1848-55 and 1867-80) such a Chairman as Mr. S. Laing, one of the ablest financiers of the day,* and, since 1869 (on the retirement of Mr. George Hawkins), such an efficient General Manager as Mr. J. P. Knight. The business of the Directors was not simply to develop a certain Railway scheme ; but to develop it judiciously, systematically, and profitably ; for they had to reconcile two things apparently incompatible with each other ; the interest of the public and the interest of the shareholders. But one thing was certain : a complete Railway scheme could not be carried out at once ; it had to be done bit by bit, as time and opportunity and money admitted. On the whole, the Directors appear to have worked upon a well-devised plan ; first securing their Main Line and Coast Branches and then gradually

[* Mr. S. Laing still occupies the post of Chairman of the Company, 1892.]

opening up such districts as formed points of radiation towards the ultimate development of their entire Railway system, taking London and Brighton as the two great poles of attraction. In some instances, however, the formation of branch lines was "forced" upon them by threatened competition, and this course of action, whether judicious or not, was not always profitable.

The details of the Railway development, up to 1879, embracing some 380 miles, are interesting. The first permanent rail was laid, as we have previously stated, at Hassocks Gate, February 4th, 1839; and about two and a half-years afterwards the Main Line was opened throughout its entire length (50 odd miles), the first carriage leaving Brighton for London, September 21st, 1841. The Coast Lines were next simultaneously developed. On November 24th, 1845, Worthing received its first Railway passengers (the West Line, as far as Shoreham, having been finished as early as May, 1840), and Chichester on June 8th, 1846. On the same day the first train from Brighton reached Lewes; and before the end of the same month the East Coast Line was opened to Hastings. In another twelve months (June, 1847), the West Coast Line was extended to Portsmouth, and thus the three great arteries of the London, Brighton, and South-Coast Railway system were completed. Including a branch to Epsom from Norwood, their extent was some 140 miles; the total cost of the works up to that time being about two and a half millions.

The Directors did not pause here. Between October and December, 1847, the Keymer to Lewes and Lewes to Newhaven Branches were completed and opened. By these a most important object was effected: the Port of Newhaven was brought to within 56½ miles of London, and enabled the Company to open a line of communication (by rail and boat) between London and Paris, the journey from one capital to another being then made in eleven or twelve hours! A few months later (February 14th, 1848), the line from Horsham to Three Bridges was opened. The Branches to Eastbourne and Hailsham were opened in the following year (May 14th, 1849); making a grand total of 187 miles available for traffic.

The Directors now rested on their oars, avoiding the construction of new Lines until they could ascertain the results of their previous labours; but devoting, in the meanwhile, a large amount of capital to the improvement of their existing plant, including stations, wharves, &c., and doing their utmost to develop the passenger and goods traffic of the various Lines. During this interval of rest (1848-54) the traffic, as well as the general business of the Company, uniformly increased. The passenger traffic rose from 2½ to 6½ millions; the value of the goods traffic from £61,000 to £150,000; the gross revenue from £453,000 to £715,000; the dividend on the capital from £3 12s. per cent. to £5 10s.; and the £50 shares from £25, or half their nominal value, to above par.

During the next eleven years (1849-60) the Directors chiefly turned their attention to the construction of Lines connected with the Crystal Palace and the West End of London. The extensions

THE CHALK HILL (formerly near New England Road)—about 1860.

Taken from the top of Shoreham Railway Tunnel.

from the Palace reached Battersea in March, 1858, and in October, 1860, they were completed (across the Thames) to the Grosvenor Basin, Victoria-street, at which point the Company's West-End Terminus is situated. These Lines were most important adjuncts to the Company's system; and their advantage also to Brighton could hardly be over-estimated: Belgravia, Westminster, and the adjacent districts,—places from which Brighton receives so many first-class visitors,—being brought by their aid to within an hour and a half's ride of it.

But whilst the Main Line was thus improved and extended, the rural districts were not neglected. The East Grinstead Branch was completed and opened in July, 1855; that of Uckfield in October, 1858; and in October, 1859, the Horsham Line was extended to Petworth. In July, 1861, the Mid-Sussex Line was opened to Partridge Green, and in the following September throughout to Horsham, opening up the beautiful and fertile districts of West Sussex.

Though the Company had had to fight a battle (with the West Sussex Landowners) in the preceding interval, its tide of success still rolled onwards. The passenger traffic (in 1861) had increased by millions, and the gross revenue by hundreds of thousands; the dividend on the capital had increased to £6 per cent. per annum, and the shares had risen to 116.

After 1861 various additions were made to the Lines, &c., at the London end of the Main Line. The most important of these was, probably, the Company's participation in the West London Extension Line between Clapham Junction and Kensington, which was opened for traffic on 1st March, 1863. This Line is the joint property of the Brighton and other Companies, and is the connecting link of several Lines, so that a passenger may, if necessary, proceed from any Station on the London and Brighton and South-Coast Lines to any station on the North London, Metropolitan, London and North Western, Great Western, and London and South Western Lines.

On August 3, 1863, the Line from Pulborough to Ford was opened, and, a fortnight after, from Ford to Littlehampton. By the opening of this Line, the Company secured, in connection with Littlehampton Harbour, an improved route for the traffic of the Channel Islands, and opened up a considerable traffic between that Harbour and Honfleur, and the coast of Normandy, to which it is the nearest port. Bognor received its first visitors by Railway on the 1st June, 1864; and on the same day was opened the Branch from Newhaven to Seaford.

From 1864 down to 1879 great strides were made in the development of the Company's Lines. In May, 1865, the section from Sutton to Epsom Downs was opened, a length of a little more than four miles, but millions of passengers have been conveyed over it to the famous "Derby" and "Oaks" Races; and in the same month the West Croydon and Selhurst "spur," a connecting and short link from West Croydon to Victoria, was used for the first time. In August, 1866, a portion of the South London Line was used for traffic, viz., from London Bridge to Brixton, the remaining portion being completed by May, 1867, to Battersea Park, thus forming a new, short, and attractive *route* between London Bridge and Victoria. This section of the Company's system is enormously patronised, trains running to and fro nearly every five minutes. A number of so-called "spurs," to facilitate traffic, and shorten or supply duplicate routes, were soon afterwards completed, making perfect a network of Railways without parallel, perhaps, in the country. In 1867-68 the new Mid-Sussex route, *viâ* Dorking to Portsmouth, was opened, obtaining for the Brighton Company a share of the Portsmouth and Isle of Wight traffic. The first portion of the East London Line was opened in December, 1869, and in April, 1876, the remaining piece, from Wapping to Liverpool-street, the latter enabling the Brighton Company to participate in the City traffic; and when this is connected with "The Metropolitan," it will render the suburban system of the Company complete from East to West. Besides the above and other important additions to the Company's Lines, enormous sums have recently been spent upon the enlargement and improvement of stations. Within the last two years (1878-79) London Bridge Station has had nearly £100,000 spent upon it, in the extension of platforms and re-arrangement of the "yard."* The Crystal Palace, East Croydon, Clapham Junction, New Cross, West Croydon, Burgess Hill, Portsmouth, Horsham, and many other stations have been added to, and greater facilities afforded them for carrying on the traffic. On the 5th of April, 1880, a portion of the new Tunbridge Wells and Eastbourne Line was opened, viz., from Hailsham to Heathfield, and the remainder, between Heathfield and Groombridge, is now (June, 1880) nearly finished. This section of the system opens up a new *route* from Kent and East Sussex to the South-Coast. The Midhurst and Chichester Line is now in the hands of the contractors; and when this is completed, Sussex and a great portion of Surrey would appear to be wholly radiated by the London, Brighton, and South-Coast Railway.

On a review of what has been done in connection with the Railway generally from its commencement, neither the Directors, nor the Shareholders, nor the public have probably much reason to be dissatisfied, either with the extent of mileage opened up for traffic or for general pecuniary results connected with its transactions.

Up to December, 1879, the whole of the Company's Lines available for traffic extended to some 380 odd miles. [Since this latter date, down to December 31st, 1891, the Company's system has been

---

* The traffic at London Bridge (says *The Builder*) has been greatly facilitated by the recent complete and costly re-arrangement of the whole of the points and signals by Messrs. Saxby and Farmer. One "cabin" contains 280 levers, and another, worked, in connection with it, has 90 levers. The object of these important changes is to give more expansive and elastic use to the platforms, especially in relation to the passenger traffic inwards by the morning, forenoon, and express trains. In addition to a new platform at the London Bridge Station, a block of buildings has been erected in front of the Station for the accommodation of the Engineering Staff and other Officers of the Company. At the outer end of the "yard," as it is called technically, appliances and accommodation of the best description have been provided for the Company's service in an immense water-tank, pumping-engine, turn-tables, guards' rooms, lamp rooms, &c. The working of the Station as remodelled is all, or almost all, that can be desired.

Year	Line	Date		Mileage		
	East London Line and S.E. Branch	26th May, 1865	...	...	1	8
1870	Eastbourne Spur	1st August, 1870	—	8		
	Portsmouth Harbour Extension	7th July, 1873	1	5		
1873	Hailsham to Heathfield	5th August, 1873	7	74	18	47
	Heathfield to Eridge		9	48		
1875	Cliftonville Spur	29th June, 1875	1	34	1	34
1876	Chichester to Midhurst	13th July, 1876	11	76	11	76
	Ryde Pier Railway	23rd July, 1877	1	18		
1877	Barcombe Junc. to East Grinstead	10th August, 1877	17	13	26	54
	Horsted Keynes to Hayward's Heath	2nd August, 1877	4	55		
	Dyke Railway		3	48		
	S. Croydon to E. Grinstead L.L.	17th June, 1878	18	70		
1878	Spur to E. Grinstead, High Level	17th June, 1878	—	55	20	64
	Ditto Edenbridge, S.E.R.	17th June, 1878	—	27		
	Ditto Eridge	17th June, 1878	—	72		
1879	§Polegate Junction, No. 1	3rd May, 1879	—	46	1	1
	Ditto ditto No. 2		—	35		
	Selsdon Road to Woodside	6th August, 1880	—	33		
1880	Fratton to Southsea	28th August, 1880	2	29	4	61
	‡Littlehampton Direct Railway		1	79		
1881	Oxted to Edenbridge	11th August, 1881	4	14	12	26
	Edenbridge to Groombridge		8	12		
1884	¶Lewes deviation	3rd July, 1884		79	—	79
				Total	481	17
				31		
* Deduct Old Line via Keymer Line, closed on opening of Lewes and Uckfield Junction		2	13			
+ Ditto ditto Shoreditch Junction to Liverpool Street, &c., not included in Lease		—	42			
§ Ditto closed on opening of Polegate New Junction, No. 1		—	3			
†† Ditto closed on opening of Direct Line		1	30	4	39	
¶ Ditto closed on opening of Lewes deviation						
				Total	476	58

†† Authorised by Chatham and Dover Co.'s (New Lines) Act, 1884.
‡‡ Closed 1st December, 1871; Re-opened 1st June, 1886; Closed again 1st September, 1890.

extended nearly another 100 miles, making a grand total of 4763¼ miles. Among the more important extensions have been the lines from Chichester to Midhurst, from Barcombe Junction to East Grinstead, from Horsted Keynes to Hayward's Heath, from South Croydon to East Grinstead, the Dyke Railway, from Oxted to Edenbridge, and from Edenbridge to Groombridge, opening up accommodation and facilities for inter-communication to districts which are not only much appreciated, but confer advantages that cannot be too highly estimated. The *annexed table*, specially compiled by Mr. H. Humphriss, the Assistant General Manager, shows the Company's entire system of Lines up to December, 1891.]

It may be stated that there were in 1879 six Stations for Brighton, viz., Brighton Central Station, London-road Station, Lewes-road Station, Kemp Town Station, Hove Station, and West Brighton Station. The traffic at these Stations is continually on the increase, particularly at those on the extreme east and west. The growth of the goods traffic at Kemp Town is extraordinary, particularly in coal, which is being diverted somewhat from the Trafalgar-street depôt; and there is every probability of the Kemp Town Station becoming an extensive goods depôt. Very large additions have been recently made to the West Brighton (formerly Cliftonville) Station; and since it has become an important junction with the main London Line at Preston Park, the traffic, both goods and passenger, has greatly increased. Not long since a few straggling passengers might be seen leaving West Brighton Station, making their way by newly-formed roads or through the fields to their homes in the sparse neighbourhood; now, every train discharges its long stream of passengers to a largely populated district. The alterations and improvements at this Station have cost the Company several thousands of pounds; but they are as yet incomplete, the frontage and other improvements being in hand. At the Hove Station the goods yard has been much enlarged to meet the daily increasing requirements of the West End.

Preston Park Station, which is now much used, has been so metamorphosed of late to adapt it to the requirements of the West Brighton Junction, that it bears now [1892] no resemblance whatever to the original Station.

The Brighton Central Station has also undergone many changes. New and commodious platforms have been constructed, and the whole interior re-arranged, both as regards passenger acommodation and alterations of lines. Thousands of pounds have been spent in improvements in the Locomotive and Carriage Departments, and new and handsome workshops are now in the course of construction. The head-quarters of the Stores Department have been removed to New Cross. In the Goods Department the traffic has been so much developed that new ground has been scheduled for an enlargement of the yard, which for a long time past seems to have been unable to stand the pressure put upon its space; but when these enlargements are completed they cannot fail to prove of much advantage to the trading community and to the town generally.

It may be added that, to facilitate the issue of tickets to passengers, not only for their own Lines but for other important Lines running from London to all parts of the country, for enquiries, &c., the Company have opened a fine office on the Old-steine (originally Donaldson's Library, at the corner of St. James's-street), which is also a telegraph station; there is also another Local Office at the old Red Coach Office in Castle-square; and there is a Brighton West End office at 73, Western-road, Hove.

THE CAPITAL OF THE COMPANY; THE RECEIPTS AND EXPENDITURE; ITS RESOURCES, &c.

An important feature in the Reports of the Railway Company is the capital account. In 1841 the capital of the Company was about £2,250,000; in 1851 it had been more than trebled, standing at £7,111,267; in 1861 it reached £10,167,786; in 1868, £20,246,666 13s. 4d.; and at the end of 1879 it amounted to £22,620,432. [In December, 1891, the total was £24,293,168 17s. 10d.] It may be regarded as a high compliment to the business qualifications of the Directors that such vast sums should be raised with the facility they were. Yet some of the amounts expended almost make one shudder at the enormous responsibility they entailed. At the outset—before a penny could be realised in return, and with the future in a state of uncertainty—the cost of works, up to December, 1841, amounted to £2,269,359. Then the cost of the Lines in Sussex averaged something like £16,400 per mile; and a few such miles "eat into money." Between 1858 and 1863 there was expended on the Lines and Stations north of Epsom no less than £3,071,475; and in the last six months of 1863 various Lines and Stations cost £550,000, upwards of £355,000 of which was absorbed by the South London Line and London Bridge Station alone!

But without entering into minor details, we will give the particulars of the general expenditure of the capital account of the Company up to December 31st, 1879, also that to December 31st, 1891:—

	Dec. 31st, 1879.	Dec. 31st, 1891.
On Lines and Works open for Traffic...	£17,053,840 15 4	£21,357,426 18 10
On Lines in progress	800,397 7 9	
On Lines abandoned under the Company's Act, 1868	217,349 0 2	216,400 4 7
On Surrey and Sussex Junction Lines	469,191 5 7	
On West Sussex Junction Line...	10,361 7 4	10,361 7 4
On Working Stock, Machinery, and Tools	1,838,592 11 6	2,553,672 1 9
On Steamboats and Dredgers ...	112,701 11 7	155,308 5 4
Total	£20,502,433 19 3	
Discount, less premium, on Stocks and Shares	572,951 16 11	
Capital unexpended...	1,545,046 17 2	
Total authorised Capital	£22,620,432 13 4	£24,293,168 17 10

Yet, enormous as these amounts are, there is strong testimony afforded to the admirable management of the Company in its Revenue returns. These returns exhibit a most extraordinary development, which, for years past, has known no decrease. In 1848, the Revenue of the Company amounted to £453,408; in 1862,

£1,025,000; in 1869, £1,266,660; and in 1879, £1,924,237. [In 1891 it reached to £2,496,705.] The amounts for 1879 and 1891 were made up as follows:—

	1879.	1891.
1st, 2nd, and 3rd Class Tickets	£1,130,360 0 0	£1,455,312 0 0
Amount of Season Tickets	145,915 0 0	220,424 0 0
Parcels, Mails, Horses, Carriages, &c.	95,487 0 0	151,047 0 0
Merchandise, Live Stock, Minerals, &c. (less Cartage Expenses)	511,688 0 0	625,574 0 0
Rental of Property (net)	37,830 0 0	46,230 0 0
Steamboats (net), Transfer Fees, &c. ...	2,957 0 0	2,882 0 0
	£1,924,237 0 0	£2,496,705 0 0

Such enormous "current receipts," of course, entailed enormous "current expenditure." The grand total of this latter in 1879 was £865,660; and some of the items are interesting:—Thus £239,417 is set down to "Locomotive Power"; and to obtain this said Locomotive Power something like £45.000 was expended for coal and coke, and about £3,500 for water! Then the "Maintenance of Way" cost £132,704; the Carriage and Waggon Department £65,092; the Traffic Charges, £263,508; General Charges, £36,883. But, as might be supposed, the greater proportion of all these sums goes for two unnamed items—wages and salaries; the staff of officers and employés generally numbering nearly 10,000. [On the 31st December, 1891, the total staff of the Company was 10,949.] And, then, for taxation! In this respect the Company cannot be said to come off lightly, as there was paid in 1879 for rates and taxes £62,359, exclusive of the Government Duty, amounting to £45,198. Some £8,388 went for law and Parliamentary charges; and that undesirable item, "Compensation," absorbed £15,189.*

But, with this great expenditure, there is associated the satisfaction of knowing that every penny appears to have been judiciously spent; the working expenses of the Company last year [1879] in comparison with the earnings being less than in any previous year, amounting only to 45 per cent. of the revenue, or 2s 6¼d. per mile run by the trains. The returns, in fact, of the eleven years up to 1879 exhibit an almost uniform progression; and the credit of achieving such gratifying results is undoubtedly due to the persistent efforts of Mr. S. Laing, the Chairman, and the Directors; and to the indefatigable General Manager, Mr. J. P. Knight,† who have been worthily supported by the executive Staff generally. In 1867 not a farthing dividend was paid to the Shareholders of the Company, the shares being quoted as low as

---

[* The "current expenditure" for the year 1891 was £2,006,259. The more important items were—Locomotive and Carriage and Waggon Charges, £460,284; Coal and Coke, £79,211 5s. 2d,; Water, £5,796 10s. 6d.; Maintenance of Way, £187,811; Traffic Charges, £240,933; General Charges, £40,575. Rates and Taxes, £100,653; Government Duty, £25,194; Law and Parliamentary Charges, £9,685; and Compensation, £28,439.]

[† Shortly after Mr. Knight's death (July 23, 1886) the duties of General Manager were undertaken by Mr. Allen Sarle, Secretary to the Company, who, at the unanimous request of the Directors, and in acknowledgment of his exceptional abilities, holds the two offices in combination. How well this high compliment was deserved has been abundantly shown by the fact that under his able régime the progress of the Company's business has known "no retiring ebb," whilst his

46½; in 1868 the dividend was 12s. 6d.; and in 1869 only 10s. In 1872 the dividend rose to £3 2s. 6d.; and in 1879 to £6; the shares being quoted at 136. These matters will, however, be more clearly seen by the following details, which extend from 1869 to 1891 (inclusive):—

Year.	Miles Open.	Miles Run. Passenger Trains.	Miles Run. Goods Trains.	Receipts. £	Expenses. £	Working Expenses. Per Cent. Revenue.	Working Expenses. Per Train Mile.	Price of Shares. December.	Dividend. Per Cent. per Ann.
1869 ...	367	3,512,335	699,172	1,266,660	670,186	53	3 2	46⅞	0 10 0
1870 ...	368¾	3,777,438	731,744	1,283,765	655,766	51	2 10¾	41½	0 15 0
1871 ...	371	3,950,902	812,115	1,382,153	646,861	46 4-5ths.	2 8½	74⅝	2 10 0
1872 ...	376¼	4,294,533	889,035	1,479,945	703,431	47½	2 8½	78¾	3 2 6
1873 ...	376¼	4,374,154	935,724	1,583,376	797,366	50 2-5ths.	3 0	89½	3 5 0
1874 ...	376¼	4,517,127	954,854	1,641,767	801,005	49	2 11	93	4 0 0
1875 ...	376¼	4,768,145	1,060,633	1,736,868	817,814	47	2 9½	118⅝	5 0 0
1876 ...	379¾	5,076,910	1,046,617	1,763,869	823,634	46¾	2 8¼	119¾	5 0 0
1877 ..	379¾	5,352,080	1,112,569	1,836,146	847,258	46 1-7th.	2 7½	126½	5 12 6
1878 ...	379¾	5,680,843	1,186,761	1,943,788	901,565	46 2-5ths.	2 7½	130	6 5 0
1879 ...	380¼	5,647,299	1,212,925	1,924,237	865,660	45	2 6¼	136	6 0 0
1880 ..	395¼	5,945,504	1,283,895	2,031,097	899,485	44⅓	2 6	145	6 10 0
1881 ...	407¼	6,249,473	1,355,829	2,086,100	963,745	46 1-5th.	2 6½	142	5 15 0
1882 ...	422	6,453,272	1,371,441	2,099,289	1,041,548	49 3-5ths.	2 8	121	4 7 6
1883 ...	433	6,521,451	1,427,306	2,135,011	1,052,472	49 3-10ths.	2 7¾	135	4 10 0
1884 ...	455	6,703,422	1,432,655	2,146,519	1,047,383	48¾	2 7	120	4 10 0
1885 ...	457	6,725,164	1,411,797	2,089,990	989,883	47⅓	2 5	117	4 7 6
1886 ...	459	6,521,618	1,400,477	2,127,975	970,553	45 3-5ths.	2 5½	133	5 2 6
1887 ...	461	6,702,903	1,412,233	2,171,936	981,874	45 1-5th.	2 5	136	5 10 0
1888 ...	471½	6,995,607	1,433,042	2,213,335	1,002,101	45¼	2 4½	144	5 12 6
1889 ...	476	7,383,046	1,466,215	2,382,209	1,061,189	44½	2 4¾	161	7 2 6
1890 ...	476¾	7,516,269	1,505,808	2,458,220	1,142,034	46 2-5ths.	2 6¼	162	7 0 0
1891 ...	476¾	7,607,008	1,570,865	2,495,705	1,212,150	48 3-5ths.	2 7¾	157	6 10 0

unvarying courtesy in dealing with matters generally in connection with his official duties has secured for him a marked esteem in every district where the Company's system penetrates. Mr. H. Humphriss, who had been for many years in the Traffic Department, is Assistant General Manager, and a more able and worthy coadjutor could not well be desired.]

To many it may probably be a source of wonder how the enormous traffic of the Line is so successfully accomplished. But look at the "Locomotive Stock" of the Company. This, on December, 1879, consisted of no less than 331 engines and 202 tenders! (the cost of construction of these alone must have amounted to nearly a million sterling). Then, its "Carriage and Waggon Stock" is almost incredible in quantity, There are in all 2,140 carriages, the 1st class numbering 483; the 1st coupé, 9; composite, 201; 2nd class, 334; 3rd class, 643; carriage trucks, 135; luggage vans, 192; horse boxes, 138; invalid carriages, 2; mail vans, 3; 6,034 goods and other waggons, trucks, &c.; 329 ballast waggons; 232 highway vehicles, and 324 horses.* With such resources, the Line would seem to be equal to almost any demand upon it. Its working powers, however, were abundantly demonstrated on Easter Monday, 1880, when, on the occasion of the Volunteer Review at Brighton, upwards of 21,000 Volunteers, with a very large number of horses, besides the general public and a heavy traffic incidental to Bank Holiday, were conveyed to Brighton and back without a single accident. [Another remarkable example of the efficiency of the working powers of the Company was afforded on the August Bank Holiday of 1888, when no less than 19,577 excursionists were booked and conveyed to Brighton, namely,—From London Bridge, 11,653; Victoria, 4,218; other Stations, 3,706. Although the numbers conveyed fall a little below those of the Easter Monday Volunteer Review of 1880, in point of hard work the August Bank Holiday of 1888 was certainly the most difficult the Company has ever had to contend with.]

But let us look a little further into the details of

THE PASSENGER TRAFFIC RETURNS.

These Returns, from the commencement, present an almost unvarying increase; the number of passengers daily, weekly, and yearly conveyed from one point to another being almost incredible. The total number conveyed in the year 1848, when the main arteries of the London, Brighton, and South Coast Railway may be said to have been completed, was about 2½ millions; in three years (to 1851) this had increased to upwards of 3½ millions; in the next three years (to 1854) to nearly 6½ millions; the increase alone between 1853 and 1854 amounting to no less than 1,847,972—upwards of three-fourths of the entire traffic of 1848, only six years previous. And so the increase went on, at a most rapid rate (during several years increasing upwards of one million per year), till, at the close of 1863, the grand total of passengers during that year reached the enormous number of 12,574,003. In another decade, in 1873, this number had nearly doubled, the numbers being 23,280,032. In 1876, the total was

[* The Locomotive Stock of the Company in December, 1891, included 410 engines; 382 first class carriages; two first coupé; 19 first bogie; 364 composite; 351 second class; 1,066 third class; 112 carriage trucks; 300 luggage and brake vans; 213 horse boxes; five invalid carriages; three mail vans; 7,248 goods and other waggons and trucks; 432 ballast waggons; 283 highway vehicles; and 366 horses.]

28,923,106; and in 1879, 32,525,341. [In 1891 it was 44,787,384.] We give in their entirety the

RETURNS OF PASSENGER TRAFFIC from 1848 to 1891 inclusive (exclusive of Annual and Season Ticket Holders).

Year.	1st Class.	2nd Class.	3rd Class.	Total.
1848	669,106	1,159,879	886,793	2,685,778
1849	544,998	1,554,716	1,159,316	2,658,989
1850	522,802	997,642	1,318,375	2,838,949
1851	651,121	1,225,789	1,736,977	3,613,887
1852	825,759	1,242,222	1,657,412	3,725,273
1853	753,684	1,321,841	2,436,106	4,491,361
1854	1,147,647	1,719,146	3,481,880	6,339,533
1855	1,215,799	1,764,383	3,368,466	6,348,938
1856	1,287,442	1,887,284	3,868,470	6,811,904
1857	1,328,763	2,114,631	3,848,743	7,241,077
1858	1,271,184	2,174,856	4,078,558	7,424,688
1859	1,254,734	2,119,744	4,874,277	8,395,615
1860	1,339,492	2,457,576	5,748,225	9,545,103
1861	1,645,072	2,768,846	6,432,717	10,786,655
1862	1,906,631	2,787,849	7,594,782	12,288,302
1863	1,841,810	2,658,787	8,072,316	12,574,003
1864	1,909,149	2,825,627	8,731,040	13,765,816
1865	2,162,455	2,872,788	9,645,630	14,669,873
1866	2,307,613	2,951,888	11,462,344	16,721,845
1867	2,222,019	3,147,888	12,272,882	17,659,589
1868	2,018,470	3,001,791	12,500,125	17,519,386
1869	1,702,013	2,668,563	12,140,855	16,560,431
1870	1,893,462	2,841,741	14,655,240	19,370,443
1871	2,079,514	2,678,321	16,820,136	21,577,971
1872	2,166,328	3,047,849	17,769,827	22,783,654
1873	2,209,968	2,840,874	18,179,190	23,230,032
1874	2,299,336	2,872,168	19,430,415	24,571,919
1875	2,355,005	2,841,963	20,274,878	25,411,786
1876	2,307,316	3,081,984	23,533,786	28,923,106
1877	2,300,617	2,854,481	22,483,933	28,799,011
1878	2,224,277	3,012,733	24,441,425	30,678,435
1879	2,140,925	3,023,487	26,790,919	32,525,341
1880	2,064,793	3,097,458	30,880,188	36,042,435
1881	2,116,000	3,883,511	22,388,045	28,379,525
1882	2,050,318	3,846,232	33,921,791	39,871,341
1883	2,008,921	3,567,554	35,519,532	41,286,007
1884	1,953,873	3,674,103	35,022,874	40,600,750
1885	1,709,989	3,625,469	35,257,306	40,692,764
1886	1,679,313	3,222,464	32,438,083	37,337,870
1887	1,715,757	3,382,777	33,439,702	38,538,236
1888	1,576,339	2,865,345	34,475,314	38,917,198
1889	1,661,381	2,873,915	36,144,487	40,679,783
1890	1,663,822	2,815,060	39,020,766	43,499,648
1891	1,764,516	3,268,737	39,754,111	44,787,364

Another interesting feature in connection with the Traffic of the Railway is the number of miles run by the trains; and the distance traversed during a single year is equally as extraordinary as the enormous number of passengers carried. In 1848 the number of ... run by trains was 1,119,308—about 48 times the circumference ... globe; in 1850, the number was 1,276,430½—the trains thus ...ishing a distance equal to the earth's circumference every week! In 1851 the miles ran exceeded 1½ millions—equal to a double journey to the moon and back, in addition to the diameter of her orbit. In 1855, the mileage exceeded two millions; and in 1860 it had reached 2,627,939—a distance almost equal to a journey round the sun! and in 1863 the miles ran amounted to no less than 3,381,082—or, daily, three-fourths of the distance between Brighton and Sydney (Australia). In the next 10 years, in 1873, the mileage had increased to 5,309,878; and in 1879, to 6,860,224. [In 1891 it amounted to 9,177,873.]

Let us now see

WHAT BRIGHTON OWES TO RAILWAY ACCOMMODATION.

There is no question that the pre-Railway decade (1831-41) was a trying one for Brighton. A crisis had come in the fortunes of the town. There was to be an ebb or a flow. It had risen to the extreme height of prosperity which one system of travelling—that of coaches—would allow; and if no improved mode of locomotion could be introduced, the channel of public favour would be turned elsewhere, and Brighton would become a modern Venice.

And yet the people of Brighton had for years hesitated, hemm'd and ha'd, and shook their heads wisely and doubtingly about a Railway. They had enjoyed so much prosperity under the stage-coach *régime* that they had not the heart to exchange it for another! They attributed the dullness of their town to other causes—to want of Royal favour—to badness of times—to over-building—to anything but the real cause, and that was, that people would not consume four or five hours in coming to Brighton when they could go with ease and in any number to other watering places in half or in quarter that time.

To show that this absence of Railway accommodation was one great reason for the decline of Brighton, both as a fashionable watering place and in a material point of view, we have only to compare its pre-Railway condition with its post-Railway condition, to compare the ten years from 1831 to 1841 with any succeeding ten years up to 1879 [and later on]. The mass of evidence in favour of its post-Railway era is overwhelming. After the year 1841—the year in which the Main Line from Brighton to London was opened throughout—Brighton experienced a very remarkable course of prosperity. The population increased with rapid strides; in fact, the population in 1863, some 20 odd years after, was nearly double that of 1839, the year previous to the opening of the Railway. The town itself had in 1863 extended in every available direction, and, instead of being "overbuilt," the better class of small property was at a premium, and no house of that description could be obtained near the centre of the town "for love or money."

As the aspect and condition of Brighton before and after the formation of the Railway offer many interesting points of comparison, we are tempted to enter into a few details respecting them.

The growth of Brighton, so far as streets and houses are concerned, has been since 1840 more extensive and rapid than is, perhaps, generally supposed. Growing up under our eyes,—a new street or erection appearing here and there, a bit of waste land being taken in, or a garden or field disappearing,—we do not, from seeing these things in detail, comprehend this extraordinary growth in the aggregate. In 1840 there were numerous gaps and openings in the line of houses forming the Marine-parade; Kemp Town was in the "Far East," and entirely disconnected from Brighton. To the westward, the sea frontage was somewhat more connected; but immediately behind it —from the Western-road looking northward—all was comparatively blank. To the north-eastward, again, and, indeed, far to the northward, there was many a broad acre "streetless, houseless."

In 1879 the centre of the town shows no very marked changes; but in all the other directions there has been an extraordinary growth of "bricks and mortar" during the past 30 or 40 years. Nowhere has the land been more rapidly absorbed by the formation of streets and building operations than in contiguity to the Railway. From Trafalgar-street to New England, in the whole slope between the London-road and the long brow of the hill on which are now the Railway Terminus and Workshops, there were not in 1840 half-a-dozen streets, and some of these were nameless. At present there are nearly fifty streets, closely lined with houses, and thickly inhabited by a thriving and industrious population, a large proportion of whom, probably, derive their subsistence from the Railway.

To the west and north-west of the Terminus, the growth of dwelling-houses has been even greater. Taking old St. Nicholas as a stand-point, and looking westward along what is now called Upper North-street to Montpellier-road, and then northward from Mount Sion-place and along the brow now occupied by the Railway and its Works to New England,—Montpelier-road forming the arc from point to point,—there was not in 1840 in all this vast area a dozen houses, save the old Workhouse (in the Dyke-road), and those of Vine-place (immediately opposite). In 1879, independently of the space absorbed by the Railway itself, this area is intersected by streets in every direction—nearly fifty in number—the houses in which are mostly of a good class and among the best paying property in the town.

To show how rapidly some portions of this area were covered, we will take the space between Vine-place and Upper North-street. This in 1838-39 consisted of two fields—Butcher Russell's—famous for pugilism and cricket. Within a quarter of a century after these fields were occupied by Clifton-place, and Clifton-terrace with its newly-formed enclosure, this latter bounded on the south by a spacious Cemetery—long since disused!

Speaking of cricket, it may be stated that, between 1830 and 1840 Trafalgar-street could boast of a cricket-field—Shoosmith's— who kept "The Union" Inn, Glo'ster-lane, from the front of which Inn the field ran to Trafalgar-street. At that time, also, Trafalgar-street had little else on each side but gardens, enclosed by elder hedge-rows, and only six streets ran from it.* Trafalgar-street can now boast of 20 streets; whilst its hedge-rows have long since been superseded by houses.

Another street-formation exclusively due to the Railway is the Queen's-road. Previous to the erection of the Terminus, there was no direct road northward from Air-street (now the southern portion of Queen's-road): Windsor-terrace, which led from it (on the opposite side of Church-street) being closed by the Hanover (now Presbyterian) Chapel garden. The opening of the Queen's-road, from the Quadrant to the Terminus, was, therefore, not only a great public improvement, but it served to uproot those abominations at the top of North-street, known as "Petty France" and "Durham," and to purify a tainted atmosphere caused by the slaughter-houses and knacker's yard at their rear.

The Queen's-road also conferred another advantage on the town by opening a new route for traffic from the north to the west,—a fact to which the great rise in the value of Western-road property may be mainly attributed. Prior to the formation of the Railway, business in the Western-road was *nil*. The North-street end was known as Regent's-place; its southern side being formed by the houses of Grenville-place and Clarence-place, which houses may be said to have literally "turned their backs" upon it. Old Jones, the pyrotechnist (who lived at the North-street corner of Grenville-place), had, indeed, a shop window of about 4ft. square looking into the Western-road; but there was little else beyond, in the way of business, till what was then known as Western-place (running from Clarence-gardens to Preston-street) was reached. At the present time, Western-road presents a very different aspect, and may be regarded as one of the leading business thoroughfares of the town.

Between 1831-41, there were but 437 houses erected in Brighton, giving an increase in rateable value of £24,427. In the succeeding 10 years (1841-51), when the Railway had given an impulse to building, and also to other trades, there were erected no less than 2,806 houses, about six times as many as in the preceding 10 years; in the next 10 years (1851-61), the increase in the number of houses was 2,396, increasing the rateable value of the town £62,363. Brighton in 1861 possessed a total of 13,339 houses; so that, in the 20 odd years after the opening of the Railway, the number of houses had increased by 5,202, and the rateable property of the town by £111,199. In 1879, the total number of houses in Brighton was 15,809; with a rateable value of £528,899. [In 1891, the number of houses had increased to 19,992, and the rateable value to £627,940 15s.]

Among other advantages which Brighton owes to the Railway is the employment it affords to a large number of persons: larger, probably, than is generally supposed. In the Coaching Department in Brighton there are 229 persons employed; in the Engineers', 110; in

---

* There were one or two better class houses at the bottom of the street, as Mr. Carter's and Mr. D. P. Hack's; higher up (at Frederick-place) were Mr. Ross's villa and the residence of Lady Hamilton; but at the top Hudson's black mill "towered in its pride of place" over the corn fields in its vicinity.

the Goods and Stores, 200; and in the Locomotive and Carriage, 1,738; making up a grand total of 2,277.* Now, if we put the salaries, &c., received by these persons at the average of 25s. weekly, it would amount to nearly £3,000 per week, or £150,000 per annum. It would not be unfair, perhaps, to assume that at least three-fourths of this sum is disbursed in the shape of food, clothing, rent, &c., which, of course, must materially benefit, directly or indirectly, the trading community of the town. Then the sums which have been expended on the works connected with the Brighton Stations, the Locomotive and other works, during the last 40 years or so, have been up to 1879 little short of £500,000 [up to 1891 this expenditure had amounted to £750,000], the major portion of which has, doubtless, been spent in the town.

It is needless, perhaps, to point out the advantages to Brighton arising from the current traffic of the Line; but in 1861 the passengers to and from Brighton (exclusive of season ticket holders) amounted to 1,689,358—upwards of one million and a half! and in 1879 it was probably little short of 5,000,000. [For the year ending June 30th, 1891, the actual numbers were 4,623,366.] Then the excursionists to Brighton average each season, we believe, over 500,000. [For 1891 they exceeded 700,000.] Supposing then that each passenger and excursionist spent during his visit to the town only a shilling or two, the total would amount to no inconsiderable sum.

Again, the Goods' traffic of the Line, by the facility which it affords for the conveyance of merchandise of every description, must act advantageously to the local consumer. The amount of stock alone which is brought into Brighton yearly by the Railway is enormous. In 1879 this included 11,000 beasts; 3,663 calves; 70,211 sheep; and 5,442 pigs—total, 90,316.† We need now no longer ask—

" Upon what *meats* does this our Brighton feed,
That it has grown so great!"

With these facts we will close our notice of "THE RAILWAY AND ITS GROWTH."

[* In 1891 these numbers were—Coaching and Goods Department, 513; Engineers', 215; Stores, 25; Locomotive and Carriage, 1898; making up a total of 2,651. Putting the salaries and wages at an average of 25s. each person weekly, it would amount to upwards of £174,000 per annum.]

[† For the year ending December 31st, 1891, the numbers were—Cattle, calves, 3,449; sheep, 59,840; pigs, 8,983; the total being 82,234.]

The Post Office.

THERE is, probably, no local public institution in Brighton wherein the Past and Present are more forcibly contrasted than the Post Office. The changes it has undergone have been so numerous—the alterations in the mode of conveying letters to a distance, Railways superseding post-horses, carts, &c., and thereby facilitating despatch—the substitution of a cheap and uniform rate of charge, irrespective of distance, in the place of the old and inconvenient, uncertain, and manifestly unequal rate—have so completely revolutionized postal arrangements, that the present generation can scarcely realise what they were in the past. A card, a letter, or a sample of goods can now be sent for ½d. or 1d., and a sum of money, a parcel, or book-packet, for a nominal charge, to any part of the United Kingdom, with such punctuality and despatch as our forefathers never dreamed of, though paying in some instances twenty times the cost. And even if the present postal facilities are not speedy enough for our requirements, we can, since the adoption of the telegraphs by the Post Office, " wire " from Land's End to John o'Groat's in much less time than a letter could formerly be sent from Brighton to Hove !

These improved postal facilities are, of course, general, affecting every town in the kingdom as well as Brighton ; but a local application of them will contribute to a better understanding of the changes which have taken place in the Post Office since the close of the last century.

At what period a Post Office was originally established in Brighton is now past finding out. Whether, in primitive times, when delivering letters was solely a private enterprise, and when " haste, poste haste," was the almost universal endorsement on letters, or whether it was in the days of Charles I., when His Majesty, " affecting the welfare of his people, and taking into his princely consideration how much it imports his state and this realm that the secrets thereof be not disclosed to forreigne nations, which cannot be prevented if a promiscuous use of transmitting or taking up of forreigne letters, &c., should be suffered,"appointed a Postmaster, and forbade all others from exercising that which to the office pertained, " at their utmost perils,"—we cannot now determine.[*] Most probably it was in the time of the

---

[*] If Charles I. had no other merit, at all events he must be allowed the credit of having been to a great extent the founder of our postal system, in which, no doubt, he saw the opportunity of establishing what promised to be at once a boon to his people and a lucrative monopoly for himself. The newly-

Commonwealth, when the Act was passed "to settle the Postage of England, Ireland, and Scotland," and which enacted that "there shall be one Generall Post Office, and one officer styled the Postmaster-Generall of England and Comptroller of the Post Office."

The first office opened in this district, under this arrangement, was, doubtless, at Lewes,* as the most important town, whence letters were subsequently despatched at stated times, to various places, among others, to the then "obscure fishing village," known as Brighthelmstone. The "Postmaster-General" had the horsing of all "through posts" and persons "riding in post"; all other persons being forbidden to "set up or employ any foot-posts, horse-posts, or pacquet-boats." The rates at this time for a single letter were:— under 80 miles, 2d.; above 80 to 140, 4d.; above 140, 6d.; and on the Borders and in Scotland, 8d. As the practice of "weighing" letters had not then come into fashion, "size" regulated the price; thus:—"Two, three, four, five, or more letters in one packet, *to pay according to the bigness of the packet.*"

The earliest Post Office in Brighton of which we know was at the bottom of Middle-street, immediately opposite Middle-street lane (now South-street). Of the character of this primitive establishment, who was the Postmaster, or what arrangements there were for the delivery of letters, there is no evidence to show.† In 1779, the Post Office was removed, for the better accommodation, probably, of the then numerous fashionable visitors to Brighton, to the Library of Miss E. Widgett, at the south of the Steine, in the premises immediately to the east of the York Hotel, now occupied by a chemist's shop, &c. The letter-box was "round the corner" (facing the old Baths in Pool Valley), two or three posts protecting the steps

---

founded office passed well and safely through the rough ordeal of a Parliamentary inquiry, and in 1644 there was a weekly post at work along all the chief lines of road, and Mr. Edmund Prideaux firmly established in the chair of control. The King, his Ministers, his Court, and afterwards his "trusty and well-beloved cousins" of the Upper House, and the knights and burgesses of the Lower House, claimed the right of sending their letters free; and hence arose the Parliamentary privilege of "franking," abolished only in our own days; but in spite of this drawback the Post Office showed a net profit of £5,000 a year at the end of Charles I.'s reign.

* In the "Calendar of State Papers" (1666-67), Samuel Rose, writing to the Navy Commissioners from Lewes, 19th March, 1667, says:—"His letters are to be sent to the Talbot, in Southwark, the Lewes Carrier is there every Thursday before 12 o'clock." The usual course of transmitting letters for nearly a century after was to leave them at some place in London, and the country carrier, calling for them, took them on. In the "Danny Papers" (*Arch. Coll.*, vol. x., p. 14) we learn that Mr. Courthope, in 1758, had two London correspondents, Mr. Ray, the botanist, and a Mr. Willoughby. Mr. Ray's letters were always deposited at "The Red Lion," in Thames-street, near Billingsgate; and Mr. Willoughby's were directed to "his most honored coson, Peter Courthope, Esq., to be left at Mr. Faye's, an apothecarie's shop, at the sign of the Sugar Loafe, neere the Conduit in Fleet-street, London."

† In the *Archæological Collections*, vol. x., p. 38, we learn that, in 1753, the Rottingdean letters were delivered from Brighton. Lady Wilson (one of the Courthopes, of Whiligh,) then resided at Rottingdean; and her son, writing to her from Scotland, after Culloden, directed his letter, "To the Lady Wilson, at Rottingdean, near Lewes, in Sussex, South Britain; by Brighthelmstone bagg."

MISS WIDGETT'S LIBRARY, SOUTH OF THE STEINE, 1779.— THE POST OFFICE.

MISS WIDGETT'S LIBRARY, SOUTH OF THE STEINE, 1779.—
THE POST OFFICE.

leading to it; for the beach at that time reached up to the house, and the sea also not unfrequently paid it a visit. *(See plate.)*

Of the local postal arrangements at the period we learn from *A Description of Brighthelmstone* (1779), published by E. Widgett, that "During Summer Post sets out from Brighthelmstone for London every morning (excepting Saturday) at nine," reaching London about seven in the evening. In the Winter the Post went out (at 11 at night!) but four days each week (Mondays, Tuesdays, Thursdays, and Saturdays); and returned only on Thursday and Saturday mornings.

A year or two later, Mr. Bowen (who succeeded Miss Widgett as Librarian) officiated as Postmaster; as did Mr. Bowen's successor, Mr. A. Crawford. From that time forth the inhabitants of the town were relieved from the penalty, as regards their letters, of the "seasons' difference," the mails being made up *every day* but Saturday for London, both in winter and in summer.

But even then postal arrangements both at Lewes and Brigbthelmstone were not altogether satisfactory; for in the *Lewes Journal* of June 6th, 1785, the following paragraph appears:—"A delay in the conveyance of the Mails from the General Post Office, London, to this town and Brighthelmstone, which has long been the subject of complaint, is at length removed, by which regulation each place is accommodated with their letters three hours earlier on a day than heretofore, a circumstance that will be found very convenient to the trading part of the inhabitants of both towns, and particularly so to the company resorting to Brighthelmstone during the season, who, in consequence, will have time to finish their diurnal epistolary correspondence before dinner, which they have long wished for."

Under Mr. Crawford's auspices, the subsequent postal arrangements were, considering the means at his disposal, excellent, though, as contrasted with modern requirements, they would in more respects than one be deemed *slow*. What they were may be learned from the following summary of the details given in the "BRIGHTHELMSTON DIRECTORY FOR 1800":—

All Mails, for whatever destination, were made up at six o'clock each evening of despatch, and seven o'clock was the latest hour letters were received.

The LONDON MAIL and the EAST GRINSTEAD MAIL was despatched every evening, except Saturday; Croydon, Bletchingley, Godstone, &c, were from the East Grinstead delivery, and received their letters *daily*; Crawley, Cuckfield, Lindfield, and "other places in that neighbourhood," were from the same delivery, but received letters "only three days in each week."

The LEWES MAIL was despatched every evening, without exception; and Eastbourne, Seaford, Hailsham, Uckfield, and adjacent places, were from the Lewes delivery, and had their letters *daily*; Ditchling, however, in the same delivery, received letters "only on Sundays, Wednesdays, and Fridays, in the morning."

The SHOREHAM and WORTHING MAIL, though made up every evening, did not "set out" till early the next morning; and it was the same with the STEYNING MAIL, which went on to Arundel, Chichester,

Portsmouth, &c.; the letters, doubtless, being delivered on the day of receipt, as Henfield, from the same delivery, is mentioned as receiving letters "only three days in the week."

The HURST MAIL was made up only three evenings in each week the letters being despatched on the following morning.

Letters for Horsham and the north-west extremity of the County, and for Battle, Hastings, &c., in the eastern extremity, had to "pass through London."

Thus much we gather as to the despatch of letters *from* Brighton at the period; but as to the arrangements for their delivery *in* Brighton, the old "Directory" is silent. *Erredge* says that "during the time Mr. Crawford was Postmaster, his son was the only letter carrier in Brighton."* One of the outlying districts, Rottingdean—then a great place of fashionable resort per "donkey" by Brighton visitors—appears to have had its special carrier, as it is stated to be "from the delivery of our Postmaster, who sends the letters there daily."

It may not be uninteresting at this point to give the rates of postage at this period, and which were, in fact, continued up to 1840, when the uniform Penny Postage system was introduced:—

				d.
For any distance not exceeding 15 miles from the Office where they are despatched				4
Above 15 miles, and not exceeding 20 miles				5
" 20 "	"	"	30 "	6
" 30 "	"	"	50 "	7
" 50 "	"	"	80 "	8
" 80 "	"	"	120 "	9
" 120 "	"	"	170 "	10
" 170 "	"	"	230 "	11
" 230 "	"	"	300 "	12
" 300 "	"	"	400 "	13
" 400 "	"	"	500 "	14

The above were the charges for single letters. No letter or packet, however, was charged as more than three letters, unless it weighed an ounce; above that weight the price of a single letter was charged for every quarter of an ounce.

What the charges were in 1800 to places less than 15 miles distant, we cannot ascertain. But just prior to the Penny Postage, the charges were:—

Brighton to Hurstpierpoint and St. John's (calling at Preston, Patcham, &c., *en route*)	1d.
Brighton to Shoreham (a mile or so nearer)	2d.
Brighton to Lewes (about the same distance)	3d.

---

* It is interesting to note that Mr. William Crawford, the "only letter carrier in Brighton" in the olden time, subsequently went to London, and ultimately became the partner of the late Mr. Farquhar, an East Indian merchant, and once the owner of Font Hill. He was an unsuccessful candidate at the first Brighton election in 1832; but subsequently represented the City of London, an honour which his son, Mr. Robert William Crawford, also had in 1870. The widow of Mr. Andrew Crawford, the Postmaster of Brighton, died some years since at 20, New-steine, leaving her property here to Mr. R. W. Crawford. Some of this property is decidedly "early Brighton,' as those to the west of Brighton-place, immediately beyond the Knab. In the centre house of the three there is a very ancient room, the ceiling being curiously festooned.

THE POST OFFICE.

These charges alone are pretty good local evidence of the anomalies and inequalities of the old rates of postage. From London to Brighton the rate was 8d.; but, wonderful to relate, up to about 1840, this ensured their delivery in Brighton only as far as 69, London-road ! If the receiver resided beyond that favoured house, "off the stones" or pavement, *an extra penny was charged ! !* Some years previous to this the "stones" ended northward at the Glo'ster Hotel, and westward at Russell-street, but subsequently the latter were extended to Cannon-place.*

Mail coaches were first put on the road between London and Brighton in 1807.† At this period the Post Office was at the north-east corner of Prince's-place (to which place it was removed from the Steine, in 1803, Mr. J. Redifer succeeding Mr. Crawford as Post-master), whence the letters were despatched at the same hours on the same days as heretofore. We learn, however, that the London Mail arrived every morning (except Monday) about seven, and "the letters are delivered, after they are sorted, in all parts of the town, with commendable despatch."

"Robbing the Mail" sounds strangely to modern ears, or, at least, is only known by tradition. In the early part of the century it was of frequent occurrence, and the drivers invariably went armed; blunderbusses, pistols, &c., being provided at the expense of the Government. For instance, in an advertisement in the *Brighton Herald*, of February 1, 1811, for a mailman between Brighton and Chichester, a paragraph states that special provision is made for "*a brace of pistols, at the expense of the Government.*"

---

* So vexatious had the "off the stones" penny become that, in March, 1830, a public meeting was called to petition the House of Commons to abolish the impost. One speaker at the meeting said that, from the information which he had collected, it appeared that, about the year 1788, by reason of the smallness of the town at that period, the salary of the Postmaster being probably insufficient, the additional charge of one penny was made on all letters delivered in the town with the view of augmenting it. This being considered an illegal charge, an action was brought by an individual against the Postmaster, and a verdict was obtained. Owing to this circumstance, a person was sent down from the General Post Office to examine the limits of the town, and he accordingly made a survey. On looking over the western part of the town, he discovered a vacant piece of ground, where Cannon-place now stands, but which was then occasionally utilised for bathing machines, and which, although at that period there were many houses beyond, he fixed upon as the line of demarcation for the boundary of the town; and from that period to 1830 one penny extra had been charged on all letters westward of that spot. To the eastward, Charlotte-street was made the boundary, and northward, Sussex-street, on the Grand-parade. The petition was presented to the House by Mr. Joseph Hume, and he could have needed little "coaching" to back up the petition; for he happened to be staying in Brighton in 1829, and his "extras" for one single morning (having received 34 letters) amounted to 2s. 10d. !

† Mr. John Palmer, manager of the Bath Theatre, about 1790, broached to Mr. Pitt the idea that the "post" might be carried by mail coaches. It is strange, indeed, that such an idea should have been a novelty in the days of our grandfathers, and that for accelerating the post from an average speed of less than four miles to a little over six miles an hour Mr. Palmer should have claimed and received—even after many a weary struggle—a Parliamentary grant of £50,000. But such really was the case. Lord Canning tells us (First Report of the Postmaster-General, 1855) that in the early part of last century a "despatch"

This protection was, in fact, absolutely necessary at this period by reason of the numerous cases of mail robbery with violence, and even murder, which had occurred in the neighbourhood, and especially between Arundel and Chichester.

But to return to the Brighton Post Office. Coming to 1818, sundry improvements had been effected in the arrangements. For instance, London letters were received until 9 p.m.; or, with an extra charge of 1d., until 9.30; and even until 10 p.m. if 6d. extra were paid. Then, too, the following accommodation was offered:— "Letters and papers (by the London Mail) may be obtained at the Post Office window, at 7.30 a.m." The postmen, it is added, "complete the delivery of letters in the town in four hours afterwards." There were, also, two mails (at 7 and 10 p.m.) to Lewes each evening and a mail to Chichester every morning at 4, leaving the London bags for Shoreham, Steyning, Arundel, and Chichester; letters to the west of England, as far as Land's End, being sent by the Cross Post *; and a peripatetic messenger (in addition to the one to Rottingdean) left Brighton at 7.30 a.m., with letters for Preston, Patcham, Piecombe, Clayton, and Hurstpierpoint. Another left at the same hour "who delivers all letters beyond No. 59, Marine-parade, to the Crescent, and to Rottingdean. The messenger brings back letters the same evening."

The "advice to visitors" issued by the Brighton Postmaster at this period is so quaint that we must quote in its entirety:—

"The infinite number of mistakes which frequently happen during the summer, in regard to letters being sent to wrong people, or lying at the Post Office many days, and, at last, returned to the dead-letter box in London, has been long complained of as a great evil at watering places.

"The only way to prevent these unpleasant circumstances is for every person, as soon as they are settled in their houses, to leave their

---

took nearly three days in reaching London from Plymouth; and even as lately as between 1730 and 1740 the London mail for Edinburgh left only thrice a week, and was equally long in performing its journey. That in bulk the country mails were wonderfully less than now may be gathered from the fact, which Lord Canning records, that on one occasion the Scottish mail carried only a single letter! and this fact is authenticated by a reward, offered in 1779, for the arrest of certain footpads who robbed the postboy of the whole north-western mail—in other words, of the letters for Birmingham, Shrewsbury, Chester, &c.—which then were easily packed up in a little leathern valise, though now, probably, they would weigh several tons. Scarcely less wonderful is the fact, recorded by Macaulay, that the whole revenue of the kingdom at the accession of William III fell short of the sum collected in pennies by the General Post Office within two or three years after the death of William IV.

* The idea of "cross posts" was suggested to the Post Office by Ralph Allen—of Prior Park, the friend of Pope—one who may be called in two senses a "man of letters." Up to his time (the early part of last century) the postal communication had been confined to the connection of London with the several larger country towns, while there were no means of sending a letter direct from Oxford to Buckingham, or from Salisbury to Southampton. Ralph Allen being a man of capital and sound sense, he farmed the "cross posts" which he suggested at a profit of £12,000 a year, and made a handsome fortune by his venture. We first learn of his scheme being adopted in 1720, and it was only at the close of the last century that the "cross posts" were absorbed into the general postal system, when it was calculated that their income was some £200,000 a year.

THE POST OFFICE IN NEW ROAD IN 1848.
(Now No. 22.)

Christian and Surname, and place of abode, at the Post Office; and, likewise, when they leave Brighton, where they wish their letters to be sent after them.

"It frequently happens that many persons of the same Surname come down to Brighton about the same time, and, therefore, too much care cannot be taken to prevent letters falling into wrong hands; and this can only be done by leaving a correct address with the Postmaster."

To act upon this advice might have been practicable in 1818; how such an arrangement could be carried out now, when our visitors during the season amount to between 60,000 to 70 000, we shall not venture to determine. At this period,—as, indeed, has been always the case with the local Post Office officials,—there was every desire to accommodate the public, and we learn that,—

"For the better accommodation of the town, the letter-carriers go round the whole neighbourhood with a bell, to collect in all letters, between the hours of eight and nine o'clock."

And this after they had done letter-carrying for the day! At one time, as many as six letter-carriers did this collecting duty, with bell, each evening, 1d. being charged for each letter so collected. In the Kemp Town District, from its then *extreme distance*, the letters were collected *free !* and numbers of the British public (residing eastward) in those days, keenly alive to the old proverb of "a penny saved is a penny earned," made a practice of walking with their letters to the boundary of the district, where the unfortunate bellman was compelled to receive their favour, *minus the fee !* His round, as may be supposed, was always the heaviest; while, on the "maiden walk," as the Grand-parade and northern district was termed, the bellman frequently returned without so much as a single letter or a single penny! The custom of collecting by bellmen ceased in 1846, when the third local delivery was established, on which occasion five extra letter-carriers were put on.

It would be beside our purpose to notice in detail the causes which led to the removal of the Brighton Post Office from one locality to another. Suffice to say that, in 1822, it was removed from Prince's-place to 67, East-street (the premises now occupied by the Messrs. Hudson), which was new fronted in classic style, and the interior adapted to the then postal requirements. In 1827 the East-street Post Office was closed, and a new Office opened at 149, North-street. Four years afterwards, 1831, there was another removal to New-road (the door above Messrs. Crunden and Sons'), whence it was again removed, in 1849, to its present situation.* Originally the Ship-street premises were somewhat confined; but, as business so much increased, it became necessary to enlarge the Office in 1858, the piazza under which the letters, &c., were formerly posted being absorbed into the front office, the room thus obtained being devoted to the money order business and the lobby for the accommodation of the public applying for stamps, making en-

---

* As an illustration of the way in which the various Manors of the town are intersected, it may be stated that the present Post Office is in the Manor of New Shoreham, *alias* Rusper!

quiries, &c.; the outside letter-boxes being flush with the street. In 1870 another enlargement took place, to accommodate the Telegraph department. We may mention that, after Mr. Redifer, the office of Postmaster was filled by Mr. Ferguson, whose successor was Mr. C. J. Whiting, who entered upon his duties in 1850.*

Having previously noted the successive stages of the early growth of the Post Office, we come now to the year 1840, when, thanks to the persistent efforts of Mr. Rowland Hill, the Penny Postage system was adopted by the Government.† In that year the entire staff of the Brighton Post Office consisted of three clerks, fourteen letter-carriers, and three rural messengers (to Hove, Rottingdean, and Hurst). Brighton had then but two deliveries,—morning and evening; but Hove and the rural districts had to content themselves with one—when the messenger arrived! In 1872 the staff of the Office consisted of seventeen clerks, one inspector of letter-carriers, four sorters, three stampers, forty letter-carriers, and three rural messengers. There were then *four* deliveries daily (except Sundays, when there was but one) in Brighton, Hove and Preston-ville, commencing at 7 a.m., 11.15 a.m., 4.30 p.m., and 7 p.m.; the 4.30 delivery was put on in August, 1869. Preston, Patcham, and Rottingdean had each two deliveries daily. Eight mails were daily (except Sundays) received from London; and no less than ten were despatched daily to London and other districts; on Sundays three mails only were despatched. In all matters connected with the despatch of mails, Brighton "moved with the times." It was among the first of those towns which received what are known as "midnight despatches," that is, "supplementary mails leaving London about midnight, so as to admit of letters posted too late for the ordinary night mails being included in the first delivery in the morning." By these midnight despatches, says the Postmaster-General (17th Re-

---

* Mr. Whiting retired on the 31st December, 1890, and was succeeded on the 27th May, 1891, by Mr. Wilson A. Hetherington, B.A., of Christ Church, Oxford, formerly one of the Surveyors of the General Post Office.

† The *Times*, a few years ago, in alluding to the history of the Post Office, gives the following particulars respecting the origin of the penny post:—"It may be fondly imagined by some of our readers that Sir Rowland Hill was the first deviser of a penny post. Nothing can be further from the truth. He took up an old idea, worked it, too, zealously, and brought it to a successful issue. As far back as 1683, one Robert Murray, an enterprising upholsterer, of London, bethought himself of a new way to make a fortune, and he set up a penny post in the City. Though there were no Spooners or Whalleys in Parliament in those days, yet the ultra-Protestant party denounced it as 'a device of the Jesuits,' and vowed that Mr. Murray's bags, if opened, would be found to be full of Roman Bulls and Papal Indulgences. Whether this outcry alarmed him we know not; but Murray appears to have assigned his idea and 'plant' to a man named Dockwra, who, though prosecuted by the Crown for invading its monopoly, contrived to hold his own so far as to get a pension of £200, and with it the Controllership of the 'London District Post,' of which Murray must be regarded as the founder. But before many years were over Mr. Dockwra was suspended on account of complaints, among which was one to the effect that 'many a time he had hazarded the life of a patient when physic was sent by a doctor or apothecary.' It appears, then, that while we send only boxes of pills and powders, the penny post of 200 years ago would carry draughts from St. Bartholomews's to the Strand or to Westminster."

port, 1871), "the number of letters which thus obtain an earlier delivery amounts to about 130,000 a week. At Brighton, for instance, about 1,500 letters arrive every night, and fall into the first delivery in the morning instead of the second, as formerly."

Unquestionably one of the greatest conveniences in connection with Post Office accommodation was the opening of "Receiving Houses" in outlying districts of the town. In 1840 there were but three of these opened: in St. James's-street, Preston-street, and at the Trafalgar-street corner of St. George's-place. In 1872 there were no less than sixteen opened; in 1879-80 there were two more, and letters collected from them four times a day (except Sundays). Pillar-boxes —an extension of similar accommodation—was an after-growth. The first four of these were put up in April, 1858: in the Western-road (corner of Montpelier-road); at the Old-steine (corner of the Marine-parade); at the corner of Marine-square; and in Sussex-square. In 1872 the Pillar and Wall-boxes were twenty-three in number, and letters were collected from them six times daily, except Sundays. In 1879-80 the Pillar and Wall-boxes had been increased to thirty-five, from which there were daily seven collections.* These collections were formerly done by two special messengers; but in 1860, by reason of the number of letters deposited, the duty was done by collecting- carts, of which in 1870 there were four.

The Post Office Savings Banks were first opened in this town in December, 1861, at the branch offices in Bedford-street, Western-road, Hove, and at Cliftonville. This business was not transacted at the Chief Office, Ship-street, till March, 1862, at which period it was also extended to other branch offices. Money Orders were first issued in Brighton in 1838 (the year when the original firm of "Stow and Co." was absorbed by the General Post Office); and Life Assurance and Annuity business in 1865. The Telegraph business in connection with the Post Office commenced in Brighton, February 5th, 1870, when there were 13 Telegraph Stations, including those at the local Railway Stations.

The public generally are probably not aware of the large amount of business transacted at the Brighton Post Office, and it appears to be continually increasing. From the Postmaster-General's Reports we have compiled the following information as to the "Amount of Postage" in Brighton for several years, commencing with 1858, when the local return was first included in the large town list, to the year 1862, when the publication of the table ceased :—

1858	1859	1860	1861	1862
£19,430	£20,884	£21,572	£21,945	£22,579

Then with respect to letters, &c., the increase in number has been enormous. We cannot, as the returns issued are not uniform, show the increase year by year; but must take them as they are. In 1840,

---

* At the present time (June, 1892) there are five Branch Offices (manned by trained Staff from Head Office); the Receiving Offices have been increased to thirty-six, and the Pillar and Wall-boxes to sixty-eight, and from most of these two latter there are from ten to twelve collections daily (Sundays excepted).

after the adoption of Penny Postage, the average weekly delivery was a little over 50,000 a week, or about 250,000 a year. In 1870 the number for one week in the March quarter reached to 101,900; in the corresponding week, 1871, it was 105,685 (in addition to 8,230 book packets, 377 pattern or sample packets, 7,743 newspapers, and 6,667 post-cards); in the last return, for a week in January, 1872, the number of letters is 142,890. In October, 1876, the week's delivery of letters amounted to 177,516, independently of books, circulars, papers, and cards. The details were as follows:—On the 9th, the delivery included 28,009 letters, 2,950 books and circulars, 2,798 papers, and 1,762 cards; on the 10th, there were 30,879 letters, 2,781 books and circulars, 2,479 papers, and 2,327 cards; on the 11th there were 27,569 letters, 1,788 books and circulars, 2,439 papers, 1,832 cards; on the 12th there were 27,611 letters, 2,396 books and circulars, 2,089 papers, and 1,747 cards; on the 13th there were 29,655 letters, 2,103 books and circulars, 3,246 papers, and 1,935 cards; on the 14th, there were 25,844 letters, 2,111 books and circulars, 4,002 papers, and 1,639 cards; and on the 15th there were 7,949 letters, 596 books and circulars, 800 papers, and 434 cards. The total deliveries of the seven days were 222,370,—an exceedingly good week's work.

In January, 1877, an important change took place in the interior arrangements of the central Post Office in Ship-street, with the view of making it the head office in the town both for postal and postal-telegraph purposes. By an exchange with the London and Brighton Railway Company, the latter offering the use of a range of offices on the upper floor of the local Terminus, in return for the use of the Telegraph Office on the Old-steine for a booking-office, &c., the Telegraph Office staff was transferred to Ship-street,—the spacious sorting-room there being adapted to its new requirements, instruments, &c., —and the Post Office staff—sorters, facers, stampers, carriers, *et hoc genus omne*—to the Railway Company's premises.*

---

* Early in the present year (1892) some important extensions and alterations were commenced at the Head Office in Ship-street, which, when completed, will afford the accommodation that has for a long time past been needed, alike by the public and the Postal and Telegraph staffs. The whole of the back portion of the building has been for some time devoted to the Telegraph staff; but, the constant growth of business in all the branches carried on at the Post Office has for a long time past made the accommodation altogether inadequate, alike for the telegraph operators, the clerks, and the public generally. All this is now being altered. The model lodging-houses which adjoined the back of the Post Office, as well as a builder's yard in front of the lodging-house in Clarence-yard, have been secured, giving a total ground space of 104 feet by 60 feet; and, under the supervision of the Postmaster, Mr. Wilson A. Hetherington, the alterations are now being carried out. The Ship-street frontage is to be much the same as now; but the letter-box will be shifted slightly nearer North-street, and a second entrance will be formed at the southern end, giving access to the public office, and, by means of an ample corridor, to a public inquiry office. The partition that now divides the public office from the telegraph operating department will be set back some twenty or five-and-twenty feet, thus considerably enlarging the public office, and giving room for a counter seventy feet long, or about double the length of that which now has to do duty for all the various branches of the Post Office work. On the new area that is to be taken in, a double-storey building will be erected; the upper floor of which will be devoted to the telegraph operating department. The floor space to be covered will be about

The staff of the Post Office in June, 1880, consisted of seventeen clerks, one inspector of letter carriers, five sorters, five stampers, six junior stampers, forty-two letter carriers, twelve auxiliary letter-carriers, and three rural messengers. There were five deliveries daily (except Sundays, when there was but one), in Brighton, Hove, and Prestonville, commencing at 7 a.m., 9.30 a.m., 11.30 a.m., 4.30 p.m., and 7 p.m.; the 4.30 p.m. delivery was put on in August, 1869, and the 9.30 a.m. delivery in January, 1880. Preston had then three deliveries daily; and Patcham and Rottingdean had each two. Eight mails were daily (except Sundays) received from London; and eight are despatched daily to London and other districts.*

We subjoin some details of a week's work at the Post Office with respect to the number of letters, &c., delivered in Brighton in "season" (November) and out of "season" (April) from 1878 to 1880 and in 1891 and 1892:—

NUMBER OF LETTERS, &c., DELIVERED IN BRIGHTON.

Week ending	Letters.	Book Packets and Circulars.	Newspapers.	Post Cards.	Total.
1878. April 13	134,592	17,073	16,631	11,233	179,529
" Nov. 16	153,975	20,480	15,602	13,343	203,400
1879. April 28	137,458	17,924	15,931	10,833	182,146
" Nov. 15	164,581	31,113	16,630	13,940	226,264
1880. April 24	151,692	22,057	13,348	12,313	199,410
1891. Nov. 14	225,205	57,068	15,063	25,757	323,053
1892. April 9	237,130	52,273	16,722	25,684	331,669

POSTED IN BRIGHTON FOR LOCAL DELIVERY
(included in the above).

1878. Nov. 16	20,986	7,970	620	6,951	36,527
1879. April 26	16,903	4,422	617	3,302	25,244
" Nov. 15	17,979	8,164	1,418	5,629	33,190
1880. April 24	19,773	7,245	402	4,734	32,154
1891. Nov. 14	42,302	12,380	993	10,883	66,558
1892. April 9	47,528	13,204	1,869	9,923	71,824

Some other statistics are also interesting:—

AMOUNT OF STAMPS—POSTAL, TELEGRAPH, AND RECEIPT— SOLD (at Head Office only).

	Postal.	Telegraph.	Receipts.	Total
1877	£18,529	£6,506	£573	£25,608
1878	19,069	6,871	631	26,571
1879	19,677	7,091	737	27,505
1891	...	...	...	47,033 †

(These amounts show smaller totals than those of former years,

---

sixty-two feet square, though about a quarter of the space will be occupied by staircases and a store room. On the ground floor, offices for the clerks, a small letter-sorting office, and other much-needed accommodation will be provided, such as will enable the busy staff behind the scenes at the Post Office to discharge their duties under conditions of comfort that are now much lacking.

* At the end of the year 1891, the Postal Staff consisted of 58 Superintendents and Clerks, 1 Inspector of Town Postmen, 108 Postmen and Stampers, 2 Auxiliary Postmen, and 2 Rural Postmen. There are six deliveries on week days (one on Sundays) throughout Brighton, Hove, and Preston, commencing at 7, 9, 10, and 11.45 a.m., and 2.30, 4.30, and 7 p.m. Patcham and Rottingdean have three deliveries. There are fourteen despatches from Brighton to London, and 13 mails from London to Brighton daily on week days.

[† The distinction between Postal, Telegraph, and Receipt Stamps has been abolished since 1879.]

but then the amounts included Stamps sold at the local Receiving Houses).

LETTERS REGISTERED (at Head Office only).

1877—21,730.   1878—32,981.   1879—40,096.

LETTERS DETECTED CONTAINING COIN, and which were compulsorily Registered (at Head Office only).

1877—847.   1878—832.   1879—838.

REGISTERED LETTERS DELIVERED IN BRIGHTON (at Head Office only).

1878—56,965.   1879—76,273.   1891—92,765.

The Money Order Office business of the Brighton Post Office is enormous. The issues and payments some years ago were exceeded by only some five or six other of the largest towns in England. *Ex gratia* :—

	1857.	1859.	1861.	1863.	1870.
Issues	£97,558	£109,780	£115,299	£129,057	£149,725
Payments	83,725	94,693	103,737	116,043	132,671

During the years 1877-78-79, and for 1891, the number of issues and payments have been as follows; but the amounts of the respective issues are, however, unobtainable, as no records of them are now kept :—

MONEY ORDERS ISSUED AND PAID (at Head Office only).

	Number Issued.	Number Paid.
1877	47,786	94,893
1878	44,245	87,190
1879	41,534	82,079
1891	8,088	24,632

POSTAL ORDERS ISSUED AND PAID (at Head Office only).[*]

	Issued.	Paid.
1891	75,960	195,849

The Post Office Savings' Bank transactions have of late years largely increased in Brighton; the business in 1877-78-79 and in 1891 being as follows :—

SAVINGS' BANK TRANSACTIONS (at Head Office only).

	Number of Deposits	Number of Withdrawals
1877	11,935	5,167.
1878	12,246	5,044.
1879	12,542	5,664.
1891	14,588	7,324.

In addition to the above, there is the Life Assurance and Annuity business to transact, Dog and Gun Taxes to receive, &c., so that, altogether, the local Post Office staff cannot say "they have got no work to do!" The Institution, in fact, is one of which the town may well be proud; for in every department there would appear to be systematic organisation and intelligent supervision, and a desire to meet the public requirements to the utmost. We can only hope that every town in the kingdom may have as good reason as Brighton has to be satisfied with its Post Office.

[* The Postal Order system was introduced in 1881, and has very largely taken the place of the Money Order system, as the above figures show.]

The "Telegraph" business has for some years past formed a special adjunct to that of the Post Office, and we, therefore, give under a separate heading some particulars respecting—

TELEGRAPHY IN BRIGHTON.

Nearly 40 years have passed away since Brighton was first connected with London by Telegraph; "The Electric and International Company" having sent the first message from the Brighton Railway Station on the 11th January, 1851. Subsequently a line of wires was laid underground from the Railway Station (by way of Trafalgar-street, St. George's-place, Glo'ster-place, and Grand-parade,) to the Old-steine, in the north-west corner of the York Hotel, where, on the 1st February, 1851, the Company opened their first office in the town itself.

As a means of communication, the Telegraph was not then so popular as it has since become; a Manager (Mr. J. W. Fourdrinier), two operators, and three messengers sufficing for the work of the local office; whilst the instrument used was "Cooke and Wheatstone's Double Needle," requiring two wires, which were used by the Railway Company in conjunction with the Telegraph Company. The charges for transmission at that period were 2s. 6d. per message of 20 words (addresses free) for every 50 miles, with a "delivery" rate (which remained in force until 1870) of 6d. per mile; but no charge for delivery was made if the address was within half a mile of the office.

Lewes folk in the olden time were apt to hold strongly to the opinion that Brighton was indebted to Lewes for "every good thing." We shall not attempt to controvert this; but it is satisfactory to know, if only by way of reciprocity, that the erst "obscure fishing village" was the medium through which the advantages of Telegraphy reached the old County town. The Telegraph Company extended its wires from Brighton to Lewes in 1853; and, up to 1870, Brighton and Lewes were the only towns in Sussex which had telegraphic communication other than that afforded by the Railway Company; but, as the Railway Company had a telegraphic system connecting their Stations, the neighbouring towns were not altogether without its advantages. What the Railway originally charged for messages, we are unable to say; but, from 1860 to 1870, it was 1s. for 20 words from one Station to another, with a charge for delivery of 6d. per mile commencing from the office door. Of the amount of "business" transacted in Brighton by the Telegraph Company up to 1855 (when Mr. J. T. Bidder had succeeded to the local management), we have no precise—no reliable—information; but 368 messages having passed in one week,—and this at a slack season of the year, namely, in February,—the annual number of messages may, in round numbers, be taken as 20,000.

In 1854 the Company arranged with three of the local newspapers to supply them weekly—on the day prior to that of publication—with "Intelligence," consisting of "Markets, Funds, Parliamentary, and General News," at a charge of £10 per annum. It also supplied (at

£10 10s. per annum) one local Club and two Libraries with a daily service of General News ; the news, in all cases, being collected by the Company. In the same year (1854) the Telegraph Company issued " Franks " or " Stamps " of various values, which were then used, as they are now, for messages, as postage stamps are used for letters; and the charge for a message from Brighton to London was reduced from 2s. 6d. to 1s. But how long this reduction lasted is doubtful; for in 1862 the lowest charge was 1s. 6d.

Two years later (in 1856) the Company's office was removed from the York Hotel to 18, Old Steine,—formerly Donaldson's Library, where Royal and Noble, and all the *beau monde* in days gone by, were wont to congregate,—which had, just previously to 1856, been transformed into a coachmaker's shop! But this by the way. In 1858, the Company, discarding the original " Double Needle " instrument, introduced the " Morse Recorder," which registered messages on a strip of paper ; and as the " Morse " system required only a single wire, the Company gained the advantage of getting two lines to London. Beyond mentioning that Mr. J. Millington was appointed local manager, *vice* Bidder, and held the office until 1861, when he was succeeded by Mr. George Field, there is little to record in connection with local Telegraphy for several years. The Company did a steady, but not an increasing business; due, probably, to the fact that for a long period Telegraphy was looked upon by the public merely as an extraordinary means of communication. It is only within the last 20 years that its advantages and convenience have come to be regarded as a necessity.

In 1864, Brighton and London were connected by a third wire. The charges for " Telegrams " (as they were now called) to London being 1s. for 20 words, and the "addresses" (limited to 10 words) free. To the other Offices of the Company the charges were from 1s. 6d. for 50 miles to 4s. for 250 miles. But in July, 1865, they were again revised : 1s. being charged for 100 miles ; 1s. 6d. for 150 ; 2s. for 300 ; and 4s. for 400 and upwards. These rates remained in force up to 1870. The Local Staff in 1864 consisted of the Manager, three operators, and four messengers; and the annual number of Telegrams had increased to 33,120, of which 213 were for the Continent. An additional operator was put on in the following year, when the aggregate amount of work done doubled that of 1855. The annual number of Telegrams was now 40,000 ; and of these 6,000 were done at the new office which had been opened, on the 1st July, at the Bedford Hotel ; 12,634 were for delivery in London, and 300 on the Continent ; whilst 455 were transacted during the August Races at the Brighton Grand Stand, to which wires had been extended some five or six years previously.*

In January, 1866, a snow storm and gale of extraordinary severity deranged the whole Telegraph system of the kingdom, and Brighton was without telegraphic communication for four days—a circumstance which had never happened before.

---

* In 1880 there were three wires to the Grand Stand, and at the August Races of that year no less than 3,394 messages were disposed of.

Sundry local changes took place in connection with the Company during the following year: the Bedford Hotel Office was removed to the East Lodge of the West Pier; and a new office was opened at Burlington-street (Marine-parade). At the close of 1867 the British and Irish Magnetic Telegraph Company extended a wire to Brighton and opened Offices at 1, Castle-square and at the Grand Hotel; Mr. J. E. Parker being local Manager. The wire was carried underground up the Marine-parade to Black Rock, thence (*viâ* East Dean and Polegate) to Battle, where it joined the South-Eastern Railway and was in connection with London. The advent of this Company at Brighton produced, however, no change of rates, as the tariffs of the Telegraph Companies had previously been assimilated; but as the Magnetic Company had a working agreement with the South-Eastern Railway Company, a modification of the charges to Stations on that Line took place.

The original Company extended their wires to Hove in February, 1868, opening an office at Hove-place, Cliftonville. The local business both of the original Company and of the Magnetic Company was generally increasing; for, in 1869, their joint staffs (exclusive of the Managers) consisted of eight telegraphists and 12 messengers; the offices were six in number (exclusive of those belonging to the Railway Company); and the number of messages dealt with during that year was no less than 73,600. Of these 184 were purely local,—that is, were sent from one local office to another; 350 were sent to the Continent; 20 to America; and 12 to India.

By virtue of an Act passed in 1868, the Postmaster-General was empowered on behalf of the Government to purchase the lines and plant of the Telegraph Companies; and, accordingly, the whole of the Telegraph system throughout the kingdom was transferred to the Post Office on February 5th, 1870. Thenceforth, Mr. C. J. Whiting, the Postmaster of Brighton, became the chief of the local offices; Mr. Field, the previous Manager, acting under him as Superintendent. The "wire" extensions to various towns and villages of the County now rapidly took place, and Brighton soon became a large Telegraphic centre; the work of the year in Brighton and Hove amounting to 110,000 messages. In 1871 new offices were opened, and the "wires" were extended from 18, Old Steine (the Head Office), to the Chief Post Office, in Ship-street; and the "business" of 1871 exceeded that of 1870 by 23 per cent.

The charge for messages under the Post Office in 1880 was 1s. per 20 words to any part of the United Kingdom or Ireland, addresses (unlimited) free; and telegrams were delivered free within one mile, or at a charge of 6d. beyond the first mile. As regards the transmission of "Intelligence," the Government, not collecting news as the Companies did, fixed the rate for news messages to Newspapers, Clubs, &c., at 1s. per 100 words if sent between 6 p.m. and 6 a.m., and 1s. per 75 words if sent at other hours; and these messages were forwarded by Associations or appointed correspondents. A very large quantity of "Intelligence" was daily telegraphed to Brighton through these sources; and, so far as Brighton was concerned, we believe that no other town in the kingdom was so amply provided with telegraphic facilities.

Brighton, it may be stated, was one of the first towns to which the system of sending telegrams in opposite directions at the same time on the same wire was applied. This system, called "The Duplex," was introduced in 1873; and in 1877, such was the increase of business, that it was deemed expedient to remove the head-quarters from the Old-steine to the Chief Post Office in Ship-street, which was re-arranged to meet the new requirements; the Old-steine establishment was, however, subsequently re-opened as a branch-office. The Service in Brighton sustained a loss by the death of Mr. George Field, in December, 1877, after holding office for 16 years. He was succeeded by Mr. F. Cox, the present Superintendent.

In 1878 more rapid means of transmission between Brighton and London was found necessary, and the Automatic System of Sir Charles Wheatstone was introduced, by means of which 130 words a minute could be telegraphed,—a speed equal to nearly five times that of a hand-worked machine; and, by the application of "Duplex" working, one wire carried in an hour and a half as many messages as were dealt with in 1854 in a week. But although the apparatus in use was extensive, there was need for additional facilities, and in June, 1880, a "Quadruplex" was fitted on one of the numerous wires to the Metropolis. By this system four separate messages passed together at the same time on one wire; and it was so arranged that the Central Office in London could send to and receive from one part of Brighton while another part of Brighton was sending to and receiving from the Central Office in London,—a vast improvement upon the system in 1851, when it required two wires to carry one message.

In June, 1880, there were eleven Telegraph Offices open in Brighton (exclusive of those of the Railway), and the staff was over 80 in number. The number of Telegrams for disposal in the town in 1879 was 320,538, or an increase over 1870 of 190 per cent., while the number of Telegrams passing through the town amounted in addition to 143,868,—a total of nearly half a million! What the increase will be in another decade, we shall not pretend to determine.

[Some idea of the growth of the work of the Telegraph Office since 1880 and up to 1892 may be obtained from the following:—
An important alteration in the charge for telegrams took place on September 1st, 1885, when the minimum charge for a telegram of 12 words (or less) was fixed at 6d., and a halfpenny for each extra word, addresses being charged for. Another important alteration took place on July 8th, 1891, in the abolition of charges for the delivery of telegrams in large towns, which included Brighton. Previously, when messages had to be delivered beyond a mile from the Office, a fee of 6d. per mile was charged for porterage, but telegrams are now delivered free at all times within the town postal delivery. A new Branch Office (*i.e.*, an office manned by a Staff from the Head Office) was opened at Hove Town Hall in June, 1882, and another in the Western-road (Hove) in June, 1885. A third was opened in

College-road (Kemp Town) in August, 1888, and a fourth at Cannon-place, in June, 1891, in place of the one at the West Pier. New Telegraph Offices have been opened in Lewes-road, Dyke-road, Cowper-street (Hove), and York-place, and it has been arranged to open shortly another office in North-road, which will make a total of 17. During the year 1891 there were 459,141 telegrams sent from Brighton, and 475,556 received for delivery in the town, exclusive of 59,267 "Press telegrams"; and there were, in addition to this, 545,289 telegrams passing through the Head Office for other places, giving a grand total of one million five hundred and thirty-nine thousand. There are now six wires to the Grand Stand at the Race Course, and in 1888, during the August Race Meeting, 7,772 messages were disposed of at that office. In 1888 the wires were extended to the Sussex County Cricket Ground at Hove, and in June, 1891, during the match between Sussex and Cambridge University, 1,949 telegrams were dealt with at the office there. To meet the enormous increase of work, additional wires have been provided and the Staff has been considerably strengthened. It now numbers 82 telegraphists and 115 messengers. There are now thirteen wires from Brighton to London, which supply the requirements of the town and district, and cross-country and local wires are numerous. They are all fitted with the most improved form of apparatus—"Duplex," "Quadruplex," "Wheatstone Automatic," and "Hexode." The "Automatic" is now worked at a speed of 375 words per minute (or 330 words per minute in opposite directions when "duplexed"), and the "Hexode" is an instrument on which six telegrams can be sent at the same time. There have been three recurrences of breakdowns such as that in 1866, the first being just twenty years after, namely, in 1886; the second in 1891; and the third on the night of Good Friday, April 15th, 1892. These were all caused by snowstorms, accompanied by gales. The "blizzard" of 1891 was very destructive; but the damage caused by the storm of 1892 has never been equalled. The Brighton district suffered heavily, and to many places the communication could not be restored for several days.]

the towns-folk; for some few years later (in 1580) the Town-Book states that there were then in the town 400 mariners (without enumerating their families), 102 artificers and husbandmen, "able to contribute to the expenditure of the town," and, independently of the constable and twelve assistants, there were 92 freeholders of land and tenements,—a total of 607. Reckoning each family only at four persons, this would give the population in 1580 at about 2,400 persons, independently of the "poor families," who, paying no rates, were not enumerated.

But to return to North-street. So early as the time of "good Queen Bess,"—and, perhaps, much earlier,—a Town Well had been made in the street (at the entrance of what was subsequently known as "The Unicorn" Yard, now Windsor-street); and the Court Rolls of the Manor of Brighthelmston-Lewes record the following respecting this Well in the days of the "most high and mighty Prince James" (1619):—"April (16 Jac.), it is ordered at the Court Leet, that a building which Richard Scrase, gentleman, has erected over the common Well in the upper end of North-street, shall not convey to the said Scrase, or his heirs, any right in the said Well, more than as an inhabitant." It may be added that the inhabitants always evinced much partiality for the water of this Well; for, in 1766, Dr. Relhan says—"The water most esteemed by the inhabitants is drawn from a Well in the middle of North-street." The extract we have given from the Court Rolls affords indisputable evidence of the antiquity of the street, which is further proved by title deeds relating to some of the earlier houses. For instance, at the south-east corner of what is now New-road there is stated to have been in 1637 "one messuage and tenement, garden, and one croft of land situate in the North-street of Brighthelmston." Then, the house which subsequently became known as "The White Lion" was erected as a farm house prior to 1675, as, most likely, was "The Unicorn," lower down the street; and the house formerly at the north-east corner of West-street, and a few others in other parts of the street, were, probably, coeval with them. These houses, on both sides of the street, were wide apart, the intervening spaces being either meadows or agricultural land; as was the case in the interior of the town itself, with the hemp-gardens, &c. So lately as 1665, the Bartholomews are described as a "parcel of pasture."

In 1700 (in the days of William III.) the Friends' first Meeting-House in Brighton was opened in North-street. What North-street, or what Brighton, was then one can scarcely venture to portray. What a contrast would each present to their respective appearances in the days of Queen Victoria! The town—then commonly called Bredhemston—was a poor, old-built fishing town, of about 1,400 or 1,500 inhabitants (their number had sensibly diminished during the previous half-century, and did not again reach 2,000 until 1766). On the beach under the Cliff were some 130 wretched-looking tenements, interspersed with capstans, stake-places, &c.,—all of which were swept away by the memorable storms of 1703 and 1705. Above the Cliff, between the Steine and West-street, were probably about as many similar tenements, in "spots or patches," or ranged along the sides of the hemp-gardens, the only imposing structures connected with the town being old St. Nicholas Church, on the hill to the north-west, and the Block House, "towering in its pride of place" on the sea cliff, with four howitzers in its front garden, bidding defiance to all invaders, even though it were a second Spanish Armada!

During the next 20 or 30 years a few more houses were erected in North-street, chiefly on the south side. These were all more or less of the "old Brighton" regulation pattern: low elevation, with entry (into the ground-floor room direct) down a step, perhaps, two,—with the risk of knocking your head on entering the front door. There was then, probably, not a shop in the street; at all events, we do not learn of the existence of one until some few years later; the more central streets, as Middle-street, Ship-street, Black Lion-street, &c., being then the chief places of business. At this period North-street was most likely unpaved and wholly unlighted; for it was only an outside street, with a couple of narrow paths (subsequently Ship-street-lane and Ironmonger-lane) leading through fields from the then centre of the town into it.

It was about the middle of the last century when North-street showed signs of "progress." More houses were built; and, in 1757, an enterprising individual—one Ambrose Austin—actually opened a shop in the street! This shop, which, we suppose, much resembled the shop of a country general dealer of the present day, must have been a curiosity in its way, judging by the miscellaneous nature of the goods which the proprietor sold, and of which he took good care, by repetition, to let the world know he had "all sorts." Austin was evidently a pushing man, who did not desire to "hide his light under a bushel," judging by the advertisement which he inserted in the *Lewes Journal* in the year above mentioned. *Ex. gratia:*—

"NOTICE IS HEREBY GIVEN, that AMBROSE AUSTIN, HEMP and FLAX DRESSER in the NORTH STREET, at BRIGHTHELMSTONE, sells *all sorts* of dressed Hemp and Flax: *all sorts* of Groceries; *all sorts* of New and Second Hand Cloaths, Hats, Stockings, Shoes, Boots, and Clogs.

"N.B. - Shoemakers may be furnished with *all sorts* of Leather, as Blackgrain, and Wax'd Skins, Dressed Hides, Boot-Legs, Over-Leathers, and Pattern Soles, at very low Prices."

As we hear no more after this of "Ambrose Austin," it is possible that his enterprise in business enabled him to "retire" speedily.

North-street at this period would appear to have included what is known as Castle-square; for a visitor to Brighton in 1766, speaking of the streets of the town, says:—"North-street runs along the end of the other five, from the Assembly House ('The Castle' Inn), kept by Mr. Shergold, almost to the Church." It was, however, gradually increasing in importance. In 1761, Selina, Countess of Huntingdon, had reared—almost opposite the Friends' Meeting House—that ever-memorable monument of her piety and womanly self-denial, her Chapel, in which Whitfield preached and the "sainted" Romaine ministered. In 1774 North-street could boast of a Theatre: a "pretty building, about the size of that of Richmond." Later on the Baptists erected their "Salem" just within New-street (now Bond-street). In 1770, however, North-street contained only 88 houses, all told ; and, as showing the estimation in which the street was then held for building purposes, there is authentic record of the fact that in 1772 a piece of land (the site of the present No. 14) was hawked about for sale for *sixteen pounds !* (Eight years later it realized 475 guineas ; and the purchaser the next day was offered 25 guineas more for his bargain.) Yet there must have been at this time some good houses in the street; for the *Lewes Journal* of November, 1775, contains the following advertisement, respecting a house (exact situation not defined) in North-street :—

TO BE LET, a HOUSE in NORTH STREET, Brighthelmstone ; stone-built ; large garden with fruit trees, walled all round ; summer house at the upper end, that commands a most agreeable view of the adjacent country, particularly the South Downs ; six bed chambers ; on first floor, five rooms ; second floor, two parlours ; ground floor, hall, kitchen, pantry, detached laundry ; vaults and cellaring. Said House is usually let for lodgings ; and generally produces £100 per annum.

So lately as 1776 there was a huge barn standing at the bottom of North-street (on the site of what is now the Capital and Counties Bank) which projected considerably across the street. Opposite to this barn (on the east side) was a lofty, hideous wooden building, called "the weigh-scale," which served to weigh hay, corn, stone, bricks, &c., on which tolls were paid when brought into the town. An old local work states that the barn "was taken down for the purpose of rendering the passage more commodious" ; the writer adding, "it must be allowed that this alteration has proved a great addition to the beauty of the place." *

In 1779 there was on the north side of the street only one street running from North-street to the Spring Walks (now Church-street), namely, New-street (Bond-street); while on the south side, if one wished to go from North-street to the Black Lion-street, it was necessary to get over a stile (at the entrance to the present Lanes, to the east of Messrs. Reed's, ironmongers,) into a footpath leading to it through the fields.

But the town some few years later, when the sunshine of Royal favour had been bestowed upon it, underwent important changes, and in those changes North-street, from its close proximity to the Royal residence, largely participated. The Friends' Meeting House was no longer in its primitive isolated position ; for, between 1770 and 1794 upwards of 60 new houses had been built in the street. The south side, in fact, presented an almost continuous line of buildings ; the large gap of garden ground previously existing

---

* The barn, &c., was purchased by Mr. Hall (subsequently of the firm of Hall, Bond, and Brewster), surgeon, who erected on a portion of the site the house in which he so long resided, and those contiguous to it, extending to what is now Carlisle House, Pavilion-buildings. These latter houses were afterwards purchased by William IV., and enclosed in the Pavilion Estate, when the Southern Entrance to the Pavilion (which ran parallel with the north side of North-street) was erected in 1831. This "Entrance" was removed in 1851, after the town had purchased the Pavilion property.

opposite Prince's-place being now covered. On the north side equal activity in building had taken place. Then, in addition to New-street, another street (King-street) had been formed; Salmon-court and Mulberry-square (opposite Ship-street) had each acquired a "local habitation and a name"; and upwards of 60 tenements were huddled in Durham and Petty France (which in later times were a "shame and reproach" to the town, and were swept away when the Queen's-road was formed) and in the slums of "The Unicorn" Yard.

From an old "Town-rate Book" for the year 1784 (formerly in the possession of Alderman Davey, but now in the Free Library) we glean some authentic and interesting particulars respecting the owners and occupiers of North-street at that date, and also the rateable value of the property in it. Amongst the names mentioned are Sir Lucas Pepys (of whose wife, Lady Pepys, the Prince of Wales purchased the Promenade Grove); Selina, Countess of Huntingdon; Mr. Charles Rudhall (whose brother erected the first bells in old St. Nicholas); Mr Joseph Walls (whose smithy faced for many a year down North-street); Mr. Fox (proprietor of the Play-house); Mr. Richard Palmer (the founder of the firm subsequently known as Palmer and Green); Mr. Salmon (who owned Salmon Court); Mr. Pimm (whose well-known gardens in Church-street were subsequently devoted to—what became one of the most disgraceful streets in the town—Pimlico, now Tichborne-street); Mr. Shergold, of "The Castle," &c. The rating of the street in 1784 contrasts strongly with what it did in 1880 and in 1892. The total amount of the assessment, for the whole street, in 1784, was £350 4s. (not more, probably, than the sum at which one house is now assessed); and if the assessment of "The Castle," which was really without the street boundary, is deducted, the assessment was only £279 14s. !* Happy tax-payers of the period! The highest assessment in the street—that of Sir Lucas Pepys—was only £19 5s. The Playhouse (including a vault and yard) was assessed only at £5 10s.! But we will give the details in full, merely adding that the rate was at 2s. in the pound :—

ASSESS-MENT.	NAMES, DESCRIPTION OF PROPERTY, &C., IN NORTH STREET, 1784.	RATING.
£ s.		£ s. d.
2 0	John Sarjeant, Sen.: a house ...	0 4 0
11 10	Richard Tillstone: a house, stable, and yard	1 3 0
19 5	Sir Lucas Pepys: a house, stable, garden, coach-house, lean-totts, and paddocks	1 18 6
2 10	John Penticost: a house	0 5 0
4 15	Mrs. Pulling: a house	0 9 6
7 10	Lady Huntingdon: a new house	0 15 0
4 15	Ditto: another house	0 9 6
6 10	Miss Horton: a house	0 13 0
7 15	Mrs. Price: a house	0 15 6
1 10	Ditto: for a stable, coach-house, and new garden	0 3 0
4 0	Henry Carter: a house, yard, and back-buildings	0 8 0

* In 1791 the rates for the whole of North-street realized on a 1s. 1½d. rate only £27 16s. 0½d , and those of the whole town, lands included, but £223 15s. 9.1. A penny rate in 1880 produced nearly £2,500. [In 1892 it produces £2,750.]

312   A PEEP INTO THE PAST.

ASSESS-MENT.	NAMES, DESCRIPTION OF PROPERTY, &C., IN NORTH STREET, 1784.	RATING.
£ s.		£ s. d.
3 10	William Yates: a house ...	0 7 0
1 5	Ann Brooker: a house ...	0 2 6
3 0	George Ellmore: a house and garden	0 6 0
1 0	Ditto: a stable ...	0 2 0
7 0	John Ackerson, Jun.: for dwelling-house and lodging-house	0 14 0
1 0	Ditto: for another house in East-street	0 2 0
1 15	Thomas Wilmshurst: a house ...	0 3 6
1 15	John Ackerson, Jun.: a house	0 3 6
7 0	Charles Rudhall: a house, yard, warehouse, &c. ...	0 14 0
1 0	George Roberts: a house	0 2 0
4 0	Thomas Chalk: a house	0 8 0
6 0	William Colbron: a house and shop ...	0 12 0
1 0	John Palmer, Jun.: a house	0 2 0
0 10	Ditto: for a shop ...	0 1 0
2 5	Thomas Adams: a house	0 4 6
5 10	Fox: for the Play-house, vault, and yard	0 11 0
4 10	Mrs. Mittens: a house	0 9 0
3 10	Thomas Webb: a house, yard, and back-buildings	0 7 0
1 5	Widow Harman: ...	0 2 6
1 5	Mrs. Viner: a house	0 2 6
9 10	Ditto: her lodging-house	0 19 0
9 0	Grace Geere: a house	0 18 0
2 10	John Gilbert: a house	0 5 0
1 0	Robert Wood: a house ...	0 2 0
1 0	Jedediah Thompson: a house ...	0 2 0
5 0	Joseph Walls: a house and shop	0 10 0
2 0	Ditto: for a stable and herring house	0 4 0
4 5	Richard Hemsley: a house and shop	0 8 6
2 0	Thomas Wigram: a house and ground, stable and shop	0 4 0
5 0	John Wigram: a house and ground ...	0 10 0
0 15	William Saunders: a house	0 1 6
3 0	Elizabeth Mighell: a house	0 6 0
0 15	John Pulling: a house ...	0 1 6
8 15	John Lulham: a house, coach-house, and stables ["The White Lion"] ...	0 17 6
7 5	Thomas Barber: a house	0 14 6
1 5	Ditto: and house, workshop, and yard	0 2 6
8 5	Richard Marchant: a house and ground	0 16 6
1 15	Widow English: a house	0 3 6
3 5	Widow Barnett: a house	0 6 6
2 10	Richard Palmer: a house and shop ...	0 5 0
4 10	Ditto: a lodging-house	0 9 0
2 10	Thomas Salmon: a house	0 5 0
1 0	Michael Compit: a house	0 2 0
1 0	William Pimm: a house	0 2 0
1 0	Widow Groavet: a house in the garden	0 2 0
17 0	Mrs. Dring: a house, coach-house, and stables	1 14 0
7 15	Ditto: for Mrs. Turner's house and stables	0 15 6
6 5	John Sicklemore: a house and ground	0 12 6
1 10	Ditto: a windmill	0 3 0
16 0	Samuel Shergold: a house, coach-house, and stables	1 12 0
2 15	Ditto: a warehouse in Black Lion-street	0 3 6
7 15	Shergold and Co.: for the stables and coach-house, late Hicks's	0 15 6
70 10	Ditto: for the Castle Tavern, &c.	7 1 0
4 15	Ditto: for coach-house and stables, late Stiles's ...	0 9 6
1 0	Ditto: for a barn and ground ...	0 2 0
350 4		

At the period of the small-pox scourge (1786) the number of the inhabitants of North-street was 529—about a sixth of those of the whole town. About 1785 the first coffee-house and tavern were erected in North-street (the original of the present "Clarence" Hotel). The first Brighton Bank was opened in North-street in 1787, the original firm being "Harben, Shergold, Scutt, Rice, and Son": the hours for transacting business were "from nine in the morning till six in the evening." (In 1800 the firm was "Shergold, Mitchell, Rice, Rice, and Mills.") This Bank was at 103, North-street (opposite the present Union Bank), and, though it withstood the "Panic" of 1825, it soon after transferred its declining business. The earliest local printing-office, that of Messrs. William and Arthur Lee, of Lewes, was "set up" in North-street, in the old Play-house, in 1789. The first local Pleasure Gardens—the Promenade Grove—opened in 1793, were entered from North-street, by what is now Prince's-place. In North-street, too (in Prince's-place), was erected, in 1794, the first Chapel of Ease to the Parish Church—the Chapel Royal—built "on account of the rapid increase of population, and the consequent complaint of room [want of?] in the Church; and not only for the accommodation of the company, but also for the use of such of the inhabitants as are disposed to become purchasers of pews." On the completion of the Chapel Royal a colonnade was formed in front of it, and afterwards continued right round Prince's-place, on the east side of which some neat shops had been erected, which at first seemed to have been utilized during the season by London tradesmen for the accommodation of the "company" visiting Brighton, but were subsequently permanently occupied by tradesmen of the town. The first-local coach-office (that is, one devoted exclusively to the business,) was opened at No. 1, North-street, about the year 1794.

But we will pass on to a little later period, 1800, when we get more definite information respecting the street and its inhabitants. It is, however, very difficult to realise now what North-street was, as a street, in 1800, so many changes in it having since taken place. It was narrow, both at top and bottom, and irregularly built throughout. At the top, in fact, for some distance above West-street, it was only about 15 or 20ft. in width, and some idea may be formed of the character of the original houses and shops there by those existing (though they are altered in some respects), and by reference to the annexed *plate*. East-street in 1800 ran through the Pavilion Grounds. Prince's-place then had a neat shrubbery in its centre. New-road did not exist. The Royal Colonnade was unformed; where it is, facing North-street, was the southern boundary wall of the old "Castle" stables, blank and sombre, pierced here and there by small and dingy half-moon stable windows. Opposite, at the east corner of the Lanes, was a little cottage, with garden plot in front, occupied by Mr Rudhall (of the firm of Rudhall and Dudlow, now Messrs. Reed's). What was formerly known as Ship-street Lane (leading from North-street to Ship-street) was a narrow and inconvenient thoroughfare, just admitting the passage of a single vehicle; the foot-path (on the west side) being a causeway, some feet above the road, running along to Duke's-court. Portland-street was then incomplete: its beginning was a large yard, extending about half way up the present street, and known as Portland

Yard,* and beyond, northward, were market-gardens. Opposite Portland Yard a few houses, with paved forecourts, stood back from the line of the street to a point which may be seen even now over No. 50, (formerly Messrs. Sayer's.) Unicorn Yard was in extent much about the same as Portland Yard; the old Barracks, subsequently "The Unicorn" stables, being entered from it on the left hand. Higher up, on the same side, immediately above "The White Lion," and in the narrowest part of the street, were the rookeries of "Durham" and "Petty France." At the top of the street (the south-west corner) was the smithy, with forge, &c., of Mr. Simon Wisden (now supplanted by the handsome Drapery Emporium of Ald. S. H. Soper); and opposite was another smithy, forge, &c., belonging to Mr. Joseph Walls. Behind this latter was Viner's coach factory (and yard), and above this ran a row of cottages (some of which were removed when Chandler's—now "North-street Brewery,"—was erected) up to a second little row of houses, which then, as now, bounded the top and faced down the street. Behind these was a huge chalk-pit, a large portion of which was filled up when Upper North-street was formed.† The Post Office was removed from the Steine to North-street (at the north-eastern corner of Prince's-place) in 1803, where it remained for nearly twenty years.

In 1800 North-street had become an active business thoroughfare, having in it between 50 and 60 shops, a bank, two coach offices, and half-a-dozen public-houses. Subjoined, however, is a complete list of the tradesmen and other residents in the street at that period, compiled from "The Brighthelmston Directory for 1800."‡

No.
1. Gourd, Boulton, Tilt, Hicks, Baulcomb, and Co., London Coach proprietors.
2. Gregory, James, medicine warehouse and toy shop.
3. Lynch and Tayler, linen drapers; Nightingale, Thomas, glover and breeches maker.
4. Smith, John, pastry cook and confectioner.
5. Irish, James, watchmaker and silversmith.
7. Wilmshurst, Thomas, watchmaker and silversmith.
8. Paine, Richard, drawing master and stationer.

---

* It owed it name, we believe, to the Messrs. Lambert, stone-masons, whose yard and business premises were there located.

† In a cave in this pit Corporal Staines (an old marine, a "character" in the olden time, who had served under Nelson at Copenhagen), resided for several years, previous to his removal to the hut which he erected near the old Manor Pound and Parish "stocks," at the back of the Parish Church, just where the entrance to the New Burial Ground now is. Staines afterwards removed to a hut at the top of Rose-hill, where he erected a flag-staff and a small battery, firing a gun every evening at sunset. *Erredge* says, "He was very crippled, and obtained his living by exhibiting miniature fortifications, constructed by himself, the soldiers and cannons which surmounted the battlements being formed of chalk; as was also a very rude model of the gallant ship, 'The Victory,' bearing, under a black canopy, a coffin containing the body of the Hero of Trafalgar." The Corporal eventually ended his days in the Workhouse.

‡ The old "Directory" gives but 105 houses in North-street proper in 1800; therefore some portion of the 150 said to have been in the street in 1794 were probably "in courts at the upper end of North-street, west of King-street." Eighteen years later (in 1818) the houses and shops in North-street had increased to 148. The number now is 173.

NORTH STREET.

No.
- 9. Grenville, Jonathan, watchmaker and goldsmith ; Grenville and Prince, music sellers.
- 10 and 11, Glaisyer, John, chemist and druggist.
- 12. Dring, William, grocer, tea dealer, and oilman.
- 13. Martin, Thomas, cordwainer.
- 14. Penticost, Thomas, plumber and glazier.
- 15. Newbold, William, linen draper.
- 17. Welsford, Roger, Esq.
- 20. Rudhall and Dudlow, ironmongers and braziers.
- 21. Thompson, Jedediah, blacksmith and greengrocer.
- 22. Martin, Lucy, haberdasher.
- 23. Morling, John, victualler ("Coach and Horses").
- 24. Henwood, Crossweller, Cuddington, Pockney, Harding, and Co., London Coach proprietors ; Henwood, William Henry, victualler ("New Inn").
- 26. Burfield, John, linen draper.
- 27. Cripps, William, coach and sign painter.
- 29. Walker, George, broker and appraiser ; Walker, Frances, mantua maker.
- 30. Martin, John, man's mercer, &c.
- 31. Collard, John, chemist.
- 32. Hargraves, John, surgeon.
- 35. Newton, John, surgeon.
- 36. Wood, James, watch maker.
- 37. Baker and Co., hatters.
- 38 and 39. Gilburd, John, hairdresser and toyman.
- 41. Gibbs, Thomas, salesman.
- 43. Harmer, Thomas, wireworker, grocer, and auctioneer.
- 44. Lee, William and Arthur, printers.
- 45. Washington, Lydia, mantua maker.
- 47. Bayley, Thomas, victualler.
- 48. Simpson, Thomas, cordwainer and leather cutter.
- 53. Goldsmith, Mary, grocer.
- 54 and 55. Chittenden, Joseph, draper, &c.
- 57 and 58. Streeter, Edward, baker, &c.
- 60. Wisden, Simon, blacksmith.
- 61. Walls, Joseph, blacksmith.
- 63. Viner, Joseph, coach and harness maker.
- 73. Sicklemore, James, grocer.
- 74. Shoubridge, John, corn chandler.
- 75. Wallis, John, victualler ("White Lion").
- 78. Davidson, Joseph, victualler ("Unicorn"), cow keeper and milkman.
- 80. Mighell, William, grocer.
- 82. Erredge, William, hairdresser.
- 83. Allen, Richard, grocer and blacksmith.
- 84. Hughes, Joseph, attorney.
- 85. Barnard, Mary, victualler ("Blacksmiths' Arms").
- 87. Elphic, John, butcher.
- 88. Palmer, Edward, whitesmith and bellhanger.
- 89. Salmon, Thomas, gardener.
- 91. Martin, Edward, linen draper and tailor.
- 92. Paine, Cornelius, school master.
- 93. Maiben, Adam, saddler and harness maker.
- 94. Grantham, George, lodging-house keeper.
- 95. Holder, Daniel, lodging-house keeper.
- 96. Furner, John and Thomas, gardeners.

No.
97. Brooker, Henry, attorney and notary public.
99. Kendall and Co., hatters.
103. Shergold, Michell, Rice, Rice, and Mills (The Bank).
104. Moron, Mary, lodging-house keeper; Morling, Philip, spruce beer merchant and brewer; Elmore, George, horse dealer and livery stable keeper.
105. Hall, John, surgeon.

As regards the business character of North-street, it was viewed with very different eyes in 1800 from what it would be by those of the present day. One writer, in 1808, says :—" In truth, Castle-square, and the half of North-street, may be said to be the Bond-street of Brighton; and in the latter there are many as well contrived and furnished shops as those of the Bond-street of the Metropolis." What these " well contrived and furnished shops" were like, it would be difficult to realise at the present time, since not one of them remains in its original condition,—

" All, all are changed, the old familiar places."

The upper storeys of some of the old houses are, indeed, still to be seen; but the old shops—which were one and all of unpretentious character—are gone. In an interesting biography of the late William Constable (written some years ago by Mr. Barclay Phillips) we get a glimpse of the original establishment from which Messrs. Hannington's subsequently sprung.* In 1802, the business (one of the three drapers then existing) was carried on by Mr. Daniel Constable (with his brother William as shopman) at No. 3, North-street.† The infant concern consisted of a "shop and one room behind"—the latter serving for all the purposes of living by day and of rest by night! From the elder Constable's diary we learn that the proprietors " opened shop," " painted shop," &c., as, doubtless, did the

---

* The late Mr. S. Hannington commenced business in North-street, July 25th, 1808. His first advertisement, published in the *Brighton Herald*, was as follows :—

LINEN DRAPERY, MERCERY, HABERDASHERY, AND HOSIERY,
No. 3, North-street.

S. HANNINGTON begs leave most respectfully to inform the Inhabitants and Visitants of Brighton, and its vicinity, that he has taken the above-mentioned Shop (late Tamplin and James) and intends OPENING on MONDAY NEXT, July 25th, with a new and elegant Assortment of Goods in the above Branches, which will be sold for Ready Money, at such unusual low Prices, as, he trusts, will ensure the future Patronage and Support of those who may be pleased to confer on him their favours.

† The Messrs. Constable disposed of their business in 1806 to Mr. Ireland (uncle of the late Alderman Ireland), the projector of Ireland's Gardens—now Park-crescent, who, on his removal to No. 9, in 1807, disposed of it to Messrs. Tamplin and James. The brothers Constable subsequently went to America, where they devoted themselves to scientific pursuits. Mr. William returned about 1825, and a year or two later made himself "famous" by performing a "flying" feat at Mr. Ireland's Gardens, descending successfully, by means of wheels attached to a cable, from the top of the Assembly Room to the north of the Grounds, though it apparently afforded little satisfaction to the spectators, the feat being performed very rapidly and differently to what had been expected. In 1841, Mr. W. Constable introduced photography to Brighton, opening a "blue room" on the Marine-parade. He died December 22nd, 1861.

other shopkeepers of the street. We get, too, in the same biography, some particulars as to the customs of the tradesmen at that early period. If a shopkeeper required a "change"—he took it and lost nothing. It was quite in order to close a shop and put up a notice "Gone for a holiday. Back next week." A not unusual notice, also, was "Gone to London for the winter." We are told, too, that, at this primitive period, the tradesmen of North-street, as did others residing in similar outside districts, closed their shops after dark in winter time! Certainly, as gas-lighting had not come into fashion, the streets, being but dimly lighted by the old oil lamps, and ill-paved, needed wary walking by promenaders, and must have been most unattractive for "shopping."

With respect to other of the earlier local tradesmen of North-street, it may be mentioned that allusion has been made (p. 137) to Mr. Richard Lemmon Gregory, assistant to Mr. James Gregory, of No. 2, North-street. But we must not pass over Mr. Thomas Nightingale (familiarly known as "Tommy" Nightingale, in his way a local "character"), glover and breeches maker. "Tommy" was an active business man. In 1791 he occupied a shop in North-street nearly opposite "The Unicorn." It must have been a very small shop; for it was assessed at only 10s. a year, and the demand upon him for a 1s. 1½d. rate made in 1791 was 6¾d.! As property in North-street is now rated, one is tempted to exclaim "Happy Tommy"! But Tommy wasn't happy; for in 1800 he had removed to No. 3, North-street (afterwards Messrs. Constable's), and even here was not content. This latter shop was perhaps still too small for him; for, be it known unto all men, Tommy manufactured the Prince of Wales's hunting-breeches! and, what is more, cleaned them after hunting, as well as those of the Royal suite. He therefore again removed over the way, into the uppermost of the shops formerly to the south of the Chapel Royal; and, though an ugly pump stood boldly out in a passage close to his doorway for several years, he settled down. Here, as regularly as morning came, Tommy placed in a chair, outside his shop-door, a huge stuffed leather glove—some 3ft. or 4ft. in height—to proclaim to all the world, Thomas Nightingale, glover, &c., liveth here! Peace to his manes!

But to pass on. An important change was made some four or five years later in the lower part of the street. The Prince of Wales, by consent of the town, absorbed that part of East-street running from North-street to Church-street into the Pavilion Grounds, and, by way of compensation, formed the present New-road, through what was then Messrs. Furner's garden, and this occasioned other changes, giving importance to the locality. North-street was now *the* business street of the town. Another Bank—the Union Bank—was opened in it in 1805 by Mr. Thomas West, in conjunction with Messrs. Brown, Hall, and Lashmar; their neighbour, Mr. Daniel Constable, being, we are told, the first to open an account with them. In 1806 the Friends' old Meeting-house in North-street (south-east corner of New-road) was removed and several shops erected on its site. During the previous 10 or 12 years, however, other important changes had been made in the neighbourhood. According to Budgen's "New and Correct Plan of Brighthelmston in 1788," property of some description ran down North-street just below the Friends' Meeting-house, and far across Prince's-place, which latter had not then its present dimensions, and was oblong in shape. This property was doubtless removed in 1793, when the Chapel Royal was built, and for some years after—down probably to 1803—there appears to have been a vacant space at the South-side of the Chapel up to the old Meeting-house, which at this period must have stood almost full out into the street.

If the "business" character of North-street in the early part of the century increased rapidly, the tradesmen of the period do not seem to have been over-burdened—as their successors are deemed to be now—with "rent and taxes." A comparison between "past" and "present" in this respect is not without interest. For instance, the houses and shops which formerly stood on the sites of what are now Nos. 15, 16, and 17, produced just before 1800 an annual rental of £17; and in 1814 their united assessments only amounted to £14 15s. The property now realizes probably a rental value of between £500 and £600 a year. Then, again, the dwelling-house, shop, &c., which formerly stood at the corner of West-street (on the site of Mr. Bull's grocer's shop, now Messrs. Baker and Co.'s), was sold in 1793-94 for £432. When Mr. Bull's new shop was erected, about 35 years ago, the town paid something like £2,000 for the privilege of merely setting it back a few feet in North-street and West-street.

A still more important proof of the rise in value of property in North-street, is, however, afforded by the "Brighton Surveyor's Book, for the year 1814" (formerly in the possession of the late Alderman H. Martin). In this book is given the amount at which every house throughout the town was assessed in 1814, and the details—so low are the assessments—are such as are calculated to make the present generation sigh for the "good old times!" The assessors of 1814 must have been either very liberal or else unfamiliar with the application of the modern "screw." Fancy forty-seven (that is the actual number) of the houses in North-street assessed at only £4 a year each, and nine-tenths of the others under £10! The assessment of the whole of the houses in the street was only £960; just one sixth of the amount for those of the whole town, namely, £5,790. (In 1880 the rateable value of the town was about £550,000; it is now £627,940 15s.) Mr. Diplock's premises, No. 4, North-street (the lower portion of what is now Hannington's best shop), were assessed at £5 5s.; Mr. John Glaisyer's (now Glaisyer and Kemp's) at £11 5s.; "The New Inn" ("The Clarence") at £34; "The Coach and Horses" (next door) at £4; "The White Lion" at £14; "The Unicorn" at £5 10s.; and "The Hammers" ("The Blacksmiths' Arms") at £4. One of the most extraordinary assessments is the Theatre (New-road), which is put at *eighteen pounds!* What would the late Mrs. H. Nye Chart have said, if, when a 2s. rate was made, she had received a "demand" for only 36s.!

OLD HOUSES IN NORTH STREET

Some of the Surveyor's notes in the above book, as to the reasons why rates were not paid by certain individuals, are worth quoting. Not a few have attached to them "Left Brighton" and "Gone"; others, "Worked" and "Worked out" (how accommodating were rate-collectors in the olden time!) By the side of several exempted names is "Poor"; of others, "Dead"; and one unfortunate man is noted as "Dead and Poor." Another ground of exemption is "Washerwoman"; then there is "Don't pay," and "Don't pay Taxes," and, *mirabile dictu!*—"Will not pay"; and the plea of this determined individual appears to have been allowed!

Among the early "events" of North-street, there is one worth mentioning, by reason of the excitement it occasioned, namely, the exhibition of Napoleon's carriage (taken at Jemappes, after Waterloo), in the old "Castle" stables, New-road. The carriage was brought to Brighton by a Mr. Bullock, who had previously exhibited it in London, as he stated, to 100,000 persons. While here, crowds daily flocked to see it, and to sit in it; and the sensation it excited elicited,—we believe, from Mr. Rickman ("Clio" Rickman, as he was called, himself a "curiosity"*)—the following lines, which appeared in the Lewes paper:—

> "What wondrous things are daily brought to view
> Produced by Time, and shown by Fortune's glasses:
> Six noble horses the great Napoleon drew,
> Now, one Bullock draws a hundred thousand asses!"

Another "event" was the singular detection of smuggled goods, in the shop of Mr. Spencer Weston, a tradesman of North-street. Mr. Weston, formerly of Seddlescombe, near Hastings, carried on the business of silk-mercer and lace-man in a shop where are now Nos.

---

* "Clio" Rickman, who adopted this cognomen from his taste for history, was a member of the old Quaker family of that name, still flourishing near Lewes. His habits were, however, anything but Quaker-like; he called himself a "citizen of the world," held extreme Republican principles, was an admirer of Tom Paine, Horne Tooke, &c., and, to the end of his long-protracted life, which was closed in London some 55 years ago, dressed in a very eccentric style. He was a man of strong original genius and great literary taste, but was extreme in his opinions and peculiar in his habits. A correspondent of the *Brighton Herald*, some years since, in paying a genial tribute to "Clio," says of his closing days:—"He enjoyed a small annuity, and died at the house in London (Upper Marylebone-street) in which he had lived many years, and where he had carried on business as a bookseller and publisher. It was from thence he fled to France in woman's attire when Thomas Paine was convicted for the publication of the 'Rights of Man' in 1792. The booksellers and publishers of it were also prosecuted and suffered judgment to go by default, for which they received the sentence of three years' imprisonment each. 'Of these,' Clio Rickman relates, 'I was one, but, by flying to France, I eluded the merciful sentence.' It was at his rooms in London that I last visited him in 1828. He was enjoying a tranquil age, surrounded by relics and memorials of the eventful years that had fallen to his lot; the table at which he sat was hallowed to him by his friend, Thomas Paine, having written thereon some of his anathematised and far-resounding works; books and objects of value and taste were around; a suit of fine chain armour hung on the walls, while the solace of the pipe, and often opium, were within reach. In Paine's will Clio's name is coupled with that of Thomas Addis Emmett—'expatriated Republican of Ireland,' as Clio calls him,—for a sum of money arising from the sale of some property in America, but the executors did not, or could not, carry out the bequest to the satisfaction of our old friend."

18 and 19. The excellence of his stock excited the suspicion of the Excise officers, who occasionally "dropped in to have a look round." On one such occasion, after the officers had made a fruitless search, Mr. Weston spread for them a bountiful luncheon, to which they were nothing loth to partake. The "host" chuckled to himself that he had "done" them again, when the Commanding officer, suddenly rising from the hospitable board, said "I think we'll look round once more before we go." They did; and the search was fatal! some goods being discovered upon which no duty had been paid, and Mr. Weston was fined £120. This, however, was a mere "flea-bite" to that in which he was subsequently mulcted, when the whereabouts of his "secret chamber" was made known to the Excise by, it was believed, a charwoman. Mr. Weston's kitchen extended the whole width of the premises in the rear, and the fire-range was so contrived as to draw out and in upon hidden wheels. Behind the range was the little room in which the smuggled stock was kept snug and dry. This time the Excise thought to "break" the delinquent; imposing a fine of no less than £10,000! Mr. Weston had, however, saved a few "pieces"—added to which he had recently been the fortunate winner of the "Grand Prize" in a lottery—*and he paid it!* Such offences as Mr. Weston's were regarded by the public in those days as very venial. The goods were "run" for Mr. Weston by the then fastest cutter on the coast, "Master Wren," of Brighton, owner; and taken from whence they were landed in carts of the huckster type to a preconcerted place in the vicinity of the shop, to await the signal that the way was clear.

Another of the early tradesmen may, perhaps, be mentioned in passing, namely, Mr. Richardson, familiarly known as "Old Richardson," silk and lace mercer, furnishing undertaker, &c., whose shop was at the East-street corner of Castle-square. He was the father of Mr. George Frederick Richardson, the Curator of Dr. Mantell's Museum, formerly on the Old Steine. There are, we suppose, "top-sawyers" in every business; and old Mr. Richardson used to boast that he was "the only man who knew how to walk in front of a funeral." And, when occasion required, the worthy tradesman invariably carried the board with the plumes thereon in front of the funeral procession.

One other North-street "character" of a little later period, was Mr. Hammond, hair-dresser, &c., whose shop was just within the New-road. None seemed to know whence he came, or whither he went. He was a mulatto, and used to dress in superb style, with "Paul Foskett" hat,—that is, a high one of huge proportions and with ample brim,—cut away coat, light coloured breeches, and top boots. He proclaimed himself "Inventor of the Antelope Oil;" and over his shop, looking up North-street, was a huge painting (in garish colours) of a negro shooting an antelope. The "Inventor" used to aver that if the Oil were dropped on the pave-stones, hair would appear in 24 hours! Whether or no he afforded ocular demonstration of the miracle is not recorded.

About 1814 Mr Choat's "Emporium of Literature," *alias* Library, was opened in North-street, at the south-east corner of Prince's-place; and a fine Library it was, the catalogue containing some 12,000 volumes (which formed the nucleus of Loder's and Folthorp's in after days). A description of it says, "it is situated in one of the most popular streets for business. * * * The gravity of its plan is never broken in upon by the lighter amusements of music, song, &c., but news, literature, and politics, are its distinguishing characteristics." A few years previously the office of the *Brighton Herald* had been removed from the top of North-street* to its present premises in Prince's-place. The Place, in fact, became a "centre" for the dissemination of news and literature; for at the upper (North-street) corner, immediately opposite Choat's, a Mr. Trowbridge opened a bookseller's shop. He was succeeded, we believe, by Mr. Taylor, a well-known bookseller in times gone by, publisher of "The Garland" (a poetic miscellany), "The Brighton Guide," and several other local works. Subsequently Genns' coach-office book-keeper, "old Jones," started at the same shop a bookstall, and turned news-vendor—the first in Brighton; his mantle later on falling on the shoulders of his nephew, William Grant, who elevated news-vending into a "business," and whose shop in Castle-square became the head centre of "news" in Brighton.

In 1823 another important improvement took place in North-street, by the formation of the Royal Colonnade (the builders being Messrs. Cooper and Lynn). When completed (the houses over the Colonnade being of good elevation) it formed a handsome addition to the street; and the shops there were soon taken. The business situation of the Colonnade was then a most desirable one. It led to the Theatre; and, after 1831, when the Post Office was opened at the north end of New-road, the Colonnade (for "business" along the King's-road was then comparatively *nil*) was regarded as one of the best places for business in the town. Among the earliest of those who "opened shop" in the Colonnade, was the late Mr. T. H. Wright, of the Colonnade Library (at the North-street corner).

Looking down the list of tradesmen in North-street in 1823, one is struck at the changes which have taken place during the last 60 or 70 years. There are not now in the street many more than half-a-dozen businesses carried on in the same name or even by legitimate successors to those who were there in 1823. Hannington's, and Hall, West, and Co.'s (Union Bank); Glaisyer and Kemp's, Bowen and Co.'s, Folkard's, and Palmer and Green's; the *Brighton Herald* and the *Brighton Gazette*; S. Ridley's and W. Cheesman's, and all are told! How many once-familiar names and businesses have dropped out of sight; and how many that are almost unknown to the present generation! Diplock, silk mercer; Wilmshurst and Philp, silversmiths; Paine, stationer; Blaker, Lashmar, Mills, Lidbetter, and "Joey" Stillwell, grocers; Harry Tuppen, butcher; Noble, sweep; Weller, broker; Plumpton, eating-house keeper; Dennis Penticost, carpenter; Hemsley, coach-maker;

---

* North-street may now (1892) be regarded as the "home" of the Press; for all the local journals, save one, are published in it.

Vollar, stable-keeper; Martin, tailor; Chapman, stonemason; Wallis, wine merchant; Chassereau, fancy shop; Loder, librarian, and many another that might be mentioned. In 1823 Mr. Lewis Slight, so potent in later days as Clerk to the Commissioners, carried on in North-street the business of ladies' shoemaker, and his wife that of stay-maker; Baxter (later on of the *Sussex Express*) sold books and stationery; Simon Wisden's smithy blazed; "honest" Jonathan Streeter sold his flour; Pitt did business as pipe manufacturer; Barns, the cutler, owned "The Brighton Royal Exchange," and "Tommy" Nightingale was ready and willing to "make breeches."

In 1827, the old "Footway to Hove" (leading from the top of North-street) was widened; in 1831 there was an important alteration at the bottom of North-street, in the erection by William IV. of the Southern Entrance (now removed) to the Pavilion; and about 1834 there was considerable improvement at the top of West-street, at which time Cranbourne-street was formed (Mr. Rickard's School, in West-street, being removed for the purpose). But *the* improvement of North-street was about 1845, when "Durham" and its offensive adjuncts were swept away for the formation of the Queen's-road. It would be difficult to realize now the state of this locality at the time. North-street at this particular spot was little more than 15ft. or 20ft. wide. "Durham" (entered by a square opening from the street) resembled an old inn yard, sunk in squalidity and filth, an old-fashioned balcony running in front of the upper rooms of some of the houses. "Petty France" (another batch of squalid tenements, behind "Durham" to the east), was reached by a long passage by the side of Mr. Caudle's chemist's-shop—the only decent house of the range. Below Mr. Caudle's was an oblong square yard, at the north-east end of which was "The White Lion" tap. In this square, by the side of Mr. Caudle's, Mr. Jolly, grocer (the predecessor of Mr. Bull) used to open his sugar-tubs—an "event" of special interest to boys of North-street and neighbourhood some 60 years ago!

In July, 1855, there was an altogether unexpected removal of property in North-street, by the falling of one of the two houses wherein the late Mr. Gregory for many years previously had carried on the business of trunk-maker, &c. These houses (then Nos. 55 and 56), were among the earliest built of those then existing in the street, their erection dating back, it is thought, to the time of the Commonwealth. With the view to rebuilding, one of the houses was taken down, business meanwhile being carried on in the other; when, a day or so after, without a moment's warning, the latter collapsed, the whole building falling in. Mr. Gregory's two daughters, a lad, and a little dog were in the shop at the time, but, though one and all went down with the falling ruins, singular to relate each escaped almost unhurt.

There "passed away" in February, 1855, one who may fairly be mentioned among the North-street tradesmen, namely, Dudley Harricks, who for years kept a hosier's shop in the Lanes, a few yards up from North-street; in fact, among the N.B.'s in his window was the following: "Take out your tablet and note that

D. Harricks's shop is — yards — feet — inches from North-street, the principal street in Brighton." The old hosier was a man of strict integrity and of irreproachable private character, but eccentric in many matters. He had, however, a keen eye to business and to the advantages of "special" advertising; the many quaintly written distiches in praise of his goods exhibited in his window, or painted on the board at the south-side of his house, being most potent in attracting the attention of passers-by. So far as we can remember, one or two of the "originals" on the outside board ran thus:—

"The Mushroom springs up in the morning, and disappears before night; but not so

D. HARRICKS,

Who has now stood his ground for — years, and always paid Nineteen Shillings in the Pound. Pray do assist him to pay Twenty."

"A WET JACKET.

A Wet Jacket is a very unpleasant Thing.

D. HARRICKS

Sells Waterpoof Overcoats, Undercoats, Ladies' Knee Caps, Welsh Flannel, Tapes, Bobbins, and Pins."

Among those in the window, not the least conspicuous was the following, pinned either on a pair of hose or a pair of garters:—

"A PRESENT FROM BRIGHTON.

One for the left leg, t'other for the right-un."

Mention may, perhaps, be made of "Billy" Spears, who kept *the* ham and beef shop of the town some 40 years since, at No. 27, North-street (the door above Messrs. Bowen and Williams', now Reed's), and whose only rival for many years was Plumpton, some 20 doors higher up, just opposite "The Hammers." In early life (Mr. Spears was born in 1774) he was apprenticed to a cook and confectioner at the West end of London, but showed his indentures a "fair pair of heels," and went with a few others on a "looting" expedition to the wars in Low Flanders. He served aboard ship subsequently; and used to tell a singular anecdote that, as his vessel was once going by Brighton, she passed a fisherman at sea in a boat. He hailed the man with, "Do you know Mr. Hicks, of 'The Old Ship'"? "Yes," was the answer, "died last night"! The vessel's sailing on prevented further question; but Mr. Spears subsequently learnt that the answer was true. "Billy" was full of anecdote, and a complete "Sir Oracle" in matters theatrical; being in early days familiar with G. F. Cooke, Jack Bannister, and other stage notabilities of the period. Bannister was very partial to him, and used to address him as "my jolly young cook-o'-cooks." Previous to settling in Brighton, Mr. Spears officiated as man-cook to the late Duke of

Northumberland, and afterwards to Lord Gage, at Firle, by whom and others to whom he was known he was supported in his declining days.

But we must pass on; and in conclusion will give a few details illustrative of the value of property in North-street in recent years, The assessment of North-street in 1784, as we have previously stated, was £354; in 1814 it had increased to £960; in 1827 to £1,386 5s.; and in 1879 to £17,673 10s. [In 1891 it was £19,581, and the gross estimated rental £24,500.] In December, 1875, Mr. Samuel Ridley submitted to auction the late Mr. Scarborow's business premises, 135, North-street, comprising dwelling-house, two shops, with stores and show-rooms, and having a separate entrance in Windsor-street. The property covered an area of about 2,500ft. It realised no less than £5,030, the purchaser being the Town Clerk, acting on behalf of the Street Improvements Committee. (So recently as 1867—only eight years previously—Mr. Scarborow had purchased the property for £2,550!) And yet, after all, the Corporation did not make a bad bargain; for when the upper portion of the property was re-sold by Messrs. Wilkinson and Son, in July, 1877, it fetched £4,060. Then, with respect to "The White Lion." In 1814, this house was assessed at £14 10s. yearly; and in 1872 at £207. In this latter year it was purchased by the Corporation, who paid for it the large sum of £8,000. Messrs. Cochran's business premises, No. 49, North-street, were sold by Messrs. Wilkinson, in February, 1877, for no less than £4,920; and the same firm, in July, the same year, sold three plots of land above "The Unicorn Inn" for very large sums. The first plot—immediately above the Inn—realised £1,620; and two other plots above this plot, £1,760 each, or nearly £95 per foot. In connection with the property lower down the street—that formerly existing between the New-road and Prince's-place—equally extraordinary prices were realised. For instance, Mr. Lulham's late premises—some three or four shops of limited area, immediately to the south of the Chapel Royal—were sold by Mr. Samuel Ridley, in 1875, for £4,200, the purchaser being the late Mr. Alderman Ireland, to whom the Corporation subsequently gave £500 for his bargain! The properties altogether (in 1841 and 1859) cost Mr. Lulham only £2,500. The shop and premises above these,—Mr. Plumer's, at the corner of the New-road, and the shop below (late Dagg's),— were purchased by Mr. Daniel Hack, in 1827, for £2,500; but the Corporation, in January, 1878, gave for the same property £7,920. On the old houses being removed, their site (less a considerable portion, taken off for widening the street,) was submitted to auction by Mr. B. Webb, in May, 1879, and, though the superficial area offered was barely 130 square yards, it realized £2,420; or about £85,540 per acre. The highest price, we believe, ever obtained for a piece of land of similar size in the town.

We may fitly conclude our notice of North-street with some particulars concerning one of its old houses,—of which, about a century ago, the Rev. Thomas Hudson (subsequently Vicar of

OLD HOUSES IN NORTH STREET.

(Formerly at the North-East Corner of West-Street.) *From a Pen and Ink Drawing.*

Brighton) was tenant. This old house (in its last days known as "The London Tavern") was situated at the north-east corner of West-street, and was removed by Mr. Joseph Smith, draper, whose fine business premises now occupy its site.

To many old Brightonians the old house has always been invested with a special interest, as being, we believe, the earliest established Commercial School in Brighton: the precursor of Mr. Paine's, Mr. Humber's, and other well-known schools. It was *the* school of the period, and among the scholars were the Tuppens, the Lashmars, and Attrees, and others, the sons of the then principal local tradesmen. *When* the house was first erected is now past finding out. From the old deeds relating to the house its possessors can be traced back 150 years or more. By the will of Diones Geere (of Heyton, otherwise South Heighton, in the County of Sussex, clerk), dated November, 1763, "the messuage or tenement, yard or backside, and piece of land, at the upper end of the West Street of Brighthelmstone," was given to trustees on trust, "to raise by mortgage or otherwise a sum not exceeding £200, for the education of his only son, Diones Geere, at school and at the University (£2,000 would scarcely suffice now) and subject thereto to his son absolutely." The Rev. Diones Geere* came into possession of the property through his wife Grace, the daughter of Richard Lemmon (High Constable of Brighton in 1732, and with whom the Whichelos, another old Brighton family, were connected.) Mr. Lemmon appears to have acquired the property of one Hardham, and, without going further, there is evidence of the existence of the old house as early as 1720-30.

The "yard or backside, and piece of land," attached to the house (this last fronted into West-street) extended for some distance down North-street, into what was subsequently known as Chapman's Yard. The limits of this Yard were apparently undefined (land in North-street was not so valuable then as now)—it was not even enclosed till 1801.

In 1784 the house was occupied, or rented, by the Rev. Thomas Hudson, who succeeded the Rev. Henry Michell as Vicar of Brighton in October, 1789. The house, with "yard or backside, land, and stables," was in 1784-92 rated at £9 5s.! It must, at that period, have been deemed an important property; for there were only some half-dozen other properties in "the West-streete" higher rated, namely, Messrs. Grover and Co.'s (subsequently Messrs. Killick's and now Messrs. Vallance, Catt, and Co.'s), Mr. Knapp's, Mr. Kipping's, Mr. Whichelo's, and Mr. Stephen Poune's. Even Mrs. Thrale's (Dr. Johnson's Thrale) and Mrs. Scutt's, at the bottom of the street, were less rated, being respectively assessed at £7 15s. and £8 10s. On Mr. Hudson succeeding to the Vicarage, the house was occupied by his Curate, the Rev. J. Mossop, who in it "opened school," with

---

* The late Mr. Geere, surgeon, of Broad-street, was a descendant of this old Sussex family, some members of which about 200 years ago resided at Ovingdean Grange.

the view probably of increasing the scanty income derived from his curacy. This could have been but small; for the value of the Vicar's own living at this period was but £100 per annum! It was augmented, certainly, by visitors' contributions in the "Vicar's Book," at the Libraries; but these rarely amounted to another £100. Mossop, however, laboured earnestly and well in his supplementary vocation, earning the respect and esteem of both parents and scholars. One of these latter (the late Mr. Samuel Shergold, son of Mr. Shergold, of "The Castle,") thus speaks of his personal characteristics :—" Poor Mossop! I remember him well: a north-countryman, of almost gigantic figure, with a foot—improperly so called; it ought, in reality, to have been called a yard; a scholar, and a deep one, no doubt; but utterly unappreciable by little boys of an age such as he had the trouble to instruct. Poor man! he is long since gone to his account; and the memory of his worth and utility mingles with the events before the Flood!" *The Gentleman's Magazine* of the period affords abundant evidence of the Rev. Mr. Mossop's local archæological research and literary ability; and his manly conduct in the disgraceful affair of "Dr. Vicesimus Knox and the Surrey Militia," in 1793, was most creditable to him. Mr. Mossop died April 7th, 1794, and *The Gentleman's Magazine* for that month contains the following valedictory notice of him :—" At Brighthelmstone, aged 38, the Rev. John Mossop, M.A., of St. John's College, Cambridge, Curate of Brighthelmstone, Master of the Grammar School of that place, and Grand Master of the Royal Clarence Lodge. Indefatigable in his professions both as a preacher and schoolmaster. As a scholar, his abilities were too well known to need repetition."

After Mr. Mossop's death, the old house "went to strangers"; and in 1801 the Rev. Diones Geere (who had succeeded his father in the inheritance) disposed of it, with the piece of ground now occupied by Mr. Smith's present shops, but then having only one messuage upon it, to Mr. Robert Ackerson, bricklayer, for £495! and the lower portion of the land (subsequently Chapman's stonemason's yard) to Mr. Richard Chapman, the parties purchasing jointly covenanting "to erect forthwith a flint wall, of the height of 7ft., to be a boundary between the properties." Later on, the house was devoted to business purposes. In 1822 it was occupied by Mr. A. Lidbetter, grocer, with whom was Mr. William Jolly, who afterwards removed to the grocer's shop opposite, subsequently Mr. Bull's. In 1857, the trustees of Mr. Robert Ackerson disposed of the property purchased in 1801, when it realised more than ten times the amount which Mr. Ackerson originally gave for it, and its subsequent value previous to its removal was estimated at £6,000. The house was for many years occupied by Mr. Juniper, ironmonger, &c. It was opened as "The London Tavern" in March, 1858, but had been, we believe, opened as a house of refreshment a short time previously.

Going over the house just previous to its removal, when it was "shorn of its fair proportions," dilapidated, falling here and there to decay, its capacious old rooms dismantled, divided and sub-divided, one could scarcely conceive how it could have been even inhabited, much less that an enormous rent should have been paid for the privilege to do so.* But "the situation's all." There was still to be seen the old school-room on the first-floor, but much curtailed; the once famous old fire grate, with "dogs," &c., was gone bodily. The ancient kitchen "chimney corner," even then of mammoth proportions,† still remained, conjuring up a thousand memories of the olden time. One thing, however, struck us as peculiar in the *old* walls of the house; rushes were used instead of laths on which to deposit the plaster. Their use in great quantities would indicate an abundance in the neighbourhood; but Brighton furnishes none such. Whence, therefore, came they? Possibly from Lewes, where there was formerly no lack of them. If so, it furnishes another item in the indebtedness of Brighton to Lewes!

---

* Some idea of the wretched and valueless condition of the materials of the old house may be formed when we state that the whole were disposed of at the auction for less than £20; one of the houses fetching no more than *twenty-four shillings*.

† The old "chimney corner" formerly projected considerably on to the present line of pavement in West-street.

Religious Edifices in North Street.

THE FRIENDS' MEETING HOUSE.

THE earliest religious edifice opened in North-street was that of the Society of Friends, in 1700-1, at the south-east corner of what subsequently became the New-road. It was not a new building; but some premises which had been acquired by the Friends were by them converted into a Meeting-house. These premises are described in a deed of conveyance, dated August 31, 1700, to "Thomas Parsons, of Cowfold, husbandman," (who paid £105 for them,) as "All that messuage or tenement, *malthouse*, out-houses, edifices, and croft of pasture land thereunto belonging, conteyning by estimation one acre either more or less, scituate, lying, and being in Brighthelmston, in the occupation of Richard Parker."* Thomas Parsons (a member of the Society of Friends, as was, doubtless, his tenant, Richard Parker) leased this property for 1,000 years, from February 8th, 1700, to sixteen persons (as trustees for the Friends), five of whom were named Beard, two Ellis, and two Scrase, the remainder being R. Verrall, John Grover, A. Galloway, B. Mosely, T. Rigge; and under their auspices the Friends' first Meeting-House was opened. The meadow-land behind the House, running northward, was enclosed, and thenceforth became known as the Quakers' Croft (or field), a square piece, however, abutting on the Spring Walks (Church-street), being set apart for a Burying Ground.†

Of the size or architectural character of the original Meeting-House little is now known. No drawing of it is, we believe, in existence. The Friends, too, entertaining a higher regard for a

---

* This property was in existence as early as 1637, perhaps earlier. The first possessor mentioned in the deed is Nicholas Jackett. He died in 1638, and the property descended to Thomas Jackett, who, on the 11th December, 17th Charles II., mortgaged it to William Humphrey, of Newhaven, merchant, to secure £50. On the 23rd March, 1675, Jackett parted with his remaining interest in the property to Humphrey, who probably left it by will to his children; for, on the 17th June, 1699, the property was conveyed by Thomas Russell and Phillis his wife and several other parties to "Thomas Beard, of Meeching, alias Newhaven, mercer, and Anne his wife," who subsequently conveyed it to Thomas Parsons.

† This ground is now occupied by the Corporation, who are, however, restricted by deed from building upon it.

"living temple" than for "one made with hands," were content with a plain structure. As to who its builder was, even tradition is silent. But, simple or ornate in character, there the old Meeting-House stood, to the south of the pretty meadow attached to it, for over 100 years or more, generation after generation of Friends worshipping in it, unmolesting and unmolested.

Previous to the Meeting-House being opened by the Friends in Brighton, their "Meetings" were held at Blatchington, in the house of some members of the Scrase family. In that parish most probably they then buried their dead; and there also their marriages were celebrated.* Blatchington, in fact, was resorted to by the Friends for "Meetings" for some years previous to those at Brighthelmstone; it was more secluded, and therefore less liable to those persecutions to which the Friends were subjected at Brighthelmstone—not the least disgraceful and virulent of these persecutors being Captain Tettersell, of "blessed memory," in connection with the escape of Charles II.† So early as 1668 a Meeting of Friends was held at Blatchington, the records of the Society containing the following:—

"At a general meeting of the Friends of Truth, held at Richard Bax his house, at Capell, in Surrey, on the 9th day of the 7th month, in the yearre 1668, for and concerning the poor and the other affairs of the Church," the names of the meeting-places for the south and east part of the County—divided into four districts—are given as follows :—"Hurst, Blatchington, Rottendean, Lewes, Marsfield Forge, and Buckstead." The first "Meeting" was to be held at John Wenham his house, near Lewes. A "NOTE" says :—"Agreed that some Friends from all the Meetings in the County do meet together once in every quarter of a yearr, the first Meeting to be kept at Blatchington, at the house of the widow Scrase, on the 2nd of ye 9th mo."—The first "Monthly Meeting" held at Blatchington was held at the house of Henry Scrase, the 17th day of the 5th mo. (16) 72.

The first "Monthly Meeting" held by the Friends in Brighton was on the 17th day of the 10th month, 1679. There were, however, Friends in Brighton and the neighbourhood who "endured and suffered for the Truth's sake" some 20 years or more previous to this date, as we learn from "An Abstract of the Sufferings of the People call'd Quakers, for the Testimony of a Good Conscience,

---

* In the "Diary" of Elizabeth Grover, a young Quakeress (1697-1726) is recorded, under date, 1697, "My Father and Mother, John and Elizabeth Grover, Married at Blatchington on the 29th of 5th month."

† Whatever merit may have been due to Tettersell in connection with the Royal escape, his conduct in after years was most despicable: he exercised his authority as High Constable of Brighton, in 1670, "with the zeal of a bigot and the malign industry of a ministerial spy." Discovering a house in the town where a few Dissenters met, the door was broken open under a warrant, and though there was no evidence against the inmates, except that it was asserted by Tettersell's minions "that they had heard from within a voice in the elevated tone of prayer or instruction," they were summoned before the Justices at Lewes, and fined in the full penalty allowed by the Statute—the master of the house, William Beard, in no less than £20; and to enforce this, it is stated in Crosby's "History of the English Baptists," Tettersell "broke open his malthouse, and took thereout sixty-five bushel sacks of malt, which he sold to one of his partizans for *twelve shillings a quarter*." Verily, Tettersell's memory deserves to be held in honour!

from the Time of their being first distinguished by that Name, Taken from Original Records and other Authentick Accounts."* Thus, 1. "FOR NOT PAYING TITHES." On principle, the Friends uniformly refused to pay tithes, and "distress" following, goods were taken from persons living in the County during the year 1655—59 of the value of £558 15s., to satisfy demands amounting to only £219 13s. 7d.! not the least unreasonable of these "distresses" being a seizure made on the goods of Nicholas Beard, of Rottingdean, to the value of £111 5s., for only one year's tithe of a farm of £100 per annum rent.† 2nd. "FOR NOT PAYING STEEPLE-HOUSE (Church) RATES." For demands on various parties for Church-rates for sums amounting to £5 9s. 5d., goods were taken worth £15 10s. 3rd and 4th. "FOR DECLARING TRUTH IN STEEPLE-HOUSES," &c., and "FOR MEETING TOGETHER, AND GOING TO MEETINGS." The details under these heads are so extraordinary, that we quote them literally from the "Abstract":—

"About the same Time (1658) John Pullatt, of Brighthelmstone, for speaking to the Priest and People in the Steeple-house there, was put prisoner into the Blockhouse, and the next day sent to the County Goal till Sessions, then sentenced to Bridewell to be whipt and kept to hard labour. The Time of his Imprisonment in the Gaol and Bridewell was about six months In the year 1659 John Snashford, of Chiltington, and Nicholas Beard, of Brighthelmstone, for going into the respective Steeple-houses of those places, were much abused, hal'd by the Hair of the Head, and the former thrown over a Seat, to the endangering of his life."

"1658. A Meeting being held at the House of William Gould, in Brighthelmstone, the Professors of that Town, coming from their Worship, first broke the Windows, which work *one zealous woman was observed to do very devoutly with her Bible!* then they flung in much Filth on those that were there met, and at length thrusting in upon them, hal'd out Joseph Fuce and some others, throwing him very dangerously on the Ground, and haling him and others out of the Town, threatening, that if he came thither again, they would throw him into the Sea. After this manner did the People there frequently abuse those who were assembled together; of which Abuses Margery Caustock had a large share. Her daughter, also of the same Name, going from a Meeting was cruelly stoned and wounded in the Face, to the endangering her Eye, and her Blood was spilt to that

---

* This work was "Printed and Sold by the Assigns of J. Sowle, at the Bible, in George Yard, Lombard-street, London, 1733."

† This Nicholas Beard would seem to have been an especial victim to persecution. How £10 was *extracted* from him is so extraordinary that we must relate it *verbatim et literatim* ("Sufferings," p. 77):—"In this year, 1667, Nicholas Beard, then of Rottingdean, was cheated on tenn pound, by Thomas Gere, of Offingdean [Ovingdean], who came to him desiring him to grant him a favour; and being demanded wherein, he replyed, thou must not deny me, for I stand in need of tenn pounds, and thou must help me if possible (or words to that purpose), and further said he would pay him or satisfy him next Saturday att furthest. So the said Nicholas, knowing nothing of his craft, did lend him tenn pounds to doe him a curtasy, as he thought, but when he had the money he pulled out his warrant out of his pocket, and said *there* was satisfaction for him, and told the said Nicholas that he was commanded to take or destrain for tenn pounds, because he did not send armes into the Trained Bands, and that he devised this way to save himself any further labour and the said Nicholas any other way of charge, because the said Nicholas could not with carnal weapons Warr nor send two men soe to doe."

Degree, that some of her wicked Persecutors boasted that they had *killed one Quaker;* as they had almost done another, namely, Richard Pratt, by stoning him."

"Richard Pratt, for giving in a Paper to the Bench of Justices at Lewes Sessions, representing the cruel Usage and stoning of his Friends at Brighthelmstone, and desiring them to exert their Authority for protecting the Innocent from such Abuses; was by them committed to the House of Correction, and ordered to be whipt there, and kept to hard labour. As they were haling him away to Bridewell, one William Hobbine, seeing him in danger from the Pushing of the People (this was probably interpreted as an Attempt to rescue the prisoner, and under that colour ensnared another innocent Man) laid hold of Him to keep him from falling; for which he was fined three Pounds, and sent to Gaol for not paying it."

"1658. Widow Katch being moved to go into the Steeple-house at Brighthelmstone, and for speaking to the Priest and People there assembled, was hailed forth and bruised in her body and very hardly used by the cruel Professors of the town, who put a rope about her neck and hailed her out of the Town."

But in spite of persecutions under the notorious Conventicle Act and other iniquitous Acts, the Friends steadfastly held fast to their principles, and many were added to the community. After the Toleration Act, 1 Wm. and Mary, which exempted Dissenters from many penalties heretofore existing, they held their "Meetings" in peace; and as their number continued to increase, it was deemed expedient that the Brighton Friends should have a "Meeting-House" of their own in Brighton. This House, as we have previously stated, was opened in North-street in 1700-1. The Friends in Brighton at this period were, probably, among the most thriving and industrious of the community. Nor were they mere "stay-at-homes"; for in the interesting "Diary" of Elizabeth Grover previously alluded to, we learn that their daughters went long journeys and their sons traded in foreign parts. *Ex gratia:*—"1723. Brother John's new Vessell in was built and went first to Sea in the 10th Month." "1724. Brother John stopped with his Vessell in Brighthelmston Road, the first time, being then bound to the Canarys, ye 2nd of 6th month." "1726. Brother William went to Ffrance in the 5th mo., and came home again in the 6th month, being gone between 5 and 6 weeks." "Brother John stopped again in this Road, being on his passage from Stockholm to Opporto, the 26th of the 6th month." "1718. My sister Mary was at school at London." "1719. My Mother and Self was in the West Country." "1723. Mary Grover went hence for Pensilvania, 10th of 1st mo." "1726. Went to Visit my Relations in Dorsetshire, and went from thence to London, and into Yorkshire and Westmoreland."[*]

---

[*] By reason of their general and local interest, we are tempted to make a few further extracts from Elizabeth Grover's "Diary":—

1703. A Terrible Storme, commonly called the November Storme, in which 2 windmills at Brighthelmstone was blown down and much damage at Sea, November the 26th.

1705. A Terrible Storme, commonly called the August Storme, wherein many trees were blown down and great damage at Sea, in or about the 9th or 10th of ye 6th mo.

There is little of special interest to record respecting the Friends during the next fifty years or more. They were unostentatious and unaggressive; ever ready to help a "weaker brother," and each and all strove to do their duty in their respective callings. As in the days before the Flood, "they married and were given in marriage"; and strange to say almost the only event recorded in connection with the old Meeting-House in North-street was a marriage which took place there. It is thus described in *The Lewes Journal*, of September 18th, 1749:—

"On Thursday last was married, at the Quakers' Meeting at Brighthelmstone, Miss Sally Snashall, of Hurstpierpoint, Sussex, an agreeable young woman with a plentiful fortune, to Mr. Elijah Warring, Surgeon, at Alton, in Hampshire. The Service was performed by Mr. Thompson, who made an eloquent and solemn discourse. There were present a great many young persons of that Society, and the ceremony was accomplished with an awful and decent regularity. They afterwards went to the Old Ship, where they had a very elegant entertainment provided."

Of the estimation in which the Quakers were held at the close of the last century, there can be no better testimony than the following, which we take from *The Lewes and Brighthelmston Pacquet*, of September 17th, 1789:—

"The time may come when a wise Legislature will condescend to inquire by what medium a whole Society is made to think and act with uniformity, for upwards of a century; by what policy they have become the only people on earth free from poverty; by what economy they have thus prevented beggary and want amongst their members, while the nation groans under the weight of taxes for the poor? Let those who please consider the Quakers fanatics; they are such fanatics as always merit esteem; they are great, illustrious, modest, intelligent, and virtuous people; animated with the most beneficent principles. They have a comprehensive charity to all mankind, and deny the mercies of God to none; they publicly aver that an universal liberty is due to all; are against impositions of every kind; though they patiently submit to many themselves, and are perhaps the only people of all mankind whose practice corresponds with their principles."

1723. The Groynes against ye Sea, Brighthelmstone, began built, September.

1723-24. A French Vessell Shipwrecked at Brighthelmstone, the 1st day of 11th month.

1723-24. John Humphery and his Wife both killed by the fall of a Wall, which Happened by a violent Storme, on the 19th of the 11th month. At the Same time a pretty Large Vessell was, by ye violence of the Wind and Tide, carryed into the Pool.

1725-26. An Exceeding Great rain and wind, which broke down and Caryed away the Bridges at Lewes and Excett in the night between the 1st and 2nd days of the 11th mo. At the same time, the King, in his return from Hanover, Landed at Rye, in Sussex.

1726. The Town Mill at Brighthelmston was Blown down on the 10th day of the 5th month.

1726. Wheat Harvest begann at Brighthelmstone on the 11th of the 5th month, and had begun in Some places a weak Sooner, was genereelly over hereabouts by the 1st of the 6th month.

1726. The 26th of the 6th month, the Turrett and Clock of the Blockhouse was Taken down.

1726. In this Year the Railes was Sett upon the Clift.

Soon after 1800 the Friends in Brighton, who had now become comparatively a numerous body, decided to erect a new Meeting-House in some open ground at the top of Black Lion-street. The change in the character of North-street may have had something to do with the removal of the Friends' Meeting-House. But a more important reason was, probably, the close proximity of the old Meeting-house, Croft, &c., to the pleasure-gardens known as the Promenade Grove. The Grove abutted on to the Quakers' Croft. In it almost daily concerts were given; there were also pic-nic parties, displays of fireworks, &c., and here the Prince of Wales and his companions and all the world of Fashion in Brighton were wont to revel during the season. The Prince, too, being desirous to extend the Pavilion Grounds, made an offer for the Croft, which the Friends parted with for £800—an act of liberality in strong contrast with the conduct of the Son of Vulcan, living near the Northern Entrance, who refused to part with his smithy, though the Prince offered for it four-fold its value.* Whatever the cause, certain it is the Friends opened their new Meeting-House in 1805,† Messrs. T. and J. Rickman, C. Spencer, W. Grover, J. Summers, J. Holmes, and J. Chantler, assigning to Wm. Verrall, "on the 20th of the fifth month (commonly called May), 1806," for £1,000—

"All that piece or parcel of ground then lately used by the people commonly called Quakers, with the Meeting-House, buildings, and premises then lately standing thereon, situate in North-street, Brighthelmston, aforesaid."

Soon after the old "Meeting-House" (with buildings, premises, &c.) was taken down, and, Mr. Verrall erecting several shops on the site, the old familiar place was "known no more."

As an appendix to the foregoing, and as throwing much light upon the early history of the Friends in Sussex, we publish the following

---

* The Prince of Wales would appear to have been on good terms with the Friends. A well-authenticated anecdote is related of His Royal Highness meeting one morning Friend Tuppen (builder), and accosting him with "How are you, Tuppen"? to which the sturdy Quaker at one replied, "Very well, thank thee, *George*"! The Friends in Brighton, it may be added, have on several occasions evinced much public spirit. The father of the late Mr. Daniel Pryor Hack (this latter gave £500 to the Free Library) in 1803 was first and foremost in securing the road through the Pavilion for the Prince of Wales; failing which the Prince would have perhaps altogether left Brighton. When Mrs. Fitzherbert's stables were erected in New-road, adjacent to the "Quakers' Burying Ground," the Friends acceded to "the request of Maria Fitzherbert to continue the window looking into their Ground" on her paying "a penny a month." To Friend Isaac Bass's liberality we owe the important thoroughfares of Prince Albert-street and the Avenue. This latter he gave to the town, at the same time offering to the town the house below (late Madame Temple's) for £1,100, which was refused! It is probably now worth thrice that sum. [The present representative of the Hack family,—Mr. Daniel Hack,—has been a generous benefactor to the cause of education in the town. He has for some years past, in addition to spending money freely in fostering manual and technical instruction, contributed £200 per annum in providing Scholarships, with the view to induce parents of poor but promising children to keep them longer at school. At the present time there is at the York-place Technical School machinery worth at least £1,000, provided at Mr. Hack's cost, of which the pupils have the free use.]

† This building was considerably enlarged in 1876; and class and lecture rooms were also added to it.

"Paper," with which we have been favoured from the private records of the Society in Brighton :—

SUSSEX FRIENDS.
ACCOUNT OF THE FIRST PUBLISHERS OF TRUTH IN Yᴱ COUNTY, WROT. IN 1706.

SUSSEX. AN ACCOUNT OF THE FIRST COMING OF THE PEOPLE OF GOD, IN SCORNE CALLED QUAKERS, INTO THIS COUNTY OF SUSSEX, and in what places they first declared the Truth, and by whom they were first received, &c. God, Whose Mercies are over all His Works, and hath had regard to the cry of the Poor, and the sighing of the Needy in all Ages, and to the breathing of His own Seed through all Generations, did in this our Day and Age send forth His Servants to preach the everlasting Gospel of Peace and bring the Glad Tidings of Salvation and Redemption, and Liberty to the Captives, and that the Oppressed should be set free, the People come to yield obedience to the heavenly gift of God, the Light of Christ Jesus, as it was made manifest to them.

This Blessed Testimony and joyful tidings of Salvation were first preached in the north side of the County of Sussex about the 3rd month in the year 1655, at the town of Horsham, by John Slee, Thomas Lawson, and Thomas Laycock, and, no man receiving them into his house, some of them declared the Truth in the open Market in a powerful manner, directing the people to yield obedience to the heavenly Gift of God, the light of Christ Jesus, as it was made manifest in them. This was to the great admiration of some : yet (as in all ages) the most part reviled, and some stoned them, others counted them madmen, yet all did not daunt them, nor stop their testimony, but they bore all with such meekness and patience as were wonderful to behold, and after having finished their testimony for that time, at that place, they came the same day to the house of Bryan Wilkinson, who then lived in a park, at Sidwick lodge, in Midhurst parish, about two miles from Horsham, who received them. He being judged the first man that gave entrance, as well to their persons as to their testimony (this Bryan Wilkinson came out of the north of England not long before), and the next day, being the first of the week, they had a meeting in his house, where, through the power that attended their testimony, the witness of God in some was revealed unto, and so from that time Truth began to spread itself in this County of Sussex.

The next meeting after that was at Ifield, the next first day following, at the house of Richard Bonwick (a weaver by trade), who was the first that received them and their testimony in that place, where was also convinced Richard Bax, senior, a labourer in the Lord's vineyard, now living at Capel, in Surrey, as also several others, and thus the Lord's work began to prosper.

Soon after that meeting held at Richard Bonwick's, the same Friends, viz., Thomas Lawson, Thomas Laycock, and John Slee, as is supposed, came to Twineham, to Humphrey Killingbrook's, and had there a meeting which was very great and serviceable, to the convincing of several, and particularly John Grover the elder, Wm. Ashford, and Elizabeth Killingbrook the elder.

And about this time, viz., the 3rd mo. in the aforesaid year, came Thomas Robinson the elder to the town of Lewes, and came to a Seekers' meeting held at Southover, near Lewes, at the house of John Russell, where he declared the Truth to the convincement of Ambros Galloway and Elizabeth his wife, and Stephen Eager, who were then members of the said meeting, and he was the means of the extinguishing of that meeting.

Soon after that came that memorable man, GEORGE FOX, and with him in company Alexander Parker, to the house of the aforesaid Bryan Wilkinson, where they met with Thomas Laycock, who being moved to go into the Steeple-house at Horsham, was for the same committed to Horsham Gaol on the 24th day of the 4th month, 1655, by Edward Mitchell and George Hussey, called Justices, where he remained about a quarter of a year. The same first day George Fox had a meeting at Hiniam Brocket's house at Beeding and Alexander Parker went to a Baptist meeting. And in the same week George Fox had a meeting at the said Bryan Wilkinson's house, where one Matthew Caffin, a Baptist Preacher, came and opposed him. And in the same week also George Fox and Alexander Parker held a meeting at Ifield, at the house of Richard Bonwick, where was a great meeting and such heavenly testimonies borne, as were to the convincement and settlement of many, and from that time and in that parish was settled a MEETING ON EVERY FIRST DAY OF THE WEEK, which was the first meeting that was gathered in this County to sit down together in silence to wait upon the Lord.

Now, at the aforementioned meeting, there was one Thomas Patching, who then lived at Bonwicke-place, in Ifield, who desired George Fox and the other Friends with him to have a meeting at his house, which was granted, and he with many of his house believed; and after that at that place were many persons meeting; and there was settled the FIRST MONTHLY MEETING that was set up in the County, which was on the last sixth day in every month; and hath since been removed to the house of Richard Bax, at Capel, in Surrey, by reason of Thomas Patching removing from that place.

Now Thomas Laycock, being brought out of prison to the Sessions, which was then held at Chichester, on his way thither he held a meeting at one William Penfold and Daniel Gitton's House, at Binstead, near Arundel, being accompanied with John Slee and Thomas Lawson, where was convinced Nicholas Rickman, Edward Hamper, William Turner, Tristrum Martin, John Sudgate, and several others. And when he came to the Sessions he was there set at liberty; but did not continue so long, for coming back, accompanied by the two aforementioned Friends, he had a meeting at the house of Nicholas Rickman, in Arundel,* where, as he was declaring the Truth to the people, there came in one George Penfold, a Constable, instigated thereto by one John Beaton, a Presbyterian Priest, and assisted by one John Pellatt, and pulled away the said Thomas Laycock and broke up the meeting, having Thomas Laycock before one Thomas Ballard, Mayor, who was also a Presbyterian, who immediately committed him again to Horsham Prison on the 3rd day of the 8th mo., 1655.

And within a little time after this George Fox and Alexander Parker, came to Steyning, where there they were received by John Blakam, and he being then Constable of the town let them have the liberty to meet in the Market-house.

---

* In the "Sufferings" (1656), it is stated " Nicholas Rickman and his wife were taken by warrant from their house and sent to prison, being accused of blasphemy, saying the Word of God was before the Scriptures were written, and kept there from Sessions to Sessions, until the case was laid before Oliver Cromwell and his Council for about half a year, and then proclamation was made in open Court that if any one had anything to accuse them of, they should come forth. Nobody coming, they were discharged."

SELINA, COUNTESS OF HUNTINGDON.
Ætat 83.

After they two, viz., George Fox and Alexander Parker, came from that meeting at Steyning to Lewes, where they had again another meeting, at the house of John Russell, in Southover, a parish joining to Lewes, and they travelled from thence eastward to Warbleton and those parts.

Quickly after which came Ambros Rigge and Joseph Fuce through this County, and travelled much amongst us by visiting all the meetings and served much to the establishing of them, and continued their labours amongst us several years.

And here in this place it may be convenient to remember the wonderful goodness of God to Richard Bonwick in particular, who, as is before observed, had the first settled meeting of this County in his house, for the particulars of which take the following relation :—

This Richard Bonwick and his wife, were both very aged and their labour done, and but low in the world (as to outward estate), and they had also a kinswoman more aged than either of them to maintain; and he was very often a sufferer in the case of tithes, as may be seen in the following relation of Friends suffering, for a little farm of ten or twelve pounds a year, in which he dwelt, and had sometimes one cow, and sometimes two at a time, taken from him by the Priest for tithes, and he was always very ready to communicate on all occasions of that substance that God had given him, and was still very free to Friends in his house, yet, like the woman's barrill of meal and the crusse of oil mentioned in the first of Kings, 17 Chap., 16 verse, *his little did never fail*, but he had more at the day of his death than he had in the day that he first received Friends into his house, which were many years asunder.

THE COUNTESS OF HUNTINGDON'S CHAPEL.

The second religious edifice opened in North-street was the little Chapel which, in the summer of 1761, Selina, Countess of Huntingdon, built behind her private residence, which then stood on the site of the front portion of the present handsome Chapel, and almost opposite the Friends' first Meeting-House. The erection of the original Chapel was brought about somewhat in this way:—The Countess had been induced to visit Brighton through the illness of her son, for whom sea-bathing was deemed necessary. Whilst here she visited many sick and needy, and, as was her wont, in administering to temporal necessities, she was not unmindful of affording spiritual instruction: Her Ladyship was, in fact, "zealous for the Lord," and deeply impressed with religious fervour, as much from conviction as from frequent association with earnest men like Wesley and Whitefield.* On the death of her son, in September, 1757, at

---

* In some MSS. of the Rev. Mr. Toplady, published after his death, appears this following singular circumstance, which was related to him by the Countess:—"A gentlewoman, who lived in the vicinity of Brighton, dreamed that a tall lady, whose dress she particularly noticed, would come to that town and be an instrument of doing much good. It was about three years after this dream that Lady Huntingdon came to Brighton. A few days after her arrival the above gentlewoman met Her Ladyship in the street, who, instantly she saw her, said—' Oh, Madam, you are come!" Lady Huntingdon, surprised at the

the early age of 18, the Countess left Brighton for a time, but returned to it a year or two afterwards. As heretofore, she at once actively interested herself in the spread of religion; and seeing how much her own efforts, though exercised in a comparatively limited sphere, were blessed, the Countess thought something more might be done, and accordingly sent for the Rev. George Whitefield, then her Chaplain. He came, and preached his first sermon in Brighton in a field at the back of "The White Lion" Inn, North-street, on Sunday, September 8th, 1760. On the following Friday he preached twice, and on each occasion there was a "very numerous audience." As a consequence, a local religious Society was formed; but the want of a meeting-place was much felt by the members. The Countess would have gladly provided it; but at the time—chiefly arising from her abundant gifts for charitable and religious purposes—her funds were well-nigh exhausted. To such a woman, however, as the Lady Huntingdon—especially when the spread of religion was concerned— the word "impossible" was unknown. With a sacrifice truly noble, she disposed of her jewels, which realized altogether £698 15s., and, with the money thus obtained, her "heart's desire" was carried out.*

The little Chapel, which was of the plainest character, was opened, as we have said, in the year 1761; the opening sermons being preached by the Rev. Martin Madan. For some time it was solely supplied by clergymen of the Established Church; and among those who successfully took charge of the congregation were the Revs. W. Romaine, J. Berridge (Rector of Everton), Henry Venn (the grandfather of the late Rev. H. V. Elliott, of St. Mary's, Brighton), and J. Fletcher. So rapidly did the congregation increase that, six years after its opening, the Chapel was found "too straight" for them. Accordingly, in 1767, an enlargement took place. The Chapel was closed during the alterations; and, on the 20th of March, "Her Ladyship gathered her Chaplains around her, and re-opened the sanctuary for the worship of God." The Rev. Mr. Madan preached in the morning, and the Rev. George Whitefield in the evening, to crowded congregations. From an old map of the period, it would appear that one entrance to the Chapel must then have been by a passage at the west side of the Countess's house, leading from North-street; another entrance also being just below what was subsequently known as Poplar-place (in the Lanes)—from a row of

---

singularity of such an address from an entire stranger, thought that the lady was bereft of her senses, asked—'What do you know of me?' 'Madam,' replied the gentlewoman, 'I saw you in a dream three years ago, *dressed just as you now appear*,' and proceeded in the relation of her dream to the Countess."

* In the *Coronet and the Cross*, we are told that Lady Ann Erskine (one of the Countess's trustees), related to a Minister a kindred anecdote, in connection with a Chapel at Birmingham :—"Lady Huntingdon had been accustomed to keep £300 in her house in order to defray the expenses of her funeral. This money was on no account to be touched. The Countess being much pressed for want of money to advance towards the Birmingham Chapel, said to Lady Ann, 'I want £300. I have no money in the house, but that put by for my funeral. For the first time in my life I feel inclined to let that go.' Lady Ann replied, 'I shall be glad when *that money* is out of the house. You can trust God with your *soul*; why not with your *funeral?*' The Countess at once took the money, and devoted it to the desired purpose."

poplars growing there—but then being a portion of the pathway through the fields from North-street to Black Lion-street. To the south of the garden in which the Chapel stood, there was at this period a large meadow (attached to a farm close by), in which for many a year after cattle were wont to graze.

The Countess took a lively interest in the welfare of the little Chapel, and personally superintended the instruction of the younger members of the congregation in singing, and also in religion. Special progress would appear to have been made in singing, as an effective choir was formed. One of its earliest members, in her youthful days, was Mrs. Humber, the wife of the once well-known local schoolmaster. An event in the history of the choir deserves notice, namely, its visit to Tunbridge Wells. The *Lewes Journal* of July 24, 1769, says:—

"Saturday last about twenty young people went through this place from Brighthelmston to Tunbridge Wells, to attend at the opening of a new Chapel built there by Lady Huntingdon: they were young people that Her Ladyship got instructed in Psalm singing, &c." *

In 1774, to meet the necessities of a constantly-increasing attendance, the original Chapel was rebuilt in a much-enlarged form (the walls of the old structure forming part of the building pulled down in 1870) the pulpit being placed in the centre of the eastern side, just opposite the spot where the Sortain memorial tablet was subsequently placed. The main entrance to the Chapel at this period was by the Lanes, as the Countess's residence (immediately north of the Chapel) completely shut it out from North-street. The expenses of this rebuilding were chiefly borne by Miss Orton, a lady who resided next door to the Countess; † and, as an instance of the feeling existing among members of the congregation, it may be stated that several mechanics gave labour free in their overtime, so that the building might be the more quickly raised. At the re-opening, on the 24th July, the Rev. W. Romaine preached; and among those who preached in the Chapel during the next few years, in addition to those who originally took charge of the congregation, were the Revs. Toplady, Bliss, Glasscott, Taylor, and Dr. Haweis, the last Chaplain of the Countess.‡ Rowland Hill also frequently ministered there,

---

* A 'Diarist,' who resided in Ship-street, Brighton, in 1780, doubtless refers to some members of the choir when he alludes to "the spiritual songs and hymns which some females (attendants at Lady Huntingdon's Chapel) in the next house are continually chanting."

† Miss Orton was an intimate friend of the Countess; a woman "after her own heart." She contributed largely towards the Countess's church-building expenses; aided her in her spiritual work, and accompanied her throughout a "preaching excursion" made by Rev. G. Whitefield, in the North of England.

‡ The Countess of Huntingdon died in 1791, and was buried in the family vault at Ashby-de-la-Zouch. With the view of erecting a monument to the memory of the Countess, a visit was made about twelve years since to her tomb by some members of the Free Church connection, and the vault, after the lapse of nearly a century, was opened for their inspection. The inscription on the coffin is as follows:—"Selina, Countess of Huntingdon, born 13-24th August, 1707; died June 17, 1791, in the 84th year of her age."

and it is a well-known fact that, on one Sunday evening when he was preaching, a quarrel took place in North-street between some of the 10th Hussars and the Gloucester Militia—then quartered in Brighton—which ultimately grew to be so serious that some of the men ran into the Chapel for refuge. Rowland Hill at once ceased preaching, and effected a peace between the men—for that occasion.

The alteration which was made in the Chapel in 1774 sufficed for some 15 years, down to 1788, when a front gallery was erected by the voluntary subscriptions of friends. Even then the congregation were at times much in need of "elbow room." In fact, for some time previous to the alteration in 1810, the children who attended the Chapel Sunday School were marched previous to the Service either to the Union-street Chapel or to the Baptist Chapel in Bond-street, so as to make room for the regular congregation at the Countess of Huntingdon's. As yet there were no pews in the Chapel, the only seating accommodation being moveable forms. On the enlargement in 1810, the interior of the Chapel was made "exceedingly neat"; but so rapidly did the congregation "increase and multiply" that further alterations were from time to time subsequently made, one of the more important being the erection of galleries. In 1822 these galleries were enlarged; the Chapel was lengthened at the south end; and the upper portion of the Chapel house (the original residence of the Countess of Huntingdon) was converted into a long gallery (in after days familiarly known as the "cock-loft"); an entrance was also made by the side of the house from North-street into the Chapel. At the re-opening services, on April 19th, 1822, the Rev. Rowland Hill officiated. The edifice thenceforth remained for some years equal to the needs of the worshippers. There was, however, no settled Pastor, the pulpit being supplied by a succession of Ministers, agreeably to the original plan of the Countess of Huntingdon. The teaching of the Chapel, at the present time, may be characterised as Evangelical; the prayers of the Church of England being read at the Sunday and other Services much in the same manner as in the Churches connected with the Establishment. At the close of the last century the congregation were styled "Methodists."[*]

In the year 1831 there was a strong desire among the congregation for a settled Minister, and the first to fill that sacred office was one whose name will ever be identified with the edifice—one whose fervid eloquence, piety, unobtrusive charity, gentleness and simplicity of manner, and large toleration, endeared him to all with whom he was brought in contact. We allude to the Rev. Joseph Sortain.

---

[*] In the Countess's time the teaching would appear to have been Calvinistic. The "Diarist"—from whom we have previously quoted, under date Sunday, 6th September, 1780, says:—"Went to Lady Huntingdon's Chapel in North-street in the evening; the Minister (a Mr. Mills, a Quietist, who strikes the pulpit violently with his hands, and thunders the bottom with his feet,) a gentleman, and scholar, but apt to wax warm, and, like some other extempore preachers at such times, capable of uttering—almost nonsense. He told us that divine grace was bestowed unmerited, nay, unsolicited; that in a book, before the beginning of the world, it was recorded who should be saved, and who should not."

THE REV. JOSEPH SORTAIN.

Mr. Sortain had come to Brighton in August of that year as an "occasional preacher." He was then but 22 years of age, thin and almost boyish in appearance; but the fire, the fervour, the earnestness, of his preaching was marvellous; and such appears to have been its effect upon the congregation, that a strong invitation was given to the gifted young man to become their settled Pastor. After much anxious consideration, Mr. Sortain decided to accept this high office, and preached his first sermon as Pastor of the Countess of Huntingdon's on February 17th, 1832. Even at this period Mr. Sortain was a brilliant and finished preacher. He studied earnestly, thought deeply, and his intellectual vigour was stimulated by warmth and intensity of feeling. Later on, Mr. Sortain's sermons may be more fitly characterised as orations: bursts of fervid, vigorous, overwhelming eloquence, which charmed the ear, satisfied the mind, and, above all, acted like a spell upon the feelings.* At his best, Mr. Sortain had to struggle against the defects of a weak and unmusical voice; but, if at times almost painful to occasional hearers, it was, strange to say, absolutely pleasing to those accustomed to it. Soon after the commencement of the ministry of Mr. Sortain, so popular was he, that the congregation again became "cabin'd, cribb'd, confined"; and "enlargement" of the Chapel in 1842 was again decided on. At this period it was thought to have been done effectually. Nearly all the old Chapel house was thrown into the body of the Chapel; the organ was removed from the south side of the Chapel to the north, the

---

* From one of the many tributes to Mr. Sortain's marvellous powers in the pulpit, we copy the following beautiful sonnet, written by the late Mr. Joseph Ellis, the gifted author of *Caesar in Egypt, Costanza, and other Poems*, and published by him in the latest edition of his works:—

SORTAIN.

AFTER HEARING HIM PREACH.

If I might envy, it should be, SORTAIN,
  Thine heritage of intellectual joy;
  For well I know that in this world's annoy
All other harbourage compares in vain:
Sweet are these earthlings! but or shine, or rain,
  Each in fruition breedeth its alloy;
  Hourling delights, born to themselves destroy!
How would we have the mutable remain?
  Oh! to *forget* them all, and, rapt, to lose
Sense of mortality; a while to rise
  Into sublimer being—as the dews
Twixt Earth and Heaven, gaining dim surmise,
  Of what, unflesh'd, we may be; this endues
Man like a god—this dost *thou* realize.

From an obituary notice of Mr. Sortain by the same author, we take the following:—"The personality of Mr. Sortain was pleasingly consistent with the ideal of a 'genius.' His habit of life was that of the student. Of child-like simplicity in matters mundane, he cared only to think, to read, and to preach. Above the middle height, with a well-proportioned frame and regular features, he might be called 'a fine man.' His cranium was 'square,' yet, to the casual observer, the frontal outline did not indicate power; nor was his facial expression unusually forcible. But his eye, full, dark, and bright, betokened the empyreal fire. When in the strong tide of 'thick-coming fancies,' he seemed to rise into the pure intellectual and for a time forget all of earth around him; then that eye blazed like a meteor and betrayed the temper of the soul that

space it occupied being converted into seats; and, altogether, the place was rendered capable of holding 1,000 persons.*

Mr. Sortain's ministry extended over 28 years—down to 1860—and it would be, perhaps, not too much to say, that during that long period he was the most popular preacher in Brighton. The "Visitors' Pew"—formerly in front of the pulpit—large as it was, Sunday after Sunday was invariably crowded. Of the then most distinguished visitors to Brighton—the high-born and the wealthy, the gifted and the great, statesmen and men of letters, divines and philosophers, actors of repute, and the educated classes generally—few failed "to hear Sortain."†

For the last ten years of his life Mr. Sortain's health gradually declined; yet he never ceased to maintain that cheerful and pleasing disposition and equanimity of temper so familiar to all who had the privilege of being intimately acquainted with him. On his last visit to the Chapel, a few days before his death, as it too sadly proved, he remarked in a pleasant way, on leaving the Vestry, "Good bye, old Vestry; I suppose I shall never see you again!" Those who stood by, and heard the exclamation, little thought how painfully soon the presentiment would be realised! Only a few days after, on July 12, 1860, he died peacefully, after a fit of paralysis, at Norwood, whither he had removed for the benefit of his health.‡

A few months after Mr. Sortain's death, the vacant pulpit of the Chapel was filled by the present Pastor, the Rev. J. B. Figgis, B.A.,

---

illumined it. Then, too, that voice, hitherto so tremulous and shrill, took the tone of a trumpet and evoked the latent sympathies of the most supine. His oratorical action was natural because impulsive, and telling because natural; so that, notwithstanding imperfection of voice, he was always impressive. * * * Some of his most powerful sermons were delivered without the aid of a single note. What that effort was, those only who have heard him in the vigour of his powers can adequately estimate. It was indeed an astonishing manifestation of abstruse 'thinking aloud,' of inductive reasoning and subtle analysis, of splendid imagery, of graceful and fervid rhetoric. Those to whom his manner was new would despair of him, and think that he must inevitably be lost in the mazes of his argument; but however involved or complicated his propositions, he escaped from them like a giant from the toils, or as the sun, after some time struggling with the mists and clouds, breaks forth at length unobscured into full effulgence."

* It was said at the time that, if the place could have held 3,000 persons, they would have been there to listen to Mr. Sortain. And we believe so. It is an interesting fact, and goes to substantiate this belief, that, though the Chapel was said to be only capable of holding 1,000 persons, there were, on the morning of the Census, in 1851, *eleven hundred* present.

† The late General Sir John Burgoyne attended the Countess of Huntingdon's Chapel every Sunday when in Brighton; and Charles Mayne Young, the celebrated actor, who spent his closing years in Brighton, was a constant attendant, as long as health permitted.

‡ The mortal remains of Mr. Sortain were interred on the 23rd July, in the Churchyard at Hove, in accordance with his own expressed wish; and, in addition to the members of his family, they were followed to their last resting-place by several Ministers of the Established Church, nearly all the Dissenting Ministers of the town, and by many members of his congregation. The Congregation subsequently placed a tomb, suitably inscribed, over the grave of Mr. Sortain; a tablet to his memory was placed in the Chapel; and later on a marble bust was placed in the Vestibule of the Pavilion, a white marble scroll at the foot of the last bearing the following inscription:—"They that be wise shall shine as the brightness of the firmament; and they that turn many to righteousness as the stars for ever and ever."—Daniel xii., v. 3.

a native of Dublin. During Mr. Figgis's ministry, there would appear to have been no diminution in the congregation, but rather an increase; and from the inconvenience to which the regular attendants were subjected from over-crowding, as well as from defective ventilation, &c., the Committee resolved, at the close of the year 1869, to take steps to erect a more commodious building. No sooner was the project mooted, than several friends promised substantial assistance; others volunteered to collect subscriptions; and though the receipts from both these sources were at the time some £1,700 short of the amount needed, the Committee felt themselves justified in proceeding with the work. Accordingly, designs were solicited from various architects; and that of Mr. J. Wimble, of London, was ultimately selected.

The ceremony of laying the memorial stone of the new edifice took place in the afternoon of Monday, August 15th, 1870, and was performed by the Right Hon. the Earl of Shaftesbury, K.G., in the presence of a large number of Clergymen both of the Established Church and of other denominations, many members of the congregation, and other friends.

The memorial stone, which forms the centre basement stone of the tower erected at the eastern porch of the Chapel, facing North-street, previously to its being lowered into its position, had placed beneath it, by the Noble Earl, in a receptacle cut for the purpose, a sealed bottle, containing one of the bills announcing the ceremony; a copy of the Centenary Services held in the old Chapel in May, 1862; a copy of the *Brighton Herald* of Saturday, August 13th, 1870, containing a history of the Chapel; a copy of the London *Times* and one or two other journals; a list of subscribers to the Building Fund; and a parchment with the following inscription:—

"In 1761, Selina, Countess of Huntingdon, erected a small Chapel behind her house in North-street, Brighton. In about 13 years it was rebuilt. Several subsequent enlargements took place; that of which this stone is the memorial, erected on the same site, with additions, was set on foot in 1869. The place has been blessed of God from the beginning. This memorial stone was laid on August 15th, 1870, by the Right Hon. the Earl of Shaftesbury, K.G. (Signed.) J. B. Figgis, M.A., Minister; T. B. Winter, Benjamin Cooke, George David Sawyer, Samuel Aylen, Frederick Tooth, Committee of Management; T. B. Winter, B. Cooke, Treasurers of Building Fund; Frederick Tooth, John Jeffcoat, Secretaries; John Wimble, Architect; George Myers and Sons, Contractors."

On the face of the stone itself was cut the following inscription:—

"THIS MEMORIAL STONE
OF THE CHURCH, ERECTED ON THE SITE
OF THAT BUILT IN 1761
BY
SELINA, COUNTESS OF HUNTINGDON,
WAS LAID ON AUG. 15, 1870,
BY
THE EARL OF SHAFTESBURY, K.G."

The new Chapel is in the geometrical decorated Gothic style; and has a handsome frontage, surmounted by a spire, and presents a very imposing appearance from the New-road and parts of North-street. The main entrance in North-street is by a triple archway, supported by capitalled columns of good design, above which are two windows, surmounted by a rich rose or wheel window, erected by the Spa Fields congregation in memory of the Countess of Huntingdon. The interior of the Chapel has a ceiled roof, with open timber supports. It is lighted on each side by five two-light windows; the south wall being pierced by three windows: the centre one—the "Sortain Memorial Window"—having five lights, with handsome head tracery. A gallery of ornamental character runs along the full extent of each side of the building. The organ is now on the ground floor to the south-east of the building. The seating accommodation of the present Chapel is about 900. The new edifice was re-opened for Divine Service on Monday, March 20th, 1871, and among those who took part in the opening services were the Rev. J. B. Figgis (Pastor of the Chapel), the Rev. T. E. Thoresby, the Rev. Paxton Hood, the Rev. S. S. England, the Rev. J. Jones, and others. The sermon in the morning was preached by the Rev. Donald Fraser, M.A., of the Presbyterian Church, Marylebone, and in the evening by the Rev. W. Allon, of Islington. The re-opening was celebrated in the afternoon by an elegant luncheon at the Pavilion, the Earl of Chichester presiding, supported by the Earl of Kintore, a large number of clergymen, and also several members of the congregation. It is satisfactory to add that, though the task of re-building and furnishing involved a total cost of some £7,000, the whole of that sum was paid off, thanks to the exertions of the Rev. J. B. Figgis and to the liberality of the congregation and friends, within about five years after the completion of the new edifice.

THE CHAPEL ROYAL.

To many, a special interest attaches to this edifice, as being the first erected Chapel-of-Ease to the old Parish Church of St. Nicholas. It is, moreover, associated with the palmy days of Royalty in Brighton, and was the most favoured Place of Worship with the throng of fashionable visitors who followed in its wake. It was also the place where so many old Brightonians were wont to worship, and in which many of their descendants—though the interior has undergone marked changes—love to do so still.

From an abstract of old title deeds we learn that the land on which the Chapel was built was, in 1721, in the possession of Mr. Richard Masters (High Constable of Brighton in 1710), who, by his will, dated 25th May, 1721, bequeathed it "unto his loving wife," it being therein described—"All that my copyhold land and premises, with their and every of their appurtenances, late Smith's, situate, lying, and being in Brighton aforesaid; and also all that my

THE CHAPEL ROYAL, WITH OLD HOUSES IN NORTH STREET,

Formerly at the South of the Chapel.

copyhold barn and land, late Harrison's, situate, lying, and being in Brighton aforesaid; and also that all my copyhold barn and land, late Paine's, situate, lying, and being in Brighton aforesaid, with their and every their appurtenances, &c."

The above land abutted on the west to the Quakers' Meeting-House and Croft, and was, probably, like the Dairy Field (now the Western Lawn of the Pavilion) devoted to farming purposes. The property eventually came into the hands of " Richard Tidy, gentln.," who married Joan, only daughter of Richard Masters ; and his successor, Richard Tidy, by will, dated 26th December, 1788, gave it " to Richard Lemmon Whichelo, the father, and Thomas Scutt as tenants in common." They, in February, 1789, " surrendered their moieties to the use and behoof of the Right Hon. George Lord Leslie," who, in October, the same year, surrendered " to use of W. W. Pepys, Esq.," with the proviso—" to be void on payment of annuity of £116 to Lady Jane Elizabeth, Countess of Rothes," wife of Sir Lucas Pepys, Bart. (Physician to George III.), and they, at a Special Court Baron, held 24th February, 1792, " surrendered to the use of the Rev. Thomas Hudson," then Vicar of Brighton.

The object of the Vicar, in acquiring this land, was to erect on it a new Chapel, as a Chapel-of-Ease to the Parish Church of St. Nicholas, " on account of the rapid increase of population, and the consequent complaint of room [want of room?] in the Church : and not only for the accommodation of the company, but also for the use of such of the inhabitants *as are disposed to become purchasers of pews.*" The Vicar's primary reason in selecting the site was, doubtless, its contiguity to the Pavilion, as being more convenient for the attendance of the Royal patron of the town than the Old Church, though it does not appear that the Prince very often availed himself of it. Be that as it may, His Royal Highness cordially supported the worthy Vicar's efforts, and graciously condescended to lay the first stone of the new building, on the 25th November, 1793, the Prince being accompanied from the Pavilion by Captain Churchill, Mr. Hudson, the Vicar, and Mr. Saunders (of Golden-square, London), the architect. The area in which the ceremony took place was surrounded by the principal inhabitants of the town and by a brilliant assemblage of beauty and fashion, among the ladies present being Mrs. Fitzherbert, Miss Vanneck, Miss Pigot, Miss Graham, &c. The proceedings were commenced by Mr. Saunders addressing His Royal Highness, and respectfully requesting that, as Grand Master of the Masons, he would be pleased to signify whether or not it met with his approbation? On receiving the assurance that it did, the stone, with the following inscription, was laid in due form :—

"THIS STONE
WAS LAID BY
HIS ROYAL HIGHNESS GEORGE, PRINCE OF WALES,
NOV. 25TH, 1793."

The " laying" was followed by some loyal speechifying ; performances by His Royal Highness's Band ; and the ringing of a joyous peal from the bells of old St. Nicholas. The Promenade Grove (then occupying the western portion of the present Western Lawn of the Pavilion, and entered through a gate at the upper portion of what is now Prince's-place), was then thrown open, and an elegant *déjeûner* was given by Mr. Hudson in the Saloon to a very large party. On the following Wednesday, a party of the inhabitants likewise celebrated the ceremony in orthodox English fashion, by a dinner at "The Castle Tavern"; and it is related, "such was the good order and harmony, under the very respectable Chairman, that every individual of the company appeared delighted with the business of the day." Some lines were composed and sung on the occasion. The world must mourn their loss, for history has not preserved them!

The building of the Chapel by Mr. Bodle was pushed on with much vigour. It was completely covered in by October, 1794, and on August 3rd, 1795, it was opened for Divine Service; a charity sermon for the children of the Sunday School and School of Industry being preached on the occasion by the Rev. Dr. Langford, Canon of Windsor. His Royal Highness the Prince of Wales and his newly-wedded wife, the Princess Caroline of Brunswick, who were then staying in Brighton, were present. Did the Prince's thoughts revert to the day when he laid the foundation stone of the building in which he was seated? Then another lady was by his side—by many still believed to have been his wife: the beautiful Mrs. Fitzherbert, the only woman he was said ever to have really loved!

The Chapel, for a few years after its completion, was only opened during the Brighton Season,—then ranging from June to September. There were, however, sacred concerts occasionally given there; Mr. Prince, the organist of the Chapel, was not only a skilled performer on the organ but was a composer of much ability, and, being known to many of the leading musical celebrities of the day, had special facilities for getting up such concerts One of the grandest concerts which he gave was in September, 1800, as a benefit concert, the advertisement of which in the *Sussex Weekly Advertiser* was as follows :—

ORATORIO.- CHAPEL ROYAL, BRIGHTON. For the BENEFIT of Mr. PRINCE, Organist.

On TUESDAY, the 9th of SEPTEMBER, 1800, will be given A GRAND SELECTION OF SACRED MUSIC from the Works of HANDEL.

Leader of the Band, Mr. G. ASHLEY. Organ by C. DUPUIS, Esq.

Principal Vocal Performers : Mrs. ILIFF, Miss CAPPER, and Miss BARNETT; Mr. DENMAN, Mr. HAYMES, and Mr. ASKER.

Principal Instrumental Performers : Messrs. J. and C. LINDLEY, SIMCOX, SALIO, MALSCH, KEILBECK, SIMPSON, BENNEWITZ, MINCKI, SHER, REHNS, senior and junior, BODENSTEIN, BEHRENS, PRINCE, &c., &c.

CHORUSES will be supported by upwards of EIGHTY VOCAL AND INSTRUMENTAL PERFORMERS, after the same manner as at Westminster Abbey, in commemoration of Handel.

Tickets 3s. 6d. each ; and Seats to be taken of Mr. Prince, at his Music Warehouse, Prince's-place, and at the Libraries. Doors to be open at Half-past Ten o'clock and the Performance to begin at Twelve precisely.

In the meantime the Vicar (the Rev. Mr. Hudson) apparently single-handed, was arranging financial matters in connection with the edifice (he enfranchised it in April, 1801, for £25), with the view of securing it to himself and his successors as a Chapel-of-Ease to the Parish Church. At length, in June, 1803—nothing standing in the way of the Chapel being opened permanently—he obtained an Act of Parliament, 43 Geo. III., c. 91, to constitute it as such Chapel-of-Ease, and "for no other purpose whatsoever." When ready, the Bishop was to be required to consecrate the said Chapel, "by the name of the Chapel Royal"; the Perpetual Curate was to be appointed; and to Mr. Hudson and his successors was secured the right of appointing such Perpetual Curate "upon occasion of every future vacancy." Among the reasons given in the preamble of the Act for the erection of the Chapel was —"the situation of the Parish Church of the said Parish of Brighthelmston *being, by reason of its distance from the greater part of the town, inconvenient to the inhabitants in general.*"

Some of the sections of the Act are peculiar, and sadly contravene the notions of the advocates of "free and open Churches." Thus, in order to reimburse the said Thomas Hudson the sums expended on building the Chapel, &c., he, his heirs, and assigns, are empowered "from time to time, and at all times from and after the passing of this Act, *to make profit of the said pews or seats, by selling or disposing thereof*, to any inhabitant of the said Parish of Brighthelmston, *for the highest and best prices that can be gotten for the same*"; and "all and every the said pews so purchased" to be vested in the purchasers, their executors, &c., and "shall and may be bargained, sold, conveyed, leased, devised, or otherwise aliened or disposed of by the Proprietors thereof for the time being." Some pews were, however, set apart for the maintenance of the Perpetual Curate, and marked with "C" (this letter remained on several pews down to the time of their removal in 1876); they were to be selected "fairly and indifferently" from the whole of the Chapel, by Thomas Hudson, with Richard Day and John Bull, of Ship-street, Esquires, and be deemed "sufficient to produce a present yearly sum or annual profit amounting to at least *One Hundred and Fifteen Pounds per annum.*" As the Curate, out of the rents, &c., arising from the letting of the said pews, was required to "find and provide bread and wine for the Holy Communion, and all other incidental charges and expenses attending the said Chapel," the Curacy could not be deemed a "fat living," even when supplemented by *half* the fees from baptisms and churchings (the other half going to the Vicar).[*] The Curacy, pure and simple, would not seem to have yielded a *living*, and all who have held it from first to last (with one exception, and his tenure of

---

[*] The Baptismal Register of the Chapel, it may be stated, does not commence till the year 1834; previous to that year the baptisms were entered in the Register of the Parish Church of St. Nicholas.

office was very brief,) have been part Proprietors of the Chapel. The list of Perpetual Curates since the opening is as follows:—

Rev. — Portis (from Bath)	1803–1818
Rev. — Lovell	1818–1822
Rev. E. R. Butcher (subsequently Pemberton), D.C.L., who exchanged with Mr. Lovell	1822–1830
Rev. H. J. Urquhart, M.A.	1830–1834
Rev. Thos. Trocke, M.A.	1834–1875

The value of their Proprietorships in the Chapel during their respective Curacies may be gleaned from the following compilation (by the late Mr. F. E. Sawyer) from the original documents:—

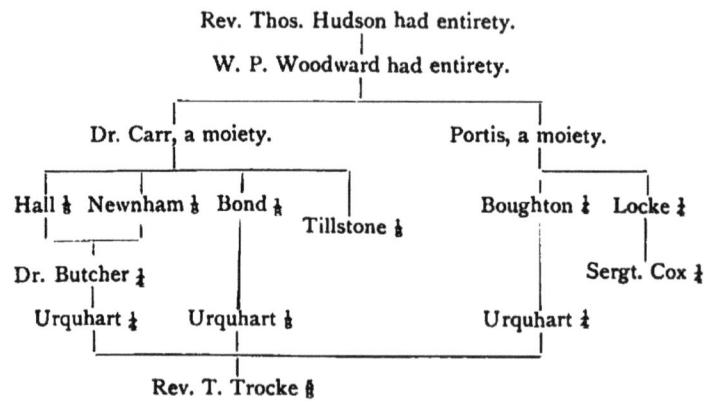

```
                    Rev. Thos. Hudson had entirety.
                                |
                    W. P. Woodward had entirety.
                                |
        ┌───────────────────────┴───────────────────────┐
    Dr. Carr, a moiety.                          Portis, a moiety.
        │                                               │
   ┌────┼────┬──────┐                           ┌───────┴───────┐
  Hall ¼ Newnham ¼ Bond ¼                   Boughton ¼      Locke ¼
   │                   Tillstone ⅛                              │
   │                                                       Sergt. Cox ¼
 Dr. Butcher ¼
   │
 Urquhart ¼      Urquhart ⅛                            Urquhart ¼
                       │
                 Rev. T. Trocke ⅝
```

It may be stated, in passing, that a special section of the Act exempts the Chapel from parochial rates, and another enacts "That no marriages shall at any time be solemnized in the said Chapel, nor shall any corpse be buried in the said Chapel or the vault thereof"; but another section gives power to "sell or let the vault under the said Chapel." This vault has long since been let to a wine and spirit merchant, and the anomaly of its being devoted to such a business in such a situation has afforded from time to time exercise for small wits. One effusion was as follows:—

> "There's a Spirit above and a Spirit below:
> The Spirit of bliss and the Spirit of woe.
> The Spirit above is the Spirit Divine;
> The Spirit below is the Spirit of Wine."

A wide-spread impression at one time prevailed that the Chapel had never been consecrated. How such an impression originated we are at a loss to conjecture; but we can state, on unimpeachable authority, that the Chapel was consecrated on the 16th August, 1803, with the usual solemn ceremonies, by the Right Rev. the Lord Bishop of Chichester.

Mr. Hudson subsequently disposed of his proprietorship in the Chapel to Mr. W. P. Woodward, and from him it came into the joint possession of Dr. Carr (who succeeded Mr. Hudson as Vicar) and the Rev. — Portis. The latter was the first Perpetual Curate of the Chapel. He appears to have been a popular Minister, for the Chapel was much frequented during his curacy by both townsfolk and visitors,—so much so, that in July, 1812, it was said to be "totally incapable of containing the crowds which repaired to it each Sunday"; and, in consequence, a meeting of the subscribers to the *Free* Chapel in St. James's-street (subsequently known as St. James's) was held at the Rev. Dr. Carr's (the Vicar), who then resided at 3, Marlboro'-place, when it was resolved "to adopt measures for the completion, as early as possible, of that much-neglected building," with the view of affording more accommodation for worshippers.*

It is difficult now to ascertain what the regulations respecting seats in the Chapel Royal were at this period; but until 1810 no servants (except the Prince of Wales's) were admitted into the Gallery; and, when the restriction was broken through by the "back seats being appropriated for their accommodation," a local journalist remarked, "How the upstairs renters of pews will approve of the alteration time must evince."

In November, 1814, a fourth part of the Chapel was announced to be sold by public auction. The Chapel was owned in equal portions at this period by Dr. Carr and the Rev. Mr. Portis; but which of the two was desirous of disposing of his quarter proprietary share does not appear. The advertisement in the *Brighton Herald* was as follows :—

CHAPEL ROYAL, BRIGHTON.

TO BE SOLD, by Public Auction (due notice of the time of Sale will be hereafter given), in small Shares, or in one Lot, ONE-FOURTH PART of all that FREEHOLD BUILDING and capacious WINE VAULTS, with the ORGAN, FURNITURE, and all the FIXTURES, &c., within the same, situated in Prince's-place, Brighton, commonly called the Chapel Royal, which will intitle the Purchaser to a proportionable share of the rentals and profits of all the pews, seats, &c., within the said Chapel, save and except a certain number of pews set apart for the maintenance of the Curate, from and out of which he is chargeable with the Clerk's salary, and other expenses thereunto appertaining, agreeable to the provision made in the Act of Parliament for building the said Chapel.

The amount of money collected at the Chapel in earlier times for charities of the town, after sermons by some of the most notable Church of England preachers of the day (as the Revs. E. Cannon, Philip Dodd, T. B. Powell, Pitman, and Moore, Dr. Rice, Dr. Holland, and the Hon and Rev. E. J. Tournour), was immense. On one

---

* This Chapel, after sundry vicissitudes, was open as a "Free Chapel for the Accommodation of the Poor," on Sunday, July 25th, 1813, by the Rev. W. Marsh, A.M., Domestic Chaplain to the Right Hon. Lady Barham, a notice being issued as follows :—"The Body of the Chapel is free to all persons, whether tradesmen, mechanics, fishermen, labourers, servants, or others, who have no other provision for their religious duties, the south side being for women and girls, and the north side for men and boys." The Gallery was "reserved' to Governors and Subscribers, the subscriptions ranging from £100 to £2 2s. "Personal admissions" were also issued for various periods.

occasion (in October, 1808,) no less than £137 8s. 6d. was collected for the Deaf and Dumb Institution. There was a singular "N.B." at the foot of the advertisement announcing the sermon: "One of the Children will repeat the Lord's Prayer." When these Charity sermons were preached, it was customary for the Proprietors of the Chapel to give the use of their pews, and notices were issued, requesting that "no money be paid for seats or given to persons who open the pews."

During Mr. Portis's Curacy, concerts were occasionally given at the Chapel for charitable purposes. On the 9th December, 1806, an oratorio from Handel was performed there, the Prince's band taking part; Mr. Bennett, of Chichester, presiding at the organ. In June, 1813, a "miscellaneous and sacred entertainment" was given in aid of the Brighthelmston Infirmary; the artists included Miss Wright and Miss Ferrari. The Prince's band (under Mr. Kramer) was also present. The grandest concert, however, was given for the same Institution in August, 1813, under the patronage of the Prince Regent, who commanded that 20 guineas on his account should be given to the Charity. The vocal performers were Mdme. Catalani, Mdme. Bianchi Lacey, Miss Giles, and Mr. Lacey, with full band and chorus (all who took part giving their services). The receipts amounted to about £150. In the Prince's pew were Lord Fortescue, Mr. and Lady Sarah Bailey, Lord Yarmouth, &c. The Vicar himself (Dr. Carr) did not disdain to call in extra musical aid in the cause of Charity; for in October, 1817, on the occasion of his preaching for the Society for Promoting Christian Knowledge, he secured, as an additional attraction, the attendance of the private band of the Prince Regent, as well as the Parish Church Choir to assist in the Psalmody.

There is not much of special interest to record during the later history of the Chapel. The Proprietors in 1834-5 gave permission for the removal of the shrubbery formerly in the centre of Prince's-place, which was their private property. This shrubbery had become a public nuisance (certainly the peacock from the Pavilion could perch upon its rails and display his "magnanimous tail" for the admiration of juveniles of the period!), and its removal was effected in a single night. Mr. Lewis Slight (then Clerk to the Commissioners), on learn-what was being done, sent round in the morning several cartloads of flints, &c., which being strewn over the vacant space, it was taken possession of "in the name of the town," and has been used ever since as a public highway.

As a building, the Chapel Royal is of very unpretentious design, and its exterior has no claims to any architectural feature. It is lighted on three sides by several very plain windows. The Royal Arms, which surmount the front of the edifice, quarter the French Arms, and indicate the date of erection at the close of last century. The interior was entirely altered in 1876 (after the Rev. Thos. Trocke's retirement); but the following description, written in 1875, will afford some idea of its original character :—

"The interior of the Chapel is lofty, and galleries run all round, supported by 12 pillars, which again carry 12 columns (the capitals being ~med by P.W.'s feathers), that support the roof. The ceiling rises from the cornice above the columns in a square tapering shaft to a lantern-light (erected in 1848), which it had had originally, but it had been supplanted by a plain ceiling, with a centre flower surrounded by the "Garter," with motto. The only ornamentation is in the West Gallery front, which is enriched with the Royal Arms (with P.W.'s feathers on each side), and two miniature caryatides, supporting a lion and shield. The front of the Royal Pew (East Gallery) is also enriched with the Crown and the Urim and Thummim of Jewish history. The original pulpit and reading desk of the Chapel were of similar design; but they were supplanted by the present structure (in which both are combined) in 1851, the originals being generously given by Mr. Trocke to St. Stephen's, which was then building. The Communion Table, &c. (under the West Gallery) is in good taste and not too ornate. Between the Decalogue over the Table, is a picture of "the Crucifixion" (by Van Veen), presented by Mr. Trocke some 35 years since.* The present organ was erected in 1834 (by Robson, London), and cost £200; the case was made in Brighton. The Chapel has accommodation for 874 worshippers, but being a distinctly proprietary chapel, only 224 seats are available to other than seat-holders. It was without a bell until the year 1822."

The Perpetual Curacy of the Chapel was held by the Rev. Thomas Trocke for forty years, he having entered upon it in 1835, and preached his farewell sermon (on his retirement, by reason of age,) in September, 1875, having deservedly earned the esteem, not only of the members of his congregation, but of his fellow-townsmen generally. As a proof of the esteem in which Mr. Trocke was held by his congregation, a subscription of £200 was raised among them in 1848, which was expended in purchasing the massive and elegant chandelier with which the Chapel was thenceforth lighted, and a piece of silver plate, as a testimonial of the "congregation's esteem for his high character, and high sense of his ministerial usefulness." Few clergymen have done more than Mr. Trocke, in the early part of his career especially, to promote Church extension in Brighton, and few took a more active part in furthering the interests of Local Charities; and in his retirement he has the best best wishes of all who have had the pleasure of his acquaintance.

One difficulty presented itself on Mr. Trocke resigning, and that was the procuration of another Incumbent, owing to the proprietary rights, which were owned by Mr. Trocke and a gentleman named Urquhart, rendering the living a very poor one. Ultimately, the present Vicar of the Parish, the Ven. Archdeacon Hannah, arranged for the abolition of these rights by purchasing them for a sum of £2,000, with the view of making the building a free and open Church; and in this effort he was laudably assisted by one of his own Curates, the Rev. C. S. Chilver, who accepted the Incumbency, and set himself to work to raise a fund for the double purpose of extinguishing the proprietary rights and reconstructing the Chapel. Plans were prepared by Mr A. W. Blomfield, architect, of London, and the work was undertaken by Messrs. G. Lynn and Son, builders, of Brighton.

* There was formerly, in the same place, a copy (by Whichelo, of Brighton) of Meng's picture at All Souls', Oxford, of "Our Saviour appearing to Mary in the Garden," or the "Noli me tangere." The figure of the Saviour becoming decayed, it was cut out, and the remains of the picture, comprising the female figure, &c., were removed to the Board Room of the National Schools.

The interior of the Chapel now presents an elegant, airy, and cheerful appearance. The old West Gallery and the Royal Pew in the East Gallery have been removed; whilst the North and South Galleries, as well as that on the east side, have been entirely reconstructed. Their façades are very neat and light, supported on octagonal wooden columns and surmounted by an ornamental arcade, from which springs the domed ceiling carrying a lantern light. The whole of the woodwork, including the seats in the galleries and on the ground floor, is stained; and the columns are crowned with small but neat illuminated capitals. The seating accommodation (open benches have supplanted the old-fashioned pews) is much about the same as it was in the old building; for, notwithstanding the West Gallery has been done away with, extra seating has been obtained under the South Gallery by the removal of one of the old vestries on that side; and the organ has been placed over the vestry on the North side. A recess is thus formed at the West end which is converted into a Chancel, in which the choir-stalls are placed, on each side of the altar-steps. The Chancel screen—which is arcaded, pierced, and ornamented, in keeping with the columns and arcades of the galleries—carries the West end of the domed ceiling. This ceiling is panelled out, and in each panel—four in number—are painted the emblems of the Four Evangelists—Matthew, Mark, Luke, and John. This work was entrusted to the Messrs. Heaton, Butler, and Bayne, of London; their chief labour, however, was spent upon the reredos, which is simply but very effectively composed of artistic mural paintings. The dado is painted in diaper pattern, and the entire Chancel wall is bordered and panelled with a pattern harmonising with the arcading of the screen. The centre and larger picture is that of "The Good Shepherd;" flanked by four lancet-shaped panels, in which are the Rose and the Lily; and on each side of these are the Lord's Prayer, the Decalogue, and the Creed. A bunch of corn and a cluster of grapes fill up two smaller panels between these; whilst the entire bordering, or tracery, is emblematical of the sacramental bread and wine, being composed of wheat and the vine. Above these, and in the centre, is a Calvary Cross, with the Alpha and Omega, and on each side are angels, in circles, emblematical of Eternity.

The Chapel is lighted with starlights round the galleries—the old chandelier in the centre being done away with; and two very handsome standard lights are placed in the Chancel. The artificial illumination of the edifice was carried out by Mr. R. Shrivell, an old Brightonian, but now resident in London. Daylight is obtained from the lantern in the roof and the side windows, all of which are glazed with stained glass in quarries, which admits a very bright but soft light; in fact each part is in thorough keeping with the other, and reflects the highest credit on the builders and architect.

The re-opening Services took place on Tuesday, the 6th February, 1877; the preachers in the morning being the Bishop of the Diocese and in the evening the Venerable Archdeacon Hannah, D.C.L., Vicar of Brighton. At the close of each there was an offertory in aid of the Restoration Fund, on which £2,000 was then due, and for which the

Incumbent, the Rev. C. S. Chilver, made himself responsible. This was in addition to the £2,000 purchase money—and until the entire debt is cleared off, one-half only of the seats can be appropriated as free; so that for the present, the Chapel retains a portion of its proprietary character.*

The Rev. C. S. Chilver resigned the Incumbency in 1879, and this was subsequently accepted by the Rev. Denwood Harrison.

[The Rev. D. Harrison held the Incumbency of the Chapel for seven years, retiring in 1886, since which time he has been Incumbent of All Saints'. He was succeeded by the Rev. W. S. Andrews, who retired in 1890, on receiving the appointment of Wicken Rectory, Stony Stratford. The present Incumbent, the Rev. H. L. Beardmore, entered upon his duties in January, 1891.]

[* On the removal, in 1879, of the old houses formerly to the south of the Chapel by the Corporation, with the view of widening North-street, the aspect of that portion of the sacred edifice which faced North-street was pitiful to behold. It had been hoped that the Town authorities would have refronted so much of the building as their improvement had laid bare. But, as this was not done, the responsibility of facing this difficulty fell upon the Vicar of Brighton and the Incumbent of the Chapel. With a boldness which did them credit, they determined to make the south front worthy of the historical traditions of the sacred edifice. Objections were offered by the Town Council to the earlier plans submitted; but eventually that, which showed the building as it now appears—with its handsome elevation, noble clock tower, and new and tastefully designed entrances--was accepted, and the work was carried out, at an estimated cost of £1,800, by Messrs. Lynn and Son, builders; the architect being Sir Arthur Blomfield. Since then the organ has been removed from the North Gallery to the south of the Chancel, and last year (1891) the reflooring of the Chapel—a much needed and almost too long delayed improvement—was carried out at a cost of £400. There remains yet one more improvement to the venerable edifice, namely, a new Eastern front, to correspond with the Southern front. As it is now, the Eastern front is a "shame and reproach," which, it is to be hoped, will speedily be removed.]

MR. WILLIAM FLEET.

A Pioneer in Local Journalism.

MR. WILLIAM FLEET.

(Reprinted from the *Brighton Herald* of April 1st, 1874, with additions.)

ON Sunday last, Mr. William Fleet, for so many years Proprietor and Editor of the *Brighton Herald*, passed to his rest at the ripe age of 87 years.

As connected almost from its origin with that journal, the first established in Brighton,* and, excepting the *Sussex Advertiser*, of Lewes, the oldest newspaper in Sussex, some few remarks are justly due to the memory of the deceased, and may not be uninteresting to our readers.

The *Brighton Herald* was founded in September, 1806, by Mr. H. Robinson Attree, one of a wide-spread Sussex family, (still represented in Brighton by Mr. George Attree, his eldest son), and Mr. Matthew Phillips, also a Sussex man, and elder brother of Mr. Henry Phillips, the well-known botanist. The original publishing office of the paper was No. 8, Middle-street, and its first number was "made up,"—a printer's technical phrase,—by Mr. Fleet's brother-in-law, the late Mr. William Mason, who for so many years afterwards carried on the business of a bookseller at Chichester. The first "leading article" was written by Mr. M. Phillips, who at that time resided at Henfield; and we have heard that such was the limited means of communication in those days, that his contributions were actually sent over to Brighton by a special messenger on horseback! The connection of Mr. M. Phillips with the Press did not, however, last very long; his genius lay in another direction, and he very soon turned his attention to road-making and surveying, and produced one of the earliest and best known maps of his native county, which may still be seen in the hall of many a country

---

* The *Lewes and Brighthelmston Pacquet* was started by T. Budgen, of Lewes, in July, 1789. But only 26 numbers were published. This paper was printed at Lewes, and was regarded more as a County paper, Brighton news occupying but a very small space in its columns.

mansion and wayside inn. In May, 1808, the partnership between Messrs. Attree and Phillips was dissolved; the paper thenceforth being published by Mr. Attree alone, who in October the same year removed his establishment to the top of North-street.* In January, 1810, Mr. Attree took Mr. William Fleet, who was a Hampshire man (educated at the then famous school of Petersfield) and a practical printer, into partnership; Mr. Fleet having previously managed the paper from 1807. In April Mr. Attree, who was also an auctioneer, withdrew from the newspaper and printing business, which was once more removed—namely to Prince's-place (the printing office being at the back of Messrs. Glaisyer and Kemp's)— and was conducted till 1811 by Messrs. Fleet and Bray, when this partnership was also dissolved, and the paper and printing business passed into the hands of the late Mr. Fleet alone. So they remained until 1843, Mr. Fleet in the meantime being assisted by his two sons, William and Charles. On the former leaving England for Canada, where a most promising career as an Advocate was cut short by death, Mr. Fleet took his second son into partnership in 1843, and, at the expiration of the full period of it, in 1864, gave it up into his hands, and retiring, at the age of 77 years, to enjoy a well-earned repose. This extended over a period of ten years, until, as we have said, his death, on Sunday last, and for the most part was passed in the enjoyment of good health. Mr. Fleet was, indeed, a man of a most vigorous constitution, strengthened by very temperate habits. He never over-stepped the bounds—we might say—of abstinence, although he never refrained from the moderate use of those stimulants which he believed to be chiefly hurtful in their abuse. Thus he hardly knew what it was to have a day's illness during his long life, and yet for more than 50 years he was daily engaged in his business, going and returning "like clockwork" between the *Herald* Office and his private residence at the north part of the town. His old apprentices (some of them, like Mr. Mitchell, of the *West Sussex Gazette*, proprietors themselves of prosperous journals) love to remind each other of his habits of punctuality, and the early hours which he encouraged in them; and by imparting a thorough knowledge of the "art and mystery" of printing, he formed many generations of skilful workmen.

In the days when the *Brighton Herald* was young, newspapers were few and dear. Its price for the first nine years was 6d.; the Stamp Duty on each copy being 3½d.; in September, 1815, when the Stamp Duty was increased to 4d., its price was 7d. Then every advertisement paid a duty of 3s. 6d.; and there was a heavy tax upon paper! In addition to all which, the laws were stringent with regard to libel, and Government prosecutions for criticisms on the

---

* Among those associated with the *Brighton Herald* at this period was the late Mr. William Shelley, for half-a-century or more parish sexton. He was, in fact, the first Brighton newsman, or rather the first person employed to supply the Brighton newspaper to country subscribers, which he did on foot,— starting early every Saturday morning to Shoreham, Lancing, Worthing, and other places westward.

acts of statesmen were of frequent occurrence, so that a Newspaper Editor scarcely dared discuss public questions without the fear and dread of a criminal information, and the dreary prospect of fine and imprisonment.

Nevertheless, the *Brighton Herald*, from its first number, steadfastly pursued its undeviating and consistent course. Started as the advocate of rational and moderate principles,—neither bowing down to senseless worship of wealth and station on the one hand, nor preaching rabid democracy on the other, it staunchly upheld Constitutional liberty, and promulgated truth and humanity in all places and on all occasions. At a time when there was no "cheap literature," the *Brighton Herald* furnished its readers with matter of higher interest and more enduring character, and so drew around it a body of contributors who could supply it with something more valuable than the description of a huge gooseberry or the doings of a mere public-house meeting.

In earlier days, it was distinguished as the paper that first made known to the British public some of the most important events in European history. At one time, during the wars of Napoleon, the only communication with France was through Brighton and Dieppe. All intelligence was brought secretly, and chiefly by the smugglers (ancestors of several now thriving local families); and an agent of the Comte de Provence, afterwards Louis XVIII., a certain Duc de Caistrés, resided in Brighton for the express purpose of managing the correspondence. The news of the great battle of Talavera (for which Lieut.-Colonel Wellesley was elevated to the Peerage) was first received here. The late Mr. Fleet was allowed the privilege of being in the Banqueting Room at the Pavilion when Lord Wellesley's despatches were delivered to the Prince Regent and read aloud by His Royal Highness amidst the loud cheers of a distinguished company. The famous proclamations of Napoleon to the French Army, on his escaping from Elba, were also first received in Brighton through this channel, and were translated for the *Brighton Herald* with a spirit and correctness which ensured their adoption by the Metropolitan Press; and, indeed, in subsequent histories. Mr. Fleet used to repeat with enthusiasm the opening words of the most famous of these addresses of Bonaparte to the French Army :—

"Tear down those colours which the nation has proscribed, and which for four-and-twenty years have been the rallying point of the enemy. Hoist the *tri-colour* cockade! You bore it in the days of your greatness!"

It may not be out of place here to observe that, in singular contradiction to the feeling of the age to which he belonged, Mr. Fleet was an intense admirer of the first Napoleon, and we doubt if there were many men better acquainted with the facts of his wonderful career, or the works which have been written about them. These loaded his library shelves and were read by him with unabating zest down to within a comparatively short time of his demise. As showing the scope of events embraced in Mr. Fleet's long life, we may add a fact to which he would often refer: that, when an apprentice at Portsmouth, he took off, "in hot haste," a parcel of stationery to "The Victory," the ship of Nelson, then about to start on that famous voyage which ended in the destruction of the French and Spanish fleets off Cape Trafalgar and in the death of the hero himself.

Coming to more recent times, we may state that the news of the French Revolution of 1830 was first published in the *Brighton Herald*. The intelligence had reached Dieppe on the Friday morning, was brought over by the late Captain Cheesman in one of the General Steam Navigation Company's vessels, which landed at the Chain Pier, and "slips" were forwarded from the *Herald* office to the London *Times* the same night. So too, by a somewhat singular coincidence, it fell to the *Brighton Herald*, 18 years afterwards, to make the earliest announcement of the arrival of Louis·Philippe as a fugitive to the shores of England, after the Revolution of 1848. The deposed monarch landed, with the Queen, at Newhaven, on the Friday morning, and the correspondent of the *Herald* at that port was the first to board the vessel ("interviewing" in those days was unknown) and to bring the news to the *Herald* office.

In conclusion, we may say that the Liberal party in Sussex has been,—little as some extreme men acknowledge the fact,—deeply indebted to Mr. William Fleet, who was the sole advocate of an enlightened policy, foreign and domestic, in this County for the first quarter of the present century. The Lewes paper of that day had no politics, and the *Brighton Herald* fought the battle single-handed. Every great measure of Reform that has made England what she now is, the wonder and envy of other nations, was supported in its turn by the late Proprietor of the *Brighton Herald*, and this liberal spirit was not confined to national politics, but extended itself to every proposal to improve the government of Brighton and to add to its beauty and prosperity. In the former work, Mr. Fleet was brought into contact with some of the earliest Reformers of the present century—among them, with Thelwall (the colleague and fellow-sufferer, at the hands of an almost despotic Government, of Horne Tooke), Sir Richard Phillips, Clio Rickman, Sir Godfrey Webster, Charles Pierson, Daniel Whittle Harvey, and other men famous in their day for their Liberal opinions. In domestic reforms he was closely allied with the late Lewis Slight, to whom the town owes so much, and aided him in his successful attempt to introduce new blood into the local government, then in the hands of an almost closed body. But, in the course of time, the same reforming spirit which clung to him through life made Mr. Fleet a supporter of the movement for a Charter of Incorporation and stopped for a time the connection, in town affairs, of the Proprietor of the *Herald* and the "Emperor" of Brighton,—as he was called by his friends,—Lewis Slight, though it never destroyed their feelings of mutual esteem.

As an interesting episode in the career of the *Brighton Herald*, it may be mentioned that on September 6th, 1856,—the jubilee of its establishment,—Mr. Matthew Phillips, one of the original Proprietors, and then in his 80th year, sent a letter of congratulation to Mr. William Fleet and his son. The employés of the establishment (through Mr. J. G. Bishop, who was then overseer), also seized the occasion to present Messrs. Fleet and Son with an illuminated address (suitably framed) as follows:—

"TO MESSRS. W. AND C. FLEET, PROPRIETORS OF THE *BRIGHTON HERALD.*

"GENTLEMEN,—With sincere respect, we, the Workmen and Apprentices in your service, beg to offer you our congratulations on the 50th anniversary of the establishment of the *Brighton Herald;* and we do so with the more pleasure from the consideration that you are still enabled to exercise that judicious supervision and direction of that journal which sustained it at the commencement of its career.

"Established at a period when the Press was subjected to the jealousy and opposition of numerous adverse and powerful influences, hampered by unwise and restrictive laws, its mission scarcely known or understood, you succeeded, by an honourable, consistent, and manly course of action, in raising the *Brighton Herald* to that eminent position it now occupies among the town and county newspapers.

"We desire also, at this opportunity, to express our thankfulness, not only for the kind consideration which, as employers, you have ever manifested in promoting our interests; but as men, in the readiness in which you have at all times afforded us assistance in seasons of difficulty or affliction.

"In conclusion, we earnestly hope that you may both long be spared to fill the position which you have for so many years occupied with such distinguished success; that the *Brighton Herald* may long retain the prosperity and influence it now enjoys; and that, under the blessing of Heaven, health and happiness may attend you and yours.

"We remain, Gentlemen,
"Yours most obediently,"
[Here follow the Signatures.]

It would be an easy, and also an agreeable task, to swell this notice with facts and associations supplied by so lengthened and so busy a career as that of the late Mr. William Fleet, and to call up recollections of the numerous men and events he was brought in contact with. Almost all of the former—that is, all who may be called his contemporaries—passed away before him. He remained, in the latter days of his life, the last of the first literary knot of men whom Brighton could boast as townsmen, and who gave expression to their opinions in the columns of a newspaper. Amongst these, in addition to those already referred to, may be named, as originally connected with the *Brighton Herald*, Mr. G. F. Richardson, Mr. John Baker, (first Editor and Proprietor of the *Brighton Gazette*), Mr. Levi Emmanuel Cohen (first Editor and Proprietor of the *Brighton Guardian*), Mr. Barnard Gregory, who began his remarkable and not very reputable career in Brighton, Dr. Styles, &c. Of the public men of Brighton, too, the Wigneys, the Faithfulls, the Slights, the Coopers, the Folkards, the Savages, the Lamprells, &c., not one, we be believe, of the original *corps* remains, though in some cases (as that of Mr. G. Attree, Mr. S. Ridley, Aldermen H. Martin and W. H. Hallett, Mr. J. A. Freeman (Town Clerk), and Mr. Folkard, the family is represented. Their labours and duties have devolved on new men, who themselves are, many of them, growing old in the service. Perhaps we may be allowed, in closing our notice, to express a hope that they, when their day of work is over, may be allowed to enjoy a season of repose, such as that which the late Editor and Proprietor of the *Brighton Herald* passed in retirement, before paying that debt of nature which we all owe and must all pay.

THE FUNERAL.

The remains of the deceased gentleman were subsequently interred in the Parochial Cemetery, Lewes-road, in the same vault as those of his wife, Mary Elizabeth Fleet, who died in 1873, at the age of 83 years, after an union of above 60 years. The body was followed by their only surviving son, Mr. Charles Fleet, and by Mr. W. H. Mason and Mr. Charles Mason, grandsons, and Mr. George Gatehouse, of Chichester, as chief mourners; also by Mr. W. W. Mitchell (of the *West Sussex Gazette*), Mr. J. G. Bishop (partner of Mr. Charles Fleet since his father's retirement in 1864),* and Mr. C. Bishop, Overseer in the *Brighton Herald* office; all three old apprentices of the deceased. At the entrance of the Cemetery Chapel, a number of gentlemen, including the Proprietors of the *Brighton Gazette*, the *Brighton Guardian*, the *Brighton Examiner*, and the *Brighton Daily Mail*, and several old townsmen, joined the funeral *cortège*, in order to pay their last mark of respect to the deceased.

From the obituary notices which appeared in various Brighton and Sussex Journals we select two: those of the Editor of the *Brighton Examiner* and of the Editor of the *West Sussex Gazette*— as coming from gentlemen who had been brought into close relation-

---

* Mr. Charles Fleet retired in June, 1880, since which period Mr. Bishop (who has been associated with the office since May, 1839) has been sole Proprietor. In 1889, when Mr. Bishop celebrated his Jubilee, he was presented by the employes (through Mr. J. W. Nias, the Editor), with a handsomely framed illuminated address, as follows:—

"To JOHN GEORGE BISHOP, Esq., Proprietor of the *Brighton Herald*.

"DEAR SIR,—It is with sincere respect that, in asking you to accept this address, we beg to congratulate you most cordially on the completion of your association with the *Brighton Herald* Office for the period of 50 years. It is appropriate that the *Brighton Herald*, the first newspaper published in Brighton, and now in its 83rd year, should have for its Proprietor the senior member of the Brighton Press, who in successive capacities has won his way by his own ability, prudence, integrity, and industry.

"Whilst your career has thus afforded a bright example to others, we gladly welcome this unique opportunity of recording our recognition of the helpful and healthful influence brought to bear on those with whom you are daily in contact by your generous and kindly spirit as an employer and the sterling worth of your character as a man.

"It is with feelings of unqualified esteem and hearty gratitude that we now offer our congratulations, whilst it is our earnest hope that, having reached your jubilee, you and yours may long be spared and blessed with health, and that your useful and honourable career may be continued in every prosperity and good fortune."

[Here follow the Signatures.]

ship with the deceased, and could speak of him from long personal experience:—

From the *Brighton Examiner*.

We regret to record the decease, on Sunday, at his residence in Park-crescent, of Mr. William Fleet, formerly Proprietor of the *Brighton Herald* newspaper. Mr. Fleet, who attained the ripe old age of 87 in January last, became attached, as manager, to the *Herald* in 1807, of which Mr. H. R. Attree, father of Mr. George Attree, auctioneer, was the founder in 1806. From that year till 1810 Mr. Fleet retained that position, and during the ensuing twelve months he, in conjunction with a gentleman named Bray, became Proprietor to the oldest-established journal in Brighton. After 1811 he was sole Proprietor, and remained so for many years, until he took into partnership his second, and now only surviving son, Mr. Charles Fleet. About ten years back (1864) the deceased gentleman entered upon a well-earned retirement, and till within the past few months was in the enjoyment of his customary excellent health. Latterly, however, he became so unwell that confinement to his room became necessary. Shortly after Mr. William Fleet severed his business connection with the *Herald*, his son took into partnership Mr. J. G. Bishop, who had been connected with the office, mostly as its Overseer, since 1839, and, under the style of Fleet and Bishop, the business has since been carried on. The energy of the deceased in the conduct of journalism was one of the most remarkable traits of his character; and, as an instance of the difficulties he surmounted in the days when there were no locomotives or telegraphs, we may mention that the *Herald* was the first paper in Sussex to publish the list of killed and wounded at, we believe, the battle of Vittoria (1813). Indeed, all through the Peninsular war Mr. Fleet was to the fore, as a publisher of the all-important news; and his energy in business matters did not desert him up to the very day that the form which had been so familiar at the *Herald* Office for over half-a-century bade it good-bye, to seek that rest and quiet so justly deserved. That he carried with him the esteem of those engaged at his establishment, may be inferred from the fact that, on the occasion of the jubilee of the *Brighton Herald*, in September, 1856, he (and his son) were presented by the employés with a handsomely-framed address of congratulation. Mr. Fleet, as Proprietor of the *Herald*—which he saw clear of all, or nearly all, the varying vicissitudes of the advertisement, stamp, and paper duties gained almost universal respect; but only those who were brought into personal contact with him could fully appreciate the thorough genuineness and good nature of his character. As one of these, the Proprietor of this journal bears testimony to the manly and straightforward business qualities of the gentleman whose death it is now our sad duty to publish.

(From the *West Sussex Gazette*.)

A gentleman honourably connected with journalism during the present century is now numbered with the dead. Mr. W. Fleet, formerly Proprietor of the *Brighton Herald*, died on Sunday last, at the advanced age of 87. The deceased gentleman first saw light in 1787; and when we reflect on the events in life, which have now become matters of history, in that period, we almost seem to have passed through more changes than occurred in the five centuries previous. To one possessing the intelligent mind of the departed gentleman this reflection must have been most striking. The *Brighton Herald*—still a flourishing and vigorous newspaper—was established in the year 1806; and Mr. Fleet undertook the management of the journal in 1807. In 1810 he became a part owner, and in the following year he was the sole Proprietor and Editor, and his interest in the journal continued until 1864. Our ancestors, who were the pioneers of journalism, are deserving from us of the most profound regard. They passed through all the struggles and difficulties which beset the newspaper Editor, leaving to the present generation a splendid inheritance in a free and untrammelled Press. Men who build houses seldom profit by the speculation; nor did those who paved the way for a free expression of opinion in the public journal realize large fortunes. They simply forced their course through the jungle, cleared away the brushwood, and left the paths clear and open for the succeeding generation. The life of the late Mr. Fleet is somewhat identical with that of the late Mr. Charles Knight. Both gentlemen started in the world at almost the same moment—one at Windsor, as the Editor and Proprietor of the *Windsor and Eton Express*, in 1812; and the other as the Proprietor of the *Brighton Herald*, in 1811. Both journals were on an equal footing; and we have understood that the Proprietors exchanged papers from a very early date, and may have done so to this time. Anyone who wishes to learn something of the snares and pitfalls which beset the journalist in the early part of the century should read "Passages of a Working Life," by Charles Knight, and he will be there amazed at the energy—indeed the heroism - of those who struggled in troubled times to make the English newspaper what it is. Take the position of the newspaper in 1821. The stamp on each sheet of paper was fourpence; each advertisement paid a duty of 3s. 6d., and a heavy tax existed on the paper itself. Perhaps the latter was of little consequence, as the direct duties were sufficient to cripple and restrain the circulation of a newspaper. But, worse than all, the Editor was hemmed round by stringent bonds and securities on his property, and all imaginable safeguards against libel; and on this subject we cannot do better than quote the work of Charles Knight (p. 262, vol. 1) on the manner in which a censorship was exercised over the Liberal Press. He says:—" In March, 1821, the 'Constitutional Association' was formed, for the purpose of prosecuting printers and publishers who went beyond what they deemed the proper bounds of political discussion. This despicable Association - despicable, however supported by rank and wealth - saw no mischief in the gross libels of one set of writers who professed to be the friends of the Government, but instituted the most reckless prosecutions against 'Liberal' newspapers. The term 'Liberal' had then begun to mark a certain set of opinions which had outgrown their former title of 'Jacobinical.' This Association acquired the name of 'The Bridge-street Gang.' After three or four months of a hateful existence—denounced in Parliament, execrated by every man who had inherited a spark of Milton's zeal for the liberty of Unlicensed Printing - this Association was prosecuted for oppression and extortion. The Grand Jury found a true Bill against its Members. They were acquitted upon their trial; bnt practices were disclosed which showed how dangerous it was for a crafty attorney and a knot of fanatical politicians to play at Attorney Generalship." It was such men as the late Mr. Fleet that struggled with heroism against this power and persecution, and landed the Press in the glorious position it occupies at this moment as the exponent of public opinion and the enemy to oppression. This was not done without suffering, both in purse and person; and we think we are not wrong in saying that the late Mr. Fleet underwent some punishment by an imprisonment, as the Hunts and other eminent and patriotic writers of the period did, for so boldly expressing his political opinions in the face of all the terrors and threats by which he was surrounded. The energy of the late Mr. Fleet in his younger days was remarkable; and were it not that the laws put every obstacle in the way of the journalist—as if he were a vendor of poison—

such energy and ability must have led to a splendid position in the County. But the vigilant eye of the courtesan was everywhere, the jealousy and revenge of the local squirearchy was soon aroused, and such was the condition of the law—of which we have quoted a specimen—that the wings of the Editor were cut at all points, and he could only flutter so far, and no farther. There were, of course, the toadies of journalism, as there are now, who did the dirty work of their tyrannical patrons, and crawled through the world, leaving their slime in their path. But the *Brighton Herald* never truckled to this, nor has it done so since. The journal has pursued the honourable paths of independence to this day; and the great and glorious career of the departed gentleman - for such we must call the life of one who has fought with his pen for our liberties is to be venerated, especially by all journalists. The deceased gentleman leaves behind him a most exemplary and clever representative, who has for many years past conducted the journal, in the person of his son, Mr. Charles Fleet; and, although the death of the venerable journalist, at the age of 87, might have been naturally anticipated, we regret to lose one surrounded by the associations of almost a century. But the laws of Nature cannot be overcome, if the vicious laws surrounding the Press are to be subdued; and we can only add to this imperfect but sincere expression of admiration at the career of the late Mr. William Fleet the simple words —' May he rest in peace.'"

A Retrospect of Twenty Years.

BRIGHTON—1850 AND 1870.

THERE are few English towns which can compare with Brighton in rapidity of growth, whether as regards extension of area or increase of population, during the successive stages of its development from the time when, as a humble fishing village, it first found favour with Royalty, until now, when it has attained a magnitude and embraces districts which, to Brightonians in days gone by, would have been absolutely inconceivable. Without dwelling upon these successive stages, we may mention that we have had an opportunity afforded us, by the perusal of two Brighton Directories,* of judging of the changes which took place during twenty years: of seeing what Brighton was in 1850,—as to its extent and population, its social and other characteristics,—and of comparing it with Brighton in 1870. The changes—social, personal, and material—which the town underwent, even in that brief period, were so remarkable that we shall make no apology for offering a synopsis of the more important of them to our readers.

The task gives rise to mingled feelings of pleasure and regret. Those associated with Brighton from an early period will feel proud to note that, in the great and manifold changes of those twenty years, there was continual progress. In all directions save one—where the sea confronts the land with an impassable barrier—we "enlarged our borders," adding house to house, and street to street, over widely-extended areas. New and important townships grew upon our skirts; noble mansions covering what were formerly green fields or gardens; and grand and palatial buildings of recent erection meeting the eye at almost every turn. Such of the charitable and other institutions as were ill-lodged or inconveniently located in 1850 were, previous to 1870, either removed to more desirable situations or their abiding places superseded by others more adapted to their increased requirements; narrow thoroughfares were widened, adding materially to the public convenience as well as to their appearance; and in one or two notable instances there were certain localities removed which had become a bye-word and a reproach to the town.

There is, it will be admitted, in every one of the changes which took place during those 20 years, much cause for congratulation;

---

* Published respectively in 1850 and 1870 by Mr. Folthorp and Mr. Page, of 173, North-street.

but, at the same time, one involuntarily reverts to other changes within the same period—changes which give rise to feelings of regret: in the losses sustained; in the "old familiar faces," now seen no more; in the earnest workers, who have ceased to toil; in the gifted and the good, who have passed away from us; in the near and dear ones, whose vacant places will for ever remain unfilled. In addition to these, too, how many pleasant spots have been covered; how many venerable fabrics removed—linked, it may have been, with some old tradition or quaint history, or some time-honoured association, around which the memory fondly clings!

Those unacquainted with Brighton in 1850 can scarcely conceive the large area which was covered by "bricks and mortar" in the subsequent 20 years, or what alterations were made within that period in various parts of the town. Brighton in 1850 had just recovered from a serious stagnation—a turning point in its history. Building operations were going on in all directions, to meet the constantly-increasing demand for houses by those who,—in consequence of the better travelling facilities which were then afforded,—had been induced to visit us. To show the extent to which these building operations were carried on, it may be stated that all the north-eastern part of the town, lying between Hanover-street (immediately behind Hanover-crescent) and the Queen's Park, and between the upper part of Sussex-street and Islingword-road,—at present covered with houses,—was in 1850 little else than garden-ground, with two windmills upon it (near the Park). The Freehold Land Society's Estate, which was comprised within a triangle formed by Elm-grove, Islingword-road, and Hampden-road, wholly covered by house property in 1870, was twenty years previously used as gardens. Wellington-villas were unknown in 1850; in fact, between Elm-grove and "The Bear Inn," Lewes-road, the only house existing at that date was Scabe's Castle, situate on a farm about midway between the two. The Extra-Mural Cemetery was just then being laid out; but the Parochial Cemetery—in 1870 tenanted by its thousands—was in 1850 *in nubibus*. Upper and Lower Lewes-roads, from their starting-points each side of Park-crescent to their junction at the Lewes-road Viaduct, had not in 1850 a single house between them! The Round Hill Estate was unknown in 1850; and the Hanover Cricket Ground—said to have been the finest piece of turf in England, and the scene of many an exciting contest between the "giants of those days," such as Slater and Brown, Box and Lillywhite, Pilch and Wenman, the Broadbridges, the Mynns, and many another wielder of bat and troller of ball known to fame—had just been broken up preparatory to building Park-crescent. "The Hanover Arms," attached to the Cricket Ground, still stood in 1850, kept, however, by its last tenant, Thomas Box, *the* wicket-keeper of the period. The gardens, too, behind the once-famous ball-room, were then undisturbed; and the glories of the "Maze," at their northern end, had not entirely departed.

Turning to the north-west of Brighton, the increase in building within the 20 years (1850-70) was equally great. In 1850 there was little else except gardens between Ann-street and the Montpellier-road, the Railway Goods Line, &c., in that locality not being formed until 1851; and the pretty triangular field at New England, in front of what was originally Murrell's (Chatfield's) Farm,—and, subsequently, Harry Pegg's, of the Royal York Hotel,—which was intact in 1850, was in 1870 covered with houses; nought remaining of its pristine state but the two or three trees growing near "The Bridge Inn," adjacent to the Montpellier-road Viaduct. Where Montpellier-crescent, &c., now is, there were in 1850 pleasant fields; and in the one nearest the Dyke-road was the once famous Murrell's Pond, whilst that to the south was later on devoted to the purposes of a cricket-ground. In 1850 such a township as Prestonville (which was projected in 1865 by Mr Daniel Friend, on land to the north of the New England Farm*), was undreamt of: the carriage-road which subsequently formed its western boundary totally obliterated the upper portion of that once pretty rural retreat—that is, some forty or fifty years ago—known as "Lovers' Walk," which was brought into terrible notoriety in 1831 by being selected by the murderer Holloway as a hiding-place for a portion of his wife's remains. The Dyke-road, again, starting from the "Seven Dials" (where it intersects the Montpellier-road), had not in 1850 a single house on it near the town, except Hove Place (Mr. Bright Smith's) and Port Hall (Sir Page Dick's). Lashmar's Mill (with its little cottage and minor adjacent buildings), was the first erection which one came to in that direction. All the handsome property now in that neighbourhood, as indeed, much of that in Buckingham-place, &c., and from Clifton-place to West Hill-road (where Mr. Hudson's once famous Black Mill formerly stood), is of modern growth, irrespective of the fine property erected, or in course of erection in 1870, on the ground formerly belonging to the Old Workhouse, &c. The open space in Vernon-terrace, for many years used as a nursery garden by Messrs. Parsons and Son, once well-known florists in the Western-road, was prior to 1870 absorbed by buildings; as, in fact, was the large field known as the Temple Field (so called from its proximity to "The Temple,"—a residence built by Thomas Read Kemp, the projector of Kemp Town. The upper portion of the western boundary of the Temple Field was prior to 1870 covered by that fine block of houses known as Denmark-terrace. It would scarcely be believed that, so recently as 1850, there was a large open field in the Western-road (immediately south of the Wick House), and extending from what is now York-road to Brunswick-place. Yet such was the fact. Upper Brunswick-place itself could then boast of but six houses, one on the Eastern side and five on the Western. In the upper one of these five houses the late Mr. J. S. McWhinnie resided; in the lower, Mrs. Cockburn (Byron's earliest love, Mary Duff, the news of whose marriage, he said, "startled him

---

* The township of Prestonville covers 6½ acres. The site—so little was borough extension in this direction then anticipated—previously to its being purchased by Mr. Friend, had been fixed upon by the Town Council for the purposes of a public Abattoir. Had that most desirable institution been built there, what a change from now would the residential character of the neighbourhood have presented!

like a thunder-clap"). Immediately to the north of these houses was the pretty field known as Chatfield's field. In 1850, aye, and even later, one might have stood in that field, and, looking westward, then seen, at the distance of a mile or so, the neat and unpretending Parish Church of Old Hove, with the little village lying to the south of it. All between it and the spectator was then green fields (with the sea to the south and the Downs to the north), dotted here and there with a house, a farm, &c., which offered but little interruption to the view. Not a house of what is now known as Cliftonville was in existence. The large pond (known as Lower Wick Pond), which was situated in Hove Fields, just beyond the south-western corner of what is now the upper portion of Lansdowne-place, had just prior to 1850 been filled up. Lower Lansdowne-place was then but half built on; and Adelaide-crescent had only a dozen houses on its south-eastern side. Palmeira-square was, in 1850, about to be laid out; and the ruins of the Antheum,—huge iron girders, &c.,—which had lain rusting in the walled enclosure just beyond "The Wick Inn" since they fell in August, 1833, had only just been removed.

The Eastern part of Brighton cannot compare with the Western with respect to the increase in the building operations of the twenty years between 1850 and 1870. The gaps in the Marine-parade, which formerly existed, were, however, filled up prior to 1870, and much property was built between the Eastern-road and St. George's-road, and thence towards Kemp Town.

Coming nearer home, the building operations in the centre of the town in that period were chiefly consequent upon improvements made by the town authorities, the most important being the widening of Duke-street and North-road. The Queen's-road, too, or rather that section of it which in 1850 was known as Air-street, was in 1870 completed and otherwise improved by the removal of those erections attached to the slaughter-houses which so long disfigured and disgraced it. Altogether, the "bricks-and-mortar growth" of Brighton between 1850 and 1870 was enormous, and such as few of even those who have been living in its midst would credit did not the facts speak for themselves. The results may be thus summarized :—In 1850 the rateable value of Brighton and Hove was about £300,000; in 1870 it might be set down as £500,000; in 1850 the two places contained 439 streets, &c.; in 1870, 620; in 1850 their respective populations were—Brighton, 65,573; Hove, 4,104; in 1870 Brighton (estimated), 100,000; Hove about 12,000. May the succeeding twenty years show equally gratifying results; and still increasing prosperity!

Having described the large additions made to the area of Brighton by the building operations in the 20 years (1850-70) under notice, we will now turn to the changes effected in various public institutions, &c., within the town itself during the same period.

Previous to the year 1850 the Pavilion, with its beautiful grounds, was to the inhabitants of Brighton as a "sealed book." It was then in the possession of the Crown. Its then south gate, with sentry-boxes on each side, stood parallel with Mr. Seabrook's house at the bottom of North-street, now the south-west corner of Pavilion-

THE WEST BATTERY AND CLIFF (with Hog-boats in front),—about 1830.

(The Flag-staff on the present Esplanade, opposite the Grand Hotel, shows the site of the old Battery.)

buildings. A huge prison-like block of buildings (over which the Pavilion clock tower peered) then formed the northern side of Castle-square, on the site of which the present Pavilion-buildings were subsequently erected.

On the Marine frontage, especially to the west of Brighton, the changes which took place between 1850 and 1870 were very numerous. About 1858 the West Battery (of which the flag-staff now alone remains), with its guns, &c., was entirely removed, having twice previously been shorn of its fair proportions, in order that the King's-road might be widened as well as to admit of the continuation of the beautiful promenade, known as the Esplanade, which—running from that point to the Western toll-house (removed in 1888)—supplanted the unprotected green slopes which, with naked steps at intervals, originally faced the sea. The Battery-house itself (which overlooked the Battery) was sold in 1861, and the Grand Hotel erected on its site; next, the Norfolk Hotel was rebuilt; and the West Pier was added to the attractions of Brighton. Not long afterwards the Grand Concert Hall in West-street was erected,* necessitating the removal of Mr. Hargraves's house, formerly Mrs. Thrale's, dear to classic memory, where Fanny Burney and Dr. Johnson visited; and with the house went the old wooden pump, respecting which old Dr. Hargraves was reported to have said that it was worth (or rather, we suppose, the water which it yielded) so many hundreds a year to him!

In West-street, consequent upon the widening of its upper portion in connection with the improvement of Duke-street, several other houses connected with local history of bygone times were removed. "The Albany Tavern," which stood at the corner of Duke-street, was formerly the residence of Townshend, the Bow-street runner; and there George IV. had frequently lunched. In the house next above lived years ago Mr. Beach Roberts, a local celebrity in his day, known as the "Walking Newspaper;" and immediately adjoining was the house of Ings, the butcher, one of the Cato-street conspirators, who was hung, at Newgate, in 1820.

Among other changes in West-street was the erection in 1868 of the magnificent Turkish Bath. With the Baths generally, there were, indeed, great changes during the 20 years we are dealing with. The Lion Mansion now stands on the site of what were formerly Williams's Baths; the site of Wood's (late Creak's) Original Baths, in Pool-valley, now forms part of Brill's Baths Company's buildings, which occupy not only that site but the site of "The Duke of Wellington Inn," "The White Horse Hotel," and of "The Rising Sun Hotel." Mahomed's once celebrated Baths, too, are gone, their place being occupied by Markwell's Royal Hotel.

In addition to those previously noted other of the public Institutions of the town underwent important changes during the twenty years treated of. The Post-office, in 1850, shifted from the New-road to its present quarters. In 1850 the Brighton Custom House was on

---

[* The Concert Hall was entirely destroyed by fire on October 7th, 1882, at 11.25 p.m., little more than the frontages in Middle-street and West-street remaining. The Hall is now (1892) being reconstructed.]

the King's-road; the Inland Revenue and Excise Office, however, was then content to do its business at "The King and Queen," a meeting being held once in six weeks! and the Stamp Office was at the corner of Broad-street. In 1853-54 our venerable Parish Church was restored; and the opportunity was then taken of planting the Church-yard with trees—following the good example which had been set in other localities, and which has been subsequently judiciously extended. In 1850 there was no opening from Glo'ster-street to Sydney-street; the space being occupied by the Female Orphan Asylum, with its neat garden in the fore-ground. Subsequently a new Asylum was built in the Eastern-road; and contiguous to it the Blind Asylum was erected, the inmates being removed thence from their ill-suited quarters in Jubilee-street. A similar judicious transfer of locality was made with respect to Swan Downer's School, which was removed from Gardner-street to the top of North-street, near Smithers's Brewery. The building of the Industrial Schools at the Warren Farm, and subsequently the Workhouse, in a well-chosen locality, must also be noted among the changes of the twenty years. Restlessness, in fact, during the period, would seem to have been the prevalent spirit of our public institutions. The County Court Office in 1850 was at 151, North-street, and, after a second removal, settled down subsequently into its present permanent quarters. At the same date the Savings' Bank was in Prince's-place; the London and County Bank (now Messrs. Potts and Co.'s music warehouse) adjoined it; the Lying-In Institution was in High-street; and the Brighton and Sussex Mutual Provident Society was at 47, East-street, at the North-west corner of Steine-lane. Both the then local Gas Companies as well as the Water Company occupied different offices in 1850 to what they did 20 years later; and the Odd Fellows of the town, wisely eschewing public-house meetings, have, since 1850, erected for themselves a Hall.

But what of the Literary Institutions which existed in 1850 in Brighton? Alas! not one remained in 1870. The Royal Literary and Scientific Institution, Albion Rooms, died a lingering death, leaving, however, a rich legacy to the town in its valuable library. The Athenæum, too (in 1850 at 64, West-street), established under very favourable auspices, subsequently passed away. And so has the Working Man's Institute, Middle-street; for, notwithstanding the support it received from Messrs. Moses Ricardo, Herbert Holtham, Cordy Burrows, &c., all staunch friends to the working classes, "its place is known no more."

The government of the town itself underwent great changes between 1850 and 1870. At the former period it was not Incorporated; but was "regulated, paved, improved, and managed" by the Town Commissioners (Lewis Slight, Clerk); the Police (T. H. Chase, Chief Officer), being also under their control. The High Constable (who appointed his own Headboroughs) was annually elected by a jury of the inhabitants, summoned by the Lord of the Hundred of Whalesbone (the Earl of Abergavenny). The Town Crier was then a recognized officer. The law was administered by County Magistrates; and if an inquest was required to be held, it was necessary to send eight miles (to Lewes) for the County Coroner! The Directors and Guardians of the Poor (R. Becher, Clerk), in 1850 had their offices at the Town Hall. There were in 1850 but three newspapers in the town (in 1870 there were seven); the electric telegraph had not been introduced; and Brighton still retained and recognised that official so important to the world of fashion in the olden time—a Master of the Ceremonies!

It would be well nigh impossible to give a detailed list of the changes which occurred between 1850 and 1870 in many localities of the town, much less those in single streets. The extent of the changes, however, among the residents of the more important streets, where fluctuations would be thought less likely to take place than in others, is almost startling. The King's-road and Marine-parade, North-street, St. James's-street, East-street, and the Steine are instances of this. North-street, for example, in 1850 contained 173 places of business; and yet, out of the whole number, there were but *eighteen* in which changes had not taken place, either by removal or in proprietorship, by death or otherwise, in the 20 years succeeding 1850. One has almost ceased to remember Cartwright and Warner's (No. 5), Whiteman and Cobbett's (No. 14), Sams's, and other grocers there in 1850. How few in 1870 knew aught of Chassereau's once famous Repository (No. 21), of Souch's (No. 52), or Wild's (No. 162)? or of Paine, the bookseller (No. 9)? Dutton and Thorowgood (in 1850 at No. 172) have migrated to East-street; and McCarroll's music warehouse (formerly No. 171) has ceased to exist, their places being occupied by Messrs. Hannington's carpet warehouse; and Wright's (in 1850 *the* shop of the Colonnade, subsequently occupied by Mr. Tozer) was, in 1870, known as Potts and Co.'s at No. 167. The names of Creasy and Baker, George Hall (upholsterer), Williams and Yearsley (ironmongers), W. Walkley and Acton and Son (butchers), T. Shales (draper), Seabrook (surgeon), T. Mussell (chemist), Charles Alderton (tailor), W. Hope (carrier), George W. Sawyer, Uriah Lane, and Richard Mighell—all more or less known as residents in North-street in 1850 sounded unfamiliar in 1870; as indeed did others of pleasant memory, as Billy Spears, Pickett, of "The Coach and Horses," Charley Briggs, of "The Unicorn," Fred. Farmer, &c., all of whom have passed away. Among the "old familiar faces" of North-street was that of Major Bayntun, the Barrack Master, whose house (No. 136, now Mr. Attree's Auction Mart), with flint facing and having plain iron railings in front, was well known to the small boys of 1850 (and of previous years) from the grape-vine which almost covered its front, the fruit of which, if pleasing to the eye, was, from an ancient cause, always *sour!*

In 1850 the Churches of the Establishment in Brighton numbered but 13; All Saints' was being built; and there was but one other Church in Hove besides the Parish Church. In 1870 there were in Brighton (including Dr. Winslow's), 22; 4 in Hove; and 1 in Cliftonville. In 1850 the Dissenting and other Places of Worship numbered 19; in addition to the Friends' Meeting-house, the Jews' Synagogue, and the Roman Catholic and Presbyterian Churches. The Pavilion Chapel (subsequently the Trinity Presbyterian Church) was then being used for a Gymnasium! Twenty years later there were no less than 35 Dissenting and other Places of Worship; the Society of Friends and the Jews still had each but one Place of Worship; but the Roman Catholic Churches had increased to 3, the Presbyterians 2, whilst in two Chapels there were French and German Services conducted. But, satisfactory as may have been the increase in the number of Places of Worship themselves, we cannot survey the list of 1850, with the names of those who then ministered in them, without a feeling of sadness at the personal losses which many flocks sustained within the 20 years that followed. Of those connected with the Establishment, it may be mentioned that, in 1850, the Rev. F. W. Robertson ministered at Trinity; James Anderson at St. George's; C. D. Maitland at St. James's; W. Du Pré at St. Margaret's; and H. V. Elliott at St. Mary's. In 1870 others occupied their places. Dissent also had to lament within the 20 years the decease of many among the more prominent of its Ministers, including the Revs. J. Sortain, J. N. Goulty, W. Savory, J. Sedgwick, J. Grace, Vinall, Sharp, and Malleson (Unitarian); and the Roman Catholic Church lost Canon Reardon.

Besides the above, many other personal changes—alas, how many!—took place in our midst during those memorable twenty years. How many worthy, how many noble, how many gifted, and how many notable persons passed away in that brief period! In 1850 Brighton was represented in Parliament by Sir George Pechell and Lord Alfred Hervey. Before 1870 we lost not only Sir George (and his brave son, who fell in the Crimean war), but a previous colleague (1837-41), Sir A. J. Dalrymple, and their immediate predecessors, Mr. George Faithfull and Mr. Isaac Newton Wigney. The father of Lord Alfred Hervey, the Marquis of Bristol—whose munificent gifts to the town as well as his unbounded private charity will cause his name to be ever held in grateful remembrance—also passed away, together with many another worthy, to whom, like him, the charitable institutions and the poor of the town were much indebted, as the Duke of Devonshire, Lady Jane Peel, Sir Ralph and Lady Grace Gore, Mr. Hanbury Tracy, Sir Thos. Blomfield, and others. What a gap do we find in 1870 in the names of those who were our principal residents in 1850: Mr. C. Craven, Major Colegrave, Mr. P. C. Cazalet, Lady Ashburnham, Count Bathyany, Mr. H. Bethune, Lady Boynton, Mrs. Bridges, Sir Edward Kerrison, Mr. E. Catt, Baron Goldsmid, Lady Hotham, the Hon. A. Macdonald (the "Lord of the Isles"), Mr. Bright Smith, Col. Kemys Tynte, Colonel Wyndham, &c. And so of others, equally well known, who then dwelt among us, as Captain Falkiner (noted for his eccentricities, and who was Second Lieutenant on board the "Shannon," when she fought and won her 15 minutes' battle with the "Chesapeake" in 1812) his brother, Sir Rigg Falkiner, Colonel Eld, M.C., Sake Deen Mahomed (who introduced shampooing into the town, and who was in 1850 an undoubted centenarian), Madame Michau (*maîtresse de danse* to the Prince of Wales and others of the family of George III.), Captain Michelet (fencing master), Paul Foskett ("Protestant"), &c. Of these,—

"Some have left us,
And some are taken from us; all are departed;
All, all, are gone, the old familiar faces."

Of public men, how many names, familiar enough in 1850, were missed in 1870! Among the Magistrates at the former date were Mr. William Seymour (one of Brighton's worthies, and amongst the most able of those who who ever sat upon the local Bench), Major Allen, Mr. G. Basevi, and Mr. John Borrer. Out of the 86 Commissioners who in 1850 managed the affairs of the town, scarcely a fourth remained to us twenty years later; their Clerk (Lewis Slight), their Solicitor (C. Cobby), and their Town-rate Collector (John Chalk), were also removed by death. With respect to the Commissioners themselves, few of the present generation know aught of the men— nearly all now passed away—who in 1850, and long antecedently, strove, each according to his light, to render Brighton, by public and other improvements, every way worthy of the high position she had then attained among the fashionable watering-places of England. Foremost among these may be mentioned Mr. Thomas Cooper (a thoroughly practical man, to whom especially we owe the formation of the Queen's-road, who built the Town Hall, the Bedford Hotel, &c.), Mr. Isaac Bass (who projected Prince Albert-street and gave the ground for the formation of the East-street Avenue, affording a new route in this direction to the Marine-parade), Mr. William Beedham (first Chairman of the Brighton Water Company), Messrs. E. Cornford, J. Colbatch, J. Bradshaw (most voluble of local "horators," and the "war-horse," as he was designated, of the Corporation movement at the time that that question was agitated), D. M. Folkard, Hyam Lewis, Samuel Ridley, R. Edwards, E. Thunder, E. Savage, John Patching, John Good, W. Lambert, J. Yearsley, &c.

The lists of "professions, trades," &c., of 1850, when compared with those of 1870, show many a hiatus. Take, for instance, the medical profession. Out of the 76 "physicians," &c., practising in Brighton in 1850,—not a few of whom were eminently skilful in their profession, as the Messrs. Lawrence (father and son), Dr. King, Messrs. H. Blaker, Vallance, Newnham, Paine, &c.,—only about 20 odd remained in 1870.

The list of solicitors in 1850 contained the names (wanting in 1870) of Messrs. T. Attree, S. W. Bennett, F. and C. Cooper, W. Penfold, T. Freeman, J. S. McWhinnie, &c. Artists, again, show the loss in the same period of F. Arundel, Leathem, Nash, and of others less known to fame. It might be added that, in 1850, the then President of the Royal Academy, Sir Martin A. Shee, was a resident in Brighton. Of the librarians of 1850, but one remained in 1870; and of all the hotels of the town in 1850 there was not one twenty years later in which there had not been a change of proprietorship, either by death or otherwise. The tavern changes within the period we are dealing with were "legion"; and an involuntary sigh escapes us as we note how many once genial spirits—men who seemed especially adapted to their vocation—are now no more: Suggers, of "The King's Arms"; Starr, of "The Castle"; Stonham, of "The Seven Stars"; Lower of "The Pelham Arms"; Briggs, of "The Unicorn"; Pope, of "The Wheat Sheaf"; &c.

But we must pass on to another section of this "Retrospect"—one which affords irrefutable evidence of the growth of Brighton, namely,—a statistical comparison between 1850 and 1870, of some of the trades, &c., of the town.

Within the period named the builders, &c., increased from 80 to 134; the architects and surveyors, from 13 to 21; the painters, from 60 to 72; and the ironmongers, gasfitters, &c., from 26 to 60. The number of stonemasons remained stationary; whilst the timber-merchants showed a decrease (almost the only trade which did so) of 5. The furnishing and upholstery warehouses increased from 38 to 53; the china and glass warehouses, from 10 to 23; the French polishers, from 5 to 8; the trunkmakers, from 6 to 10; and the Tunbridge-ware, dressing-case, &c., makers, from 14 to 46. The house-agents in 1850 numbered 42, an increase in the 20 years of 15; the the auctioneers, 28, an increase of 11; and the brokers, 29, an increase also of 11.

The increase between 1850 and 1870 in the number of those who comprised the local commissariat department, &c., appears, to have kept pace with the growth of the town. Thus, the butchers increased nearly 50 per cent., from 100 to 142; the bakers and pastry-cooks, from 124 to 185; the grocers, tea dealers, &c., from 108 to 215; the fruiterers and greengrocers from 91 to 160; the fishmongers, from 15 to 27; and the poulterers, from 14 to 16. The hotels exactly doubled their number, increasing from 16 to 32; the boarding-houses increased by 4, numbering 29; the coffee and dining rooms increased from 14 to 33; and there were, in addition, 8 restaurants. The lodging-houses increased from 486 to 721. The brewers more than doubled their number, increasing from 14 to 29; the wine and spirit merchants increased from 32 to 60; the ale and porter agents from 6 to 10; and the taverns and public-houses from 97 to 398! The ginger-beer and soda-water trade was scarcely so progressive; the manufacturers increasing but 2 in the 20 years. The dairymen, too, were a very stationary class during the double decade; in 1850, when the population was about 70,000, they numbered 42; in 1870, when it was about 120,000, they numbered 43! We are unable to furnish information as to the source whence the necessarily increased supply of milk was obtained; *possibly* more cows were kept! or ——the reader's experience or imagination must supply the omission.

The provision for clothing, &c., for the increased population in the 20 years appears to have fully kept pace with the requirements. Thus the tailors increased from 73 to 116; the clothiers and outfitters, from 9 to 18; the boot and shoemakers, from 78 to 144; the linen and woollen drapers, from 46 to 94; the lace warehouses, from 7 to 16; the baby-linen warehouses, from 4 to 12; the mantle warehouses, from 1 to 8; and all trades of a kindred character show more or less increased numbers. The straw-bonnet makers, however, were exceptional: they actually decreased from 21 to 9. Oh! Fashion—which just previous to 1870 brought chignons, &c., into favour with the ladies—what have you to answer for!

The Schools in Brighton during the 20 years increased in a much greater ratio than the population, the boarding schools numbering 165 in 1870—an increase of 64 over those of 1850; the day schools showed an equal satisfactory return, increasing during the same period from 17 to 44. The number of professors of various kinds also increased from 101 to 165; and the booksellers, printers, newsvendors, &c., showed a more or less satisfactory increase.

The legal profession, so far as the solicitors were concerned, did not much increase between 1850 and 1870: the latter year, when there were 46, showing but four in number over those of 1850. The law stationers actually decreased 50 per cent.: they were 6 in 1850, and in 1870 but 3. In the former year not a single barrister resided in the town; in the latter it was blessed with seven! The medical profession since 1850 appears to have well thriven: the medical practitioners increasing from 76 to 106; the chemists and druggists, from 38 to 64; and the dentists from 12 to 28. There was only one surgical instrument maker in 1850; in 1870 there were 5. With respect to a trade—which to some minds has a close connection with the medical profession—that of undertaker, the numbers increased in the 20 years from 19 to 27.

We must here close our "Retrospect" of the changes which 20 years brought about: a chequered one, it may have been; but one which, we trust, has not proved altogether uninteresting to our readers.

Hove.

A STORY is told of an ancient philosopher, who was so intent upon watching the stars that he overlooked the well at his feet. Something analogous to this may be said as regards Brighton and Hove. As a body corporate, Brightonians are so occupied with their own affairs that the rapid growth of their nearest neighbour, Hove, has been, with the majority, entirely overlooked. The facts, nevertheless, are too prominent to be ignored, that the once comparatively secluded village of Old Hove is now still more secluded by the fine streets, &c., in its vicinity; that the once rural walk through pretty meadows which led to it has been supplanted by a spacious carriage road; that, between Hove and Brighton, squares, avenues, &c., skirted by palatial mansions, have been formed; and, though really in a separate township, they have come to be regarded, by reason of their close association with Brighton, as part of it.

Old Hove, or, as it is now called, West Hove, some 40 or 50 years ago consisted of a single street, about 100 yards long, running from the beach-gap to the road leading (eastward) to the Church. There were two or three goodly houses in it (occupied chiefly by owners of land in the neighbourhood), and a few others contiguous to it along the sea frontage. Besides these, there were at the lower part of the street, a few cottages, a smithy, and the inevitable "public" ("The Ship Inn"); the upper part of the street being devoted to agricultural buildings, &c. As it was then, so it has been, we suppose, from time immemorial; for in the drawing, showing the attack of the French on the "towne of Brithampston," in 1545, "Hove village" consisted of a single street. What the number of inhabitants was at that period, we know not—whether celibacy prevailed—whether the Malthusian doctrine was in force— or other causes operated adversely to increase; but the population amounted in 1800 to only 101, the ladies being in a minority of three—a disproportion which the subsequent 10 years but little diminished, as in 1811 the population had not increased more than a dozen, the ladies still being in a minority of one.

The stationary character of Old Hove was, doubtless, attributable to its isolated situation. It lay a long way south of the old Shoreham road, the once main artery from Brighton to London by Steyning; and it is, perhaps, owing to this fact that all the old "Guides," while eloquent on Aldrington, make little or no mention of Hove. The inhabitants, or, at least, the lower stratum of them, did not, probably, repine at this. They lived and enjoyed themselves in their own way;

and any shortcomings were, doubtless, atoned for by the annual "bull-bait" on Easter Tuesday, with an occasional "one in," when the landlord of "The Ship" could arrange it.* The isolation of Hove, too, suited a section of the community who carried on a little "private business" on their own account, *i.e.*, smuggling. It was, in fact, a most convenient spot for carrying on this illicit commerce, as, in former times, the sea at high tides washed up to the bottom of Hove-street, and tubs could be run in, "slung," and carried off with comparative impunity.†

The "bide as we be" principle for many a year ruled in Old Hove. Some 60 years ago the only observable new erections were posts and rails! enclosing the pleasant fields which lay between Lower Wick Pond and Hove Church, and once a favourite rural resort of Brightonians. These erections were an eye-sore both to "foreigners" and residents; and, for special reasons, to no one more than the then Churchwarden of Hove, Mr. S. Webb, himself. He was a very portly man, and being unable, by reason of his size, to get through the posts each side of the footpath through the fields, he was prevented going his accustomed road to Church! He took an early opportunity of complaining to the County Magistrates; but to no purpose. Captain Heaviside (a gentleman standing some 6ft. 6in. in height) was on the Bench when the complaint was made, and no little mirth was occasioned by the Captain remarking,—"If you are too stout, Webb, to get through the posts, do as I do—step over them!" ‡

But this by the way. In noticing, however, the growth of Hove, we shall not pretend to make an archæological excursion into what we believe would prove an "uneventful historie." The discovery in January, 1856, of what were considered to be the remains of an ancient British chieftain, and of some Celtic antiquities in the once well-known barrow in Coney-burrow field (subsequently cut through

---

[* The ring to which the bulls were attached was to be seen within the last 50 or 60 years on the beach south of the lower path of the road to Shoreham, just to the west of "The Ship."]

† *Apropos* of smuggling at Hove, there is an anecdote worth repeating. Hove and Preston were formerly ecclesiastically conjoined: the Service being conducted at each Parish Church on *alternate* Sundays. One *Hove Sunday*, the worthy Vicar, in full canonicals, went to the Church to "do duty." To his astonishment, the bell was not going; and, on enquiring the reason of the Sexton, that individual coolly informed him that he had made a mistake—that, in fact, it was *Preston Sunday!* The Vicar felt certain he was right; the Sexton as stoutly asserted he was wrong. But the Vicar would not give in, and ordered the bell to be rung forthwith. The Sexton said, "It's no use, Sir, you can't preach to-day." "Why not"? exclaimed the Vicar indignantly. "Because," rejoined the Sexton, "*the Church is full of tubs, and the pulpit's full of tea.*" This incident must have occurred under an improved state of ecclesiastical affairs in Hove; for, in a description of Hove, by the Rev. J. Mossop, published in *The Gentleman's Magazine*, in February, 1792, it is stated "Divine Service is only performed in the Church *once in six weeks*," the writer adding, "and, by the appearance of the ruinous state in which it at present is, that will soon be entirely neglected."

‡ Captain Heaviside was a gentleman well-known in fashionable circles in Brighton some 50 years since. He resided in Brunswick-square, and it was from thence that, in 1840, his wife eloped with Dr. Lardner (author of the *Cyclopædia* and other eminent scientific works). In August of that year, there was a *crim. con.* trial at the Assizes, Heaviside *v.* Lardner, the plaintiff obtaining a verdict for £8,000 damages.

by the road formed from the eastern corner of St. John's-terrace to the present Railway goods station) would lead to the inference that the locality was once peopled by the "Ancients."* This, barrow, however, had little to do with Hove proper, which was situated fully half-a-mile to the westward. Hove, we may state, was one of the many lordships in the County belonging to Godwin, Earl of Kent; and after the Conquest William Fitz-Board held it of William de Warenne. The Domesday account of Hove is somewhat confused; but there appear to have been in it " 14 villeins, 8 bondmen, and 6 salt-pans!" It was then designated *Hou*.† In the reign of Edward I. some of the Pierpoint family possessed the Manor. The village subsequently appears to have grown considerably; but it suffered much by encroachments of the sea. In 1340, according to the return of the *Nonarum Inquisitiones*, there were no less than 150 acres of land, worth 10 marks a year, submerged in the Parish of Hove, and at Aldrington and Middleton 40 acres were inundated. In 6th James I., Mr. M. A. Lower says the "Manor belonged to the Crown, and from 1638 to 1712 to the family of Scrase."‡ William Scrase, the new Lord of the Manor, was evidently "before his age," in being a staunch "Conservative"; for at a Court held December 1, 1647, it was ordered that "no tenant farmer or occupier within the Manor, shall hereafter take to keep or depasture any horse, &c., of any forraigneurs or strangers, but only of the cottagers or poor inhabitants." What was the extent of Hove or the number of its inhabitants at this period is now past finding out. The village was larger, probably, than it

[* From some particulars respecting the antiquities discovered in the barrow, we learn, from a paper communicated to the *Sussex Archæological Collections* (vol. ix., pp. 119-24) by Mr. Barclay Phillips, that the labourers who were removing the earth of the barrow, on reaching the centre, about nine feet below the surface, struck upon a rude coffin, between 6ft. and 7ft. long, lying nearly east and west. In the earth with which the coffin was filled were fragments of various bones, apparently charred, and about the centre, as if they had rested on the breast of the body interred, were—1. An "amber cup," hemispherical in shape, with a "lip" or "nich,' and ornamented with a band of fine lines running round the outside, about half an inch from the top. It has a handle, large enough for the insertion of a finger, ornamented with a fillet on each side of the surface, which is flat, similar to that on the cup itself. The cup would seem to have been made and carved by hand. 2. A "celt," or head of a battle axe, made of iron-stone, some 5in. long, 1·9in. wide in the broadest part, and ·8in. thick. It is in perfect preservation, with a hole neatly drilled through the centre for the insertion of a handle. 3. A small "whetstone" (apparently), 2·7in. long, ·6in. wide, and ·35in. thick, tapering off slightly at each extremity. 4. A "bronze dagger," very much oxydised. Two of the rivets, with fragments of a bone handle, remain attached to the lower end of the blade. It is 5·5in. long, 2·4in. wide, and ·3in. thick at the lower end. These interesting relics were subsequently presented by Baron Goldsmid to the Town Museum, where they now are."]

† From time immemorial and down to within the last 30 or 40 years the name was pronounced *Hoove*; but now the prevailing fashion is to pronounce it Hōve. Both, however (with Cliftonville), would seem to be in danger of extinction by a newer designation (which is being very generally used), namely, West Brighton,—a name "invented" by the London and Brighton Railway Company, and given to their new passenger station at Hove.

‡ In 1723 Philip Tredcroft, who, we believe, married Elizabeth, the only child of William Scrase, was the Lord of the Manor, and subsequently it passed through the hands of Edward Tredcroft and Nathaniel Tredcroft until 1808, when William Stanford, of Preston Park, became the Lord. These Lords were,

was at the close of the last century, and, like Brighton at a former period, consisted of an upper and lower town; for, at a Court of the Manor, held April 8th, 1651, it was stated that "The two town wells, one at the upper end and the other at the lower end of Hove, for the benefit of the tenants, are in sad decay, for want of curbs and other necessaries," and an order was given "that the same shall be repaired by John Scras, gent., and Walter Bailie," *who were authorized to tax,* and "any one refusing shall forfeit and pay for every such refusal vi. s. viii. d." The well "at the upper end" of Hove-street was filled up about the year 1876 or 1877; but the other was probably submerged by the sea during the storms of 1703-5. The Court Rolls in 1704 record several instances of cottages "eaten in by the sea" at the lower end of the "Ville de Hova." Early in the present century a portion of the "stein" of the old lower town well was to be seen about 20 or 30 yards down the beach, immediately opposite the western side of Hove-street.

What was the condition of the Old Parish Church of St. Peter—which appears to have been erected at a very early date, and was subsequently destroyed by fire—in the middle of the 17th century—it is difficult to conjecture. It was then, most likely, as it was at the close of last century—in ruins; a portion of the old nave—about 50ft. in length—serving the villagers for the purposes of worship; and the remains of the original handsome tower affording accommodation for a couple of bells. This tower fell in 1801, when a "wooden pigeon-house steeple" was erected as a substitute, and did duty until the restoration of the Church in 1834. Hove would seem to have been at one period of some ecclesiastical importance; the remains of some once beautiful tracery, &c.,—still to be seen in 1880 in the barn at the top of Hove-street,—leading to the inference that the building was originally a "religious house." Scant provision was made, however, in the latter part of the last century, for the performance of religious services in Hove Church; and "opposition" was in existence in 1779 in the shape of a "Presbyterian Meeting-House," though where this was situated is now unknown. One Mr. Johnson ministered in this Meeting-House; but we are told by a "Diarist" in 1779, that this gentleman, "who blended reason with religion," is "but very slenderly attended."

[As a matter of special interest in connection with the records of the old Church, we insert the following from a "Historical Retro-

---

however, only Leaseholders of the Manor, the freehold belonging to the Prebendaries of two Stalls in the Cathedral Church of Chichester, viz., the Prebend of Hova Villa and the Prebend of Hova Ecclesia. In August, 1810, these two portions of the Manor were kept distinct for a Lease of part of the Prebend of Hova Ecclesia, and, including the Manor, was made to William Stanford; while in April, 1816, the Prebend of Hova Villa was leased to William Marshall, of Hurstpierpoint, and Charles Marshall, of Steyning. From this time the Manor continued in the same families until 1874, when the freehold of both Manors, which had been acquired by the Ecclesiastical Commissioners, as well as the leasehold interests, became vested in George Gallard and William John Williams. The only records of the Manor now available would appear to have commenced with Mr. Scrase's possession, the first entry being dated January 2, 1638. Among the names mentioned in the first Court transactions are Parker, Fowle, Whichelo, Mighell, Blaker, Scras, Farncombe, Woolgar, and Bradford.

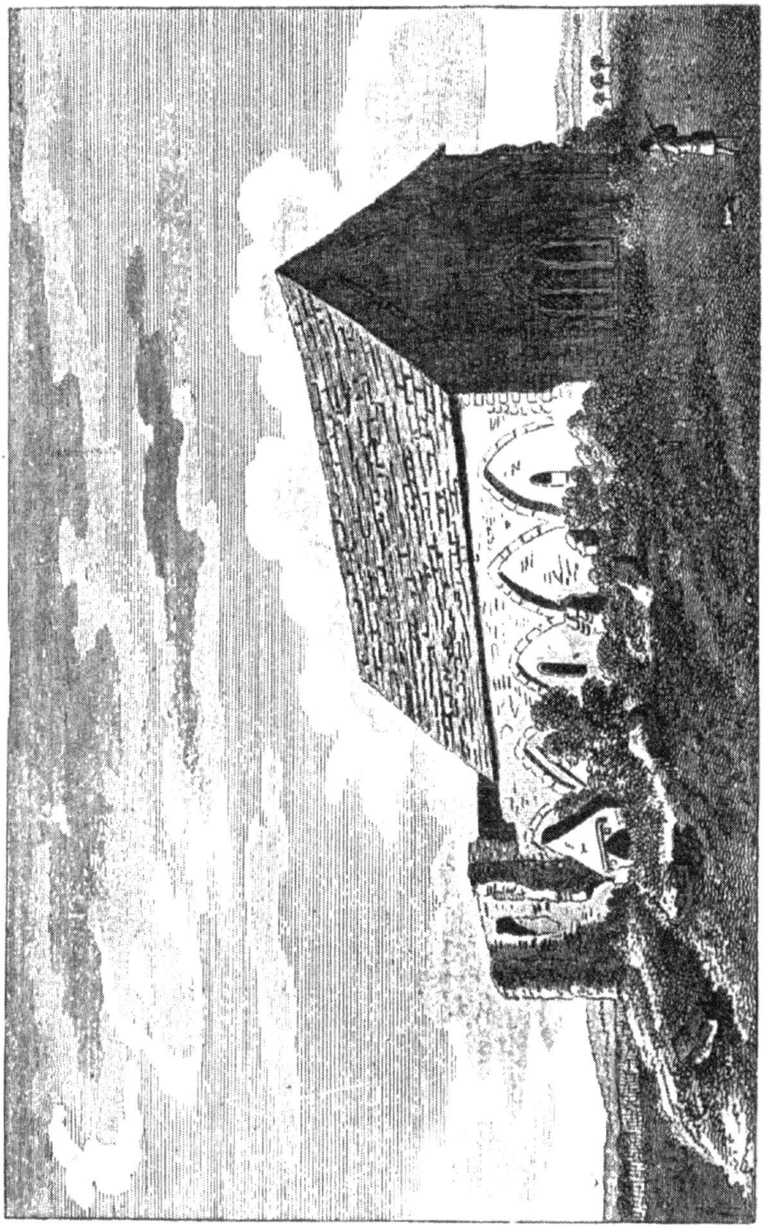

spect of Hove," specially collated by Mr. H. C. Porter for the *Brighton Herald* a few years ago : —

" But little appears to have been known of the Ministers in charge of the Parish till the Reformation, when the Prebendary of Hova Villa in the Registry of Chichester was valued at ten pounds, the Vicar being ordered to pay seven shillings and sixpence a year to the Vicar of Brighton. The living of Hove being annexed to that of St. Peter's, Preston, by order of the Vicar-General, Thomas Cromwell, the registers of births, marriages, and deaths were kept at Hove.

" Before the Reformation, the parish priests of St. Andrew's, Hove, were appointed by the Prior of St. Pancras, at Lewes, the last being Guy Rolf, in 1508. The first Vicar was the Rev. Eno Mason, admitted in 1538, the same year as that of the initial entry of a matrimonial contract, dated October 20th, between Thomas Browning and Eda Jefferye. The buryalls (burials) commence December 12th, 1539, with that of Emily Smith. The introductory baptismal records have been obliterated prior to August 22nd, 1635, when the christening of Thomas, son of Thomas Sherly, or Shirley, is given. The following is a list of the Vicars of Hove-cum-Preston, with the dates of their confirmation :—Robert Whillak, September, 1542 ; Thomas Saull, May, 1553; Edmund Stotuda, January, 1562 ; Ashmead Henry Short, November, 1566 ; John Beason, 1580 ; Fitz Maurice Cox, February, 1586 ; Winifred Shook, 1618 ; Humphrey Shoots, 1624 ; Richard Turner, 1650 ; James Purse, 1660 ; Francis Cox, October, 1673 ; James Bowens, January, 1686 ; Henry Alleyn, 1690 ; George Orton, July 2nd, 1692 ; George Baznesley, 1695 ; George Orton, 1702 ; John Barksholl, 1720 ; George Orton, 1731 ; John King, May 8th, 1749 (the former Vicar being interred at Preston, April 10th, 1749); William Hayley, 1754 ; Joseph Francis Fearon, 1789 ; James Stainer Clarke, 1790 ; Walter Kelly, 1834 (who retired December 16th, 1878*), and with him terminated the annexation of the Parishes, Hove being on April 2nd, 1879, allotted to the Rev. Thomas Peacey, and Preston to the Rev. A. D. Freeman a few weeks later.

[* The Rev. Walter Kelly died in January, 1888, after having been Vicar of Preston-cum-Hove between 40 and 50 years. There was no more worthy Minister of the Gospel, nor one more revered by his parishioners, than the Rev. Walter Kelly, and it was only fitting that a memorial of him should be erected in the venerable Church wherein he so long and so faithfully ministered. Not only was his tenure of office distinguished by its exceptional duration, but he has left behind him a record fraught with good works and a memory cherished by all who had the privilege of coming in contact with him. The memorial, which was carried out by subscription, at a cost of rather more than £200, consisted of the erection of a white marble tablet, enclosed in a frame of pink-veined marble, and the embellishment of the Chancel. The inscription on the tablet is as follows :—

"To the Glory of God and in Loving
Memory of the Rev. WALTER KELLY,
The Sanctuary was Adorned by many Parishioners
And Friends.
He was Vicar of Hove and Preston
From 1834 to 1878,
And fell asleep in Christ
On the 29th January, 1888,
In the 85th year of his age."]

"The parochial registers are very curious. Each volume consists of slips of vellum about eighteen inches long and four or five inches in width, folded and stitched in a cover of like material. The caligraphy is similar to that in the Bishop's Act Books, and is of a miscellaneous character; sometimes neat and clear, but in the older books more fantastic, and in Latin, a language much in vogue for registers long after the Reformation. The leaves are written on on both sides, a margin being left at the sinister hand, containing notes of the entries. They are in tolerably good preservation. The first volume dates with considerable precision from 1538 to 1643, excepting a few omissions from 1607 to 1619. Civil marriages would appear to have been performed for several Parishes by Mr. Anthony Shirley, from April 19th, 1656, to November 17th, 1657. The break that takes place in these records of ancestry is accounted for by the Puritans holding power. The Preston books begin about the same date. There are some items inserted as follows:—" Begun 29th September, 1653, by order of Parliament"; another register is also commenced later on, dated April 19th, 1656, as the register for marriages in Preston, by Anthony Shirley, Esq., one of the Justices of the County.*

"June 12, 1656.—The purpose of marrige between Nicholas Wisdome, of Wodmancote, in Sussex, husbandman, and Sarah Brale, of ye same County and Pish., spinster, was published three severall Lor-days in ye Pish. Church of Woodmancote, viz., ye 11, 18, and 25 days of May, Ano 1656, and they were married here ye 12 of June, —56.

"June 17, 1656.—The purpose of marrige between Jno. Kennard, son of Jno. Kennard, both of Patching, yeoman, and Mary Parson, of Plumpton, daughter of Gregory Parson, of the same place, hath been published in Lewes market on three severall market days, and they were married at Hove the 17th of June, 1656; John Fowler, of Hurst-per-point, Taylor, and Mary Warwick, of Shermanbury, had their purpose of marrige published 3 severall Lor-dayes in ye pish. churches of Hurst and Shermanbury, and they were maried at Hove August 5th, 1656.

"June 14, 1657.—William Wignans, of Hove, and Elizabeth Adams, of Brighthelmstone, had their purpose of marriage published 3 severall Lord's dayes in ye congregation at Brighthelmstone, and no exception made agnst it, and they were married here the 14 of June, Ano. 1657.

"The entry of November 17th, 1657, is the last of the regular records, and shows that George King and Mary Moore, both of Hove, had their 'purpose of marrige published three severall Lor-dayes,' and they were married by Richard Turner, minister, November 17th, Ano. 1657. The Puritan form of contract was not entirely discarded for about eight years after, as in 1665 appears the entry—'Thomas Payne and Mary Holmwood, having their purpose of marriage published on three several Lord-days in Patcham Church, were maried May 1st, 1665.'

"The entries are supplemented by a marginal note, recording: 'All above were married by Anth. Shirley, Esquire.' A few other

---

* Some further particulars respecting the Shirleys will be found in the chapter relating to "Preston."

extracts from the registers, which bring the four books up to 1773, are unique. Among the 'christenings' figure that of

"Anthony, sonne of Richard Sherley, baptised January 6th, 1582.
"Henry, the sonne of Mr. Anthony Sherley, was born on Frydaye, about 3 o'clock in the morninge, being the 6th daye of March, 1590.
"Phillip Scras, daughter of Walter Scras, baptised on the 31st day of December, 1646 (not the only instance of a female child being christened with a man's name).
"Margrot, daughter of Walter Scras, baptised August 30, 1650.
"Richard Scras, baptised September 20, 1653.
"John Scras, baptised June 24, 1656.
"William Scras, baptised June 29 1659.
"Mary, daughter of Richard Turner and Mary his wife, baptised November 4, 1650.
"Thomas, the sonne of Richard Turner, minister, was born ye 21st day of February, at almost 12 at noon, 1656,—baptised the one day of March in the same year.
"Richard, the sonne of Richard Turner, minister, was born ye 24th day of January, at almost 2 in ye morning, and baptised ye 8th day of February following, 1659.
"John and Benjamin, two sons of John Bradford, both baptised January 21, 1662, by Mr. Bonner—'is no mint here.'
"Richard, the son of Thomas Winchester and Mary his wife, was baptised about Michaelmas, in the year 1652.
"Sarah, daughter of George Orton and Mary his wife, baptised February 9, 1704.
"George, son of George Orton, vicar, and Mary his wife, baptised (being 14 dayes old) September 23rd, 1706.

"The 3rd register has the baptism of Anna, daughter of Nathaniel and Anna Kemp, April 20th, 1716, and George, son of Nicholas and Susanna Beard, March 24th, 1719-20. Grace and Sarah, daughters of Richard and Mary Stanford, were received into the Church, being of riper years, by the Revd. William Weston, December 25th. 1765. Henry Cummings, a negro, from the Barbadoes, W.I., was baptised by the Rev. Wm. Weston, curate, July 25th, 1769, at Preston, in the presence of Ann Potter; William Crowe and John Markwick, the witnesses.

"That the descendants of the Ministers have been interred in the churchyard of Preston is undisputed fact. 'Elizabeth ye daughter of Humphrey Shoots, minister, buried ye July 4th, Anno. Dom. 1626.' Later occurs the burial of Dorothy, sixth wife of John Brooker, Ano. December 21st, 1677. It was not till the eighteenth century that the ages of the dead were recorded, the first being that of John Bradford, senr., August 29th, 1703. aged seventy-four or thereabouts. A little earlier the custom of the Searcher's affidavit being necessary at a burial is shown:—Mary Ade, wife of Thomas Ade, was buried on ye 25th day of February, 1682; affidavit brought to me, James Purse, curate. Mrs. Grace Cheynell, burrde May ye 4th, 1683; affidavit brought; signed James Purse, curate. Sir Anthony Shirley, Bt., buridd June 22nd, 1683; affidavit brought within ye time limitted. Mary, wife of Nathaniel Savage, with her two Twins, both still born, was burried Oct. ye 9th, 1704. Jno.

Cheynell, of this parish, was buried Oct. 5th, 1715. Mrs. Cheynell, late wife of John Cheynell, buried Jan. 15th, 1716.*

"A stamp duty on the registering of burials, &c., was commenced on October 2nd, 1783; the new register book was bought in 1812. By the will of Edward Scras, who died in 1576, he gave ten shillings to the Church at Hove, and John Scras gave by his bequest 6s 8d. on June 8th, 1619, to be divided among nine of the poorest inhabitants in the Rape of Lewes. William Scras, about 1650, received ten pounds per annum for the lease of Hove Parsonage from the Prebendary.

"The fragment of scarcely legible writing that appears on the last page of the Preston Register (vol. 3) relates to some announcement of convocation meetings, and what is left runs as follows:—

>   ded upon by
>   both provided
>   convocation holden
>   our Lord God 1562, was
>   ye Parish Church of . . .
>   of Preston and Hove in the time
>   of Divine service being the 17th
>   the other half the 24 (day in the
>   year of our Lord 1619 in the
>   presence of Churchwardens named
>   (writon . . . .
>   . . and . . . of the former
>   publisshed by me Winifred Shook Vicar of
>   oresaid Preston *cum* Hove . . . .
>   Anthony Shirley
>   Test.   Thomas Shirley.
>   Richard Scras (Scrase).
>   James Buckall
>   Anthony Jeffary.
>   John Ffriend.
>   Robert Buckall (Churchwarden).
>   Andrew Death (Churchwarden)."

The formation of the Brighton Camps at Hove in 1793-94-95 doubtless served to bring the latter village into prominence, though at that time the dwellings in it were only "about a dozen." We should like to have entered fully into the history of the Brighton Camps; to tell of the patriotic ardour and enthusiasm which they evoked; to recount the doings of the Prince of Wales; to notice the grand reviews and field days; also the tragic and the mirthful episodes associated with the Camps; but we must forbear.

In 1802 an event, at which "all the world wondered," took place off Hove. This was the supposed foundering of the good ship "Adventure," Captain William Codlin, commander. The morning of Sunday, August 8th, 1802, was bright and beautiful; towards noon, however, there was a dense fog, which lasted the whole afternoon. There was little or no wind; the sea was calm; and in the evening,

---

* See further reference to Cheynell in the chapter relating to "Preston," under the heading of Preston Church.

A VIEW OF THE INTENDED FISHERY AT HOVE—about 1814.

Designed for Sixty Dwellings for Fishermen.

as the fog cleared, a brig, evidently abandoned by her crew, was seen coming heavily, as if water-laden, westward. Just as she reached opposite the bottom of Hove-street, the water was up to her bulwarks, when down she sank, and was wholly lost to view. Strong suspicion of foul play was excited, as there appeared to be nothing to account for such a disaster. This suspicion proved to be true—the object of the Captain evidently being to obtain the insurance money. All was apparently well-planned ; but

"The best laid schemes o' mice and men,
Gang aft a gley."

As the tide receded, the top of one of the brig's masts appeared above water, indicating her whereabouts ; and Mr. S. Stepney, of Brighton, was employed to raise her. A day or two after the occurrence Dr. Hargraves was on "the Bank," at the bottom of West-street, Brighton, and Captain Codlin happened to be standing near him. The Doctor said, " Don't you think, Captain, they'll get her up ?" " I'll swallow h--ll fire, if they do," replied Codlin. The four fishing-boats engaged by Mr. Stepney, however, did their work successfully ; and when "The Adventure" was towed ashore, a hole was discovered in the ship's bottom ; and the auger with which it was bored was lying near it ! Codlin, anticipating this discovery, had previously taken the coach to London, going thence to Dover, where he got on board a vessel, with the view of getting across the Channel. But justice was on his track. Another vessel was dispatched, which overtook the former, and he was brought back to London—a prisoner. Codlin was subsequently tried for the offence, found guilty, and, as was then the custom, hung for his crime at Execution Dock, Woolwich. The raising of "The Adventure" cost Mr. Stepney £30, for which he was never reimbursed one farthing! His sole memento of the transaction was a dirk, found on board the ship ; and this is still in the possession of a member of his family.

About 1813-15 there was an attempt to establish a new Fishery at Hove. Plans were got out; prospectuses were issued ; meetings were convened ; but all to no purpose. The promoters reckoned "without their host "—the Brighton fisherman, true to his instinct of clinging to his native shore, could not be made to comprehend the advantages of the "happy fishing grounds" at Hove. And so the scheme fell through. In after days the site, with sundry erections, was known as "Jack Smith's Rookery" (so named after the principal promoter, Mr. Smith, a local "character," familiarly known as "Jack" Smith); but it left a legacy which, probably, will never cease to be lamented by the inhabitants of Hove. The "Deizes and Curing Houses," erected on the beach in connection with the New Fishery, were subsequently occupied as dwelling-houses.[*]

---

[*] The folly of erecting these houses on the beach, without the protection of groynes, &c., was proved in November, 1824, when, during the storm, the sea washed completely over them, and the poor families lodging in them had to flee for their lives, and were ultimately accommodated in a barn. They were kindly cared for by Sir Edward Kerrison, who sent money and other necessaries to Mr. Buckwell, of the once famous old "Bun-house" at Hove, for their relief. In later days the "Bun-house" was kept by Mr. Arnold.

Hence the idea arose of building to the south of the road, which was subsequently consummated by "Sergeant" Mills, in building Mills's-terrace; and this example being followed, an open Beach in front of Old Hove and the continuation of the beautiful terraces now in front of Brunswick-terrace and West Brighton is, most probably, lost for ever!

At the time "The Hove and Brighthelmston Fishery" was projected, Hove itself would appear to have been looking-up; the houses in it had actually increased since 1792 cent. per cent.! namely, to "between 20 and 30," and the inhabitants to "about a hundred and twenty." Sicklemore, in his *Epitome of Brighton* (1815), says of Hove :—" Several charming lodging-houses have been built here of late years, and present appearances indicate that at no very distant period Hove will extend an arm of brick and mortar to meet the advancing one from Brighton, until the two places may figuratively be represented as shaking hands." This "salutation" has taken place; but it took upwards of half-a-century to accomplish it!

But in spite of "charming lodging-houses," Hove still maintained its old repute for smuggling; and possibly a more daring act was never perpetrated than that which took place in its vicinity early on Sunday morning, October 10th, 1819. A suspected "smuggling boat" being seen off Hove by some of the Custom House Officers, they, with two of the crew of "The Hound" revenue cutter, gave chase in a galley. On coming up with the boat their suspicions were confirmed. They at once "boarded" her; but, while intent on securing their prize, nine of the smugglers leapt into the "Hound's" galley, and, thus escaping, "rowed off rejoicing"! They, however, "hallooed before they were out of the wood"; for, landing at Hove, seven only escaped, two being taken prisoners by some other officers who were in waiting for them. This fact becoming known through the village, the cry was—"To the rescue." Upon which a large company of smugglers assembled, and, according to the advertisement respecting the affair issued by the Custom House authorities, " commenced a desperate attack upon the officers, and, having overpowered them, assaulted them with stones and large sticks, knocked them down, and cut the belts of the Chief Officer's arms, which they took away, and thereby enabled the two prisoners to escape." With the view of bringing the offenders to justice, the Commissioners of His Majesty's Customs, were "pleased to offer a reward of £200"; but, as a matter of course, without effect. The cargo of the "smuggling boat" consisted of 225 tubs of gin, 52 tubs of brandy, and 1 bag of tobacco.*

---

* Cases of smuggling at Hove might be multiplied *ad infinitum*. On the 20th October, 1827, a smuggling boat succeeded in running 500 tubs opposite Brunswick-terrace. The Blockade were overpowered, disarmed, and several of them severely wounded, whilst it is supposed that two or three of the smugglers were either severely wounded or killed. So recently as 1835, there was an attempt made to run "a crop of goods" near Hove turnpike gate, as many as between 40 and 50 men waiting there with *bats* ready to carry off the tubs when landed. The attempt was defeated by the vigilance of the Coast Guard, and a large number of the tubs secured, which were landed on the Chain Pier.

THE ANTHEUM—1838. ADELAIDE TERRACE.

The subsequent extension of the "brick and mortar arm" was almost wholly on the side of Brighton. Gradually the houses extended westward along the sea front. But the crowning work was the building, in 1822-3, of Brunswick-square and terrace.* On their completion, almost every house was at once occupied; and this naturally gave a strong impetus to building in the neighbourhood. For the accommodation of the district, a new Market was erected in in 1825; but, with the subsequent growth of shops in the vicinity, this gradually fell into desuetude.† A new Church—or rather Chapel-of-Ease to the old Parish Church, which was altogether inadequate to accommodate the now numerous fashionable residents of Hove (West Brighton)—St. Andrews, was erected in 1828.‡ About 1830 Adelaide-crescent (to the west of Brunswick-terrace) was projected. Some few houses were built at the south-eastern side; and with these it seemed as if extension westward was to be "thus far and no farther"; for there was no addition to them for nearly a quarter of a century after. The grounds (now in the centre of Palmeira-square) were prettily laid out and enclosed; but the property of the Crescent being in little demand scant attention was paid to them; and the enclosing iron palisading and the roadway round it were for years in a most neglected condition. Lansdowne-place was also up to a certain point similarly "stayed"; its upper portion being houseless. Brunswick-square and terrace were, however, well occupied; and in 1829, at a meeting of the owners and inhabitants at "The Kerrison Arms,' Sir W. Freemantle presiding, steps were taken to procure an Act of Parliament to regulate the paving, watching, lighting, &c., the Rev. J. Scutt contributing liberally towards the expenses.

But the material development and social progress of Hove might have been altogether different from what it was—its present new era of prosperity might have been antedated by some forty years—but for the accident which resulted in the total destruction, on the 30th August, 1833, of the Antheum.§ This noble structure—which was erected on a piece of land now absorbed by the enclosure of Palmeira-square

---

* The major portion of the land on which these handsome houses were built was used as a "sheep run," and was at one time within memory leased so low, we believe, as 6s. per acre! Singular to relate, when the ground was being dug out for the foundations of the first house in Brunswick-square—at the south-east corner—the sea one day reached so high as to wash into them; a most unusual occurrence, which has never since recurred.

† This Market has for some years past been used as a riding-school; and, with the improvements carried out by the former proprietor, the late Mr. A. DuPont, is regarded as one of the best riding-schools in Brighton.

‡ This Church was consecrated and opened on July 5th, 1828, by the Bishop of Chichester, Dr. Carr; the prayers were read by the Rev. J. Townsend, and the sermon preached by its founder and first incumbent, the Rev. E. Everard. Mr. Everard retained the incumbency until 1838, his successors being the Rev. O. Marden (1838-56), the Rev. W. H. Rooper (1856-63), the Rev. W. H. Karslake (1863-66), the Rev. H. Beaumont (1866-68), in which latter year the present incumbent, the Rev. Dan Winham, entered upon the duties. Under Mr. Winham's auspices, the Church has since been thoroughly renovated, and the interior in many respects considerably altered.

§ From the Greek *Anthos*, a flower, and meaning *a place of flowers*.

—was projected by Mr. Henry Phillips, the well-known botanist. It originated out of the Oriental Garden which had preceded it, in 1825, at the top of Oriental-place, Brighton, so called after it, and which had also been projected by Mr. Phillips, but was never actually erected. About an acre and a half of land was devoted to the Antheum and grounds. The Antheum itself was a grand dome, intended to be glazed, and was the largest in the world—exceeding in diameter that of St. Peter's, at Rome, by 36 feet; its width at bottom being 164ft., and its height from the ground to the top of the ring 64ft. With the cupola it would have been 80ft. or more on the outside. This magnificent building—the massive iron girders supporting it rising direct from the ground — impressed all beholders with its grandeur and beauty. Doubts had from time to time been expressed as to its security, owing to the faulty design of the engineer, a Mr. English, the dome not being the section of a perfect sphere, but of an oblate spheroid. Mr. Phillips himself was desirous before the interior scaffolding was removed of obtaining the opinion of Mr. Rennie, the celebrated engineer; but the builder, without orders, removed the major portion of this scaffolding, and the building may be said to have stood of itself. On that day more persons than ever visited the wonderful structure, all admiring the boldness of mind that had projected it, and the marvellous skill with which it had been reared. The effect on entering the interior was especially grand and beautiful; the walks were partly formed, and many thousands of plants, some of them extremely curious and rare, covered the walls and mounds of earth, enabling the visitor to judge of the effect which would be produced when it was finished. The same evening, the remainder of the scaffolding was removed, and the next morning the Antheum was again opened to the public. Mr. Phillips was himself occupied during the greater part of the day under the very centre of the Dome, marking out and superintending the formation of an aquarium. At six o'clock all had left, excepting a man named Wyatt and the head gardener. A little before seven, the gardener was alarmed by a loud cracking noise. Wyatt exclaimed, "Save yourself; it is not safe," and they had barely escaped without, when the whole top part of the dome fell in with an awful rapidity; the huge ribs collapsing one after another, like a pack of cards, accompanied by a sound resembling the continued firing of cannons. Nearly half the girders remained standing naked in the air; but subsequently these also fell, and the ruin of the fair fabric was complete! General sympathy was expressed for Mr. Phillips, who, at the very moment when his most sanguine expectations seemed about to be realised and certain success apparently awaited him, saw all ruthlessly destroyed for ever. The shock to his system was such that, within a fortnight, Mr. Phillips, though only 53, was struck blind. For years after, the huge iron girders lay where they had fallen, amid the *débris* of the structure. Such was the wonder and admiration which the Antheum excited, and so many visitors were attracted to it, that, had it been completed, and the idea of its skilful projector been fully carried out, there is every reason to suppose that it would have influenced in a hundred ways the fortunes of Hove. It may be added that, when the

HOVE (WEST) SEA FRONT, ABOUT 1833.

From Horsfield's "Sussex."

late Sir Joseph Paxton was designing his building for the Great Exhibition of 1851, he came down specially to Brighton to see whether he could obtain any of the old plans of the Antheum, that structure having probably suggested to his mind the idea of the original Crystal Palace.

In 1834, soon after the Rev. Walter Kelly was inducted to the Vicarage of Preston-cum-Hove, active steps were taken to restore the old Parish Church. The condition of the Church was, in fact, at this period, scarcely creditable to the wealthy community which now resided in the parish. The interior, entered by a small porch on the south side—was not only uninviting, but altogether unfitted for the decent celebration of Divine Worship. Though the original aisles had long previously disappeared, there yet remained on each side the Church four out of the five original Early Gothic arches, supported on cylindrical columns, with curiously ornamented capitals; the Chancel was also entered by a Gothic arch. Once mooted, the restoration of the old Church was warmly taken up by the parishioners: a Vestry meeting, in February, 1834, voting £2,000 towards the work. This was subsequently carried out upon the plans of Mr. Basevi, architect, and the Church re-opened for Divine Service on the 17th June, 1836. Accommodation was provided for 481 seats, 350 being free. In 1839, the West End gallery was erected, giving accommodation for 200 more worshippers. There are now some handsome coloured memorial windows in the Church, which also contains some interesting mural tablets: to various gallant Officers; to the Rev. Thos. Rooper and Mrs. Rooper, and their son, Major Rooper; to Lady Westphal; to Mr. G. Basevi, and to his son, Mr. G. Basevi, the architect of the Church, who lost his life by falling from the tower of Ely Cathedral in 1845. There are also others, including one to Copley Fielding, the celebrated artist, with some lines beneath which were written by the Rev. C. Townsend. In the Churchyard—which is a model of order and neatness—are many interesting and beautiful monuments, notably one (on the north side of the Church) to the memory of the Rev. Joseph Sortain, erected by the congregation of the Countess of Huntingdon's Chapel.

It may be of interest to mention in passing that the late Rev. J. P. Malleson, Minister of the Unitarian Chapel, New-road, Brighton, on which chapel originally appeared the inscription in Greek characters, "Mono Theo dia Jesou Christo doxa" ("Glory to the only God through Jesus Christ"), carried on a school in one of a row of three houses facing the sea at West Hove,—a row of houses with fronts of shiny black bricks,—Mr. Malleson's being a double house, with balconies. It was originally built and occupied by a Roman Catholic family, named Corney, gold lace manufacturers in London. At the north end of the dining room was a secret little hemispherical room, designed and used as a private oratory. The door was disguised as a looking-glass, and opened with a spring; in fact, there were two looking-glasses in the panels. Mr. Peter Taylor, for many years M.P. for Leicester, and who died at Brighton in December, 1891, was educated when a boy at Mr. Malleson's school.

There is little to note during the next 15 years or so concerning the growth of Hove. Old Hove was almost stationary, and as isolated, comparatively, as ever; little or nothing being done to extend the "brick and mortar arm" Brightonwards. All building vitality was, in fact, on the side of Brighton; and here the "straw did not begin to move" with much vigour until about 1850. On August 4th of that year the first house in York-road, at the south-east corner of the Western-road field, was commenced; and soon after the greater portion of the old familiar field was absorbed by streets and houses; Chatfield's field (on which the west side of Upper Brunswick-place was built) "followed suit," and by and bye a new Church, dedicated to St. Patrick, was erected in Cambridge-road by the Rev. Dr. O'Brien.* In other portions of the neighbourhood houses were fast being erected, and a compactness was given to its residential character which had hitherto been wanting, and auguring well for the future.

But East and West Hove were as yet "wide as the poles asunder"; the intervening space (a portion of which was subsequently devoted to the Brunswick Cricket Ground)† being at the east end devoted to brick-fields, or was otherwise in a most neglected condition, and more especially on the "front," where were several old brick-kilns, mud huts, &c.; while to the west there were still the meadows attached to the Wick Farm; "Long Barn Cottage," the neat residence for so many years of Mr. W. Rigden, being the only house to the right of the pathway between "The Wick Inn" and the Church, if we except the little low-roofed cottage (with sweets, &c., in the window) standing at the corner of the hedge-row which led from the pathway at the end of Mr. Rigden's meadows to the old Parish Church and to Old Hove.‡

The first substantial extension, or rather addition, to Old Hove was Cliftonville.§ This Estate, which consists of some 16 odd acres, was projected in 1851-2 by Mr. George Hall, Mr. Richard Webb Mighell, Mr. William Kirkpatrick, and Mr. George Gallard. The projectors may be said to have been endowed with a "long sight"; and if they did not at the outset realize the fruit of their labours,

---

[* The Church of St. Patrick's, at Hove, which was already rich in artistic embellishment, has recently (May, 1892,) been further beautified by an extensive work of decoration. The three walls of the chancel have been painted with a bold and finely executed subject, representing "The adoration of the Son by the Angels and the Church."]

† This Cricket Ground was formed after the Hanover Ground was devoted to building purposes by the formation of Park-crescent. It was closed after the season of 1871, on the Stanford Estate coming into the market; provision was, however, made by the Surveyor to the Estate, with the sanction of Mr. Benett-Stanford, for the formation of another Ground—the present County Ground—which was opened in 1872.

[‡ The land immediately north of this hedge-row was devoted to market-gardens. The one near the Church-yard was occupied by Mr. Bartlett; but that more easterly was kept, about 1830, by one Coppin, a bit of a character in his way. He kept his coffin standing on end for some years in a corner of his bedroom. He liked John Barleycorn, and whether he had imbibed too much, or whether he had over-eaten, or both, it happened that one Sunday afternoon he fell asleep during Divine Service, and, awaking in the midst of the sermon, gave utterance to a loud "Amen!" He was at the time Parish Clerk.]

§ Cliftonville owed its name to a cottage, known as "Clifton Cottage," which was situated by the roadside in the lower part of what is now Albany-villas. It was built about 1825 for Mr. Lashmar, of Middle-street.

they richly deserved to do so; for, notwithstanding the earlier drawbacks to which it was subjected, Cliftonville—seeing the present enhanced value of the property on the Estate—must be regarded among the best of the earlier building speculations in the neighbourhood of Brighton. It was judiciously laid out; the streets, originally twelve in number, being broad and open, running regularly from north to south and east to west. Cliftonville may be said to have sprung into existence with the rapidity of a transatlantic town. House after house, villa after villa, seemed to rise as if by magic. Some of the latter, particularly the more southern of Medina and Albany-villas, which are detached, displaying externally much architectural beauty. Of the earlier drawbacks of Cliftonville, the more serious of these were that it was "cabin'd, cribb'd, confin'd," which tended much to detract from its character as a marine residence. Leaving out of the question the buildings on the south side of Shoreham-road,—in a line with Mills's-terrace, which almost entirely shut out its view of the sea,—Cliftonville was enclosed on the north by an ugly strip of wall, which effectually prevented egress in that direction, not only of carriages and other vehicles, but even of foot passengers! Again, there was no outlet for carriages or other vehicles either to the north-west or to the north-east: the then Church-street—between the Church and Hove Fields—being abruptly closed at each end to all but pedestrians; and, shortly after the formation of Cliftonville, the pretty walk through Hove Fields to Brighton was supplanted by a narrow gravel path, bounded on each side by a wall of tantalizing height.

The formation of Cliftonville opened a new era in the history of Hove. Houses and inhabitants increased and multiplied, not only in the new Western district, by the subsequent erection of the noble property known as St. Aubyn's, and other handsome property along the front; but also in the Eastern. In the Brunswick-square and terrace district; on the Northern side of the Western-road; and also on the Goldsmid Estate building activity was everywhere apparent. Palmeira-square (a continuation of Adelaide-crescent), projected by Baron Goldsmid,* was being rapidly developed, and when completed, formed a worthy rival, as a Western termination to the Queen of Watering Places, to Kemp Town, which formed the Eastern. At the north-western corner of Palmeira-square a new Church was erected in 1852, and dedicated to St. John. (This was, unfortunately, built right in the centre of the carriage road from Brighton, which for this reason was compelled to be diverted on its extension westward.) The beautiful lawn in front of Brunswick-square and terrace was widened and improved, and subsequently, on the completion of Palmeira-square, was extended to its western extremity. To illustrate the increase of the respective districts, it may be stated that in 1851 Old Hove contained but 125 houses, the inhabitants

---

* Palmeira-square was so named after a then newly-acquired title of the late Sir Isaac Lyon Goldsmid, Bart., who, by Royal license, under date June, 1846, "was authorized to accept and use in this country the title of Baron De Goldsmid and De Palmeira, conferred upon him by the Queen of Portugal in recognition of the important services rendered by him on various occasions to the Portuguese nation."

being 778 (the ladies however being in a minority of 50!); but in 1861, after Cliftonville had been built, the houses were more than treble that number, amounting to 506, while the inhabitants had quadrupled, numbering 3,291. Singularly enough at this period the disproportion of the sexes was reversed, the ladies having a majority over the gentlemen of 583! In the Brunswick-square and terrace district, during the same decade, the houses had nearly doubled in number, increasing from 446 to 863, and the inhabitants from 3,326 to 6,327. By the Census return of 1871, it appeared that the two districts united contained 1,587 houses, an increase over 1861 of 218; and 11,249 inhabitants, an increase of 1,631 over those of 1861, the gentlemen numbering 3,886 and the ladies 7,363, or, nearly two to one! Blissful Hove! no wonder there was then such a demand for houses in the locality. The rateable value of the parish also showed a corresponding increase. In 1857, the rateable value of the whole parish of Hove was £63,225 (the proportion of Cliftonville being £19,000); in March, 1872, it was £101,252 5s., and the gross estimated rental no less than £126,326 6s., amounting to over one-fourth of that of the whole of Brighton for the same year, viz., £488,656. A special census of Hove was taken in February, 1878 (under the direction of Mr. Packwood, Town Clerk). By this it appears that the total number of inhabitants in Hove was then 17,387 (residents, 16,069, and visitors, 1,318), or an increase of 6,138 over the number in 1871, namely, 11,249. The number of inhabited houses was 2,452 against 1,184 in 1871; the increase, therefore, was 968. The average number of inhabitants per house was 7·1; in 1871 it was 7·5. In November, 1880, the number of houses on the rate-book was 3,120; their rateable value being £189,867 6s. The population at the same period was estimated at about 19,000. [In 1891 the number of houses was 4,600: and their rateable value £250,903, whilst the number of inhabitants, according to the Census of 1891, was 26,097.]

In 1871 Hove entered on a new phase of development, by reason of the coming into the market of that portion of the Stanford Estate which lay along the sea-frontage between Adelaide-crescent and Palmeira-square and Cliftonville; its appropriation to building purposes effecting the long-predicted junction,—at least, so far as "bricks and mortar" were concerned,—between Brighton and old Hove. Some 40 acres of the Estate—subsequently known as the West Brighton Estate—were leased to a well-known London firm. Other portions of the Stanford Estate were soon after in the builders' hands. To the north-east of Cliftonville, between Holy Trinity Church (erected in 1863) and Hove Drove, Mr. George Gallard,— one of the original projectors of Cliftonville, and a gentleman who more than any other developed West Hove, — secured several acres, on which building operations were actively carried on: new roads being formed and opened; one, especially, for which he deserved the thanks of the community—that running from the top of George-street to Hove Drove, which up to that time had been effectually closed both to foot passengers and vehicles by the ugly strip of wall

LILLYWHITE AT HOME.—"A Reminiscence of the Past."

SKETCHED FROM THE COTTAGE WHERE THE FAMILY WERE BORN.

(The Building to the left is the late Mr. W. Rigden's Residence, "Long Barn House," which, together with the Cottages, &c., in the rear, have been supplanted by Melrose Hall and Grounds, Wilbury Road).

previously alluded to. Mr. Gallard also subsequently secured another five acres, north of the Hove Drove Estate—substantial evidence of what he, the most experienced man in the district, thought of the Drove portion of the Stanford Estate as a building speculation. South of Mr. Gallard's property, the Olliver Estate (the property of Messrs. Ireland and Savage), was next in progress; and eastward of it, running up to the West Brighton Station, some pretty semi-detached villas were built under the direction of Mr. H. J. Lanchester, the first architect of the Stanford Estate itself. Coming further eastward, the land along the Church-road, each side of Mr. Rigden's picturesque villa and its agricultural surroundings, was soon after marked out for building, together with the pretty field east of it, where the little Lillywhites once tumbled and played, and at the north-east corner of which the "nonpareil" bowler's old cottage residence formerly stood. "Long Barn Cottage" (Mr. Rigden's) soon after disappeared, and with the rise of handsome buildings and the formation of fine streets in the vicinity, " its place was known no more."

It would be beyond our purpose to speak in detail of the rapidity with which the Hove portion of the Stanford Estate was absorbed by "bricks and mortar;" and with a completeness altogether unparalleled " down South." Its "avenues" and "gardens" and streets— all more or less skilfully laid out according to situation—were developed, too, apparently regardless of cost; and more especially along the sea-frontage; those erected there being reputed to have occasioned an outlay before completion of something over half-a-million sterling.*

Simultaneously with building progress, it was only natural to expect that the governing bodies of the various districts of which Hove was formerly made up should be aroused into activity, and bestir themselves to decide what was to be the local governing power of Hove in the future. The old anomalous condition of things— some half-a-dozen different bodies of Commissioners, acting independently of each other—was undoubtedly inimical to the best interests

---

* An idea of the value of this sea-frontage property—which doubtless is enhanced by the tastefully designed gardens to the south of the road—may be formed by the fact that in 1879-80 Messrs. Jenner and Dell (of Regency-square, and of Church-road, Hove), the well-known auctioneers and house and estate agents, sold by private treaty:—Nos. 1, 4, 7, and 8, Queen's-gardens, for the aggregate sum of £32,000; No. 2, Adelaide Mansions, for £6,250; and some residences in First Avenue, for £17,800; No. 4, Adelaide Mansions. for £8,500; No. 4, Queen's-gardens, in the adjoining block, for £7,500; Nos. 9, 10, and 12, Queen's-gardens, for the aggregate sum of £20,250; and a detached freehold villa residence in Wilbury-road, West Brighton, for £3,350 More recently the same firm have sold upon this Estate, among other transfers, the following:—Nos. 3, 6, 9, and 12, Queen's-gardens, for the aggregate sum of £27,400; No. 1, King's-gardens, undecorated, for £12,700; No. 15, King s-gardens, for £10,000; No. 1, Victoria Mansions, for £10,000; and plot of land adjoining, with frontage of 130 feet to Grand Avenue, for £6,000. Also No. 2, Victoria Mansions, for £9,500; No. 7, Victoria Mansions, for £6,000; No. 21, Second Avenue, for £6,500; No. 23, Second Avenue, for £6,000; No. 6, Third Avenue, for £7,500; No. 2, Third Avenue, for £5,500; No. 1, First Avenue, for £5,500; Nos. 58, 60, and 71, The Drive, for the aggregate sum of £17,800; and Nos. 1, 3, and 4, Adelaide Mansions, for £23,000.

of Hove; and steps were early taken to promote a "fusion"; for, will'ee or nill'ee, it was either "fusion" or—"joining Brighton!" Brighton twice essayed to woo the coy maiden, Hove, into wedded bliss; but each time she successfully resisted; and, as if to repel further advances, she immediately after the last essay "set up house" for herself. She subsequently "mended her ways," and did many things needful for the well-being of her community. Of late (in 1879-80), she has shown a tendency to indulge in some expensive luxuries; and what the ultimate result will be, we will not venture to predict. It is said that the single blessedness of Hove will last only for a time; that, at length, she will unresistingly yield herself up to Brighton. We shall see. But, whether single or mated—"FLOREAT HOVA."

[We are unable to enter fully into the manifold details of the marvellous progress, both social and material, which Hove has made during the last 10 or 12 years; but a brief summary of the more important of these will not be altogether uninteresting. It is indisputable that Hove within the period named has achieved for herself a position among latter-day fashionable marine resorts which can scarcely be paralleled. In all directions, save where the sea puts a limit, she has enlarged her borders. In 1800 a single street sufficed for her 100 residents; but now, in the Year of Grace, 1892, her streets, roads, and other like places,—flanked for the most part by palatial mansions and houses of handsome elevation, and not a few of which possess charming verdurous surroundings,—stretch for 25 miles! whilst "The Drive"—the heart's desire of one of Hove's early pioneers, the late Mr. George Gallard—now embraces a circumference, extending round Brighton, of between eight and nine miles. A few years ago there were gloomy forebodings that young Hove, in the first flush of her newly-awakened vigour, was going ahead too fast, and was about to indulge in some expensive luxuries, which would be likely to entail upon her residents heavy burdens and regrets in the future. But these forebodings have not been realised. Rather the reverse; for, notwithstanding her enormous expenditure since 1880 on public works and various necessary improvements, so skilfully have the financial arrangements of Hove been managed that the rating for the past ten years has not averaged more than 4s. in the £. Those who have of late years "ruled the roost" in Hove must be credited with having acted on a well-defined plan in meeting public requirements, and their course of action has been fruitful of good results. There could be no question—so rapidly was Hove increasing in population and extending its "bricks and mortar"—that a new Town Hall,—where the governing powers of the community could be carried on with something like decency and convenience,—had become of paramount necessity. The miserable makeshift, which had done duty for so many years in an inconveniently-situated "back-slum" (as it was characterised), had become altogether inadequate for the accommodation so urgently needed. The ⁁ once mooted, there was no delay in carrying it out. A piece of ground between Tisbury-road and Norton-road was acquired from the Stanford Estate Trustees for £6,000. The design of Mr. A. Waterhouse, A.R.A., of London, for the new building was accepted, together with Mr. J. T. Chappell's contract to erect it for £31,933. The first stone was laid with due ceremony, on the 22nd May, 1880, by Mr. James Warnes Howlett, Chairman of the Hove Commissioners. Two years and a half were occupied in the building, and on Wednesday, December 13th, 1882, at noon, Mr. Howlett "declared it open — not merely for the Commissioners in the performance of their important duties; not merely for the Magistrates in that handsome Court where justice could be administered with dignity and convenience; but for the town at large, for all those many occasions of a social, political, religious, festive, or Masonic character, which in a town like Hove must be constantly arising,—open, in fact, for the use and enjoyment of the inhabitants at large." He added that his most fervent wish was that the Hall might long stand the pride of their town, "A thing of beauty and a joy for ever." The opening ceremony was followed by a banquet in the Grand Hall; and a grand ball was given on the following evening. The whole cost of the Hall, land, building, and furnishing, may be set down at about £50,000. The clock over the main entrance has a set of chimes and carillons, the bells and chiming apparatus having been fixed by Messrs. Gillett and Bland, of Croydon, at a cost of £1,567 10s. Having thus provided, as it were, for the living, the inhabitants of the growing township had next to provide for another pressing necessity, a place for the repose of the dead. After some difficulty, a piece of land, of about 25 acres, was secured in the neighbouring parish of Aldrington, on the Shoreham-road. This was judiciously and tastefully laid out, and with the erection of chapels and lodge, the total cost of the Cemetery amounted to about £17,000. It was consecrated by the Bishop of the Diocese, and opened, in May, 1882. And now another important work had to be faced, namely, the construction of a sea wall. The havoc made by the sea along the front had occasioned much anxiety, and had involved heavy expenditure on more than one occasion, with very little permanent results. In 1884 it was determined to deal with the matter effectually—once and for all. A substantial wall, of some 2,000 feet in length, and extending from the eastern boundary of the town to the west of Adelaide-crescent, was constructed. It is faced with flint blocks, backed with concrete, and has a granite coping surmounted by a strong ornamental railing. The cost was about £40,000. Some £7,000 was also spent on groyning and improvements on the foreshore; and Hove may now truly boast of a sea frontage, which, so far as it extends, with its broad asphalted promenade and well-kept lawns, it would be difficult to outvie. Within the last year Hove has acquired and laid out a new Western Lawn, adjoining Aldrington, at a cost of about £6,000; and it is to be hoped that ere long steps will be taken to extend the eastern promenade from the end of Adelaide-crescent that ever-to-be-regretted western barrier,—Mills's-terrace. directions the "powers that be" in Hove have evinced a com spirit with a view to "meet the times." Hove has now, in addition to the Church Schools, its School Board,—which was first elected in December, 1876,—with three schools in full working order, and another large school, with swimming bath, in course of erection. In 1886 there was opened, at a cost of £12,070, a Hospital for Infectious Diseases. In 1887, some 20 acres of land were acquired and laid out for that great desideratum, a Recreation Ground, which was opened in May, 1891 ; its total cost being £14,000. Another useful acquisition to Hove is the establishment of a Free Library ; the town being polled on the question on the 28th March, 1891, when the voting was—For 1,197 ; against, 502. Premises were thereupon secured in the Grand Avenue; the News-room was opened December 14th, 1891 ; and both the Reference and Lending Library are being stocked, the latter starting with 3,000 volumes. Cottage Baths were opened in May, 1892, in Livingstone-road ; at prices (1d. and 2d.) which should ensure a further extension. But unquestionably the greatest public effort in Hove of recent years has been the erection of a new Parish Church, in the Drive and Eaton-road, which was necessitated by reason of the deficient accommodation in the old Parish Church of St. Andrew. The Church (the foundation stone of which was laid by Dr. Durnford on 25th April, 1889,) was consecrated on the 1st May, 1891, and was legally constituted the Parish Church of Hove on and from January 1st, 1892. The building is constructed of Sussex sandstone ; is in the Early Decorated style of architecture ; and is being built from the design of Mr. J. L. Pearson, R.A., the architect of Truro Cathedral. As yet only a portion of the fabric is to be completed, at an estimated cost of £17,667 ; but, thanks to the indomitable zeal of the Vicar, the Rev. Prebendary T. Peacey, and his equally zealous Building Committee, over £17,000 of that amount has been raised, and the remainder will, doubtless, be soon forthcoming. At no distant date, therefore, it may be expected that an attempt will be made to complete the sacred edifice. Hove may be regarded now as an independent and well-regulated community, with a form of government, consolidated in 1872-73, which has so far satisfied its requirements. As yet it retains its old attachment to the Steyning Union, as a medium for the relief of the poor ; and it is also dependent upon the County Magistrates for the administration of justice ; but the Police Force is exclusively under the control of the Commissioners. It has a well-equipped Volunteer Fire Brigade, to whose funds the Commissioners contribute £120 a year ; and it also furnishes a Company to the Brighton Rifle Volunteers. Independently of the Hove Banking Company, Limited, each of the Brighton Banks has a Branch in Hove. In other respects,—as regards the School of Science and Art, Reading Rooms, Clubs, the Regatta, &c., the sister town is "up to date." It may be added that, for the purposes of government, Hove is divided into six Wards, represented by 51 Commissioners ; it is also represented upon the East Sussex County Council by two Aldermen and six Councillors. Some changes in the local governing powers within the last year or two may be noted. Mr. Howlett, who had been Chairman of the Commissioners for 13 successive years, retired in 1891, and in recognition of his services was presented with a piece of plate, value 120 guineas, and a memorial portrait, by T. Blake Wirgman, at a cost of 300 guineas, which is to be hung in the Commissioners' Board Room. He has been succeeded by Mr. G. B. Woodruff, a gentleman whose geniality, accessibility, and sterling business capacity eminently qualify him for the post he so worthily fills. There has been one other official change, namely, the retirement of Mr. C. A. Woolley, the Town Clerk, but who still retains his connection with the Commissioners, as Consulting Solicitor. His successor is Mr. H. Endacott, whose well-deserved appointment was a graceful recognition of his "perseverance in well-doing," both as Clerk to the Commissioners for so many years, and for his untiring services in helping forward all that has of late appertained to the welfare of Hove.]

Preston.

BRIGHTONIANS, as a rule, used formerly to take small account of Preston. Their town, favoured for many a year by the presence of Royalty, increased so rapidly that the little village to the North was all but ignored. Yet, in ancient times, Preston was quite as important a place as its now overgrown neighbour. Brighton might once have boasted of being patronised by Royalty; but Preston, almost from time immemorial, had the "privelege"—if privilege it was—of *supporting* Royalty. It was one of the 54 Manors which the Conqueror gave Robert, Earl of Moreton, his mother's son, when he made him Earl of Cornwall; and under several succeeding monarchs, down even to the days of "Good Queen Bess," Preston enjoyed the same unenviable privilege. The privilege, in fact, continued during the next reign; as, in 7 James I., certain lands in the Manor, of £39 per annum value, were assigned towards the maintenance of Prince Henry.

The existence of the Manor and village of Preston is well authenticated as far back as the days of Edward the Confessor, at which early period it was, and long previously had been, in connection with Chichester. For distinction's sake, there being other Prestons in the County, it was always called *Preston Episcopi*. *Domesday Book* says of it:—

"The Bishop holds Prestetone, which was always attached to the Monastery. Twenty hides have been and continue its assessment. The arable is 12 plough lands. There is a plough and a half in the demesne; and 30 villeins, with 20 bondsmen, have 12 ploughs, and three houses in Lewes, yielding 1s. 6d. Here is a church, 15 acres of meadow, and a wood yielding two hogs of pannage" (food for two hogs).

Following this, we are told,—

"Lovel holds two hides of this Manor, and has there two ploughs, and nine villeins, with three bondsmen, having two ploughs and a mill there. The value is 40s."

The whole Manor, in the time of Edward the Confessor was valued at £18; the amount at which it was appreciated under the Conqueror. The land in the latter's time had been farmed at £25; but would not yield this rental. The Canons of Chichester (it is added in *Domesday*) hold 16 hides in common, which were never assessed to the Land Tax, *according to their account (!)*, and have there four ploughs in the demesne. The value of this is £8.

Of the actual extent of the Manor we obtain little further authentic information till the time of Queen Anne, when it appears that the Manor extended into Brighton, Hove, Patcham, Westmeston, Middleton, Slaugham, and Bolney. In the fine levied in the 13th Anne, the Manor was said to consist of "5 messuages, 3 dove houses, 9 gardens, 550 acres of land, 30 acres of meadow, 400 acres of pasture, 40 acres of wood, and 680 acres of furze and heath."*

Reverting to its early history, the son of the Earl of Cornwall, mentioned above, being "a religious person, after the mode of those times, gave the Lordship of Preston to the Abbey of Bec, in Normandy." We hear, however, no more of it till Edward III., when Thomas, Lord Poynings, died possessed of it. In the reign of Henry VI., John Duke of Bedford, the King's uncle, who was then Regent of France, died seized of it.

We now come to an interesting episode, in the history of the old Manor; namely, its association with Anne of Cleves, the repudiated wife of Henry VIII. Anne's connection with Henry and her subsequent repudiation are among the most extraordinary of Royal romances. No sooner had Henry buried Jane Seymour, the most beloved of all his wives, than he immediately began to cast about for another. He set his heart on the daughter of the Duke of Guise; but—heavy blow and sad discouragement to the Royal suitor—she was betrothed! Henry next thought of a German alliance, which Cromwell warmly seconded, from motives of national policy, and proposed to him Anne of Cleves. Henry was much pleased with a portrait of her, painted by the celebrated Hans Holbein. After some months' negotiation, the marriage was arranged, and, towards the end of December, 1538, Anne arrived at Dover. Henry was impatient to be satisfied with regard to the person of his bride, and posted off privately to Rochester to get a sight of her! He found her big and tall as he could wish; but he said she was utterly destitute both of beauty and grace, and very unlike the pictures he had received. He swore, in fact, that she was a great "Flanders mare," and declared that he never could bear her any affection. Matters were not improved when he found that she could only speak Dutch, of which he was entirely ignorant; and he returned to Greenwich very melancholy. Henry, notwithstanding his aversion, resolved to "put his neck into the yoke." But the morning after the marriage he told Cromwell that he hated his new consort worse than ever. For a brief period, however, the King kept up a show of civility to Anne; but at last, breaking all restraints, he determined to seek a dissolution

---

* In 1649, the yearly value of lands, quit rents, tithes, &c., in the Parish of Preston, was given as £378. Brighton, in the same return, is put at £801 15s. Horsfield says:—"In 1663, the annual rent reserved out of the Manor of Preston, of £63 3s. 11., was returned to the Lord Treasurer Southampton, as a fee farm rent, within the survey of the Exchequer, to make part of the provision intended for Queen Catherine's jointure. The same authority adds:— "By the custom of the Manor, the descent is to the *youngest son*, and the widow is entitled to her free bench."

of the "odious marriage." The real cause for this suddenness of action was, that he had fixed his affections on another—the ill-fated, fickle, but beautiful Catherine Howard; and, to gratify this new passion, there was no expedient but a divorce from Anne of Cleves, who was packed off to Richmond, in pretended anxiety for her health, while Henry was preparing his creatures to act out the farce of legalizing the divorce. He told his "faithful Commons" that, in prosecuting the affair, he had nothing more at heart than the *Glory of God* and the *Good of the Realm !* and to the Convocation he added two more reasons; that when he espoused Anne he had not *inwardly* given his consent, and that he had not thought proper to consummate the marriage! The Convocation was satisfied, and annulled the marriage; Parliament ratified the decision; and, two days after, the sentence was notified to Anne, who heard it without emotion.

Poor Anne! She was blessed, we suppose, with a happy insensibility of temper, even on those points which most nearly affect her sex. On being offered £3,000 a year, and to be adopted by the King as his *sister*, she, under her hand, declared her acquiescence in the sentence and the settlement ! On the 8th day of the succeeding month she saw Catherine Howard, her rival, raised to the Throne, and—soon afterwards carried to the scaffold !

Anne's dower chiefly consisted of the Manors and estates forfeited by the attainder of Cromwell (the Minister who had proposed her to Henry) and among these were Brighthelmston-Lewes, Falmer, and Preston, and they were to be held "without rendering an account from the Lady Day foregoing the same grant, which was dated January 20th, 1541." After her divorce, Anne took up her abode in Preston Place (in a room of which her portrait, we believe, still hangs—whether Holbein's or not, we cannot say).* She subsequently lived in seclusion in an old monastery at Falmer; and, after spending the remainder of her life in tranquillity, she died at Chelsea in July, 1557, and was buried on the 3rd August in Westminster Abbey.

Following the fortunes of the Manor, it appears that, by an Act of Parliament, passed early in the reign of Elizabeth, empowering that Sovereign to take into her hands any Bishopric, Preston, with others, was seized by the Crown. In the 34th Elizabeth, Sir Thomas Shirley, of Wiston, became possessed of Preston;† and Anthony, the younger son of the William Shirley, who succeeded to Wiston in 1540, settled there. He obtained the estate through the interest of his mother, her second husband, Richard Elrington, Esq., having "remitted no care to her first progeny." Anthony married Barbara, the daughter of Sir Thomas Walsingham, of Sedbury, Kent,

---

[* A favourite resort of Anne's, when residing at Preston Place, was the copse known of late years as Hollingbury Copse, situated to the east of the bungalow residence built by the eminent Shakespearean scholar, Mr. J. O. Halliwell-Phillipps. In the plan attached to the title deeds of the Hollingbury Estate, the copse is described as " Anne of Cleves' Copse."]

† Sir Thomas was one of the four gentlemen, who, in 1578, were appointed by the Crown to inspect the " Auncient Customs" of Brighton, to settle every disagreement between the inhabitants, with regard to admission into the Society of Twelve, the assessment of town-rates, &c.

and by her had a large family. He died in 1624, and was buried in Preston Church. This Anthony was uncle to the celebrated "Three Travellers,"* whose romantic lives and adventures in the reign of James I., are remarkable even in the history of the times, and, as the late Rev. Charles Townsend said, "in the history of Sussex, should form a little 'Odyssey,' to which all the poetic and distinguished spirits of the County might well look up, and be proud of."† In the reign of Charles I., the Shirley who owned Wiston and Preston sacrificed the former estate to the cause of loyalty, Preston only remaining to him when the troubles of the time were ended; and the fate of this gentleman, who sorely pined at the losses he had sustained, is still preserved in a rustic distich—

"Shirley of Preston
Died for the loss of Wiston."

In 1654 a Baronetcy was conferred on Anthony Shirley, who does not appear to have emulated his predecessor's loyal qualities, for he took a very active part in public affairs in the time of the Commonwealth. Only two Shirleys afterwards lived to "endure the enfeebled splendour of their house"; and, in 1705, on the death of Sir Anthony's grandson, Richard Shirley, the male branch and baronetage became extinct.

Sir Richard Shirley devised the Manor of Preston to his three daughters, Judith (who died in 1711, unmarried); Ann, who married Robert Western, Esq.; and Mary, who married Thomas Western, Esq., of Rivenhall, Essex. On the death of Judith, the Manor became vested in her sisters, in equal moieties; and on the marriage of Mary, in 1712, Ann's moiety was released, in consideration of £6,275, to Thomas Western, Esq. (Mary's husband), and the whole Manor became vested in him. Thomas Western, Esq., died in 1766, leaving as his heir Charles Western, Esq. The end of this latter gentleman was of the most melancholy character. Whilst taking an airing in a carriage

---

* For further particulars concerning the "Three Travellers," see "The Shirley Brothers; an historical account of the lives of Sir Thomas, Sir Anthony, and Sir Robert Shirley, Knights," by Evelyn Philip Shirley, Esq., M.A., M.P. Printed for the Roxburghe Club, 1848.

† Charles Townsend was the last of a *coterie* of eminent men in the world of arts and letters, who lived, flourished, and had their day some forty, fifty, aye, even sixty years ago. He was the friend of Turner, Copley Fielding, Wordsworth, Rogers, and a welcome guest amongst the galaxy of *savans*, artists, poets, and sculptors with which the late Lord Egremont used to delight to surround himself when at Petworth, and which has since made famous, and will, for many years to come, render classical, that lovely spot in the western portion of our lovely County. Mr. Townsend was a man of highly educated and refined taste. He had a singular appreciation of the beautiful, and his judgment was eagerly sought by poet and painter. He was, during the Vicarage of Dr. Carr, a curate of Brighton; he subsequently became curate of Preston-cum-Hove, which post he held until the late Lord Egremont presented him with the living of Kingston-by-Sea. The parsonage house at that time was nothing better than a very poor cottage, and so for many years Mr. Townsend lived in Brighton. After 1848, however, he lived at Kingston-by-Sea, having added some rooms, which were built and fitted up according to his own antiquarian notions, to the old cottage which served as the parsonage. He died there on Saturday, January 29th, 1870, in his 81st year. His remains were interred at

along the Goldstone-road with his wife and eldest son, Charles Callis Western, it being very hot, he ordered the coachman to stop to water the horses at a sheep-trough, he himself meanwhile getting out of the carriage and standing by their side. Mrs. Western, having occasion to use her pocket-handkerchief, shook it, which startled the horses; and Mr. Western, attempting to stop them, was dragged down, and, the carriage wheels going over his head, he was killed on the spot. The affrighted horses still running on, Mrs. Western, on passing some furze, threw the child into it, and thus probably saved its life; whilst she herself jumped out of the carriage shortly after and escaped without injury. This occurrence took place on the 19th July, 1771. The widow, with her two children, shortly after left Preston, and never more returned to it.

The Manor House was then occupied "by strangers." In 1784 Thomas Read Kemp, Esq., M.P. for Lewes, resided there. It has been from time immemorial the custom of the Lord to reside at the House; but when this was first built it would be difficult to determine. From exterior appearances the present House does not seem of great age, and was, probably, a rebuilding on the old site in the latter half of the last century.

In 1794 Charles Callis Western, Esq.,* conveyed the Manor, with the Hundred of Preston, and several valuable farms in the Parishes of Hove and Preston, containing about 980 acres, to William Stanford, Esq., in consideration of £17,600. The new Squire was a man of great energy, and, under his auspices and judicious management, the value of the Manor was considerably augmented. He died at the ripe age of 77, in March, 1841, and was succeeded by his son William, who died on the 11th April, 1853, leaving as sole heiress to his now valuable estates his daughter Ellen, then only some four or five years of age. Miss Stanford married, in 1867 (by permission of the Court of Chancery, she being at that period a minor), Vere Fane Benett, Esq., of Pythouse, Wiltshire, who has since assumed the name of Benett-Stanford. What the value of the Stanford Estate was in 1880, how much it has of late years realised, and what it will ultimately realise, seeing how favourably it is situated for building, it would be difficult

---

Preston, in the same grave with those of his father and mother. A biographer says of him:—"He had many offers of rich Church preferment from his numerous influential friends; but he steadily declined them all. He was happier by himself, in his little hermitage by the sea, where, with his books, his statues, his pictures, and his quaint old wainscoating and chairs, he could live and dream—dream and live—in a world of his own imaginings. But, besides the charm of this anchoritish life.he had a horror of the artificial conventionalities of society. He had an honest love for that which is noble and good and true, and an utter disgust of the vanity, humbug, and time-serving nonsense, which is almost inseparable from the life of the courtier, the place-seeker, and the man of the world. He could not bring himself into harmony with what he considered ridiculous conformities. Particularly eccentric was he in dress. The present ritualistic parson would have been horribly scandalised to have seen this little old clergyman with a blue coat, a yellow waistcoat with mother of pearl buttons, a black neck-tie, and nankeen gaiters."

* Charles Callis Western, Esq., who was descended from both the elder and younger line of the Shirleys of Preston, was created Baron Western, on the 28th January, 1833. He died, unmarried, in 1841, and (his brother being dead) the title became extinct.

to estimate. Something like £30,000 was paid by the Railway Company in 1839 to the late William Stanford, Esq., for the privilege of passing over certain portions of the Estate ; and we have heard that, before the West Brighton Estate was laid out, as much as £250,000 was offered for the piece of land lying between the eastern portion of the Cliftonville Estate and Palmeira-square. What it eventually realised we do not know; but enough to make it pardonable in a man to wish that he had been " to the Manor born."

Thus much respecting the Manor of Preston. Let us now briefly glance at the old village and its associations. Visiting it some years since, after a long absence, we were struck with the changes which were everywhere visible, and we involuntarily recalled the happy time,—alas! so long gone by,—when in boyish days we used to count the posts and rails running along the Preston-road ; to swim our "flat-bottomers" in the stream under the wall when Patcham well overflowed; or to mount on a chum's back to peer over the wall at the pretty white house with the green meadows and trees in front, with the venerable Church close by, and were scared by the cry of "Stanford's coming!"

But times are changed! and the village and its surroundings too. The changes in these latter, however, are such that the old village itself was in 1880 simply "nowhere." There remained, as of old, the noble trees on each hand (though on some Time had left its traces in ruined trunks and broken branches) as you entered the village by the road from Brighton*; there was still the grand old Shaw to the left, which the local fashionable world in the days of George III. and later on desired to make a rural retreat ; the same charming and picturesque view from the road of the ivy-clad old Church tower, with the Manor House, Preston Place, close by, both embosomed in trees. The neat and substantial Manor farm-house, &c., was yet existing on the left of the road leading up to the Railway arch. In the village itself, the ancient hostelry of "The Crown and Anchor," so well known in the old coaching days as the first halt out of Brighton, still hung out its sign. Then, the old Rookery appeared to be as flourishing as ever, if the vocal strains of the sable colonists in "Valentine time" are any criterion.† The "Drove" wore much of its old familiar aspect, though a wall had lately been built to the right of it, some distance up. In and about the village some few spots remained unaltered. The old

---

* Within these seventy years there were hedge-rows each side of the road between Brighton and Preston. The walls, of which a portion only now remain, were built in 1817 by the late W. Stanford, Esq. Formerly, a path ran from the right-hand side of the road across the fields in front of Preston Place to the Church and Drove. This path was originally a continuation, we believe, of the Lovers' Walk, running formerly from the Dyke-road, at a point now known as the Seven Dials.

† A good joke is told in connection with this Rookery. A once well-known Brightonian, seeing a number of "loafers" hanging about some buildings looking out for a job, told them he knew for a certainty that a large amount of building was at that time going on at Preston. A dozen or so of the men started off immediately. On arriving there they looked about in vain for building ; and, on enquiring of a countryman, were told—" He knew nawn't about buildings, except the Squire's rooks a-making their nests!" We never heard whether they ...ed for a job!

village "smithy" and wheelwright's shop, we may mention, succumbed to the Railway, which runs over their site. Two other pieces of antiquity—twin-blots on the escutcheon of the village—the Workhouse and the "black-hole," were soon after removed. The Workhouse was simply a thatched building, with flint and brick walls, and stood immediately to the west of "The Crown and Anchor." On its being pulled down in 1844, the poor thenceforth found their "last home" —but one—in the poor-house of the Steyning Union at Shoreham. The "black-hole" adjoined the Workhouse,—meet companionship, truly! This "black-hole" was of very primitive construction. There were, certainly, four walls and a roof, and it had two cells; but no provision was made for windows—as being too luxurious, perhaps, for the destined inmates; and all the light obtainable within came from between some bars inserted in the door. This door was itself a curiosity; at least, inside: the whole of the back of it being completely studded with hob-nails, to prevent, it was said, its being sawn through! Some woodwork lined the inside walls of the "black-hole," and this was as thickly studded as the door with the hob-nail adornment.

But let us turn to a more pleasant theme—the original Tea Gardens at Preston. *When* these were originally formed, or who was their projector—their first "General Manager"—is now probably past finding out. The Gardens were "doing a good trade" so early as 1769, when they were a favourite fashionable resort by visitors to Brighton; and it may be presumed that they were in existence for some time previous. *Why* Tea Gardens should have been formed in such a place, so "remote from towns," is a singular circumstance. The "house for the reception of company" being immediately opposite the entrance gates of the road leading to the Manor House, it is probable the Lord was in some way associated with the formation of the Gardens, or derived a revenue from them; and more especially as visitors had the privilege of entrée to the Grove of "ancestral elms" in close proximity, known as "The Shaw." The records respecting the Tea Gardens are very scanty. Down to the close of last century they would seem to have been as popular as ever. *The Brighthelmston Directory* for 1788 says:—"At Preston, there is a house for the reception of company; and in the gardens a very handsome tea room has been lately erected. The great neatness in which the house and gardens are kept, the excellence of the accommodations, the delightful situation of the place, and the obliging disposition of the proprietor, ensure him frequent visits from Brighthelmston and the places adjacent."

Later on—in the early part of the present century—the tea and coffee rooms were in the house itself. In 1809 the landlord of "The Crown and Anchor," opposite, was the proprietor; and the entrance to the rooms—which were on the ground floor and first floor,—was then at the north side of the house—opposite the door of the inn. A staircase behind the house led from both rooms into the gardens, which at this period were shorn somewhat of their original proportions. A few years later, in 1815, a local chronicler says,—"There are at Preston a small tea garden and tea rooms; but they are seldom resorted to by the higher classes of Society"! Subsequently —*sic transit gloria mundi*—the Gardens were built upon, and the rooms were altogether closed; the house being opened as a general shop, which also did duty as the first Preston Post Office.

There was, however, in 1809, a "revival" of the ancient glories of "The Shaw," as would appear from the following advertisement in the *Brighton Herald*:—

PUBLIC BREAKFAST, &c.- In honour of the Brilliant and Decisive Victory recently obtained by Sir Arthur Wellesley in Spain, and of the Successful Efforts of the Grand Expedition.

BY SUBSCRIPTION.—TICKETS, 3s. 6d. EACH.

It having been suggested by various Ladies and Gentlemen in Brighton, that a Public *Dejeune* be held in the pleasant, romantic, and rural situation, called PRESTON SHAW, about a mile to the North of the Town, would be an agreeable addition to the amusements of the place, the Nobility and Gentry are, therefore, respectfully informed, that the Proprietor of the Grounds, W. STANFORD, Esq., has kindly yielded his sanction to the measure, and the entertainment will consequently take place there, of which due notice will be given.

A select Band of Music is engaged for the occasion, together with Vocal Performers of acknowledged merit; and a Platform will be constructed for those who may choose to Dance.

Subscriptions to be received at the Libraries, and at the Royal Circus, where Tickets may also be procured.

The "Dejeune" was subsequently arranged for Monday, September 4th; but the weather proved so wet that it was put off till the next morning, when we are told, "many *elegantes* from this town were present, among whom were the Duchess of Marlborough, &c. Two bands of music gave cheerfulness to the rural scene, and a third was in readiness for country dances; the latter, however, found no employment."

A notice of Preston would be incomplete without some allusion to the Prince's Dairy—which formerly stood embosomed in trees in the angle formed by New England-road and the London-road. The Dairy has a local historic interest from its association with the Prince Regent, in the days when Brighton basked in the brightest sunshine of Royal favour. The Prince's Dairy and its surroundings, some 50 or 60 years ago, presented one of the loveliest rural pictures imaginable. It was best seen from the top of New England Hill— "Constitution Hill," as it was formerly familiarly called—now wholly removed or partly covered by the Railway workshops and by New England-street and other streets, but then reached by a bridle-road (on each side of which corn-fields waved) running from what is now the top of Trafalgar-street. The house and adjoining picturesque erections, with trees and gardens, lay immediately beneath you, its pretty orchard to the left, and the freshest of green meadows beyond; while to the west, on a rising ground—now covered by the goods line of the Railway—was the once well-known castellated building, partly covered with ivy and enclosed by shrubs, and said to have been the favourite resort of the Prince whenever he visited the

Dairy. Then there was the old Indian figure—with turbaned head, black face, and long earrings, and holding a drawn bow and arrow in his hands—placed among the lovely trees in front of the house, in order to frighten away the birds ; but he was also a terrible scarecrow to the smaller Brighton juveniles of the period !

The Dairy was erected about 1805-6, and was, we believe, originally merely rented by the Prince of Mr. Stanford; and this belief is strengthened by a paragraph in *Attree's Topography of Brighton* (1809), which states, after alluding to the Dairy, " A part of the enclosed lands hereabout is also *rented* by His Royal Highness, which affords pasture for cows, though seldom more than two or three are kept there." The fact was, that for mere dairy purposes, the levies on the Dairy by the establishment at the Pavilion do not appear to have been of a very onerous character. The spot was more frequently used by the Prince and his friends as a rural retreat, and here were held several of those *fêtes champêtres*, &c., so much in fashion at the time, and of which local tradition has not preserved the most creditable memorials. Whether such memorials be true or not, it is not for us to say ; but the Dairy was at one time reputed to be the residence of Lucy Howard,* the Prince's " Fair Rosamond," the knowledge of whose presence there excited the jealousy of Lady Jersey (who then " ruled " at the Pavilion, and deemed herself " first favourite " of the fickle Prince), and led to one of the most discreditable acts which the Prince ever committed. It was the custom of the Prince to leave the Pavilion at twilight, ride along the Lewes-road, and then strike back over the Downs to visit the "retreat" of Miss Howard. Lady Jersey's suspicions being aroused, she employed a stable-boy to watch the Prince. In an ill-fated hour the boy was caught at his work of espionage by the Prince, and, hesitating in his explanation to him of his object, was so unmanfully and so unmercifully chastised by him as to be rendered a cripple for life. The boy was subsequently removed to the home of his parents, at Horsham (where he died twelve years after), his parents being allowed by the Prince £50 per annum for his support. The excitement caused by this occurrence led to Miss Howard's immediate removal from the neighbourhood, to which she never returned.†

---

* A child of Miss Howard, who, it is said, survived to its second year, was buried in St. Nicholas Churchyard, under the name of George Howard.

[† In the original edition of this work the *locale* of this discreditable episode in the Prince's career was stated to have been the Prince's Dairy, to which place local tradition had generally assigned it. Subsequent research leads to the inference that this is incorrect, and that the true *locale* was Patcham Place. Huish (*Memoirs of George IV.*, vol. L., 262) says that Miss Howard resided at a "comfortable mansion, which stands about three miles from Brighton, at the foot of a wood, on the right hand of the road leading from London." The Prince's Dairy was not a mansion ; it was not three miles from Brighton ; and there was no wood near it ; all of which, however, would apply to Patcham Place. But the most important evidence against the Prince's Dairy is the date of the occurrence. According to Huish the episode took place previous to 1800. The Prince's Dairy was not built till 1805. The same writer adds :—"Lucy Howard afterwards became the wife of Mr. Smith, a gentleman of independent property in Yorkshire, and was the mother of a numerous family, and died respected by all who knew her."]

On the Prince giving up the Dairy, it was occupied as a private residence, down to the year 1871, when, with all its picturesque surroundings, it was wholly removed prior to the building (by Messrs. Ireland and Savage) of what was subsequently known as the Dairy Estate.*

To pass on. In the old coaching-days, about the year 1807-8, when "time" was becoming an object with travellers, the direct road between Brighton and London, by Cuckfield and Reigate, was formed, and Preston set up a turnpike-gate! This gate was for many years a grievance to Brighton, as it effectually barred its visitors from the enjoyment of one of the prettiest rural drives in the vicinity. From time immemorial, in fact, almost from its first erection, and down even to modern times, the gate bore on its top the friendly greeting —"No Trust!" Owners of carriages used frequently at that time to drive as far as the "Shaw," and then return to Brighton, much to the chagrin of the pikeman. Sometimes they would alight at the "Shaw," and *walk* through the gate on to Withdean. But Cerberus would not always be deprived of his "sop" by such means; and so lately as 1848 one shilling was actually demanded of two ladies, who so alighted, before the toll-keeper would allow them to pass through the gate! However, in 1853, when it became known that the Trustees of the road were applying to Parliament for a renewal of their powers, active and energetic steps were taken both by Brighton and Preston to get the gate removed farther northward; and, thanks to the arduous labours of the Committee appointed—Messrs. W. Hallett, J. Cordy, Lewis Slight, Daniel Friend, and others—this long-standing incubus, after five days' fight in the House of Commons, had to be removed (in May, 1854,) by the Trustees 100 yards north of Withdean.

It is impossible to estimate the advantages of the removal both to Brighton and Preston; to the latter especially it may be said to have opened a new era of prosperity. The "straw had begun to move" some two or three years previously. Far-seeing people saw in Withdean a most desirable residential district; and so early as 1851, Messrs. D. Friend and Saunders had each erected a villa in what is now Harrington-road (opposite the well-known Tivoli Gardens, which were opened as pleasure gardens under their new Italian name in 1851-52, though they had done duty as the Strawberry Gardens for some 20 years previously).† When the turnpike gate was actually removed, all the more available sites for such residences along the London-road were rapidly secured. A few years later, and other

---

* A joke in connection with the building of this Estate may be mentioned. The estate was laid out on the wedding-day of the Princess Louise and the Marquis of Lorne; and all the streets were originally named after the "styles and titles" of the Marquis. Roseneath-terrace, for instance, was intended to have been called Lorne-terrace. A board was put up with this name upon it; but some wag, having put "For" before Lorne, making it *For-Lorne*-terrace, the intended name was at once abandoned, and Roseneath-terrace substituted.

[† The Tivoli Gardens ceased to exist as public pleasure gardens early in 1888, the land having been bought by Mr. R. C. Gazeley, whose residence adjoined them.]

districts of Preston began to be built upon. Mr. Daniel Friend, with one or two coadjutors, projected, in 1866, the Clermont Estate, in Withdean, containing some 200 houses, and building, some three or four years after, proceeded so rapidly in other directions, that none could then predict where it would stop. The best proof, however, of the "past and present" of Preston up to this period is afforded by the Census returns. In 1801, it contained 222 inhabitants; and in 1821 the population had only increased to 319, the number of houses being 53. In 1831, the inhabitants were 429. In another 30 years, down to 1861, these had increased only to 569, the houses being 111. From this period the stationary character of Preston may be said to have ceased; for in the next ten years—1861-71—the houses had increased to 409, and the population to 2,019,—more than threefold! In 1880 there were probably upwards of 1,000 houses in Preston; their rateable value being £50,820 10s. The inhabitants then numbered about 5,400. [In 1892 the houses had increased to 2,242, their rateable value being £78,484. The inhabitants have more than doubled since 1880, the number being now 12,694.]

Some particulars respecting the rating of Preston some 50 or 60 years ago are worth quoting from an old rate-book (in Mr. Daniel Friend's possession). The village at that period was not a "paradise" for ratepayers. If the rating at Preston were as high in 1880 as it was in the years 1826-33, we opine there would be an exodus *en masse* from that pleasant neighbourhood. For instance, in 1828, the poor rate was 12s. in the £: the land and houses in the parish being assessed at a total of £338 5s.; the land of the Stanford Estate being put at £128, the house at £20. In 1828 the poor rate was 18s. in the £; in 1830, 20s.; in 1831, 30s. (in two rates of 17s. and 13s.); in 1832, 33s. (in two rates of 24s. and 9s.); in 1833, 31s. (in four rates, respectively 14s., 5s., 6s., and 6s.), and so on. The burden of these rates was very grievous to the poorer ratepayers, and some of the collector's "observations" on non-payment are not to be wondered at, as,—"A large family and very poor," "Refusing on account of being very poor and having a large family," &c. Things came to a crisis in 1837, when a meeting of the parishioners was held with the view of procuring a "re-valuation" and "re-measuring" the parish.* This was subsequently done, and the result was that the new assessment was upwards of seven times more than the old, namely, £2,217; the land of W. Stanford, Esq., being assessed at £660; and his house and land at £106 more. In 1846 the assessment of the parish reached £3,615; the Railway Company being assessed at £1,000 and the Waterworks Company at £150.

---

* Though the "re-valuing" of the parish was the primary object of the meeting, the parishioners did not at the same time neglect other matters. For instance, Mr. W. Stanford, jun., proposed (and it was carried unanimously) "that two pairs of handcuffs be purchased for the use of the Parish of Preston"; it was also resolved unanimously "That the Black Hole be hired of W. Stanford, and cleaned out, and the key delivered to John Still, High Constable."

Between 1861-71, the old village itself, though somewhat isolated from its more vigorous offshoots, showed some signs of vitality. In the midst of its diminutive and ill-constructed dwellings, many of which were in unhealthy proximity to agricultural erections, National Schools were built. South-lane (a very poor locality) could boast of some new houses! The village, too, actually enjoyed the privilege of a Post Office! Where one public-house formerly sufficed for the accommodation of the neighbourhood, in 1871 it had two; and,—sure sign of the "march of civilisation,"—a new and commodious Police-station was erected!

Within the last few years (in 1873) Preston elected to "join" Brighton; and whether due to the "union" or not, the northern suburb increased and multiplied with marvellous rapidity. Without entering into the details of this growth, suffice it to say that the whole area between the south of the Viaduct and the Brighton northern boundary (which in 1868-70 was "houseless") is now covered with "bricks and mortar." North of the Viaduct a large number of houses have also been erected; while, on the western side of the Preston-road, handsome villas extend along the whole distance up to the ancient "Shaw," rendering this district (which overlooks Preston Park) one of the most picturesque in the neighbourhood of Brighton. Preston had in 1880 two Railway Stations (though some "knowing ones," some 20 years before, had said there would be no necessity for even one); and the formation of the new "Drive," which extends from Preston to Hove, opened up an additional attraction to Brighton visitors and residents.

THE CHURCH.

The Church is a plain and unpretending building. In 1870 it underwent some judicious improvements, more especially in the interior arrangements. The building, which is dedicated to St. Peter, was erected in the time of Henry II., and additional interest attaches to it from the fact that it is entirely in one style, Early English. Prior to the improvements, the interior of the Church was simple and homely. In ornamental scrolls,

"O'er either door, a sacred text, invited to godly fear."

The walls were whitewashed, and all scrupulously clean. There were no aisles, and a plain stone arch led into the Chancel. The east window of the Chancel had three lancet lights, placed side by side within a large arch. Two of the three windows on each side the Chancel were filled in with bricks and compo! In the south wall of the Chancel was an ambry (for the reception of alms) and three sedilia (stone seats), separated by slender shafts, and canopied by trefoiled arches. The south door was bricked up, though it was undoubtedly at some former period the chief entrance to the Church; and this is confirmed by the fact that, in 1857, there were discovered, in the churchyard, a portion of a paved pathway, the door-stone, and the solid foundations of the old porch. Possibly, the pathway to "The Drove," from the Preston-road, which we have previously alluded to (p. 404) was the "old way to Church."

LONDON ROAD AND NEW ENGLAND VIADUCTS—about 1860.

Taken from the Chalk Hill.

PRESTON CHURCH (before restoration).

Reverting to the interior. There were previous to the late improvements but 22 pews in all in the Church! and one of these was appropriated to the Vicar and another to the Churchwardens. These pews were ranged on each side; they were of all sizes: their construction was of the plainest character (and the pulpit was of a piece with them), and all sorts of shifts were resorted to in the vain endeavour to make them comfortable. Then, as to the Vestry: well, it was, probably, as large as a sentry-box.

Among the more interesting features of the interior of the old Church are the mural paintings (now much obliterated) on each side of the Chancel arch. Taking as a criterion the costumes in the principal painting, "The Murder of Thomas A'Becket," their date (says their discoverer, the late Rev. Charles Townsend) cannot be later than Edward I. The discovery of these paintings in 1830 was by a singular accident. The "Commandments" had been, it appears, painted on the whitewash and plaster which covered the pictures; and Mr. Townsend, in endeavouring to scrape away the letters, which had been greatly decayed by damp and age, and after removing many thick coats of plaster, discovered the interesting old paintings. The question almost involuntarily arises—why they should ever have been covered up? One possible solution may be found in the fact, that it was prompted by fear. Henry VIII., in the latter part of his reign, issued a proclamation which commanded "all images and pictures of Bishop Becket through the hole realme to be put down and avoided out of all Churches, Chappels, and other places." The bruit of the cannon with which Henry's myrmidons shattered the walls of the beautiful Priory of Lewes, may, probably, have reverberated thence over the hills to Preston; and, a panic spreading among the inhabitants, the old paintings were obliterated by whitewash, and, to make assurance double sure, they "laid it on thick"!

Of the paintings on the Northern side of the Chancel arch, the details of A'Becket's murder would appear to be faithfully pourtrayed in accordance with historic details. There are the altar and cup, with A'Becket beside them, turned towards his murderers, with hands stretched out, as if resigned to his fate. The first murderer (de Tracy) is, with his sword, striking his head and also the hand of Grim, his friend, which is held out to protect him; the second (Fitzurse) is stabbing A'Becket from behind; the third (Morville) is prepared to strike a third blow; while the fourth (Brito) is turning aside, as if in remorse; and we read that "he broke his sword." The divine hand descending towards the "martyred Saint" is significant. The paintings above this represent "St. Catherine," and the instrument of her martyrdom—the wheel; the Emperor Maximinius (in whose reign she perished) being beneath her feet. The other subjects to the left appear to be Christ at the Sepulchre after He had risen, asking Mary, "Why weepest thou?" and Christ convincing "unbelieving Thomas," one hand being turned towards the wound in His side.

The paintings on the Southern side of the arch consist of an angel in the act of weighing a departed soul: the Devil on one side endeavouring to raise the scale by his weight, and the Virgin Mary at the other scale striving to counteract his influence. Above is a female figure in a Gothic niche, piercing a dragon with the point of a cross; the other two figures, with foliage, &c., associated with it are undefinable.

Only two colours appear to have been originally employed in the paintings, viz., a reddish brown and yellow ochre; but evident subsequent repaintings, rudely done, have much disfigured and confused one or two of the original pictures.

One of the most interesting features of the Chancel is the beautiful altar tomb, on the north side. It is of the Perpendicular period, and the sides are richly carved. The slab, which is of Wealden marble, bears the following inscriptions:—

"Here lyeth the body of Anthony Shirley, Esq., 2nd son of William Shirley, Esq., of Wiston, who died December 7th, 1624. Also, his Wife, Barbara, daughter of Sir Thomas Walsingham, Knt., of Sedbury, in Kent, who died 2nd January, 1623." [Followed by 12 Christian names]

Over the tomb is another sepulchral monument, of which the brasses, which were small, are lost. Before defacement by whitewash, there could be seen on it the effigies of a gentleman and lady, kneeling at a desk. Beneath them were seven boys and five girls, having their Christian names over them. The names showed that the two figures at the desk were intended to represent Anthony Shirley and his wife, and their family of twelve children.*

On the South wall of the Chancel is a white marble tablet on black ground to the memory of William Stanford (who purchased the Manor of Preston in 1794), who died in 1841; also to that of his first wife and relict, and to some children who died in infancy; and another beautiful white marble tablet to William Stanford, son of the above, who died in 1853, and on the North wall are other tablets relating to members of the Stanford family. The remains of all the members of the family are deposited in a vault in the Chancel, a prescriptive right being obtained by their possession of the Lay Rectorship of Preston.

---

* The present inscription on the slab is comparatively modern, and doubts have arisen as to those over whose remains the tomb was erected. The Rev. Charles Townsend attributes the tomb to be that of Anthony Shirley; but the learned historian of the Shirley Family (Mr. E. P. Shirley), speaking of this tomb, says it is that of "Edward Elrington, Esq., whose son Richard, by Beatrice, the third daughter of Sir Rauff Shirley, of Wiston, bequeathed his freehold, in Preston, to Marie, his wife, whose first husband was William Shirley, Esq. It is to her that Sir Richard Shirley alludes, when he says that the Manor of Preston 'came to Anthony Shirley'—her second son by her first husband—by the gift and procurement of his mother, she being unwilling to alienate it from the ancient and renowned family of Shirley.'" [Whilst touching upon the Shirley tombs, one cannot help expressing regret that a stone erected to a member of the Shirley family, which was formerly in the chancel, was on the restoration of the Church in 1870 removed outside, and made to do duty as a *pavement slab* of the pathway at the east end of the Church! It might, at least, have been stood in an upright position. As it is, it is cracked across, and the inscription, which is as follows, will probably soon be obliterated:—"HERE LYETH BVRIED THE BODY OF ELIZABETH THE DAVGHTER OF Sr. RICHARD SHIRLEY BARRONETT WHO DEPARTED THIS LIFE THE 23D DAY OF APRILL ANNO DOMINI 1684."]

The old Church contained one stone which readers of ecclesiastical history who visited it were sure to enquire for—that of Francis Cheynell, D.D., the well-known theological controversialist, and the bitter and persistent opponent of Chillingworth. His remains repose beneath a slab, which was in the nave leading to the Chancel; but the stone was so foot-worn that the inscription was illegible, and it would have been deemed a plain slab but that it was known that Cheynell's stone was next his wife's, which was better preserved by being in the then first pew left of the Chancel. The original inscription on Cheynell's stone was—

"Here lyeth the Body of Francis Cheynel, Doctor in Divinity, who deceased May 22, An. Dom. 1665."

The stone over his wife's grave read thus:

"Here lyeth the body of Grace Cheynell, Wife of Francis Cheynell, D.D., who deceased January 15, 1696."

We cannot enter into the details of Cheynell's chequered career or his violent controversies. The virulence he displayed towards Chillingworth's writings was most extraordinary, though singularly enough Cheynell treated the *man* himself, when in evil case, in his last days, with much attention. When he died, however, Cheynell "refused to bury his body, though he thought it fitting to bury his book," which he did by throwing it into his grave, and at the same time uttering a tirade of the most bitter character. Subsequently, when stripped of his possessions and worn out with controversy, Cheynell ended his days in peaceful seclusion at Preston.

Over the doorway of the old Church was a pithy epitaph in Latin (written by the late Rev. Charles Townsend), to the Rev. James Douglas, author of "Nenia Britannica," and at one time Curate of Preston. It has been translated thus:—

"Sacred to the memory to James Douglas, M.A, who in his work called 'Nenia Britannica,' has most learnedly explained all that relates to the burial of the early inhabitants of Britain. He died, November 5, 1819, aged 67. He was a disturber (though not without due reverence) of other men's sepulchres; may he rest quietly in his own."

Mr. Douglas originally entered the military profession, but abandoned it after a few years and took holy orders. His zeal and ability as an archæologist were untiring, as his numerous valuable works testify, and these were only equalled by his skill as an artist, the whole of the fine plates in the "Nenia" having been executed by himself. His fame as an antiquary secured him favour among Church patrons; and in a notice of him, in *Sussex Worthies*, Mr. M. A. Lower says, though not displaying any peculiar fitness for the clerical profession, he received from the Prince of Wales the compliment of being made one of his chaplains; and the fact of the Prince being often at Brighton, doubtless induced Mr. Douglas to accept the curacy of Preston. Mr. Lower adds—" His habits were simple, and his manners unaffected and popular. But genius will have some eccentricities; and he is said to have kept a white pony, which he occasionally ornamented with spots and touches of lemon-colour, brown, and other hues." Mr. Douglas died November 5, 1819, and was buried south of the Church, near the western wall of the churchyard, close to the spot where now lie the remains of one who has so highly extolled his labours, the Rev. Chas. Townsend. The remains of Mr. Douglas's once fine collection of antiquities were purchased of his widow by Sir Richard Colt Hoare, and presented to the Ashmolean Museum at Oxford, where they now are.

The bells of the venerable old Church were till the recent improvements in a very unsatisfactory condition, only one having been for a long time available for duty. Time out of mind, two lay useless on the belfry stage; and so long ago as 1686, when a Commission was appointed to inquire into the state of the bells of the different churches in the County, it was reported of Preston as follows:—"One of ye bells is cracked." The bells were three in number. The first bore the date 1714, the initials of the maker being "S. K." (probably Samuel Knight, who erected the bell in Poynings Church in 1715). The second (the only perfect bell) was without a date, but bore the following inscription:—"Sancte Botolfe Ora Pro Nobis," and had also on it an octagonal medallion and two shields. In a circle within the former were the words, "Ihu merci ladi help;" one shield having in its centre a pair of cross-keys, each angle being fitted respectively with a dolphin, a wheat-sheaf, a bell, and a ewer; the other, the monogram "T. M.," doubtless Thomas Meares, who, between 1791 and 1804, "cast 16 bells in Sussex." The third bell was inscribed "Gloria Deo in excelsis." 1631. "B. E." The initials being those, probably, of Bryan Eldridge, who put up several bells in Sussex about that period.

The parish registers appear to have been carefully looked after. They go back as far as the middle of the 16th century. In the churchyard are several interesting memorials: some of local celebrities, and others of ancient date.

A year or two since, on the retirement of the Rev. Walter Kelly, Vicar of Preston-cum-Hove, the respective parishes were ecclesiastically divided: the Rev. Thomas Peacey being appointed to the Vicarage of Hove, and the Rev. A. D. Freeman, for several years Curate of Preston, to the Vicarage of that parish.

In 1876 some interesting archæological discoveries were made at Preston. On digging out the ground for the houses of the Springfield-road, about 50 yards east of the London-road, the workmen came upon what were apparently rudely-formed graves, with bones, fragments of pottery, &c.; a coin was also found, which would seem to fix their date at about A.D. 160. Subsequently, at a short distance from the above, the site of a Roman villa was discovered; with hundreds of small blocks of various colours (indicating that some of the floors were laid with mosaic work), bronze and copper coins, jars, &c., affording indubitable evidence of occupation. Some of the discoveries have found a place in the local Museum; but the site of the ancient villa itself is now covered by modern erections.

[Preston "up to date" affords abundant evidence of prosperity, and especially as an attractive residential district. Unquestionably an important factor in its prosperity has been its association with the Municipality of Brighton. Previously Preston had lacked vitality, but during the past 20 years or so the township may be said to have advanced by "leaps and bounds." The population has increased more than six times since 1871; and the number of houses also in a similar proportion. These latter now cover a wide area, and stretch in some directions to distances that some years ago would have been deemed almost inconceivable. Beautiful villas now run along each side of Preston-road far into Withdean; houses are gradually extending to the east of Preston Park on towards Hollingbury; and there are strong indications that the Tivoli Estate, embracing the area from the back of the Tivoli Gardens right up to the Dyke-road, will be soon wholly given over to "bricks and mortar." In one respect Preston has of late been showing a most commendable vitality, namely, in "mending its ways." The broad and pleasant road to Brighton—from the Vicarage to the Stanford Avenue—is a marked and welcome change from the old order of things. The old hostelries—the historic "Crown and Anchor," dating back to 1711, and the "Black Lion"—have been rebuilt and set back in the line with the improved road, and alterations with a similar view have been made in adjacent properties, notably, in the Vicarage garden enclosure, which formerly impinged considerably on the thoroughfare. Preston Drove has also been opened out and otherwise improved; and the same may be said of the Ditchling Road and those roads in the region of Hollingdean, where, some day, the long-expected Abattoir is to be erected. On the western side of the main line of Railway, near the Preston viaduct, road improvements have also been made, not the least important being the formation of a new Drive past the Tivoli and the residence of the late Lady Ogle, up to the Dyke Road, which will assuredly prove of much advantage to the district in the near future. But the most important event in the later history of Preston, and equally so in the history of Brighton generally, has been the purchase by the Brighton Corporation, in 1883, of the sixty acres of meadow land now known as Preston Park (why should it not have been called *Brighton* Park?). The proposal that the site should be purchased from Mr. Vere Fane Benett-Stanford, for the purpose of a public recreation ground, came before the Brighton Town Council in 1876; but on the 6th of September in that year the proposal was rejected by 19 votes to 12,—the majority, actuated by mistaken motives of economy, being of opinion that Brighton ought to content itself with its magnificent marine front and its breezy downs; that young Brighton's aspirations in the way of a cricket field and playground ought not to soar beyond the serviceable but ragged Level; and that pure air was a minor matter compared with low rates. And not only so, but there were not a few sagacious ones who were satisfied that in wet weather the proposed Park would be little better than a swamp. So the "land of promise" was left to the undisputed possession of the cows; and the buttercups and daisies that have since given delight to hundreds of children remained for another seven years hidden away behind the bare wall that separated the meadows from the Preston-road. Events have shown that, although an undoubted mistake was made, it was not an irreparable mistake. It was, however, a very costly one. In 1876 the land could have been purchased for something under £30,000 By the 5th of April, 1882, when the Council, this time by 25 votes to 20, agreed to the purchase of the site, its market value had risen from £30,000 to £50 000. Thus, the delay cost the town £20,000. Still, by a rare stroke of fortune, the Park was, in a sense, destined never to cost the ratepayers a farthing. About the time that the purchase was agreed upon, the Council received the munificent bequest of no less than £70,000 from the late Mr. William Edmond Davies, whose transactions on the Race Course had won him the title of "The Leviathan of the Turf." The sum which Mr. Davies left to the town in which his closing days were spent more than sufficed to cover the cost of the purchase and the laying out of the ground. It was not until the September of 1883 that the purchase of the Park, together with what is popularly known as the "Rookery," on the opposite side of Preston-road, was completed; and no sooner was this effected than the ground was opened to the public; the date of this informal opening being Monday, September 10th, 1883. By that time the wall enclosing the land had been partly removed, and the foundations were being laid for the iron fence, which was set back inside the line of trees that now so pleasantly rise from the outer pathway. The ceremonial opening it was resolved to defer until the laying out of the ground had been practically completed. This took some considerable time. At length, when the carriage drives and intersecting footpaths had been made, and the flower-beds had been formed and trees had been planted, and when, with the aid of a belt of trees already in existence there, the winding rustic avenue had been constructed, on the east side of the Park, and the "rotten row" for the equestrians had been formed close by, a little further to the east,—when all this had been done, and the Park had been entirely enclosed with an iron fence, then Alderman A. H. Cox, on the last day of his second year of Mayoralty, namely, on the 8th November, 1884, gave the Park a ceremonial opening. The chief feature of the ceremony, which took place on a Saturday, in brilliant weather, and in the presence of from 12,000 to 15,000 spectators, was a procession round the Park. The cavalcade, which was formed in Stanford-avenue, was headed by a carriage containing the Mayor and Mayoress (Alderman and Mrs. Cox), Alderman E. Martin (Chairman of the Recreation Grounds Committee), and the Town Clerk (Mr. F. J. Tillstone). Afterwards came the members of the Corporation, the Naval Artillery Volunteers, the Yeomanry Cavalry, the 1st Sussex Artillery, and the 1st Sussex Rifles, the last two Corps being accompanied by their Bands, the Police Fire Brigade and the Brighton Volunteer and the Railway Brigades, residents of the town in private carriages, and lastly the members of the various cycling clubs. After a tour of the

Park had been made, the Mayoress, who had some time previously planted a tree given by the Right Honourable W. E. Gladstone, performed, with exemplary freedom from political bias, a similar operation in respect of a chestnut tree that had been obtained from the Marquis of Salisbury. To enable her to perform this service, the Mayoress was presented with a silver spade, with polished oak handle. Then a silver key was handed to the Mayor, who, after he had been invested with this symbol of authority, declared the Park to be duly opened for the benefit of the public for ever. The declaration was received with cheers, and, a little later, the performance of the National Anthem by the combined Bands denoted that the ceremony was at an end. At the centre of the by no means imposing entrance at the southern end of the Park a couple of granite tablets were subsequently erected, that on the inside, facing northwards, bearing an inscription commemorating the opening, and that on the outside, facing southwards, chronicling the "munificent bequest by William Edmond Davies of Seventy Thousand Pounds to the Corporation of Brighton, a portion of which sum was applied towards the purchase and laying out of this Park." From this time the Park has enjoyed unquestionable popularity amongst persons of all ages and all classes. For the children it has been a happy playground, and it has proved scarcely less attractive to adults. Sweethearts have been by no means insensible to a certain romantic charm about the shady avenue; its roads have been the favourite haunt of cyclists; and as a carriage drive it has provided a pleasant variation from the marine front. Military Tournaments for the Charities, Police and School Sports, and Fire Brigade and other Fêtes have in due course been witnessed there; the Volunteer Corps have found in it a splendid drill ground; the Officers of the Cavalry Regiments stationed at Brighton have resorted there for the purpose of polo practice, bringing with them their Band, and thus providing many an afternoon's agreeable entertainment for the inhabitants; whilst on Wednesdays and Saturdays throughout the winter months football teams have waged war there under the eyes of hundreds of interested spectators. For cricketers and cyclists the best of provision was made in 1887; a large tract of ground in the northeastern part of the Park being levelled for the purpose of a cricket field, surrounded with a cinder track for bicycle racing. This part of the Park was opened with a match between the Sheffield Park Eleven and the Brighton Brunswick Club, on the 12th May, 1887. By way of an opening ceremony, Mrs. Reeves (Mayoress), Mrs. H. Davey, Mrs. Saunders, and Mrs. Wood hauled up a flag on a staff given by Mr. Councillor J. J. G. Saunders, one of Brighton's staunchest patrons of athletics and sports of all kinds; and, to further signalise the event, Mr. Councillor E. Booth, an ardent cricketer, entertained a large company at luncheon in the newly-erected pavilion. The County Cricket matches have continued to be played on the ground of the Sussex County Club at Hove; but the Park ground has been a favoured meeting place for the various Brighton Cricketing Clubs; whilst the cycling track has been used over and over again for race meetings, mostly on Bank Holidays. The ground gives accommodation for several thousand spectators; facilities for a good view being furnished by the formation on the eastern side of banks and terraces which add much to the picturesqueness. Subsequent to that date, a refreshment chalet of ornamental design was erected under a knoll of trees on the slope rising from that part of the ground always selected for the purposes of sports and other exhibitions. At the top of the slope, in a more central position, stands a clock tower, erected at the expense of Mr. Councillor Edward White. The first stone was laid by the donor on August 13th, 1891, when he was presented by the Mayor (Alderman S. H. Soper), on behalf of the Corporation, with a silver trowel and mallet. Mr. White took the opportunity of acknowledging the interest shown in the matter by Mr. Councillor W. Marchant, through whom the offer of the clock tower was made to the Town Council. The opening ceremony is to be performed by the Mayor (Alderman Dr. Ewart) on the 17th of June, 1892. The clock tower, a handsomely designed structure of red brick, enriched with terra cotta of two shades, forms a welcome feature in the Park, as an object alike of ornament and utility. It also serves as a monitor, for, in addition to the commemorative tablets, is one bearing the following verse :—

> "Here I stand, with all my might
> To tell the hours by day and night.
> Therefore, example take by me,
> And serve thy God as I serve thee."

Mr. White's example is one that may well be imitated by other townsmen. A gateway worthy of the Park would, for instance, be an acquisition. Of this donors may rest assured, that anything that tends to the beautification of the place would be cordially welcomed; for, although opinion on the subject was at the outset divided, it would probably be difficult now to find a person in Preston or Brighton who does not regard Preston Park as one of the town's most treasured possessions.]

At this point we will bid our readers "farewell," and close "A PEEP INTO THE PAST."

ADDENDA.

A Relic of Captain Nicholas Tettersall.

The following Indenture, relating to Captain Tettersall, who was associated with the escape of Charles II., has an exceptional interest. It has been transcribed for us by Mr. F. W. Madden, Librarian to the Brighton Public Library, from the original which has been recently presented to that Institution by Mr. Somers Clarke :—

This Indenture made the fowerteenth day of November in ye yeare of the reign of our Sovereign Lord Charles the second by the grace of god King of England, Scottland, France and Ireland, Defender of the Faith &c. the twenty fowerth* & in ye yeare of our Lord Christ one thousand six hundred seventy and two Betweene Nicholas Tettersall of Brighthelmstone in ye County of Sussex Esquire of the one part and John Geering of the same place and County Joyner on ye other part Wittnessith That whereas the sd Nicholas Tettersall in the day of the date hereof lawfully seised in his Demeanes as of ffee of &c in one parcell of Land with a house there upon builded situate lying and being in the street called ye Hempshares of Brighton aforesd conteyning in Length eighteene Paule and in breadth six Paule and lyeth to ye house and Lands which was formerly Bakers on the South to the house and garden now in the tenure and occupation of Benjamin Martens on the North to ye King's highway on ye west & to ye Land of Charles Humby on the East Now ye Sd Nicholas Tettersall for and in consideration of the Fatherly loue and affection which hee beareth unto Susanna Geering wife of the sd John Geering ye naturall and only Daughter of him ye sd Nicholas Tettersall and for divers other good causes and considerations him heerunto especially moueing hath given, granted aliened enfeoffed and confirmed & by the sd presents doth fully, cleerly & absolutely give grant alien enfeoffe & confirme unto ye sd Susanna Geering her heires & Assignes for ever all ye cottage formerly a stable adjoyning unto ye Messuage of Benjamin Martens aforesaid together with a parcell of Land lyeing to ye eastward of the sd cottage conteyning in length from east to west an hundred & nineteen feet & in breadth from North to South thirty ffeet with all & singular ye priviledges & appurtenances thereunto belonging That is to say with free ingress egress & regress to in & from the well lately built and belonging to ye sd ffreehold paying therefore an equall proportion towards ye repaires thereof as alsoe free liberty of ingress egress and regress betweene ye sd cottage & the house comonly called ye Old Shipp for ye convenience of bringing & laying in Timber & other necessaryes on ye ground afore sd, To Have & to Hold the sd cottage and parcell of ground with all and singular ye premisses with theire & every of theire priviledges & appurtenances before by these presents granted & confirmed or meant mentioned or intended to bee granted & confirmed & every part and parcell thereof unto ye sd Susanna Geering her heires and assignes to ye only use & behoofe of her ye sd Susanna Geering & her heires for ever. And ye sd Nicholas Tettersall for himselfe his heires Executos & Administratos and for every of them doth covenant promise & grant to and with ye sd John Geering his heires Executos Administratos & Assignes & to & with every of them by these presents That shee the sd Susanna Geering her heires & Assignes shall & may from henceforth for ever peaceably & quietly have hold use occupy possess & enjoy the sd cottage and parcell of land and all other ye premisses aboue by these presents mentioned to bee given granted & confirmed and every part & parcell hereof & ye rents issues and proffitts thereof shall and may receive and take without Lett interruption or contradiction of the sd Nicholas Tettersall his heires or Assignes or of any other person or persons claiming from by or under him them or

---

* Reckoned from 1649, the date of the death of Charles I.

any of them or by his or theire meanes rights title consent privity or procurement In Witness whereof the parties to these presents interchangably have putt theire hands & seales The day & yeare first above written.

                                  NICHOLAS X TETTERSALL
Signed Sealed & Delivered   his   mark
  in presence of   (Seal missing.)
    EDW. LOWE *
    ROBERT R SAUNDERS
       his   mark /

A Relic of Charles Mathews.

The following "relic" of the elder Mathews, which it was intended to incorporate with the associations of "The Old Ship" was by accident omitted therefrom. It was communicated to the Author by the late Mr. T. C. Noble, author of *Memorials of Temple Bar* and other valuable historical works :—

A very interesting letter has recently come into my hands, which, by some of the "ancient" inhabitants of Brighton, may be considered particularly curious, especially if they ever had the friendship or reminiscences of the well-known comedian, Charles Mathews. The letter is dated November 25, 1832 ; is in the writing of, and signed by, the world-famous George Robins, and is directed to "Charles Mathews, Esq., Old Ship, Brighton," for which the receiver had to pay a postage of 8d. (now it would be 1d.) ! I do not intend to give a full transcript of the contents, which relates to money matters, but a few quotations from it will be of interest :—

"MY DEAR FELLOW,—When you think of your misfortunes turn for a moment to the other part of the picture : in the little million of actors during your long career you stand alone. Is there nothing for self-congratulation in this? The Theatres are deserted but the Adelphi. Is this nothing? Actors put on half-pay and with a prospect of absolutely nothing. Is not this a source from which, as opposed to yourself, you take (or ought to do) great comfort? I consider you a fortunate man, and I will illustrate my arguments by one fact worth 100 assertions—there is nothing like you either as regards talent or success. And now adieu to my sermon. . . . . Turn over a new leaf, my dear boy. You are yourself a host - the most popular man in the world, with a charming wife and the best son in Europe. What more is needed ? Shall I tell you ? Do you give it up ? A little anti-cholera in the shape of old Strangard's best port, not too much, but enough to enable you to distinguish and value your good fortune (in spite of a little blot or two) as opposed to that of all your brethren."

In the top corner of the letter, the writer adds, "Don't burn this, but read it every Sunday morning, when you are not up in time to go to Church or have a sudden fit of the spleen." The "elder" Mathews was born in 1776, and died on his birthday, the 28th June, 1835. He was twice married, but had only one son. After leaving Merchant Taylors' School, he turned actor, and, during the last sixteen years of his life, his "Mathews at Home" was one of the sights of "the town." The son, Charles James, was born at Liverpool on the 26th December, 1803. He, too, was educated at Merchant Taylors' School and at Clapham, and subsequently became the pupil of Pugin and Nash, the two eminent architects of their day. He, however, turned actor and wrote plays, became manager of the Adelphi, of Covent Garden, and the Lyceum successively. In 1838 he married one of the most popular actresses of the time—Madame Vestris, who was the daughter of the famous engraver, Bartolozzi. She was born in 1797, and was first married at the age of sixteen to Armand Vestris, the ballet master of the King's Theatre, Haymarket, who died in 1825. She died at Fulham the 8th August, 1856, and her husband, "Charles Mathews the younger," died at Manchester the 23rd June, 1878.

---

* Vicar of Brighton at the period referred to.

Index of Contents.

ABDUCTION and Pursuit of Miss Max, an Irish Heiress, in 1777, 119.

ABORIGINES—Opposition of the Fishermen to the Enclosure of the Steine, in 1822, 144—Fight between "Landsmen" and "Fishermen" on the Opening of the Junction-road, 1827, 175—"Betty Mash" and the Stocks, 185- Fisherwomen's "Toy Fair,' 191—Custom of "Strewing" with Sugar Plums and Wheat, 196—Quaint Costume of the Ancient Fishermen, 199—Ancient Custom of "Crying Down," 201.

ACCIDENTS—"Single-speech" Hamilton's, 161 ; Coach, 255, 260-1-2—First Railway, 270.

ALBION ROOMS - Literary and Scientific Institution, 156—Romantic history of one of the frequenters of, 156.

ALMS HOUSES—Foundation of Howell's, 20.

AMUSEMENTS—Fashionable and Popular, 25 to 106—Ball at the "Castle," 1758, 28—Card Playing Fashionable in 1788, 32—Theatrical Entertainments, 40 to 66—Public Breakfasts at the Promenade Grove, 68—Concerts at the Promenade Grove, 70—Fireworks at the Promenade Grove, 72—Loyal Festivities, Sports, &c., 81—Pugilism patronised by Royalty, 83—Celebration of Admiral Boscawen's Victory in 1758, 81—Celebration of the Prince of Wales' Birthday, 1789, 82 ; and of the Prince of Wales' and Duke of York's Birthdays in 1790, 82—Celebration of the Ratification of Peace in 1801, 84—Foot Racing, 84, 85, 86—Horse Racing from 1770 to 1850, 86 to 92—Pony Racing at the Promenade Grove, 74—Pugilism in 1788, 91 ; in 1811, 204—White Hawk Fair, 92—Cricket, 93 to 102—Bowling Green on the Steine in 1665, 93 - Women Cricket Players in 1747, 94—First mention of Brighton Cricketers in 1758, 94—Rules of the present game of Cricket framed in 1774, 95—Cricket Ground at Ireland's Gardens opened 1823, 102—Cock-Fighting in 1746, 102—Cock-Throwing, 105—Bull-Baiting in 1758, 105—Skating on the Steine, 111—Sea Bathing a fashionable amusement in 1769, 111—Hind, Stag, and Fox Hunting, 112, 115—Ladies at Billiards in 1769, 114—Boating and Bathing in 1769, 115—Raffling at Libraries and Shops, and "Pam" or "Loo" at the Libraries, in 1777, 118—Gambling in 1779, 119—Whimsical Races in 1786 and 1805, 127, 141—Practical Joking in 1787, 128—Mr. Barrymore's Equestrian Freak, 129—Curious Diversions of the Prince's Associates in 1805, 141—Donkey Riding in early part of century, 142—Trinket Auctions, 1806, 143 -"Pam" in 1810, 143—Toy Fair under the Cliff, 191—First Fancy Fair in aid of the Sussex County Hospital, 1827, 190—Cock-Fighting, 201, 211, 221—Prize-Fighting in 1788, 91 ; in 1811, 204—Tea Gardens at Preston, 115, 404—The "Tivoli" Gardens, Preston, 408 - Sports and Fêtes at Preston Park, 417.

ANNE OF CLEVES—Her connection with Preston Manor, 400.

ANTIQUITIES—Celtic, discovered at Hove in 1856, 378, 379—Mural Paintings at Preston Church, 411—The Collection of the Rev. James Douglas, of Preston, presented to the Ashmolean Museum, Oxford, 414—Romano-British Discoveries at Preston, 414.

ANTHEUM—Erection and Fall of the, in 1833, 387, 388.

ARCHÆOLOGICAL DISCOVERIES—At Hove, 378, 379 ; at Preston, 414.

ASSEMBLIES, BALLS, &c.—Recognised as Fashionable Institutions in 1758, 28, 29—Announcement of, 29—Race Ball, 1807, 34—Birthday Ball of the Prince of Wales, 1807, 34—Dancing on the Green at the Promenade Grove, 1794, 71—The first Race Ball, 90—Ball in honour of the Prince and Princess of Wales in 1796, 136—First Tradesmen's Ball, in 1823, 149—"Dejeune" at Preston Shaw, 406.

INDEX.

ASSEMBLY ROOMS—At "The Castle," built 1761, 27—At "The Old Ship," erected 1767, 27—Mr. Noel's Concert at "The Castle" in 1768, 27 - Public Ball at "The Castle," August 19th, 1758, 28—Closing of "The Castle" Rooms in August, 1816, 36—Raggett's Subscription House, 110.

AUSTIN, W.—Landscape Painter in 1800, Memoir of, 8.

AWSITER, DR.—His remarks concerning Sea Bathing and drinking Sea Water, 224 to 226.

BADDELEY, Mrs.—Actress; Notice of, 46.

BAKER--First Librarian on the Steine, in 1760, 112, 113.

BANKS in 1800, 7—Robbery of Brighton Union Bank Notes, 253—The first Brighton Bank opened, 1787, 313—Union Bank opened 1805, 317—Savings' Bank in Prince's-place, in 1850, 370.

BARRYMORE, EARL—Anecdotes of, 48, 129—His death in 1793, 131—His Brother's Equestrian Freak, 129.

BASEVI, G.—Architect of Hove Parish Church, 389—Death of, in 1845, 389.

BATCHELOR, JAMES—A Pioneer of the Coaching Era, 242, 243—Batchelor's "Hearse," 245.

BATHING, SEA—223 to 239—A Fashionable Amusement in 1769, 111—Dr. Russell's Recommendation of Brighton, 221—Dr. Awsiter on, 224—Description of Bathing Machines in 1770, 225 - Bathing Stations, 227—Bathing Women, 228—Ladies Bathing, 228—Demand for Machines in 1778, 228—Martha Gunn and the "Opposition," 229—Mrs. Thrale's love of, 231—Miss Burney's Early Bathing, 231—The Use of Queues, 231—The Duke of Cumberland's dog "Turk," 231—"Smoaker" Miles and the Prince of Wales, 233—List of Bathers in 1790, 233—Smoaker II., 234—"Doctor" Tattersall, 235—Mrs. Cobby and the "Three Black Crows," 235—Anecdotes of Martha Gunn, 236—Nuisance of open Bathing, 1806, 237—Baths in Brighton, Past and Present, 237—Visit of Brighton Bathers to the Great Exhibition in 1851, 238.

BATHS—Erection of, in Pool-valley, 1769, 226—Rates of Subscription, 237—Williams's Baths, opened 1803, and other Private Baths subsequently, 237—Sake Deen Mahomed's Baths, 175 - Turkish Bath, erected in 1868, 237, 369—Baths at Hove, 396.

BATTERY—The Old, formed in 1761, 111—Undermined by the Sea in 1786, 111—The West Battery, removed in 1858, 369.

BEAUCLERK, LORD F.—His skill at Cricket, 99.

BEGGARS—Punishment of, 10.

BELLS—Of old St. Nicholas, cast in 1777, 207—Bell Ringers' Society, 206—"Volunteer" Ringer, 207—Bells of Preston Church, 414—Chimes and Carillons at Hove Town Hall, 395.

BILLIARDS—Lady Players in 1769, 114—Mr. Edwin Kentfield's skill at, 165.

BLIND ASYLUM—Erected about 1850, 370.

BLOCK HOUSE—Description of the, 173.

BOATS, Pleasure—Boating in 1769, 115.

BOTTING, JEMMY—Hangman, Anecdote of, 203.

BOUNDARIES—Of Brighton, in 1800, 11 to 13.

BREWERIES—The Black Lion, 186—Wichelo's, 197—Lucas's, 198—Vallance, Catt, and Co.'s, 200.

BRIGGS AND KNOWLES, Messrs.—Fatal accident to, in 1822, 178.

BRIGHTON BEAUTIES in 1785, 121.

BROADBRIDGE, "JIM"—A famous Cricketer; his *début*, 101, 102.

BRUNTON, MISS—Daughter of Manager of Brighton Theatre, married to Earl Craven in 1807, 64.

BULL-BAITING—At Rottingdean, in 1758, 105—At Preston, in 1759, 106—At Lewes, in 1781, 106—At Hove, 106 and 378.

BURKE, EDMUND—In Brighton, 54.

CAMPS, MILITARY—Formed near the Steine, at Brighton, in 1792, 134—Formed at Hove, in 1793, 384.

INDEX.   423

CAPPS, Mr. T. W., and "The Age," 258.

CAROLINE, QUEEN—Her Trial, reported by Mail Coachmen, 259—Princess Caroline at "Single-speech" Hamilton's, 162.

CARRIERS—Thomas Smith and Mary Smith, of Lewes, in 1746, 242—Difficulty of Travelling in Sussex, 1751, 242.

CARVER, DERRICK—Founder of Black Lion Brewery; Martyrdom of, 186.

CATLIN, "BILLY"—Shooting Exploit of, 212.

CEMETERIES—Extra-Mural, laid out in 1850, 366—Hove Cemetery made at a cost of £17,000, and opened in 1882, 395.

CHANTREY—The Sculptor; his loss on Statue of George IV., 221.

CHEYNELL, FRANCIS, D.D.—Notice of, 413.

CHURCH HISTORY—Of Hove, 381 to 384.

CHURCHES—(See "Religious Edifices.")

CLERICETTI, COUNT—His bequest to the Museum and Library, 1888, 159.

CLEVES, ANNE OF—her connection with the Manor of Preston, 400.

CLIFTONVILLE—commenced in 1851, 390.

CLUBS—Raggett's Subscription House, 1792, high play indulged in, 133—Raggett's succeeded by Bedford's Club House, about 1815, 133 - Catch and Glee Club held at the "Golden Cross,' 221.

COACHES—"Machines," introduced prior to 1750, 113—Upwards of 40 in 1821, 149—"The New Ship," the Original Coach Office in 1741, 192—The "Coaching Era," 241 to 264—The Enervating Effect of, 242 - Difficulty of Travelling, 242—Batchelor's Lewes Coach, 243—Tubb's "Flying Machine," 243 - Batchelor's "Hearse," 245—Tubb and Davis in 1767 introduced "Flys" to and from London daily, 245—The "Stage Waggon," in 1777, 246—Mail Coaches started 1791, 247—Number of Coaches in 1788, 247—Packets in Connection with Coaches in 1788, 247; in 1814, 256—Coach Roads in 1790, 248—Description of a Coach Ride to London in 1790, 248 to 250—Coaches in 1800-1802, 250, 251—Ride from London to Brighton in 1801, 251—Mr. Hine, sen., a famous Brighton Coachman, 251—Profits in 1808, 252—Mail Coaches Established in 1810, 253—Coach Robberies, 1812 and 1821, 253, 254—Fast Coaches started in 1813, 254—Fast Travelling in 1830, 1834, 255—Coach "Racing" Accidents, 255, 260, 261, 262—Number of Coaches in 1822 and 1839, 257—Anecdote of the "Preserver" Coach, 257—Returns of Coaching Business in 1828, 256—Mr. T. W. Capps—his "Model" Coach "The Age," 258 Sir St. Vincent Cotton, Anecdote of his love of Gambling, 258—Description of the Old Blue Coach Office, 259—Castle-square in the Coaching Era, 259—Queen Caroline's Trial Reported by the Mail Coachmen, 259—List of Famous Coachmen, 260—End of the Coaching Era in 1841, 262, 263—Revival of Coaching in 1866, 264—Mail Coaches Introduced in 1807, 293—First Coach Office Opened in North-street, 1794, 313—The "Criterion" brings down King's Speech, in 1834, in 3 hours and 40 minutes, 255—Remarkable Coaching performance by James Selby, in 1888, 255, 256.

COBB, MR.—Proprietor of the Brighton Theatre in 1793, 55.

COBBY, EDWARD—Directory for 1800 (see commencement of work), Compiler of Brighton Directory, 3, 16.

COCK-FIGHTING—Matches in 1746 and 1772, 102—In 1776 and 1780, 104—Subsequent matches, 104—Cock-throwing, 105—Cock-fighting at "The Half Moon" in 1786, 201—At "The White Lion," 203—At "The Coach and Horses" in 1785, 211—At "The King's Arms" in 1811, 221.

CODLIN, CAPTAIN, and "The Adventure," 384.

CONCERT HALL, West-street—Destroyed by Fire, 1882, 366.

CONCERTS—Summer; held at the Promenade Grove, 1794, 70—Oratorios and Concerts at the Chapel Royal, 346, 350.

COPPIN—A "Character" at Hove, in 1830, 390.

COTTON, SIR ST. VINCENT—Anecdote of, 258.

COUNTY COURT—In North-street in 1850—370.

COURT-MARTIAL—Upon Oxford Militiamen in 1795, 189; at "The Castle" in 1810, 220.

COURTS, YARDS, &C.—Peculiarity of Building, and great number of, 14—Description of Saunders's Buildings, 14.

CRANE, Mr. E. and MISS AGNES—Their aid to Museum, 159.

CRICKET—93 to 102—Women Players, 94—Introduction of the Third Stump in 1775, 95—First mention of Brighton Players in 1758, 94—The present Rules, framed in 1774, 95—The Prince's Cricket Ground, formed in 1791, 96—The "White Lion," a Cricketers' House in 1765, 96—The Duke of York's Match in 1789, 96—Hammond first played in Brighton, 96—First Match between Sussex and Kent in 1790, 96—Match between Brighton and Mary-le-bone, in 1792, lasting four days, 97 - Lord Frederick Beauclerk's splendid batting, 99— G. Osbaldeston's "Play," 100—"Jim" Broadbridge's *début*, in 1815, 101— Match for 1,000 Guineas on the Level, 101 - Last Grand Match on the Level, in 1822, 101—Ireland's Ground, opened in 1823, 102—Brunswick Cricket Ground, closing of, 390—The Sussex County Ground, opened in 1872, 390 - Preston Park Cricket Ground, 417.

CROUCH, MRS. ANNA MARIA—Vocalist ; Memoir of, 52.

CUSTOMS—Ancient, 196, 201.

DAIRY, THE PRINCE'S—Reputed Residence of Miss Howard, 407—The Prince of Wales's treatment of a youthful Spy, 407—The Old Indian at, 407 - Its removal in 1871, 408.

DAVIDSON, DR.—Memorial to, 159—His Fossils of the Paris Basin, 159.

DAVIES, WILLIAM EDMOND—His bequest of £70,000 to the town, 416.

DIARY OF ELIZABETH GROVER - 332, 333.

DIDDEAR, MR. - Lessee of the Theatre in 1796, 58.

DELAWARR, EARL—Fête on Coming of Age, 219.

D'EON—Appearance of the "Chevalier" or "Mdlle." at the Brighton Theatre, in 1793, 54.

DIRECTORY, COBBY'S, FOR 1800—(see commencement of work) the Brighthelmston Directory for 1800, 3 to 22.

DOUGLAS, REV. J. (of Preston), 413.

DUELLING—Dr. Kipping's duel, 87.

DUNVAN—Author of " History of Lewes and Brighton," his opinion of Brighton in 1795, 4.

ELD, LIEUT.-COLONEL, Last " M.C." of Brighton—Account of, 37 to 39.

ELECTIONS—Anecdotes of, 177—Consolation Dinner to Colonel Warden Sergison, 1807, 219.

EMERY - Actor ; Memoir of, 56.

ENCLOSURES, NORTH STEINE—Formed in 1817, 215.

ESPLANADE—Improved in 1858, 369.

FAIRS—White-Hawk Fair, 92—Fishermen's Toy Fair, 191—First Fancy Fair in aid of the Sussex County Hospital, 1827, 190—Highest Prosperity of Brighton Fair, 1825 to 1835, 191.

FASHIONS The Gipsey Hat, 1791-93, 132—Ladies' Tails, 1794, 133—The Theft of a "Tail," 133—The Disuse of Queues in 1791-93, 132—Costumes for Ladies and Gentlemen in 1807, 140—Queues and Bathing, 231.

FISHERMEN—(See Aborigines).

FITZHERBERT, MRS.—Description of her Mansion, 165 - Her Distinguished Visitors, 166—The Will of, 167—The later Occupiers of her Mansion, 110 and 167.

FLEET, MR. WILLIAM—See "A Pioneer in Local Journalism," with obituary notices from *Brighton Herald, Brighton Examiner,* and *West Sussex Gazette,* 355 to 363.

FLOGGING (MILITARY)—190, 220.

FLOODS, POOL VALLEY—135, 183.

FONTENELLE, MISS—Actress; Notice of, 52.

FORTH, W.—The Second "M.C." of Brighton, appointed 1808, 34- Resignation of, in 1828, 37.

FOX, GEORGE—(Quaker) in Sussex, 336.

FREE LIBRARY—Donors to, 158—Bequest by Count Clericetti in 1888, 159.

FREEMASONS—First Lodge opened in Brighton at "The White Horse," in 1789, 177.

FRIENDS' MEETING HOUSE—329 to 334—Memoirs of the Sussex Friends, 335—Prince of Wales and the, 334.

FULLER, JOHN—In the Pillory, 214.

GAMBLING, by Ladies of Fashion, 119.

GARDENS, PUBLIC—The Promenade Grove, opened 1793, 67, 313—Balloon Ascent at the Promenade Grove, 1802, 77—Ireland's Gardens, opened 1823, 102—Tea Gardens at Preston in 1769, 115, 404 The "Tivoli" Gardens at Preston, 408.

GAS · The Steine lit by Gas in 1824, 142.

GREGORY, RICHARD LEMMON—"Dick Gregory," a noted Local "Character," Memoir of, 137.

GROVER, ELIZABETH—Diary of, 332, 333.

GUNN, MARTHA—Mistress of the Bath, in 1750, 228—Opposition to, 229 - Anecdotes of, 236.

HACK, Mr. D. - Donation of £1,000 to the Victoria Lending Library, 159.

HAMILTON, W. GERALD—"Single-Speech" Hamilton, 160—His House on the Steine (description of), 160, 164.

HANGER, MAJOR - Notice of his "field-day" on the Steine, 127.

HARRICKS, DUDLEY—An eccentric Tradesman; Notice of, 322, 323.

HAYMES, MR.—Actor; Failure at the Theatre in 1810, 64.

HEAVISIDE, CAPTAIN—Anecdote of; Trial, "Heaviside v. Lardner," 378.

HERALD, BRIGHTON—Founded in 1806, 355—Memoir of Mr. W. Fleet, 355 to 363—Stamp Duties, 356—Early Information of Important Events obtained by the, 357—Eminent Liberals connected with the, 358—Prosecution of the Press by "The Bridge-street Gang," 362—Mr. Fleet Imprisoned for Expressing his Political Opinions, 362—Mr. J. G. Bishop, the present Proprietor, celebrates his Jubilee in 1889, 360.

HINE, MR., Senior—A Famous Brighton Coachman, 251, 252.

HILTON, JOHN—His trading enterprise, 14.

HOAX—The "Hunter Hoax" in 1810, 210—Local Hoaxes in 1804 and 1810, 210 and 211.

HOLMAN, MR.—Actor; the rival of John Kemble, Memoir of, 56.

HOSPITALS—The Sussex County, Foundation Stone laid 1826, 190—Fancy Fair in aid of the Sussex County Hospital in 1827, 190 - Hospital for Infectious Diseases opened at Hove in 1886, 396.

HOTELS—Assemblies at "The Old Ship' and "Castle,' 26—"The York," formerly the Manor House, 147—Opened in 1819, 148—History of "The York," 147 - "The Albion," erected on the site of "Russell House," opened in 1826, 154—The "White Horse," 177- "The New Inn," subsequently "The Clarence," 209 - The "Gun' (Harrison's), 174 - Markwell's Royal Hotel, erected on site of Mahomed's Baths, 175.

HOUSES—Number of, in Brighton, from 1761 to 1879, 5—Assessment of value from 1784 to 1891, 5—In Hove, 392—In Preston, 409.

HOUSES, NOTABLE—Curious old houses, 3, 4—Mrs. Thrale's house in West-street, 7—Rock House, the first house erected on the East Cliff, 13—"Blue and Buff" Houses on the Steine, 13, 110—Neville House, removal of, 13, 14—The "Manor House" on the Steine, 110, 147—"Grove House,' the Residence of the Duke of Marlborough, 110—"Single-speech" Hamilton's and Lady Anne Murray's 160—Mrs. Fitzherbert's House on the Steine, 110, 165—Mr. Kemp's House, 126—On the Steine, 147 to 168—Russell House, 110, 150—Marlborough House, 160—Old House in Black Lion-street, 185—Old Houses in North-street, 324 - The Old "London Tavern," 325—The "Temple," built by Thos. Read Kemp, Esq., 367.

HOVE—An Outlying Village in 1800, 5—Bull-baiting at, 106—History of, 377 to 397—Stationary Character of Old Hove, Smuggling at, 378—Trial, Heaviside v. Lardner, 378—Lords of the Manor, 379, 380—Celtic Relics Discovered in 1856, 378—Church of St. Peter, 380 - List of Vicars from 1538, 381—Camps formed at, 384—Scuttling of the "Adventure" off, in 1802, 384—Abortive Attempt to establish a Fishery at Hove in 1813-15, 385—Erection of Mills's-terrace, 386—Brunswick-square and Terrace built in 1822, 387—St. Andrew's Church built in 1828, 387—Adelaide-crescent commenced in 1830, 387—Mr. Henry Phillips, Projector of the Antheum, 387, 388—Erection and Fall of the Antheum in 1833, 388—Restoration of the Parish Church in 1836, 389—Death of Mr. Basevi, the Architect, 389—York-road commenced in 1850, 390—Erection of St. Patrick's Church, 390—Cricket Ground opened in 1872, 390—Cliftonville projected in 1851-52, 390—The Goldsmid Estate, 391—St. John's Church built in 1852, 391—Increase of Population from 1851 to 1891, 391, 392—The Stanford Estate, 392—Holy Trinity Church erected in 1863, 392—Value of Property in Hove from 1879 to 1892, 393—Notice of and Extracts from Parish Registers, 382 to 384—Termination of the annexation of the Parish with Preston, in 1879, 381—Memorial to Rev. Walter Kelly, 381—Development of Hove in 1871, 392—The County Cricket Ground opened in Hove, 390 - Marvellous Progress of Hove from 1880 to 1892, 394—Erection of the Hove Town Hall, in 1880, at a cost of about £50,000, 395—Formation of the Sea Wall, the Cemetery, and the Recreation Ground, 394, 395—Free Library, Opening of, 395—Erection of a New Parish Church, 396.

HOWELL, THOMAS—Founder of Howell's Alms Houses, 20.

HUNTING—Hind, Stag, and Fox Hunting, 112 to 115—Hind and Stag Hunting in 1779 and 1780, 124, 125—Sensational Stag Hunt by Duke of Cumberland, 124 - Curious Stag Hunt (Lord Barrymore's) in 1788, 129.

HUNTINGDON, COUNTESS OF—Account of her Chapel, 337 to 344—Chapel built by the Sale of her Jewels, and Opened 1761, 338—Singular Dream in connection with the, 337, 338—Chapel Enlarged in 1774, chiefly by Miss Orton, 339—Death of, in 1791, 339—The Rev. Joseph Sortain commenced his ministry in 1832, 341—Reconstruction of present Chapel, 1870, 343.

ILLUSTRATIONS (for list of, see back of "Contents").

INCLEDON—Notice of, 54.

INHABITANTS—Distinction between "Inhabitants" and "Residents," 6—Principal in 1800, 6.

INOCULATION—Practised in 1786, 7.

INNS—"The Black Lion," kept by Mr. Saunders in 1784, 15—"The White Lion," a Cricketers' House in 1765, 96—Inns in 1800 and their Associations, 171 to 221—Beer in 1618 sold without a License, 171—Number of Hotels and Public-houses in 1879 and in 1892, 171 - Value of Licenses in 1819, 172—Price of Brandy in 1749, 173—Number of Inns in 1800, 173—Accommodation at "The Gun" in 1792, 174—Exhibition of Giants at "The Star and Garter" in 1785, 174—First Lodge of Freemasons opened at "The White Horse" in 1789, 177—Election Anecdotes, 177—Inquest at the White Horse" in 1822, on Messrs. Briggs and Knowles, 178—"The Rising Sun," "Ye Haunte of Olde Strike-a-Lighte," 179—Removal of "The White Horse" and "The Rising Sun" in 1869, by Mr. Oliver Weston, 178, 179—"The St. Catherine's Wheel," popularly designated "The Cat and Wheel," afterwards known as "The Duke of Wellington," and the Great Storm of 1850, 182—Right of Way through "The Thatched House," 184—"The Cricketers," formerly known as "The Last and Fish Cart," 187—"The Old Ship" the "business" house of the Town, 189—Court Martial held at "The Old Ship," 1795, 189—Sale of "The Old Ship" in 1878, increase in Value of Property, 191, 192—Mysterious

Affair at "The New Ship" in 1770, 193—Suicide of the Chevalier Maupeau, 1789, 193—Visit of Fugitive Nuns to "The New Ship" in 1790, 193—Frequenters of the Inns divided into the "East Streeters" and "West Streeters," 195—"The Sea House," formerly "The Ship in Distress," 197—Visit of William IV. to Viscountess Bronté at "The Sea House," 197—"The Spotted Dog," 197—The Town "Fire Cage" suspended opposite "The George," 198—Prince Leopold, in 1816, at "The George," 199—"The George" rebuilt 1892, 199—"The King's Head," West-street, Escape of Charles II. from doubted, "A Tale of a Shirt," 199, 200—Cock Fighting at the Half Moon," 201—"Crying Down" at "The Carpenter's Arms," 201—Penderell, J. R., Host, 201—Inquest on James Smith, killed in a Prize-fight, at "The Bell," afterwards called "The Lord Nelson," 202—"The White Lion," custom of the Manor, "Borough English," 202—Mr. Robert Wigney, known as "Gipsy Bob," 203—The "Soldiers' Room," 203—Anecdote of Jemmy Botting, the Hangman, 203—Increase in Value of Property, 204—Prize-fighting at "The Unicorn" in 1821, 205—"The Unicorn" rebuilt in 1892, 205—"The Horse and Groom," subsequently "The Bricklayers' Arms," 206—"The Hen and Chickens;" Mr. John Pocock, Parish Clerk, Host; "The Change Ringers;" "The Bells of St. Nicholas;" The name changed to "The Running Horse," 206, 207—"The New Inn," now "The Clarence Hotel," Birth-place of Miss Phillips, a popular Actress; Dinner given to Mr. Philip Mighell, who feasted 2,300 Poor in 1809 (Jubilee year), 209; First Local Magistrates' Sitting held, 1808; Undiscovered Murder of Mr. Williams in 1823; the "Hunter Hoax" in 1810, 208 to 211—"The Coach and Horses"—Cock-Fighting; Curious Exhibition; "Who Shot the Billy-Goat?" 211 to 213—"The King and Queen." Mr. Polito, the "Modern Noah"; John Fuller in the Pillory; the "Hole in the Wall," 213 to 215—"The Castle Inn," the Residence of the First Royal Visitor, 1765; Subscription Balls: Opposition of the "M.C."; Conversion of the Ball Room into the Pavilion Chapel in 1821; Parish Business; Fête on Coming of Age of Earl Delawarr, 1806; Consolation Dinner to Colonel Warden Sergison, 1807; Court Martial in 1810: Visit of Louis XVIII.; the Eccentric Mr. Webb; Demolition of "The Castle" in 1823, &c., 216 to 220—"The Golden Fleece," formerly "The Chimneys," 220—"The Marlboro'," formerly "The Golden Cross;" the old Catch and Glee Club, 221—"The King's Arms;" Cock-fighting in 1811; Tandem Drive from London to Brighton, 1816, 221—"The Crown and Anchor," at Preston, in 1811, 415—"The Black Lion," at Preston, 415.

JOHNSON, MR., Proprietor of the first Brighton Theatre, 40.

JOHNSON, DR.—His Visit to Brighton in 1782, 121—Amusing Description of his Discussion with "Parson" Michell, 181—on the want of Trees in Brighton, 231.

JORDAN, MRS.—Actress; Memoir of, 63.

JOURNALISM—A Pioneer in Local -355 to 363.

JUNCTION ROAD- Formation of in 1829, 175.

KELLY, REV. WALTER—Memorial to, 381; inducted Vicar of Preston-cum-Hove, 389.

KEMBLE, MR. and MRS. C.—Appearance of at the opening of the New-road Theatre in 1807, 65.

KEMP, THOMAS READ—Projector of Kemp Town, 367.

KENTFIELD, MR. EDWIN—His Skill at Billiards, 165.

LAMBERT, JAMES—Painter of View of Brighthelmston in 1765; Advertisement of, 112.

LARDNER, DR.—Trial, "Heaviside v. Lardner," 378.

LEVEL—in 1779, 213—Menagerie on the, in 1807, 213—Sparring Match on the, in 1807, 213—Famous Cricket Matches on the, 96.

LIBRARIES—Baker's, on the Steine, the first Library, opened in 1760, 112, 113—afterwards carried on by Thomas, Dulot, Gregory, Donaldson, &c., 112—Woodgate's Library, in 1767, 113—Rivalry between Mr. Thomas and Mr. Bowen, 118—Raffling, 118—Notice of Richard Lemmon Gregory, 137, 138—Mechanics' Institution, 155—Literary Society, 155—Mantellian Institution,

156—Albion Rooms Institution, 156—Free Public Library and Victoria Lending Library, 157 to 159—Count Clericetti's Bequest to Museum and Library, 159—Donation of £1,000 by Mr. Hack to Victoria Lending Library, 159.

LILLYWHITE—Famous Cricketer, "At Home," 393.

LITERARY AND SCIENTIFIC INSTITUTION, Brighton Royal—Establishment of, 157.

LOCAL EXAMINATIONS, Sussex Board for—Establishment of, 157.

LODGING HOUSES—in 1800, 18—Terms in 1736, 18—Number of Visitors in 1761, 18—Accommodation in 1779, 19—Names of Owners of, in 1800, 19—Details of, Published in Directory, 20—Accommodation in 1800, 29.

LYNN, "POSS"—The local Dogberry, 9.

MAHOMED'S BATHS—Supplanted by Markwell's Royal Hotel, 175.

MANTELLIAN INSTITUTION—Formation of, 156.

MAILS—Mail Coaches, 247, 253, 293—Queen Caroline's Trial reported by Mail Coachmen, 259—London and Country Mails in 1779, 291.

MALLESON, REV. J. P. (Minister of New Road Unitarian Chapel)—School at Hove, 389.

MANORS—The old "Manor House," 109, 147—Goodwyn's rental of Brighthelmston Manor, 110—Mr. Richard Scrase, his connection with the Manor of Brighton. 147—Custom of the Manor, "Borough English," 202—Fines paid to the Lord of the Manor, by Proprietors of "White Lion" in 1705 and 1851, 202—The present Post Office in the Manor of New Shoreham, 295—Lords of the Manor of Hove, 379—of Preston, 399—Extent of Preston, 400.

MARKET—New Market erected in 1774, 192—The first Charter, date of Edward II., 185, 311—The usual Place for Proclamations, 185.

MARKWELL'S ROYAL HOTEL—Discovery of Old Battery in digging-out the foundations of, in 1869-70, 111.

MARLBOROUGH, DUKE OF—His residence on the Steine, in 1771, 116.

MARTYRS—Sussex—Account of Derrick Carver and John Launder, 186.

"MASH," BETTY—Her husband in the stocks, anecdote of, 185.

MATHEWS, MR. H. J.—Association with Victoria Lending Library, 159.

MAX, MISS—Abduction of, 119.

"M.C.'s"—In 1800—v. Brighthelmston Directory, W. M. Wade, Esq., the first, 29—Powers of the, 30—Public Notices issued in 1787 by the, 30—Regulations of the, 31—Duties of the "M.C." and his Fees, 33—Waning influence of the "M.C." in 1806, 33—Mr. Wade's death in 1808, 34—W, Forth, Esq., the Second "M.C." appointed, 1808, 34 Opposition by Mr. Wilson in 1815, 36—Emoluments of in 1827, 37—Resignation of Mr. Forth, and Election of Lieut.-Colonel John Eld, in 1828, 37—Decline of the office of, 38—Death of the last "M.C." in 1855, 39 Description of the "M.C." by the Rev. Sydney Smith, 39—Influence of the "M.C." upon the Theatre, 40 Ball given by Mr. Wade in 1796 in honour of the Prince and Princess of Wales, 136—His Edict upon Shoe Strings in 1796—136.

MELLON, MISS (subsequently Duchess of St. Albans)—Actress; Notice of, 62.

MUNDEN—Actor; Notice of, 59.

MURRAY, LADY ANNE—Notice of, 163.

MUSEUM—Mantellian, 156—Literary and Scientific, 156—Pavilion, 1862, 158—Corporation Museum and Picture Gallery, 1871-73-91, 158, 159—Chairmen of Sub-Committee, list of, 159—Bequest by Count Clericetti, 159—Davidson Collection of Fossils of the Paris Basin, 159—The Willett Collection of Chalk Fossils, 159.

NATURAL HISTORY SOCIETY, Brighton and Sussex—Foundation of, 157.

NIGHTINGALE, "TOMMY"—Notice of, 317.

NORTH-STREET—311 to 327—Probably formed in the 14th century, 311—The Town Well in 1619, 308—The Friends' Meeting House, opened 1700, 308—"Bredhemston," the common name of the Town in 1700, 308—The First Shop in North-street, opened 1757, 309—Countess of Huntingdon's Chapel Erected, 1761, 309—Theatre Built, 1774, 43, 309—Value of Property in 1772, 310—The

Weigh Scale in 1776, 310—Alterations between 1770 and 1794, 310—Owners and Occupiers, with their Assessments in 1784, 311—First Bank Opened, 1787, 313 -First Printing Office in 1789, 313—First Pleasure Gardens in 1793, 313—Chapel Royal Erected, 1794, 313 - First Coach Office Opened, 1794, 313 Description of in 1800, 313—Inhabitants of in 1800, 314 – Corporal Staines' Cave in the Chalk Pit, 314 - Constable's Shop, now Hannington's, 316 - Tradesmen's Holidays, 317—Nightingale's Shop Assessed at 10s. a-year, in 1791, 317—The New Road formed, 317—Brighton Union Bank Opened, 1805, 317 - Removal of the Friends' Meeting House in 1806, 317—Value of Property in 1800, 318—Exhibition of Napoleon's Carriage, 319—"Clio" Rickman's Career, 319 - Detection of Smuggled Goods, Heavy Fine, 320—Early Tradesmen in, 320—Alterations in, 321—Fall of Houses in, 322—Removal of Houses South of the Chapel Royal, in 1879, 353—Dudley Harricks, Hosier, 322— "Billy" Spears, 322—Increased Value of Property in, 324—Particulars of the Old House, latterly "The London Tavern,' 325—Rushes used instead of Laths in Building, 327—Rebuilding of "The Unicorn," 205.

ORTON, MISS—A large Contributor to the Countess of Huntingdon's Church, 339.

OSBALDESTON, Mr. G.—A celebrated Cricketer, 100, 101.

PACKETS—Pacquets sailing from Brighton in 1788, 247—To Dieppe in 1814, 256.

PALMER, JOHN—Temporary Manager of the Brighton Theatre in 1792, 53— His Singular Death, 53.

PANTOMIME—Not always a Christmas Treat, 49—Programme of, September, 1795, 57—In 1782 and 1823, 49.

PARIS, MR. G. DE—His Association with the Art Gallery, &c., 160.

PARISH OFFICERS—In 1800, 8.

PASSENGER TRAFFIC OF RAILWAY, 281.

PATCHAM PLACE—Miss Lucy Howard at, 407.

PENDERELL, J. R. (descendant of "Trusty Dick"), at "Carpenters' Arms," 201.

PHILLIPS, HENRY—Projector of the Antheum at Hove, in 1833, 387, 388—Blindness through grief, 388.

PHILLIPS, MISS—Popular actress; born at the "New Inn," "Clarence Hotel," 208.

PHILLIPS, MR. BARCLAY—His association with the Celtic discoveries at Hove, 378; and Sussex Board for Local Examinations, 157.

PICTURE AND ART GALLERY—Mr. W. J. Wilson's presentation to, 160—Pocock Collection, purchase of, 160— Furner Collection, 160.

PIER, ROYAL SUSPENSION—Decision to erect it, 191.

PILLORY—John Fuller put in the, 1811, 214.

PITT, WILLIAM—in Brighton, 127.

POOL VALLEY—Great Flood, in 1795, 135—in 1850, 182.

POPULATION—In 1580, 308—In 1700, 308—Preceding 1770, 5—From 1761 to 1891, 5 - Increase in 50 years from 3,000 to 40,000, 38—Of Hove in 1800 and 1811, 377—Of Hove in 1891, 392 - Of Preston in 1891, 409.

POST-OFFICE—In 1800, 18, 19 (Old Directory), and 14—In the Time of Charles I., 289 - First Post Office at Lewes, 1667, 290—First Post Office at Brighton, about 1753, 290 Postal Arrangements in 1779, 291 - Rates of Postage, 1800 to 1840, 292—The "Off the Stones" Penny, 293—"Robbing the Mail," 293—Mail Coaches introduced, 1807, 293 - Improvements in 1818, 294 —"Cross Posts" suggested by Mr. Allen, in 1720, 294—Successive Removals of the Post Office, 295—Penny Postage adopted, 1840, 296 - A Penny Post Started in 1683, 296—Staff of the, 297—"Receiving Houses," 297—Savings Banks introduced, 1861, 297—Increase of Business, 297 Statistics of Business, 297 to 305—Telegraph Business added, 1877, 297 - Staff in 1880, and in 1891, 299—Statistics of Registered and other Letters, Money Orders, Postal Orders, and Telegrams, 299 to 305—Postal Orders introduced in 1881, 300.

PRESS-GANG—In 1779, Kindly Act of the Duke of Cumberland, 122—In 1787, Routed by the Fishermen's Wives, 122.

PRESTON—399 to 418—An Outlying Village in 1800, 5—Extent and Value of the Manor of, 399—Its Association with Anne of Cleves, 400 - The "Shirley Brothers," 402, 412—Notice of the Rev. Charles Townsend, 402 – The Western Family, Melancholy Death of Charles Western, 402—Conveyance to William Stanford, Esq., in 1794, 403—"The Workhouse" and "Black-hole," 405—Preston Grove - Tea Gardens in 1769, 115 and 405 · Public Breakfast in 1809, 406—Anecdotes in connection with Patcham Place, 407 · The Turnpike at, 408—The " Tivoli Gardens," 408—The " Clermont" Estate projected in 1868, 409—Population of, from 1801 to 1892, 409 - Rating of, 409 - Description of the Church before restoration; Mural Paintings and Monuments, 410 to 414 - Notice of Francis Cheynell, D.D., 413 - Notice of the Rev. James Douglas, M.A., 413 - The Church Bells, 414— Interesting Archæological Discoveries in 1876, 414—Wonderful Growth of Preston, 415—Preston Park, 415 to 418—Purchase of Park from Munificent Bequest of £70,000 by Mr. William Edmond Davies, 416—Opening of the Park, November 8th, 1884, 416—Laying-out of the Cricket Ground : Opening of ditto in 1887, 417—Gift of a Clock Tower by Mr. Edward White, 1891, 418.

PRESTONVILLE—Projected by Mr. Daniel Friend in 1865, 367.

PROFESSIONS—In 1800, 6 to 15—In 1850, 373.

PROMENADE GROVE—67 to 80.

PUGILISM—Patronised by Royalty, 83—Fatal Encounter in 1788, 91—Fatal Prize Fight in 1800, 202—Sparring at " The Unicorn Inn " in 1811, 205—Sparring Match on the Level in 1807, 213.

QUAKERS—See " Friends."

RACES—Foot Race on the Steine, July 30, 1787, 31—Pony Races at the Promenade Grove, 1796, 73, 74—and in 1802, 78—Foot Races, 84 to 86—The first Brighton Races in 1783, 87—Horse Racing, from 1783 to 1850, 86 to 92—The Race Course in 1790, 91—Race Stand burnt in 1803, 92 Race Stand Trustees appointed, 1849, 92—The present Stand erected in 1851, 92—Race between " a Military Gentleman " and a Bullock in 1786, 127—Whimsical Races in 1803, 141—Donkey Races in 1805, 141—Sir St. Vincent Cotton's Maggot Race, 258.

RACE STAND TRUSTEES—Presentation of East End Park by Race Stand Trustees, 92.

RAILWAY—267 to 286—Mr. Vallance's Atmospheric, 268 - The first Railway opened in 1825, 267 - Agitation in Brighton in 1835, 268 - The first Permanent Rail of the Brighton Line, laid by Mr. Alfred Morris in 1839, 269 - Laying Foundation Stone of the New England Viaduct, 269—Brighton and Shoreham Line opened 1840, 270—First accident on, 270 - Opening of, to Hayward's Heath, 1841, 271—Completion of the London Line in 1841, 271 - growth and development of the, 273 to 278—Saxby and Farmer's Points and Signals, 276—London, Brighton, and South Coast complete System of Lines, 276—Capital of the Company ; Receipts and Expenditure ; and tabular statements of Miles open, Miles run, Value of Shares, Dividends, Returns of Passenger Traffic, &c., to December, 1891, 278 to 283—What Brighton owes to Railway Accommodation, 283 to 286.

RATES—Assessments from 1761 to 1891, 5—Assessment of property in North-street, 1784, 311, 312—Curiosities of Rating in 1814, 318, 319—Of Preston, 409.

RELIGIOUS EDIFICES—St. Peter's Church, Founded in 1824, 191—In North-street, 329 to 353—The Friends' Meeting House Opened, 1700, 329—Captain Tettersall a Persecutor of the Friends, 330—Friends' Meeting held at Blatchington, 330—Persecutions of the Friends, 330 to 332—Diary of Elizabeth Grover, 332, 333—Friends' New Meeting House Erected in 1805, 334 - The Prince of Wales and the Friends, 334—Memoir of the Sussex Friends, 335—The Countess of Huntingdon's Chapel Opened in 1761, 337 to 344—The Chapel Built by the Sale of the Countess's Jewels, 338 - Chapel Enlarged in 1774, 339—Alterations in 1788, 1810, and 1822, 340—Rev. Rowland Hill Officiated at the Re-opening in 1822, 340 - The Rev. Joseph Sortain's Ministry, 340 to 342—Enlargement of Chapel in 1842, 341—Opening of the New Chapel in 1871, 344—Bust of Sortain placed in the Pavilion, 342—The Chapel Royal, 344 to 353—The First Stone Laid by the Prince of Wales in 1793, 345—Opened in 1795, 346—Oratorio at the Chapel Royal in 1800, 346—Act passed in 1803, constituting it a Chapel-of-Ease, 347—List of Perpetual Curates, 348—Vaults, *jeu d'esprit* upon being let to a Wine Merchant, 348—St. James's Opened as a Free Chapel, 1813, 349—Consecration of the Chapel Royal in

1803, 348—One-fourth Sold by Auction in 1814, 349—Concerts and Oratorios at, 350—Description of the Interior of the Chapel Royal, 350 to 352—Alteration of the Chapel Royal in 1876, 350 - The Rev. Thos. Trocke, Curate for 40 years, 351—Parish Church Restored in 1853, 370—Number of places of Worship in 1850 and 1870, 371 - St. Peter's Church, Hove, 380 - Restoration of the Parish Church of Hove in 1836, 399—St. Andrew's Church, Hove, erected in 1828, 387—Erection of St. Patrick's Church, Hove, 390—St. John's Church, Hove, Built in 1852, 391—Description of Preston Church, its Mural Paintings and Monuments, 410 to 414—Termination of the annexation of the Parish with Hove in 1879, 381—Erection of a New Parish Church in Hove, 396.

RESIDENTS—Principal, in 1800, 6- Notable, in 1850, 372, 373.

RETROSPECT OF TWENTY YEARS—Brighton in 1850 and in 1870, 365 to 375.

REVIEWS (MILITARY) - In 1791, 130. In 1796, 136.

RICKMAN, "CLIO"—Notice of, 319.

RINGERS, CHANGE - Meetings at "The Hen and Chickens," 206 - Opening of the Peal at St. Nicholas, in 1778, 207.

RIOTS—5th of November, 1817, Sergeant Rowles killed, 176 - Corn, in 1756, 188—Mutiny at East Blatchington, in 1795, 189.

ROADS - Coach Road across the Steine, made 1836, 145 Junction-road made 1829, 175 - Road made between West-street and Middle-street, in 1822, 196—Roads in Sussex in 1751, 242—Coach Roads in 1790, 243.

ROBBERIES—Stage Coach, 1812 and 1821, 253, 254.

ROBERTS, BEACH - The "Walking Newspaper," 369.

ROBINSON, MRS. - ("Perdita"), Notice of, 47.

ROGERS, SPENCER, ESQ.—Romantic Story of, 156.

ROYALTY - First visit to the Theatre in 1779, 47 - Patronage of the Races, 90 - The Duke of York's Cricket Match in 1789, 96 - First visit to Brighton of the Duke of Gloucester in 1765, 113 - Visit of the Duke of York in 1766, 114 - Visit of the Duke of Cumberland to Duke of Marlborough in 1771, 116 - First visit of George Prince of Wales, 1783, 125 Kindly act of the Duke of Cumberland respecting Press-ganging, 122 - Visit to Brighton of Princess Amelia (sister of George III.) in 1782 ; Anecdote of, 123—Visit of the Princess Amelia (daughter of George III.) in 1798, 137 - Visits of Royalty from 1800 to 1807, 138, 139 - Visit of the Duke and Duchess of Clarence in 1829, 150 - Opening of the King's-road by George IV. in 1822, 196 The Duke of York and the Oyster Woman, 1822, 197—Visit of William IV. to Viscountess Bronté at "The Sea House," 197—Prince Leopold at "The George Inn," 1816, 199 Charles II.'s Escape from Brighton : " A Tale of a Shirt," 199, 200 —Duke of Cumberland patronises Prize-fighting in 1811, 205 - Duke of Cumberland's dog, "Turk," 232. See also "Wales, Prince of."

RUSSELL, DR. - His recommendation of Brighton, 3—Memoir of, 141—Dr. Relhan, successor to Dr. Russell, 153 Dr. Russell's idea of a Sea-bathing place, 151 - His portrait, by Zoffany, presented to the Town in 1887 by Mr. Robert Bacon and Alderman S. Ridley, 188.

SAUNDERS'S BUILDINGS, Description of, 14, 15.

"SAVING CLAUSE" of the old Carriers, 242.

SCHOOLS—Number of, in 1800, in contrast with 1878, 16 Union School, Mr. Sharp, the First Master of Union School, Middle-street ; Primitive Modes of Punishment, the "Sand Alphabet," 17.

SCRASE, MR. RICHARD—His connection with the Manor of Brighton ; his friendship for the Thrales, 147.

SEA WATER—The Practice of Drinking, 225 ; sending to London and selling of in Southwark in 1756, 224.

SELBY, JAMES—Remarkable Coaching Performance, 1888, 255, 256.

SERGISON, COLONEL WARDEN—Consolation Dinner given to, in 1807, 219.

SESSIONS—Petty Sessions first held in 1812, 16—At "The New Inn," 209.

SHARP, Mr —First Master of Union School, Middle-street, 17.

SHIRLEYS, of Preston—382, 401, 402, 412.

SHOE STRINGS—Edict upon, by the "M.C.," in 1796, 136.

SHOPS—In 1774, Goods disposed of by throwing Dice, 118—(see also "North-street").

SIDDONS, MRS —Her various Appearances at the Brighton Theatres, 53, 60, 66— Her Performances at Brighton, Bath, and London in 1798, within the space of 96 hours, 53.

SMALL-POX—Inoculation Practised in 1786, 7.

SMUGGLING - French Lace Smuggled in 1776, 118 - In "The Old Ship" Yard in 1821, 190 Smugglers and Landlords, 252—Detection of Smuggled Goods in North-street, heavy fine, 301 - At Hove; Hove Church a Smugglers' Depôt, 378, 386.

SORTAIN, REV. JOSEPH—Sonnet to the, 341—His Ministry at Lady Huntingdon's Chapel commenced in 1832, 341—Monument to the memory of in Hove Churchyard, 389.

SPEARS, "BILLY."—Anecdote of, 323.

STANFORD, WILLIAM Conveyance of the Manor of Preston to, in 1794; the present Stanford Estate, 403.

STEINE—The, and its Associations, 109 to 145—Skating on the, 111—Libraries on the, 112, 113 - Residence of the Duke of Marlborough, in 1771, 116— Enclosure of the, in 1776, 117 - Ladies Gambling, 119—Practical Joking on the, in 1786, 128 --Major Hanger's Steine Races, 127—A Sewer built and the "Pool" filled up, in 1791, 133—Anti-Republican Meeting on the, 1792, 134— Small Camp formed near the, in 1794, 135—Great Flood in 1795, 135—Attack on Mr. Finlason, on the, 142—Donkeys on the, 142—Lit by Gas, in 1824, 142 —Important Changes on the, in 1805-8, 143, 144—Opposition of the Fishermen to the Enclosure of the, in 1822-23, 144, 145—Coach Road formed across the, in 1836, 145—Notable Houses on the, 147 to 168—North Steine Enclosures formed, 1817, 215 - The Statue of George IV., Chantrey's Loss on, 221.

STORMS—Great Flood in 1795, 135—Great Flood in 1850, 182—Telegraph Damaged in 1866, 302—in 1703 and 1705, 308.

SUETT, "DICKEY"—Actor; Anecdotes of, 62.

SUSSEX BOARD FOR LOCAL EXAMINATIONS—Establishment of, 157.

TELEGRAPH—Business added to Post Office, 1877, 298—Connected with London, 1851, 301; and with Lewes in 1853, 301—Charges for Messages, 301, 302— Market and other News supplied in 1854, 301—Local Staff, 302—Damaged by Storm in 1866, 302—Changes from 1867 to 1892, 303 to 305.

TEMPLE, THE—Built by Thomas Read Kemp, Esq.; the Temple Field built upon, in 1870, 367.

TETTERSALL, CAPTAIN NICHOLAS—Bigotry of; his virulent persecution of Dissenters, 330.

THEATRE—Regulations as to opening, 1788, 31—Influence of the "M.C.," 40— Old Brighton Theatres, 40—Mr. Johnson, the first Proprietor, 40, 41—Performances in the original Theatre, 41, 42—Theatre in North-street opened in 1774, 43—Performances at the new Theatre, 43 to 45—Change of Management in 1777, 45—Hours of Closing in 1777, 46—Notice of Mrs. Baddeley, 46 —The "Candle-Snuffer," 46—Royal visits to the, 47, 48 - Notice of Mrs. Robinson, "Perdita," 47—Anecdote of Quick, 47, 48—Earl Barrymore's appearance at the, 48—Half Prices introduced in 1789, 49—Pantomimes in 1782 and 1823, 49—Theatre in Duke-street opened 1790, 50 - Performers and Performances at the Duke-street Theatre, 50 to 53—Mr. Wilde's management in 1793, 54—Appearance of the "Chevalier" or "Mdlle." D'Eon, 54— Incledon's career, 54—Mr. Cobb, Proprietor of the Theatre in 1794, 55— Programme of Pantomime in 1795, 57—Notices of Holman and Emery, 56— Interior of Theatre re-modelled in 1796, 58—Mr. Diddear, Lessee in 1796, 58 Engagements in 1797 and 1798 of Incledon, Ellison, Munden, and Mrs. Siddons, 59, 60—Career of Munden, 59 Suett's only appearance, 62—Miss Mellon's career, 62—Messrs. Blogg and Archer, Lessees in 1779, 61—Appearance of Charles Kemble in 1799, 62—Mrs. Jordan's career, 63 - Mr. Haymes, Lessee in 1802, 63—Mr. Brunton's management in 1804, 64 Engagements of Braham, Madame Storace, Dowton, Munden, Bannister, Quick, &c., 63, 64

—Sale of the Duke Street Theatre by Mr. Attree in 1807, 65 – Opening of the New Road Theatre in 1807, 65 - Appearance of Mr. and Mrs. Kemble in 1807, 65—Appearances of Mrs. Siddons, 53, 60, 66—Engagements of Edmund Kean and of Miss O'Neill, 66 - Extraordinary Receipts, 66.

THELLUSON, PETER ISAAC – His Extraordinary Will, 164.

THRALE, MRS.—Her House in West Street, 7—Her love of Sea-Bathing, 230.

TOWNSEND, REV. CHARLES—Notice of, 402, 403.

TRADESMEN – Details of Trading Community, 16 to 18 – Extraordinary Junction of Trades by Various Individuals, 18 – Prince s Place, a Favourite Rendezvous for Migratory, 16 – First Tradesmen's Ball in 1823, 149 Early Tradesmen in North Street, 314 to 316, 320 to 322, 371—Increase of Tradesmen from 1850 to 1870, 373 to 375.

TRAVELLERS, THE THREE—Or the "Shirley Brothers," their connection with the Manor of Preston, 402.

TUBB, J.—Introduction of a "Flying Machine," 243, 244.

TURRELL, MR. STEIN—Joint Hon. Secretary with Mr. Cordy Burrows to the Literary and Scientific Institution, 156.

VAGRANTS—Punishment of, in 1819, 10.

VERSES—On "Poss" Lynn, the Town Crier, 9—On leaving the Steine, 27, 28—On Mr. Forth, "M.C.," 35—Prologue spoken on Opening the first Brighton Theatre, 41—Epilogue spoken at the North-street Theatre, Nov. 7th, 1774, 44 —Lines on Miss Fontenelle, 52—Poetical Playbill, 1796, 59—Lack of Trees in Brighton, 67—From the "New Brighthelmston Directory,' 1769, 114, 115—On Music at Baker's Rotunda, 116 - Lines on the Steine, 117—Couplets on ten Brighton Beauties in 1785, 121—On a Stag Hunt, 124—Rhyme on Tommy Onslow, 126—Lines on Brighton, 130—The origin of Veils and Gipsey Hats, 132—On Ladies' Bathing, 227, 228—Lines on "Smoaker" and Martha Gunn, 235, 236—Lines on the Exhibition of Napoleon's carriage, 319—Sonnet to the Rev. Joseph Sortain, 341—Lines on the Vaults of the Chapel Royal, 348 – Monitorial lines on the Clock Tower at Preston Park, 418.

VESTRY—Mr. Attree, Vestry Clerk in 1790; Mr. Somers Clarke elected in 1830, 6—Vestry Minute in 1701, Proclamation of Queen Anne, 185—Vestry Meeting, March, 1823, resolution to erect St. Peter's Church, 190.

VICTORIA LENDING LIBRARY—Opening of, in 1889, 159—Munificent Donation by Mr. D. Hack, 159.

VISITORS, distinguished - Edmund Burke in 1793, 54—The Duchess de Noailles, her escape from France, in 1792, 98—Lord Chief Justice Wilmot in 1763, 113 —Lord Bute in 1769, 114—John Wilkes in 1770, 114 - List of, in 1771 and 1772, 116—List of, in 1778 and 1782, 120, 121—Dr. Johnson in 1782, 121—List of, in 1779, 122—List of, in 1784, 126—Pitt's visit, and his reception, in 1785, 127—Large number of Visitors in 1786, 128 - The Princess de Lamballe, and her fate, 128—Lord Barrymore, and his Brother's Frolics, in 1788, 129—List of, from 1789 to 1793, 130—Lord Barrymore's death in 1793, 131—3,000 Visitors in 1793, 132 — List of, in 1796, 136—Great increase of Visitors in 1802, 137—General Dumourier in 1804, 139—List of, from 1800 to 1807, 139 – Number of Visitors, 1821-1822, 20,000, 149 – Fugitive French Nuns, 193.

VOLUNTEERS—Embodiment of the first Brighton, in 1792, 134—The "Sea Fencibles" raised in 1798, 134.

WADE, CAPTAIN—"M.C.," 29—his last Ball, 34.

WAGGONS, STAGE—In 1777, 246—in 1800, 250.

WALES, GEORGE, PRINCE OF—His Residence on the Steine, 26—His Associates, 26—Birthday Ball in 1807, 34—His connection with Mrs. Robinson, "Perdita," 47—Anecdotes of Earl Barrymore, 48, 129, 131—Patronized the "Public Breakfast' in 1793, 73 - His Ride from Brighton to London and Back in Ten Hours, 89 – His Splendid Racing Stud, 89—His Love of Horse Racing and Expulsion from the Jockey Club, 90—His First Visit to Brighton in 1783, 125—His Second Visit in 1784, 126—Major Hanger, His Companion, 127—His Joke on the name of Lenox, 128—His Visit in 1796, with the Princess, 135—Curious Diversions of his Associates in 1805, 141, 142—Visit to Mr. W. Gerald Hamilton, in 1789, 162—Visit to Fugitive Nuns at "The New Ship," 193—Purchase of "The Castle Tavern," 217—"Smoaker" Miles, the Bather, 233—His behaviour to the "Friends," 334 - First Stone of the Chapel Royal laid by, in 1793, 345—Anecdotes in connection with Patcham Place, 407—Appointment of the Rev. James Douglas, as Chaplain, 413.

WESTERN, CHARLES—Melancholy Death of, in 1771, 402, 403.

WHITE, EDWARD—Donor of the Clock Tower at Preston Park, 418.

WIGNEY, ROBERT—Known as "Gipsy Bob," 203.

WILKES, JOHN—In Brighton, 122.

WILLETT, MR. H. -Collection of Chalk Fossils, 159.

WITNEY, BETTY and SALLY—Notice of, 185.

WOMBWELL, CAPTAIN—His famous ride to Brighton, 221.

WORKHOUSE—Old Workhouse taken down in 1870, 367—Advertisements for Contracts in 1790, and also for a Governor, 218—Erection of Fine Property on the Site of the old Workhouse in 1870, 367—At Preston, 405.

ADDENDA.

A Relic of Captain Nicholas Tettersall, 419.

A Relic of Charles Mathews, 420.

J. G. BISHOP, Printer, "Herald" Office, Brighton.

BRIGHTON & SUSSEX
Mutual Provident Society,

Established January, 1847, and Enrolled as a Friendly Society.

Head Office—11, PRINCE ALBERT STREET, Brighton
(OPEN DAILY).

Branch Office—119, CHURCH ROAD, Hove
(OPEN EVERY TUESDAY EVENING, from 7 till 9).

OBJECTS:

THIS SOCIETY ASSURES, AS PROVIDED IN ITS RULES AND TABLES,—

Weekly Allowances in Sickness, with Medical Aid.

Life Assurances, from £5 to £200; and Assurances for the sums to be payable either on attaining Age 50, 55, or 60, or at Death if occurring sooner.

Endowments. Sums from £5 to £200, for Children and Persons of any age—a profitable Fund for Savings or Investments.

Deferred Annuities, to commence at Age 65 or 70, either in connection with or without Sickness Assurance.

Loans advanced on Mortgage of Freehold, Leasehold, or Copyhold Property, at FIVE per cent. only, either repayable in any term from 2 to 15 years, by easy Monthly Instalments, Principal and Interest included, similar to Building Societies,—or to remain on Mortgage.

The TOTAL AMOUNT OF BONUSES declared by the Society to the close of the last Quinquennium, on 31st December, 1896, was £25,522 17s. 8d. From this it will be seen that every department of the Society offers pronounced attractions for the thrifty.

President:
THE RIGHT HON. THE EARL OF CHICHESTER.

Trustees:
MARRIAGE WALLIS, Esq., J.P., R. A. BEVAN, Esq., J.P., and Rev. PREBENDARY J. J. HANNAH.

Treasurer: HENRY THOMAS WEST, Esq., J.P., Brighton Union Bank.

Directors:
Mr. THOS. TUGWELL, *Chairman.*   Mr. ALFD. HABENS, *Vice-Chairman.*

Mr. ALLEN ANSCOMBE,	Mr. JOHN GEO. BISHOP,	Mr. A. P. DOLLMAN,
" RICHD. ALABONE,	Ald. WILLIAM BOTTING,	" SAMUEL DENMAN,
" FREDK. J. BEVIS,	Mr. THOS. BULLOCK,	" FRED. HART,
" J. BILLINGHURST,	" JOHN CORNEY,	" W. DAVID SHAW.

All the above Honorary Officers are also Members of the Society.

Medical Officers:
EASTERN DIVISION—Mr. CHAS. J. JACOMB HOOD, 8, St. George's Place, Brighton.
WESTERN DIVISION—Mr. LAWRENCE W. K. PHILLIPS, 109, Church Road, Hove.

Surveyor: Mr. ALFRED CARDEN, Ship Street Chambers, Ship Street.

Secretary: Mr. GEORGE GOLDSMITH.

TELEPHONE, No. 152.

MESSRS.
JENNER AND DELL,

Auctioneers, House and Estate Agents and Appraisers.

CHIEF OFFICES,

(ESTABLISHED MORE THAN FIFTY YEARS),

22, REGENCY SQUARE,

(OPPOSITE THE WEST PIER),

BRIGHTON.

West Brighton Branch Office—
52, CHURCH ROAD,

(At the CORNER OF THE GRAND AVENUE).

Both Offices being in <u>direct</u> Telephonic Communication.

All Business is transacted under the immediate personal supervision of the Principals.

Messrs. JENNER AND DELL have the largest selection of <u>PRIVATE RESIDENCES</u> TO LET FURNISHED IN BRIGHTON, and intending Tenants are respectfully invited to send to Messrs. JENNER AND DELL a full description of their wants, when they will be pleased to forward, gratis, a Special List, with Orders to View. Messrs. JENNER AND DELL would also direct attention to their <u>LISTS OF UNFURNISHED HOUSES AND OF FREEHOLD AND OTHER PROPERTIES FOR DISPOSAL</u>, which are to be had on application.

Auction Sales conducted; Valuations made for Probate and other purposes; Inventories made and checked; Mortgages negotiated; Agents to the London Life and Fire Assurance. A.D. 1720.

County Fire Office,

20, REGENT STREET, W., and 14, CORNHILL, E.C.,
LONDON.

FOUNDED 1807.

The Premium Income of the Office, which now amounts to a QUARTER OF A MILLION STERLING ANNUALLY, is derived from Home business only, no foreign risks being undertaken. In the comparative Return of Insurances effected by all the Fire Offices in the Metropolitan District, rendered annually to the authorities for the purposes of Taxation, the COUNTY FIRE OFFICE stands fourth in the amount of business transacted.

The Rates of Premium charged by this Office are the same as those adopted by other leading Companies.

Claims are settled with promptitude, and in a fair and liberal spirit. The Payments made by the COUNTY FIRE OFFICE for Losses alone amount to Three and a Half Millions. Losses by Lightning and Explosions by Gas made good.

AGENTS IN BRIGHTON.

Mr. W. J. BRAMWELL	17, Prince Albert Street.
Mr. F. BUTLER	2, Prince's Street.
Mr. H. J. DAVIS	15, Ship Street.
Messrs. DURTNALL & CO.	149, North Street.
Mr. W. FURSE	3, Eaton Terrace, Kemp Town.
Mr. S. STEWART GAMBLE	The Bank Office, Park Crescent.
Mr. F. E. HARRISON	2, Chatham Place.
Mr. R. B. HOMEWOOD	27, Clifton Street.
Mr. B. H. NUNN	129, Queen's Road.
Mr. H. NYE	35, Duke Street.
Mr. G. D. SAWYER	100, North Street.

ROYAL EXCHANGE ASSURANCE,

INCORPORATED A.D. 1720, BY ROYAL CHARTER.

For Sea, Fire, Life, and Annuities.

CHIEF OFFICE: **ROYAL EXCHANGE, LONDON.**

Accumulated Funds Exceed £4,000,000.

LIFE DEPARTMENT.—

Large Bonuses.   Moderate Rates of Premium.   Improved Conditions of Assurance.

ANNUITIES

Granted on one or more Lives.

MARINE ASSURANCES

at the current rates of Premium.

LIGHTNING.—

The Policies of this Corporation now extend to cover Loss or Damage by Lightning, whether the Property insured be set on fire thereby or not.

To prevent trouble and hazard to the Assured, any person may pay for several years beforehand, and a discount of 5 *per cent.* is allowed for every year except the first; but all receipts for more years than one must be witnessed by two of the Directors.

Prospectuses and all information may be obtained on application at the Offices of the Corporation, or to its Local Agents,

SAMUEL RIDLEY, LEDGER, & HOLLIS,

Auctioneers, Valuers, and Estate Agents,

155, NORTH STREET, BRIGHTON, & 76, CHURCH ROAD, WEST BRIGHTON.

THE MUTUAL LIFE INSURANCE COMPANY OF NEW YORK.

INSURANCE FOR THE WEALTHY.
£116,000 was recently paid by a Leading Merchant for an Investment Policy in this Company.

SEND for NEW PROSPECTUS.

LONDON OFFICE—17 and 18, CORNHILL, E.C.

D. C. HALDEMAN, General Manager.

Bankers: THE BANK OF ENGLAND.

Accumulated Funds exceed	£33,230,654.
Bonuses paid in 1891	649,493.
Being an increase over the amount paid in Bonuses in 1890 of	73,745.

THE MUTUAL OF NEW YORK is a purely Mutual Company, and there are no Shareholders to absorb any of its profits, while the Accumulated Funds and Surplus all belong to the Insured. At the same time there is no liability to the Policy Holder whatever, beyond the payment of Premium named in his Policy.

ACTUAL RESULTS.

A LARGE BONUS—

The Company have recently forwarded to the holder of Policy No. 278,127 a Cheque for **£1,099 13s. 6d. in payment of the Cash Value of the Bonus for 1891,** the Policy being for £10,000, **and issued in 1886** on the five year distribution plan. This return is equal to an annual cash bonus of **£2 4s. 0d. per cent.** Many of these Policies are reaching the bonus period with results very gratifying to the insured.

The total payments to Policy-holders to December, 1891, amounted to **£68,215,248** of which upwards of **£17,032,676** were bonus payments—more than **twice the amount of Bonuses paid** by any other Company.

ANNUITIES GRANTED ON MOST FAVOURABLE TERMS.

For Premium Rates and other Information, please apply to

MESSRS. **RIDLEY, LEDGER, & HOLLIS,**
LOCAL AGENTS,
Branch Office - 155, **NORTH STREET, BRIGHTON.**

General Life & Fire Assurance Company.

Established] LIFE—FIRE—MORTGAGES—ANNUITIES. [A.D. 1837.

| CAPITAL | ... | ... | ... | ... | £1,000,000. |
| FUNDS IN HAND exceed | | ... | ... | £1,350,000. |

Chief Office—103, CANNON STREET, LONDON, E.C.

BOARD OF DIRECTORS.

Sir ANDREW LUSK, Bart., *Chairman.*
Principal ANGUS, D.D.
JOSEPH BOLTON DOE, Esq., J.P., D.L.
The Most Hon. the MARQUIS of EXETER.
Hon. R. C. GROSVENOR.
Lieut.-Col. F. D. GREY.

GEORGE PITT, Esq.
WILLIAM STRANG, Esq., *Deputy-Chairman.*
Lord GILBERT KENNEDY.
JAMES S. MACK, Esq., J.P.
HENRY WILLIAM RIPLEY, Esq.
Rt. Hon. C. PELHAM VILLIERS, M.P.

The Company undertakes Life Assurance of every kind at moderate rates, and on terms and conditions which compare favourably with those of other Companies.

Policies are made indisputable after five years.

Regulations are in force for securing to the Assured the benefit of the surrender value of a Policy in the event of its lapse.

Fire Insurances are accepted at Tariff Rates.

All claims settled with liberality and despatch.

Prospectuses and Proposal Forms may be obtained on application at the Chief Office, or any of the Branches.

Double advantage Policies issued securing TWO PAYMENTS of the amount assured —one payment on the attainment of a specified age, and a second payment at death thereafter. HENRY WARD, *Secretary and Manager.*

AGENTS FOR BRIGHTON AND DISTRICT—

ELLIOTT & SONS, Auctioneers and Valuers, 54 and 55, SHIP STREET, BRIGHTON.

"WEST END" CLOTHING DEPOT,
131, CHURCH ROAD, HOVE.

THOMAS TUGWELL,
Proprietor.

LARGE AND VARIED STOCK OF YOUTHS', BOYS', AND JUVENILES' CLOTHING,

In all Materials for the Season.

MEN'S CLOTH AND TWEED SUITS,

Suitable for Office, Business, or Best Wear, at low and reasonable Prices, or made to measure.

HARD & SOFT FELT HATS, in all SHAPES & COLOURS.

𝕮ricket 𝕿rousers, 𝔖hirts, 𝔍ackets, 𝔅elts, and 𝕮aps.

BOOTS and **SHOES** in great Variety, from well-known and Good Makers. **TENNIS** and **BEACH SHOES** in all Sizes.

A SMALL QUANTITY OF

LIEBIG

"COMPANY'S"

EXTRACT OF BEEF

ADDED to any **SOUP, SAUCE,** or **GRAVY,** gives Strength and fine **Flavour.**

See Signature (as annexed), in Blue Ink across the Label on each Jar of the Genuine Extract.

Keeps for any Length of Time, and is Cheaper and of Finer Flavour **THAN ANY OTHER STOCK**

Makes Cheapest, Purest, and Best BEEF TEA. FORTY POUNDS of Prime Lean Beef are used to make ONE POUND of this Extract.

COOKERY BOOKS (Indispensable for Ladies) sent **FREE** on application to

LIEBIG'S EXTRACT of MEAT COMPANY,
LIMITED.
9, FENCHURCH AVENUE, E.C.

By Special Authority of the Brighton Town Council.

THE SEVENTH EDITION, WITH PORTRAITS AND ILLUSTRATIONS.

PRICE TENPENCE (NETT).

THE

BRIGHTON PAVILION

AND ITS ROYAL ASSOCIATIONS,

WITH A

Descriptive Guide to the Rooms

AND COMPLETE

Catalogue of the Collections of Old Brighton Prints and Drawings

IN THE

SUPPLEMENTARY MUSEUM,

BY

JOHN GEORGE BISHOP,

Author of "A Peep into the Past!—Brighton in the Olden Time," "Strolls in the Extra-Mural Cemetery," &c.

ACCEPTED BY T.R.H.

The Prince of Wales,   The Princess of Wales.

AND OTHER MEMBERS OF THE ROYAL FAMILY.

OPINIONS OF THE PRESS.

A little local history is this, which has all the charm of a romance with all the value of an historical record.—*London Standard*.

There is a charm about Mr. Bishop's little history which is irresistible. . . It is a thorough *multum in parvo* of Brighton history.—*Daily Mail*.

It is most pleasant and agreeable reading, and quite apart from its great value as an historical record, will maintain its position in public estimation by pure force of its own charm.—*Brighton Gazette*.

To be had at the "Brighton Herald" Office, or at the Ticket Office (Grand Entrance), Royal Pavilion.

TELEPHONE 223.

NORTH STREET BREWERY,

BRIGHTON.

OFFICES - 201, WESTERN ROAD.

Smithers and Son,

FAMILY

PALE ALE, STOUT, AND PORTER

BREWERS AND MALTSTERS.

FAMILIES SUPPLIED WITH 4½, 6, 9, and 18 GALLON CASKS.

Vans deliver to All Parts of Town Twice Daily.

DISCOUNT FOR CASH.

THE LEADING AND BEST FAMILY PAPER SOUTH OF LONDON.

The Brighton Gazette

And Sussex Telegraph,

Published every Thursday & Saturday, contains

LEADING ARTICLES

ON LOCAL AND GENERAL EVENTS.

LONDON NOTES (by our SPECIAL CORRESPONDENT).

BRIGHTON CHIT-CHAT.

| ECCLESIASTICAL & RELIGIOUS, | GOSSIPS OF THE CLUBS, |
| DRAMATIC, ART, & MUSIC. | SPORTS, &c. |

HOVE NEWS AND NOTES.

TOWN COUNCIL SKETCHES.

BRIGHTON & HOVE POLICE COURTS.

LECTURES AND DEBATES.

FULL FASHIONABLE VISITORS' LIST.

List of Auction Sales. Local Amusements.

COUNTY JOTTINGS.

TO BE HAD OF ALL NEWS AGENTS.

WILLIAM JAMES TOWNER, Proprietor and Publisher,
150, NORTH STREET, BRIGHTON.

FREMLIN BROS.,

Family Ale and Stout Stores,

MANCHESTER STREET,

BRIGHTON.

ALE and STOUT from 2s. 6d. per Dozen Imperial Pints, in Screw Stoppered Bottles.

Also in 4½ Gallon Stone Jars with Lock Taps, and in Casks from Nine Gallons upwards.

BREWERY - MAIDSTONE.

The Great Brighton Book Store,
41, 42, 43, NORTH STREET,
WILLIAM J. SMITH, Proprietor.

150,000 VOLUMES IN STOCK—New and Second-hand.

BRIGHTON OLD BOOK CIRCULAR, GRATIS.

BOOKS Bought in any quantity for Cash, or Exchanged.

BOOKS and other Literary Property Catalogued, or Valued for Probate.

BOOKS BOUND in Best Styles by Competent Workmen.
Work and Charges defy Competition.

BOOKS, PRINTS, and DRAWINGS relating to Sussex and Brighton, on Sale.

ESTABLISHED 1806.

THE OLDEST, THE BEST, AND
MOST POPULAR WEEKLY JOURNAL
ISSUED IN BRIGHTON.

The Brighton Herald,
PUBLISHED
EVERY SATURDAY MORNING,
PRICE ONE PENNY, WITH
"Local Guide" Monthly, Gratis.

A HIGH-CLASS FAMILY NEWSPAPER.

**ALL THE NEWS of the WEEK CAREFULLY CONDENSED.
NO LONG AND TEDIOUS REPORTS.**
DRAMATIC, MUSICAL, & ART CRITICISMS.   LITERARY NOTICES.
LATEST NEWS BY SPECIAL TELEGRAMS.

BEST MEDIUM FOR ADVERTISEMENTS.

PUBLISHING OFFICE:
PRINCE'S PLACE, NORTH STREET, Brighton.
JOHN GEORGE BISHOP, Proprietor.

Geo. F. ATTREE,

Auctioneer, Valuer, & Estate Agent,

THE ESTATE AUCTION MART,

136, NORTH STREET, BRIGHTON.

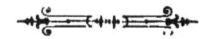

The FURNITURE SALE ROOMS, situate in NORTH STREET, are OPEN DAILY for the reception of HOUSEHOLD FURNITURE, MUSICAL INSTRUMENTS, PAINTINGS, SILVER PLATE, BOOKS, and ORNAMENTAL ITEMS, for immediate Sale. For Terms and Entry Forms, apply at above Address.

ATTREE, UNDERTAKER,

Proprietor of Modern Carriages,

136, NORTH STREET, BRIGHTON.

Telegraphic Address, "ATTREE, BRIGHTON."   Telephone, No. 126.